Living
Our Stories,
Telling
Our Truths

Living
Our Stories,
Telling
Our Truths

Autobiography and the Making

of the African-American

Intellectual Tradition

V. P. Franklin

OXFORD UNIVERSITY PRESS
New York   Oxford

Oxford University Press

Oxford   New York
Athens   Auckland   Bangkok   Bombay
Calcutta   Cape Town   Dar es Salaam   Delhi
Florence   Hong Kong   Istanbul   Karachi
Kuala Lumpur   Madras   Madrid   Melbourne
Mexico City   Nairobi   Paris   Singapore
Taipei   Tokyo   Toronto

and associated companies in
Berlin   Ibadan

Copyright © 1995 by V. P. Franklin

First published in 1995 by Scribner,
1230 Avenue of the Americas, New York, NY 10020

First issued as an Oxford University Press paperback, 1996

Oxford is a registered trademark of Oxford University Press

Library of Congress Cataloging-in-Publication Data
Franklin, V. P. (Vincent P.), 1947–
Living our stories, telling our truths : autobiography and the
making of the African-American intellectual tradition / V. P.
Franklin.
p.   cm.
Originally published: New York : Scribners, 1995.
Includes bibliographical references and index.
ISBN 0-19-510373-4 (Pbk.)
1. Afro-Americans—Biography.   2. Autobiographies—United States—
History and criticism.   3. Afro-Americans—Intellectual life.
I. Title.
[E185.96.F74   1996]
920'.009296073—dc20   96-22441

1 3 5 7 9 10 8 6 4 2
Printed in the United States of America

Dedicated to the memory of
Cecelia S. Franklin
Eloise Owens Strothers
Ernest Batchelor III
Ronald Batchelor
Maurice J. Bennett
Sylvia A. Boone
Larry Harris
A. Wade Smith
Cecil Ivory
Tony Morton
Raymond H. Brown

CONTENTS

PREFACE

WHEN I DECIDED to examine the African-American intellectual tradition using the autobiographies of black leaders and literary artists, I was soon confronted with an embarrassment of riches. Given the numerous important autobiographical works, the most difficult task was trying to decide which ones to use. As a historian, I was primarily concerned with those works that dealt with recurring themes in African-American cultural and intellectual history, but I also wanted to make sure that I discussed some of the more influential works in the autobiographical literary genre. Even with these criteria, I still found that I had to be selective, and the works I ultimately chose to examine were those I found most helpful to me in trying to explain the evolution of the larger intellectual tradition.

Over the last three decades there has been a virtual explosion in research and writing on African-American leaders, artists, and spokespersons. Thousands of journal articles, books, monographs, literary analyses, and biographical studies have appeared on individual artists, literary themes, ideological debates, and political movements in which African-American intellectuals have been involved. I have utilized this extraordinary outpouring of historical and literary research as a guide in pursuing this historical synthesis. At the same time, because I was also interested in documenting the intricate relationship between experience and ideology, I have decided to include extended excerpts from the primary sources—the autobiographies themselves. Many of these literary artists were masters of the English language and I want the reader to gain an appreciation of not only what these writers said, but also how they said it. Style and content, text and context are what I have attempted to present in this overview of African-American intellectual history.

I began working on this topic over a decade ago and this is the first full-length version that has made it to the printed page. While I have attempted to be relatively comprehensive, I am under no delusion that this is definitive or "the last word" on the subject (not even from me). The initial research for this project was conducted while I was a Scholar in Residence at the Schomburg Center for Research in Black Culture in 1985–1986, funded by the National Research Council's Ford Foundation Postdoctoral Fellowship Program for Minorities. The administration and entire staff of the Schomburg Center were extremely supportive, and I want to thank in particular Howard Dodson, Sharon Howard, Diana Lachatenere, and Mary Yearwood for their assistance.

Over the years I have presented bits and pieces of this work at various symposia, conferences, and forums and have benefited from the comments and criticisms of many artists and scholars. I would like to express my thanks to my colleagues and friends in the departments of history and African-American Studies at Yale, Arizona State, the University of Pennsylvania, and Drexel University. My students at these institutions often taught me as much as my colleagues (sometimes more), and I also want to express my thanks to them. Some of the most fruitful intellectual exchanges occurred at the annual meetings of the Association for the Study of Afro-American Life and History, and I want to thank the officers and members of that organization for finding a place for me on the program year after year. And there are those who read and commented on the entire manuscript or various chapters, or provided me with the intellectual sustenance needed for the long haul. I wish to thank Sandra Bowen Motz, Gloria Naylor, June O. Patton, Sigmund Shipp, Bettye Collier-Thomas, Jack T. Franklin, Nancy Grant, Mary Frances Berry, Genna Rae McNeil, Lillian S. Williams, James Turner, Linda M. Perkins, Malinda Chateauvert, Charlotte Sheedy, Dick Dretsch, Julie Mostov, Patricia Cooper, and Gilbert Ware. Some of the people who have been most important to me spiritually and intellectually over the years are no longer here to share in the fruits of our collective labor. This work is dedicated to their memory.

INTRODUCTION

I found that to tell the truth is the hardest thing on earth, harder than fighting in a war, harder than taking part in a revolution. If you try it you will find at times sweat will break upon you. You will find that even if you succeed in discounting the attitudes of others to you and your life, you will wrestle with yourself most of all, fight with yourself, for there will surge up in you a strong desire to alter the facts, to dress up your feelings. You'll find that there are many things you don't want to admit about yourself and others. As your record shapes itself, an awed wonder haunts you. And yet there is no more exciting adventure than trying to be honest in this way. The clean, strong feeling that sweeps you when you've done it makes you know that.

—RICHARD WRIGHT, 1944

FROM THE PUBLICATION of the *Narrative of the Life of Frederick Douglass, An American Slave* in 1845 to Lorene Cary's *Black Ice* and Brent Staples's *Parallel Time: Growing Up in Black and White* in the 1990s, the autobiography has been the most important literary genre in the African-American intellectual tradition in the United States. For the former slaves who wrote their life stories, the act of writing was often considered an act of self-liberation. The struggle for freedom is a core value in the collective experience of African Americans in the United States and the autobiography provided a personal account of what freedom meant and how it could be achieved. African-American intellectuals and artists in the late nineteenth and twentieth centuries wrote their autobiographies with the political and social circumstances for African Americans in mind, and used their personal experiences as a mirror to reflect that larger social context for Afro-America. In some instances, again reminiscent of the slave narratives, these African-American intellectuals used the autobiographical form to examine ideological issues and to situate their personal preferences within that larger political context.[1]

The slave narratives laid the foundation not only for the African-American autobiographical tradition, but also for novels and short fiction produced by black writers in the nineteenth century. There was a close resemblance in structure and organization between the slave narratives and the earliest black novels, such as William Wells Brown's *Clotelle; or the President's Daughter* (1853), Martin Delany's *Blake; or the Huts of America* (1859), and Frances E.W. Harper's *Iola Leroy; or The Shadows Lifted* (1893). In both the slave narratives and the early novels, the heroes or heroines were introduced, subjected to certain types of cruelty and oppression that were dramatized for the reader, made aware of the fundamental injustice inherent in their condition, fled the oppressive circumstances, and subsequently became involved in larger movements to end the injustice and oppression. Moreover, many of the so-called protest novels produced by W. E. B. Du Bois, Richard Wright, Chester Himes, and other African-American writers in the twentieth century structurally have much in common with the slave narratives.[2]

In the twentieth century, although hundreds of novels have been written, the autobiography remained the preferred literary form for many African-American artists and intellectuals. Henry Louis Gates, Jr., in the introduction to *Bearing Witness: Selections from African American Autobiography in the Twentieth Century* (1991) argued that "the will to power for black Americans was the will to write; and the predominant mode that this writing would assume was the shaping of the black self in words." Gates admitted that even though fiction in general, and the novel in particular, is the most practiced literary genre today, "the impulse to testify, to chart the peculiar contours of the individual protagonist on the road to becoming, clearly undergirds even the fictional tradition of black letters, as the predominance of the first person form attests." The autobiography fulfilled the need to define the individual "black self" to a society that denied the existence of a black reality. The literary artist was attracted to the possibility of using language to define the self in an autobiographical text. The artists were preoccupied with literary styles and forms out of the past that could provide models for those who wanted to participate in this intellectual tradition of "bearing witness."[3]

Unlike the literary artists who were preoccupied with "shaping their public 'self' in language," many African-American intellectuals and leaders turned to the autobiographical form primarily for ideological and political purposes. These were exceptionally gifted and highly educated individuals who had demonstrated over and over again that they were superior intellectually and culturally to the vast majority of black and white Americans with whom they came into contact. The autobiographical text was used to serve ideological purposes, and the intellectual's personal experiences were related to particular matters of principle that were important in their lives.

For the literary artists the autobiography often was their first book, and it was used to establish their careers as writers. African-American intellectuals trained in theology, the sciences, law, or journalism, however, turned to autobiography only after their professional reputation had been established. In a life devoted to challenging the discursive structures created to define African-American social reality, these scholars had experienced the freedom of writing—the need to define a literary self—very early in their careers. Having mastered written English at a young age, the "attainment of literacy," which figures so prominently in the slave narratives and in autobiographies by literary artists, is rarely an issue for African-American intellectuals.

At the same time, poets, playwrights, novelists, and other literary artists closely associated with important political movements and specific ideological positions sometimes produced autobiographical texts full of their personal experiences in political struggles and ideological debates. This preoccupation with ideology and matters of principle emerges as a major theme in the autobiographical texts produced by African-American intellectuals. Indeed, the autobiographical act defined the nature of the relationship between ideology and personal experience for these intellectuals.

The autobiographical work produced by African-American artists and intellectuals occupies the central position in the African-American literary and intellectual tradition because oftentimes personal truth was stranger than fiction. It was not so much that the things these artists and intellectuals experienced were miraculous or supernatural. It was that, in declaring that these things occurred, and that they lived to tell them, these authors challenged American society's perceptions about itself and undermined its prejudices about black people. But there were usually significant objectives beyond shocking and challenging white American perspectives on "the Negro." One finds that African-American autobiographers had serious ideological preoccupations and that these intellectual issues changed from decade to decade and from one generation to another.

The *Narrative of the Life of Frederick Douglass* is generally considered one of those classic works produced during the American Literary Renaissance of the 1840s and 1850s. Along with Herman Melville's *Moby-Dick* (1851), Henry David Thoreau's *Walden; or Life in the Woods* (1854), and Walt Whitman's *Leaves of Grass* (1855), Douglass's *Narrative* set a literary standard that would be used for evaluating autobiographical works before and afterward. In the *Narrative* and *My Bondage and My Freedom* (1855), Douglass described his personal experiences to assist the political movement aimed at the abolition of slavery in the United States. *The Life and Times of Frederick Douglass,* published in 1881 and 1892, as well as Booker T. Washington's autobiography, *Up from Slavery,* published in 1901, were written to show how high a former slave could rise in American society. Over the last two decades, Douglass's *Narrative* and his two later autobiographies have been the subject of perceptive and probing critical analyses by Robert Stepto, Houston A. Baker, William Andrews, Henry Louis Gates, Jr., Robert O'Meilly, and other literary critics; and the result has been a renewed appreciation of Douglass's formidable contribution to the African-American autobiographical tradition. These critics have concluded that if the slave narratives can be considered the United States's unique contribution to the autobiographical form, then Douglass's *Narrative* represents the most noteworthy example of this distinctly American literary creation.[4]

While Frederick Douglass's contribution to American and African-American literary traditions has been generally acknowledged and praised, the importance of his ideas and works to the evolution of the African-American intellectual tradition has also been examined. Historian Waldo E. Martin in his book, *The Mind of Frederick Douglass,* presented a detailed analysis of Douglass's more important ideological positions, including his belief in "racial assimilationism." "Douglass's ideal nation-state, society, and culture would have been raceless," Martin observed. "Even if different races had coexisted in this utopia, it would have been raceless in the sense that race would not be an issue." In one of his most famous speeches, "The United States Cannot Remain Half-Slave and Half-Free," delivered to black audiences throughout the 1870s and 1880s, Douglass made clear his belief that "there is but one destiny, it seems to me, left for us and that is to make ourselves a part of the American people in every sense of the word. . . . Assimilation and not isolation is our true policy and our natural destiny. Unification for us is life; separation is death."[5]

Martin found that "Douglass unequivocally advocated total Negro assimilation into the white, Anglo-Saxon Protestant-dominated political culture." But Douglass did not stop there; he also preached (and practiced) miscegenation, or "the amalgamation of the races." In another famous address of the 1880s, "The Future of the Colored Race," Douglass predicted that African Americans "will be absorbed, assimilated, and will only appear finally, as the Phoenicians now appear . . . in the features of a blended race." For Douglass racial assimiliationism was a progressive development, and Americans "easily adapt themselves to inevitable conditions, and all their tendency is to progress, enlightenment, and the universal." Douglass looked to the creation of a "composite American nationality" and a "cosmopolitan nation, the grandest and most comprehensive illustration of the human race." Waldo Martin concluded that while Douglass was aware that the United States at the end of the nineteenth century was "no racial assimilationist haven, ideologically . . . he could not separate the interdependent ideal and reality of a composite American nationality because his vision of Americans transcended race and encompassed humanity."[6]

Waldo Martin and other historians have characterized Frederick Douglass's racial assimilationism as "integrationist." As we shall see, however, while many other African-American intellectuals and spokespersons in the nineteenth and twentieth centuries considered themselves integrationists, only a very small number expressed as part of their social vision the advocacy of the total absorption of the African race in the United States into the white American majority.

As W. E. B. Du Bois put it in one of his most famous works, *The Souls of Black Folk* (1903), the African American "would not bleach his soul in a flood of white Americanism, for he knows that Negro blood has a message for the world. He simply wishes to make it possible for a man to be both a Negro and an American, without being cursed and spit upon by his fellows, without having the doors of Opportunity closed roughly in his face."[7]

While Frederick Douglass should be the leading candidate for designation as "father of the African-American autobiographical tradition," we must look to Rev. Alexander Crummell as the progenitor of the dominant ideological concerns and preoccupations of African-American intellectuals. Throughout the nineteenth and early twentieth centuries, African-American intellectuals demonstrated an overarching commitment to "race vindication." Given the overwhelmingly negative conceptions in the larger society about African and African-American character and capacity, these intellectuals lived lives that were personal vindications of racist notions about black people. When white racists claimed that Africans were incapable of mastering Greek, Latin, or higher mathematics and science, these individuals not only mastered these subjects, but excelled at them. When these highly intelligent individuals sought additional training beyond that available within the black community, and were barred from white institutions, they often left the country and studied at European colleges and universities. In the nineteenth century Alexander Crummell, W. E. B. Du Bois, Francis Cardozo, Mary Church Terrell, and other African-American intellectuals attended and received degrees from European universities that had reputations and standards far higher than those of schools in the United States. Thus their personal experiences undermined racist perceptions about the "educability of the Negro."[8]

Once they received their advanced training, these intellectuals then engaged in activities to vindicate the race from the distortions and misconceptions about people of African descent rampant throughout American society. Through their scholarly research and writing, African-American intellectuals challenged the white "experts" on the Negro and the "Negro Problem" by presenting what they considered was "the truth" about the race. Their well-documented articles and books were a marked contrast to the works produced by white researchers that many times were built almost entirely upon racist assumptions.

As we move into the twentieth century, we find that African-American intellectuals chose particular areas of the "race problem" to investigate and to which they devoted their political lives and intellectual energies. Ida Wells-Barnett exposed the truth about lynching and through her investigations was able to demonstrate that in only a few instances was the rape of a white woman even mentioned as the reason for these brutal crimes. James Weldon Johnson was committed to documenting the significant artistic contributions of the

African-American masses to American life and culture. Johnson firmly believed that the only *original* contributions to world culture coming from the United States were those made by African Americans. Harry Haywood joined the Communist Party at a young age because of its commitment to the advancement of the working classes. However, within the party Haywood was determined that the leadership recognize the revolutionary potential of the black working class. For Haywood this became a matter of principle and he forced the party to recognize the unique history and circumstances for black workers in the United States and to support policies and programs that reflected that distinctness.

African-American intellectuals' ideological commitments were not based on faith or ideals alone, but were reinforced and solidified by their personal experiences. Thus the autobiography served as a personal tapestry upon which they wove those events and movements that shaped their personal beliefs and identity. In some instances these intellectuals turned to the autobiographical form to clarify the reasons they adopted particular ideological positions during their lives, while others used their autobiographies to present what they perceived as the missing chapters in the story of the collective experience of African Americans in the United States. In either case the resulting work became a touchstone, sometimes a classic in the emerging African-American intellectual tradition.

Alexander Crummell in *Jubilate,* Ida Wells-Barnett in *Crusade for Justice,* James Weldon Johnson in *Along This Way,* Harry Haywood in *Black Bolshevik,* and W. E. B. Du Bois in his three major autobiographical works, *Darkwater, Dusk of Dawn,* and *Soliloquy* clearly demonstrated an intellectual preoccupation with race vindication as well as other specific ideological issues with which they were closely associated and identified throughout their lives, and which eventually became important elements within the emerging African-American intellectual tradition. The personal narratives produced by African-American artists and intellectuals after 1940 were generally less concerned with "defending the race" and more reflective of contemporary issues facing blacks and whites in the United States. The autobiographical works by Richard Wright, Zora Neale Hurston, Malcolm X, James Baldwin, Gwendolyn Brooks, Amiri Baraka, and Adam Clayton Powell, Jr., were personal testaments by highly visible spokespersons who felt a need to address particular social and cultural issues of which they had some personal knowledge and experience. It was rarely the case that they saw their lives as vindication against the negative perceptions of black people in the society at large, but their experiences provided important insights into pressing and controversial issues currently under debate among black and white Americans.

Novelist Richard Wright's experiences as a member of the John Reed Club and Communist Party in Chicago helped shape his major theoretical statement on the social purposes of African-American literature. In "Blueprint for Negro Writing," published in 1937, Wright called upon black literary artists to adopt Marxian approaches to their craft, and in *12 Million Black Voices* he expressed his profound appreciation of the cultural beliefs and practices of the rural and urban black masses. After his break with the Communist Party, however, Wright emphasized in his major autobiographical work, *Black Boy*, published in 1945, the "pathologies of black life" that resulted from legal segregation. Zora Neale Hurston, on the other hand, distrusted both black and white communists, ignored Marxist literary theories, and used her autobiography, *Dust Tracks on a Road* (1942), to describe those aspects of her personal background that made her a unique individual. More importantly, Hurston's autobiography presented a portrait of rural black folk entirely different from that found in Wright's *Black Boy*. Hurston not only described her personal experiences while growing up that underpinned her integrationist ideological perspectives, she also made clear her appreciation for the religion and folk practices of southern blacks.

Like Frederick Douglass, the eminent scholar and intellectual W. E. B. Du Bois wrote three major autobiographical works. And also like Douglass, Du Bois was considered an "integrationist" (among other things). However, in his ideological perspectives Du Bois was much closer, particularly in his early years, to Alexander Crummell than to Frederick Douglass. In his first autobiography, *Darkwater*, published in 1920, race vindication was an overarching theme. At the same time, however, Du Bois made clear his belief that "The Souls of White Folk" would be saved by the "Children of the Moon." The moral destiny of the United States, Du Bois believed, would be determined by the way it dealt with its darker citizens.

In 1940 Du Bois published his second major autobiographical work, *Dusk of Dawn,* and he again emphasized his belief that the way that the United States solved the so-called Negro Problem would determine whether or not it could truly be considered a democratic nation. More importantly, Du Bois used this autobiographical work to explore the meaning of the African-American experience in the United States. "Why are we here?" became a fundamental question to be asked and answered by African American intellectuals in the United States. Alexander Crummell many times expressed his belief that Africans were in this country to take on the advantages of "civilized society," to advance themselves, and to serve as an example and model for other Africans and oppressed colored peoples throughout the world. In *Darkwater* and *Dusk of Dawn,* however, Du Bois argued that in improving themselves and their social and political circumstances, African Americans would be serving the cause of democracy in the United States and the Western world.

No one was as surprised as Du Bois himself that he would live to write his third major autobiographical work, *Soliloquy,* which was not published until after his death in August 1963 at the age of ninety-five. This work is very different from the earlier autobiographies and expressed Du Bois's profound disillusionment with democratic processes as they operated in the United States during the McCarthy era, sometimes referred to as the period of the "American Inquisition." Du Bois was a victim of the U.S. government's attempt to silence the critics of its Cold War policies and repressive anti-communism. In the *Soliloquy* Du Bois made clear his support for the communist governments in the Soviet Union, China, and Eastern Europe; and he denounced those members of the black elite, the so-called Talented Tenth, who refused to speak out and even shunned those such as himself who were wrongfully accused of being "anti-American." An analysis of the autobiographical legacy of W. E. B. Du Bois provides important insights into why the most important African-American intellectual in the twentieth century joined the Communist Party in 1961 and died in exile in Ghana in 1963.

In the early 1960s James Baldwin was considered by many to be the leading African-American spokesperson for the integration of African Americans into the mainstream of American society. Although Baldwin over and over again made good on his claim that he was a "literary artist," it was in his nonfiction, most of which was autobiographical, that he examined the intimate relationship between experience and ideology. Baldwin believed that there would be no progress in black-white relations in the United States as long as white Americans continued to tell lies and construct elaborate fantasies about themselves and the nature of the society they had created. In the essays in *Notes of a Native Son* (1955) and *Nobody Knows My Name* (1961) Baldwin confessed his murderous rage over the way he and his brothers and sisters were treated by white Americans, and he appealed to his white oppressors to change their wicked ways, for their own good. Otherwise, Baldwin predicted, those who were similarly situated would respond violently to these oppressive conditions and practices.

In *The Fire Next Time* (1963) and *No Name in the Street* (1972) Baldwin made clear the similarity in the ideological positions of integrationists, such as himself, and militant black nationalists, such as Elijah Muhammad and Malcolm X. The major objective for both integrationists and nationalists was black liberation. The answer that Baldwin gave to the question "Why are we here?" was the same as that of Dr. Martin Luther King, Jr.: "To redeem the soul of America." However, Baldwin understood that Elijah Muhammad and the Nation of Islam sought the redemption of Allah's chosen people in America, and he viewed this as a worthwhile goal. In fact, in his autobiographical essays Baldwin emphasized the point that the only matter of principle that separated him from the Black Muslims was their belief in black liberation "by any means necessary."

In 1967 Harold Cruse declared that the emergence of the Black Power movement precipitated what he called the crisis of the Negro intellectual. In the ideological debates between integrationists in the civil rights movement and militant nationalists associated with Black Power during the second half of the 1960s, the local police, agents for the FBI, conservative black and white politicians, and other members of the political and economic establishment inadvertently did all they could to ensure that the black militants gained the upper hand. It was not primarily the militant rhetoric of the black nationalists that brought about the ideological conversions of many older and young African Americans, it was their day-to-day experiences with white racist institutions and practices that pushed the masses into the waiting arms of the Black Power advocates.[9]

In *The Autobiography of Malcolm X* the personal experiences that served to justify Malcolm's rejection of integrationist doctrines were described in vivid detail. Although Malcolm emphasized the mental and physical changes he underwent throughout his life, there is still great ideological continuity in this work. From the beginning to the end Malcolm emphasized self-determination and his belief that if African Americans are going to triumph over the mental and spiritual death to which they are subjected in the United States, then they will have to develop the discipline, self-respect, and pride that were the foundation for the success of the Nation of Islam with the "lowest of the low" in the black community. Given the oppressive conditions and the self-destructive behaviors exhibited by too many African Americans, the only way black liberation will be achieved is through "the resurrection of the dead."

The description of the religious conversion experience at the center of *The Autobiography of Malcolm X* represents a narrative strategy found in many other "spiritual autobiographies." Literary scholars who have examined the Western autobiograpical tradition from *The Confessions of Saint Augustine* in the fifth century to the present have identified a type of "conversion discourse" that is not confined to the "religious" sphere. Peter A. Dorsey in *Sacred Estrangement: The Rhetoric of Conversion in Modern Autobiography* (1993) found that, over the last three centuries in particular, "conversion became a model for many kinds of pyschological changes, yet the secular autobiographies of the period continued to respond to the socializing function implicit in conversion rhetoric: like the works in the Christian tradition, many of these narratives are centered on the acceptance of vocation." These secular writers "departed from Christian models by using conversion rhetoric to affirm the dignity of their inner selves, but they nevertheless were also engaged in a process of reform—whether social, philosophical, or cognitive. They may have distrusted the kind of unquestioned submission associated with religious conversion, but they continued to affirm the value of community—even if the communities they valued became quite elusive."[10]

Within the African-American autobiographical tradition from the slave narratives to *The Autobiography of Malcolm X,* the conversion rhetoric, preoccupation with reform, and search for community are readily apparent. The ideological conversion experience was important in the autobiographies of Ida Wells-Barnett, Harry Haywood, W. E. B. Du Bois, Richard Wright, Gwendolyn Brooks, Amiri Baraka, and Adam Clayton Powell, Jr. In *Report from Part One,* poet Gwendolyn Brooks detailed her conversion to the literary styles, content, and objectives of the Black Arts Movement of the second half of the 1960s. Poet and playwright Amiri Baraka described his transformations from Greenwich Village bohemian to cultural nationalist to Marxist-Leninist-Maoist in his 1984 autobiography. Following his attendance at the Bandung Conference in Indonesia in April 1955, Adam Clayton Powell, Jr., the most powerful black elected official in the United States at the time, moved away from what he considered a narrow black nationalism to a more internationalist or Third World position. Like the autobiographies of Gwendolyn Brooks and Amiri Baraka, *Adam by Adam* presented a detailed examination of the personal experiences that led to this profound ideological conversion.

More important, in the second half of the twentieth century, the autobiographical works produced by African-American artists and intellectuals generally reflected the dominant ideological issues and concerns that went into the making of the African-American intellectual tradition. While there was less emphasis on race vindication, it was still an issue addressed in the autobiographical works by Baldwin, Baraka, Brooks, and Powell. Each of these writers emphasized the need to tell the truth to the powerful, praised their working-class family background and encounters with black workers, expressed their appreciation for the cultural gifts of rural and urban black folk. Whether they believed that African Americans were destined to save America from itself, or that black people in the United States must be liberated "by any means necessary," they made clear their understanding of the need for self-determination and independent black leadership.

When we begin to explore systematically the autobiographies of African-American artists, scholars, and leaders, we find they provide an incomparable intellectual legacy for African Americans entering the twenty-first century and seeking answers to the question "Why are we here?"

1

Alexander Crummell

Defining Matters of Principle

———

We have seen, to-day, the great truth, that when God does not destroy a people, but, on the contrary, trains and disciplines it, it is an indication that He intends to make something of them, and to do something for them. It signifies that He is graciously interested in such a people. In a sense, not equal, indeed, to the case of the Jews, but parallel, in a lower degree, such a people are a "chosen people" of the Lord. . . .

With all these providential indications in our favor, let us bless God and take courage. Casting aside everything trifling and frivolous, let us lay hold of every element of power, in the brain, in literature, art, and science; in industrial pursuits; in the soil; in cooperative association; in mechanical ingenuity; and above all, in the religion of our God; and so march on in the pathway of progress to that superiority and eminence which is our rightful heritage, and which is evidently the promise of our God!

—ALEXANDER CRUMMELL, 1877

Photographer unknown. Reprinted by permission of the Schomburg Center
for Research in Black Culture, New York Public Library.

AFTER ALMOST twenty years as an Episcopal missionary in West Africa, Rev. Alexander Crummell arrived in Boston from Freetown, Sierra Leone, in April 1872 and by the middle of May he had made his way to New York City, where he had been born in 1819. He was fifty-three years old, but he appeared older due to constant bouts of ill health. In his autobiographical work, *Jubilate: Shades and Lights of a Fifty Years' Ministry, 1844–1894,* Crummell claimed that he had enjoyed good health during most of the almost twenty years he had spent as a missionary in Liberia. "After my acclimation, I entered into health, such as I never had before, and such I have never had since," Crummell exclaimed. "Under the tropical sun I became vigorous, elastic, life-enjoying. If I had not gone to Africa, I am quite sure I should have died years ago" (20).[1]

Rev. Crummell's letters to the Episcopal Church's Foreign Missionary Committee in Boston, however, told quite a different story. He had trouble adjusting to the West African climate each time he returned from abroad, he had severe problems with his liver, and could barely walk sometimes due to varicose veins. On numerous occasions Rev. Crummell complained about the impact a move to a missionary station located in the interior would have upon his already precarious health, and at times the Episcopal officials actually rescinded the transfer for health reasons. There were of course numerous other discrepancies between the documentation unearthed by his many biographers and what Crummell wrote in his major autobiographical work. Whereas the letters and correspondence were immediate and private, his numerous essays, sermons, and books were meant for posterity. His public life was committed to certain ideals and principles, which he expressed in his writings, and it was through these public pronouncements and activities that Crummell came to be considered the most influential African-American intellectual in the late nineteenth century.

Although Alexander Crummell was an Episcopalian priest, lecturer, educator, and scholar, his life was also full of trials, tribulations, death-defying adventure, and political intrigue. More importantly, his educational pursuits set the stage for intellectual performances by later artists and scholars. Crummell not only founded institutions to carry out intellectual and literary activities, but his concerns and approaches prefigured literary and academic approaches among African-American intellectuals in the twentieth century. Alexander Crummell

23

was one of the founding fathers in the African-American intellectual tradition, and his ideological principles were brought together with his personal experiences in his autobiographical sermon first delivered in December 1894, at the celebration commemorating his half century as an Episcopal priest. Several biographers have commented negatively on Crummell's only major autobiographical statement, claiming that he was "dishonest," "inaccurate," and "misrepresented certain events." However, the autobiographical text served many purposes within the African-American intellectual tradition, and Rev. Crummell's *Jubilate* was representative of the black intellectual's use of this literary form to explore the nexus between personal experiences and ideological development.[2]

Alexander Crummell inherited his commitment to education and intellectual pursuits from his father, Boston Crummell, who had been born in West Africa, but was brought to the United States as a young child, and sold into slavery. Born in New York City in 1819, Alexander Crummell grew up in a home environment where he was taught to be proud of his "pure African heritage." Alexander was also told that his father upon reaching maturity merely walked away from his slave master, who decided not to pursue him. While less is known about Alexander's mother, Charity Hicks, who was born of free parents on Long Island, we do know that she was also of pure African ancestry. When Alexander was a young child, Boston Crummell, who worked as an oysterman, hired private tutors to instruct his son in mathematics, science, and Western literature, but within his family he was schooled in his African heritage. Alexander Crummell understood that the numerous wars and violent conflicts that took place in West Africa were encouraged by the European and African slave traders, and that his father, as well as thousands of other Africans, had been captured and brought to America against their will. It was the darkness that had befallen Africa and African peoples that prevented them from joining together in liberating themselves from mental and physical oppression.[3]

As an individual Boston Crummell had resisted the oppression of American slavery and when he came to New York City in the 1790s he became intimately involved with the organized movements to end the practice in New York state. Through the efforts of the New York Manumission Society, founded in the city in January 1785, legislation had been introduced into the state assembly for the gradual end of slavery. This measure would not precipitously free those Africans enslaved in the Empire State, but called for the manumission of the sons and daughters of slaves at the ages of eighteen and twenty-one respectively. Similar to the gradual manumission law passed in Pennsylvania in 1780, the measure nonetheless sparked fierce debate. The greatest opposition came from Dutch slaveowners in Kings, Richmond, and Ulster counties, who saw the measure as an infringement on their "property rights" by depriving them of the slaves' labor in cotton, wheat, or corn cultivation once they reached the age of manumission. The bill was defeated in the assembly by pro-slavery forces, but the anti-slavery efforts continued to push the issue. When John Jay, the president of the Manumission Society, became governor in 1795, a new bill was introduced into the state assembly and there was furious activity in local communities to generate support. Again slaveowners claimed slave emancipation without compensation violated their property rights, and over the next three years a compromise bill was agreed upon that called for the emancipation of all *children* of slave parents born after July 4, 1799 at the age of twenty-eight (males) or twenty-five (females). An "abandonment clause" allowed owners, financially unable to take care of slave children, to abandon them to the state, which would bound them out in service to "overseers," who more often then not turned out to be their former owners. Under the pretext of caring for unwanted children, slaveowners received windfall profits from the New York state government to care for these "abandoned slaves."[4]

Although slavery was on its way out in the northeastern states at the turn of the nineteenth century, free black New Yorkers and former slaves were soon confronted by another political and physical challenge: the founding of a national society whose purpose was to raise money for the repatriation of the entire free black population to West Africa. The American Colonization Society (ACS) was organized in December 1816 in Washington, D.C., and its Board of Directors was a virtual who's who of early American politics. Bushrod Washington, the nephew of George Washington, was elected the first ACS president, and during the antebellum period James Madison, Henry Clay, Daniel Webster, Francis Scott Key, John Marshall, Roger George, and Andrew Jackson were included among its officers.[5]

The formation of the American Colonization Society served to divide the free black community in New York City, with some favoring and others opposing the repatriation scheme. Despite his pride in his African heritage, Boston Crummell opposed the colonization efforts as a threat to black freedom in the United States. The eminent bishop Richard Allen of the newly organized African Methodist Episcopal (AME) church led the free black opposition to the Colonization Society from his pulpit at Bethel Church in Philadelphia. Bishop Allen and others organized mass rallies at the church where the colonizers were denounced in no uncertain terms. At the one held on January 17, 1817, James Forten, a prominent sailmaker, chaired the meeting and when he asked those in the audience who desired repatriation to signify by saying "aye," a hush fell over the church. When Forten asked those who opposed the scheme to respond, according to one account, "one, loud, tremendous 'No' went up which . . . seemed as it would bring down the walls of the building." A few months later in New York City, Boston Crummell's pastor and close friend, Peter Williams, preached a sermon at St. Philip's Church on African colonization and made it clear that "we are *natives* of this country; we only ask to be treated as well as the *foreigners*. Not a few of our fathers suffered and bled to purchase its independence; we ask only to be treated as well as those who fought against it."[6]

But there were other black New Yorkers, friends of Boston Crummell, who supported the efforts to found an American colony in West Africa for free blacks from the United States. Through financial support from wealthy slave-owners and military assistance from the government of President James Monroe, the American Colonization Society was able to organize its West African settlement in what was later called Liberia, with Monrovia as its capital. The ACS immediately began to issue pamphlets and brochures trying to attract free black settlers. The group's official magazine, *The African Repository,* carried news and information about the African colony and became a major propaganda vehicle distributed widely among free blacks.[7]

It was not until 1829 that white colonizers in New York City were able to get their first highly educated African-American intellectual, John Russwurm, a close friend of Boston Crummell, to convert to the cause of free black colonization. Considered one of the first African Americans to receive a bachelor's degree from an American college (Bowdoin, 1826), John Russwurm was one of the original founders and publishers of the first African-American newspaper in the United States.[8]

Meeting regularly in the home of Boston Crummell during the winter of 1826, John Russwurm, Samuel Cornish, a Presbyterian minister, and several others came to the conclusion that free blacks needed their own newspaper to answer the scurrilous and unfair attacks launched against them in the daily and weekly press. On March 16, 1827, the first issue of *Freedom's Journal* appeared and Russwurm and Cornish made it clear that through the newspaper, "we wish to plead our own cause." It would not only publish pieces that would educate its readers in their best interests, but would also press for black "civil rights" and an end of slavery in the United States.[9]

In December 1828 *Freedom's Journal* published the earliest version of the most militant proposal for dealing with the problems facing African Americans in the United States, *Walker's Appeal.* David Walker had been born in North Carolina of a free black mother and slave father, but traveled widely throughout the South, eventually settling in Boston where he established a clothing business. Walker became involved in anti-slavery activities in the city, and spoke at meetings and rallies. Then in 1829 he put his orations together into a pamphlet that called upon the oppressed African peoples in the United States, the Caribbean, and South America to rise up in violent revolution against their oppressors. The slaveowners were the "natural enemies" of African peoples and it would be considered wrong for the slave *not* to take up arms against them.

Walker's black nationalism maintained that African Americans individually and collectively must take their destiny into their own hands if they are to achieve true liberation. "Your full glory and happiness," declared Walker, "shall never be fully consummated, but with the entire emancipation of your enslaved brethren all over the world."[10]

David Walker and other contributors to *Freedom's Journal* came down heavily on the colonization movement. Even after Samuel Cornish left the newspaper and Russwurm became the sole editor, a great amount of space was devoted to anti-colonizationist statements and articles. But to the surprise of the entire literate free black community, John Russwurm announced in the February 14, 1829, issue that he supported black self-determination in Africa as well as the Caribbean and looked to the day when an independent black nation would exist in West Africa. Shortly thereafter, Russwurm abandoned the paper and sailed for West Africa. He landed in Liberia in November 1829 where he remained for the rest of his life. John Russwurm's conversion to colonization was a shock to his friends and colleagues, but he was only the first of many African-American intellectuals who turned their back on the United States because of the way people of African descent were treated by the white citizens of the country.[11]

As a youth Alexander Crummell was exposed to another important vehicle for African-American intellectual expression, the national black conventions, which began to be held regularly beginning in 1830. The immediate cause for the calling of the first national black convention was the renewed enforcement of the notorious "black laws" by the state of Ohio. In 1804 and 1807 the Ohio legislature had passed several statutes placing severe restrictions on the legal rights of free blacks, and demanding that those who entered the state post a $500 bond as a guarantee of "good behavior." The laws were basically unenforced until 1829 when there was a severe economic downturn. Unemployed white workers in Cincinnati, feeling threatened by free black competition for fewer and fewer jobs, confronted African Americans on the streets, and demanded their freedom papers. If the black person could not produce a certificate or bond, he or she was told to get out of town or be run out. The confrontations escalated in August and white mobs formed and began physically attacking free black men, women, and children on the streets and in their homes. One free black man was killed and many suffered severe injuries; an exodus began and hundreds of African Americans from throughout Ohio fled to central and western Canada.[12]

Fearful that this type of repression would spread to Pennsylvania and other eastern states, Bishop Richard Allen and James Forten issued a call for a meeting of "leading colored men" to draw up contingency plans in case free blacks had to flee the United States in large numbers and become refugees in Canada.

The meeting was held in Philadelphia in September 1830, and forty delegates were in attendance representing all of the northern and midwestern states. The convention endorsed a proposal to send an agent to Canada to locate land for a free black settlement. Boston Crummell attended the national black convention in Philadelphia in 1831, and his son, Alexander, played a prominent role in both the national and state conventions held in the 1840s. The black convention movement provided an important intellectual forum for African-American intellectual and political leaders to debate and define positions on pressing issues facing the black population in the United States. Educated and eloquent African-American elites recognized their responsibility to utilize their skills and learning in charting the future for people of African descent in the increasingly hostile white-dominated society.[13]

The young Alexander Crummell learned that "knowledge is power" first-hand at the feet of his father, Boston Crummell, and his father's friends Samuel Cornish, John Russwurm, and Rev. Peter Williams, all of whom were at the center of the free black community's efforts to educate and uplift themselves and their brethren. Boston Crummell was so committed to Alexander's intellectual development that he not only hired private tutors but also enrolled his son at the Free African School No. 2 at a very young age. And because there were no secondary schools available for free blacks in New York City, Boston Crummell and several other parents opened the Canal Street High School in 1831 and hired white teachers to instruct the children in Latin, Greek, and other more advanced subjects.[14]

Among Alexander Crummell's classmates at the Free African School and Canal Street High School was Henry Highland Garnet, who later became a Presbyterian minister and one of the most militant African-American intellectual leaders in the nineteenth century. Although he was born on a slave plantation in Maryland, when he was nine years old, Henry and his family escaped slavery and settled in New York. During the summers Henry worked as a cabin boy on merchant ships, and in 1829, while he was at sea, slave catchers attempted to recapture his family. The Crummells lived next door to the Garnets and the ten-year-old Alexander witnessed the entire event. He recalled that when George Garnet, Henry's father, was confronted by the slave catchers at his front door, he made his escape through an open window. "Between the two houses was an alley about four feet wide; the only escape was to leap from the side window of the bed-room to my father's yard. How Mr. Garnet made this fearful leap, how he escaped breaking both neck and legs, is a mystery to me to this day, but he made the leap and escaped." Even Boston Crummell's "ill-tempered dog, the terror of the neighborhood" remained quiet throughout the incident. When young Henry Garnet returned later that summer, he was in a panic over the scattering of his family. Eventually, Henry obtained employment in the home of Captain Epenetus Smith on Long Island. Unfortunately, during his stay there Henry injured his leg in a sporting event, which made him a cripple for the rest of his life. Alexander Crummell commented that the injury and dispersion of his family had a noticeable effect on Henry's character. "The anguish of this family calamity gave birth to a giant soul! . . . The soberness which comes from trial, the seriousness which is the fruit of affliction, the melancholy and the reflection which spring from pain and suffering, for he was now a cripple, soon brought Garnet to the foot of the cross."[15]

In demonstrating their strong commitment to advanced study and higher education, Alexander Crummell, Henry Garnet, and a much-admired third classmate at the Free African School, Thomas J. Sidney, became involved in one of the most interesting and dangerous incidents generated by the new radical abolitionist movement. In the early 1830s free Africans were joined in their struggle against American slavery by radical white reformers, led by William Lloyd Garrison, publisher of *The Liberator* in Boston beginning in January 1831. Garrison, born in Massachusetts in 1805, had gained firsthand knowledge about the brutality associated with slavery when he went to Baltimore in the late 1820s to work for Benjamin Lundy's anti-slavery magazine, *The Genius of Universal Emancipation*. The opponents of American slavery had previously been supporting the "gradual manumission movement" that was important in bringing about the end of slavery in most of the northern states. But William Garrison, having witnessed the cruelty and inhumanity of the peculiar institution in Maryland, a slave state, decided to return to Boston and launch a radical abolitionist newspaper, *The Liberator.* Garrison militantly called for no compromise with slaveholders and denounced the practice of slavery as sinful, immoral, and anti-Christian. He wanted the immediate end of slavery and used newspapers, magazines, pamphlets, books, and most importantly, lecturers in his campaign to persuade the public of the evils of American slavery.[16]

The Dangerous Pursuit of Higher Learning

IN OCTOBER 1834 a notice appeared in Garrison's *Liberator* announcing that abolitionists in New England had started a secondary school in Canaan, New Hampshire, Noyes Academy, that would be open to "colored youth of good character on equal terms with whites of like character." In their idealism, Alexander Crummell, Henry Highland Garnet, and Thomas J. Sidney hoped that their successful matriculation and graduation from Noyes Academy would dispel the commonly held view of whites that African Americans were intellectually deficient and incapable of absorbing advanced learning. The demonstration of their individual intellectual abilities could be considered an important element in the overall vindication of the black race from the charge of mental inferiority.[17]

The three took a steamboat from New York City to Providence, Rhode Island, and were forced to sleep on the open decks. The remainder of the trip was equally unpleasant because they were not allowed inside the stagecoaches or inns or hotels along with paying white customers. Crummell later commented that "the sight of three black youths, in gentlemanly garb, traveling through New England was in *those days* a most unusual sight; it started not only surprise, but brought out universal sneers and ridicule." There were about forty white students at the school when they arrived and the new black students were well received. Unfortunately, the white citizens of Canaan were not so cordial and decided they did not want a "nigger school" in their community. On August 10, 1835, a white mob of over three hundred attacked the school, and brought over ninety oxen to drag the school building into the town commons. The black students were hidden in a nearby boardinghouse during the rampage, but they were later fired upon by the mob. Garnet, using a double-barreled shotgun, returned the fire, which was enough to drive off their attackers. The black students were told to get out of town, which they did within days, finally returning to New York City a month later.[18]

What was most astonishing was that this violent, dangerous incident in New Hampshire in no way dampened the youths' strong desire for learning and intellectual advancement. Only a few months later when they were informed that Beriah Green's Oneida Institute in Whitesboro, New York, was accepting black students, the three set off again and this time were able to enroll and remain at the institute for almost two years. During that time the young Crummell underwent a "religious conversion experience" and in 1838 with the support of his pastor, Peter Williams, declared his intention to seek ordination as a priest in the Episcopal church. Although his classical training at Oneida Institute had prepared him well for holy orders, Crummell always remained bitter over the fact that he was denied admission to the Episcopal Church's General Theological Seminary, located in his hometown, New York City, solely because of his race.

In his autobiographical work, *Jubilate,* Crummell devoted many pages to a discussion of his interactions with white Episcopal officials who were racist and discriminatory in the dealings with the young priest or those who were helpful and acted in his behalf. "I became a candidate for [Holy] Orders in 1839, and at once, under my Rector's direction, applied for admission to the General Theological Seminary in New York." Benjamin T. Onderdonk, seminary trustee and bishop of New York, did not want to alienate southern Episcopalians who had been generous toward the school and convinced the other board members to reject Crummell's petition for admission. Not satisfied with this outcome, Bishop B. T. Onderdonk and later his brother, Henry Onderdonk, bishop of Philadelphia, felt it necessary to summon and then humiliate the young Crummell in person. Following the trustees' debate over Crummell's petition, "Bishop [B. T.] Onderdonk sent for me; and then and there, in his study, set upon me with a violence and grossness that I have never since encountered, save one instance in Africa." In effect, Crummell was causing trouble by his request for admission and "the Bishop was determined that South Carolina should not be offended by the presence of a Negro in that Seminary" (8–9). Crummell was astounded that such abusive behavior came from a high church official and man of the cloth. White friends and supporters, most notably William Jay and John Jay, "the son and the grandson of the illustrious John Jay, the first Chief Justice of the United States," recognized the injustice of the trustees' decision and assisted Crummell in making his way to Boston, where he became a candidate for orders in 1840, and after studying with several prominent Episcopal clergymen, was ordained in St. Paul Church, Boston, in May 1842 (9).

After briefly serving two small black congregations in Providence with very little support or success, young Rev. Crummell applied for a position in a black Episcopal church in Philadelphia, and Bishop Henry U. Onderdonk, Benjamin's brother, tried to get the young deacon to agree to several humiliating demands. Crummell recalled the bishop's words verbatim fifty years later: "I cannot receive you into this Diocese unless you will promise that you will never apply for a seat in my Convention, for yourself or for any church you may raise in this city." This Crummell refused to do as a matter of principle. Vindictively, the bishop went to the Episcopal church's Pennsylvania Convention and got the members to accept a canon law "that no such church, or its minister, should be admitted to the Convention" (10). Although without official representation, Rev. Crummell worked with several black congregations in Philadelphia, but had little success overall. In his autobiography he attributed his failure to the hostility of the "reverend divines," who were insulting, rude, and offered little support or assistance.

It should be noted that Alexander Crummell was unsuccessful in Providence and Philadelphia not merely because of the hostility of the racist Episcopal church officials who refused to allow African Americans to participate in denominational activities as equals, but also because of the young pastor's relations with his black parishioners. It appears that Rev. Crummell could not throw himself into the daily activities of a parish priest, such as tending to the needs of his communicants and raising funds for programs and improvements in the church. Indeed, there were numerous reports to church officials from parishioners about their dissatisfaction with their minister, and it is very likely that the feeling was mutual. In 1845 Crummell returned to New York City and became rector of the Church of the Messiah, whose congregation was made up of mostly poor black servants. This was another unsuccessful experience in the Episcopal pastorate. In one of the few comments about those years, Crummell suggested that "it would be useless as well as tiresome to enter into the particulars concerning my work in New York," for it would merely be "a repetition of the misfortunes of Providence and Philadelphia" (10).[19]

Although he was having all kinds of problems with his Episcopal superiors and members of his church, Rev. Crummell's reputation as a scholar and intellectual was growing and this served him well in the movements to gain civil rights for free blacks in the northern states. When the New York State Colored Convention met in Albany, in September 1840, Crummell was only twenty-one years old. Not only was he in attendance, but young Rev. Crummell drafted the convention's official address to the New York state legislature demanding equal rights for African-American citizens, including the right to vote. Crummell also served on the committee that drew up a petition asserting the right of suffrage for all citizens without special property qualifications. More importantly, Crummell sided with the free black leaders from New York who opposed William Whipper and other black Philadelphians' suggestion that the creation of all-black institutions and societies was a form of "self-segregation" and directly contradicted the demand to become fully integrated into American society. Crummell fully supported the convention's resolution condemning racial discrimination, but also endorsed the position that free blacks must work together for racial uplift. This included the development of black-controlled institutions that would be geared toward the social, economic, and political advancement of free and enslaved African Americans in the United States.[20]

Alexander Crummell and his close friend Henry Highland Garnet made public statements that clearly demonstrated their commitment to the African American cultural value of self-determination—the belief that African Americans must take primary responsibility for their survival and advancement in American society. However, when Garnet issued public statements calling for massive slave uprisings and the violent overthrow of the southern slave regime, Garnet and Crummell parted company. When Henry Garnet completed his studies at Oneida Institute, he settled in Troy, New York, and studied privately for the Presbyterian ministry. In 1842 he was licensed to preach and became pastor of the Liberty Street Presbyterian Church, the city's only black Presbyterian congregation.[21] In the late 1830s Rev. Garnet had been active in William Lloyd Garrison's American Anti-Slavery Society, but when a split developed within the organization between those abolitionists who wanted only to use education, propaganda, and moral suasion to bring about the end of slavery and those who wished to enter politics and launch a third political party committed to abolitionism, Garnet sided with the latter group. At a convention held in Albany, New York, in April 1840, politically minded abolitionists organized the Liberty Party. In May 1840 at the annual meeting of the American Anti-Slavery Society, held in New York City, the political abolitionists, led by Salmon P. Chase, James Birney, and Theodore Weld, walked out when it became clear there would be no support for the Liberty Party or any political action. The dissidents reconvened three days later and launched the American and Foreign Anti-Slavery Society, which was committed to political strategies to bring about the end of American slavery. Rev. Garnet not only joined the new organization, but he also became one of the leading African-American spokespersons for the Liberty Party, traveling around New York state speaking in support of the party's candidates.[22]

The launching of the Liberty Party caused a second split within the ranks of the black abolitionists. Not only were they divided over the issue of all-black versus integrated organizations, but some remained Garrisonians, while others, such as Henry Highland Garnet, became allied with the new political abolitionist camp. The young Frederick Douglass was clearly the most prominent black abolitionist associated with the Garrisonians. Born a slave in Tuckahoe, Maryland, Douglass was sent by his owner to Baltimore in 1826 to work as a houseboy. Thirteen years later, with the help of Anna Murray, a free black, Douglass escaped slavery, later marrying Murray and settling in New Bedford, Massachusetts, where he soon became involved in William Lloyd Garrison's abolitionist campaigns. Because of his exceptional speaking ability (and the fact that he was tall, dark, and handsome), Douglass almost immediately became a star in the radical anti-slavery firmament.[23]

The next meeting of the national black convention was held in Buffalo, New York, but the debate over whether or not to support the Liberty Party was overshadowed by the delegates' response to Rev. Henry Highland Garnet's "Address to the Slaves of the United States." Although it is unclear when and exactly why Rev. Garnet shifted his ideological position, the speech he gave at the 1843 black convention was the most militant (some said radical) anti-slavery statement put forward by an African-American intellectual leader since the publication of *Walker's Appeal* in 1829. Garnet called on enslaved African Americans to violently resist their oppression. "The diabolical injustice by which your liberties are cloven down neither God, nor angels, or just men command you to suffer for a single moment," he declared; "therefore, it is your solemn and imperative duty to use every means, both moral, intellectual, and physical that promises success." In one of the most famous passages in nineteenth-century African-American thought, Garnet proclaimed the slaves' moral obligation to resist.

> Brethren arise, arise! Strike for your lives and liberties. Now is the day and the hour. Let every slave throughout the land do this, and the days of slavery are numbered. You cannot be more oppressed than you have been—you cannot suffer greater cruelties than you have already. *Rather die free men than live to be slaves.* . . . Let your motto be resistance! *resistance!* RESISTANCE! No oppressed people have secured

their liberty without resistance. What kind of resistance you had better make, you must decide by the circumstances that surround you, and according to the suggestion of expediency.[24]

Rev. Garnet's address caused an uproar at the Buffalo convention. While some delegates believed that such a statement was long overdue, others found it incendiary and ill-timed. Frederick Douglass felt that should this message get to the slaves it could lead to widespread bloodshed, and following Douglass's advice, the convention refused to endorse Garnet's statement.[25]

Although Alexander Crummell was a longtime friend of Henry Garnet, he did not attend the 1843 national black convention, and there is no evidence that he endorsed Garnet's militant call for slave insurrection. Crummell did attend the 1847 black convention held in Troy, where Garnet delivered a similar "Address to the Slaves," but it was again rejected by the delegates and Crummell appears to have sided with the majority. Perhaps Crummell was unwilling to take sides publicly in the debate between Garnet and Douglass because he felt that this was an issue that former slaves would know better. Crummell had never been a slave; indeed, he had never even visited the slave states, and thus he had no firsthand knowledge about the advisability or possibility of widespread slave rebellion. What Crummell did know on the basis of his experiences was that free blacks needed access to higher education to develop their intellectual abilities. In a "Treatise on Education" written in 1844 and in a report he wrote for the Committee on Education at the 1847 national black convention, Crummell argued that the failure to allow African Americans access to education would not only perpetuate their ignorance and intellectual stagnation, but force them to languish in the throes of barbarous superstition where they would remain unresponsive to enlightened moral principles. Crummell believed that "the objects of the intellect are unlimited," and that all human beings are capable of grasping the right moral principles. As far as the African Americans were concerned, Rev. Crummell admitted that although there had been physical and spiritual development over the previous years, they "are still lacking intelligence, scholarship, and science." And given the fact that African Americans were denied admission to the vast majority of white institutions of higher education, Crummell's report to the black convention in 1847 called for the opening of a black college.[26]

In light of the debate among black abolitionists over the advisability of all-black institutions, Crummell's recommendations were significant for identifying his particular position in this ongoing ideological debate. The committee's report was accepted by the majority of the delegates at the 1847 black convention primarily because, as was the case in 1843, the Philadelphia integrationists decided to boycott the meeting. Alexander Crummell's advocacy of black-controlled institutions aimed at African-American advancement would continue throughout his life and made him the leading ideological spokesperson for the self-determinist cultural values that were embraced by the African-American masses and elites in the last quarter of the nineteenth century.

From as early as 1845 there is evidence that Alexander Crummell was interested in advancing his education by study at an English university. In 1847 when it was suggested by several Episcopal clergymen that he travel to England to raise money for his Church of the Messiah, he decided to pursue that option. When Crummell and his family arrived in England early in 1848, he was merely the latest in a long and distinguished line of African-American intellectuals and orators who lectured and studied in Europe. During the 1840s and 1850s among the many African Americans on the British anti-slavery lecture circuit were Frederick Douglass, Henry Highland Garnet, Charles Lenox Remond, William and Ellen Craft, Samuel Ringgold Ward, James McCune Smith, and Martin R. Delany. These black abolitionists visited the British Isles to raise funds and solidify ties between the American and British movements. Alexander Crummell, however, was one of only a handful of African-American visitors to enroll in a British university and take a degree.[27]

Throughout 1848 and most of 1849, Rev. Crummell lectured before British audiences on the horrors of the institution of slavery and the need to support the anti-slavery movement in the United States. He solicited funds for his church, and by the summer of 1848 he was also seeking contributions to support his studies at an British university. The young minister spoke in Birmingham, Liverpool, Bath, Manchester, as well as London, and visited various other parts of the British Isles with his family. It is believed that in 1841 Alexander Crummell married his wife, Sarah, when he was twenty-two and she was eighteen. Their first child died young, but two boys, Alexander Jr. and Sydney, survived and accompanied them to England. A daughter, Frances, was born in England on June 18, 1849; but the younger son, Alexander, died in 1851 after swallowing a button. A second daughter, Sophia, was born later that year, and a third, Dillwinna, was born in 1853. These were all difficult pregnancies for Sarah Crummell, who suffered serious health problems throughout her life. Sarah's poor health meant that there were several pregnancies that she was unable to take to term.[28]

In the fall of 1849 Crummell enrolled in Queen's College, Cambridge University. For Crummell this was a dream come true, for he believed that "no seat of learning in the world has done more, for human liberty and human well-being, than this institution [Cambridge]." Before beginning his university studies, Rev. Crummell received tutoring in Latin and Greek. Although he had studied classical languages at Oneida Institute, it was mainly religious texts; he needed to become familiar with the works of Aristotle, Plato, Horace, and the

other secular writers. At Cambridge an undergraduate student had to take a series of examinations in specific subjects in order to qualify for a degree. Upon
entrance Crummell passed the university examination, and then he sat for examinations in several other subjects at the "ordinary," or "honors," level.
Crummell studied Old Testament history, the New Testament in original
Greek, Euclidian mathematics, moral philosophy, and several authors in Latin
and Greek, including Plato, Tacitus, and Horace. He took his final examinations in January 1853, but did not pass at a high enough level, so he took them
again in February and qualified for the BA degree.[29]

During his years of study at Cambridge, Crummell continued to travel
throughout England lecturing and soliciting funds for the Church of the Messiah. What is significant is that the subject matter of his talks moved beyond the
campaign to abolish slavery in the United States to encompass Pan-African issues and "black international unity." For example, in a speech before the Ladies'
Negro Educational Society, a British group dedicated to the support of educational programs for African Americans in the West Indies, Crummell spoke of
the importance of solidarity among all African peoples, and the need "to raise
up the great African family, in its several sections to civilization and enlightenment." He also began to speak more and more about the need to "bring the
gifts of civilization to Africa." "There is no spot, of all this wide world, to which
my heart travels with more ardent affection than Africa," Crummell declared in
1851, right before he announced his decision to become a missionary to
Liberia. "Although born in the United States . . . I should think myself privileged [to spend] . . . the small measure of [my] ability in efforts in the salvation
of those to whom I am connected by descent in that benighted land."[30]

As early as September 1851, Crummell expressed to his close friends the
likelihood that he would not return to the United States once he had completed his studies. The reasons he gave included his poor health (he had been
under a doctor's care virtually the entire time he was in England), and the need
to live in a warmer climate, and his fear that he would be unable to find a suitable position that would allow him to support his large family. It is also likely
that Crummell was aware of the deteriorating social and economic circumstances for free blacks in the United States during the early 1850s. The increasing threats to withdraw from the union being made by leaders from the
slaveholding states forced northern politicians to acquiesce to the southerners'
demands for greater protection of the slaveowning interests. When the issue
came to a head in 1850, a compromise was worked out by Senator Henry Clay
of Kentucky that allowed for a balance in representation from the slave and
nonslave states in the U.S. Congress and temporarily doused the flames of suc-
cession being fanned by southern firebrands. The Compromise of 1850 also included a new Fugitive Slave Law, which called upon law enforcement officials
in the so-called free states to assist slave catchers in capturing and returning

runaway slaves to their legal owners; anyone caught assisting fugitives was liable to fine and imprisonment for up to six months. The legislation caused fear and in some instances panic among free blacks in the North, and following the recapture of the first fugitive slave under the new legislation in September 1850, there was a mass black exodus from Pittsburgh, Cleveland, and Boston to Canada by former slaves and their families.[31]

A surprising development was the fact that Frederick Douglass, who had strongly opposed Rev. Henry Highland Garnet's call in 1843 and 1847 for violent insurrection by the slaves to bring down the slave regime, now called for armed self-defense by former slaves threatened by slave catchers. "We must be prepared should this law be put into operation," Douglass exclaimed to large crowd at Faneuil Hall in October 1850, to see "the streets of Boston running with blood" (preferably the blood of slave catchers). At the same time, there was renewed interest on the part of free blacks in pursuing the possibility of a mass emigration to West Africa, particularly Liberia. The issue of free black emigration dominated several black state conventions held in 1853 and a National Emigration Convention was convened in Cleveland in September 1854, after the national black convention held in Rochester, New York, the month before failed to consider seriously the emigrationist alternative for oppressed African Americans in the United States.[32]

One of the reasons Alexander Crummell gave for not wanting to return to the United States following his graduation from Cambridge University was the violence and demagoguery of the white majority. "My hopes are not bright ones even for the white men and their children in America controlled as [they] are by an unscrupulous and boisterous Democracy, which neither fears God, nor regards man; and by a demagogic priesthood, who devote their best energies in maintaining the sanctity of slavery and the infallibility of the state." But he was also unsure about going to Liberia. From his earliest days in the home of his father, Boston Crummell, Alexander had imbibed anti-colonizationist sentiments, and the idea of emigrating to Liberia would be anathema to many of his radical abolitionist friends in the United States. But by 1853 circumstances had changed. Liberia had been an independent nation for over five years, and Rev. Crummell had been in touch with Episcopal church officials in the United States who were interested in founding a college there. It appears that what finally convinced Crummell to become an Episcopal missionary was a meeting he had in England with the new president of Liberia, Joseph J. Roberts, who emphasized the great influence a man of his education and background could command in the shaping of the new black nation.[33]

Black Missionary in Liberia

WHEN REV. ALEXANDER CRUMMELL and his family arrived in Monrovia, Liberia, in August 1853 there were only about eight thousand citizens who had been born in the United States and had emigrated to the new republic over the previous thirty years. For the first twenty-five years of settlement, white agents for the American Colonization Society ran the colony's affairs. The ACS was able to gain funds from the U.S. government to purchase lands from the native peoples. Unfortunately, the Africans did not realize that they were "selling" the land to the settlers; the natives thought they were giving the newcomers the right to use the lands along with the indigenous people in the area. This cultural misunderstanding led to serious and deadly conflicts between the settlers and the natives. As groups of settlers moved away from the Atlantic coastline into the interior, the likelihood of conflict with native peoples increased and on several occasions the settler communities on the frontier were almost completely wiped out. In the case of the Vai and Dei peoples, who used only spears and arrows to assert their claims to the land, they were subdued and pushed aside by settlers who used guns and cannons. But the Gola, Kru, and Grebo peoples had been given guns and other modern weapons by European slave traders, and the African-American settlers were only able to establish their authority after many years of armed conflict that resulted in great loss of life and property.[34]

In many ways the conditions and circumstances for the African-American settlers, or Americo-Liberians as they came to be known, resembled that of the European colonizers in North and South America and southern Africa in their relations with native peoples. Indeed, this very point was made by the black opponents of African emigration and the colonization movement in the United States. Alexander Crummell addressed this criticism by pointing out that these settlers were not really "foreigners" but African descendants who were returning to the "land of their forefathers." Rev. Crummell made the point that "I have come back to within a day's journey of the very spot whence my own father was stolen in his boyhood and where my poor ancestors lived from time immemorial. Who has a better right to emigrate to Africa than me?" The second reason Crummell emphasized in justifying African-American emigration was to aid in bringing about the end of slave trading along the west African coast. In the 1840s and 1850s slave trading was still actively pursued, even after most European governments banned participation in the inhuman practice by its citizens. Americo-Liberians worked closely with the British and American navies in destroying "slave factories" where captives were kept until they were loaded onto slave ships. The Liberians also launched military expeditions against native Africans in the interior who raided villages and captured men, women, and children to sell into slavery. For Crummell this was a strong moral argument for African-American emigration.[35]

But what was most troubling in the nature of the interactions between settlers and native Africans was the disdain and condescension that the New World men and women exhibited toward the indigenous people. The Westerners viewed the natives as primitives and savages whose cultural practices they considered "uncivilized." Within a few years following the American settlement, a well-delineated class structure developed in the colony with Americo-Liberians of mixed racial heritage perched at the top. They used their Christian religion, Western dress, and English language to set themselves apart from the native population as well as the sizable number of recaptured Africans who had been taken from slave ships stopped on the open seas and brought to the American colony. This group became known as the Congoes and remained at the bottom of the Americo-Liberian social structure. By the early 1840s the Americo-Liberians from the United States and the West Indies controlled the governmental and political institutions in the colony and when the agents of the American Colonization Society were unsuccessful in gaining protection of their commercial rights from challenges by British traders from the neighboring colony of Sierra Leone, they declared their independence in 1847. Liberia thus became the first independent black republic in Africa.[36]

Rev. Crummell would become intimately involved in the social, economic, and political relationships that were developing among the various classes and groups in the new Liberian nation, and the positions he took on the various conflicts that arose involved matters of principle that would define his intellectual legacy in both Liberia and the United States. Crummell's concern about institution building, his belief in the unity of all African peoples, his appreciation for the cultural values and practices of the uneducated black masses began with his upbringing in the United States. His experiences in Africa crystallized these beliefs and values so that they became the guiding principles in the formulation of his strategies and programs for African and African-American advancement.

As a missionary, Rev. Crummell's primary responsibility was supposed to be teaching in the Episcopal missions in Liberia. However, upon his arrival he set about the task not merely of establishing in Monrovia a mission school, but also a church. There were already several Episcopal churches in the settlement, but Crummell was convinced that another was needed. At first, he received the support of Rev. John Payne, the missionary bishop for the Episcopal church in Liberia, but within a year several conflicts arose between Rev. Crummell and Bishop Payne over Crummell's handling of the finances for the new Trinity Church. Relations between the two soon became strained.[37]

There was a dispute over the salary that Rev. Crummell was to receive from the Episcopal Foreign Mission Committee, located in the United States and a branch of the Episcopal church. Bishop Payne often castigated Crummell for overdrawing his church accounts and his failure to supply annual financial records to church authorities. But these were only the more obvious areas of conflict between the two churchmen. At various points Alexander Crummell, a very proud and well-educated black man, made it clear that he resented having to take orders from a white person in a black-controlled nation. For his part Bishop Payne felt threatened by Rev. Crummell's education and the reports he received that Crummell wanted to be the next missionary bishop in Liberia.

In March 1857 when the Foreign Missions Committee of the church refused to raise his annual salary, Crummell resigned from his position. For several months, however, he continued to work with the various missions at St. Paul's River and asked for no compensation because he had already made certain commitments to the parishioners. Convinced that Rev. Crummell was truly devoted to his missionary work, Bishop Payne offered him a teaching position at Mount Vaughn High School in Cape Palmas at his old salary. Unlike Monrovia where many of his communicants were from the New World, Cape Palmas was in the interior and the boys attending the secondary school were native-born Africans. This was an extremely important experience for Crummell because it convinced him that the native Africans had important gifts to contribute to the civilizing process and economic advancement of African peoples. Rev. Crummell continued to work with the various missionary churches and schools, but it was the intimate association with Africans at Cape Palmas that supported his ideological positions in subsequent political debates with Liberian public officials.[38]

Meanwhile, Crummell was kept apprised of the increasingly volatile conditions in the United States following John Brown's raid on the arsenal at Harpers Ferry in 1859, the complicated presidential election campaign in 1860, and subsequent withdrawal from the union by several southern states following Republican Abraham Lincoln's election victory in November. Rev. Crummell was also aware of increasing interest among free blacks in emigration to Liberia as conditions for them went from bad to worse. He had been contacted by several organizations and offered the opportunity to lecture on the benefits of emigration to the free black population. The deciding factor in his decision to return to the United States, however, was the deteriorating health conditions of his aged parents. In the spring of 1861 Crummell and his family embarked for the United States, arriving in April 1861 at the onset of the Civil War. Greeted in New York City by Rev. Henry Highland Garnet and other friends, he first attended to his parents. Then, leaving his wife to take care of the family in New York City, Crummell embarked on a wide-ranging speaking tour sponsored by the New York Colonization Society and other African emigrationist groups. He traveled to Philadelphia, Washington, Baltimore, Chicago, Toledo, Detroit, and even Canada promoting Liberian emigration and his first book, *The Future of Africa,* which was published early in 1862.[39]

The book contained essays and addresses that Rev. Crummell had delivered during his time in Liberia. The overriding theme stressed in the ten essays was race vindication. In the preface Crummell declared that "the Author feels that they [the essays] are somewhat fitted to two important ends; namely, first, to show that the children of Africa have been called, in Divine providence, to meet the demands of civilization, of commerce, and of nationality; and second, that they are beginning, at last, to grapple with the problems which pertain to responsible manhood, to the great work of civilization, to the duties and requirements of national life, and to the solemn responsibility of establishing the Christian faith amid the rude forms of paganism."[40]

During his stay in the United States, Rev. Crummell was joined in these Liberian recruitment efforts by Edward Wilmot Blyden, who, though born in St. Thomas in the West Indies in 1832, came to Liberia 1850 through the support of the New York Colonization Society. Blyden journeyed to the United States specifically to have access to secondary training but he found all educational doors closed to him because of his race; so he took up the colonizationists' offer to support his education at Alexander High School in Monrovia. Blyden was an outstanding student, and immediately upon graduation in 1856 began publishing the *Liberia Herald,* the nation's only newspaper. After several years of study with private tutors, Blyden was ordained as a Presbyterian minister. In February 1861 Rev. Blyden was sent by the Liberian government to England to raise money and support from philanthropists and humanitarians, among them former British Prime Minister William Gladstone, for the opening of Liberia College. Blyden joined Crummell in the United States in June 1861 and both men traveled throughout the eastern part of the country trying to raise funds for Liberia College and support for African emigration. Rev. Blyden returned to Liberia later that year, but in April 1862 the Liberian government appointed him and Rev. Crummell "commissioners for the Government and people of Liberia" for the purpose of recruiting African American emigrants to Liberia, and he was back in the United States by May 1862.[41]

Initially, Crummell and Blyden were enthusiastically embraced by African Americans. However, as the circumstances for the Union forces deteriorated and it became a military necessity for President Abraham Lincoln to issue the preliminary Emancipation Proclamation in September 1862, freeing all the slaves in the rebelling states, enthusiasm for emigration schemes decreased significantly as thousands of African Americans were recruited as soldiers in the Union Army. Crummell returned to Liberia in January 1863, leaving two of his daughters enrolled in the preparatory department at Oberlin College. Although at that time the future status of the African population in the United States was unclear, Crummell understood that the opening of the first institution of higher education in a black-controlled nation would be important for the vindication of the race from the charge of innate intellectual inferiority. Crummell viewed his life and educational experiences as a personal repudiation of that charge against African peoples, and he hoped that Liberia College would become the vehicle for the dissemination of the treasures of civilization on the African continent.

Mulattoes versus Pure Negroes at Liberia College

AFRICAN-AMERICAN intellectuals were not only preoccupied with debunking the theories and ideas about black inferiority, they also tried to place their learning and intellectual prowess in service to the race. Alexander Crummell had succeeded in demonstrating his intellectual superiority to the vast majority of Europeans and European Americans through his mental discipline and university training. He had come to Liberia as a missionary to bring the advantages of "civilization" to "barbaric" Africans who were still caught up in paganism. However, Crummell's positive interactions with the native Africans at Cape Palmas, as well as his negative encounters with the Americo-Liberian mulatto elite, convinced him that the cultural practices and moral beliefs of the indigenous African peoples would be important to the development of a strong black civilization. The native African's "love of trade" as exhibited in the marketplaces that were the center of commercial activity in every large settlement demonstrated the desire for economic advancement and self-sufficiency. These commercial values would be essential for the development of a powerful black nation-state. As we shall see, in the 1860s Rev. Crummell became embroiled in several bitter conflicts with the Americo-Liberian leaders who wanted to exclude the indigenous peoples from citizenship and direct access to the political and economic institutions being developed within the society.[42]

The individual intellectual's attitude toward the cultural beliefs and practices of the African and African-American masses—southern peasants, sharecroppers, domestic servants, skilled and unskilled laborers—emerges as an extremely important issue in the development of the African-American intellectual tradition. The issue came to involve critical matters of principle; thus it is important to understand the dialectical relationship between the personal experiences of the intellectuals and their ideological positions. Alexander Crummell laid the foundations for the development of the African-American intelligentsia in the United States and his experiences in Africa demonstrate the impact his direct contact with the African masses and "mulatto elites" had upon his ideas and perceptions. Rev. Crummell came to Liberia intending to bring the gift of civilization to the primitive and backward natives. But he felt compelled to change these elitist, Western notions in favor of a Pan-African vision that recognized the strengths of indigenous African cultural beliefs and practices.

Rev. Crummell's experiences teaching native Africans at the Mount Vaughn High School in Cape Palmas between 1857 and 1861 helped determine his position in the acrimonious dispute over the site for the new college. Authorized by legislation in 1851, the Liberia College was not opened until January 1863 due to differences among the Americo-Liberian officials about where the college was to be located. As one of the most highly educated members of the community, Crummell was immediately offered a professorship. Rev. Crummell and his "pure Negro" colleague, Rev. Edward Blyden, who also accepted a professorship, favored a more inland site for the school so that native Africans would have greater access to the institution. Former Liberian President J. J. Roberts was appointed president of the college, and he and other mixed-blood Americo-Liberians on the college's executive committee not only wanted the school located in Monrovia, the capital, but they also wanted enrollment limited to the children of the Americo-Liberian elite. They wanted no native Africans at all at the college and they got their way.[43]

For Alexander Crummell, the decisions made by President Roberts and the executive committee reflected a sinister aspect of Liberian life and society. If Liberia was to develop as strong black nation, it would have to extend the fruits of civilization to the native Africans. However, the Americo-Liberians opposed any attempt to integrate the natives into the society and viewed African Americans' lighter skin color and admixture of white blood as signs of their cultural superiority. Moreover, the "mulatto clique" looked down upon and distanced themselves from the pure-Negro Americo-Liberians, many of whom advocated closer relations with the Africans. As a result, the college was opened in Monrovia and the student body remained small (never more than thirty students) because of the narrow-mindedness of the president and college officials.

Throughout his three and one-half years at Liberia College Crummell felt he was being tormented by the decisions of the president and the executive committee, backed by the white Episcopal Board of Trustees located in Boston, because he was a "pure Negro" and proud of it. Rev. Crummell was the only faculty member with university training, and yet every effort was made to undermine his effectiveness by making additional demands on his time, while paying him the same salary he received as a missionary. In a series of letters to the Board of Trustees Crummell complained about the salary and the fact that whenever he was unable to attend his classes, due to either ill health (which was too frequent) or foul weather and impassable roads during the rainy season, President Roberts made deductions from his already meager salary. Even with funds from his ministerial duties, Crummell's extreme financial state meant that he was unable to support his two daughters enrolled at Oberlin College in Ohio. In March 1865 he received a letter from the girls, aged four-

teen and sixteen, asking him to come and get them. Although the president
and executive committee opposed granting him a leave of absence because this
meant more work for them, Crummell left Liberia to retrieve his daughters in
May 1865, and was gone for almost six months.[44]

President Roberts and the executive committee filed formal charges
against Rev. Crummell in April 1866 for failure to perform his professorial duties. At a meeting of the faculty held subsequently, Crummell refused to tem-
per his criticisms of President Roberts and the mulattoes running the college.
He defended his teaching record, and denounced the anti-black attitudes and
actions of the college administration. Both he and Rev. Blyden were victimized
because they were pure Negroes, "and as Negroes, [we were] determined to
uphold the honor of the race against the efforts and intrigues of some who
[had] no confidence in the African, and whose malignity ever [was] at work in
Liberia to humble and disgrace *black men.*" The college officials were of the
opinion that "the true black man is inferior, and can't do anything." It was understandable that he would be the object of prejudice and discrimination at the
hands of white Americans, but even in this black-controlled nation he felt pursued "by a filthy class . . . who hate the Negro more intensely that any slave-
dealer at the South ever did—men whose whole life has been spent crushing
out black men." Eventually, Rev. Crummell made it clear to the Board of
Trustees that he would resign his position if J. J. Roberts was to remain as college president. On July 11, 1866, the board informed Rev. Crummell that his
services were no longer needed; he remained attached to the institution without compensation until November of that year.[45]

With the loss of his college position Crummell became more dependent on
his ministerial duties as a source of income. Unfortunately, Crummell's participation in an abortive attempt to create an independent Liberian church in-
curred the wrath of Missionary Bishop John Payne, who already felt threatened
by Rev. Crummell's earlier activities. Eli Stokes, a black Methodist minister in
Monrovia, launched a campaign in the early 1850s to create an interdenomina-
tional union among Christians in Liberia. Appealing to the nationalistic feelings of the Americo-Liberians, Rev. Stokes denounced the continuing control
exercised over Liberian religious affairs by white clergymen. Initially, Crummell
rejected the plans advocated by Rev. Stokes and favored black autonomy within
larger white-controlled Christian denominations, such as the Episcopal or
Presbyterian churches. As a black Episcopalian priest, Alexander Crummell recognized the value of the traditions, religious order, organization, and the financial resources available within the denomination to which African and
African-American members had access in bringing about the advancement and
"civilization" to African peoples.[46]

By the early 1860s, however, following numerous conflicts with the white
missionary bishop for the Episcopal church, Rev. Crummell had changed his

mind and in 1864 he signed a letter, written by black Liberian clergymen, denouncing what they considered was overtly racist behavior. Bishop John Payne
was accused of being an apologist for slavery and slaveholders, and in his interactions with black religious people, often tried to convey to them the "idea of
[their] personal inferiority." "We came to this country hoping to find *one* spot
on earth where an American black man could entertain feelings of self-
respect. . . . It is our right in this land . . . ecclesiastically, as well as politically,"
the black ministers declared, "we cannot yield it." The Foreign Mission Committee did not respond to the accusation hurled at Bishop Payne, and in his annual report for 1864, the bishop took the opportunity to attack Crummell for
failing to carry out his ministerial duties at St. Peter's Church in Caldwell
where he had been assigned as rector in 1863 upon his return from the United
States.[47]

While Rev. Crummell was involved in the disputes with Roberts and the
mulatto clique at Liberia College, Bishop Payne decided in September 1864 to
move against Crummell's ministerial position and appointed a mulatto, Rev.
Alfred Russell, to the pulpit at St. Peter's. Rev. Crummell fought back, however, and organized his parishioners to reject the appointment of the new rector. In letters to the Foreign Mission Committee Crummell defended his
record at St. Peter's, describing the advantages he had brought to the congregation, which had once driven him from the pulpit because of the vehemence
of his denunciations of their drinking and carousing. The committee nonetheless went along with the bishop and reassigned Crummell to a remote missionary station in Crozerville, Liberia. Although Crummell agreed to obey the
order, he also detailed the hardships that such a move would have on him and
his family, for which the committee would be responsible. The committee relented and allowed Crummell to remain at St. Peter's in Caldwell, but Bishop
Payne continued his attacks, this time with new ammunition supplied by
Crummell's son, Sydney.[48]

Despite Alexander Crummell's attempts to provide the best possible social
and educational opportunities for his son by sending him to England to study,
Sydney refused to follow the righteous path laid out by his stern and autocratic,
though generous, father. Upon his return to Liberia in 1864, Rev. Crummell
discovered that Sydney had an alcohol problem and he and his drinking buddies provided a bad example for the young people in his parish and school. The
reverend was forced to ask Sydney to leave his home. Unable to find and keep
work, Sydney returned fourteen months later, the prodigal son begging his father's forgiveness. Crummell took him back and gave him a position as a
teacher in the church's school. Within months rumors reached the reverend
not only that Sydney was drinking again, but that he was giving liquor to the
children in the school. Rev. Crummell was outraged and confronted the
drunken Sydney; he dismissed him from his position.

Sydney turned on his father, denouncing him and his educational enterprise. He even tried to get the parishioners to withdraw their children from the
school. When this failed, Sydney then wrote a vicious letter of denunciation to
Rev. Crummell's main antagonist, Bishop John Payne, accusing his father of
tyrannical behavior with members of the family, while denying them sufficient
funds for food and clothing. Rev. Crummell was said to have publicly humiliated his children, whipping them in the streets for some minor offense. And although the charge was not included in the letter, rumors circulated that Rev.
Crummell was a wife-beater. All these charges Crummell vehemently denied,
but the bishop immediately turned the letter over to Episcopal priest Alfred
Russell, who wanted Crummell's position. Rev. Russell took the issue to the
Liberian government and a grand jury investigation was held. Numerous
Liberian friends and acquaintances of Crummell subsequently submitted documents and petitions attesting to the reverend's fine character and disputing the
vile inaccuracies presented in Sydney's letter. When one of Crummell's daughters appeared before the jury and denied all the charges in Sydney's letter (Mrs.
Crummell did not testify since the wife-beating charge was not included in the
letter), the indictment and charges were thrown out by the court, but the entire affair was a scandal of major proportions for which Crummell blamed
Bishop Payne, whom he denounced to Episcopal authorities as a racist and
liar.[49]

Sydney Crummell eventually recanted the accusations he made against his
father, and the two came to a reconciliation. Ultimately, it was Sydney's later
imprisonment by ambitious mulatto politicians that led to Alexander Crummell's ultimate decision to leave Liberia altogether. In 1868 and 1869 Rev.
Crummell returned to his ministerial work at St. Peter's in Caldwell and his
missionary activities in the interior. His work with the native Africans made
these the most fulfilling years during his entire sojourn in Liberia. Unfortunately, political turmoil soon engulfed Liberia and Crummell was eventually
forced to flee for his life. Throughout his nineteen years in Liberia Rev. Crummell had been offered numerous political positions, all of which he refused.
However, Crummell was closely associated with the "black faction" in Liberian
politics and when that group was violently removed from power, Rev. Crummell's life was threatened, even though he was not a political official.

In the presidential elections of 1870, Edward Roye, a pure-Negro
Americo-Liberian and associate of Rev. Crummell, was elected president. During his early months in office, Roye went to England to negotiate a $500,000
loan for the government, but the terms for interest and the repayment schedule were seriously disadvantageous to Liberia. The mulatto-controlled Liberian
Senate objected to the terms of the loan and accused President Roye of impropriety in the matter. Under the terms of a referendum held in 1869, Roye was
to serve as president for four years. However, the Liberian Senate refused to al-

low the amendment of the constitution, and a violent political struggle ensued.[50]

At the outset in April 1871, Alexander Crummell remained above the political fracas intellectually and personally, even taking a side trip to Freetown, Sierra Leone, where he visited an old university acquaintance. But by late August 1871, through members of his congregation and his own family, Rev. Crummell was quickly drawn into the now violent struggle for political power between the True Whig (pure-Negro Americo-Liberians) and the Republicans (mulatto Americo-Liberians). Former President J. J. Roberts returned to politics to lead the mulatto faction during the crisis, and the battles that were fought at Liberia College with Edward Blyden and Alexander Crummell were extended to the Liberian government. The murder of Samuel Finley, the Liberian postmaster in Monrovia and a black political appointee of President Edward Roye, sparked a political reversal and change in the control of the government. The True Whigs were disunited in their response because one of the accusations hurled by mulatto Republicans at the Negro government was that Rev. Edward Blyden, the secretary of state, had committed adultery with President Roye's wife. The disunity and indecision among the True Whigs allowed Republicans to succeed in their efforts to remove Roye from the presidency, and incite mob action. Ultimately, Blyden and Crummell were forced to flee for their lives.[51]

Alexander Crummell was a very moralistic person, and his experiences over the years on three continents supported a strong Christian value system that had as one of its most fundamental principles, "Thou shalt not covet they neighbor's wife." Rev. Crummell believed the rumors and charges, even though Rev. Blyden denied them all. Meanwhile, the mulatto-inspired black mobs began attacking the black members of Roye's government, including Edward Blyden, who fled to Sierra Leone, and later Sydney Crummell, who was appointed acting secretary of state. Then the black mobs moved on to others who were friends and associates of President Roye, and Alexander Crummell finally came to the conclusion that he would have to leave as well.

Fully reconciled with his son, after Sydney penned letters of recantation about his earlier characterizations of his father, Rev. Crummell made arrangements for him to store and look after his books and personal papers. Crummell had been verbally assaulted several times on the streets and received numerous threats on his life; his friends and parishioners urged him to leave as soon as possible. He went to Freetown, Sierra Leone, first, and in early March 1872 he booked passage for Boston. He arrived there in April and then headed for New York City, his hometown.[52]

Several of Alexander Crummell's biographers have been critical of the account of the nineteen years in Liberia found in *Jubilate: Shades and Lights of a Fifty Years' Ministry, 1844–1894*, published in 1894. They strongly suggested that Crummell, who wanted to be known for his attachment to "Christian righteousness," had deliberately misrepresented his experiences as a missionary. However, Crummell used his autobiography to describe the personal experiences that were important in understanding the ideological positions he assumed throughout his long and active life. In the autobiography Rev. Crummell emphasized the point that while he was residing in Liberia, he kept himself "abstinent entirely from politics, but I felt myself forced by the condition of the country and the demands of the people, to take my place as a public Teacher. . . . The people wanted my opinions concerning national life, and as a devoted Negro, I was glad to advise and give counsel by public speech." Rev. Crummell told the truth in this autobiographical work; in Liberia he was a "public Teacher" and intellectual leader, not a politician. In *Jubilate* Rev. Crummell also responded to the common criticism that he was too inflexible, moralistic, and rigid in his beliefs. "I am proud of this criticism," Crummell proclaimed. "It is in evidence that I tolerated no iniquity, and that I rebuked depravity." As former slaves, the Americo-Liberians had been subjected to "the galling discipline of slavery"; what they needed was "the sober discipline of freedom." "I told the people of Liberia the naked truth, on all occasions, without flattery, and as a censor of great faults. All peoples, on their first passage from slavery to freedom, need moral rigidity. Restraint, moral and political restraint, is and will be . . . the great need of such a democratic system as that of the Republic of Liberia" (20–21).

The American Negro Academy

ALEXANDER CRUMMELL had functioned as an intellectual and "public Teacher" in Liberia and he continued these activities when he returned to the United States in 1872. Crummell was instrumental in creating organizations and structures for carrying out intellectual debate among various spokespersons for the national African-American community. For Alexander Crummell institution building was a matter of principle. He had pastored African-American churches in Providence, Philadelphia, and other cities, he built churches in Liberia, opened schools that were attached to the churches, and founded black literary and reading societies. Upon his return to the United States, Crummell pursued institution building with a vengeance. He was asked to become rector of St. Mary's Church in Washington, but when he arrived, he found that St. Mary's was really only a chapel, located in the rear of St. John's Episcopal Church, where black parishioners held separate services. The black congregation had long expressed its desire for a black minister, and by November 1879 under the leadership of Rev. Crummell, they went on to build an impressive religious structure, St. Luke's Episcopal Church. From the pulpit of one of the most influential black churches in the District of Columbia, Crummell preached black self-help and racial solidarity for African-American advancement in the United States and throughout the world.[53]

Although Alexander Crummell often spoke out in favor of African-American missionary activities to Liberia and throughout Africa, it was also clear from statements and actions after 1873 that he no longer believed that African emigration was a viable collective solution for the problems facing blacks in the United States. In an essay entitled "The Race-Problem in America," published in 1891, Crummell declared: "when a RACE, i.e. a compact homogeneous population of one blood, ancestry and lineage—numbering perchance, some eight or ten millions—once enters a land and settles therein as its home and heritage, then occurs an event as fixed and abiding as the rooting of the Pyrenees in Spain or the Alps in Italy." In the new environment racial groups interact culturally, but physical assimilation does not necessarily occur. Crummell disputed that idea that an "amalgamation of the races" would take place if Africans remained in the United States. "Do the indications point to amalgamation or to absorption as the outcome of race life? Are we to have the intermingling of our peoples into one common blood or the perpetuity of our diverse stocks with the abiding integrity of race, blood, and character?" Crummell subscribed to the contemporary views on the significance of racial contributions to the advancement of "civilization" and held firmly the ideal of black "racial integrity." As a "pure Negro," and one of the leading intellectuals in the United States at the time, Rev. Crummell made clear his opposition to "amalgamation or absorption."[54]

> Amalgamation in its exact sense means approach of affinities. The word applied to human beings implies will, and the consent of two parties. In this sense there has been no amalgamation of the races; for the Negro in this land has ever been the truest of men, in marital allegiance, to his own race. Intermixture of blood there has been—not by the amalgamation, which implies consent, but through the victimizing of the helpless black woman. But even this has been limited in extent.[55]

Happily, in the 1890s "intermixture has had a wide and sudden decline, and . . . the likelihood of the so-called amalgamation of the future is fast dying out."[56]

Rev. Crummell also argued that the "race problem" is "the only question now remaining among us for the full triumph of Christian democracy" in the United States. The crucial test for the American democracy was "the civil and political rights of the Negro." "If this nation is not truly democratic then she must die! Nothing is more destructive to a nation than an organic falsehood! This nation cannot live—this nation does not deserve to live—on the basis of a lie!"[57] Thus by the early 1890s, for Christian and democratic reasons, Rev. Crummell had come to the conclusion that the race problem had to be solved *within* the United States.

Alexander Crummell also opposed "amalgamation" because of his experiences with mulattoes in Liberia. As far as Crummell was concerned, mulatto intellectuals were only indirectly involved in the vindication of the black race, if at all. Any intellectual or literary achievements they made would be attributed to the admixture of white blood. Indeed, for Rev. Crummell the intellectual achievements of "pure Negroes" was important in convincing the mulatto elites to participate in the civilizing process for the black masses. The conflict between his experiences with the mulatto elite in Liberia and his desire to create an institution for African-American intellectual advancement came to a head with the creation of the American Negro Academy, the first national learned society among African-American intellectuals in the United States.

The original idea for the American Negro Academy was attributed to Richard Robert Wright, Sr., then president of Georgia State Industrial School for Colored Youth in Savannah, and William Crogman, a West Indian–born professor of Greek and Latin at Atlanta's Clark University. Alexander Crummell had been involved in the sponsoring of black learned societies from the 1870s. Rev. Crummell was among the founders of the Negro Historical Society in Washington in 1877. Its purpose was "the promotion of culture, civilization and progress among the people of the United States." But in 1893 when first contacted by Professor Crogman about the need to establish a national society for "black scholars and thinkers . . . to formulate strategies for solving the problems of their people and to respond to the attacks of white intellectuals," Crummell was unwilling to make a commitment. But by 1896 he had changed his mind and came to view the learned academy as an "imperative necessity." Biographers and historians have suggested several possible reasons for Crummell's change of heart. The deterioration in the social, economic, and political conditions for African Americans was continuing during the 1890s, but "apologetics justifying their mistreatment emanated from respected intellectual, political, and religious figures." According to historian Alfred A. Moss, Jr., Crummell "may have come to believe that an organized group of educated blacks, committed to a reasoned defense of their people, was a necessity."[58]

The rise of Booker T. Washington to prominence following his address at the Cotton States Exposition in Atlanta in September 1895 was very likely another factor that influenced Rev. Crummell's decision. As was discussed above, Crummell had been dismissed from his position at Liberia College in 1866 by J. J. Roberts and other "mulatto officials"; now in 1896 Crummell was fearful that a "mulatto elite" was rising in the United States and was becoming the leading spokespersons for the African-American community. In a letter early in 1896 to "pure Negro" journalist John Edward Bruce, also known as "Bruce

Grit," Crummell complained that "American race prejudice is waxing . . . but lo and behold, just at this juncture up rise a fanatical and conceited junto, more malignant than white men, pushing themselves forward as leaders and auto-crats of the race and at the same time repudiating the race. And what is the basis of their superiority? Bastardy!"[59]

In creating the American Negro Academy, Alexander Crummell set out purposely to avoid "black opportunists who jump at anything the white man says, if it will give him notoriety and have him jingle a few nickles in [his] pockets." The nine originators of the academy, which included four ministers, three professors, one publisher, and one poet, met in Washington in December 1896, and drew up the original list of individuals to be invited to membership. The list included four lawyers and seven college professors, including the young W. E. B. Du Bois, then in Philadelphia working at the University of Pennsylvania on his classic work *The Philadelphia Negro*. There were eight educational administrators (excluding Booker T. Washington) and the journalists were represented by John Edward Bruce and Benjamin F. Lee, editor of the AME *Christian Recorder*. The largest group of professional elites recommended for membership in the academy, however, was the clergy. There were thirteen ministers listed, some of whom were also college professors or administrators, while others worked solely within various religious denominations.[60]

The founding of the American Negro Academy was an important event in the internal development of the African-American intelligentsia in the United States. But the academy was much more significant as the *ideological expression* of certain intellectual currents within Afro-America. The academy was similar in membership and purpose to the intellectual structures being created in the late nineteenth century by various American ethnic groups, including the Irish, Polish, Italian, and German Jews, to combat racist attacks and propaganda. But the academy was even more important as the institutional expression of certain ideological commitments made by the intellectuals who organized it. Given the personal experiences and ideological background of its founders, matters of principle determined who was and who was *not* offered membership in the academy.

At the March 1897 meeting, for example, when the name of Richard T. Greener, the first black graduate from Harvard College, was brought up for consideration, Alexander Crummell was outspoken in his opposition. Although Greener was a well-known lawyer who had served as dean of Howard University Law School between 1878 and 1880, Greener and his wife had Caucasian features and very fair skin. Crummell believed the reports that the Greeners passed for white whenever it suited them. Richard Greener was a typical example of the "black opportunist," according to Crummell, and in the debate he made it clear that it was not the passing for white that he found so objectionable, but the passing back and forth, and becoming "Negro" when convenient or beneficial. "I . . . object to his coming back to our ranks, and then getting on my Negro shoulders, to hoist himself, as a Negro, into some political office." Crummell's objections were sustained and Richard T. Greener was not invited to academy membership.[61]

Booker T. Washington's name was also omitted from the list of the thirty-one black leaders and intellectuals originally recommended for membership in the American Negro Academy. The well-known principal of Tuskegee Institute in Alabama was later offered admission along with five others, probably at the suggestion of Rev. Francis J. Grimke, his close friend and one of the academy's originators. But Washington never attended any meetings, and was dropped from membership in December 1898 for failure to pay dues. However, it was unlikely that Washington would want to participate in this particular African-American intellectual institution, since during the eighteen months of Crummell's presidency, he continually denounced Washington as the ringleader of "the opportunistic mulattos," associated in his mind with Richard T. Greener. Privately, Crummell considered Booker T. Washington a "white man's nigger" who "will betray you and sell you"; publicly, Rev. Crummell forcefully challenged the Tuskegee principal's claims that industrial education was the most appropriate form of schooling for southern blacks.[62]

Throughout the 1870s and 1880s there was enthusiastic support for the inclusion of some form of "industrial education" in the American public or "common" schools, especially those serving lower-class children. Industrial and manual vocational institutes, schools of engineering, and institutes of technology sprouted up in virtually all the large urban areas, and students and teachers were spurred forward by the strong desire to participate in the ongoing industrial expansion. The activities of General Samuel Armstrong at Hampton Institute and Booker T. Washington at Tuskegee were considered part of this larger industrial education movement. In actuality, however, the particular type of "Negro industrial education," consisting primarily of moral training, instruction in basic literacy, manual labor, and handyman skills developed at Hampton and Tuskegee, reflected the views of the larger white society about the mental inferiority of African Americans and African peoples throughout the world. The Hampton model was considered part of the "vogue of industrial education" and wealthy capitalists used philanthropic foundations to provide funding to spread the Hampton-Tuskegee form of industrial education among black public and private high schools and colleges. The fact that the Hampton program was backed by the immense wealth of the Southern Education Board, the General Education Board, and various other foundations meant that for many struggling black schools and colleges seeking financial support, "the Tuskegee Machine," as it came to be known, led by Booker T. Washington, would become a force with which to be reckoned.[63]

Initially, in the late 1870s and 1880s, Alexander Crummell had been one of the leading supporters of industrial education for the black masses. In an 1881 address on "The Dignity of Labor," Crummell stressed the idea that work, even menial, servile labor, was good for the black masses because it helped develop character, dignity, and discipline.[64] But in his inaugural address as president of the American Negro Academy in March 1897, Crummell stated not only his current views on the vogue of industrial education, but also outlined a few more of the guiding precepts that defined his ideological positions. Crummell believed that "civilization is the primal need of the Negro race," and that race advancement depended upon "the scholars and thinkers, who have secured the vision which penetrates the center of nature, and sweeps the circles of historic enlightenment; and who have got the insight into the life of things, and learned the art by which men touch the springs of action."[65]

Rev. Crummell's overriding concern was group or collective advancement, not individual achievement. "As a race in this land, we have no art; we have no science; we have no philosophy; we have no scholarship. Individuals we have in each of these lines; but mere individuality cannot be recognized as the aggregation of a family, a nation, or a race; or as the interpretation of any of them." Crummell firmly held that "until we attain the role of civilization, we cannot stand up and hold our place in the world of culture and enlightenment. And the forfeiture of such places means . . . inferiority, repulsion, drudgery, poverty, and ultimate death."[66]

Crummell drew a contrast between "man's material needs . . . for feeding the body," and the need to feed "the living soul." Quoting the New Testament: "Man cannot live by bread alone, but by every word that proceedeth out of the mouth of God"; he declared that "civilization is the *secondary* word of God, given for the nourishment of humanity," and Crummell sought "the very highest art in the shaping and moulding of human souls."[67]

As an Episcopalian minister, Crummell's "social idealism" should be considered an integral part of his "religious idealism." At the same time, he was clear about the differences between his cultural ideals and the capitalistic strategies associated with Professor Booker T. Washington. Rev. Crummell admitted that there were alternative strategies being suggested for achieving "civilization." There were "large schools of thought" interested in

> suggesting remedies for the master-need of the race . . . the surest way to success. . . . Some of our leaders and teachers boldly declare, now, that *property* is the source of power; and then that *money* is the thing which commands respect. At one time it is *official position* which is the masterful influence in the elevation of the race; at another, men are disposed to fall back upon *blood* and *lineage* as the root (source) of power and progress. Blind men! For they fail to see that neither property, nor money, nor station, nor office, nor lineage, are fixed factors,

in so large a thing as the destiny of man; that they are not vitalizing qualities in the changeless hopes of humanity.[68]

Crummell and the vast majority of late-nineteenth- and early-twentieth-century American and European intellectuals subscribed to the contemporary ideas about "race," "national destiny," and "peoplehood"; and they accepted social Darwinist conceptions of the "struggle for existence" and "the survival of the fittest" among the various "races." According to these notions, the stronger, more resourceful groups and nations survive and come to dominate weaker, less inventive peoples. For Crummell the spread of "Anglo-Saxon civilization" in the late nineteenth century to numerous parts of the world demonstrated the greatness of the Anglo-Saxon people.

> The greatness of people springs from their ability to grasp the conceptions of being. It is the absorption of a people, of a nation, of race, in large majestic and abiding things which lifts them up to the skies. These once apprehended, all the minor details of life follow in their proper places, and spread abroad in the details and the comfort of practicality.

Crummell believed that without the "gift of civilization" women and men "are sure to remain low, debased and groveling."[69]

As far as Alexander Crummell was concerned, the industrial education provided at Hampton and Tuskegee institutes and schools like them would not provide the "civilization" or "leadership" necessary for African-American advancement in the United States. In his annual address to the American Negro Academy in December 1897, entitled "The Attitude of the American Mind Toward the Negro Intellect," Crummell pointed out that the stifling of African-American intellectual development was one of the prime objectives of white Americans from the earliest settlement and establishment of the institution of slavery. "'Put out the light, and then put out the light,' was their cry for centuries." The participation of the Christian churches and state legislatures was needed "to stamp out the brains of the Negro." Contrary to later denials, this was done with the full knowledge "that the Negro had brain power. That denial was an after thought. Besides legislatures never pass laws forbidding the education of pigs, dogs, and horses. They pass such laws against the intellect of *men*."[70]

Following emancipation the systematic denial of access to public schooling and literacy training further slowed black intellectual advancement. Now it was being suggested that industrial education was the most appropriate schooling for African-American advancement. "'The Negro must be taught to work' . . . 'Industrialism is the only hope for the Negro' . . . 'Send him to Manual Labor Schools' . . . 'You must begin at the bottom with the Negro.'" To accept these views put forward by Dr. Samuel Wayland of Philadelphia and Booker T. Washington that "they should have industrial education" because that would lead to "self-support and elevation of their condition" was, according to Crummell, to engage in "half truths."

> For to allege "industrialism" to be the grand agency in the elevation of a race of already degraded labourers, is as much mere platitude as to say, "they must eat and drink and sleep"; for man cannot live without these habits. But they never civilize man; and *civilization* is the objective point in the movement for Negro elevation. . . . He needs the increase of his higher wants, of his mental and spiritual needs. *This,* mere animal labor has never given him and never can give him. But just in proportion as the higher culture comes to his leaders and teachers, and so gets into his schools, academies, and colleges.[71]

Crummell vehemently opposed the currently fashionable ideas about the need for "caste education" and "a Negro curriculum."

> The Negro Race in this land must repudiate this absurd notion which is stealing on the American mind. The race must declare that it is not to be put into a single groove; and for the simple reason (1) that *man* was made by his Maker to traverse the whole circle of existence, above as well as below; and that the university is the kernel of all true civilization, of all race elevation. And (2) that the Negro mind, imprisoned for nigh three hundred years, needs breadth and freedom, largeness, altitude, and elasticity.[72]

Unlike Booker T. Washington, who became the black spokesperson for African-American industrial education, Rev. Crummell viewed this latest educational campaign as just another element in the larger conspiracy to stifle African-American intellect and prevent civilization.

The Intellectual Legacy of Alexander Crummell

ALEXANDER CRUMMELL'S role in the founding of the American Negro Academy served as the culmination of a distinguished career as minister, educator, lecturer, and intellectual leader. Upon his death in September 1898, numerous memorials and eulogies praised him as a "great man" and "prophet." The most famous eulogy was that of W. E. B. Du Bois, who later published it as a chapter in *The Souls of Black Folk* (1903). "I saw Alexander Crummell first at a Wilberforce commencement. . . . Tall, frail, and black he stood with simple dignity and an unmistakable air of good breeding. . . . Instinctively, I bowed before this man, as one bows before the prophets of the world. Some seer he seemed, that came not from the crimson Past or the gray to-come, but from the pulsing Now, — that mocking world which seemed to me at once so light and dark, so splendid, and sordid." Du Bois waxed poetic on the trials and tribulations Crummell suffered at the hands of officials in the Episcopal church; how he was able to overcome the prejudices and racism he encountered.[73]

Both Du Bois and Crummell emphasized the physical effects that racist practices had upon the young minister. In *Jubilate* Crummell expressed his belief that church officials forced him to live in poverty. Denominational financial support for the activities Crummell desired was not forthcoming and his communicants were too poor to help. "The clergy stood aloof from my work. . . . On one occasion I was in a state of starvation." Crummell became ill and he recalled that "if it had not been for Rev. S.H. Tyng [of St. George's Church in Philadelphia], and the unfailing generosity of my great patron, Hon. John Jay, I think I must have died; for poverty, want, and sickness had well nigh broken me up" (10). Du Bois noted that Crummell labored for his congregation "in poverty and starvation, scorned by his fellow priests."

The young Du Bois leaned heavily upon *Jubilate* for the details of specific events and incidents in Crummell's life. More important, Du Bois demonstrated that he clearly understood the larger ideological concerns and matters of principle for Crummell's generation of African-American scholars and intellectuals. Crummell had devoted his entire intellectual life to the vindication of the black race. Black scholars and intellectuals would not only defend the race, but would also provide the leadership for the uplift of the masses. But how does one account for Crummell's failure to reach the black masses in Providence and Philadelphia? In *Jubilate* Crummell blamed the racism and bigotry of Episcopal church officials for his failures. Du Bois was more concerned about the effect of this defeat upon Crummell and his assessment of his people. There was of course the "temptation to doubt" the capacity of African peoples to accomplish specific objectives needed to bring about their own advancement.

> To doubt the destiny and capability of the race his soul loved, because it was his; to find listless squalor instead of eager endeavor; to hear his own lips whispering, "They do not care; they cannot know; they are dumb driven cattle—why cast your pearls before swine?"—this, this seemed more than man could bear; he closed his door, and sank upon the steps of the chancel, and cast his robe upon the floor and writhed.[74]

Rev. Crummell may have suggested personally to the young Du Bois that there were times of doubt and despair over the race's ability to rise; however, in his autobiography Crummell mentioned what life's experiences had taught him, and there was nothing but optimism expressed.

One large truth I wish to put before you, namely, that standing now more that three score and ten in age; the scars of bitter caste still abiding, I am nevertheless a most positive OPTIMIST. All along the lines of my own personal life I have seen the gracious intrusions of a most merciful providence. Every disaster has been surmounted and eclipsed by some saving and inspiring interposition. It is not merely a personal experience. It is a wider truth. It is a fact and a principle which pertains to the large and struggling race to which we belong. There is a Divine, an infinite, an all-powerful hand which moves in all our history; and it moves for good (24).

While most nineteenth-century European and American intellectuals subscribed to this progressive view of history, sometimes referred to as Positivism, it was primarily African and African-American scholars and thinkers who believed that peoples of African descent would progress as fast or faster than other groups in Western societies. Crummell dedicated his life to demonstrating the African's ability to advance to higher levels of civilization.

Alexander Crummell should be considered the Father of the African-American intellectual tradition not merely for the institutions and structures supporting intellectual activity he helped to create, but because his preoccupation with race vindication, black nationalism, and integration prefigured the predominant ideological concerns of African-American intellectuals throughout the twentieth century. Crummell's autobiographical essay was not a political statement; but the celebration of his fifty years in the ministry provided him the opportunity to state what he learned politically, the political knowledge he had acquired from his life experiences. "And now you may ask me—What is the conception of life which my experiences have wrought within me?" (22). In the early part of the century "when it was a reproach for any man to show devoted interest in the Negro race," there were white Americans inside and outside the Episcopal church who extended "generous brotherhood" to him and his people (22–23). Christian philanthropy had saved Crummell on numerous occasions and he not only wanted to thank those who were so generous, but to encourage them to continue with these "noble generosities." The greater part of Crummell's autobiographical statement was devoted to explaining how he faced the challenges that racism presented him within the Episcopal church and to naming those white Americans who helped him to succeed. Throughout his lifetime and since, friends and relatives, scholars and biographers have wondered out loud why Crummell maintained his affiliation with such a racist institution as the nineteenth-century Episcopal church in the United States. Since he supported black self-determination throughout his life and founded numerous black-controlled institutions, why did he remain obedient to the white authorities in the Episcopal church?

In *Jubilate* Crummell wanted to put that issue to rest; African Americans needed civilization and on the basis of Christian brotherhood, many whites within the Episcopal church had committed themselves to "Negro advancement." "The age of chivalry is not gone! Never in all the history of the world has the Almighty been wanting of the gallant spirits, ready, at any sacrifice, to vindicate the cause of the poor and needy, and to wax valiant in the fight for the downtrodden and oppressed" (23). Those white Christians who devoted their lives "to philanthropy by vindicating the cause of the down-trodden Negro," (24) who provided all manner of personal assistance to Crummell throughout his life, served as the major justification for his commitment to African-American integration into larger social and cultural institutions in American society. For Alexander Crummell, African-American autonomy within larger white-dominated social institutions and structures became a matter of principle and he used his autobiography to examine the personal experiences that went into his acceptance of that ideological position.

Alexander Crummell understood that one of the major activities of the African-American scholar and intellectual was to vindicate the black race from unsubstantiated charges of mental inferiority and unjustified attacks on its religious practices and morality. Crummell also understood that white Christian scholars, reformers, and philanthropists who participated in this process of race vindication were to be commended and that their books, articles, pamphlets, and speeches on this topic should be considered part of the emerging African-American intellectual tradition in the United States.

2

Ida B. Wells-Barnett

To Tell the Truth Freely

~

Like many another person who had read of lynching in the South, I had accepted the idea meant to be conveyed—that although lynching was irregular and contrary to law and order, unreasoning anger over the terrible crime of rape led to lynching; that perhaps the brute deserved death anyhow and the mob was justified in taking his life.

But Thomas Moss, Calvin McDowell, and Henry Stewart had been lynched in Memphis . . . and they had committed no crime against white women. This is what opened my eyes to what lynching really was: An excuse to get rid of Negroes who were acquiring wealth and property and thus keep the race terrorized and "keep the nigger down." I then began an investigation of every lynching I read about. I stumbled on the amazing record that every case of rape reported in that three months became such only when it became part of the public record.

—IDA B. WELLS-BARNETT, 1928

Photographer unknown. Reprinted by permission of the Schomburg Center for Research in Black Culture, New York Public Library.

As TEACHER, journalist, reformer, and women's rights advocate, Ida B. Wells-Barnett became one of the most influential African-American intellectuals in the late nineteenth and early twentieth century. As was the case with Alexander Crummell, Wells-Barnett decided to write her autobiography after a long life dedicated to the vindication of her race. However, unlike Rev. Crummell, whose autobiographical work was relatively brief, Wells-Barnett's autobiography was several hundred pages and documented many of the important incidents in her life. Although the work was written in the late 1920s, it was not published until 1970 under the title *Crusade for Justice: The Autobiography of Ida B. Wells*, and edited by her youngest daughter, Alfreda Duster. Part of the work was handwritten, other sections were dictated to a secretary, proofread, and revised, and almost completed by Wells-Barnett before her death in Chicago on March 25, 1931, at the age of sixty-nine. Many of her personal papers, published writings, and diaries, including the manuscript for the autobiography, came into the possession of the members of the family at that time.[1]

The occasion for the publication of Alexander Crummell's autobiographical work, *Jubilate*, was the celebration of his fifty years in the Episcopal ministry. For Ida Wells-Barnett there was an incident that took place in Chicago in the late 1920s. A twenty-five-year-old black woman was asked during a Young Women's Christian Association meeting to describe someone she knew who had the characteristics of the fifteenth-century French peasant girl and military leader, Joan of Arc. The young woman mentioned Ida B. Wells-Barnett, but when she was asked why she chose her, the woman was unable to respond precisely. She then came to Ms. Wells-Barnett and inquired, "I have heard you mentioned so often by that name [Joan of Arc], so I gave it; I was dreadfully embarrassed. Won't you please tell me what it was you did, so the next time I am asked such a question I can give an intelligent answer?" (3).

Wells-Barnett was struck by the question and the reality that most of the crusading against lynching for which she became internationally known had taken place before this young woman was born. "I then promised to set it down in writing so those of her generation could know how the agitation against the lynching evil began, and the debt of gratitude we owe to the English people for their splendid help in that movement." In the preface she also gave several ideological reasons why she had decided to write her autobiography. The story of the South from the end of the Civil War through the early twentieth century has been dominated by the "southern white man's misrepresentations." "The gallant fight and marvelous bravery of the black men of the South fighting and dying to exercise and maintain their newborn rights as free men and citizens, with little protection from the government which gave them these rights and with no previous training in citizenship or politics, is a story which would fire the race pride of all our young people if it had only been written down." Most of the leading black politicians "who made the history of that day were too modest to write of it, or did not realize the importance of the written word to their posterity." Wells-Barnett believed that "our youth are entitled to the facts of race history which only the participants can give"(5).

Ida Wells-Barnett's autobiography was not merely the story of her life, it was an ideological lesson based on personal experiences. While the period from the Civil War to the turn of the century was riven by turmoil and racial conflict, none of the leading African-American political figures wrote his own version of what happened; "we have only John R. Lynch's *Facts of Reconstruction.*" Her autobiography was to fill the gap in the historical record because "there is such a lack of authentic race history of Reconstruction times written by the Negro himself"(6).

Judge John Roy Lynch's autobiography, first published in 1913, was in the intellectual tradition of "race vindication" and was the result of his desire "to tell the truth freely." Born in slavery in Concordia Parish, Louisiana, in 1847, Lynch was the mulatto offspring of his owner, Patrick Lynch. Following the death of his father, John Roy Lynch was sold to a slaveowner in Natchez, Mississippi, but was emancipated by the Union Army in 1863. At the end of the war, Lynch immediately became involved in Republican politics, eventually serving in the U.S. Congress from 1874 to 1878 and 1882 to 1884 as the representative from Mississippi's Second Congressional District. In the preface to his autobiography Lynch declared that "the author of this work has endeavored to present *facts* as they were, or are, rather than as he would like to have them, and to set them down without the slightest regard to their effect upon the public mind, except so far as that mind may be influenced by the truth, the whole truth and nothing but the truth." The contemporary interpretations of the Reconstruction era describe it as "a disappointment and a failure," a period of "Negro domination" in which corruption, graft, and fraud were rampant. As far as Lynch was concerned these perspectives were completely inaccurate, and his job was "to furnish the readers and students of the present generation with a true, candid, and impartial statement of the material and important facts based upon his own personal knowledge and experience."[2] In presenting this autobiographical statement, however, the former Mississippi congressman chose to emphasize the larger-than-life political figures and events of the era, and only focused on his own personal experiences in relation to these broader issues. Ida Wells-Barnett's autobiography was different, much more personal, and focused primarily on how these larger political events affected her personal life and how she had an impact on national and international political movements and campaigns.

It is clear that Wells-Barnett intended her autobiography to be a political and ideological statement. While she was generous with information about her family, friends, and personal life, the major topics and issues addressed were political, and her experiences in these political activities and movements encompass the major part of the autobiographical work. The first three chapters are devoted to her early years in Holly Springs, Mississippi, and Memphis, Tennessee. She was the oldest of the seven children of James Wells and Elizabeth Warrenton, former slaves who following the war were able to support their large family through their father's skill in carpentry and their mother's fame as a cook. Unfortunately, when Ida was only fourteen years old, a yellow fever epidemic hit Holly Springs, killing her parents and the youngest child, Stanley. Rather than allow the six remaining children to become scattered among family and friends, Ida Wells decided to keep them all together. She went on to finish her course of studies at the local American Missionary Association school, Shaw University (later Rust College), and eventually secured a teaching position in a rural area. Initially, her grandmother came to watch the children when Ida was away teaching, but her grandmother soon suffered a paralytic stroke and was taken away to be cared for by her only living daughter. A friend of the family was hired to look after the Wells children until the family received an invitation from her mother's sister Belle to come and live in Memphis. Ida's aunt was a widow with three young children, and after securing apprenticeships for her two younger brothers, Ida and her three younger sisters went to Memphis.[3]

"The Princess of the Press"

IDA WELLS soon found a teaching position in Shelby County, Tennessee, several miles outside of Memphis, and an incident occurred in May 1884 when she was traveling home that served as the spark for her career as a journalist and militant fighter for the rights of her people. She was riding in the ladies' coach of the Chesapeake and Ohio train headed for Memphis when the conductor told her to leave that coach and go to the smoking car. She refused. Despite the passage of the Civil Rights Act of 1875, which banned discrimination on the basis of race, creed, or color in theaters, hotels, transportation, and other public accommodations, several railroad companies, with or without legislative sanctions from the states, began segregating black passengers on the trains. The conductor returned and tried to physically remove Wells from the car; "he tried to drag me out of the seat, but the moment he caught hold of my arm I fastened my teeth in the back of his hand. I had braced my feet against the seat in front and was holding to the back, and as he had already been badly bitten he didn't try it again by himself. He went forward and got the baggageman and another man to help him and of course they succeeded in dragging me out" (19). Rather than sit in the smoking car, she decided to get off the train at the next station.

Ms. Wells returned to Memphis, hired a black lawyer, sued the Chesapeake and Ohio Railroad Company, and won her suit in the local circuit courts. She was awarded $500 in damages in December 1884. But on appeal to the Tennessee Supreme Court in December 1887, the decision of the lower court was reversed, and Ida Wells was forced to pay court costs.[4] The reason she lost when the railroad company appealed the verdict had more to do with the changes occurring for the African-American population in the United States in the mid-1880s than with the particular merits of the case.

On October 15, 1883, shortly before the Wells incident, the U.S. Supreme Court had declared several sections of the Civil Rights Law of 1875 unconstitutional. This meant that rules and regulations issued by the owners of private businesses and enterprises calling for separation of the races in accommodations open to "the public" were not in violation of the Fourteenth Amendment to the Constitution, which prohibited discriminatory actions by the *states*. The Supreme Court ruled that, in the absence of direct state action, the U.S. Congress in a civil rights law could not mandate "social equality" in public accommodations owned by private individuals. The Court's decision was vehemently denounced by the vast majority of African-American intellectual and political leaders. The preachers preached fiery sermons with strong protests against the judicial betrayal, and argued that private companies had always been subject to regulation by the states in which they were located. Black publications were awash with editorials and articles denouncing the Court's "narrow interpretation of the Fourteenth Amendment," which was intended to guarantee "equal protection of the laws" to all citizens. Mass protest meetings were organized in black communities throughout the country where each speaker tried to capture the disappointment and fear for the future of African-American citizenship rights.[5]

One of the first African-American journalists to respond to the Supreme Court declaration was T. Thomas Fortune, who proclaimed in the *New York Globe* on October 20, 1883, that "the colored people of the U.S. feel today as if they had been baptized in ice water." Fortune believed that the mass protest rallies being held throughout the country will give "expression to the common feeling of disappointment and apprehension for the future." This same Supreme Court earlier that year had ruled that there could be no federal protection against "organized vigilante groups," such as the Ku Klux Klan, that attempted to interfere with a citizen's right to vote. "Having declared that colored men have no protection from the government in their political rights," wrote Fortune, "the Supreme Court now declares that we have no civil rights—declares that railroad corporations are free to force us into the smoking cars or cattle cars; the hotel keepers are free to make us walk the streets at night; that theater managers can refuse us admittance to their exhibitions for the amusement of the public."[6]

An even more radical response came from Henry McNeal Turner, bishop of the African Methodist Episcopal (AME) church. A former army chaplain and Republican politician in Georgia until he was denied his seat in the Georgia legislature in 1868 by anti-black Democrats, Rev. Turner had traveled throughout the South organizing churches for the black-controlled denomination and he had recently been raised to the bishopric for his efforts. Stopped by a reporter for the *St. Louis Globe-Democrat* and asked for his comments, Bishop Turner declared that this decision "absolves the Negro's allegiance to the general government, makes the American flag to him a rag of contempt instead of a symbol of liberty." He believed that "it reduces the majesty of the nation to an aggregation of ruffianism, opens all the issues of the late war, sets the country to wrangling again, puts the Negro back into politics, revives the ku klux klan and white leaguers, resurrects the bludgeons, sets men to cursing and blaspheming God and man, and literally unties the devil." Bishop Turner understood the purpose of the Thirteenth and Fourteenth Amendments was "to equalize the black and white races." The U.S. Congress had been given the power to define the rights of citizens under the amendments, and did so in the Civil Rights Act of 1875. Now, "seven men in Washington put their little will in opposition to the will of 50,000,000 people." Bishop Turner became more committed than ever to the voluntary repatriation of hundreds of thousands of African Americans to west and southern Africa.[7]

At the time Ida Wells was not aware of the significance of the Supreme Court decision and in the lower court she had won her suit. Thus when the lawyers for the Chesapeake and Ohio Railroad offered to settle the suit out of court, she refused. It was a matter of principle, she knew she was right. Unfortunately, when the Tennessee Supreme Court heard the case in April 1887, the impact of the U.S. Supreme Court's 1883 ruling was already being felt and the Tennessee court found that the railroad company's regulations were not unreasonable and that Wells filed the suit merely to harass railroad officials. She was ordered to pay the two-hundred-dollar court expenses. This experience of challenging the large railroads and Tennessee court system had a profound effect upon Ida Wells.

The suit against the Chesapeake and Ohio Railroad attracted the attention of the African-American press nationwide. The twenty-five-year-old school-teacher from Memphis was asked to write about the experience and the story was taken up by several religious and nonreligious newspapers. Wells then continued to send in articles written in a "plain, common-sense way on the things which concern our people," she later wrote in her autobiography. "Knowing that their education was limited, I never used a word of two syllables where one would serve the purpose. I signed these articles 'Iola'" (34). This was the beginning of her career in the field of journalism. After several unrewarding years as a teacher, Wells welcomed the opportunity to write regularly for various African-American publications. She was hired to write a weekly column for the National Baptist Convention's publication, *Our Women and Children,* and over the next three years her articles were reprinted in over twenty newspapers and magazines. Fellow journalists and publishers in the National Negro Press Association soon dubbed Iola "the Princess of the Press."

In 1889 Wells acquired one-third interest in the *Free Speech and Headlight,* being published in Memphis by two friends, Rev. F. Nightingale and J. L. Fleming. Rev. Nightingale was pastor of Beale Street Baptist Church, one of the largest congregations in the state, and he made sure that his parishioners supported the newspaper. Wells successfully traveled throughout the region selling subscriptions. "At Greenville, Mississippi, I attended the state bar association, made a short appeal to them, and came out with the subscription of every man present. In Water Valley, Mississippi, the state grand master of the Masonic lodge suspended the session for half an hour to let me appeal to them for subscriptions. When I came out of the meeting I was weighted down with silver dollars and had to go straight to the bank." The *Free Speech* became financially viable and she happily gave up her teaching position. Wells later confessed, "I never cared for teaching" (39).

The next four chapters of the autobiography were devoted to the other set of personal experiences that defined who Ida B. Wells was to become and the ideological stances she would take. On March 9, 1892, three friends, who had been arrested for shooting a white man while protecting their own property, were forcibly taken from the Memphis jail by a white mob and brutally murdered. "While they slept a body of picked men was admitted to the jail, which was a modern Bastille. This mob took out of their cells Thomas Moss, Calvin McDowell, and Henry Stewart, the three officials of the People's Grocery Company. They were loaded on a switch engine of the railroad which ran back of the jail, carried a mile north of the city limits, and horribly shot to death" (50). Although eyewitness accounts of the victims' last moments appeared in the Memphis daily newspapers, no one was ever arrested for the crime. Ida Wells was in Natchez, Mississippi, at the time of this vigilante action, and when she returned, in the *Free Speech* she offered this advice to African Americans in Memphis:

The city of Memphis has demonstrated that neither character nor standing avails the Negro if he dares to protect himself against the white man or become his rival. There is nothing we can do about the lynching now, as we are out-numbered and without arms. The white mob could help itself to ammunition without pay, but the order is rigidly enforced against the selling of guns to Negroes. There is therefore only one thing left that we can do; save our money and leave a town which will neither protect our lives and property, nor give us a fair trial in the courts, but takes us out and murders us in cold blood when accused by white persons (52).

The black citizens of Memphis not only heeded the advice of the *Free Speech* and began to leave the city, but those who remained organized an economic boycott against white-owned businesses. "For the first time in their lives the white people of Memphis had seen earnest, united action by Negroes which upset economic conditions." But mob action against the *Free Speech* itself was finally carried out when Wells told the truth about the reasons African-American men and women were being lynched throughout the South. The common excuse given by southern white leaders as a defense for lynchings and other mob violence was the outrage generated among southern whites over the rape of white women by black men. The white mobs were merely "defending the honor of their women." Wells understood and accepted "the idea meant to be conveyed—that although lynching was irregular and contrary to law and order, the unreasoning anger over the terrible crime of rape led to the lynching; that perhaps the brute deserved death anyhow and the mob was justified in taking his life" (64).

But Thomas Moss, Calvin McDowell, and Henry Stewart had *not* been accused of committing "crimes against white women." Indeed, these men were attacked because the People's Grocery Company had taken away customers from competing white businesses in the area, and the white businessmen were resentful. Wells decided to investigate other incidents of lynching in the region, and reported her findings in the pages of the *Free Press.* She found that black men who were caught having consensual sexual affairs with white women were accused of rape and subsequently lynched to protect the reputation of the woman involved. Wells interviewed the relatives of eight blacks who were victims of "lynch law" in April and May 1892. "Three were charged with killing white men and five with raping white women. Nobody in this section believes the old thread-bare lie that Negro men assault white women. If Southern white men are not careful they will over-reach themselves and a conclusion will be reached which will be very damaging to the moral reputation of their women" (65–66).

This editorial statement served as the excuse and justification for white mob action against the *Free Press.* Luckily, J. L. Fleming, the business manager, was warned that the mob was on its way and he was able to flee to safety. Ida Wells was traveling in the Northeast, and was informed of the attack by T. Thomas Fortune, who was then publisher of the *New York Age*. Fortune provided front-page coverage for the article based on Wells's investigations of lynchings for alleged rape. Since Wells could not return to Memphis, Fortune offered her a position as columnist and reporter on the newspaper.[8]

Ida Wells's experiences in Memphis supported her ideological commitment to telling the truth. The lynchers "had destroyed my paper, in which every dollar I had in the world was invested. They had made me an exile and threatened my life for hinting at the truth. I felt that I owed it to myself and my race to tell the whole truth." Illicit sexual relationships between white men and black women were common in the South during the slave era and accepted as a matter of course. Unfortunately, "I found that this rape of helpless Negro girls and women, which began in slavery days, still continued without hinderance, check or reproof from church, state, or press until there was created this race within a race—and all designated by the inclusive term 'colored'" (70).

In her autobiography in the chapter entitled "To Tell the Truth Freely," Wells branded the southern white men hypocrites. "They could and did fall in love with the pretty mulatto and quadroon girls as well as the black ones, but they professed an inability to imagine white women doing the same thing with Negro and mulatto men. Whenever they did so and were found out, the cry of rape was raised, and the lowest element of the white South was turned loose to wreak its fiendish cruelty on those too weak to help themselves." But more often than not, mob action was generated by white fear of black competition. Moss, McDowell, Stewart, and hundreds of other African Americans were lynched because they had acquired wealth and property and were viewed as an economic threat to certain whites. Because the primary excuse given for the lynchings was the rape of white women, "an entire race" was "branded as moral monsters and despoilers of white womanhood and childhood." This in effect "rob[s] us of all friends we had and silence[s] any protests that they might make for us" (71).

The publishers of the *New York Age* printed over ten thousand copies of the issue containing Ida Wells's lynching investigations and statistics. Wells received invitations to speak in Philadelphia, New York City, Wilmington, and Washington. After a lecture in Brooklyn, New York, in October 1892 a group of black women agreed to finance the publication of the series that appeared in the *New York Age* in pamphlet form. *Southern Horrors: Lynch Law in All Its Phases* was issued in November 1892 and included a prefatory letter from Frederick Douglass thanking Wells for her work. "You give us what you know and testify from actual knowledge," Douglass noted. "You have dealt with the facts with cool, painstaking fidelity and left those naked and uncontradicted facts to speak for themselves. Brave woman! you have done your people . . . a service which can neither be weighed nor measured."[9]

In Philadelphia when the pamphlet was just issued, Wells was interviewed by Catherine Impey of Somerset, England, editor of *Anti-Caste,* an English magazine published on behalf of the native peoples of India. Immediately upon Impey's return to England, reports began to circulate about another particularly gruesome lynching that took place in Paris, Texas. A black man accused of ravishing and murdering a five-year-old white girl was imprisoned, tried, and sentenced to death by public burning. Notices were sent out in the area announcing the public torture, "the school children had been given a holiday to see the man burned alive, and the railroads ran excursions and brought people from the surrounding country to witness the event." There were also reports that the crowd "fought over hot ashes for the bones, buttons, and teeth as souvenirs." Isabelle Fyvie Mayo, Scottish author and active opponent of the Indian caste system, asked Catherine Impey to recommend someone who could explain "why the United States of America was burning human beings alive in the nineteenth century" (84). Impey mentioned her recent interview with Ida Wells, and subsequently at the request of Mayo, Wells was forwarded an invitation to visit and lecture in England on behalf of the cause of "racial justice."

Actually Wells made two lecture tours to England in the 1890s, the first between April and June 1893 and the second between March and July 1894. In her autobiography, *Crusade for Justice,* Wells-Barnett included entries from her travel diaries and extended excerpts from newspaper accounts from throughout England about both lecture tours not merely to support her personal reminiscences, but to document the English response to her message. For example, copies of the original dispatches sent to the United States and later published by the *Chicago Inter-Ocean* were included in the autobiography, conveying the impression that there was widespread and growing support for the anti-lynching crusade due to her visits. But what Wells-Barnett chose to dwell on were the personal consequences for telling the truth. The speaking engagements in England went well, the audiences were responsive, and her hosts were charming and attentive. But right at the end of her first stay in June 1893, Wells was answering questions from the audience after a speech and was asked whether social reformers Rev. Dwight Moody and Frances Willard should be included in that list of prominent and influential Americans who refused to speak out against lynching. Rev. Moody was an internationally renown preacher and founder of the Moody Bible Institute in Chicago. Wells had personal knowledge that Rev. Moody generally preached to segregated audiences in his trips to the South, and never condemned mob violence against southern blacks.[10]

Frances Willard was president of the Women's Christian Temperance Union (WCTU), the largest organization dedicated to the passage of state and federal legislation prohibiting the sale of liquor in the United States. As such the WCTU was also the leading supporter of "home protection" through the passage of legislation giving equal rights to women. As the spokesperson for the leading temperance group, Willard was asked to comment on various reform issues, and was asked about the explosive racial conflicts in the South between blacks and whites.[11]

Ida Wells was asked during her first visit in 1893 what she thought about these two white social reformers, and Wells told the truth as she knew it. There were reports in black newspapers that "no Negroes had ever heard of Rev. Moody's refusal to accept these jim crow [segregated] arrangements, or knew of any protest of his against lynching." As far as Frances Willard was concerned, Wells recalled an interview with her "in which she practically condoned lynching," and despite protests by black leaders, never retracted her statements. "Having this in mind I could not truthfully say that Miss Willard had ever said anything to condemn lynching." Wells's statement was challenged by temperance workers in the London audience, and "not having a copy of the interview with me, I could not verify the statement" (112–113).

The same issue came up during her second trip to Great Britain in June 1894; "remembering those challenges, I made it a point to get a copy of the *New York Voice* containing the [October 23, 1890] interview." Wells not only quoted from the interview in that presentation, it was subsequently published in its entirety, along with Wells's response, in the British newspaper *Fraternity*. Frances Willard was in England at this time as the guest of Lady Henry Somerset, who was then president of the British Women's Temperance Association. After Willard's 1890 interview appeared in *Fraternity*, Lady Somerset decided to publish her own interview with Willard in the *Westminster Gazette*. This time Willard claimed "that neither by voice or pen have I ever condoned, much less defended, any injustice toward the colored people." Regarding the recent increase in lynchings, Willard believed that "all good people, North and South, white and black, [are] practically united against the taking of any human life without due process of law." However, Willard reiterated her support for efforts to disfranchise uneducated blacks and "alien illiterates" in the United States.

> [O]n my return from a temperance tour through the South four years ago I was interviewed as to the colored vote, and I frankly said that I thought we had irreparably wronged ourselves by putting no safeguard on the ballot box in the North that would sift out alien illiterates, who rule our cities today with the saloon as their palace, and the toddy stick as their scepter. It is not fair that they should vote, nor is it fair that a plantation Negro who can neither read nor write . . . should be entrusted with the ballot. We ought to put an educational test upon that ballot from the first. Would be demagogues are leading the

colored peoples to destruction; half-drunken white roughs murder them at the polls or intimidate them so they do not vote. That is what I said (206–7)

According to Willard, the 1890 interview in question "did not touch upon the subject of lynching" (208).

Ida Wells sent a letter to the *Westminster Gazette,* reponding to this latest interview with Frances Willard and making it clear that this was "the first time to my knowledge that Miss Willard has said one single word in denouncing lynching or [in] demand for law." Wells also pointed out that if Willard was so interested in letting the British public know about her opposition to lynching,

why was she so silent when five minutes were given me to speak last June at Prince's Hall, and in Holborn Town Hall this May? I should say it was because as president of the Women's Christian Temperance Union of America she is timid, because all these unions in the South emphasize the hatred of the Negro by excluding him. There is not a single colored woman admitted to the Southern W.C.T.U., but still Miss Willard blames the negro for the defeat of prohibition in the South!

Wells concluded that "the fact is, Miss Willard is no better or worse than the great bulk of white Americans on the Negro question" (209).

The matter may have been dropped at this point but at the WTCU's annual meeting in Cleveland in November 1894, Frances Willard decided to bring up the issue of Ida Wells and her campaign against lynching in her major address to the convention. Willard believed that in her zeal to expose the "abomination of lynching" Wells had besmirched the reputation of white women throughout the United States. "It is my firm belief that in the statements made by Miss Wells concerning white women having taken the initiative in nameless acts between the races she has put an imputation upon half the white race in this country that is unjust, and save in the rarest exceptional cases, wholly without foundation." In *A Red Record: Lynchings in the United States—1892, 1893, 1894,* a pamphlet Wells published early in 1895, she included excerpts from Willard's address and her response to these latest charges. Wells claimed that

at no time, or place nor under any circumstance, have I directly or inferentially "put an imputation upon half the white race in this country" and I challenge this "friend and well wisher" to give proof of this charge. . . . What I have said and what I now repeat . . . is that colored men have been lynched for assault upon women, when the facts were plain that the relationship between the victim lynched and the alleged victim of his assault was voluntary, clandestine and illicit. For that very reason we maintain that in every section of our land, the accused should have a fair, impartial trial so that a man who is colored shall not be hanged for an offense, which if he were white, would not be adjudged a crime.[12]

The unwillingness of the WCTU to go on record in opposition to lynching was again demonstrated in Cleveland at the November 1894 meeting. Ida Wells was in attendance and although an anti-lynching resolution was proposed, it was not offered to the delegates for a vote. Subsequently, a version of the proposed anti-lynching resolution was published in the December 6, 1894, issue of the *Union Signal,* the WCTU's official newsletter. While it proclaimed that the WCTU "is utterly opposed to all lawless acts in any and all parts of our common lands," it also stated that the members were "praying for the time . . . when the unspeakable outrages which have so often provoked such lawlessness shall be banished from the world, and childhood, maidenhood and womanhood shall no more be the victims of atrocities worse than death."[13] Ida Wells was incensed by the statement, which "reiterates the false and unjust charge which has been so often made as an excuse for lynchers." The facts behind lynchings showed that "nearly a thousand [blacks], including women and children, have been lynched upon any pretext whatsoever, and that all have met death upon the unsupported word of white men and women."[14]

In a private meeting with Ida Wells during the Cleveland meeting, Frances Willard explained she had made the statement in her official address because "somebody in England told her that . . . [Wells] attacked the white women of America." Wells responded that Willard had acted solely on the basis of "hearsay," and Wells wanted "an unequivocal retraction of her statements." In the same issue of the *Union Signal* where the proposed anti-lynching resolution was printed, the editors included a statement intended to clarify the points Willard raised in her annual address. Willard feels she "has been misunderstood and she desires to declare that she did not intend a literal interpretation to be given to the language used, but employed it to express a tendency that might ensue in public thought as a result of utterances so sweeping as some that have been made by Miss Wells."[15]

But Ida Wells found

this explanation . . . as unjust as the original offense. I desire no quarrel with the WCTU, but my love for the truth is greater than my regard for an alleged friend who, through ignorance or design misrepresents in the most harmful way the cause of a long suffering race, and then unable to maintain the truth of her attack excuses herself as it were by the wave of the hand, declaring that "she did not intend a literal interpretation to be given to the language used." When the lives of men, women and children are at stake, when the inhuman butchers of innocents attempt to justify their barbarism by fastening upon the whole race the obloquy of the infamous crimes, it is little less than criminal to apologize for the butchers today and tomorrow to repudiate the apology by declaring it a figure of speech.[16]

Several biographers of Frances Willard have concluded that Willard responded the way she did because she truly believed that Wells had attacked the reputation of white women. But the historical reality was that during the 1880s and 1890s it was black women who were being blamed for the alleged assaults by black men upon white women. The argument was made that black men lusted after "virginal" white women because black women were lustful, immoral, and licentious.

Slighted Womanhood

IDA WELLS-BARNETT'S attachment to the truth meant that she not only published her version of the acrimonious international debate with Frances Willard in a pamphlet in 1895, but she also included the documents in her autobiography in the late 1920s. The anti-lynching campaign became an international movement due primarily to Ida Wells's activities in England. In *Crusade for Justice* Ida Wells-Barnett discussed the origins of the British Anti-Lynching Committee and included the names and affiliations of the over one hundred distinguished English citizens and social reformers who became members. Over five thousand pounds in financial contributions had been made to carry out the work of informing the British public about this barbarous social practice (216–17).

Upon her return to the United States in July 1894 several celebrations were held and Wells traveled around the country talking about the response to her anti-lynching campaign in England. However, she made it clear that her message was still not well received, even among some "representative colored men." When she came to speak in New York City in August 1894,

> I was waited on by a delegation of the men of my own race who asked me to put the soft pedal on charges against white women and their relations with black men. I indignantly refused to do so. I explained to them that wherever I had gone in England I found the firmly accepted belief that lynchings took place in this country only because black men were wild beasts after white women; that the hardest part of my work had been to convince the British people that this was a false charge against Negro manhood and that to forsake that position now . . .

would be to tacitly admit that the charge was true, and I could not promise to do that (220).

But Wells also could not abandon her activity because the denigration of "Negro womanhood" was part of the rationalizations for lynchings. As part of the social and moral reform impulse of the Progressive Era of the late 1880s and 1890s thousands of "women's clubs" had been formed to deal with the depressing social conditions, particularly in large American cities. The Club Movement was responsible for the opening of playgrounds, nurseries, day-care centers, and homes for single working women and took the lead in addressing the social problems facing families in urban America. The middle-class reformers went beyond noblesse oblige in justifying their activities and argued that in protecting the family in this dangerous and deadly urban environment, they were, in effect, strengthening the entire society.[17]

Women's clubs were also formed by middle- and upper-class African-American women who believed that these organizations could work for "race advancement." Fannie Barrier Williams, one of the leaders in the black women's club movement, explained that the "club movement among colored women reaches into the sub-social condition of the entire race. . . . [It] is the effort of [the] few competent in behalf of the many incompetent."[18] In 1893 the Chicago Women's Club was organized by Ida Wells, with the assistance of Mrs. John Jones, the wife of the wealthiest African American in the city. Following her triumphant return from the lecture tour of England in 1894, the club was renamed the Ida B. Wells Club and sponsored numerous political and cultural programs to raise the consciousness and social status of African-American women.

The impulse behind the formation of a national black women's organization was provided by the desire to tell the truth about the conditions and circumstances for African-American women in the face of widespread attacks on Negro womanhood. As we have seen, part of the mythology surrounding lynching was the assertion that the immorality of black women was part of the reason why black men raped white women. For example, in 1889 Philip Bruce, a white southerner, published a book entitled *The Plantation Negro as a Freeman,* in which he claimed that "a plantation negress may have sunk to a low point in the scale of sensual indulgence, and yet her position does not seem to be substantially affected even in the estimation of the women of her own race." Bruce also asserted that "the rape of a negress by the male of her own color is almost unheard of [because the black male] is so accustomed to the wantonness of the women of his own race that it is not strange that his intellect, having no perception of personal dignity or the pangs of outraged feeling, should be unable to gauge the terrible character of this offense against the integrity of virtuous womanhood."[19]

When the first public statement and protests against lynchings in the

United States were issued in 1895 by the newly formed British Anti-Lynching Committee, James W. Jacks, president of the Missouri Press Association, was incensed and he released a widely circulated response in defense of the white South. "This plea [from the British] seems to us to take the form of asking us to make associates for our families of prostitutes, liars, thieves, and lawbreakers generally, and to especially condone the crime of rape if committed by a negro." In her autobiography Ida Wells-Barnett recounted how this statement so enraged Josephine St. Pierre Ruffin, president of the New Era Club, a black women's group in Boston, that Ruffin issued a call for a national gathering of black women's clubs because Jacks "had libeled not only me, but the Negro womanhood of the country through me." Subsequently, at the meeting held in Boston where over three thousand were present, the groundwork was laid for the creation of a "national organization of colored women's clubs." The following year representatives from black women's organizations from all over the country attended a second meeting, this time in Washington, where the National Association of Colored Women (NACW) was founded. Mary Church Terrell, an educator, lecturer, and close friend of Ida Wells from Memphis, was elected the NACW's first president. The new national organization saw "the defense of black womanhood" as one of its highest priorities.[20]

On June 27, 1895, Ida B. Wells married Ferdinand L. Barnett, an attorney and publisher of the *Chicago Conservator.* Ferdinand was a widower with two sons, Ferdinand Jr. and Albert, age nine and seven, when he married Ida Wells. Between 1896 and 1904 the couple had four children: Charles, Herman, Ida B. Jr., and Alfreda. Afterward, Mrs. Wells-Barnett cut down her outside work significantly, though not completely, to stay home and raise her children. She continued to work with the Ida Wells Barnett Club in Chicago and the new NACW, wrote articles for the *Conservator,* and lectured and spoke out against lynching, sometimes taking her youngest child along with her to speaking engagements. The social and political circumstances for African Americans in the United States were deteriorating even further in the 1890s and Ida Wells-Barnett could not remain completely on the sidelines.

Ida Wells-Barnett and the National Afro-American Council

BY 1895 the organized campaign to remove African Americans from the southern electorate was forging ahead in full force. Beginning with the Mississippi constitutional convention in August 1890, state after southern state rewrote or amended its constitution to include poll taxes and literacy qualifications for voting. The measures not only were effective in eliminating all but a very small number of black voters, but they also prevented almost half the otherwise eligible white males from voting as well. Complaints were registered with local white politicians so that when Louisiana held its constitutional convention in August 1898, a loophole was included in the form of a "grandfather clause" that exempted from literacy requirements those state residents whose father or grandfather had voted on or before January 1, 1867.[21]

White supremacist campaigns spread to the organized labor movement and hundreds of workers' organizations raised new barriers to prevent membership by African-American workers. As part of their negotiations with employers, union officials sometimes included the elimination of black workers from the workplace as one of their demands. When unions that discriminated against black workers went on strike, as was the case in Chicago in 1894 at the Pullman Railroad Car Company, black workers became strikebreakers, thus gaining additional opprobrium of organized white labor. Following the unsuccessful Pullman strike, a concerted effort was made by railway unions across the country to prevent blacks from obtaining employment on the railroads. After 1894 the only job made available to blacks on the railroads was as porters on the Pullman sleeping cars. Striking white workers at the coal mines in Pana and Virden, Illinois, in 1898 received the assistance of the state government and local militia in preventing exploited and jobless black workers from crossing picket lines and gaining desperately needed employment.[22]

After the U.S. Supreme Court decision in 1883 upheld the right of private agencies, such as railroads and theaters, to issue rules and regulations calling for the separation of the races, the southern states also began passing Jim Crow legislation mandating segregation. The failure of Republican politicians, black and white, to challenge this new legislative development led to a call in May 1887 by journalist T. Thomas Fortune for the creation of a new national leadership organization whose purpose would be to guarantee the protection of basic citizenship rights for African Americans. Although Fortune received positive responses from professors, politicians, and preachers as well as publishers about the need for such an organization, and a few local leagues were formed it was not until November 1889 that a call went out for a national meeting, signed "in the main by the young and progressive newspaper element."[23]

The national conference was held in Chicago in January 1890 and was attended by 141 delegates from twenty-three states. In his keynote address to the meeting Fortune made it clear that the delegates considered themselves "representatives of 8,000,000 freemen who know our rights and have the courage to defend them." The purpose of the organization was "to protest against taxation without representation; to secure more equitable distribution of school funds; to insist upon fair and impartial trial by judge and jury of peers . . . to resist by all legal and reasonable means mob and lynch law. . . . And [to] assist healthy emigration from terror-ridden sections to other more law-abiding sections."[24]

Contrary to recent interpretations, the National Afro-American League was not an "integrationist" organization. Although its methods were similar to those of the later white-sponsored National Association for the Advancement of Colored People (NAACP), and used the courts to challenge legislation aimed at restricting black civil rights, the objectives of the Afro-American League were self-determinist.[25] T. Thomas Fortune made this clear in an essay on the league published in the *AME Church Review,* the most important scholarly journal among African Americans during that period. In the past African Americans were afflicted by "the sentiment of the slave," Fortune suggested; but "it is being supplanted by a manlier and more rational sentiment—a sentiment of self-reliance and self-help and mutual dependence." He viewed the Afro-American League as "the first fruits of this new sentiment. It will hound the old sentiment to its death, and dance and make a joyful noise upon its grave."[26]

Fortune felt it was "the people" who were "arousing themselves from the lethargy of centuries, conscious that they alone are competent to work out for themselves the great destiny a righteous God has in store for them." He merely wanted this groundswell to "march resolutely forward" under the "proud banners of the Afro-American League." These self-determinist sentiments reflected those of the black journalists and publishers associated with the league, as well as the core cultural value system of the southern black masses.[27]

Unfortunately, in the early 1890s as things went from bad to worse for southern blacks, the Afro-American League made virtually no progress on pressing civil rights issues. Local leagues had been formed and were active in various locations, and T. Thomas Fortune traveled around the country lecturing before public meetings and social gatherings. But because Fortune refused to allow black politicians, specifically those who were running for and serving in public office, to play an active role in determining the activities of the league, they withheld their support and this undercut the organization's credibility in many circles. The National Afro-American League was to be independent of both the Republican and Democratic parties, and thus black politicians were prohibited from serving in leadership positions within the organization because it was felt they had divided loyalties. Most of the black politicians were wedded to the Republican Party, but it was the Republicans who needed to be denounced for assisting white supremacist campaigns in the South through their legislative and political decisions.

Fortune traveled around the country, speaking on behalf of the league, but membership dues and financial contributions were small and did not even cover his personal expenses. There was no way financially for the league to sustain the costs for several court cases against discriminatory treatment and forced separation on public conveyances, not even a case involving Fortune himself. Only a few league branches sent delegates to the January 1891 annual meeting in Knoxville, Tennessee; and by July 1891 Fortune announced that the league's treasury was empty.[28]

Then in March 1898 following two particularly grisly lynchings of southern black postmasters in Georgia and South Carolina, Bishop Alexander Walters, a prominent leader in the second largest black religious denomination, the African Methodist Episcopal Zion (AMEZ) church, in an open letter, co-signed by a number of other black leaders, pleaded with Fortune "to call a meeting of the leaders of the race at an early date to take into consideration the present condition of affairs and suggest a remedy for the same." But Fortune showed skepticism in his reply of August 24, 1898. "There is just as much need of the Afro-American League today as there was in 1890; there is even more need for such an organization; but I do not believe that the masses of the race are any more ready and willing to organize local and state leagues of the National league and to sustain them by moral and financial support than they were in 1890 and 1892."[29]

After receiving over one hundred letters endorsing Bishop Walters's statement, Fortune finally relented and agreed to call a meeting of black leaders and professionals, which took place in Rochester, New York, on September 15, 1898, following the unveiling of a monument there to the late Frederick Douglass, who had died in February 1895 at the age of seventy-eight. Over one hundred met, and instead of reactivating the league, the participants decided to found the National Afro-American Council, whose objectives mirrored those of the league. The council would investigate lynchings and southern outrages, and bring legal action on behalf of oppressed African Americans. It would encourage "migration out of the terror-stricken sections of this land," and would promote "both industrial and higher education," as well as "business enterprises among the people."[30]

Ida Wells-Barnett attended this meeting and in her autobiography, *Crusade for Justice*, she recalled that "many white people of Rochester were at our initial meeting and seemed to be willing to help us. But the pugnacious attitude of Mr. Fortune did not win their support." Later that same day when the nominating committee put forward Fortune's name for the presidency of the council, Wells-Barnett asked him if he believed the organization would gain widespread support in the African-American community. "He arose and answered . . . that he did not have any confidence in the race's support and that he declined the presidency." Someone then nominated Bishop Alexander Walters as president and he was elected. Ida Wells-Barnett was elected the council's national secretary. "So despite my best intentions, when I got back home to my family I was again launched in public movements" (255–56).

When the American Negro Academy was formed in 1897, under the leadership of Rev. Alexander Crummell, no women were offered membership. At the time Ida Wells-Barnett was busy with the black women's club movement and her anti-lynching campaigns. However, Ida Wells shared the same ideological position with the anti-Bookerite element within the academy, and thus when Bishop Walters invited her to the meeting in Rochester in September 1898, she decided to attend. Booker T. Washington was becoming more and more famous for his conservative pronouncements on the problems facing African Americans in the 1890s. As described in Chapter One, Alexander Crummell criticized Washington for advocating educational programs that would stifle the African-American intellect; Ida Wells-Barnett also criticized Washington for suggesting that African Americans should forgo college and university training, and pursue industrial training and skills. And when Washington failed to speak out against the disfranchisement campaigns and even suggested that African Americans should withdraw from politics and concentrate their efforts of developing viable business enterprises, Wells-Barnett understood that this position threatened black civil rights and she made clear her ideological differences with Washington. What was particularly unnerving to her was Washington's opposition to public protest and agitation against lynching and other outrages committed against southern blacks.[31]

Washington and his supporters were frozen out of the American Negro Academy, but his views were well represented among leaders in other national black organizations. Mary Church Terrell, the first president of the National Association of Colored Women, was on very good terms with Washington; and in May 1898 her husband, Robert Terrell, who was then principal of the M Street Public School in Washington, was appointed to the U.S. Board of Trade through Washington's support and influence. Due either to personal predilection or political expediency, when the NACW held its biennial meeting in Chicago in July 1899, Mary Church Terrell decided not to invite Ida Wells-Barnett. While Terrell claimed that the reason Wells-Barnett was not contacted was because of objections to her presence at the meeting coming from the Chicago women on the Program Committee, it was also the case that Wells-Barnett was a potential opponent for Terrell's reelection to the presidency of the organization.[32]

At the time, Mary Church Terrell told Ida Wells-Barnett that she went along with the objections coming from the Chicago women because she knew Wells-Barnett would have her hands full in making arrangements for the National Afro-American Council meeting.[33] While that was indeed the case, there was still great ideological distance between the social and political positions assumed by the NACW under Terrell's presidency and the public positions taken by Ida Wells-Barnett. For example, in her first presidential address, Terrell argued that believing that it is only through the home that a people can become really good and truly great, the NACW shall enter that sacred domain to inculcate right principles of living and correct false views of life. Homes, more homes, purer homes, better homes, is the text upon which our sermons to the masses must be preached. . . . Let us not only preach, but practice race unity, race pride, reverence and respect for those capable of leading and advising us. Let the youth of the race be impressed about the dignity of labor and inspired with a desire to work. . . . Let us purify the atmosphere of our homes till it becomes so sweet that those who dwell in them carry on a great work of reform.[34]

There was no mention in Terrell's speech of women's suffrage, equal rights, female autonomy, or any of the other issues and themes associated with the black feminist thought of that era. Josephine St. Pierre Ruffin, Fannie Barrier Williams, Ida Wells-Barnett, and other leaders of the black women's club movement had always emphasized women's rights and female equality as important objectives of the national club movement. However, Terrell's positions were much more traditional and conservative and had more in common with the views associated with Booker T. Washington than Ida Wells-Barnett and other black women's rights activists. Terrell's biographer Beverly Jones concluded that "her conservative ideology could not be called feminist. Terrell's advocacy of the domestic role of women did not unequivocally espouse the social equality of women." While the NACW was important in assisting lower-class women and children through its charitable programs, the ideological positions espoused by Terrell in no way challenged the traditional beliefs about the role of black women or "the Negro's place" in American society.[35]

When Mary Terrell was giving her speech at the NACW convention, Ida Wells-Barnett was indeed busy making preparations for the upcoming meeting of the National Afro-American Council. The group was convening in Chicago in August 1899 and Wells, as national secretary, wanted things to go smoothly. Over the previous year T. Thomas Fortune had begun to espouse the same conservative positions associated with Booker T. Washington (in hopes of gaining a Republican political appointment), and in interviews, speeches, editorials, and letters, Fortune attempted to deflect the increasingly strident denunciations of Washington coming from the more radical black publishers, professors, and preachers. The Republican Party's failure to address these serious black concerns meant that most black Republican politicians and appointees decided to skip the council's meeting in Chicago. Fortune even advised Washington to avoid attending the sessions. On the third day of the meeting, however, AME minister Reverdy C. Ransom openly denounced Washington for failing to attend the meetings even though he and his wife were in the city. The Chicago newspapers were filled with details of the council's deliberations and differences, but several delegates, including W. E. B. Du Bois, later apologized for the denunciations and supported a resolution commending Washington's "noble efforts." Nonetheless, in his presidential address to the council, Bishop Alexander Walters not only condemned President William McKinley and the Republican Party for its failure to protect the rights of southern blacks, but also suggested that African Americans should look to favorable Democratic politicians for support and pursue a course of "political independence" in electoral affairs.[36]

As was the case with the American Negro Academy, because of significant differences in the values and ideological principles of the leadership, Booker T. Washington was unable to control the pronouncements and direction of the National Afro-American Council in 1898 and 1899. It was not so much the potential incompatibility of the so-called radical ideological positions enunciated by the academy and council as opposed to the accommodationism and the petit bourgeois capitalist objectives espoused by Washington, but the fact that Washington could not control the leadership of these two organizations. By the turn of the century Washington was slowly but surely moving into the position of final arbiter for black Republican political appointments. Statements issued by the council condemning the Republican Party were impolitic (to say the least) from Washington's point of view, so he followed the advice of T. Thomas Fortune and others who suggested that he steer clear of this new leadership group.[37]

At the same time, however, Booker T. Washington shared with Alexander Crummell, Ida Wells-Barnett, and other leaders a strong belief in institution building for African-American advancement. Thus Washington decided he needed to form his own national organization, which he would control and would disseminate his petit bourgeois capitalist views and conservative ideology. Beginning in 1892 Washington had launched the annual Tuskegee Negro Conferences in which hundreds of southern rural blacks learned important farming techniques and other agricultural information from the Tuskegee faculty, government officials, and knowledgeable individuals, black and white.[38]

The idea for the National Negro Business League (NNBL), however, appears to have grown out of the annual conferences on the "Negro Problem" held at Atlanta University beginning in 1895. W. E. B. Du Bois had come to the school in 1897 to take charge of the conferences, and in the spring of 1899, the meeting was devoted to "The Negro in Business," and several of the participants suggested that local, state, and national black businessmen's organizations be formed. Du Bois had compiled a list of black businessmen for the conference, and later that year at the Afro-American Council's meeting in Chicago, he was named head of the council's Business Bureau. Du Bois later supplied Washington with the list of black businessmen who were eventually invited to the first meeting of the NNBL, which was held in Boston in August

1900, just one week before the third annual meeting of the Afro-American Council in Indianapolis, Indiana.[39]

Ida Wells-Barnett noted in her autobiography that "having gotten the idea of what it would mean to have a national organization of his own people at his back, he [Washington] had taken a leaf out of our book to organize what would be a non-political body and yet would give him the moral support that he had begun to feel he needed in his school work." The NNBL would demonstrate to white people of the North "the interest colored people were showing in his work" (264). *Crusade for Justice* presented a much more moderate assessment of Washington's actions than when she first heard about the conference in Boston. At the time Ida Wells-Barnett editorialized in the *Chicago Conservator* that Washington had "ample opportunity to suggest plans along business lines and Prof. Du Bois, the most scholarly and one of [the] most conservative members of the Council, who is chairman of the Business Bureau, would have been glad to receive Mr. Washington's cooperation." Du Bois had indeed cooperated with Washington and supplied him with a long list of potential members. Wells-Barnett was also upset that the inaugural National Negro Business League meeting was scheduled for Boston less than a week before the Afro-American Council meeting in Indianapolis. She was very close to the mark when she declared that Washington "will not go anywhere or do anything unless he is 'the whole thing.' He can't be 'all in all' in the Council for there are others who are as anxious as he is to find the right, and equally anxious to do it." In the new business league Washington could be "president, moderator and dictator."[40]

With the advice, guidance, and financial backing of Andrew Carnegie, William L. Baldwin, and other wealthy white capitalists, Washington hoped that the NNBL could serve as the vehicle for disseminating his conservative capitalist views beyond the black and white business elites to the black masses. In his opening address before the meeting in Boston on August 23, 1900, Washington made it clear he wished to attract "those of our race who are engaged in various branches of business, from the humblest to the highest, for the purpose of closer personal acquaintance, of receiving encouragement, inspiration, and information from each other." And just as the leaders of the National Afro-American League and Afro-American Council were interested in establishing branches throughout the country to generate local support for the maintenance of black political and civil rights, Washington in his closing remarks to the three hundred NNBL delegates urged that "in each community you try to plant the spirit to form an organization that will result in the employment of colored people where you live." The conference disseminated information on how "local business organizations" could be formed "in all parts of the country."[41]

In public pronouncements Washington echoed the sentiments expressed in private correspondence to Bishop Alexander Walters, the head of the Afro-American Council. "Politics and other general matters are dealt with in the National Afro-American Council which meets in Indianapolis," declared Washington in an interview with the *Boston Journal*. "This meeting [in Boston] is to be a purely business one, and not a political affair."[42] And by all accounts of what took place, that was the case. The well-attended sessions were devoted to the "ups and downs" of successful black capitalists. And despite the fact that the newspapers that week were filled with the grotesque details of a brutal race riot in New Orleans, in which the homes and churches of African Americans were attacked and burned, and many blacks were killed, the black business-men's deliberations did not include any discussion of black political rights or the appropriate responses to such violent outrages.[43]

At the National Afro-American Council's meeting the following week in Indianapolis, however, the overriding issues were lynching and racial violence, disfranchisement, civil rights, and political action. Supporters of Washington, however, were well positioned, and when he arrived in the city only one-half hour before he was to speak, he was taken directly to the hall. In his speech Washington consciously avoided the political issues under debate earlier at the meeting and emphasized "the need for more business ventures" and argued that "I do not believe that in any large degree any race has been permitted to share in the control of the government till a large number of the individual members of that race have demonstrated beyond question their ability to suc-ceed in controlling successfully their own business affairs."[44] Washington made no mention of politics, civil rights, or mob violence, and left the meeting im-mediately after his address. When questioned by a reporter from the *Indi-anapolis Journal* about his failure to discuss or even mention politics or mob violence, Washington "declined to answer."[45]

Although he refused to discuss politics in his public utterances or in his ad-dress to the National Afro-American Council, behind the scenes Washington's energies beginning in late August 1900 were almost completely absorbed in generating support among African Americans for Republican politicians, espe-cially the presidential and vice presidential candidates, William McKinley and Theodore Roosevelt.[46] T. Thomas Fortune, still hoping for a Republican polit-ical appointment, publicly recanted his earlier attacks on McKinley's record and hit the campaign trail. He addressed numerous African-American groups throughout the Midwest on behalf of Republican candidates. Washington felt relieved when the Afro-American Council decided not to issue a statement supportive of either the Democratic or Republican candidates. But this was due primarily to the efforts of Fortune, who headed the council committee ap-pointed to draw up the statement.[47]

Although Booker T. Washington avoided political appointments through-out his career, with the election of McKinley and Roosevelt in November 1900

he became the most important black political "boss" in the United States. In
her autobiography Ida Wells-Barnett noted that

> when later on President McKinley was assassinated [in 1901], Theo-
> dore Roosevelt became president in his stead. It is a matter of history
> that Booker T. Washington became his political advisor so far as the
> colored people of this country were concerned. There were those of us
> who felt that a man of no political strength in his own state and who
> could do nothing whatsoever to elect a president of the United States
> was not the man to be the advisor as to the political appointment of
> colored men from states which not only could, but did cast votes by
> which the Republican president had been placed in office (265).

Ida Wells-Barnett was explicit in her autobiography about why she opposed the leadership of Booker T. Washington. Everything Washington stood
for was at variance with what she had come to accept on the basis of her personal experiences. "Mr. Washington's theory had been that we ought not to
spend our time agitating for our rights; that we had better give attention to trying to be first class people in the jim crow car than insisting that the jim crow
car should be abolished; that we should spend more time practicing industrial
pursuits and getting education to fit us for this work than going to college and
striving for a college education. And of course, fighting for political rights had
no place whatsoever in his plans" (265).

In the spring of 1903 W. E. B. Du Bois's *The Souls of Black Folk* was published and contained among other things an explicit attack on Washington's
ideological positions. In the chapter "Of Booker T. Washington and Others,"
Du Bois criticized him for not following in the footsteps of principled black
leaders like Frederick Douglass, Charles Remond, and Alexander Crummell,
and argued that Washington "represents in Negro thought the old attitude of
adjustment and submission, but adjustment at such a peculiar time as to make
his program unique." "In other periods of intensified prejudice all the Negro's
tendency to self-assertion has been called forth," observed Du Bois. "At this
period a policy of submission is advocated. In the history of nearly all other
races and peoples the doctrine preached at such crises had been that manly self-
respect is worth more than lands and houses, and that a people who voluntarily surrender such respect, or cease striving for it are not worth civilizing."[48]

The book caused quite a stir in African-American intellectual circles. Ida
Wells-Barnett recalled that Celia Parker Wooley, a Unitarian minister in
Chicago and close friend, had a gathering of the literati at her home to discuss
the work.

> Most of those present, including four of the six colored persons,
> united in condemning Mr. Du Bois's views. The Barnetts stood almost

alone in approving them and proceeded to show why. We saw, as perhaps never before, that Mr. Washington's views on industrial education had become an obsession with the white people of this country.
We thought it was up to us to show them the sophistry of the reason-
ing that any one system of education could fit the needs of an entire
race; that to sneer at and discourage higher education would mean to
rob the race of leaders which it so badly needed; and that all the industrial education in the world could not take the place of manhood.
We had a warm session but came away feeling that we had given them
an entirely new view of the situation (281).[49]

The following year (1904) Ida Wells-Barnett expressed her ideological differences with Booker T. Washington in another public forum. The editors of
World Today, a leading news monthly, asked her to participate in a symposium
on "The Negro Problem from the Negro Point of View." Booker T. Washington led off with a discussion of "The Tuskegee Idea." Washington reminded
his readers that the Tuskegee Institute was located in the heart of the Black
Belt that extended from Baton Rouge, Louisiana, in the south to Memphis,
Tennessee, in the north and from central Mississippi through Alabama and
Georgia and into South Carolina in the east. Over sixty percent of the population there in 1900 was African-American, the vast majority of whom were
farmers and agricultural laborers. The major problem for these farmers, according to Washington, was an absence of "industrial efficiency."

> The Negro farmer looks upon the soil as a mine rather than a labora-
> tory and accordingly he takes out but does not put in. Planting the
> same crop in the same soil year after year, using implements of ridicu-
> lous antiquity, leaving every operation to the very last moment and
> conducting it then in the crudest way, with the last spark of hope al-
> most trampled upon by the merciless crop-lien system, the average
> Negro farmer in the black belt is in a miserable plight.[50]

The Tuskegee Institute through its educational program that emphasized
training in agriculture and through the annual farmers conferences was committed to the "industrial regeneration" of the Black Belt counties. The vast majority of its students were "taking professional courses in agriculture" or were
taking "agriculture as a regular part of their academic work." In contrast,
Washington mentioned that he had recently attended "the commencement exercises of a Negro 'university' in the South, and there I listened to the disquisitions of students who had been admitted to the fellowship of educated men
and women or, more accurately, had just received A.Bs." One of the student
speakers, who presented a talk on "The Genius of Shakespeare," Washington
later found out "came from a log cabin on the outskirts of a sleepy town in Al-

abama, where her surroundings were the most wretched." She had taken courses in Latin, Greek, and trigonometry, but none in dressmaking, house-keeping, or gardening. "I felt a wondering admiration for the ambition and pluck that led her so many miles away to the 'university,' but was saddened to think that her education had probably not brought her into the most helpful relation to her surroundings." Tuskegee's students, on the other hand, were provided training for "real life" and "the fundamental principle of Tuskegee's endeavor . . . [was] to use the curriculum and influence of the school explicitly as instruments of social and industrial regeneration."[51]

W. E. B. Du Bois in his contribution to the symposium, "The Parting of the Ways," summarized the major points he had made the year before in *The Souls of Black Folk*. He commented upon the increasing materialism in the United States. "The gospel of money has risen triumphant in church and state and university. The great question Americans ask to-day is, 'What is he worth?' or 'What is it worth?'" When African Americans see this, they conclude that

> the one end of our education and striving should be moneymak-ing. . . . What is personal humiliation and the denial of ordinary civil rights compared with a chance to earn a living? Why quarrel with your bread and butter simply because of filthy jim crow cars? Earn a living; get rich, and all these things shall be added unto you. Moreover con-ciliate your neighbors, because they are more powerful and wealthier, and the price you must pay to earn a living in America is that of hu-miliation and inferiority.[52]

There were those leaders (Du Bois mentioned no names) who have em-phasized industrial education and suggested that blacks should "get out of pol-itics and let the ballot go." Unfortunately,

> in their advocacy of industrial schools, the unimportance of suffrage and civil rights . . . [they] have been significantly silent or evasive as to higher training and the great principle of free self-respecting manhood for black folk—the plain result of this propaganda has been to help the cutting down of educational opportunity for Negro children, the legal disfranchisement of nearly 5,000,000 of Negroes and a state of public opinion which apologizes for lynching, listens complacently to any in-sult or detraction directed against an eighth of the population of the land and silently allows a new slavery to rise and clutch the South and paralyze the moral sense of a great nation.[53]

Du Bois believed that the vast majority of blacks opposed these positions.

> Black men in this land know that when they lose the ballot they lose all. They are no fools. They know it is impossible for free workingmen

without the ballot to compete with free workingmen who have the ballot; they know there is no set of people so good and true as to be worth trusting with the political destiny of their fellows, and they know that it is just as true to-day as it was a century and quarter ago that "Taxation without representation is tyranny."[54]

Du Bois concluded with a statement of what to him were matters of principle.

I believe that black men will become free American citizens if they have the courage and persistence to demand the rights and treatment of men and cease to toady and apologize and belittle themselves. The rights of humanity are worth fighting for. Those who deserve them in the long run get them. The way for black men to-day to make these rights the heritage of their children is to struggle for them unceasingly, and if they fail, die trying.[55]

Whereas Du Bois was general in his criticisms and confined himself to broad differences of opinion, Ida Wells-Barnett was very specific in her essay "Booker T. Washington and His Critics." She took the "Wizard of Tuskegee" to task for both the style and the substance of his ideological positions. What was particularly distressing to her was Washington's tendency to insult the average black man and to hold him up to ridicule before white audiences because he knew this was what the whites wanted to hear.

Some will say Mr. Washington represents the masses and seeks only to depict life in the black belt. There is a feeling that he does not do that when he will tell a cultured body of women like the Chicago Women's Club the following story:
"Well, John, I am glad to see you are raising your own hogs."
"Yes, Mr. Washington, ebber sense you done tole us bout raisin our own hogs, we niggers round here hab resolved to quit stealing hogs and gwinter raise our own." The inference is that the Negroes of the black belt as a rule were hog thieves until coming to Tuskegee.[56]

Wells-Barnett made it clear that "there are those who resent this picture as false and misleading, in the name of the hundreds of Negroes who bought land, raised hogs and accumulated those millions of which they were defrauded by the Freedmen's Savings Bank long before Booker T. Washington was out of school."[57] The Freedmen's Saving and Trust Company was chartered by the federal government in April 1865, to encourage the freedpeople to save their money. With its headquarters in New York City, branches were opened in Philadelphia, Washington, New Orleans, Nashville, Vicksburg, Louisville, and Memphis; and with only African Americans as depositors, by 1874 its assets totaled over $3 million. Unfortunately, the white managers in charge were incompetent and criminal and made huge loans at five percent interest to wealthy financiers, such as Jay Cooke. Following the Panic of 1873, there was a run on the bank by the depositors. The U.S. Congress made an effort to liquidate the bank's assets and reorganize it, but this came too late and it was forced to close in 1874 and the black depositors lost most or all their savings.[58]

Wells-Barnett also expressed her and others' resentment at Washington's continual attacks on higher education for African Americans. "The men and women of to-day who are what they are by grace of the honest toil on the part of such parents, in the black belt and out, resent also the criticism of Mr. Washington of the sort of education they received and those who gave it." As was the case in his contribution to this symposium, Washington often punctuated his speeches with gibes and detractions against the "college-bred Negro."

> The result is that the world which listens to him and which largely supports his educational institution, has almost unanimously decided that college education is a mistake for the Negro. They hail with acclaim the man who had made popular the unspoken thought of that part of the North which believes in the inherent inferiority of the Negro, and always the outspoken southern view to the same effect.[59]

Not only that, because of Washington's criticism of black education in general, there has been "a cutting down of the curriculum for the Negro in the public schools of the large cities in the South, few of which have ever provided high schools for the race." When this actually happened in New Orleans, where the schools for blacks were reduced to the first five grades only, Washington wrote a letter denying that was the intention of his criticisms. "But the main point is that this is the deduction the New Orleans school board made from his frequent statement that the previous systems of education were a mistake and that the Negro should be taught to work."[60]

With regard to the evil of lynching, an area where Ida Wells-Barnett had the greatest personal experience, Washington's suggested solution emerged from his ideological stance, but was completely out of accord with the political and economic realities. "Mr. Washington says in substance: Give me money to educate the Negro and when he is taught how to work, he will not commit the crime for which lynching is done. Mr. Washington knows when he says this that lynching is not invoked to punish crime but color, and not even industrial education will change that."[61] As we have seen, Ida Wells-Barnett's investigations had uncovered the fact that it was the educated, property-owning southern blacks who were being lynched and it was black social and economic advancement that served as a major justification for the enactment of Jim Crow laws.

Wells-Barnett had no objection to Washington's advocacy of industrial education, but most African Americans "object to being deprived of fundamental rights of American citizenship to the end that one school for industrial training should flourish. . . . They know that the white South has labored since reconstruction to establish and maintain throughout the country a color line in politics, in civil rights and in education, and they feel that with Mr. Washington's aid the South has largely succeeded in her aim." She concluded by asserting that "thinking Negroes" demand that Washington "refrain from assuming to solve a problem which is too big to be settled within the narrow confines of a single system of education."[62]

Ida Wells-Barnett and the Rise of the NAACP

THE PERIOD of Booker T. Washington's ascendancy as *the* Negro leader corresponded not only with the large increase in the number of lynchings, but also widespread mob violence aimed at African Americans. Racial confrontations leading to mob action and lynchings occurred in Springfield, Ohio, in 1904 and Greenburg, Indiana, in 1906. Then a major race riot took place in Atlanta, Georgia, in September 1906, after several local newspapers reported alleged assaults of black men on white women. On Saturday, September 12, an outraged mob of whites began attacking all black persons they encountered on the streets, dragging some from streetcars and wagons. The next day was quiet, but on Monday, September 14, violence flared up again and innocent blacks were beaten on the streets. When the police arrived, they began to arrest only the blacks; and when the police opened fire, it was returned by the blacks and one police officer was killed and another wounded. This sparked increased violence and massive destruction of property in black neighborhoods. At least four blacks were killed and several hundred were injured.[63]

The incident that did the most to undermine Booker T. Washington's credibility as a black leader, however, was President Roosevelt's dismissal of three companies of black troops in the aftermath of what was termed "the Brownsville riot." Black soldiers stationed in the Texas border town had been continually harassed by local whites. When a rumor circulated that white townspeople were preparing to attack the soldiers, they armed themselves and on August 13, 1906, a shootout occurred in which one white man was killed and one police officer wounded. After a hasty investigation was conducted by the U.S. Army, President Roosevelt decided to dishonorably discharge all sixty men in the regiment, even though only a few could have been involved in the incident. Both blacks and whites called Roosevelt's action an "executive lynching."[64]

Initially, Booker T. Washington collected information on the incident and was summoned to the White House to discuss it. But Washington could do nothing to prevent the President's action. After the soldiers' dismissal, mass protest meetings were held by blacks and liberal whites throughout the country. Unfortunately, Washington used his operatives to attack any African-American leader or intellectual who criticized Roosevelt's decision. Biographer Louis Harlan observed:

> Washington could have walked out on Theodore Roosevelt and the whole political game after the Brownsville affair. . . . The twin disasters of Atlanta and Brownsville showed the systemic flaws of an accommodationist racial policy for any other purpose than survival of the minority group or the power of its accommodating leader. . . . Washington might appear better in the light of history if he had seized the moment, conceded the inevitability of conflicting objectives of white and black, and challenged the rampant white supremacy of these two incidents. To do that, however, he would have had to be someone other than Booker T. Washington, schooled in slavery, trained to moderation, accustomed to compromise.[65]

A race riot in Springfield, Illinois, the birthplace of Abraham Lincoln, ultimately led to organized action and protest by blacks and whites against the increasing racial violence and injustice. The incident began when the wife of a streetcar conductor claimed that she was dragged from her bed and raped by George Richardson, a black man. Even though she later admitted that her assailant was a white man, after the local police decided to remove Richardson to another town, a white mob outside the jail became enraged and began attacking black businesses and homes. In her autobiography Ida Wells-Barnett noted that

> three Negroes were lynched under the shadow of Abraham Lincoln's tomb during these three days. Not one of them had any connection whatever with the original cause of the outbreak. One of them was an old citizen of Springfield who had been married to a white woman for twenty years and had reared a family of children by her. When the mob could do nothing else, they went to his home and dragged him out, and hanged him in his own yard (299).

Articles and editorials denouncing the riot appeared in many black and white periodicals across the country. White journalist William English Walling went to Springfield to investigate the incident and reported in his article "Race War in the North" that the white citizens felt no shame about the violence and continued a policy of intimidation and violence in hopes of driving all blacks from the city. Walling saw this kind of mob violence as a threat to political democracy in the United States and declared, "either the spirit of the abolitionists, of [Abraham] Lincoln and of [Elijah P.] Lovejoy, must be revived and we must come to treat the Negro on a plane of absolute political and social equality or [James] Vardaman and [Ben] Tillman [white supremacist politicians] will soon have transferred the race War to the North. . . . Yet who realizes the seriousness of the situation and what large and powerful body of citizens is ready to come to their aid?"[66]

Oswald Garrison Villard, editor of the *New York Post* and grandson of abolitionist William Lloyd Garrison, Mary White Ovington, a New York social worker, and Dr. Henry Moskowitz, a New York surgeon, saw the article, met with Walling, and decided to issue a call for a "national conference for a discussion of the present evils, the voicing of protests, and the renewal of the struggle for civil and political equality." The original call went out with the names of over sixty prominent individuals attached, and the National Negro Conference, which eventually led to the founding of the National Association for the Advancement of Colored People was held in New York City on May 31, and June 1, 1909.[67]

There have of course been numerous historical accounts of the origins of the NAACP. In her autobiography, Ida Wells explains why she had so little to do with the organization once it came into being. Wells-Barnett used the autobiography to explain her differences (more personal than ideological) with the early leaders of the organization. Writing in the late 1920s, she suggested that the NAACP had not been effective and "had fallen short of the expectations of its founders." While this view would not likely be shared by historians for the NAACP, it is an understandable position for Ida Wells-Barnett, given "the treatment I had received at the hands of men of my own race" who were associated with the group at its founding (327–28).

Ida Wells-Barnett was among the signers of "the Call" for a national conference on the Negro and race relations issued in January 1909, and she was listed as a member of the NAACP's first Executive Committee in 1910. However, her problems with the organization began at the founding conference in May 1909. "There was an uneasy feeling that Booker T. Washington and his theories, which seemed for the moment to dominate the country, would prevail in the discussion as to what ought to be done." Oswald Garrison Villard was one of the conveners of the conference, and was known as "an outspoken admirer of Mr. Washington." On the other side, some of those in attendance were equally outspoken in their criticism of Washington. For example, William Monroe Trotter, editor of the *Boston Guardian,* had been accused of disrupting one of Washington's speeches in 1903 and was prosecuted and subsequently served time in jail for his actions in what the Bookerites later termed "the Boston Riot." Afterward Washington's operatives in the city did what they could to destroy Trotter's newspaper and reputation in the national and local movement for black civil rights.[68]

At the founding conference a subcommittee was created, headed by

W. E. B. Du Bois, to come up with the list of individuals to serve on the Committee of Forty that would work over the next year on the establishment of a permanent organization. Amazingly, when Du Bois read the names of those to serve, Ida Wells-Barnett's was not included. "Then bedlam broke loose," Wells-Barnett recalled in *Crusade for Justice*; "for although I had assured my friends that my name had been among those chosen, when Dr. Du Bois finished his list, my name had not been called. I confess I was surprised, but I put the best face possible on the matter and turned to leave." John Milholland, a liberal white attorney from Boston, stopped her in the hall, "Mrs. Barnett, I want to tell you that when that list of names left our hands and was given to Dr. Du Bois to read, your name led the rest. It is unthinkable that you, who have fought the battle against lynching for nearly twenty years single-handed and alone when the rest of us were following our own selfish pursuits, should be left off such a committee" (324).

Ida Wells-Barnett left the building with a friend; then May Nerney, who would later serve as the secretary for the NAACP, came running out and begged her to return. Wells-Barnett refused, but her companion, Harvey Thompson, went back to clarify what they wanted. Thompson came out and told her they did indeed want her to return. She was met by Milholland, William English Walling, Charles Edward Russell, and Du Bois, who made the lame excuse that he had felt that she would be represented by Celia Parker Wooley of Chicago, and thus substituted Dr. Charles Bentley's name for hers. Wells-Barnett asked why he would put someone on the committee who did not even bother to attend the conference. Du Bois then offered to add her name, but she refused to allow him to do so because she knew that he had originally left her name off the list on purpose. Wells-Barnett left New York City the following day, "but somehow when the committee sent out its letterhead they added my name to the list" (324–26).

Historian Charles Kellogg's account of the early years of the NAACP corresponds closely with that presented in Ida Wells-Barnett's autobiography. Kellogg noted that several of the white conveners of the founding conference were on friendly terms with Booker T. Washington and wanted him appointed to the national committee. "They feared that without Booker T. Washington's name the organization would have difficulty getting funds from white philanthropists." However, the vast majority of the black participants at the conference were "bitterly anti-Washington." Thus the committee on nominations decided to take a middle course and omitted Washington's name as well as those of his severest critics, William Monroe Trotter and Ida Wells-Barnett. Kellogg also pointed out that "when Mrs. Wells-Barnett complained to [Charles Edward] Russell after the meeting, he illegally (but wisely according to [Mary White] Ovington) put her name on the committee." But the damage had been done, and neither Trotter nor Wells-Barnett ever had anything to do with the national organization, although they did on occasion support the activities of the Boston and Chicago branches.[69]

In its early years the NAACP became the most important national organization involved in the anti-lynching campaigns. It published reports and investigations of lynching and other mob violence leveled against African Americans and worked to gain the passage of federal anti-lynching legislation by the U.S. Congress. It is ironic that the person who had gained an international reputation for her anti-lynching crusade would have nothing to do with what became the most important anti-lynching organization. Ida Wells-Barnett used her autobiography not only to document her experiences in exposing the true nature and reasons behind these social outrages, but also to explain why she would have nothing to do with the major organization that took up the cause to which she had devoted so many years of her life.

After the founding meeting of the NAACP, Ida Wells-Barnett returned to Chicago and continued to work for women's rights and against the racial discrimination that was endemic to American life and culture.[70] In *Crusade for Justice* she made it clear that African-American leaders and intellectuals had a responsibility "to tell the truth freely" and this is what she attempted to do throughout her public life. Her autobiography is a major contribution to the African-American intellectual tradition because it provides a detailed account of the personal experiences that formed the basis for the particular ideological stances she assumed throughout a life heroically devoted to race vindication and the advancement of her people.

3

James Weldon Johnson

The Creative Genius
of the Negro

—

A people may become great through many means, but there is only one measure by which its greatness is recognized and acknowledged. The final measure of the greatness of all peoples is the amount and standard of the literature and art they have produced. The world does not know that a people is great until that people produces great literature and art. No people that has produced great literature and art has ever been looked upon by the world as distinctly inferior.

The status of the Negro in the United States is more a question of national mental attitude toward the race than actual conditions. And nothing will do more to change that mental attitude and raise his status than a demonstration of intellectual parity by the Negro through the production of literature and art.

—JAMES WELDON JOHNSON, 1922

Photographer unknown. Reprinted by permission of the Schomburg Center for Research in Black Culture, New York Public Library.

JAMES WELDON JOHNSON'S only novel, *The Autobiography of an Ex-Colored Man,* published in 1912, was *not* an autobiographical work. After a long and distinguished career as educator, poet, lawyer, songwriter, diplomat, journalist, civil rights leader, essayist, historian, and novelist, Johnson decided to write his autobiography. *Along This Way* was published in 1933 and received considerable critical acclaim. The book told the story of the "full and fortunate life" of a "New Negro." Johnson seemed to have lived a charmed life; he took up numerous professions and careers and excelled at all of them. Unlike the autobiographies of Alexander Crummell and Ida B. Wells-Barnett, which overflowed with descriptions of racial slights and ideological battles, Johnson managed to maintain a "spirit of detachment" throughout the work. In his adult life, Johnson had assumed the air of the "cosmopolitan gentleman" and his autobiography was in keeping with this personal style.[1]

Interestingly, there is no preface or introductory statement to *Along This Way,* but then Johnson was hardly an obscure person, having published at least one major book of poetry or nonfiction almost every year throughout the 1920s. But about two thirds of the way through the work, Johnson did mention one reason why he felt it was necessary to write his autobiography. When his novel, *The Autobiography of an Ex-Colored Man,* was issued, it was published anonymously to give it an air of authenticity as primarily a "human document." He later admitted, "I did get a certain pleasure out of anonymity, that no acknowledged book could have given me. The authorship of the book excited the curiosity of literate colored people, and there was speculation among them as to who the writer might be—to every such group some colored man who had married white, and so coincided with the main point on which the story turned, is known." But it did lead to some confusion. Even after it was republished in 1927 under his own name, Johnson wrote, "I continue to receive letters from persons who have read the book inquiring about this or that phase of my life as told in it. That is, probably, one of the reasons why I am writing the present book" (238–39).

The novel's protagonist was a fair-skinned Negro who was born and grew up in the South, traveled to Europe where everyone assumed he was white, then returned to the United States and became appalled by the treatment of black Americans. He soon falls in love with a white woman and decides to

marry her and pass for white. This novel recounts an "American" tragedy because the character felt guilt and remorse about his decision to flee his race, especially after having discovered the value and true contributions of blacks to
American and world civilization. This is one of the earliest statements of an issue that would become a matter of principle for James Weldon Johnson
throughout his life. In the novel he writes:

> It is my opinion that the colored people of this country have done four
> things which refute the oft-advanced theory that they are an absolutely
> inferior race, which demonstrate that they have originality and artistic
> conception, and, what is more, the power of creating that which can
> influence and appeal universally. The first two of these are the Uncle
> Remus stories, collected by Joel Chandler Harris, and the Jubilee
> songs, to which the Fisk singers made the public and the skilled musi-
> cians of both America and Europe listen. The other two are rag-time
> music and the cake walk. No one who has travelled can question the
> world-conquering influence of rag-time, and I do not think it would
> be an exaggeration to say that in Europe the United States is popularly
> known better by rag-time than anything else it has produced in a gen-
> eration. In Paris they call it American music.[2]

While reviewers and commentators on Johnson's autobiography have all
suggested that he was successful in avoiding ideological issues that may have
alienated potential white or black readers, this did not mean that he avoided
the discussion of important issues to which he had devoted his entire adult life.
Indeed, from 1912 with the publication of *The Autobiography of an Ex-Colored
Man* through the 1920s with his publication of African-American folk songs
and poetry, and particularly in *Along This Way,* Johnson presented his interpretation of the significance of black folk traditions to American and Western culture and its use in the creation of a truly "American" art. In these works
Johnson made his most important contributions to the African-American intellectual tradition in the United States.[3]

In *Along This Way* Johnson described in fine detail his middle-class family
background and West Indian cultural roots. Like Alexander Crummell, James
Weldon Johnson was raised in a family that valued education and learning
above the acquisition of material possessions. Professional services they provided to their racial brethren provided the basis upon which they rose to middle-
class status. James Weldon Johnson's mother, Helen Louise Dillet Johnson,
was born in Nassau, Bahamas, in 1842. Her father, Stephen Dillet, was the ille-
gitimate son of a Frenchman, Etienne Dillet, and a Haitian woman, Hester
Argo, who came to Nassau in 1802 with her three children during the Haitian
Revolution. Johnson's grandfather started out as a tailor, but later entered politics and eventually served for thirty years in the Bahamian House of Assembly.

Helen Louise's mother, Helen Dillet, one of nine children by a white planter and an African woman, moved to New York City with her only child in the mid-1840s. Helen Louise Dillet attended the New York public schools and studied music. "When she was eighteen or nineteen she sang at a concert," James Weldon Johnson noted in *Along This Way;* "James Johnson, who was in the audience, fell in love with the singer." Born free in Richmond, Virginia, in 1830, James Johnson came to New York City as a child and worked as a waiter. When the Civil War broke out, fearing that free blacks in the North would be enslaved if the South won the war, Helen Dillet returned to Nassau, taking Helen Louise with her. James Johnson followed them, obtained a job at a local hotel, and they were married there on April 22, 1864. They had a daughter, Marie Louise, and soon after James Johnson decided to return to the United States, this time Jacksonville, Florida, in 1869, and later sent for his family. Marie Louise died in June 1870, but James Jr. was born on June 17, 1871, and a second son, John Rosamond, on August 11, 1873.[4]

James Johnson, Sr., soon obtained the position as headwaiter at the Saint James Hotel, a luxury resort for winter visitors to Jacksonville; and Helen Louise Johnson became a teacher in the Stanton School, the largest black grammar school in the then small but prosperous town. Both parents impressed upon their sons the importance of learning and education. At a very early age James Jr. and John Rosamond were given reading and music lessons by their mother. "My father gave me my first own books, a 'library' consisting of seven volumes packed in a cardboard case four and a half inches high, three inches wide, and two inches deep." James Jr. read voraciously throughout his years as a student at the Stanton School (12).

Cosmopolitan Encounters

WHEN JAMES GRADUATED from Stanton School, there was some talk of sending him to Tuskegee Institute for a "practical education," but his mother insisted upon Atlanta University, where he entered the preparatory department in 1887. Unfortunately (or fortunately for Johnson), there was a yellow fever epidemic in Atlanta in 1888 and 1889, which kept James out of school for a year. However, it was during that year that he made the acquaintance of the two men who would have the greatest influence on his character. The first was a West Indian whom his father hired as his tutor.

> We went to see this man and found him in a small, dingy, cobbler's shop that he ran, pegging away at old shoes. He was a little man, very black, partially bald, with a scraggly beard, and but for bright, intelli-

gent eyes an insignificant presence. At the sight of the surroundings
my heart misgave me, and I was embarrassed both for my father and
myself. I wondered if he misunderstood so much as to think that I
wanted to be coached in spelling and arithmetic and geography. I was
reassured when the little cobbler began to talk. He spoke English as
no professor at the University could speak it (92–93).

The man was indeed a scholar who had obviously attended one of the
British colleges in the Caribbean. Johnson studied geometry and Latin with
the old cobbler, who often offered insightful asides about Roman leaders and
politics when Johnson read aloud from the classical texts. This additional enlightenment about the history and peoples he was reading about particularly
impressed Johnson. Recalling the man almost fifty years later, Johnson found
that "in the whole course of my school work the only other teacher who made
a subject as interesting to me as did this little cobbler was Brander Matthews at
Columbia. I wonder just what it was that kept him down on the cobbler's
bench?" (93).

The second influential person young James Johnson met that summer was
Dr. T. O. Summers, a white surgeon in Jacksonville. Having been convinced
that Johnson was suitable to serve as the receptionist in his medical office after
he read and accurately translated a passage from the Latin version of the Roman Missal, the two spent several months together, not merely as employer
and employee, but as friends and equals. Dr. Summers was Johnson's ideal of
the "cosmopolitan gentleman." He had studied in Europe, spoke French and
German, traveled throughout most of the world, and had a literary reputation
locally as a result of the regular publication of his poems in the *Jacksonville
Times-Union*. The doctor recommended books to his young assistant and even
gave him access to his library of what was then considered erotica, including
the works of Balzac and Boccaccio and other European intellectuals. "Between
the two of us, as individuals, 'race' never showed his head. He neither conde-
scended nor patronized; in fact, he treated me as an intellectual equal"
(94–95).

Johnson accompanied Dr. Summers on a trip by ship from Florida to
Washington, D.C. The ship's captain was a good friend of Dr. Summers and
Johnson was allowed to sit with the two at the captain's table where the otherwise moody and morose physician became quite "gay and talkative." "He
matched the captain with stories of travels to far, strange places. He gave a
thrilling recital of his experiences during the bombardment of Alexandria
[Egypt] seven years before." One behavior, however, that caused Johnson a
great deal of anxiety was Dr. Summers's practice of regularly sniffing from a tin
of ether that he carried with him all the time. "I dared not speak to him about
so personal a matter because from the beginning the relation between us was

on a high level." When Johnson had to return to his studies in Atlanta at the end of the summer, both were filled with regret. "I had made him my model of all that a man and a gentleman should be. The question rose in my mind whether I was not gaining more through contact with him than I would gain in going to school." The two corresponded for years, even though Johnson eventually decided against a career in medicine. "Then one day I was shocked to learn that Dr. Summers had committed suicide. I was deeply grieved, for I had lost an understanding friend, one who was, in many ways, a kindred spirit" (98–99).

When Johnson returned to Atlanta University's preparatory school, he petitioned to do two years' secondary schoolwork in one year, and by the fall of 1890 he entered the university's freshman class. During his four undergraduate years Johnson received a classical undergraduate education that included Latin, Greek, mathematics, science, and English; and worked in the university printing office, gaining valuable experience for his later work as an editor and journalist. But the most important experiences for understanding his later appreciation of African-American folk culture were those as a teacher during the summer in rural black schools in Georgia.

Encounters with the Folk

ACCOMPANIED BY his more experienced Atlanta University roommate, Henry M. Porter, Johnson managed to secure a position as teacher in the heart of the Black Belt during the summer of 1891. Johnson devoted a number of pages in *Along This Way* to details about his first experiences with the cultural practices of rural black folk. He lived with a family of three in their two-room cabin and was impressed by their kindness and consideration. His school was held in a shanty attached to the local church. It contained neither desks nor a blackboard. On the opening day he had about two dozen pupils, but after canvassing the district and the cotton crop had been "laid by," more and more started coming in so that Johnson soon had over fifty students and eventually had to hire an assistant.

The ministers, parents, and pupils impressed Johnson with their enthusiasm for education and their personal kindness to him in these crude circumstances. But not all the students were eager to learn. Johnson recalled a young boy with the strange name of Tunk who would not apply himself enough even to learn the alphabet. After several attempts to teach him, "I made the easy discovery that by the time he got familiar with X, Y, Z, he had forgotten A, B, C," Johnson recalled. "Tunk was not stupid; he consciously or unconsciously made up his mind that he wasn't going to study. . . . I used to watch the little rascal,

his book held up in front of his face, his brow wrinkled as though grappling
with some Einsteinian problem, peeping at intervals around the corner of the
book to see if I was watching" (111). Johnson later immortalized his recalcitrant young student in his poem "Tunk."

> Look heah, Tunk!—Now ain't dis awful! T'ought I sont you off to
>   school.
> Don't you know dat you is growin' up to be a reg'lah fool. . . .
> W'ile I'm t'inkin' you is lahnin' in de school, why bless ma soul!
> You off in de woods a-playin'. Can't you do like you is tole? . . . .
>
> Heah I'm tryin' hard to raise you as a credit to dis race,
> An' you tryin' heap much harder fu' to come up in disgrace.
>
> Dese de days w'en men don't git up to de top by hooks an' crooks;
> Tell you now, dey's got to git der standin' on a pile o' books.[5]

In his autobiography Johnson described his interactions with the children,
the church trustees who oversaw the school, and the families with whom he
lived. "In all of my experience there has been no period so brief that has meant
so much in my education for life as the three months I spent in the backwoods
of Georgia. I was thrown for the first time on my own resources and abilities. I
had my first lesson in dealing with men and conditions in the outside world. I
underwent my first tryout with social forces" (118–19).

But these personal experiences in rural Georgia were even more important
in understanding Johnson's intellectual and artistic appreciation of the black
masses. He had learned several important lessons, even though he was supposed to be the "'fesser." "I was anxious to learn to know the masses of my
people . . . and in trying to find out, I laid the foundation of faith in them on
which I have stood ever since. I gained a realization of their best qualities that
has made any temptation for me to stand on a little, individual peak of snob-
bish pride seem absurd. I saw them hedged in for centuries by prejudice, intol-
erance, and brutality; hobbled by their own ignorance, poverty, and
helplessness; yet not withstanding, still brave and unvanquished. I discerned
that the forces behind the slow but persistent movement forward of the race
lie, ultimately, in them; that when the vanguard of the movement must fall
back, it must fall back on them." He came to appreciate their "power to survive" and the "firm confidence" that comes from having survived "every degree of hardship and oppression to which any race may be subjected"
(120–21).

Johnson now understood the meaning of black laughter. At first, "their
deep, genuine laughter often puzzled and irritated me. Why *did* they laugh so?
How *could* they laugh so? Was their rolling, pealing laughter merely echoes
from mental vacuity or did it spring from an innate power to rise above the

ironies of life? Or were they, in the language of a line of the blues, 'Laughing to keep from crying'? . . . Were they laughing at themselves? Were they laughing at the white man?" Johnson was only sure of one thing, "a part of this laughter, when among themselves, was laughter at the white man. It seems to me that for the grim white man in the backwoods of the South this deep laughter of the Negro should be the most ominous sound that reaches his ears" (120).

And most importantly Johnson learned from these rural folks in late-nineteenth-century Georgia that "black is beautiful," especially black women. He saw "strong black men" and

> handsome, deep-bosomed, fertile women. Here, without question was the basic material for race building. I use the word "handsome" without reservations. To Negroes themselves, before whom "white" ideals have so long been held up, the recognition of the beauty of Negro women is often a remote idea. Being shut up in the backwoods of Georgia forced a comparison upon me, and a realization that there, at least, the Negro woman, with her rich coloring, her gaiety, her laughter and song, her alluring, undulating movements—a heritage from the African jungle—was a more beautiful creature than her sallow, songless, lipless, hipless, tired-looking, tired-moving white sister (121).

The Johnson Brothers Broadway Bound

EARLIER IN *Along This Way,* Johnson explained how the yellow fever epidemic in Atlanta that kept him out of school for a year allowed him to meet the two most influential people of his entire adult life. A similar unfortunate event, in this case a disastrous fire that destroyed the school in Jacksonville where Johnson was principal, allowed him to pursue a successful career in songwriting on New York's Great White Way. Upon graduation, rather than pursuing a possible scholarship to Harvard Medical School, Johnson returned to his hometown and became principal of the Stanton School, which at the time had twenty-five teachers and over one thousand students. Johnson brought numerous improvements in the educational program over the three years he worked there, including the introduction of ninth and tenth grades for students interested in pursuing a secondary education. Johnson also began publishing the first black daily newspaper in Florida, the *Daily American.* Unfortunately, it only lasted for about eight months and left Johnson heavily in debt. During this same period he made the acquaintance of Thomas A. Ledwith, a white Jacksonville attorney, whom he asked to help him prepare for the Florida bar examination. Despite the presence of a racist lawyer on the panel of examiners, Johnson passed the examination and was admitted to the bar. He and an Atlanta University classmate, Douglass Wetmore, opened a law office and thus Johnson divided his time between teaching in the daytime and the law practice at night.[6]

But in 1901 there was a fire that completely destroyed the building where the school was located. While he was waiting for the new school to be built, James and his brother, John Rosamond, visited New York City trying to sell some songs and the comic opera they had written together. Rosamond had studied for several years at the New England Conservatory of Music and returned to Jacksonville in 1897 after having spent some time working in a traveling musical comedy company. The two brothers then collaborated and wrote a comic opera, *Tolosa; or The Royal Document,* and while in New York trying unsuccessfully to sell it to producers, they met Bob Cole, a black songwriter and performer. At the end of the summer of 1899 the three collaborated again, this time on a love song, "Louisiana Lize," which represented movement beyond the raucous and bawdy "coon songs" of the era. This signaled Johnson's first attempt "to grope toward the realization of the importance of the American Negro's cultural background and his creative folk-art, and to speculate on the superstructure of conscious art that might be reared upon them" (152). They sold the song to May Irwin, a musical comedy star, for fifty dollars. This was the trio's first money earned for their musical compositions.

In the winter of 1900 James and Rosamond Johnson were back in Florida and were asked to help stage a celebration for Abraham Lincoln's birthday. At first, James was going to write an address but it soon turned into a poem, and Lincoln no longer was its subject. The words to "Lift Every Voice and Sing" came as "I paced back and forth, repeating the lines over and over to myself, going through the agony and ecstasy of creating" (154). The resulting poem, with music by his brother, was first performed by a chorus of five hundred schoolchildren and was a huge success. It was later adopted as the anthem for the NAACP and subsequently came to be considered the "Negro National Anthem" and has been sung and recorded ever since. While Johnson was particularly proud of the religious imagery of the last stanza, it was the middle section that directly reflected upon the history and conditions of African Americans that had the greatest cultural significance.

> Stony the road we trod,
> Bitter the chastening rod,
> Felt in the days when hope unborn died;
> Yet with a steady beat,
> Have not our weary feet
> Come to the place for which our fathers sighed?
> We have come over a way that with tears has been watered,

> We have come, treading our path through the blood of the
>   slaughtered,
> Out of the gloomy past,
> Till now we stand at last
> Where the white gleam of our bright star is cast.[7]

During the summer of 1900 and the summer and fall of 1901, James and Rosamond Johnson and Bob Cole worked on a number of songs together and by the winter of 1902 they had begun to sell. For the first six months of 1902, their royalties totaled over $1,500. Rosamond and Cole decided to put together a vaudeville act and urged James to join them in New York City. Earlier when James returned to Jacksonville in 1902, he was disappointed with the building erected to replace the Stanton School. He later learned that it was to be a temporary structure because the city school board planned on building several other schools for black children in other parts of the city, and was going to sell the land on which the Stanton School was located to private developers. Johnson investigated the matter, however, and found a stipulation in the original deed that stated that this particular piece of land could only be used for the provision of schooling for black children. Thus the "huge, crude, three-story frame building that looked more like a mill or granary than a schoolhouse" became the new and permanent Stanton School (184).

Johnson decided to resign his principalship when it became clear that he would be able to support himself in New York City on the income from his songwriting. When he arrived in the city in the summer of 1902, he was surprised by the lavish apartment that Bob Cole and Rosamond had found, which contained several large living rooms and an area in the back that served as a workshop/studio. Initially, Johnson was concerned about his finances, but after a minor disagreement was settled amicably over the royalties they were receiving from their publisher, Joseph Stern and Company, the team earned over twelve thousand dollars annually from their songs alone. Within a year, "we were at a height of popularity and success, equal, at least, to that of any other writers of popular songs in America," Johnson recalled.

> We had a clean business record and a list of hits that included: *The Maiden with the Dreamy Eyes; Mandy, Won't You Let Me Be Your Beau; Nobody's Lookin but the Owl and the Moon; Tell Me, Dusky Maiden; The Old Flag Never Touched the Ground; My Castle on the Nile; Under the Bamboo Tree;* and *Oh, Didn't He Ramble.* We had written a new song for Miss [May] Cahill, *The Congo Love Song,* that she was to sing and to make as famous as *Under the Bamboo Tree;* and there were others still to follow. In the fullness of our vogue there were times when songs of ours were being sung in three or four current musical productions (191).

Cole and the Johnson brothers became the toast of Broadway. They were soon asked by the leading Broadway producer, A. L. Erlanger, to write songs for his new show, *Humpty Dumpty,* which opened at the New Amsterdam Theater and was a big hit, and the unsuccessful *In Newport,* at the new Klaw and Erlanger Theater. The trio was invited to and gave lavish parties, where the guest list was a virtual who's who of the American musical theater at the time. They were often written up in the newspapers and were dubbed by one journalist "those ebony Offenbachs." Since Rosamond and Cole were often on the road with their vaudeville act, James decided to fill his spare time by enrolling at Columbia University where he took courses in English literature under Brander Matthews, which laid the basis for a lasting friendship between the two men.

In the spring of 1905, James decided to accompany his brother and Bob Cole on the Orpheum vaudeville circuit, but was put off by the Jim Crow arrangements they were subjected to in several places. When they returned to New York, they learned that Cole and Rosamond were booked to play at the Palace Theatre in London. The trio decided to spend the entire summer in Europe and make the Grand Tour, starting in Paris. For the first time since his early childhood, James Johnson experienced the freedom of "just being a human being."

> I need not try and analyze this change for my colored readers; they will understand in a flash what took place. For my white readers . . . I am afraid that my analysis will be inadequate, perhaps futile. . . . I was suddenly free; free from a sense of impending discomfort, insecurity, danger; free from the conflict within the Man-Negro dualism and the innumerable maneuvers in thought and behavior that it compels; free from the problem of the most obvious or subtle adjustments to a multitude of bans and taboos; free from special scorn, special tolerance, special condescension, special commiseration; free to be merely a man (209).

The experience was a delight. They stayed at the Hotel Continental in Paris, attended the Olympia Theater where Johnson was not only impressed by its size and beauty, but the fact that the orchestra played several of their hit songs. They visited Antwerp, Amsterdam, and Brussels, where they attended a musical at the Palais d'Eté, and met one of the dark-skinned performers who turned out to be an American Negro who lived in Europe with his daughter and wife, who had a German father and black mother but spoke only German. The high point was the engagement in England. "London blotted out the rest of Europe, for London was a city not to be visited but captured." Johnson quickly learned to love the city: "I grew aware of the beauty in the ruggedness of London. I rode atop busses for hours, not knowing or caring where they went, and was grateful for the intrinsic quality in so teeming a city that enabled a man to be alone" (215).

In the spring of 1904 Charles E. Anderson, the most important black politician in New York City, came to James Johnson with a proposition and request. He wanted Johnson to assist him in opening a Colored Republican Club on 53rd Street, and Johnson would head up the club's executive committee. Johnson was surprised and flattered, but pointed out that he had no experience in politics. Anderson, however, was more interested in Johnson's social connections. Indeed, Johnson was an attractive candidate for the position because he was *not* an aspiring politician. The proposal sounded exciting and Johnson agreed. The elegantly furnished club opened with much fanfare in the fall of 1904 and the major activity during those initial months was the reelection of Theodore Roosevelt as president. Johnson not only entertained visiting political dignitaries at the club, but also wrote a campaign song, "You're All Right Teddy," that became quite popular.[8] With Roosevelt's election victory in the fall, Charles Anderson accepted the political appointment as collector of internal revenue for southern Manhattan, which included the Wall Street district. At this time Anderson suggested to Johnson that he apply for a position in the Consular Service, which had been recently reorganized so that appointments were based on merit examinations and not solely on political connections. Johnson found the suggestion interesting, but he was too busy with his musical career and did not pursue the matter.

Upon Johnson's return from his European tour, Charles Anderson again brought up the possibility of the foreign service, and this time Johnson took the suggestion more seriously. His brother and Bob Cole had decided to form their own musical company and travel around the country. For Johnson the idea of traveling around the United States in a road company was not overly appealing, but "the lure of adventure and life on a strange continent" was exciting. He took the examination and passed, and through the assistance of Booker T. Washington, the unofficial black Republican boss, and Charles Anderson, Johnson was appointed the American consul in the Caribbean port of Puerto Cabello, Venezuela.[9]

In His Government's Service

JAMES WELDON JOHNSON arrived in Caracas, the capital of Venezuela, in the spring of 1906. Initially, he had trouble adjusting to the climate; but once he reached Puerto Cabello and became acclimated, he set about his consular duties and mingled on equal social terms with the local elite. Although he spent much time in Caracas, his assignment was in Puerto Cabello, a sleepy port town and backwater, and thus Johnson's most productive activity there was the completion of several poems and several chapters for his novel, *The Autobiography of an Ex-Colored Man*. After two years in Venezuela he applied for another station, and asked Charles Anderson and Ralph Waldo Tyler, a close associate of Booker T. Washington, to use their influence to get him a European post, preferably on the French Riviera.[10]

Although he was promoted, Johnson was assigned to a Central American post, in Corinto, Nicaragua, the country's most important Pacific port. In Puerto Cabello Johnson's living conditions had been semiluxurious, he had a large home with several servants, and there were secretaries to carry out most of the daily operations of the consular office. By way of contrast, Corinto resembled "a shanty town, built entirely of wood. There were less than a half-dozen attractive houses in it. The streets were unpaved; there was no electricity. Except for a couple of primitive grocery stores, there was not a shop in the place" (255).

Because of its strategic location near the Panama Canal, which was then under construction, Johnson spent much more time on consular affairs and less time on his writing. There had been threats of revolution against José Santos Zelaya, the longtime dictator, and fighting eventually broke out on the Caribbean coast. When the rebellion was crushed, things quieted down and Johnson applied for a leave of absence. On his return trip to New York City, Johnson married Grace Nail, whom he had met several years earlier. Her father, John B. Nail, owned a great deal of real estate and was considered one of the wealthiest black men in New York City. The couple had corresponded regularly and Johnson had visited her during his trips to the United States in 1907 and 1909, when they announced their engagement. They were married in a lavish ceremony in New York City on February 10, 1910.

When Johnson and his young bride arrived in Corinto in March, there was another insurrection underway, with the United States supporting the leader of the rebel group, General Juan Estrada, who eventually assumed power in August 1910. Very little of the fighting touched Corinto, however, and life for Johnson was more pleasant due to Grace's presence. Once she was set up in a new home, and began to learn Spanish in earnest, Grace Johnson adjusted to most things very well. Then one day, the earth began to shake under the house, lamps tumbled, the furniture began to move, and James immediately shouted to Grace:

> "Get out to the street, get out to the street". . . . In cataloguing for
> Grace the things she might expect in Nicaragua, I had failed to include
> the item of earthquakes; and my statement that it was because of their
> frequency that they were not regarded with great concern did not, for
> the time wholly reassure her. In truth, the question, "Did you feel the
> earthquake last night?" was asked with scarcely greater agitation than,
> "Did you hear the rain" (269).

Johnson requested and received another leave of absence in the summer of 1911 and he personally sought the assistance of Ralph Tyler, a personal friend of President William Taft, and Charles Anderson in getting another consular post. Unfortunately, he only received renewed assurances that he would get one "as soon as practicable." He returned to Corinto in March 1912, this time without Grace on the assumption that his stay would be brief. Another rebellion had broken out in Nicaragua while Johnson had been away, and the United States was supporting the new president, Adolfo Díaz, who sought American military assistance. The rebellion was led by General Luís Mena after the president removed him from his position as minister of war. General Mena refused to hand over his authority and launched an insurrection beginning with the bombardment of the capitol at Managua. As refugees fled south toward Corinto, Johnson, as the highest ranking American official, worked with American military commanders to protect the port until the arrival of U.S. battleships carrying military reinforcements.

The rebel forces were successful in capturing León and Chinandega to the north and were headed for Corinto. To avoid bloodshed Johnson let the leaders of the rebel forces know that he was willing to negotiate the terms of surrender for the city. Johnson had been notified that it was only a matter of days before the arrival of U.S. Marine reinforcements. When rebel leaders entered Corinto to discuss the terms of surrender, Johnson stalled the negotiations long enough for the USS *Denver* to arrive carrying five hundred marines. Johnson then broke off further negotiations with the rebel commanders. The next day the USS *California* arrived carrying another five hundred marines, and one day later the *Annapolis* brought an additional seven hundred to Corinto, which was now fully protected from rebel attack. Within two weeks the rebel leader, General Mena, surrendered to government forces, and soon afterward the cities captured by the rebels were retaken by troops loyal to President Adolfo Díaz, with the assistance of the American military.[11]

Because he was able to forestall the rebels' capture of the port, Johnson received high praise for his diplomatic efforts in the dispatches sent to Washington by the American military commanders in Nicaragua. Johnson hoped that his performance in this crisis would improve his chances of gaining a transfer to a European post within a year. Unfortunately, in July 1912 James Johnson, Sr., died in Jacksonville, and when his brother, Rosamond, informed him that his father's estate was in shambles, Johnson requested another leave of absence that fall to return to Florida to help straighten out the family's affairs (Rosamond was on tour in London). Upon arriving Johnson found that there had been considerable impropriety in the handling of his father's investments by a local bank that eventually went bankrupt; and that it would take much more time than he anticipated to deal with the situation. Moreover, with the election of Woodrow Wilson as president in November 1912, the possibility of Johnson gaining a promotion and transfer became significantly more remote, and even the likelihood that he would be able to remain in the foreign service greatly decreased. The Democrats were purging the government of white Republican appointees in the State Department, and Johnson was a black. Johnson met with the new secretary of state, William Jennings Bryan, who informed him that as a Republican he should feel lucky that he had any position at all in the U.S. foreign service. "I left the Secretary of State with this clearly in mind: I was up against politics plus race prejudice; I might be allowed to remain at my post; if so, I should be there for another four years at least, perhaps another eight. I came to the definite conclusion that life was too short for me to spend eight more years in Corinto. I wrote out my resignation" (293).[12]

Literary Pursuits

JAMES WELDON JOHNSON—lawyer, musician, composer, poet, educator, diplomat, and journalist—was not completely without employment alternatives when he made the decision in October 1913 to resign from the foreign service. He would have liked to have been able to earn a living through his writing alone, but that was not yet in the offing. Before leaving New York City for Puerto Cabello in 1907 Johnson had made several important literary connections. He had met Richard Watson Gilder, editor of *Century* magazine and William Hayes Ward of *The Independent*, where several of his early poems were first published. These poems in form reflected the conventional rhymed verse of the period; the subject matter was alternately universal and race-specific. "Mother Night" waxed poetic about the "brooding mother" of the universe out of which "the first sun fledged his wings of flame"; while "O Black and Unknown Bards" celebrated the enormous cultural contribution of the anonymous authors of the Negro Spirituals. The latter was a particularly moving evocation of the beauty and strength of these slave songs "which stirs the soul or melts the heart to tears."

> Not that great German master in his dream
> of harmonies that thundered amongst the stars
> At the creation, ever heard a theme
> Nobler than "Go down, Moses." Mark its bars,
> How like a mighty trumpet-call they stir
> The blood. Such are the notes that men have sung
> Going to valorous deeds; such tones there were
> That helped make history when Time was young.[13]

The Autobiography of an Ex-Colored Man was published by Sherman, French and Company in 1912. Although it received some favorable reviews, it did not sell very well and did little to advance Johnson's literary reputation since it was published anonymously. However, as part of the commemoration of the fiftieth anniversary of Abraham Lincoln's Emancipation Proclamation, which freed all the slaves in the rebelling states, Johnson wrote his poem "Fifty Years," which appeared through the efforts of his former instructor Brander Matthews in the *New York Times* on January 1, 1913. The spirit of the poem reflected that found in "Lift Every Voice and Sing," in that it was meant to inspire the African Americans' faith in the United States. It was patriotic and declared that "never yet has come the cry/When that fair flag has been assailed/For men to do, for men to die,/That have we faltered or failed." Johnson also declared that African Americans have more of a claim to the country's resources than "outcasts" and "aliens" from other lands.

> This land is ours by right of birth,
> This land is ours by right of toil;
> We helped to turn its virgin earth,
> Our sweat is in its fruitful soil.[14]

Johnson's return to Jacksonville in March 1913 signaled his reintroduction to the southern way of life and his wife's first experiences with the region and its distressing racial mores. While there were many parties and celebrations held in their honor by the black residents, the couple's interactions with local whites, some of whom Johnson had known since childhood, were disturbing and difficult. Some blacks had suggested that the discourtesies and slights, such as the failure of southern white men to tip their hats when greeting black women, were "trivial things" that did not matter. But to Johnson this was merely another indication that there was "no common ground" between southern blacks and whites. Then one day when he went into his father's bank to conduct some business, the president abruptly asked, "Do you intend to stay in Jacksonville?" Johnson replied he was not sure. The elderly bank president than exclaimed, "You can't do it. If you had never gone away, it would be a different matter. But Jacksonville is not the Jacksonville you used to know. Don't try it" (299).

Indeed in the early 1900s the entire South and nation had changed and racial discrimination and conflict was yet once more on the upsurge. The number of lynchings increased dramatically, and African Americans found more and more aspects of their social life proscribed by legally mandated segregation. The election of Woodrow Wilson signaled the return of southern Democrats to positions of power in the federal government. They moved quickly to segregate black employees in federal offices and dining areas. African American officeholders were systematically removed from their positions throughout the federal establishment and Republican politicians made only halfhearted efforts to oppose these changes. Johnson recalled in *Along This Way* that "in several communities near Jacksonville, newly appointed postmasters cut 'Jim Crow' windows at the side, through which Negroes were to get their mail, *without coming into the post office.* There they had to stand in sun or rain until the last white person on the inside had been served" (301).[15]

In the face of this discrimination James and Grace Johnson were happy to leave Jacksonville and return to New York in the fall of 1914. Grace's brother, Jack Nail, had become one of the most important real estate agents in Harlem, which was then attracting thousands of southern blacks who were migrating to the city and in need of housing. Earlier African Americans were concentrated in the southern part of Manhattan, the Five Points area, but beginning in the 1910s Harlem was opened up to black residents. The Johnsons followed this new trend and moved there as well. Within weeks of their return to New York, Johnson was offered (again through the intervention of his close friend Charles Anderson) a position as head of the editorial page on the *New York Age,* the largest and most important weekly black newspaper in the city. Struggling under severe financial burdens, T. Thomas Fortune had sold the newspaper in 1907 to Fred Moore, a confidant of Booker T. Washington. Moore became one of the most vigilant defenders of Washington's conservative ideological positions and lost no opportunity to use the pages of the *Age* to excoriate those who questioned the quality of Washington's leadership.[16]

In September 1914 Johnson returned to New York specifically to press ahead on his career as a writer, and the editorship at the *Age* would assure that his name was kept before the black reading public. In the issue announcing Johnson's appointment, it was also revealed for the first time publicly that Johnson was the author of *The Autobiography of an Ex-Colored Man* and the newspaper was praised widely for adding a man of Johnson's repute and ability to its staff. Johnson's weekly column, "Views and Reviews," became popular with black New Yorkers because of the honest and forthright manner it addressed pressing issues facing African Americans.[17]

Despite the *Age's* close association with Booker T. Washington and his Tuskegee Machine, Johnson managed to chart a middle course in his weekly columns between Washington's conservatism and the "racial radicalism" associated with Du Bois and the leaders of the NAACP. With Washington's death in October 1915, there was less need for Johnson to concern himself with the possibility of alienating conservative readers and he became even more outspoken about the deteriorating race relations and increasing racial violence throughout the country. When the NAACP led the campaign against the distortions and misrepresentations of the Reconstruction era depicted in D. W. Griffith's path-breaking epic film *The Birth of a Nation,* Johnson not only supported this action, but Du Bois published Johnson's poem "White Witch" in *The Crisis* magazine at the height of the campaign. The film had depicted black politicians lusting after white women whose virtue was saved only through the intervention of the Ku Klux Klan. Johnson's poem, however, warned black men about the "white witch" who "has seen your strong young limbs and heard your laughter loud and gay," but who also "has marked you for her prey."

> O, brothers mine, take care! Take care!
> The great white witch rides out to-night.
> O, younger brothers mine beware!
> Look not upon her beauty bright;
> For in her glance there is a snare,
> And in her smile there is a blight.[18]

In *Along This Way* Johnson noted that the poem "figured rather sensationally in a court scene in Boston, where colored citizens were attempting by legal steps to prohibit the exhibition of the moving picture, *The Birth of A Nation*. One of the attorneys for the picture people rose in court, waving a copy of *The Crisis* in his hand, and tried to make the poem evidence that such a picture as *The Birth of A Nation* was an absolute necessity in the United States" (306).[19]

Johnson had his own experience with the racial distortions and stereotypes that could be disseminated broadly through motion pictures. When he was in Jacksonville, which at the time was making a bid to become a capital of the motion picture industry, he had written several scripts for short films, and sold three of them to white filmmakers. When he and his wife saw "the first picture, [they] were so disappointed in it that [they] were actually ashamed to see the others" (298). *Aunt Mandy's Chicken Dinner* was labeled a "darky comedy" and presented black mammies and "pickaninnies" in the most ridiculous situations. While Johnson's script was much like the dialect poetry and song lyrics he had written for Broadway, the film was crude and offensive and depicted blacks in a most unfavorable light. Johnson vowed never to write for the motion pictures again.[20]

The Artist As Social and Political Activist

WHEN BOOKER T. Washington died in October 1915, W. E. B. Du Bois and Joel E. Spingarn, as members of the NAACP's Executive Committee, hit upon the idea of a national conference between the NAACP leadership and Washington's associates to effect a reconciliation between the two ideological camps. In planning the conference, which took place at Joel Spingarn's estate in Amenia, New York, in August 1916, the NAACP worked closely with Emmett J. Scott, Washington's private secretary, and Robert R. Moton, the new principal of Tuskegee Institute, in choosing those to be sent invitations. Charles Anderson, Fred Moore, and James Weldon Johnson were among those invited, and during the conference Du Bois purposely remained in the background. The meeting went well, and ultimately the statement issued afterward reflected positions supported by both radicals and conservatives. All forms of education, not just industrial, were recommended as appropriate for racial advancement; and the more moderate stances taken by southern black leaders on political rights and protest were endorsed.[21]

James Weldon Johnson not only attended the Amenia Conference but was involved in planning the program. He was also a major participant, presenting a paper on "A Working Programme for the Future." During that summer and fall of 1916 he was actively working for the election of Supreme Court Justice Charles Evans Hughes as president of the United States. Johnson was hired to write speeches for Hughes and other Republican candidates and he traveled around New York state speaking on their behalf. Right before the election, Johnson received a letter from Joel Spingarn asking him if he was interested in a new position as field secretary for the NAACP. At first Johnson demurred for several reasons. He was also considering a position with the National Urban League, which was working with the thousands of southern migrants moving into cities in the North. Moreover, if Charles Evans Hughes was elected president, there was also the possibility of a political appointment. Hughes, however, lost by a very narrow margin, which crushed that possibility. Mary White Ovington, a member of the executive committee on the NAACP board, openly opposed the hiring of Johnson as field secretary because she believed he was "hopelessly reactionary." But at the December 1916 meeting, after much debate and some maneuvering, the Board of Directors voted to offer Johnson the position and he later accepted.[22]

When James Weldon Johnson joined the NAACP staff in December 1916, it was hardly a smooth-running bureaucratic operation. The major source of friction was Du Bois, the only black in an executive position. Du Bois as editor of *The Crisis* had made the magazine the most popular and influential black publication in the country. But some members of the NAACP Board of Directors, particularly Oswald Garrison Villard, chafed at the fact that Du Bois often published editorials and articles in the magazine without first submitting them to the board's publications committee. While Du Bois had his defenders on the board, among them Mary White Ovington and Joel Spingarn, the day-to-day operation of the national headquarters was often disrupted by personal disagreements that ultimately led to the resignations of the first two executive secretaries, Frances Blascoer and May Childs Nerney.[23]

At the time of May Nerney's resignation in January 1916, several members of the staff suggested that an African American be appointed to the executive secretary position. Nerney and others felt that since the organization was increasingly supported by its growing black membership, it was appropriate to have more blacks in administrative positions. The board disagreed, and hired Royal Freeman Nash, a white writer who headed the branch in northern California. By November 1916, however, it had become clear that while Nash was good as an office administrator, he was a poor organizer and representative of the organization in public. The decision was then made by the board to hire a field secretary who would work to expand the number of NAACP branches, and only blacks were considered for this position.[24]

When James Weldon Johnson began his work in December 1916, the organization had sixty-eight branches in northern and western cities, and only three in the South, located in New Orleans and Shreveport, Louisiana, and Key West, Florida. Johnson believed its greatest potential for growth lay in the South, and he submitted a plan for organizing groups there. He set out on his campaign and traveled to hundreds of locations, meeting with local black and white leaders and professionals and ultimately setting up numerous branches. By 1919 the NAACP had over 100,000 members and 310 branches, with 110 located in the South. One of the reasons for this success was the increased economic prosperity that came on the heels of the U.S. entrance into World War I in April 1917.[25]

During the war years NAACP officials were kept busy with a number of issues relating to African Americans and the war effort. Although the organization was criticized for turning its back on the strong integrationist positions of the past, NAACP officials worked successfully with U.S. Army officials for the opening of a separate black officers' training camp at Des Moines, Iowa. Within the first six months, May to November 1917, 639 African Americans were commissioned as officers. In *Along This Way* Johnson observed that "the common sense of the matter and the pride the race took in the results snuffed criticism out" (319).[26]

Racial violence and lynchings increased during the war, and the NAACP launched a full-scale investigation of the race riot in East St. Louis, Illinois, in which over fifty blacks were killed and hundreds wounded. In order to dramatize the indignation and outrage over this mass slaughter of innocent black men, women, and children, NAACP officials organized a "silent protest parade" in New York City. "On Saturday, July 28, [1917]," James Weldon Johnson recalled in his autobiography,

nine or ten thousand Negroes marched silently down Fifth Avenue to the sound only of muffled drums. The procession was headed by some children, some of them not older than six, dressed in white. These were followed by women dressed in white, and bringing up the rear came the men in dark clothes. They carried banners, some of which read:

MOTHER, DO LYNCHERS GO TO HEAVEN?

GIVE ME A CHANCE TO LIVE.

TREAT US SO WE MAY LOVE OUR COUNTRY.

MR. PRESIDENT, WHY NOT MAKE AMERICA SAFE FOR DEMOCRACY?

Just ahead of the man who carried the American flag went a streamer that stretched across the street and bore the inscription: YOUR HANDS ARE FULL OF BLOOD! (320–21).[27]

Within ten days of the march in New York City, there was a shootout in Houston, Texas, involving black soldiers of the Twenty-fourth Infantry. Two blacks and twenty-five whites, including five police officers, were killed. Sixty-three black soldiers were subsequently court-martialed, tried, and sentenced to death for the murders. On the morning of December 10, 1917, thirteen were hanged. At a second court martial, of the fifty who were retried, sixteen were condemned to death and the remainder were given life sentences. Johnson headed a delegation of four who visited Washington in hopes of meeting with President Wilson. After some difficulty and delay they were finally able to meet with the President and to present him with a petition that asked him to "speak against these specific wrongs. . . . Our people are intently listening and praying that you may find it in your heart to speak that word" (324). The President decided to act and immediately brought an end to military executions (on the homefront) and ordered that no more were to take place until after court martial proceedings were reviewed by the War Department. As result of the review, of the sixteen black soldiers condemned to death, five were executed on the basis of the new investigation and eleven had their sentences commuted to life imprisonment.[28]

When the United States entered the war in April 1917, Royal Nash, the NAACP executive secretary, asked for a leave of absence to join the army. In the interim Johnson served as acting secretary. Nash later decided to resign his position, and in looking for a permanent replacement, the Board of Directors did not even consider an African American for the position, not even Johnson, who had demonstrated over the previous year that he could do the job. John R. Shillady, a well-respected New York social worker, was brought in as executive secretary in February 1918 and Walter White was hired by the Board of Directors as assistant secretary. During one of his speaking tours in 1917, Johnson had met the young Walter White, who came from a prominent black family in Atlanta. Johnson was impressed by the young man's intelligence and energy and asked if White would be interested in working for the national organization. At the time White was not sure about his draft status, so he did not respond immediately. He was later rejected by the draft board. In his autobiography, *A Man Called White,* published in 1948, he suggested that the reason U.S. draft officials rejected him was because he was light enough to "pass for white." When the United States entered the war, White recalled, "fantastic stories were believed that as soon as white soldiers went off to war, Negroes would rise up and massacre white people in their beds under the direction of the Kaiser's agents. Obviously, light-skinned Negroes who could easily pass as white would be the kind the Kaiser would use."[29]

Walter White's physical appearance was an asset in the NAACP's investigations of lynchings, particularly in the South. He was able to infiltrate white supremacist groups and organizations, including the Ku Klux Klan, to gather information about attacks on African Americans. Because he was a southerner and appeared to be one of their own, he was even more effective than northern white NAACP officials in gaining the confidence of local whites.[30]

In the immediate postwar years there was a significant increase in race riots, mob violence, and lynchings, many of which were investigated and publicly exposed by NAACP officials. White executive secretary John Shillady learned personally the gravity of the situation facing African Americans in the United States only after he began working for the NAACP. When the Texas attorney general attempted to seize the membership lists and books of the NAACP's Austin branch, Shillady went to the city in August 1919 to discuss the matter with local officials. On his way to his hotel following the meeting, he was stopped by a group of whites, taken away, and interrogated about his racial views. After being released, Shillady was attacked physically and badly beaten by another group of white men, including some who had questioned him earlier. Psychologically, he never recovered from the assault and soon submitted his resignation as NAACP executive secretary. In his letter of resignation, Shillady wrote, "I am less confident than heretofore of the speedy success of the Association's full program and of the probability of overcoming within a reasonable period, the forces opposed to Negro equality by the means and methods which are within the Association's power to employ."[31]

African Americans inside and outside NAACP circles assumed that James Weldon Johnson, who had demonstrated his administrative skills while serving as acting secretary, would soon be appointed to replace John Shillady. Although he was finally given the position, the NAACP Board of Directors took almost a year to finalize the appointment. Indeed, it was only after Du Bois and several other blacks on the Board pushed the issue that the official vote was taken. As the association's chief executive officer, Johnson fully supported the use of publicity to expose the brutality of lynching and mob violence. In his autobiography Johnson provided important details about the activities of the NAACP in the postwar period, particularly its efforts to expose the truth about lynchings and the causes of racial violence. In 1920, the association published and widely circulated the pamphlet *Thirty Years of Lynching in the United States, 1889–1919,* which presented the grisly details of numerous assaults and murders, and corroborated the earlier findings of Ida B. Wells-Barnett that in less than eighteen percent of the cases was the alleged rape of a white woman by a black man even suggested as the reason for the attacks.[32]

In *Along This Way* Johnson also described his personal experiences in Washington lobbying U.S. congressmen for the passage of a bill aimed at protecting the rights of potential victims of lynch mobs. Since local police officials rarely pursued the perpetrators of these heinous acts, in April 1921 Congressman L. C. Dyer of St. Louis, Missouri, introduced a bill that would make lynching a federal crime and the perpetrators guilty of murder. Johnson worked conscientiously over the next two years to gain passage of the bill. Although it managed to pass the House of Representatives in January 1922, southern Democrats blocked the measure in the Senate. What was most disturbing to Johnson was the decision of Republican senators in December 1923 to abandon the measure, after having given him assurances of their full support. "It would be difficult for me to tell just what my feelings were," he wrote in *Along This Way.* "I think disgust was the dominant emotion." Johnson felt betrayed by the Republican leadership and "my thoughts were made more bitter by a fact which I knew and which every Senator admitted, the fact that the bill would have been passed had it been brought to a vote" (371).

Politically, the 1920s witnessed the abandonment of the struggle for black rights by the Republican Party throughout the nation. In the 1920 presidential election, Republican Warren G. Harding called for a "return to normalcy," and made no overt efforts to seek the support of black voters. Republicans Calvin Coolidge in 1924 and Herbert Hoover in 1928 even made inroads into the solid Democratic South by promoting a type of "lily-white Republicanism" in their successful campaigns for the White House. The economic prosperity of the 1920s extended even into parts of the South, and Republicans were not about to alienate southern white voters by supporting "radical" leaders, black or white, who advocated "social equality."[33]

For African Americans and other oppressed people of African descent, active participation in World War I raised their political and cultural consciousness. While the slogan "Africa for the Africans" gave voice to a new ideological perspective that would serve as the rallying cry for the African liberation movements by the middle of the twentieth century, in the 1920s there were few political advancements along these lines by Africans either on the continent or in the diaspora. But the radical shift in consciousness would have profound cultural and ideological consequences in the postwar years. Indeed, in the most influential artistic and cultural circles in New York City in the Roaring Twenties, African Americans represented the *nouvelle vague* in that flamboyant era "when the Negro was in vogue."

Disseminating the Gifts of Black Folk

JAMES WELDON JOHNSON found time during and after World War I to pursue his career as a literary artist despite his heavy schedule of activities associated with his duties as executive secretary for the NAACP. Johnson continued to write his weekly column in the *New York Age* between 1916 and 1923 and of-ten reviewed the latest literary, dramatic, and musical productions offered to the American and African-American public. In January 1915 Johnson inaugu-rated a regular "Poetry Corner" in his column and requested and published verses sent to him by aspiring poets. The column laid the foundation for the publication in 1922 of *The Book of American Negro Poetry*, the first major an-thology of African-American verse. At the time very few of the artists included in the volume were known to even the black reading public, and its publication marked a milestone in the African-American literary tradition. "America as a whole knew something of [Paul Laurence] Dunbar," Johnson wrote in *Along This Way*, "but it was practically unaware that there were such things as Negro poets and Negro poetry. So I decided to write an introduction; and the intro-duction developed into a forty-two-page essay on 'The Creative Genius of the Negro' " (374). This essay elaborated upon ideas and issues with which John-son had been preoccupied for over a decade. The same points raised by the un-named protagonist in *The Autobiography of an Ex-Colored Man* were discussed in this influential essay in *The Book of American Negro Poetry*.[34]

As was the case with Alexander Crummell and Ida B. Wells-Barnett in the nineteenth century, race vindication was a major preoccupation for James Wel-don Johnson. "The status of the Negro in the United States is more a question of national mental attitude toward the race than actual conditions. And noth-ing will do more to change that mental attitude and raise his status than a demonstration of intellectual parity by the Negro through the production of literature and art." By presenting the history and development of Negro po-etry, and demonstrating the high intellectual and artistic standards achieved, Johnson hoped to prove the Negro worthy of inclusion on an equal basis with other races and ethnic groups in American civilization and society. "A people may become great through many means, but there is only one measure by which its greatness is recognized and acknowledged. The final measure of the greatness of all peoples is the amount and standard of the literature and art they have produced." Johnson believed that "no people that has produced great lit-erature and art has ever been looked upon by the world as distinctly inferior."[35]

Johnson was convinced that "the creative genius of the Negro" had "uni-versal appeal and influence." With the Uncle Remus folktales, the spirituals, ragtime, and the cakewalk, "the Negro has already proved the possession of these powers by being the creator of the only things artistic that have yet sprung from American soil and been universally acknowledged as distinctive American products."[36] Johnson also argued that this creativity was continuing and the latest example (1920) was "the several varieties of 'The Blues.' " As was the case with much of the ragtime music, "these Blues had their origin in Memphis, and towns along the Mississippi. They are a sort of lament of a lover who is feeling 'blue' over the loss of his sweetheart."[37]

While many professional musicians discount ragtime and the blues as "lower forms of art," with the spirituals "the Negro has given America not only its only folk songs, but a mass of noble music." The themes for the spirituals were taken from the Bible, "but the melodies, where did they come from? Some of them so weirdly sweet, and others so wonderfully strong." Johnson believed that "in the riotous rhythms of Ragtime the Negro expressed his irrepressible buoyancy, his keen response to the sheer joy of living; in the spirituals he voiced his sense of beauty and his deep religious feeling." Although Harry Burleigh, Will Mercer Cook, Nathaniel Dett and other black musicians had already incorporated the spirituals in concert and orchestral works, Johnson predicted that "there will yet come great Negro composers who will take this music and voice through it not only the soul of the race, but the soul of America."[38]

The purpose of *The Book of American Negro Poetry* was to bring to light certain accomplishments in the literary realm. In his history of Negro poets and poetry, Johnson concluded that in the early nineteenth century, with the exception of Phillis Wheatley, Jupiter Hammon, George M. Horton, Frances E. W. Harper, James M. Bell, and Alberry M. Whitman, many of these poets "must be considered more in light of what they attempted than what they accomplished. Many of them showed marked talent, but barely a half dozen of them demonstrated even mediocre mastery of technique in the use of poetic material and forms." And even the six whom he believed excelled above the others failed to "sound a distinctly original note." "But the same thing may be said of all American poets down to the writers of the present generation, with the exception of [Edgar Allan] Poe and Walt Whitman. The thing in which these black poets are mostly excelled by their contemporaries is mere technique."[39]

According to Johnson, Paul Laurence Dunbar was the first African-American poet to obtain mastery of poetic material and technique. "He was the first to rise to a height from which he could take a perspective view of his own race. He was the first to see objectively its humor, its superstitions, its shortcomings; the first to feel sympathetically its heart-wounds, its yearnings, its aspirations, and to voice them in a purely literary form." Dunbar did this in his poems in Negro dialect for which he was best known. But Dunbar's early poems were not in this style and "showed no distinctive Negro influence," and reflected the contemporary American poetic forms and styles. Johnson also believed Dunbar was important because, like Alexander Crummell and Liberian intellectual Ed-

ward Wilmot Blyden, "he was of unmixed Negro blood, so as the greatest figure produced, he stands as an example at once refuting and confounding those
who wish to believe that whatever extraordinary ability an Aframerican shows is
due to an admixture of white blood."[40]

But Johnson decided to include very few poems in Negro dialect by Dunbar or other black poets in this anthology because he believed that few true poets in the early 1920s wrote in Negro dialect. The younger poets wanted to
move beyond "the artistic niche" carved out for the Negro "as a happy-go-
lucky, singing, shuffling, banjo-picking being or as a more or less pathetic figure." The problem was not in Negro dialect itself, which Johnson felt had great
poetic potential, but the literary conventions associated with it, "the mode of
convention in which Negro dialect in the United States is set." Johnson cor-
rectly predicted in 1922 that, in time, "the colored poet . . . may sit down to
write in dialect without feeling that his first line will put the general reader in a
frame of mind which demands that the poem be humorous or pathetic. In the
meantime, there is no reason why these poets should not continue to do the
beautiful things that can be done, and done best, in the dialect."[41]

Johnson's conclusion made clear his integrationist ideological perspective.
He did not endorse the idea that these younger poets should be moving toward the creation of a distinct African-American artistic and literary aesthetic.

> In stating the need for Aframerican poets in the United States to work
> out a new and distinctive form of expression, I do not wish to be un-
> derstood to hold any theory that they should limit themselves to Ne-
> gro poetry, to racial themes; the sooner they are able to write
> *American* poetry spontaneously, the better. Nevertheless, I believe
> that the richest contribution the Negro poet can make to the Ameri-
> can literature of the future will be the fusion into it of his own individ-
> ual artistic gifts.[42]

This idea that American art would be greatly improved by an infusion of
African-American cultural materials was very popular in the 1920s, not merely
among black artists and writers, but among white artists as well. But the problem that arose and became the subject of intense debate was whether or not the
"artistic" works produced by blacks and whites reflected accurately the African-
American experience or were merely newly minted racist distortions and misrepresentations. From Eugene O'Neill's popular play *The Emperor Jones,*
produced on Broadway in 1920, to Claude McKay's novel *Home to Harlem,*
published in 1928, the "New Negro" intellectuals debated the most appropriate content for artistic works claiming to represent the African-American experience.

New Negro Ideological Slugfests

ONE OF the major reasons for the fierce intellectual debate among the New Negroes over the depictions of Africans and African Americans in art and literature was the reality that there were so many different types of "New Negroes," each with their own particular ideological preoccupations. Most black intellectuals at the time agreed with the black masses that "the old Negro" who had been unwilling to stand up for his rights and acquiesced to the social proscriptions imposed on him by white America had been a casualty of the war. Black soldiers who had gone to Europe "to make the world safe for democracy" became committed to making the United States safe for African Americans, or would die trying. During and after the war there was an unmistakable shift in the response of young blacks to unjustified attacks by whites. Before World War I racial conflicts were more like pogroms than race riots and enraged white mobs attacked generally defenseless blacks, burning their homes and businesses, forcing them to flee the area. During and after the war, particularly during the violent summer of 1919, blacks fought back and as a result there was less damage to black property and as many whites were killed and wounded in these incidents as blacks. African-American newspaper and magazine editors urged African Americans to fight back because a "brand New Negro" who stood up for his rights had now appeared on the scene.[43]

There was also a significant rise in the number of African-American magazines and newspapers, all competing for support among the increasingly literate black masses. Many editors and publishers used the concept of the "New Negro" to bolster a particular ideological position that they believed would advance both African-American elites and masses. At the beginning of the decade the NAACP's *Crisis* magazine was the largest and most influential black publication in the country, with a circulation of nearly 100,000. The magazine pushed its integrationist positions each month in articles, reviews, and particularly the editorials by W. E. B. Du Bois. A. Philip Randolph and Chandler Owen began publishing *The Messenger* magazine in 1917, and although they too supported integration, they were socialists and more concerned about integrating African-American workers into the organized labor movement. While Du Bois in his editorials often referred to himself as "a socialist of the path," and supported the redistribution of wealth from rich capitalists to the exploited working class, *The Messenger* was avowedly anti-capitalist, and its publishers believed that with the end of capitalism in the United States would come an end of conflicts between black and white workers. At its peak in 1923, *The Messenger*'s monthly circulation topped fifty thousand. The *Crusader* magazine, the official publication of the African Blood Brotherhood, militantly called for an end of capitalist exploitation of the working classes and wanted a Bolshevik-type revolution in the United States. The magazine achieved its peak monthly circulation of close to 35,000 in 1921. The editors, Cyril V. Briggs and W. A. Domingo, were closely linked to the emerging communist movement in the United States and came to advocate black nationalist positions in many ways similar to those adopted by Marcus Garvey's Universal Negro Improvement Association (UNIA).[44]

Marcus Garvey arrived in the United States from Jamaica in April 1916, and by 1924 the UNIA had several hundred thousand members, far more than the NAACP or any other black nonreligious organization. The Garveyite newspaper, *Negro World,* became the largest circulating newspaper among African Americans in the United States and abroad. Garvey was able to build the largest mass movement among African Americans before the coming of the civil rights movement in the 1950s and 1960s because the UNIA program appealed to the core values of the African-American experience. As result of their experiences as an oppressed people in American society, African Americans came to value freedom, resistance, education, and self-determination, and the UNIA, in its black-controlled stores and factories, steamship line, fraternal organizations, reading rooms, newspapers, and other publications, exemplified these beliefs and values. The black nationalist ideology espoused by the Garveyites reflected the self-determinist values of the black masses and thus the organization gained mass support.[45]

Garvey himself was arrested in 1921 on trumped-up charges of mail fraud by officials from the U.S. Department of Justice, and was tried, convicted, and eventually deported from the United States in 1927. At the time the Garveyites firmly believed that the leadership of the NAACP, particularly Du Bois, was involved in this conspiracy and miscarriage of justice. While recently released federal records reveal that federal officials under the leadership of J. Edgar Hoover were out to "get Garvey," there is no evidence that NAACP officials or other black leaders were part of the government operation. Robert Bagnall, the NAACP director of branches in the early 1920s, was a member of Friends of Negro Freedom, a small group that sought the deportation of Garvey following his ill-advised meeting with the Grand Kleagle of the Ku Klux Klan in August 1922. But federal officers had decided that "Garvey Must Go" long before the Friends of Negro Freedom's campaign ever got off the ground.[46]

The Garveyites, however, were convinced that NAACP officials were part of the federal government's program of surveillance and harassment because Du Bois, James Weldon Johnson, William Pickens, and other NAACP officials publicly expressed their ideological differences with Marcus Garvey in editorials, articles, and speeches sometimes calling for his deportation. The debate between the integrationists and nationalists reached its lowest point in 1923

following the appearance of an article in *Century* magazine by Du Bois, entitled "Back to Africa." Full of sarcasm and condescension, the article ridiculed
Garvey and his movement.

> It was upon the tenth of August, in High Harlem of Manhattan Is-
> land, where a hundred thousand Negroes live. There was a long, low,
> unfinished church basement, roofed over. A little, fat black man, ugly,
> but with intelligent eyes and a big head, was seated on a plank plat-
> form beside a "throne," dressed in a military uniform of the gayest
> mid-Victorian type, heavy with gold lace, epaulets, plume, and sword.
> Beside him were "potentates," and before him knelt a succession of
> several colored gentlemen. These in the presence of a thousand or
> more applauding black spectators were duly "knighted" and raised to
> the "peerage" as knight-commanders and dukes of Uganda and the
> Niger.[47]

Du Bois suggested that the entire ceremony looked like a "dress rehearsal
of a new comic opera." But these men were serious and, according to Du Bois,
to many American Negroes "it seemed . . . sinister, this enthroning of a dema-
gogue, a blatant boaster, who with monkey shines was deluding the people and
taking their hard-earned dollars; and in High Harlem there rose the insistent
cry 'Garvey Must Go.' " The description of Garvey was insulting and Du Bois
even tried to argue that the UNIA program "took no account of the American
Negro problem; he knew nothing about it. What he was trying to do was settle the Jamaican problem in the United States." But given the fact that hundreds of thousands of American blacks joined the UNIA and supported its
activities, Garvey must have been doing something right. The reality was that
the UNIA was much more successful in the early 1920s in gaining the support
of the black masses in the United States than was the NAACP.[48]

In any case Du Bois's article was the opening salvo in a prolonged and
dirty war of words. The headline in the Garveyites' *Negro World* read: "W. E. B.
Du Bois As Hater of Dark People." In calling Marcus Garvey "black" and
"ugly," Du Bois was clearly using white standards of beauty. Garvey declared
that "this so-called professor of Harvard and Berlin ought to know by now that
the standard of beauty within a race is not arrived at by comparison with another race; as, for instance, if we were to desire to find out the standard of
beauty among the Japanese people, we would not judge them from the Anglo-
Saxon viewpoint, but Japanese." Garvey went on to argue that if there was any
ugliness in the race, it was reflected more in Du Bois's family background than
in Garvey's physical appearance. In his autobiographical work, *Darkwater:
Voices from Within the Veil,* published in 1920, Du Bois proclaimed that he was
born "with a flood of Negro blood, a strain of French, a bit of Dutch, but,
thank God! no 'Anglo-Saxon.' " Garvey declared that Du Bois himself "tells us

he is a little Dutch, a little French, and a little Negro. Why, in fact, the man is a monstrosity." Du Bois's description of Garvey as black and ugly "only goes to show how much hate Du Bois has for the black blood in his veins. Anything that is black, to him, is ugly, is hideous, is monstrous."[49]

Du Bois in the *Century* article was critical of the UNIA's Liberty Hall, where the group's activities took place. "Out of this squat and dirty old Liberty Hall he screams his propaganda. . . . Garvey's basement represents nothing in accomplishment and only waste in attempt." Garvey fired back: "Here we have this 'lazy dependent mulatto' condemning the honest effort of the race to create out of nothing something which could be attributed to their ownership." The NAACP in general and Du Bois's salary in particular were dependent on "the charity and philanthropy of white people." Garvey asked what was the NAACP's program for Negro advancement? "Now what does he [Du Bois] mean by advancing colored people if he hates black so much? In what direction must we expect his advancement? We can conclude in no other way than that it is in the direction of losing our black identity and becoming, as nearly as possible, the lowest whites by assimilation and miscegenation." The following year, when Garvey sent out letters and pamphlets questioning the desire of African Americans for first-class citizenship rights in a "white man's country," Du Bois declared, "Marcus Garvey is, without doubt, the most dangerous enemy of the Negro race in America and in the world. He is either a lunatic or a traitor."[50]

In the ideological bouts between the nationalists and integrationists during the 1920s, the main event was "Battling Du Bois v. Kid Garvey." But when we examine the intellectual debate over the most appropriate purposes and subject matter for African-American literature and art, we find a very different lineup. Indeed, in terms of the positions they took on this very controversial and volatile issue, it becomes clear that Du Bois and Garvey had more in common ideologically than did Du Bois and his NAACP colleague James Weldon Johnson.

Truth, Beauty, or Propaganda?
"The Criteria for Negro Art"

HISTORIAN DAVID Levering Lewis in his important book *When Harlem Was in Vogue* points out that James Weldon Johnson was one of the six major promoters of the works produced by young African-American writers in New York City during the New Negro literary renaissance. Lewis also included Johnson's assistant at the NAACP, Walter White, and Jessie Fauset, who served as an assistant editor for *The Crisis* magazine, among the most important supporters of

"New Negro literature." Fauset published so many of the early poems and short stories of the younger writers in the magazine that Du Bois feared it would become a "literary journal." Charles Spurgeon Johnson, editor of *Opportunity,* a magazine sponsored by the National Urban League, also published the younger writers and offered prizes for the best literary works produced by young artists. Howard University professor Alain Locke, who put together a special issue of writings by New Negroes for *Survey Graphic* magazine, and later published it in book form as *The New Negro,* used his connections with upper-class whites to gain financial support for struggling young artists. Casper Holstein, born in the Virgin Islands, had become a millionaire through the numbers racket he started in Harlem after the war. Although forced to remain on the fringes of respectable society, Holstein contributed generously to the Urban League and other organizations involved in race uplift. According to David Levering Lewis, without these six supporters, the New Negro literary movement in New York City "would have been little more than a larger version of Philadelphia or Washington, places where belle-lettres meant Saturday night adventures in tidy parlors, among mostly tidy-minded literati."[51]

Many of the young black writers from all over the country received their first recognition through the literary prizes offered by *Opportunity* and *The Crisis.* First announced by *Opportunity* in September 1924, the prizes were meant to reward "outstanding artistic achievement" in literature "both by Negro authors and about Negro life." A distinguished panel of black and white writers and publishers was assembled as judges of short stories, poetry, drama, essays, and personal autobiography. Among the early prize winners who later became well-known writers were Langston Hughes, Countee Cullen, Eric Walrond, Zora Neale Hurston, Sterling Browne, and E. Franklin Frazier. The gala banquet held for prize winners served to bring together the young artists with influential white publishers and writers who could help them with their careers. However, the interracial contacts in New York City served the purposes of white artists and publishers as well, and for many African-American intellectuals the increased white interest in the folkways of "primitive and savage Negroes" was merely the latest form of white racist exploitation of Afro-America.

James Weldon Johnson stated over and over again his belief that African-American folk materials and the "black experience" in general should be used in the creation of *American* art and literature. In *The Book of American Negro Poetry* he maintained that

> there are phases of Negro life in the United States which cannot be treated in the dialect either adequately or artistically. Take, for example the phrases rising out of life in Harlem, that most wonderful Negro city in the world. I do not deny that a Negro in a log cabin is more picturesque than a Negro in a Harlem flat, but the Negro in the Harlem

flat is here, and he is but part of a group growing everywhere in the country, a group whose ideals are becoming increasingly more vital than those of the traditionally artistic group, even if its members are less picturesque.[52]

Johnson believed that white as well as black artists should be encouraged to use "the stuff of Negro life" in the creation of artistic works. Carl Van Vechten, novelist, music critic for the *New York Times,* and close friend of James Weldon Johnson, was a white man who was a self-professed fan of every-thing Negro. Van Vechten and his wife, Fania Marinoff, often escorted by Johnson or Walter White or Langston Hughes, became regulars at Harlem nightspots during the decade and threw swanky parties at their West Side apartment that brought black jazz artists, musicians, and writers together with New York's white upper crust. Van Vechten gained the reputation as an impor-tant contact person for starving black artists and he used his literary connec-tions to have the works of Langston Hughes, Eric Walrond, Claude McKay, and other black writers published by the major white publishing houses.[53]

By 1926 after *Opportunity* and *The Crisis* began awarding the annual liter-ary prizes, Du Bois became increasingly disturbed about the subject matter cho-sen by younger black writers. Rather than writing about middle-class blacks and the Talented Tenth, there seemed to be a growing preoccupation with the black lower class among these writers and Du Bois felt the depictions were meant to excite the prurient interests of the white reading public. The stories about black numbers runners, prostitutes, bootleggers, and other degenerates were not only offensive to Du Bois's more genteel sensibilities, they also presented the race in an unfavorable light that resembled much too closely the distortions and stereo-types found in the works by white writers. Between March and November 1926 Du Bois decided to publish a symposium on "The Negro in Art," and asked writers and artists to respond to several questions, among them:

> When the artist, black or white, portrays Negro characters is he under any obligations or limitations as to the sort of character he will por-tray? Is not the portrayal of the sordid, foolish and criminal among Negroes convincing the world that this and this alone is really and es-sentially Negroid, and preventing white artists from knowing other types and preventing black artists from daring to paint them? Is there not a real danger that young colored writers will be tempted to follow the popular trend in portraying Negro character in the underworld rather than seeking to paint the truth about themselves and their own social class?[54]

The first response published was that by Carl Van Vechten, who stated that he understood why some African Americans were "sensitive in regard to fiction which attempts to picture the lower strata of the race," but this attitude will force black artists "to refrain from using valuable material. . . . The squalor of Negro life, the vice of Negro life, offer a wealth of novel, exotic, picturesque material to the artist." Besides, "there is very little difference if any between the life of a wealthy or cultured Negro and that of a white man of the same class." Then Van Vechten posed a question that hinted at why he had recently become so enamored of things Negro. "Are Negro writers going to write about this exotic material while it is still fresh or will they continue to make a free gift of it to white authors who will exploit it until not a drop of vitality remains?"[55]

Van Vechten understood the value of this material because he had been working for some time on a novel about the low life in Harlem. His friends James Weldon Johnson and Walter White had read several chapters before it was published in the late spring of 1926. *Nigger Heaven* told the story of a young aspiring black writer, Byron Kasson, who comes to Harlem in search of fame and fortune. He meets Mary Love, a highly cultured librarian, who takes him under her wing. He also meets Lasca Sartoris, a black femme fatale, who excites Byron's baser instincts. After a white editor castigates the young writer for failing to write about the black underworld and "primitive exotics," he is dejected and accepts Lasca's offer to become her lover. When Lasca later tires of him and takes Robert Petijohn, a numbers runner, as her new lover, Byron, despondent and seeking revenge, hunts the couple down, finally locating them in a Harlem cabaret. Before Byron is able to act, another underworld figure, the Scarlet Creeper, shoots Petijohn. Byron runs over and empties his revolver into Petijohn's prostrate body, just as the police arrive. Byron is taken away and charged with the murder.[56]

While the novel became an immediate best-seller, African-American intellectuals became sharply divided over the merits of the work and the accuracy of its depiction of Harlem blacks. For many the title, *Nigger Heaven,* which referred to the balcony section of theaters where black patrons were forced to sit, was extremely offensive. By that time the use of the term "nigger" was no longer acceptable in most literary circles. But even beyond the title, many African Americans recoiled at the portrayal of the black underworld filled with criminal characters, and the suggestion that this was typical of black life in the city. While some black newspaper editors refused to accept advertisements for the book, Alain Locke, Countee Cullen, and other black intellectuals expressed their dissatisfaction with the work only in private correspondence for fear of alienating their white patron.[57]

Publicly, Du Bois led the chorus of naysayers. "Carl Van Vechten's 'Nigger Heaven' is a blow in the face. It is an affront to the hospitality of black folk and to the intelligence of white." He did not accept Van Vechten's suggestion the title referred to a "a haven for Negroes—a city of refuge for dark and tired souls." Du Bois viewed the "nigger heaven" as "a nasty, sordid corner into which black folk are herded" and which some are "fools enough to enjoy." He found the novel of little artistic merit because it was filled with "half-truths"; it was "a caricature" that was "ludicrously out of focus and undeniably misleading." Even if judged solely as a "work of art," he found it came closest to "being nothing but cheap melodrama." Du Bois even questioned Van Vechten's artistry: "his women's bodies have no souls; no children palpitate upon his hands; he has never looked upon his dead with bitter tears. Life to him is just one damned orgy after another, with hate, hurt, gin and sadism." Du Bois concluded that "I cannot for the life of me see in this work either sincerity or art, deep thought or truthful industry." Van Vechten had succeeded in writing something "bizarre," but Du Bois advised readers "who are impelled [to buy it] by a sense of duty or curiosity to drop the book gently in the grate and to try the *Police Gazette*."[58]

Van Vechten had his defenders, however, and foremost among them was James Weldon Johnson, Du Bois's NAACP co-worker. Johnson's lengthy review in *Opportunity* was titled "Romance and Tragedy in Harlem." "An absorbing story," full of "dramatic intensity," *Nigger Heaven* was "the most revealing, significant and powerful novel based exclusively on Negro life yet written," according to Johnson. The Negro characters are diverse and complex, "people rather than puppets." Johnson believed the novel should not be prejudged because of its title and hoped that with the Negro's rise and development that this "race epithet" will lose "its power to sting and hurt him." Johnson detailed the characters and the plot and pointed out that the story of an ambitious young man's seduction and destruction by life in the big city had been the theme of Paul Laurence Dunbar's novel *The Sport of the Gods*, published in 1901, but Van Vechten's work possesses "an innate light touch and brilliancy" of its own. It is a work of realism, and "in every line of the book he shows he is serious. But however serious Van Vechten may be, he cannot be heavy. He does not moralize, he does not over-emphasize, there are no mock heroics, there are no martyrdoms."[59]

In a direct dig at Du Bois, Johnson suggested that *Nigger Heaven* was "full of propaganda." Although he believed that Van Vechten himself "would view this as a defect," Johnson felt that through the various characters "every phase of the race question, from Jim Crow discriminations to miscegenation, is frankly discussed. . . . If the book has a thesis," Johnson concluded, "it is this: Negroes are people; they have the same emotions, the same passions, the same shortcomings, the same aspirations, the same graduations of social strata as other people."[60]

Earlier that year (1926) in his published review of Alain Locke's *The New Negro*, Du Bois had criticized Locke for putting forward the idea that Beauty rather than Propaganda should be the object of Negro literature and art. His book proves the falseness of this thesis. This is a book filled and bursting with propaganda for the most part beautifully and painstakingly done; and it is a grave question if ever in this world in any renaissance there can be a search for disembodied beauty which is not really a passionate effort to do something tangible, accompanied and illuminated and made holy by the vision of eternal beauty.[61]

Then at the NAACP annual meeting, held in Chicago in September 1926, Du Bois gave a speech on "The Criteria of Negro Art," which was published in *The Crisis* the same month (October 1926) Johnson's favorable review of Van Vechten's *Nigger Heaven* appeared in *Opportunity*. In the speech and essay Du Bois questioned the underlying premise behind Charles Johnson's, Walter White's, Jessie Fauset's, and James Weldon Johnson's promotion of art and literature by younger African-American artists as a way to deal with the reality of racial discrimination in the United States. "With the growing recognition of Negro artists in spite of the severe handicaps, one comforting thing is occurring to both white and black. They are whispering, 'Here is a way out. Here is the real solution of the color problem. The recognition accorded Cullen, Hughes, Fauset, White and others shows there is no real color line. Keep quiet! Don't complain! Work! All will be well!' "
Du Bois condemned this trend of thought.

> I will not say that already this chorus amounts to a conspiracy. Perhaps I am naturally too suspicious. But I will say that there are today a surprising number of white people who are getting great satisfaction out of these younger Negro writers because they think it is going to stop agitation on the Negro question. . . . And many colored people are all too eager to follow this advice; especially those who are weary of the eternal struggle along the color line, who are afraid to fight and to whom the money of philanthropists and the alluring publicity are subtle and deadly bribes.

Du Bois pointed out that the black writer still had to write things acceptable to whites; otherwise he or she would not be published. "The white publishers catering to white folk would say, 'It is not interesting'—to white folk, naturally not. They want Uncle Toms, Topsies, good 'darkies' and clowns."[62]
The black artist, however, must be the seeker of beauty, goodness, *and* truth. For Du Bois, truth must be considered "the highest hand-maiden of imagination, as the one great vehicle for universal understanding." And "goodness in all its aspects of justice, honor and right" must be sought

> not for the sake of ethical sanction but as the one true method of gaining sympathy and human interest. The apostle of Beauty thus becomes

the apostle of Truth and Right not by choice but by inner and outer compulsion. Free he is, but his freedom is ever bounden by Truth and Justice; and slavery only dogs him when he is denied the right to tell the Truth or recognize an ideal of Justice. Thus all Art is propaganda and ever must be, despite the wailing of purists. I stand in utter shamelessness and say that whatever art I have for writing has been used always for propaganda for gaining the right of black folk to love and enjoy. I do not care a damn for any art that is not used for propaganda. But I do care when propaganda is confined to one side while the other is stripped silent.[63]

Thus the differences between W. E. B. Du Bois and James Weldon Johnson over Carl Van Vechten's *Nigger Heaven* were not over whether or not the novel was "full of propaganda," but the fact that Du Bois found Van Vechten's depiction one-sided and confined itself to the black lower strata and underworld. But there was another important issue that both Du Bois and Johnson raised in their statements about the purposes of black art. Du Bois completely disagreed with Johnson's position that black artists should seek infusion into the mainstream of *American* art, should attempt to use black folk materials to make contributions to the development of *American* literature. For Du Bois, African-American art and literature must be distinctive because the black artists are involved in the larger task of race vindication.

I do not doubt that the ultimate art coming from black folk is going to be just as beautiful, and beautiful largely in the same ways, as art that comes from white folk, or yellow or red; but the point today is that until the art of black folk compels recognition, they will not be rated as human. And then when through art they compel recognition then let the world discover if it will that their art is as new as it is old, and old as new.[64]

The differences in the ideological positions on black art between Johnson and Du Bois become even clearer when we examine the artistic principles espoused by the Garveyites. Only recently have the contributions of "literary Garveyism" been included in assessments of the New Negro literary movement. Historian Tony Martin examined UNIA publications, especially its weekly newspaper, *Negro World,* and documented a preoccupation with drama, poetry, and literature comparable to that in *The Crisis* and *Opportunity* magazines. *Negro World* regularly published book reviews and began a "Poetry for the People" section in 1918. The newspaper also published the early works of several of the younger New Negro authors, including Claude McKay, Eric Walrond, and Zora Neale Hurston; and sponsored literary contests, with cash prizes, beginning in 1921, four years before Charles Johnson's *Opportunity* magazine.[65]

Garvey believed that "we must encourage our own black authors who have character, who are loyal to the race, who feel proud to be black, and in every way let them feel that we appreciate their efforts to advance our race through healthy and decent literature." The literary editor of the *Negro World*, William Ferris, saw propaganda as a desirable element in a literary work of art, but the main objective was to produce great literature. "Novels which can powerfully picture the civilization of Africa during the Middle Ages, novels which can powerfully envisage the struggles of an aspiring Negro in a hostile Anglo-Saxon civilization, will undoubtedly add to the prestige and standing of the Negro Race."[66]

While the subject matter in poetry and prose produced by Garveyites was overwhelmingly related to some aspect of the history and contemporary circumstances for Africans and people of African descent, the style was generally that of the English poetic masters, such as William Shakespeare, Alexander Pope, and John Dryden. Tony Martin surveyed the poetry published by the Garveyites and found that, "like their better known contemporaries, they turned their backs on Afro-American dialect poetry, despite a general fondness for Paul Laurence Dunbar. Indeed, the absence of such dialect verse was more nearly total among the *Negro World* group than among the white-published group. Such fiercely race-conscious men and women were unlikely to use a form so steeped in connotations of white condescension and Black belittlement."[67] Also, among the Garveyites there was very little experimentation with the avant garde forms becoming popular during the decade, such as free verse and prose poems.

Despite their ideological opposition to integration, some white poets and writers were regularly published in the *Negro World*. Mary White Ovington, one of the founders of the NAACP, authored a column, "Book Chat," in the newspaper in 1921 and 1922. She generally reviewed books on the race issue written by white authors. Poems and articles by J. M. Stuart-Young, a white Briton, appeared regularly between 1922 and 1929. However, the Garveyites were basically separatists who saw the value of propaganda in art, while James Weldon Johnson and W. E. B. Du Bois were integrationists who agreed with the Garveyites that art and propaganda were entirely compatible. But the one topic where W. E. B. Du Bois and Marcus Garvey most shared common ideological positions, and vehemently disagreed with the perspective of James Weldon Johnson, was their response to the publication of Claude McKay's *Home to Harlem* in 1928.

Claude McKay was born in Jamaica in 1889 and educated there before he emigrated to the United States in 1912, and attended Tuskegee Institute and Kansas State University. He came to New York City and met several white leftist writers, eventually obtaining a position as an editor for Max Eastman's *Liberator* magazine in 1919. Also that year he traveled to London and became involved with several leftist groups, finally working for Sylvia Pankhurst's Marxist journal, *Workers' Dreadnought*. Upon his return to New York City in 1920, McKay again worked for the *Liberator,* this time as co-editor of the magazine. He also published a book of poetry, *Spring in New Hampshire*. In 1922 James Weldon Johnson included McKay's most famous poem, "If We Must Die," in *The Book of American Negro Poetry* and McKay published another book of poetry, *Harlem Shadows*. In his *New York Age* column, Johnson declared that

> Mr. McKay is a real poet and a great poet. . . . No Negro has sung [more] beautifully of his race than McKay and no poet has ever equalled the power with which he expresses the bitterness that so often rises from in the heart of the race. . . . The race ought to be proud of a poet capable of voicing it so fully. Such a voice is not found every day. . . . What he has achieved in this little volume sheds honor upon the whole race.[68]

The Garveyites were equally impressed with McKay's poetry and published several works in the *Negro World*. In 1922 and 1923 McKay traveled to the Soviet Union, addressed the Third Communist International in Moscow, and visited other parts of Europe and North Africa. McKay remained abroad for several years, but in 1928 his first novel, *Home to Harlem,* was published and caused even more debate and dissension within black literary circles than Carl Van Vechten's *Nigger Heaven*. The novel described the adventures of Jake, who lives for life's sensual pleasures—sex, drugs, food, and music; and Ray, a Haitian-born would-be writer, struggling with his own black identity and his love-hate relationship with "white civilization." The novel's action takes place in bars, cabarets, brothels, and other Harlem dives populated by social outcasts, gamblers, and other low-life characters. Jake indulges his "primitive instincts" while he searches for Felice, the prostitute with a heart of gold. McKay through the character of Ray was extremely critical of American and European civilization for its materialistic ethos and social oppression of black peoples, but his portrayal of Jake's fun-loving, sexually liberated antics was sensational and lurid and helped to make the book a best-seller.[69]

Du Bois found the novel nauseating, and "after reading the dirtier parts of its filth, I feel distinctly like taking a bath." While he found parts of the work "beautiful and fascinating," he believed that "McKay has set to cater for that prurient demand on the part of white folk for a portrayal in Negroes of that utter licentiousness which conventional civilization holds white folk back from enjoying—if enjoyment it can be called. That which a certain decadent section of the white American world, particularly centered in New York, longs for with fierce and unrestrained passions, it wants to see written out in black and white, and saddled on black Harlem." McKay had satisfied white publishers' demand for black depravity, and has presented "drunkenness, fighting, lascivious sexual promiscuity and utter absence of restraint in as bold and as bright colors as he can."[70]

Reviewers in the *Pittsburgh Courier, Norfolk Journal and Guide, Chicago Defender,* and other black newspapers were unanimous in their condemnation of *Home to Harlem,* denouncing it as "more *Nigger Heaven.*" The *Negro World* labeled it "an Insult to the Race." Marcus Garvey warned his readers that "our race within recent years has developed a new group of writers who have been prostituting their intelligence, under the direction of the white man, to bring out and show up the worse traits of our people." The novel was thought to be part of a larger racial conspiracy. "Under the advice of white publishers" the younger writers have produced books "to portray to the world the looseness, laxity and immorality that are peculiar to our group, for the purpose of these publishers circulating the libel against us among white peoples of the world, to further hold us up to ridicule and contempt and universal prejudice." Garvey advised African Americans to boycott the works of these "literary prostitutes" to make them understand "that we are not going to stand for their insults indulged in to suit prejudiced white people."[71]

On the other hand, Langston Hughes and Countee Cullen praised the novel in letters to McKay. Hughes congratulated McKay on the audacity of the work. "Undoubtedly, it is the finest thing 'we've' done yet. . . . Your novel ought to give a second youth to the Negro Vogue." James Weldon Johnson was alone among writers of the older generation to praise McKay's novel, writing privately, "I think you've written a wonderful book." In a letter to Du Bois defending himself and his book, Claude McKay claimed that from childhood he had been "an artist in words" and criticized Du Bois for advocating propagandistic art. "Propaganda [was] but a one-sided idea of life. . . . I should not be surprised when you mistake the art of life for nonsense," McKay responded indignantly, "and try to pass off propaganda as life in art."[72]

In *Along This Way* James Weldon Johnson discussed the critical response to *Nigger Heaven* and *Home to Harlem,* but did not address the issues raised by Du Bois and other black reviewers of the novels. Johnson defended both works as important literary achievements and dismissed certain complaints voiced by black and white reviewers. White reviewers objected to *Nigger Heaven* because "the story was a Van Vechten fantasy." "They could not be expected to believe that there were intelligent, well-to-do Negroes in Harlem who lived their lives on the cultural level he described." Black reviewers saw it "as a libel on the race," and suggested "that the dissolute life and characters depicted by the author were non-existent." McKay's book on the other hand dealt with the same "low levels of life . . . but entirely unrelieved by any brighter lights" and McKay "made no attempt to hold in check or disguise his abiding contempt for the Negro bourgeoisie and 'upper class.' Still, *Home to Harlem* met with no such criticism from Negroes as did *Nigger Heaven.*" Johnson went on to mention that Van Vechten maintained an affectionate and "warm interest in colored people before he ever saw Harlem," which often made him the butt of jokes among his white literary friends (381–82).

Perhaps Johnson was unaware of the universal condemnation of McKay's *Home to Harlem* in the black press, which in many cases dismissed Van Vechten's work as just another vicious portrait of Afro-America coming from the pen of a white writer out to make a fast buck. More important, Johnson said nothing about the common complaint made by black reviewers of both books: they were written primarily to appeal to the prurient interests of white readers and to make money for the publishers and authors. Du Bois, Garvey, and other black intellectuals saw these novels as part of a larger trend, and believed that the younger black writers were trying to make their literary reputations by telling white folks what they wanted to hear (and what they already believed) about the "primitive Negroes."

James Weldon Johnson's personal experiences on Broadway as a composer for white musicals that utilized black-inspired musical forms, as an author whose works were published by the leading white publishing houses, and as a black member of the powerful white literary circles in New York City colored his response to black complaints about how the Negro was portrayed on stage and in literature during the 1920s. Johnson firmly believed that black folk art and music had made the most original contributions to American culture, and he did everything he could to make those folk materials available to the larger society. Along with songwriter Lawrence Brown and his brother, Rosamond, he published *The Book of American Negro Spirituals* in 1925 and *The Second Book of American Negro Spirituals* a year later, and argued that this folk music was important as art as well as religious music. "These songs [are] unsurpassed among folk songs of the world and, in the poignancy of their beauty, unequaled! . . . This music which is America's only folk music and, up to this time, the finest distinctive artistic contribution she has to offer the world."[73]

Johnson utilized black folk expressions in his poetry and other writing and encouraged other artists to do the same. In many ways *God's Trombones: Seven Negro Sermons in Verse,* published in 1927, was Johnson's crowning achievement as a poet and his most influential contribution to the emerging black intellectual tradition. Unlike his earlier poetry, these sermons are presented in free verse and although they were meant to convey the rhythms of the black minister's preaching style, Johnson chose not to write the sermons in dialect. In the preface Johnson stated that he found Negro dialect "a quite limited instrument" only capable of conveying two emotions, "pathos and humor." And given its association with the "Negro as a happy go lucky or forlorn figure . . . practically no poetry is being written in dialect by colored poets today." "In my opinion," Johnson suggested, "*traditional* Negro dialect as a form for

Aframerican poets is absolutely dead," so the black poet "needs now an instrument of greater range than dialect." Individual sermons in *God's Trombones,*
such as "The Creation" and "Go Down Death," became immensely popular
with African-American readers; however, Johnson's prediction about the death
of Negro dialect was premature.[74]

Langston Hughes, Sterling Brown, and Zora Neale Hurston had been utilizing black folk expressions, including a form of Negro dialect, in their poetry
throughout the 1920s. When he published the second, expanded edition of *The
Book of American Negro Poetry* in 1931 and included several dialect poems by
Hughes and Brown, Johnson suggested that these younger writers had returned
to the "genuine folk stuff," rather than the "artificial folk stuff of the dialect
school. . . . Langston Hughes has gone to such folk sources as the blues and the
work songs; Sterling A. Brown has gone to Negro folk epics and ballads like
'Stagolee,' 'John Henry,' 'Casey Jones,' and 'Long Gone John.' These are unfailing sources of material for authentic poetry." These writers, as did Johnson,
understood that poems that utilized African American rhythms and language
would be important in creating an authentic black voice in American poetry.[75]

Throughout his literary career James Weldon Johnson celebrated the "creative genius of the Negro," especially black folk expressions; and wanted these
folk traditions and practices to be used by both black and white artists in the
creation of a truly distinctive American art and literature. In an essay on "The
Dilemmas of the Negro Artist," published in 1928, however, Johnson discussed the problems created for black artists in particular in trying to write for
either a white or black audience. When the black artist writes about African
Americans with the white audience in mind, "he is bound to run up against
many long-standing artistic conceptions about the Negro; against numerous
conventions and traditions which through age have become binding; in a
word, against a whole row of hard-set stereotypes which are not easily broken
up." When the black artist writes for a black audience, "there are certain phases
of life that he dare not touch, certain subjects that he dare not critically discuss,
certain manners of treatment that he dare not use—except at the risk of rous-
ing bitter resentment." In an obvious, though unstated, reference to Claude
McKay's *Home to Harlem,* such works will "bring down on his head the wrath
of the entire colored pulpit and press, and gain among the literate element of
his own people the reputation of being a prostituter of his talent and betrayer
of his race—not by any means a pleasant position to get into."[76]

For Johnson the way out of this dilemma was to attempt to write for both
audiences. Discounting the possibility of developing and appealing solely to a
black audience, Johnson wanted the artist to come up with some type of "fusion" in artistic perspective that would appeal to both blacks and whites.
"There needs to be more than a combination, there needs to be a fusion. . . .
By standing on his racial foundation, he must fashion something that rises

above race, and reaches out to the universal in truth and beauty," Johnson declared. "When a Negro author does write so as to fuse white and black America into one interested and approving audience, he has performed no slight feat, and has most likely done a sound piece of literary work."[77]

Johnson's integrationist ideological position differed in important ways from that of W. E. B. Du Bois, his NAACP colleague. Johnson celebrated the use of black lower-class life as the material for use in the literary imagination, such as in the works by Carl Van Vechten and Claude McKay; Du Bois rejected this position, arguing that it tended to perpetuate traditional stereotypes about the Negro. The Garveyites agreed with Du Bois about the inappropriateness of the black underworld and criminal element as subject matter for works of art, and their literary works were aimed solely at the black audience. It was not until 1940 and the publication of Richard Wright's novel *Native Son* that a literary work by a black author dealing with lower-class black life would be embraced by both black and white audiences.

The Great Depression did much to dampen the enthusiasm of white publishing houses for works submitted by younger literary artists, black and white. By the early 1930s the economic conditions in the American publishing industry reduced the flood of books by African-American authors to a trickle and even well-established writers had difficulties finding commerical outlets for their work. The collapse of the capitalist economy in the United States ushered in a searching reappraisal of socialist and communist economic alternatives by black and white intellectuals, while communist organizers used the critical social circumstances for African Americans in the United States to recruit blacks into various leftist organizations. James Weldon Johnson was well aware of the activities of American communists and decided to address the issue in his autobiography.

"Will the Negro turn to Communism?" Johnson asked in the final pages of *Along This Way;* "I do not think so," was his response. Johnson believed that despite the current failure of the capitalist system, not only were there "no indications that the United States will ever adopt Communism," but it will also "continue to be an outlawed political and economic creed." Thus for African Americans to add this burden to their already burdensome circumstances in this country would be "sheer idiocy." Johnson placed his faith in the integrationist principles he espoused throughout his life. Despite the clamor for blacks to become a separate, self-sufficent group, Johnson argued that there were "elemental forces" at work that would lead to "the blending of the Negro into the American race of the future. It seems probable that, instead of developing them independently to the utmost, the Negro will fuse his qualities with those of the other groups in the making of the ultimate American people; and that he will add a tint to America's complexion and put a perceptible permanent wave in America's hair" (412).

Johnson reiterated these views in *Negro Americans, What Now?*, published in 1934, his last book before his untimely death in a car accident in Maine in June 1938. When the choices have been narrowed to "integration or isolation," Johnson concluded, "wisdom and farsightedness and possibility of achievement demand that we follow the line that leads to equal rights for us, based on the common terms and conditions under which they are accorded and guaranteed to the other groups that go into the making up of our national family." On the economic front, among other things, Johnson advocated that organizations such as the NAACP take up the cause of the exploited black sharecroppers of the South. "Close to seventy-five percent of Negro American farmers are share croppers. . . . The majority of them are held in peonage, a system under which they are as unscrupulously exploited as under the system of slavery." These black sharecroppers were burdened with debt by greedy landlords year after year without the possibility of clearing it off. The NAACP needed to carry out "the investigation of practices of peonage and placing the findings before the proper federal authorities, and the securing of true accountings from landlords through action in the courts."[78]

In the 1930s black and white communists began working with black sharecroppers and helped to organize sharecroppers' unions. As was the case with the defense of the Scottsboro Boys, the communists far outpaced the NAACP in their support of the rights of oppressed lower-class blacks and attracted the support of many African-American intellectuals. While these black communist and socialist intellectuals shared James Weldon Johnson's integrationist ideals, the American mainstream into which African Americans would move was conceived as a refuge from capitalist exploitation, a place where the workers and their representatives would control the means of production.

4

Harry Haywood

In Defense of the
Black Working Class

The further industrialization of the South, [and] the migration of Negro peasants from farms into industrial centers of the North and South [have] led to
the strengthening of class differentiation among Negro peoples. The political
awakening of the Negro workers is going on apace. The period since the postwar crisis has been marked by the emergence of a Negro proletariat upon the
political arena as an independent class force. The age-long isolation and par-
ticularism is being broken down in the crucible of sharpening class struggle.
This development has been given added momentum by the present crisis and
the growth of the revolutionary movement.

In this situation the Negro bourgeoisie finds that its leadership over the
Negro masses is no longer undisputed. The growth and maturing of this
"most important driving force" of the Negro liberation movement, the Negro
working class, is a direct threat to the hegemony of the Negro bourgeoisie.

—HARRY HAYWOOD, 1931

Photographer unknown. Reprinted by permission of the Schomburg Center for Research in Black Culture, New York Public Library.

THERE ARE many reasons why the autobiography has become the most important literary genre in the African-American intellectual tradition. In the face of widespread apologies for the peculiar institution of slavery produced by southern writers in the early nineteenth century, the formerly enslaved Africans and African Americans presented the "truth" from the perspective of those who were supposed to have been uplifted and "civilized" by American slavery. In the late nineteenth century when numerous scholarly and "eyewitness" accounts of the so-called Tragic Era of Reconstruction were being disseminated promulgating a new southern orthodoxy on the inability of black people to participate in "civilized society" as free citizens, African Americans who participated in the social and political struggles of the period wrote autobiographical works that presented their version of "the true facts of Reconstruction." And when ideological differences developed among spokespersons for the African-American population about how best to advance themselves in this increasingly hostile environment, these leaders turned to autobiography to present the personal experiences that led them to adopt a particular set of ideological principles.

Regardless of the particular intellectual position that was presented and defended, the autobiography became the preferred literary form for African-American intellectuals and leaders. Conservative leaders, such as Booker T. Washington and Mary Church Terrell, radical spokespersons W. E. B. Du Bois and Ida B. Wells-Barnett, and moderates James Weldon Johnson and Walter White all turned to the autobiography to explore important matters of principle that guided their lives and defined the nature of their contributions to the vindication of their race. Harry Haywood was one of the most important African-American intellectuals and theoreticians in the Communist Party U.S.A. (CPUSA) during the height of its influence on the American political scene in the 1930s. Like James Weldon Johnson, as a result of his personal experiences while growing up and living in Europe, Haywood opposed separatist solutions to the so-called Negro Problem, and committed himself to integrated movements and organizations that sought social justice and equal rights for African Americans. However, unlike Johnson, who upheld the capitalist economic system as part of the solution to the problem of black poverty and economic distress, Haywood became committed to an anti-capitalist ideological position and sought to convince African Americans to join and perhaps lead the movement for a socialist revolution in the United States.

In *Black Bolshevik: Autobiography of an Afro-American Communist,* published in 1978 at the age of eighty, Harry Haywood announced at the outset that his was a "political autobiography" that was "shaped by experiences over the years." Haywood was a member of the CPUSA for over thirty-five years. However, in 1958 he was expelled from the party for his unwillingness to accept its revisionist position on the "Negro question." Throughout his political life Haywood not only defended the black working class against the racist attacks of white workers, but he also emphasized its revolutionary potential in the long-term struggle to abolish American capitalism and imperialism. Haywood was one of the leading proponents of the party's support for "the right of self-determination" for African Americans in the Black Belt section of the southern United States. For Haywood it was a matter of principle that reflected his well-researched and long-held position on the nature of American imperialism and the road to socialist revolution in the United States.[1]

The role of African-American intellectuals as defenders of the interests of the black working class was well defined by the end of the nineteenth century. Although African American spokepersons, such as Alexander Crummell, T. Thomas Fortune, Ida Wells-Barnett, and Mary Church Terrell, were members of the black professional or middle class, they recognized that the vast majority of African Americans in the United States were skilled, semiskilled, and unskilled workers; and these black intellectuals espoused ideological positions that emphasized the interests of labor over capital. However, very few of these intellectuals adopted anti-capitalist ideological positions; rather they wanted African Americans to be allowed to pursue capitalistic enterprises without fear of discrimination and repression from white capitalists who felt threatened by these activities.[2]

There were some black leaders in the nineteenth century who viewed capitalism as part of the problem in the movement by African Americans "up from slavery" and supported socialist ideologies and movements that called for a redistribution of society's wealth from captialists to workers. Theodore Holly and Reverdy Ransom supported a kind of "Christian socialism" that saw in the teachings of Jesus Christ justification for the establishment of a "cooperative commonwealth" in which housing, transportation, communications, and other services would be owned by the state rather than private individuals. For Holly, Ransom, and other Christian socialists, capitalism was viewed as "highway robbery" and "organized thievery," antithetical to the tenets of "true Christianity." With the formation of the Socialist Party in the United States at the turn of the century, W. E. B. Du Bois, George Washington Woodbey, Hubert Harrison, and other black intellectuals supported the Socialist Party's anti-capitalist objectives, but were put off by racist practices within the party, and the white leadership's failure to recognize the unique circumstances for black workers in capitalist America. However, almost from its inception, the Workers (later Communist) Party not only championed the cause of the working class in the face of capitalist exploitation, but also emphasized the distinct form of "super-exploitation" that oppressed African-American workers in American society.[3]

In his autobiography, *Black Bolshevik*, Harry Haywood not only presented the personal experiences that led him to his anti-capitalist ideological positions, but also offered an explanation why the Communist Party, which led the struggles for black civil rights and social justice in the 1930s, played no significant role in the Civil Rights–Black Power movement of the 1950s and 1960s. In the face of attacks by publicity-seeking conservative politicians in the late 1940s, the more radical leaders of the CPUSA were incarcerated, went underground, or were forced to flee the country. Those leaders who remained were placed under a great deal of pressure to shape the party's strategies and programs to conform with those of organizations considered part of the American political mainstream. In the post–World War Two era the goals and objectives of the American Federation of Labor, United Auto Workers, and other large labor unions were considered legitimate by the political establishment, and indeed union leaders were quickly becoming members of that establishment. The leadership of the CPUSA openly sought an alliance with the liberal members of the political establishment and this new "labor aristocracy." According to Haywood, "this small elite section of American labor, based among the upper strata of skilled and higher paid workers, has through its leadership in the trade unions, inundated the working class with bourgeois ideology, promoting reformism, narrow self-interest and rampant jingoistic chauvinism." The ruling capitalist class used its money, prestige, and political power to cultivate this labor aristocracy, which served "as the lieutenants of capital within the labor movement." These labor leaders were also "susceptible to the imperialist propaganda of white chauvinism which has served to intensify the antagonisms between white and Black workers, dividing and splitting the working class into hostile groups, retarding the development of revolutionary class consciousness" (625–26).

In the early 1950s when the CPUSA moved toward a "bourgeois reformist" position on African-American advancement in the United States that differed little from the strategies and programs pursued by the leadership of the NAACP and National Urban League, Haywood voiced his objections and was later expelled by party leaders. The new CPUSA leaders allied the group with the "liberal bourgeois element" in the labor movement, and communists played no distinct role in the campaigns for civil rights and black empowerment of the 1960s. "The CPUSA did not even attempt to mobilize labor support for the Black struggle, and the labor aristocracy maintained hegemony over the workers' movement." This was a very different situation in comparison with the 1930s when the communists were in the vanguard of the movement for black and white working class solidarity and championed the cause of black civil rights. Haywood believed that their failure to assume an important role in the black protest movement in the 1960s "was in clear contrast to the unity built by communists in the thirties when the Party and the [white] working class had played a leading role in fighting for the special demands of Blacks, making the Scottsboro Boys a household word" (630).[4]

For Harry Haywood personally the communist movement was attractive even earlier, in the 1920s, because of its opposition to racial discrimination, lynching, and the anti-black mob violence that had become commonplace in post–World War One America. Haywood traced his political awakening to the Chicago race riot of 1919. "On July 28, 1919, I literally stepped into a battle that was to last the rest of my life. Exactly three months after mustering out of the Army, I found myself in the midst of one of the bloodiest race riots in U.S. history. It was certainly a most dramatic return to the realities of American democracy." What Haywood witnessed during the rioting made him realize that "I had been fighting the wrong war. The Germans weren't the enemy— the enemy was right here at home. These ideas had been developing ever since I landed home in April [1919], and a lot of other Black veterans were having the same thoughts" (1).

"A child of slaves," Haywood Hall (later Harry Haywood) was born in South Omaha, Nebraska, on February 4, 1898. His parents, Harriet and Haywood Hall, had migrated to South Omaha in the late 1880s. Haywood Sr. was born in 1860 in Madison County, Tennessee, on the plantation of Colonel Haywood Hall, who was remembered as a kind and benevolent man. Haywood Jr. never knew his grandfather because he died before he was born. But during his youth, Haywood Jr. was regularly schooled in the family folklore. Upon emancipation Grandfather Hall with the consent of his former master took his surname and remained on the plantation after the war. Grandfather Hall also became active in local Republican politics and eventually became the victim of white terrorism. "One night the Klansmen rode onto the plantation and headed straight for Grandfather's cabin. They broke open the door and one poked his head into the darkened cabin. 'Hey, Hall's nigger—where are you.' " His grandfather was ready for them, "and fired his shotgun point blank at the hooded head. The Klansman, half his head blown off, toppled onto the floor of the cabin, and his companions mounted their horses and fled. Grandmother, then pregnant, fell against the iron bed" (7).

They could not remain in Tennessee after the incident and fled to Des Moines, Iowa, where the family had friends. Haywood's grandmother gave birth prematurely to her son George, who survived and lived to the age of ninety-five. Unfortunately, his grandmother never fully recovered from the flight and premature birth and died a few years later. Haywood's father was about fifteen at this time and remained in Des Moines through the late 1880s when he left for South Omaha. There he found a job as janitor in the Cuddahy's Meat Packing Company where he was employed for the next twenty years.

Harriet Thorpe was born in 1860 on the Squire Sweeney plantation in Howard County, Missouri. Jerry and Ann Thorpe, her parents, had been born in slavery in Missouri, and lived on adjacent plantations. During the Civil War they were married and eventually had seven children. After the war the family moved to Moberly, Missouri, and Harriet Thorpe worked for a white family in the town. Harriet left Moberly in her early twenties and settled first in St. Louis, then Kansas City, and finally in South Omaha, where she met and married Hall's father. The couple had three children: Otto, born in 1891; Eppa, born in 1896; and Haywood Jr.

Although she never went to school, Harriet Hall was active in the African Methodist Episcopal church and was "a virtual repository of Black culture." Haywood recalled that "my brother Otto taught her to read and write when she was forty years old. She told stories of life on the plantations, of the 'hollers' they used. When a slave wanted to talk to a friend on a neighboring plantation, she would throw back her head and half sing, half yell: 'Oh, Bes-sie, I wa-ant to see you.' Often you could hear one of the 'hollers' a mile away" (13). Mrs. Hall worked as a caterer for wealthy whites in North Omaha. Haywood recalled that "she would bring us back all sorts of goodies and leftovers from these parties. Sometimes she would get together with her friends among the other domestics, and they would have a great time panning their employers and exchanging news of the white folks' scandalous doings" (14).

In contrast to his mother's "great fighting spirit," Haywood Hall, Sr., was "not much of a fighter, or so it seemed to me. In later years, some of the old slave psychology and fear remained. He was an ardent admirer of Booker T. Washington who . . . called on Blacks to submit to the racist status quo." In South Omaha at the turn of the century race relations were quite fluid, probably because there were so few black families. The town was populated primarily by European immigrants, mostly Bohemians, Irish, Poles, Russians, and Serbs, with a small sprinkling of Germans, Greeks, and Italians. The Halls were the only African Americans in their neighborhood, which was predominantly Bohemian. Haywood remembered the Bohemian celebrations, beautiful music, parades, and colorful costumes and found the people very friendly. "Our family got along well with all the immigrant families in our immediate neighborhood." One incident in particular involving his Bohemian neighbor and the local black policeman provides a sense of the interracial camaraderie that existed.

There was a Bohemian couple living next door. On occasion, Mr. Rehau would get a bit too much under his belt. He'd come home and

really raise hell. When this happened, Mrs. Rehau scurried to Officer
Bingham, the Black cop, to get some help. I remember one afternoon
when Bingham came to lend a hand in taming him. The Bohemian
was a little guy compared to him. Officer Bingham threw him down
out in the yard and plunked himself on Rehau's back. Dust flew as he
kicked and thrashed and tried to get out from under the Black man.
Bingham just "rode the storm" and when Rehau raised his head, he'd
smack him around until the rebellion subsided (17).

Haywood Hall, Sr., was extremely well-read and "had an amazing store of
knowledge which he had culled from his readings." He possessed an extensive library, quoted passages from the Bible from memory, and was well versed in
the exploits of Toussaint-Louverture during the Haitian Revolution, Shaka
Zulu in South Africa, and black soldiers during the U.S. Civil War. His father's
teachings served to counter the racist propaganda in the society at large about the
"innate inferiority of the Negro" and his cultural backwardness. Haywood Jr. was
one of only three African-American students in the public elementary school
he attended and only rarely encountered racist insults and slurs. But he did recall
one female substitute teacher from the South who was lecturing on the Civil
War, condemning Ulysses S. Grant as a "cigar-smoking, liquor-drinking
roughneck," and praising Robert E. Lee as "a gentleman." Haywood was disturbed. "I don't know about General Grant's habits," Haywood blurted out,
"but he beat Lee. Besides, Lee couldn't have been much of a gentleman; he
owned slaves!" The teacher was livid: "That's enough—what I could say about
you!" "Well," Haywood shot back, "what could you say?" She decided not to respond, realizing that the students would not sympathize with racial slurs. After
school, the white students crowded around Haywood: "You certainly told her
off." His mother felt he had done the right thing, but his father was not so
sure; "you might have gotten into trouble" (24–25).

Haywood Jr. mentioned that even as a youngster, "racist notions of innate
Black inferiority left me cold," basically because the academic achievements of
his brother, Otto, exploded such myths. Otto Hall had skipped one grade in elementary school and another in high school, was a gifted poet, and had won
many scholastic awards and prizes. As far as Haywood was concerned, Otto was
the most brilliant person in South Omaha, black or white. However, for some
unexplained reason, Otto dropped out of high school his senior year and decided to give up on the struggle of trying to make it in the "white world."
While growing up Otto had been independent and difficult to discipline; after
leaving school he took up "the sportin' life" in North Omaha and began hanging out in pool halls and gambling dens. Eventually, Otto Hall was attracted to
radical political movements and introduced his younger brother to leftist
groups and causes to which both were to devote many years of their lives.

In the summer of 1913, when Haywood was in high school, an incident occurred that was to disrupt his entire family's life. Haywood Hall, Sr., was attacked and beaten by a group of whites as he left his job at the Cudahy packing plant. The thugs told him to get out of town or they would kill him. "I remember vividly the scene that night when Father staggered through the door," Haywood wrote half a century later. "His face was swollen and bleeding, his clothes torn and in disarray. He had a frightened, hunted look in his eyes. My sister Eppa and I were alone. Mother had gone for the summer to work for her employers, rich white folks, at Lake Okoboji, Iowa." His father refused to call the police, "That ain't gone do no good;" and was determined to flee the town and join his two brothers, Watt and George, in Minneapolis. He packed his things, said he would telegraph their mother to return, and he left. "Our whole world had collapsed. Home and security were gone. The feeling of safety in our little haven of interracial goodwill had proved elusive. Now we were just homeless 'niggers' on the run" (32–33).

Within a week they had packed up their belongings and joined their father in Minneapolis. He had found a job for himself and his wife at the Minneapolis Women's Club as janitor and cook. A friend of his father who worked for the railroad brought Haywood to Minneapolis. His mother and sister followed a few days later. Eventually, the family was resettled in a new home, but Haywood soon dropped out of school. On the first day he arrived at his new school and entered the room, "the all-white class was singing old darkie plantation songs. Upon seeing me, their voices seemed to take on a mocking, derisive tone. Loudly emphasizing the Negro dialect and staring at me, they sang:

> Down in De Caun fiel—HEAH DEM darkies moan
> All De darkies AM a weeping
> MASSAHS in DE Cold Cold Ground.' "

Given all that had recently happened in his life, "I was in no mood to be kidded or scoffed at. That was my last day in school. I never returned. I made up my mind to drop out and get a full-time job. I was fifteen and in the second semester of the eighth grade" (35).

A Taste of Freedom

WHEN THE United States entered World War I in April 1917, Harry Haywood was nineteen years old. He was then living in Chicago, where he and his family had moved in 1915. Haywood found Minneapolis to be a beautiful city, but boring. His father and mother decided to leave Minneapolis because the employment opportunities were better in Chicago's wartime industries. Over the next two years Haywood worked as a busboy for several restaurants and railroad lines and he traveled throughout the North and Midwest. Some of his friends in Chicago were members of the Eighth Illinois, a black National Guard regiment. Fascinated by the stories of their exploits and adventures, he decided to join early in 1917, several months before the United States entered the war. "The regiment, officered by Blacks from the colonel on down (many of them veterans of the Four Black Regular Army regiments), gave me a feeling of pride. I didn't regard it just as a part of a U.S. Army unit, but some sort of big social club of fellow race-men. Still, I knew that we would eventually get into the war" (42).

The Eighth Illinois was called up in July 1917 and by late summer the unit was headed for Camp Logan near Houston, Texas. The journey was filled with much apprehension because of the shootout that had recently occurred in Houston between black soldiers in the Twenty-fourth Infantry and the local police. As the train carrying the black soldiers made its way through southern towns and cities, "we were at our provocative best." Haywood recalled that "we threw kisses at the white girls on the station platform, calling out to them 'Come over here, baby, give me a kiss.' " While they were on the train, one soldier from Mississippi, Willie Morgan, who recalled numerous "red-neck" persecutions and insults, "took advantage of his first opportunity to bait a cracker in his own habitat. He reached a big ham-like hand through the window, grabbed the fellow's face and shouted, 'What the hell you staring at, you peckerwood motherfucker?' The man pulled back, his hat flew off. Bending down, he recovered it and then moved quickly to the other side of the car, a frightened and puzzled look on his face. Our whole car let out a big roar" (46).

When they entered stores and shops at stations along the way, shopkeepers would of course ignore the black soldiers and continue to wait on white customers. This provided the soldiers the opportunity to pocket whatever was in reach. In one store when a soldier named Jeffries put down his money and asked for a Coca-Cola, the storekeeper said,

> "I'll serve you one, but y'all can't drink it in heah."
> "Why?" Jeffries asked, innocently.
> "Cause we don't serve niggahs heah."
> Just as we were about to jump him and wreck the place, Jeffries, a comedian, decided to play it straight. He turned to us and said, "Now wait, fellahs, let me handle this. What this man is saying is that you don't know your place." Jeffries told the storekeeper he knew *his* place and would drink the coke outside. "Thank goodness," the man replied, "This nigger's got some sense."

When the man handed him the Coke, "Jeffries snatched up the bottle and immediately hit him on the head, knocking him out cold." The others proceeded to ransack the store (47).

In Tyler, Texas, when a similar incident occurred, the local sheriff showed up and demanded to search the train for stolen goods. Major Hunt, one of the black officers, informed the sheriff that this was a military train and he could not enter. With a crowd of white onlookers nearby, the sheriff pushed the major aside and walked forward. At that point Jimmy Bland, the soldier on guard, shouted, "'Back! Get back or I'll blow you apart!' Jimmy pushed the sheriff in the belly with the barrel of his gun." The sheriff doubled over from the blow, finally uttered something about reporting this incident to army authorities, and left. "We all let out a tremendous roar" (49).

At Camp Logan the regiment became part of the Thirty-third Illinois National Guard division and entered intensive training. The soldiers were committed to their own form of "race vindication" and were determined to do well for their black officers because of the belief among whites that "Black soldiers could be good, but only when officered by whites." The regiment won numerous division championships in boxing, baseball, and other athletic competitions and had the highest number of sharpshooters and expert riflemen. More importantly, in the wake of the mutiny-riot by the Twenty-fourth Infantry, the racial atmosphere in the city was much less hostile. Haywood recalled no racial clashes between local police and black soldiers. "The cops had obviously learned to fear retaliation by Black soldiers if they committed acts of brutality and intimidation in the Black community. Houston Blacks were no longer the cowed, intimidated people they had been before the mutiny. They were proud of us and it was clear that our presence made them feel better. A warm and friendly relationship developed between our men and the Black community" (50).[5]

When the regiment was shipped out and sent to Camp Stewart near Newport News, Virginia, an incident occurred, involving the beating of several black soldiers by local police and whites, that almost resulted in a repeat of the Houston riot. Fortunately, violence was averted by black officers who intercepted the men, forced them to return to their barracks, and promised to investigate the incident. All of the black soldiers who were arrested returned the next day. The unit was separated from the Thirty-third Illinois division and became the 370th Infantry and sailed for France in April 1918. To their surprise, the unit was attached to the French Army because white commanders felt this was necessary "to avoid friction" between black and white American soldiers. Once they were attached to the French Army, white officers replaced the black officers, who were sent back to the United States.[6]

The U.S. Army attempted to impose upon French Army officers and soldiers white American beliefs and values about "Negro inferiority." A pamphlet was distributed entitled *Secret Information Bulletin Concerning Negro Troops,* which pointed out that "although a citizen of the United States, the black man is regarded by the white American as an inferior being with whom relations of business or service only are possible." It went on to claim that the Negro had to be censured constantly because of a lack of intelligence and discretion. "The vices of the Negro are a constant menace to the American who has to repress them sternly." The worst of these was the rape of white women by black men. In order to prevent this from happening in France, there should be no "intimacy or familiarity" between black men and white women. The French officers were asked to "make a point of keeping the native cantonment population from 'spoiling' the Negroes." Harry Haywood found, however, that "apparently this classic statement of U.S. racism was ineffectual with the French people, even though it was supplemented by wild stories circulated by U.S. white troops" (54–55).[7]

The regiment was given French weapons, underwent a brief period of French military training, and in June 1918 was sent to the trenches at Saint-Mihiel Salient near the Swiss frontier as part of the Tenth Division of the French Army. When the black regiment passed through the town of Bar-le-duc, near the Argonne sector, Haywood recalled that "we were deeply pleased by the hospitality and kindness extended to us by the townspeople there. They invited us into their homes and plied us with food and wine." In a small town in the Department of the Meuse, however, they encountered "the long arm of American racism." They were told that a black soldier had recently been hanged in the town square; "his crime was the raping of a village girl." After a few days in the town, Haywood discussed the hanging with local Frenchmen who thought it was "*très brutale, très horrible!*" They could not understand why the white officers responded as they did since "she had been raped many times before." The black soldiers later learned that the hanging of the black soldier was part of a deliberate campaign by the white American commanders "to build up the Black rapist scare among them [the French]" (62–65).

The unit entered the battle along the Hindenburg line at the Oise-Aisne Triangle, where they sustained their greatest losses. The regiment participated in the liberation of the fortified city of Laon, which had been occupied by the Germans for four years. Highly praised by the French command, the unit had over five hundred killed and wounded in battle and "won twenty-one Distinguished Service Crosses, sixty-eight Croix de Guerre, and one Distinguished Service Medal" (64). It was ironic that the number of American soldiers in Europe who succumbed to the worldwide outbreak of the "Spanish Flu" was higher than the number that died on the battlefield. On the march back after the German surrender and the signing of the armistice, Haywood collapsed along the road and was taken to a hospital in Mantes-sur-Seine outside Paris where his influenza was diagnosed. He remained there almost a month before being transferred to a hospital inside Paris where he stayed for over two months.

The hospital in Paris was located on the Avenue Neuilly near the Boulevard de Grande Armée and the Arc de Triomphe. Haywood recalled that "it was a veritable palace." He was assigned to a ward where there were only four other patients, three Australians and one white American. "They were having a ball seeing Paris, taking in all of the events, theaters, race tracks, boxing and girls. I don't believe that I saw a real sick man in that hospital." They had no money, but they developed a scam in which they sold the gifts showered on them by rich American women working with the Red Cross. "Every morning we would gather all our presents, take them to the gate, and sell them for a good price to the French who had gathered there to buy them" (71). Haywood had a high old time and took full advantage of the pleasures that Paris had to offer; then one day the hospital administrator called him into his office and announced that they were sending him back to his unit, which was stationed in Brest waiting to embark for home.

In Brest Haywood found his unit barracked in tents "in what seemed to me like a swamp. The weather was miserable, a steady cold rain. The mud was ankle deep." Haywood soon developed a fever and was sent to the hospital in Brest where he remained for over a month. While in Paris he had "become less used to the American nigger-hating way of life." But he was abruptly thrown back into that reality in Brest. Although there were no Jim Crow signs, the hospital wards were segregated, and black and white patients were physically separated. Black soldiers were regularly insulted and humiliated by the white staff. After witnessing these incidents, Haywood became increasingly depressed. "I felt that I could never again adjust myself to the conditions of Blacks in the States after the spell of freedom from racism in France. I did not want to go back and my feelings were shared by many Black soldiers" (74).

Harry Haywood did return along with thousands of other black soldiers, but their social consciousness was irrevocably altered by their experiences in Europe during the war. In Chicago Haywood managed to get a job as a waiter on the Central Michigan Railroad. When the race riot broke out on July 28, 1919, he was just returning from the *Wolverine* run to St. Thomas, Canada. After his train arrived Haywood took a circuitous route home to his family. He then went to the Regimental Armory where several army buddies were planning some defensive action. Gangs of armed whites were driving their trucks through black neighborhoods and firing indiscriminantly. The black veterans set up an ambush for the next truck that came through the area around Thirty-fifth and State Streets. "When the whites on the truck came through, they pulled behind and opened up with a machine gun. The truck crashed into a telephone pole at Thirty-ninth Street; most of the men in the truck had been shot down and the others fled. Among them were several Chicago police officers—'off duty,' of course" (82).[8]

For Haywood the Chicago riot was "a pivotal point in my life. . . . My ex-

periences in the Army abroad and at home with the police left me totally disillusioned about being able to find any solution to the racial problem through
the help of the government; for I had seen that official agencies of the country
were among the most racist and most dangerous to my people." Haywood's
response was typical of thousands of other black World War I veterans. "My
spirit was not unique—it was shared by many young Blacks at that time. The
returned veterans and other young militants were all fighting back." On a personal level Haywood understood that "I had to fight; I had to commit myself
to the struggle against whatever it was that made racism possible. Racism,
which erupted in the Chicago riot—and in the bombings and terrorist acts that
preceded it—must be eliminated" (83).

African Blood Brotherhood

AS HE SEARCHED for political alternatives, Haywood continued working at a
number of unskilled jobs on the railroad and in the restaurant at the Chicago
Athletic Club. It was also at this time that he met his first wife, Hazel. "She belonged to Chicago's Black social elite, such as it was. Her father had died and
her family was on the downgrade. Her mother was left with four children,
three girls and a boy, of whom Hazel was the oldest." A high school graduate,
Hazel was then employed as an office clerk at Montgomery Ward, while her
mother did domestic work. Harry and Hazel were married in 1920; he was
twenty-one and she was twenty-five. Unfortunately, when he quit his job at the
Athletic Club following a confrontation with his white managers, "my marriage went down the drain along with the job." Due to the postwar economic
downturn, jobs were hard to come by. The change in employment circumstances meant that "I was no longer the same man that Hazel married, and the
truth of the matter was that I wanted it that way" (92).

Haywood's veteran status helped him land a job as a mail sorter in the
Chicago Post Office late in 1920. Although for African Americans this was
considered a high-status position because of its security and benefits, Haywood
found the work extremely boring. The one positive element was the intellectual stimulation provided by his fellow black workers. There were many poor
black students and university graduates employed there and they decided to
form a literary society among themselves that met regularly and discussed important books and issues. Haywood recalled that one of the major discussions
revolved around the significance of the Garvey movement. While Haywood
and the Post Office intellectuals recognized that Garveyism was a mass response to white racism and social, economic, and political oppression, they
viewed it as an unfortunate development because the UNIA diverted this black

resistance "into the blind alley of utopian escapism." "We applauded the cultural aspects of the movement—Garvey's emphasis on race pride, dignity, self-reliance, his exultation of things Black. . . . However, we rejected in its entirety the Back to Africa program as fantastic, unreal and a dangerous diversion which could only lead to the desertion of the struggle for our rights in the USA" (107).

But there were other elements of the Garvey movement that Haywood objected to on the basis of his personal experiences. Haywood could not accept "Garvey's idea about inherent racial antagonisms between Black and white." Haywood had wavered at times on the point, "but I was not prepared to accept the idea as a philosophy. It did not jibe with my experience with whites." Haywood was familiar with the pseudoscientific works produced by William Graham Sumner, Herbert Spencer, Madison Grant, and other social Darwinists who "conducted raids upon the sciences, especially upon the new disciplines—anthropology, ethnology, and psychology—in an attempt to establish a scientific foundation for the race myth." Darwinian notions of the "struggle for existence" and the "survival of the fittest" were used to justify European and American imperialism and colonialism in the nineteenth century. "In this struggle, the Nordic, Anglo-Saxon, or Aryan civilizations naturally survived as the fittest" and imposed their will on lesser peoples and civilizations (94).[9]

"The dogma of the inherent inferiority of Blacks had permeated the national consciousness to become an integral part of the American way of life," Haywood noted. "Racist dogma, first a rationale for chattel slavery and then plantation peonage, was now carried over to the north as justification for a new system of de facto segregation." Even before he studied and thoroughly investigated the issue, Haywood understood that "this propaganda was a tissue of lies." "I reject racism—the lie of the existence in nature of superior and inferior races—and its concomitant fiction of the intuitive hostility between the races. For one thing, it ran counter to my own background in Omaha" (95–96).

Haywood began his reading and formal study of this topic through the direction provided by his brother, Otto, who had also served in the U.S. Army in Europe during the war and returned home a New Negro. Otto Hall had been drafted and served in a stevedore battalion first in the southern United States, then in France. In the army camp in Newport News, black draftees were subjected to the most indecent conditions. For months during the winter of 1917–1918 they were forced to sleep in tents and were given no bathing or toilet facilities. It was only after numerous protests were lodged that they were provided clothing and other supplies. When they were taken to France, they unloaded ships, repaired roads, and built barracks. Army discipline was ferocious and many men spent much time in the guardhouse. Otto Hall spent a great deal of time in army jails for fighting, and once when he was released and asked for a weekend pass to visit Paris, he was refused. So he decided to go

AWOL, but was arrested soon after arriving in the city. He spent most of his time in Paris in the army jail at the Hotel St. Anne.

Otto returned to the United States in 1918 completely disillusioned about white American democracy and was attracted to the Garvey movement, moving up the ranks in the African Legion, the UNIA paramilitary group. But he left the Garveyites and became involved in the radical workers' organization, the Industrial Workers of the World, or Wobblies. It was through this organization that he met several black communists who had formed their own secret group, the African Blood Brotherhood (ABB), which he subsequently joined. When Haywood mentioned to his brother the anti-racist books the Post Office intellectuals had recommended he read, Otto said, "You ought to quit reading those bourgeois authors and start reading Marx and Engels" (97–98).[10]

In 1921 Haywood quit his monotonous job at the Post Office, and found work on the Santa Fe Railroad as a waiter. The run was to Los Angeles and back, and each month he had a twelve-day layover, which allowed him to read and participate in a full social and political life. He read the books his brother recommended, Karl Marx and Friedrich Engels's *Communist Manifesto*, Marx's *Value, Price, and Profit*, and Engels's *Origins of the Family, Private Property and the State*. "The first stage of my political search was near an end. I had come from being a disgruntled Black ex-soldier to being a self-conscious revolutionary looking for an organization with which to make revolution" (117).

In the spring of 1922 when Haywood announced his intention to join the recently formed Workers (Communist) Party, Otto told him to hold off; it was not a good time because the few black members of the Chicago branch had complained to the Central Committee about the "paternalistic attitude" of their white comrades, and the issue had not yet been settled. Otto suggested instead that he join the African Blood Brotherhood, a black revolutionary group founded in New York City in 1919 by Cyril Briggs. Born on the Caribbean island of St. Nevis in 1887, Cyril V. Briggs was educated in St. Kitts and also worked for several local newspapers. In 1905 he emigrated to the United States and when the *Amsterdam News* began publication in 1911, Briggs was hired as an editor and worked for the newspaper until 1914 when he resigned to start his own magazine, *The Colored American Review*. The magazine was short-lived and by June 1916 he was back at the *Amsterdam News*. During the war, Briggs wrote several editorials critical of African-American support for the war effort. The editorials were reprinted widely in black newspapers and soon drew the attention of the U.S. Military Intelligence. Pressure was put on James H. Anderson, the publisher, to censor these statements, but Briggs resigned rather than accept the censorship. Eventually, through the financial support of J. Anthony Crawford, owner of a steamship company, Briggs launched the *Crusader* magazine in September 1918.[11]

The *Crusader* reflected the radical New Negro consciousness of the era. The magazine published literature, theater, and music reviews as well as news and political commentary. Briggs's publication not only became the "Publicity Organ of the Hamitic League of the World," a Pan-African organization founded in 1917, but also supported the successful Bolshevik revolution in Russia and eventually adopted an anti-capitalist ideological stance. Briggs maintained close ties with the two original black members of the Workers (Communist) Party, fellow West Indians Otto Huiswood and Arthur Hendricks, and in numerous editorials in the *Crusader* in 1919 Briggs championed the cause of the Bolsheviks because of their denunciations of imperialism and support for the liberation of colonized peoples. With the numerous race riots and mob action launched against African Americans during the "Red Summer" of 1919 Briggs founded the African Blood Brotherhood in October of that year as a secret, fraternal organization that would serve as "an elite revolutionary cadre" committed to black liberation and self-defense.[12]

Recent analyses have concluded that from its inception the ABB was formed as a black auxiliary to the nascent Communist Party (CP). Otto Huiswood joined the party in 1919 and was the first black delegate to attend the Comintern Congress in Moscow, and Edward Doty, commander of the ABB post that Harry Haywood joined in 1923, was an early black communist and organizer of the American Consolidated Trades Council in Chicago.[13] In its statement of aims it was clear that the ABB sought to link the struggle for black advancement and liberation with that of the white working class. Among its objectives were the following:

1. A Liberated Race
2. Absolute Race Equality
3. The Fostering of Racial Self-Respect
4. Organized and Uncompromising Opposition to the Ku Klux Klan
5. A United Negro Front
6. Industrial Development
7. Higher Wages for Negro Labor, Shorter Hours and Better Living Conditions
8. Education
9. Co-operation With other Darker Races and With the Class-Conscious White Workers.[14]

At its peak it has been estimated that the ABB had seven thousand members in posts located in the eastern United States and the West Indies.

At the suggestion of the leadership of the Communist Party, Cyril Briggs initially tried to establish an alliance with Marcus Garvey's UNIA. Through the efforts of the ABB one of the founders of the CPUSA, Rose Pastor Stokes, was invited to address the UNIA convention in New York City in August 1921.

Stokes called for cooperative efforts between blacks and communists to end "capitalistic imperialism" at home and abroad. "You want Africa," she declared. "Africa should be yours. . . . But you want a free Africa; you don't want an enslaved Africa, do you? If your eyes are open to the conditions that prevail under capitalistic imperialism, you know . . . that there can be no freedom in the farthest parts of the world so long as capitalism maintains its power in the world." Stokes declared that capitalism exploits white as well as black workers and "there is a class conflict coming on in the world, and that conflict overshadows every other element in the conflict of peoples and races and humanity. We must stand together as workers." She concluded that "it is essential for you, as workers, to struggle with the workers of the world against the powers that oppress us all."[15]

ABB members at the convention attempted to rally support behind the communist position, but were not only unsuccessful in their efforts, but also alienated Marcus Garvey when they distributed a circular suggesting that the convention itself was a failure. Briggs and the ABB members were expelled from the meeting and from that point on Briggs supported the efforts of the U.S. Department of Justice and the Friends of Negro Freedom to destroy the UNIA. From the September 1921 issue onward, the *Crusader* was filled with anti-Garvey editorials and articles. When Garvey fired back in the *Negro World*, charging that the fair-skinned Briggs was a "white man . . . claiming to be a Negro for Convenience," Briggs sued Garvey for criminal libel and the *Negro World* was forced to print a retraction. When Garvey was eventually tried and convicted of mail fraud in 1923, Briggs gained the reputation as "one of the fellows who sent Marcus Garvey to prison."[16]

Harry Haywood's brother, Otto, had joined the ABB post in Chicago in 1921. In the summer of 1922 Otto took Harry to a brotherhood meeting where he met the commander, Edward Doty, and he was subsequently initiated into the group. "This consisted of an African fraternization ritual requiring the mixing of blood between the applicant and one of the regular members. The organization took its name from this ritual. Doty performed the ceremony; he pricked our index fingers with a needle (I hoped it was sterilized!) and when drops of blood appeared, he rubbed them together." Haywood then took an oath of loyalty in which he pledged never to divulge any secrets of the organization under punishment of death. The only task that he was asked to perform for the group was to sell several dozen copies of its magazine, the *Crusader* (122).[17]

Joining the brotherhood was significant for Harry Haywood's overall ideological development. The organization was made up of black working-class intellectuals who were generally self-educated, as opposed to having been college-trained. They were "political activists," according to Haywood, who represented "the politically advanced section of the Black working class." It was in the brotherhood, Haywood recalled years later, "that I forged my first active association with Black industrial workers. I found them literate, articulate and class conscious, a proud and defiant group which had been radicalized by the struggles against discriminatory practices of unions and employers." Edward Doty, for example, was a plumber by trade, but was one of the founders of the American Consolidated Trades Council (ACTC), a federation of independent black unions in the construction trades industry. The purpose of the council was to protect the rights of black workers and improve the relations between black and white labor organizations. Doty and his followers in the Trades Council "were pioneers in the struggle for the rights of black workers" (131).[18]

Haywood remained in the ABB for only six months, but before he was to join the Communist Party officially, he was asked to become a member of the Young Communist League (YCL). H. V. Philips and John Harvey, leaders of the league, approached him because they felt he could be effective in recruiting black youths to the party. Haywood agreed and attended the Fourth Convention of the CPUSA, held in New York City in August 1925, as a representative of the YCL. There he was exposed to the most prominent factions, "Ruthenberg-Pepper vs. Foster-Bittleman," within the party at the time. The major differences between the two centered around the degree of support they received from the Communist International (CI) in the campaign to "bolshevize" the party. At this time, the CI put more faith in the Ruthenberg group's ability to strengthen the party through organizing the black and white working class in the factories, shops, and on the streets.[19]

At some time in 1924 the party's central committee decided to liquidate the African Blood Brotherhood. Beginning in 1922 Cyril Briggs worked in New York City for the communist-sponsored group Friends of Soviet Russia, and the ABB was absorbed into the party. By 1924 he became a labor organizer paid by the party and the ABB went out of existence as a separate organization. At this fourth annual convention, however, the CP leadership decided to support the formation of an American Negro Labor Congress (ANLC). It was the party's first attempt to build a "left led united front among blacks." Its purpose was to work with black organizations and unions to bring black workers into the trade union movement, to encourage the formation of black and white industrial unions, to work for the abolition of legal segregation and political disfranchisement of the black population, and to organize the black masses against imperialist oppression. This was indeed a grandiose program, and the group's inability to carry it out was suggested as early as the organizing meeting in Chicago in October 1925.[20]

Harry Haywood worked on the arrangements for the congress and Lovett Fort-Whiteman, an early black convert to communism who had recently returned from Moscow, was chosen by party officials to head up the organization. "Fort-Whiteman was a truly fantastic figure," Haywood recalled. "A brown-skinned man of medium height, Fort-Whiteman's high cheekbones gave him a somewhat Oriental look." Dressed in traditional Russian style clothes, including long shirt, wide belt, boots, and fur hat, he appeared to be a "Black Cossack." A hall on Chicago's South Side was rented for the conference, and on the opening night, a "Russian ballet" had been scheduled to be performed by an American dance troupe. Unfortunately, when one of the ballerinas peered out from behind the curtain and saw the audience, she exclaimed in a thick Texas accent, "Ah'm not goin' ta dance for these niggahs!" An uproar began in the audience, and someone shouted, "Throw the cracker bitches out!" The ballet troupe beat a hasty retreat (143–44).

The next act did not mind performing for blacks; they were Russian actors and they presented a one-act play by Alexander Pushkin, the great Russian writer of African heritage. Unfortunately, the play was in Russian. Although speeches and readings by Fort-Whiteman, Richard B. Moore, and Otto Huiswood were well received, it was an inauspicious beginning for the conference. While over 550 people attended the opening night session, only about forty were present during the deliberations the next day. A constitution was written and an elaborate program of activity was adopted, but for Haywood the entire affair had an "Alice in Wonderland quality" about it. The ANLC did received some favorable notice in black publications at the time, but Haywood's overall assessment corresponds very closely with that of later researchers. "Despite our effort and work," Haywood concluded, "the ANLC never got off the ground. Few local units were formed, resolutions and plans were never carried into action. Only its official paper, the *Negro Champion,* subsidized by the Party, continued for several years" (145–46).[21]

Black Student in Moscow

EVEN BEFORE the convening of the Fourth Annual Convention of the CPUSA in August 1925, the leadership was demonstrating its commitment to organizing black workers and hopefully recruiting them into the party. Immediately after that annual convention, Haywood's brother, Otto, left the United States for Moscow with a group of Americans to study Marxist-Leninist doctrine. There were ten African-Americans among the one hundred Americans who went to Russia for training in 1925, and each year a new contingent was sent by the CPUSA. In the early spring of 1926 Haywood was informed by party leaders that he too would be sent to Moscow. Because the U.S. Department of Justice discouraged the State Department from granting passports to "known radicals," Haywood Hall decided not to apply for a passport under his own name. Instead, he used the masculine version of his mother's name, Harriet,

Garvey's Movement
utopia + real

and his first name became his surname—Harry Haywood (148). Rather than leaving from the United States, Haywood made his way to Canada via Detroit, and took a ship from Quebec to Hamburg, Germany.

From Hamburg he went to Berlin where he stayed with Hazel Harrison, the wife of a friend from Chicago, who was there studying to be a concert pianist. She took him all over the city and he witnessed firsthand the devastation and depression caused by the postwar economic crisis. In an attempt to pay off its war debt the Weimar government had printed great amounts of paper money causing rampant inflation that wiped out the savings of the German middle class. "It was common to see shabbily dressed men still trying to keep up appearances by wearing starched white collars under their patched clothing" (149). Haywood went to the headquarters of the German Communist Party and met Ernst Thaelmann, the chairman, who inquired about the American communists he knew from various international meetings. Haywood remained in Berlin for a month until his visa was processed.[22]

It was late April 1926 when Haywood took a small Soviet ship to Leningrad where he was met by a member of the security police who escorted him to a hotel and made arrangements for his train trip to Moscow later that evening. The two arrived the next morning.

> Moscow at last! We drove from the station into the vast sprawling city—once capital of old Russia and now the new. It was a bright, sunny morning and the sun glistened off the golden church domes in the "city of a thousand churches." It seemed a maze of narrow, cobblestone streets, intersected by broad boulevards. While Leningrad had been a distinctly European city, Moscow seemed a mixture of the Asiatic and the European—a bizarre and strange combination to me, but a cheerful one. Moscow was more Russian than the cosmopolitan Leningrad. Crowds swarmed in the streets in many different styles of dress (152).

Haywood was soon reunited with his brother, Otto, but the meeting was sadly overshadowed by the news that Jane Golden, the wife of John Golden and one of the two black American women in the group, was in the hospital with a serious illness. After briefly stopping by the school, known as KUTVA, they went to the hospital and were informed that Jane Golden had died that morning. The funeral was held a few days later and the entire student body and most of the American colony was in attendance at the cemetery. Eulogies were read by school administrators as well as friends and acquaintances. "Jane Golden's funeral and the school's collective response to her death made a profound impression on me," Haywood recalled. "Through these events, crammed into the first three days of my stay in the Soviet Union, I came to know something about my fellow students and the new socialist society I had entered" (155).

"The University for the Toilers of the East Named for Stalin" (KUTVA) had been open for only two years. Its purpose was to train communist organizers to work among the various national and ethnic groups within the new Soviet Union and among colonized and subject peoples abroad. At the time of Haywood's enrollment there were representatives of seventy nationalities and ethnic groups attending the school. While the "inner section" of the school trained students from nationalities within the Soviet Union, the "outer section" comprised the student representatives from abroad, with the largest contingent coming from China. Since the new Soviet Union contained over one hundred national and ethnic groups, the leaders' objective was to build a multinational socialist state and "to bring about the unity of the laboring masses of the various nationalities for the purpose of waging a joint struggle—first to overthrow czarism and imperialism, and then to build a new society under a working class dictatorship." To accomplish this, it was necessary to declare the absolute equality before the law of all nationalities and the right of former colonies and oppressed nations to separate. One of the original guiding principles in the establishment of the Soviet Union was "the right of self-determination" of nations and nationalities.[23]

Students at KUTVA received full room and board and a small monthly stipend. The course of study lasted three years and focused on the teachings of Karl Marx and Friedrich Engels as developed by V. I. Lenin, or "Marxism-Leninism." The emphasis in Marxist ideology was placed on the exploitation of the workers under capitalism and the expropriation by the owners of the means of production, or "bourgeoisie," of the "surplus value" or wealth created by the laboring classes. According to Lenin, imperialism is the "highest stage of capitalism" where both the natural resources and the labor of colonized peoples is expropriated for the benefit of the metropolitan and colonial bourgeoisie. A socialist revolution would result in a redistribution of the wealth in the society from the capitalists to the workers, especially the industrial working class, or "proletariat." The members of the Communist Party in capitalist societies serve as the revolutionary vanguard that prepares the way for the ultimate "dictatorship of the proletariat" and the creation of a classless society.[24]

Once he learned to speak, read, and understand the Russian language, Haywood enjoyed his studies at KUTVA. He became close friends with other English-speaking students, especially those from India. He also became close with several of his instructors, who oftentimes were refugees from various parts of Eastern Europe. During most of the first year there were only six black students in attendance at the school, and when they were together on the streets of Moscow they attracted great attention. One member of the group, Bankole, was an Ashanti from the Gold Coast (now Ghana). He was born into an elite African family, and had lived in England and studied in the United States where he was recruited into the Young Communist League. Although he was sent to the Soviet Union to learn how to bring about a "workers' revolution," Bankole still assumed the appearance of a British aristocrat, complete with finely tailored suit, monocle, and cane. Haywood recalled that once when the group was walking in Moscow, some Russian children began following them shouting, "Jass Band . . . Jass Band!" All were amused except Bankole, who, "shaking with rage at the implication, jerked around to confront them. His monocle fell off as he shouted 'Net Jass Band! Net Jass Band!' As he spoke, he hit his cane on the ground for emphasis. Evidently, to these kids a jazz band was not just a group of musicians but a race or tribe of people to which we must belong" (170).

In December 1926 Haywood met Ekaterina—Ina—who became his second wife. She was born in Vladikavkaz in northern Russia, but fled the city with her mother during the revolution after her father was arrested by the Red Army and accused of collaborating with the czarist government officials. Mother and daughter settled in Moscow, and after an investigation was completed that exonerated her father, Ina was allowed to join a ballet school. Harry Haywood met Ina at a party given by British members of the Communist International. Following a brief vacation in the Crimea during the summer of 1927, they were married. At this time Haywood was sent to the newly established Lenin School in Moscow. It was opened by members of the Comintern to train advanced students "in theoretical and practical subjects." Haywood was the first black among the sixty students enrolled, all of whom had substantial experience and previous training as party operatives or officials.[25]

It was while a student at the Lenin School that Haywood was first exposed to the communists' latest position on the "Negro Question" in the United States. African Americans were essentially "an oppressed nation within a nation" and the movement for black liberation should be channeled toward the realization of "the right of self-determination" for African Americans in the Black Belt sections of the southern United States. Ultimately, this could possibly lead to the creation of a separate black nation. Haywood recalled that at the time (1927), "to me, the idea of a Black nation within the U.S. boundaries seemed far-fetched and not consonant with American reality. I saw the solution through the incorporation of Blacks into U.S. society on the basis of complete equality." The path to freedom for African Americans was through a socialist revolution. "The unity of Black and white workers against the common enemy, U.S. capitalism, was the motor leading toward the dual goal of black freedom and socialism" (219).

Besides, according to Leninist theory, a nation was a "historically constituted community of people" linked by four elements: a common territory, a common economic life, a common language, and a national culture. Upon first being presented the new position by N. Nasanov (Bob Katz), one of the leaders of the Young Communist International (YCI), Haywood agreed that "one could argue that among Blacks there existed elements of a special culture and also a common language (English). But this did not add up to a nation, I reasoned. Missing was the all important aspect of a national territory. Even if one agreed that the Black Belt, where Blacks were largely concentrated, rightfully belonged to them, they were in no geographic position to assert their right to self-determination" (220).

Haywood debated the issue with several other communist theoreticians and students at the Lenin School, including his brother, Otto. In preparation for the Sixth Congress of the Communist International, to meet in Moscow in July 1928, Otto Hall, Harry Haywood, and several other American students were appointed to a special "subcommittee on the Negro question." There were six members and each prepared reports on some aspect of the topic. Otto Hall was assigned the Garvey movement and in his presentation before the committee, "he concluded that the nationalism expressed in that movement had no objective base in the economic, social and political conditions of U.S. Blacks. It was, he asserted, a foreign importation artificially grafted on the freedom movement of U.S. Blacks by the West Indian nationalist Garvey." American blacks were not an oppressed nation, but an "oppressed minority" and the long-range goal should not be "the right of self-determination," but "economic, social, and political equality to be won through a revolutionary alliance of Blacks and class-conscious white labor in joint struggle for socialism against the common enemy, U.S. capitalism." Thus any type of nationalism manifested by African Americans was viewed from this perspective as reactionary (228–29).

After his report to the subcommittee, Harry Haywood felt obliged to challenge his brother's analysis because this assessment, which merely reflected the CP's earlier positions, did not correspond with Haywood's personal experiences with the African-American masses. Haywood disagreed with his brother that black nationalism in the United States was some kind of "foreign importation" from the West Indies. "On the contrary, it was an indigenous product, arising from the soil of Black super-exploitation and oppression in the United States. It expressed the yearnings of millions of Blacks for a nation of their own." Garvey with his "Back to Africa" slogans had merely diverted this nationalism onto "a reactionary separatist path." "To the slogan of 'Back to Africa,' I argued, we must counterpoise the slogan of . . . 'the right of self-determination in the South, with full equality throughout the country,' to be won through revolutionary alliance with the politically conscious white workers against the common enemy—U.S. imperialism" (230).

After his years as a black worker and student of Marxist-Leninist thought, Harry Haywood had come to the conclusion that "Afro-Americans are not only 'a nation within a nation,' but a captive nation suffering a colonial-type oppression while trapped within the geographic bounds of one of the world's most powerful imperialist countries." The doctrine of "inherent Black inferiority perpetrated by ruling class ideologues" was accepted by the white working class and prevented the integration of blacks into the American labor movement on terms of equality. At the same time, "bourgeois assimilationist illusions" were nurtured and "kept alive by the nascent Black middle class and the liberal detachment of the white bourgeoisie" in organizations such as the NAACP and National Urban League (233).

African Americans are engaged in a "struggle for national liberation" against imperialism in the United States, while the entire working class is involved in the "struggle for socialism." According to Haywood, the two are natural allies.

> The Black freedom struggle is a revolutionary movement in its own right, directed against the very foundations of U.S. imperialism, with its own dynamic pace and momentum, resulting from the unfinished democratic and land revolutions of the South. It places the Black liberation movement and the class struggle of U.S. workers in their proper relationship as two aspects of the fight against the common enemy—U.S. capitalism. It elevates the Black movement to a position of equality in that battle (234).[26]

When Haywood presented his assessment, "the only real persistent opposition in the subcommittee . . . came from Otto, the other students were somewhat ambivalent on the question." When the Sixth Annual Congress of the Comintern met, the report of the subcommittee was taken up on August 6, 1928, by the congress's Negro Commission, which was to examine the conditions for blacks in the United States and in South Africa. "It was a memorable day, particularly for us Black communists—a day to which we all looked forward. At last there would be a full-dress discussion on the question." Several high-ranking American communists, including Alexander Bittelman, William Z. Foster, and William Dunne, presented arguments favoring the new party position on the black liberation struggle in the United States. "The strongest opposition to the self-determination thesis both in the commission and on the floor of the congress was from Black comrades James Ford and Otto Hall." They continued to insist that American blacks were a "racial minority," not an "oppressed nation," and argued that all black nationalist movements "were led by the 'chauvinistic' Black bourgeoisie who wanted a freer hand to exploit the black masses." Black striving in the United States was for "intermingling and amalgamation." Haywood was "astounded and dismayed." To him this seemed "to be a bourgeois, liberal assimilationist position cloaked in pseudo-Marxist rhetoric" (262–63). It echoed the sentiments of racist white chauvinists in the party who Otto and James Ford had earlier complained downgraded the black liberation struggle.

Haywood cornered his brother in the hall during one of the sessions. "How, I asked him, did he expect to fight those responsible for the neglect of work among Blacks when he accepted their main premise—that the struggle of Blacks was not itself revolutionary and that it only becomes so when they (the Blacks) fight directly for socialism?" Although Otto denied this view, the discussion became too heated and emotional to continue. "I was terribly saddened by this growing rift between my brother and me. True, I no longer thought of him as my political mentor, but nevertheless I felt he was a serious and dedicated revolutionary" who unfortunately failed to recognize "the revolutionary element in black nationalism" and who only saw nationalism as "a block to labor unity" (265).[27]

When the full resolution of the Negro Commission was released in January 1929 and a summary was published on "the Revolutionary Movement in Colonies and Semi-Colonies," it declared that "the oppression of the Negroes . . . concentrated mainly in the so-called Black Belt provide[s] the necessary conditions for a national revolutionary movement." The party was to champion the black struggle "for complete and real equality . . . [and] for the abolition of all kinds of racial, social, and political inequalities." It endorsed "an energetic struggle against any exhibition of white chauvinism, active resistance against lynching," and "the acceptance of Black workers into unions from which they were barred and . . . the organization of separate trade unions when necessary." For Haywood the most important declaration was the statement that "in those regions of the South in which compact Negro masses are living, it is essential to put forward the slogan of the right of self-determination. . . . [A] radical transformation of the Agrarian structure of the Southern States is one of the basic tasks of the revolution" (268–69).[28]

Over the next year Haywood continued to work with the Negro Commission of the Communist International and attended the Fifth Congress of the Red International of Labor Unions (RILU), which was held in Moscow in August 1930. The RILU was an international association of trade unions, and labor organizers from twenty-five countries arrived for the congress. Several members of the International Trade Union Committee of Negro Workers (ITUCNW), organized in Hamburg in July 1930, also attended the RILU convention and reported on the first attempt of black workers from Africa and the Americas to join together in support of a revolutionary socialist movement. George Padmore, a black member of the Comintern whom Haywood met in Moscow in 1929, was one of the guiding forces behind the international black trade union organization and made a long presentation on the group at the RILU convention. Financed primarily by the Comintern, the main purpose of the ITUCNW was "to promote trade union organization in Africa and the West Indies."[29]

Although it established its headquarters in Hamburg and in 1931 began publishing its monthly magazine, *Negro Worker*, in a move to placate Western colonial powers the Comintern decided to disband the ITUCNW in August 1933, and Padmore was later expelled from the Comintern. By that time the *Negro Worker* had made its way into several colonial territories in Africa and the West Indies and came to be viewed as a threat to Western imperialist power. In the wake of the rise of fascist Adolf Hitler in Germany, the Soviet leadership, desirous of closer relations with West European nations, curtailed its support of working-class movements in Europe's colonial territories in Asia and Africa.[30]

In 1930, however, the Comintern and the RILU supported closer contacts between "colonial slaves" and "the proletariat of the Soviet Union." Moreover, at a meeting of the Comintern's Negro Commission, held in Moscow in August 1930 and attended by Harry Haywood, the Comintern reiterated its support for the "right of self-determination" for African Americans in the Black Belt. This included the unlimited right "to exercise, if they so choose, governmental, legislative and judicial authority over the entire territory and to decide upon the relations between this territory and other nations, including the United States" (336).

After four years' residence and study in the Soviet Union, Harry Haywood returned to the United States in November 1930. Having played a substantial role in the formulation and adoption of the Communist International's position on "Black Belt Self-Determination," Haywood returned as one of the Communist Party's leading theoreticians on the Negro question.

Red Star Rising

THE EFFECTS of the Depression, which had begun less than a year earlier, were already apparent among New York blacks when Haywood arrived home. "I caught a taxi to the national headquarters of the Party, which was then located on East 125th Street in Harlem. I looked at people along the way. Despair seemed to be written on their faces; I don't believe I saw a smile all the way uptown. What a contrast to the gay and laughing crowds in Moscow and Leningrad!" Haywood felt "overwhelmed by Harlem's shabbiness and the expression of hopelessness on the faces of the people." At the headquarters, party leaders Earl Browder, Robert Minor, Jack Stachel, and Ben Amis, the head of the Negro department, were hard at work on preparations for the upcoming anti-lynching conference called by the American Negro Labor Congress, to be held in St. Louis on November 15. The party officials informed Haywood that they planned to disband the ANLC and create a new organization because it was not only nonfunctioning, but the leadership proved reluctant to support the party's new position on blacks in the United States.[31]

The failure of the ANLC to recruit new black members to the party had been an issue raised at the Sixth Congress of the Comintern in 1928. Moreover, when the new position on the right of self-determination was adopted at that meeting, ANLC officials published statements openly at odds with the new line. Otto Huiswood, an ANLC officer and the first black communist to actually meet with V. I. Lenin in Moscow, published an article in February 1930 in the CP's official magazine, *The Communist,* entitled "World Aspects of the Negro Question." Huiswood denied the appropriateness of "self-determination" as an objective of the black liberation struggle in the United States because the black minority was not a nation, and "its only distinguishing feature is its racial origin." Writing from Moscow Harry Haywood responded to Huiswood's position in a later issue of *The Communist,* but other members of the ANLC, including Richard B. Moore, echoed Huiswood's sentiments in their speeches and articles.[32]

In 1930 party leaders decided to create a new organization that would reflect the party's latest line and they asked Harry Haywood to draft the manifesto and program for the new group. The League for the Struggle for Negro Rights (LSNR) was to be a "united front around the Party's program for Black liberation" (343). On his way to the conference in St. Louis, Haywood stopped off in Chicago to visit his family, whom he had not seen for over four years. His mother had passed away while he was in Moscow, but he did get to see his sister, Eppa, and her son, David, and his three aunts. In St. Louis he met for the first time Cyril Briggs, the founder of the *Crusader* and the African Blood Brotherhood, and Harry also was reunited with his brother, Otto, who filled him in on the details about his narrow escape from a lynch mob in North Carolina the year before.

Upon his return to the United States from his studies in the Soviet Union, Otto Hall was sent to Gastonia, North Carolina, as a labor organizer for the National Textile Workers Union, an affiliate of the CP's Trade Union Educational League (TUEL). The workers at the Loray Textile Mill had gone on strike because of low wages and poor working conditions; mill owners used the police to harass and attack striking workers and their supporters. Female strike leader Ella May Wiggins was actually shot down in broad daylight by the police during the strike. After being evicted from their company-owned homes, the strikers formed a tent colony outside one of the mills, but it was attacked by the local police who wanted them to disperse. In the ensuing shootout the Gastonia chief of police was killed and several deputies were wounded by the striking workers. Otto Hall was in Bessemer City when the attack came, and a group of striking workers went to warn him before he reached the town that a posse had been formed and was out to get him. The union members caught up with him two miles outside the city, and took him to Charlotte where he stayed until money was collected to pay his train fare to New York City. According to the account in the *Daily Worker*, "no sooner had Hall embarked on the train [than] a mob broke into the house where he hid before his departure. It was only the timely action on the part of these white workers that saved the life of their Negro comrade" (319).[33]

In St. Louis in November 1930 the LSNR was officially formed on the third day of the ANLC anti-lynching conference. Haywood's manifesto and program of action were submitted to and approved by the Resolutions Committee and adopted by the 120 delegates. The manifesto declared that "Blacks were an oppressed nation struggling against U.S. imperialism and called for unity of Black and white workers in the fight against the common oppressor." The LSNR's program called for the abolition of Jim Crow segregation and other forms of racially discriminatory practices and urged "the establishment of a united trade union movement to include Black workers on the basis of complete equality." The LSNR was to be a communist organization aimed at defending the interest of black workers in the American labor movement. Richard B. Moore was elected the national secretary and Harry Haywood was appointed to the ten-member national committee.[34]

Upon his return to New York City, Haywood was put on the CP payroll and soon became head of the district's Negro Department. Haywood was also placed on the CP's National Negro Commission, which oversaw the party's work among African Americans. Racist behavior and practices among union workers, many of whom were communists, led to numerous complaints to the Negro Commission from black communists. Cyril Briggs, who was then a member of the CP's central committee, Maude White, an organizer in the needle trades industry, and Haywood brought these complaints to the Politburo, made up of the heads of the party's various sections, and demanded that the issue of "white chauvinism" be addressed. Maude White had found that black workers in the needle trades were receiving lower wages than white workers doing the same jobs and there was strong white opposition to attempts to deal with the situation. "She became so emotionally upset," Haywood recalled, "she burst into tears and asked to be relieved of her responsibilities in the needle trades unless she were given more support" (353).

An incident at the Finnish Workers Club was typical of the racist behavior of white workers who were members of the party. Located in a racially changing section of Harlem, the club and hall served as a social center for Finnish residents and the Finnish baths were quite popular. One evening when a dance was held there, blacks who showed up were turned away by the janitor, August Yokinen, who was also head of the party's unit at the Finnish Club. When confronted about his actions, it was reported that Yokinen stated, "[If] Negroes came into the Club . . . they would soon be coming into the bathroom [Finnish baths and sauna] and [I] for one did not want to bathe with Negroes." Briggs, White, and Haywood argued that the party had to make clear its position on white chauvinism if it was to gain the support of African-American workers.[35]

In response the Politburo issued a detailed set of resolutions in February 1931 calling for the "greatest degree of fraternization" between blacks and whites in communist-sponsored social affairs, dances, and concerts. "The closest association of the white with the Negro comrades in social life inside and outside of the Party is imperative." They also announced the holding of a public trial of August Yokinen for behavior unbecoming a communist, with possible expulsion from the party if convicted. Great amounts of advance publicity were heaped upon the upcoming trial in the communist and noncommunist press. Held at the New Harlem Casino on March 1, 1931, with over two thousand people in attendance, Clarence Hathaway, editor of the *Daily Worker*, served as the prosecutor; and the LSNR's Richard B. Moore, also head of the Negro Department of the International Labor Defense (ILD), was the attorney for the defense. Although during the trial Yokinen recanted his "white chauvinistic tendencies," the jury found him guilty and ordered his expulsion from the party. They did recommend his reinstatement if he performed a number of tasks, including leading a demonstration against a restaurant in Harlem that barred blacks. Yokinen agreed. Harry Haywood, who had worked hard on the preparation and publicity for the trial, recalled that when it ended, and the crowd left singing the "Internationale," "it dawned on me that I had witnessed and participated in a historic event in the battle for Black rights. . . . It represented a breakthrough in understanding the importance of the struggle of the Afro-American people. It was the first time the revolutionary movement clearly and openly declared war on this pillar of American imperialism" (357).[36]

The CP position on white chauvinism and social equality was radical and much ahead of its time. But it was necessary to demonstrate that "they practiced what they preached." In the everyday interactions between white communists and blacks in Harlem, it was important to know what the official position of the party was. Overt racist behavior was not to be tolerated, but the communists had their own agenda and African Americans who joined the movement were expected to go along with it or they too would be expelled. Unfortunately, there were areas where the party's position diverged from that within the black community, and when black communists supported the black position, they were expelled for espousing "petit bourgeois nationalism." Even during the period of the CP's offensive to attract black members, some blacks were expelled for their ideological deviations.[37]

The communists made their greatest inroads into the black community as a result of the leadership they assumed of the campaign to save the Scottsboro Boys. When nine African-American youths who had stolen a ride on a freight train bound for Chattanooga were arrested in Painted Rock, Alabama, and later tried and convicted in Scottsboro for the rape of two white women on the

train, it was primarily through the efforts of the CP's International Labor Defense (ILD) that the original sentence of death in the electric chair for eight of
them was not carried out. The communists not only exposed the "legal lynching" about to take place and generated a national and international campaign
to "Free the Scottsboro Boys," but they also openly competed with the
NAACP lawyers to provide the defense attorneys for the beleaguered youths.
The NAACP leadership accused the communists of using the case for its own
political purposes, but the ILD attorneys were eventually able to get new trials
and the boys' release from prison.[38]

As the head of the Negro Department for the CP's New York District and later
for the national central committee, Harry Haywood participated in organizing
Scottsboro meetings, rallies, protests, and other aspects of the campaign. The first
major meeting, the "All-Southern Scottsboro Defense Conference," held in
Chattanooga in May 1931, was completely organized by members of the
Communist Party. Haywood attended and spoke at the meeting. "I remember the
enthusiasm and militancy of the two hundred delegates, especially the local
people." Haywood believed that "Scottsboro marked the first real bid of the
Party and the Black working class for leadership in the Black liberation movement."
He viewed the participation of black workers in the Scottsboro movement, unemployed councils, sharecroppers' unions, and other militant labor organizations as another form of race vindication that should not be diffused by "liberal
reformist policies" of traditional black organizations, such as the NAACP and the
National Urban League. "Black workers emerged as a force independent of the
reformists and [were] greatly strengthened by their role as part of the working class
generally" (375).[39]

But the problem remained of the racist practices of white workers and the overall weakness of the organized labor movement. These realities decreased the
likelihood that African Americans would depend upon communist-led movements to bring about black advancement and liberation. This was made clear to
Haywood when he was sent as an organizer for the communist-dominated National Miners Union (NMU), which had called a strike against the coal mining
companies around Pittsburgh. In some areas black workers were integrated
into the union structure and supported the strike. Haywood concluded that
this was due primarily to the fact that the majority of miners were foreign immigrants who could not speak English and thus black miners were able to assume
leadership positions. However, in other parts of the region black miners refused to go on strike. Haywood recalled that the white miners "seemed to expect
that the Black miners should forget about racist incidents that occurred during the
last strike, job discrimination in the mines and segregation in the company
patches (areas where mines built company-owned housing and company
stores)" (366).[40]

Haywood used the Scottsboro incident to break down the resistance of black workers to the union's demand that they participate in the strike. At the rally, where virtually the entire black community turned out, Richard B. Moore, who was then touring the country speaking on behalf of the Scottsboro Boys, spoke for two hours and held the audience spellbound by his oratory linking the miners' strike to Scottsboro and the international economic situation. Although the black miners joined the strike after the rally, by the eleventh week a back-to-work movement had begun among striking workers. Many were on the edge of starvation and just could not hold out any longer. The union leaders were not prepared for this "strategic retreat" by the miners and when they began to return to work the leadership was left isolated. "Thousands of the most militant and courageous fighters were locked out (blacklisted and evicted) by the coal operators. The NMU was decimated by the coal operators, and thenceforward, we were unable to build it into a powerful independent union" (374).

Despite this setback, the CP remained in the vanguard of protests against poverty, unemployment, and social injustice in 1932. Given this high profile, the party decided to nominate and run candidates in the presidential election. William Z. Foster, party chairman, was nominated for president, and James W. Ford, a black communist who was instrumental in the launching of the international black trade union organization, ran as vice president. The CP candidates were on the ballot in forty states, but they received only 103,000 votes out of a total of sixty million cast. This was not, however, an accurate indication of the party's influence at the time, particularly in the South, where the vast majority of black citizens were denied the right to vote.

In the summer of 1932 the communists gained even greater credibility among southern blacks for their defense of Angelo Herndon, a young black communist who was arrested in Atlanta for leading a demonstration by unemployed workers seeking public relief. Herndon was arrested and charged with "incitement to insurrection" under a fugitive slave statute enacted in 1861. In his defense black attorney Benjamin J. Davis made it clear that "the only offense Herndon committed was that he asked for bread for children; his only crime is his color." Convicted by the all-white jury, he was sentenced to eighteen to twenty years in prison, but the communists fought for Herndon's release, and in 1937 the U.S. Supreme Court finally reversed the earlier conviction.[41]

Haywood's work on the Herndon Defense Committee was interrupted in August 1932 by a return trip to Moscow to attend the Twelfth Plenum of the Executive Committee of the Communist International (ECCI). Haywood was one of three American delegates, and actually addressed the conference delegates (in Russian) at one of the sessions where Soviet Commissar Josef Stalin was in attendance. Haywood was also happy to be reunited with his wife, Ina, and many of his friends from his student days. The ECCI delegates assessed the current international situation and made recommendations to Comintern sections and affiliates around the world about how best to deal with the growing fascist movements in Germany, Italy, and other European countries.

Haywood was desirous of bringing his wife back with him to the United States. While Soviet officials quickly issued her an exit visa, when they went to the nearest American embassy, in Riga, Latvia (the Soviet Union was still not recognized by the United States at this time), Haywood was interrogated by the officials. "The ambassador himself took part in the questioning. I could tell by his accent that he was a polite Southern gentleman. Behind the mask, I could sense hostility towards me" (387). They wanted to know why Haywood was in the Soviet Union. He told them that he was a writer who had spent some time in the Soviet Union when he met his wife. The officials then announced that this office did not handle visas; he would have to return to the United States and apply for one through the Department of Immigration.

Haywood returned via Berlin to the United States and immediately applied for the visa. "Who is she—a communist?" The immigration officials in New York City were rude and hostile. "We're not letting in communists, you know." Haywood said she was just a Soviet citizen, but the officials did not move on the application for months. Haywood knew the holdup was because he was black and decided to seek legal assistance from attorney William Patterson of the ILD, the American Civil Liberties Union, and other liberal organizations. Finally, Haywood received a letter from the Immigration Department asking him to come to Washington to discuss the matter. He and Patterson met with the commissioner, who claimed that the reason the visa was not granted was not because he was black, and she was white; but because they had no evidence that Haywood had been divorced from his first wife, Hazel. He promised to get the documentation (389).

When Haywood was living in Moscow, his sister had written him that his wife had divorced him, remarried, and had several children. However, when he went to Chicago and met with Hazel, she said she had not divorced him because it was "against her religion. My church doesn't approve of divorces." "I was astounded," Haywood recalled. "Here she was living with someone else and with children, but she couldn't approve of divorce!" (390). Haywood wrote Ina that he would try and get the divorce as soon as possible. Unfortunately, he had no money for it. The two exchanged letters for years, but Haywood was unable to return to the Soviet Union for over a decade and they eventually lost contact.

Although Haywood was busy planning and coordinating the Scottsboro protests and other demonstrations in New York City, as head of the Central Committee's Negro Department he knew he had to stay on top of organizing activities in the South where the African-American population was concentrated. He made a southern tour beginning in April 1933 that took him to Al-

abama, Georgia, and Tennessee. In Birmingham, Alabama, he met with Hosea
Hudson, Nate Ross, Joe Howard, and the other members of the Sharecroppers
Union formed there in 1931 under the leadership of communist organizers.
The city was oppressive for African Americans, who were regularly victimized
by racial violence, brutality, and exploitation. Centered in Tallapoosa County,
southeast of Birmingham, the Sharecroppers Union sought to gain the right of
tenants to market their own crops and the continuation of food advances to
prevent starvation. For farmworkers the union sought a minimum cash wage of
one dollar per day for all laborers—men, women, and children; small personal
gardens for resident farm laborers; and nine months of public schooling for the
children of farmworkers. When the local sheriff learned from an informer
about a meeting of union organizers in July 1932 near Camp Hill, a shootout
occurred in which Ralph Gray, a local union leader, was killed and five others
were wounded. In December 1932, Cliff James and Milo Bentley were killed
by the sheriff's men for their union activities and the homes of other union
members were attacked in an attempt to end "communist agitation." When
Haywood went to Dadeville, where he addressed a clandestine meeting of
union leaders at the home of Tommy Gray, "there were guns of all kinds—
shotguns, rifles, pistols" that had been brought to the meeting. Assassination
attempts had been made against Gray and other union leaders and they were
determined to protect themselves (401–2).[42]

In Atlanta Haywood met with Benjamin J. Davis, the black lawyer who
gained national attention for his defense of Angelo Herndon. Although he
came from a prominent Atlanta family, after he received his law degree from
Harvard and returned home, he was limited in the types of legal work he could
pursue because of racial discrimination in the Georgia court system. The Herndon case not only allowed him to gain entrance to the courts as a defense attorney, it radicalized him and he subsequently joined the Communist Party.
Davis became a local leader of the Herndon and Scottsboro protests and as a
result was regularly threatened by the Ku Klux Klan and other racist white
groups. When Haywood arrived and was informed about the volatile situation,
"I was worried about Ben Davis, about his safety. . . . I sized him up as an up-
and-coming young communist, with great leadership potential. He would be a
good addition to our growing body of cadre—we didn't need another martyr,
we needed living activists" (406). Haywood subsequently brought the issue to
the Politburo, which agreed with his assessment. Davis came to New York City
and worked for the *Liberator* and other communist publications. In the 1940s
Davis was elected to the City Council representing Harlem and later became a
member of the Politburo himself.[43]

In March 1934 Haywood found himself in Memphis, Tennessee, which at
the time had the dubious distinction of being "the murder capital of the nation" primarily because of police murders of African Americans. Haywood trav-

eled to Memphis at the invitation of left-wing members of the local Jewish community to explore the possibility of starting an International Labor Defense branch. He was accompanied by Forshay, an ILD organizer, and Boris Israel, an investigative reporter for the *Daily Worker*. At a meeting of the International Workers Order (IWO), which provided workers with low-cost insurance, it was agreed to use the recent killing of seventeen-year-old Lavon Carlock to generate support for a branch of the ILD. Although the police claimed that he was killed while resisting arrest when he was taken into custody for allegedly raping a white woman, Boris Israel's investigation turned up a witness who said she saw the police beat the young man to death.[44]

Under the slogan "Stop Police Murder of Negroes in Memphis," the city was showered with leaflets; telegrams from all over the country were sent to the notorious mayor, Boss Crump, calling for an end to police violence and brutality. The ILD and IWO campaign was supported by the publisher of the local black newspaper, the *Memphis World*, which carried news regularly about the case. A delegation of black community leaders met with Mayor Edward Crump and pleaded for some concession on the issue of police brutality, but were not only told that he would "brook no rebellion from the niggers," but also that the dozen or so "reds" in the city "would be taken care of when the time came" (414).

Subsequently, when the witness to the brutal slaying of Lavon Carlock disappeared (probably frightened by the police into leaving town), the case fell apart. At this point the situation for Haywood and his colleagues became threatening; the police came to the *Memphis World*'s offices looking for them. They decided to leave town immediately after picking up some money wired to them by the ILD chairman William Patterson. While Forshay and Israel were in the telegraph office, two policeman came up and noticed the car's Alabama license tag. When Haywood's friends came out, they recognized the seriousness of the situation, so Israel yelled out, using a thick southern accent, " 'Come on, Sam! Let's get out of heah.' 'Yessuh,' I drawled, and climbed in the back. We kept driving until we got to Mississippi" (415).

Upon his return to New York City, Haywood prepared for the Eighth Convention of the CPUSA, to be held in Cleveland in April 1934. As the head of the Negro Department, Haywood was asked to make a report on current activities to the Central Committee and convention in general. The report, later published in pamphlet form under the title *The Road to Negro Liberation*, was Haywood's most important statement during the decade of his ideas and theories about the relationship of the communists to the movement for black advancement. The three ideological issues addressed in the report were black reformism, bourgeois and petit bourgeois black nationalism, and black nationalist deviations among black members of the Communist Party. According to Haywood, the black upper class is wedded to the capitalist system and is interested in pursuing "liberal reforms" of that system to allow the inclusion of African Americans on a basis of equality. Associated with the leadership of the NAACP and National Urban League, their objective is assimilation and believe that "the fate of the Negro masses is bound up with the maintenance of capitalism." The party must oppose these leaders and organizations because their program stands in direct opposition to "the rising movement of Negro and white toilers" to bring about a socialist revolution.[45]

The bourgeois and petit bourgeois nationalists also favor capitalism and use black nationalist ideology for their own personal advancement. Appealing to race pride and solidarity using slogans such as "Race First" and "Buy Black," these black nationalists encourage a type of racial exclusivism that runs parallel to the legal segregation enforced by the white ruling class. In the early 1930s black boycott movements arose in many northern cities calling for "Jobs for Negroes" and "Don't Buy Where You Can't Work" campaigns. While these activities clearly reflected the self-determinist cultural tradition, they ran afoul of the CP's objectives when the success of these protests resulted in the firing of white workers. Haywood believed that these "neo-Garveyite movements" represented "an attempt on the part of petty bourgeois leaders to seize the leadership of the rising movement of the Negro masses against oppression in order to throttle it by diverting it into reactionary utopian channels, away from the revolutionary struggle and hence back into the fold of the bourgeois reformists" (424). The petit bourgeois nationalists were a definite threat to the CP's bid for leadership of the black liberation movement.[46]

Petit bourgeois nationalist sentiments had developed among some black communists in the face of continual exhibitions of racial chauvinism by whites within the party. These black communists came to believe that very little could be accomplished by the party in bringing about black liberation until these white racist behaviors had been eliminated. Haywood rejected this notion and argued that indeed white chauvinism was the major tendency undermining the party's influence among African Americans, but that petit bourgeois nationalism was "the main obstacle to advancing our work among Blacks." Haywood concluded that "the struggle against white chauvinism and petit bourgeois nationalism went hand in hand. It was necessary to struggle on two fronts, for both deviated from the line of proletarian internationalism" (430–31).

Haywood received a standing ovation from the delegates to the Eighth Party Convention for his presentation and was subsequently placed on the Politburo, the party's highest executive committee. Haywood was the second African American appointed; unfortunately, James Ford, the other African American on the committee and then head of the party's Harlem district, disagreed with Haywood on a number of issues and viewed him as a threat to his own personal ambitions. Haywood found the environment in New York City increasingly hostile, but more importantly, he resisted the attempts to make him a "party bureaucrat." He requested a transfer to Chicago and in late fall of 1934 Haywood was installed as head of the party's district on the South Side of Chicago at a huge banquet held in his honor and attended by hundreds of his personal friends and comrades.[47]

The Popular Front Against War and Fascism

IN THE EARLY 1930s fascist-led movements were on the move in various parts of the world, sweeping away liberal or democratically elected governments, and launching attacks against independent nations. In September 1931 the Japanese found an excuse for invading northern China, where they set up a puppet government in their newly created nation of Manchukuo. Hitler and the National Socialists came to power in Germany in 1933 and the following year they participated in the unsuccessful attempt to overthrow the newly installed government in Austria. In October 1935 the Italians launched an invasion of Ethiopia. In each of these incidents the major Western powers and the League of Nations did little beyond making strong verbal protests. Mussolini's attack on Ethiopia was particularly disturbing to African Americans because the country had been a longtime symbol of black independence and nationhood. The Seventh Congress of the Communist International denounced Mussolini's campaigns and called upon communists around the world to build "a broad people's front" or "Popular Front" against fascism and work to prevent another world war. The parties were asked to join in coalitions and alliances with noncommunist organizations to try to halt the spread of fascist and other right-wing governments.[48]

Immediately upon his arrival in Chicago Harry Haywood began working with a broad spectrum of organizations, black and white, on a "Hands Off Ethiopia" parade and demonstration that was to take place on August 31, 1935. Leading black ministers, Christian youth groups, the Socialist Party, and the executive council of the Chicago American Federation of Labor joined the coalition in support of the demonstration. Unfortunately, Chicago mayor Ed Kelly, who had recently returned from Italy where he had received an award from Benito Mussolini, refused to give the sponsors a parade permit on the grounds that the march would be an affront to Italy, "a friendly power." When liberal ministers and others were unable to convince the mayor to reverse his decision, Haywood and the other communist leaders decided to go ahead with the protest, which was to take place around Forty-seventh and South Parkway, in the heart of the South Side black community.[49]

Hundreds of police were stationed in the area to prevent any demonstrations. Protest leaders tried to blend in with the shoppers and workers at the busy intersection, handing out leaflets, raising placards, and shouting anti-fascist slogans until the police came running and they tried to flee. Haywood was on the roof of a hotel that faced the intersection. "From this vantage point, I could see the scene unfolding. Pandemonium broke loose—the streets were crowded with demonstrators and shoppers alike. As arrests were made, people began shouting protests and slogans." From rooftops speakers with megaphones rallied the protesters and taunted the police until they were able to arrest them. "Just as they arrested the speaker on the rooftop opposite me, I leaped up and began speaking. . . . I exhorted the crowd that they had the right to march and parade, scoring Chicago's Mayor Kelly and Chief [of Police James] Allman for importing Mussolini's tactics into the Southside. . . . Then I felt a blow on the back of my head and spun around to face four plainclothes cops with riot clubs. They started to beat me but one said, 'Careful, don't bloody him up. We have to get through that crowd down there.' " They dragged Haywood down the steps of the hotel, punching and kicking him all the while, and out into the streets where they commandeered a taxi to take him to the Wabash Avenue Station. Once in the cab, "they turned their attention to me, methodically beating my legs and knees, cursing me with every blow" (454).

Haywood was thrown into a cell with many other protesters, but within minutes his legs gave out from under him. "I could no longer stand. My fellow cell mates began yelling and chanting, demanding that they take the more severely injured out to the hospital." Haywood was taken to the city hospital where a young doctor looked him over and decided he would be all right. He was then taken back to the police cell. Only thirty-five of the hundreds arrested were actually charged with a crime. Haywood was released late that evening after his bail was posted. He was carried out by one of his comrades and had to remain on crutches for over a month. The party decided to capitalize on the police violence and called a rally for the following Wednesday in the same neighborhood. Despite large numbers of police, there were hundreds of people. "Speaking to the audience from a chair, as I was unable to stand, I told the audience that our demonstration had been a brilliant success in showing that the people of Chicago were ready to unite against war and fascism, both foreign and native, and in defense of their right to speak for peace" (456).[50]

From the outset of the economic depression, the traditional black leadership groups were criticized from within and without about their failure to put forward a viable economic strategy and program for African Americans. From the pages of The Crisis W. E. B. Du Bois openly questioned the integrationist strategies of the NAACP and called for the development of business cooperatives and other all-black economic ventures to pool the financial resources within the community to produce goods, services, and jobs. Walter White and other NAACP officials denounced Du Bois's "separatist notions," and he was forced to resign from the organization and the editorship of its official magazine.[51]

Several young black intellectuals, including Abram Harris, Ralphe Bunche, John P. Davis, E. Franklin Frazier, and Robert C. Weaver, not only criticized the failure of the older civil rights organizations to respond effectively to the economic crisis, but also denounced the Democrats' New Deal programs for operating in a racially discriminatory fashion. A conference on "The Position of the Negro in the Present Economic Crisis" was called by John P. Davis and Ralphe Bunche and held at Howard University in May 1935. Speaker after speaker condemned the New Deal programs as opposed to the interest of the masses of black workers because they were aimed at perpetuating the capitalist exploitation of the working classes in general. Emphasizing the reality that the vast majority of African Americans were workers, the participants concluded that there was a need for greater cooperation between black organizations and the organized labor movement to deal with the depressed conditions for blacks. The Joint Committee on National Recovery was formed to monitor and report on the conditions for African Americans under the New Deal programs and this committee issued the call for the creation of a new organization, a National Negro Congress (NNC) that would serve as an umbrella organization for black groups and develop closer ties between black workers and the trade union movement.[52]

Several of the sponsors of the Howard University conference had close ties with the Communist Party, particularly John P. Davis and Abram Harris, but were not involved in the League for Struggle for Negro Rights (LSNR), the predominantly black communist group at one time headed by Harry Haywood. By 1935 the LSNR consisted of a few branches scattered across the Northeast and Midwest where black communists gathered together. Very few branches did any active recruiting for members, and little attempt was made to build a "black united front" by securing active support from other black organizations. In some instances issues involving African Americans in the party were passed on to the LSNR leadership and not directly confronted by the party itself. According to Haywood, "this allowed many comrades to neatly side-step dealing with white chauvinism and the revolutionary importance of the Black struggle" (440). Thus when the new popular front position called on communists to participate in alliances and coalitions with other groups, black communists embraced the call for a National Negro Congress and soon the party leadership let the LSNR go out of existence.[53]

The National Negro Congress's founding meeting was held in Chicago in February 1936, and Harry Haywood as the CP district leader for the South Side was active in making the local arrangements. "We were glad that Chicago had been chosen as the host city," Haywood recalled, "because it provided impetus for consolidating and extending our contacts and associations." There were over five thousand delegates and visitors representing over 245 organizations from twenty-eight states. Held at the Eighth Illinois Regiment Armory

(Haywood's former regiment) beginning on February 15, greetings were sent from Mao Tse-tung, chairman of the Chinese Soviet Republic; and Lij Tesfaye Zaphiro, Ethiopia's special envoy to London, addressed the meeting. Although resolutions were passed supporting the Ethiopian struggle, anti-lynching legislation, Social Security benefits, and increased unemployment relief payments, the major emphasis was on improving ties between black workers and organized labor. A. Philip Randolph, head of the Brotherhood of Sleeping Car Porters, was elected president of the congress and his keynote address denounced the advance of fascist movements at home and abroad and called for "breaking down of the color line in trade unions" and the formation of industrial unions on a nondiscriminatory basis.[54]

The passage of the Wagner Act in 1935, giving workers in most areas the right to organize and bargain collectively with their employers, split the American Federation of Labor (AFL). When the AFL leadership was asked to alter its structure to allow the participation of workers in mass production industries, it refused, thus leading to the formation of the Congress of Industrial Organizations (CIO). Under the leadership of United Mine Workers president John L. Lewis, the CIO was committed to organizing semiskilled and unskilled workers, black and white, in the meat packing, tobacco, steel, automobile, and other basic industries. John P. Davis, the secretary of the National Negro Congress, worked closely with CIO officials to break down the anti-union biases of black workers and the anti-black feelings among white workers.[55]

The formation of the CIO and NNC dovetailed nicely with the new Popular Front stance of the Communist Party. At least ten communists were appointed to the seventy-member national council for the NNC. At the Ninth Convention of the CPUSA, held in New York City in June 1936, party leaders praised the opportunities now available for organizing workers in the basic industries with the founding of the CIO. Party chairman William Z. Foster, who had suffered a heart attack during the presidential campaign in 1932, had recovered enough to briefly address the 1936 meeting, but party general secretary Earl Browder became the communist candidate for president, and James Ford was his running mate. In his acceptance speech, however, Browder moved away from the party's revolutionary positions and suggested that communism should be considered "Twentieth Century Americanism," and argued that socialism could come to the United States utilizing the traditional democratic processes. Harry Haywood recalled that "at the time I doubt that any of us understood the full implications of Browder's formulations." Missing from the party platform was any mention of support for "the right of self-determination" for African Americans, while an indirect endorsement of Franklin Roosevelt's New Deal programs was included. Harry Haywood addressed the convention, and pointed out "that it is we [communists] who have to demonstrate in theory and practice how the struggle for self-determination is at the very heart of the struggle for unity of Negro and white" (465). However, Browder was beginning to move the party's ideological positions to the right and soon Haywood's preoccupation with African Americans' right to self-determination would lead to his removal from a leadership position and eventual expulsion from the party.[56]

Harry Haywood's decision to go to Spain in 1936 to join other leftists in the unsuccessful struggle against the fascist armies of rebel General Francisco Franco did little to improve his standing among party leaders in the United States. "The Spanish Civil War was part of the worldwide drive for fascism," Haywood noted. "Spain had become the next item on their agenda, after north China and Ethiopia. The Soviet Union called for collective action to stop the aggression in Spain, but the western capitalists responded with a so-called non-intervention pact which allowed Hitler and Mussolini to flood men and munitions into Spain while the U.S., France and Great Britain refused to sell war supplies to either side" (467–68). Communist parties around the world rallied to support the newly elected republican government in Spain, and organized International Brigades to fight with the republican forces. Over three thousand Americans volunteered to go to Spain and made up the Lincoln and Washington Brigades of the Fifteenth Battalion in the Spanish Republican Army.[57]

Haywood was active in the recruiting efforts in the United States, but decided that he would volunteer to fight. "I was acutely aware of the threat of fascism. . . . I felt the presence of Black communists in Spain would help emphasize the solidarity between the Afro-American and Spanish people in the struggle against fascism." Despite the fact that he was a high-ranking communist official in the United States, a member of the Politburo, and almost forty years old, Haywood went to Spain with hundreds of other Americans and was made deputy brigade commissar for one of the English-speaking units. The role of the political commissar was to keep up the morale of the soldiers by keeping them informed about the progress of the war as well as making sure they received adequate food, clothing, supplies, their mail, and adequate rest. Haywood arrived after the disastrous Battle of Jarama in February 1937, and had to take the soldiers' complaints about the military incompetence of the commander, Lieutenant Colonel Vladimir Coptic, to military headquarters. This action eventually led to his undoing because Colonel Coptic moved to undermine Haywood's authority within the military command. Haywood participated in the Loyalist Army's attempts to break the rebel siege of Madrid and his autobiography included a detailed account of the Battle of Brunete, located just outside the city. Unfortunately, during the battle Haywood clashed verbally with the brigade commander, Jock Cunningham, who accused Haywood of incompetence. This incident eventually led to his leaving the front. Although he was offered the position of political commissar in Madrid, he rejected it because it was really a demotion. Haywood left Spain bitter and frustrated after only six months.[58]

When he returned to the United States in the fall of 1937, Haywood was dogged in party circles by rumors that he had left the front without permission. Machinations that he eventually traced to his old nemesis James Ford led to the excising of Haywood's name from articles he wrote for communist publications, his removal from his salaried position on the Politburo, and his dismissal from a public relations position at the Soviet pavilion at the New York World's Fair in 1939. When Haywood was subsequently sent to Baltimore as a party organizer, he was soon withdrawn after being accused by the party's local leader of misusing district funds. Whenever he was demoted or removed from a position, party officials often brought up "that Spanish business" as one of the reasons he was now considered a liability to party activities. But there was more to it than that.

In October 1939 after returning to New York City from Baltimore, Haywood suffered a serious heart attack. He was hospitalized for several months and then went to San Pedro, California, to recuperate. There he met Belle Lewis, a communist organizer from Kentucky. After finally getting his divorce from Hazel, he and Belle were married, and moved to South-Central Los Angeles and organized a branch of the Communist Party in their neighborhood. With the American entrance into World War II in December 1941, and the increase in war-related employment in California factories, young workers were attracted to the pro-labor position of the communists and Belle and Harry Haywood's home became a center of political activity. The CP officials downtown, however, became jealous of their success and began to denounce the "uptown braintrust." Fed up with the overt and covert attacks, and fully recovered from his heart attack, Haywood became a civilian seaman in the Merchant Marine and between 1943 and 1945 served as crew messman, baker, and cook on several merchant ships that sailed to the Far East, Africa, and Europe, thus renewing his credentials as a working-class intellectual.

Revisionism, Repression, and Promises Unfulfilled

WHILE ON SHORE leave in Capetown, South Africa, in May 1944, Haywood ran into an old friend from his days in Moscow who asked about the dissolving of the Communist Party in the United States. At that time Haywood of course knew nothing about it. Earl Browder, the party general secretary, who had begun to move the party to the right in 1936, had engineered the dissolution of the CPUSA as a revolutionary vanguard party committed to Marxist-Leninist principles and replaced it with the Communist Political Association, which was committed to "national unity" and to working within the two-party system to bring about the peaceful transition to socialism. By 1945, however, when it had become clear to French communists that in the postwar world the United States and West European countries viewed communism in general and the Soviet Union in particular as their major opponents, they sent a letter to American communists criticizing Browder's revisionist positions and leadership. The publication of the "Jacques Duclos letter" sparked furious debates within party circles and finally at an emergency convention held in July 1945 Browder's political errors were exposed and the party was reconstituted.[59]

When Harry Haywood returned to New York City in September 1945, the party was still in disarray and due to age and ill health party chairman William Z. Foster seemed unable to cope with the problems. He had remained silent during the period of Browder's revisionism and even presided at the convention that led to the dissolution of the party in May 1944. According to Haywood, Foster's unwillingness "to rock the boat" and "his failure to fully break with the right opportunism of Browder, with revisionism, left the door open for the resurgence of a line which eventually liquidated the Communist party as the revolutionary vanguard of the working class once and for all" (542–43). As part of Browder's revisionism the party dropped the slogan of "the right of self-determination" for southern blacks and liquidated the Sharecroppers Union on the argument that it was an obstacle to unity between southern black and white farmers. In December 1945, however, Harry Haywood was called to a meeting of party officials following Browder's ouster and they apologized to him for the malicious rumors spread by party comrades and for his demotion in the party organization. They asked him to write a comprehensive restatement of the party's revolutionary position on the African-American situation. Haywood agreed and over the next three years he worked on his book *Negro Liberation*, which was a detailed and updated presentation of the Black Belt thesis.[60]

Although the work was well received in communist circles and eventually translated into a number of languages, it came out at the beginning of the U.S. government's anti-communist crusade. The Smith Act, passed in 1940, called for the imprisonment of the members of any group or society that teaches or advocates "the overthrow and destruction of the Government of the United States of America by force or violence." Communists and so-called fellow travelers were summoned to hearings before the House Un-American Activities Committee (HUAC) and accused by ambitious and unscrupulous politicians of violating the Smith Act. In January 1949 eleven of the top leaders of the CPUSA were indicted under the act, and were subsequently convicted and sentenced to terms in jail. Loyalty oaths began to be required of teachers and other public employees, and blacklists were compiled of communists and communist sympathizers that kept many actors, directors, and writers in Hollywood from finding jobs.[61]

In the fall of 1950 the McCarran International Security Act was passed and declared that communism was a "foreign conspiracy" and that communists were "agents of a foreign power" who had to register with the U.S. Department of State. This legislation assisted in bringing about the deportation of communists or their prosecution under the Smith Act. The anti-communist hysteria pushed the CPUSA further and further to the right in an attempt to make its policies and programs more acceptable to the increasingly conservative white middle and working classes. The party was racked by internal divisions among those on the right who either called for the liquidation of the party altogether or the adoption of liberal reformist positions, to those on the left who wanted to maintain the party's anti-capitalist, revolutionary stance. In the area of black rights, the party openly supported the bourgeois reformist policies of the NAACP, whose Supreme Court victories culminated in *Brown v. Board of Education* in 1954, which outlawed legal segregation in public education.

Struggles and debates over charges of "white chauvinism" leveled by blacks against white members (including Belle Haywood) continued to divide the party and had a negative effect on Harry and Belle Haywood's marriage (590). After a separation and divorce, Haywood continued to oppose revisionist positions on black liberation within the party and became involved in mass organizing on New York City's waterfront. In the early 1950s Haywood worked with Gwendolyn Midlo, whom he had met earlier in Paris. She was then a party leader in Brooklyn and they eventually were married and had two children, Haywood Jr. and Becky (623). Unfortunately, Harry and Gwendolyn Midlo (Hall) became active members of the leftist, anti-revisionist caucus within the party, led by Al Lannon and Armando Roman, whose members were expelled by the bourgeois reformist leadership that gained control following the Seventeenth Party Congress in 1958. The couple was then living in Mexico City where they learned that they had been expelled from the party for their "left sectarian views" (624).

In reflecting on his thirty-six years in the party, Haywood concluded that "my experience . . . confirmed what the history of the working class struggle has shown, that in order to develop a revolutionary vanguard, the CP must constantly struggle against the powerful pressures of bourgeois ideology within its own ranks." While political repression and imprisonment did much to advance the forces of revisionism within the party during the Cold War era, it was the party leadership's "illusions about the possibility of a continued alliance with the liberal bourgeoisie" that ultimately kept the CP from making a major contribution to the black liberation struggles of the 1960s (626).[62]

Throughout his political life Harry Haywood was committed to the defense of the black working class not merely against the racist and chauvinist beliefs and practices of the white working class, but also against leftist denials of the revolutionary potential of the grassroots nationalism of the oppressed black masses. Haywood was a product and remained a member of the black working-class while he served as one of its major spokespersons within communist circles. His personal experiences reinforced his ideological stances emphasizing black working class leadership in the struggle for black liberation. "Negro labor, organically united with the militant and politically conscious section of white labor," declared Haywood in 1948, "is the only force which can rally and unite the scattered segments of the Negro people in its fight for freedom. The Negro industrial working class, in alliance with the masses of the oppressed agricultural population of the Black Belt, and leading them, is the *main driving force* of the Negro national liberation movement."[63]

After rising to the highest positions within the Communist Party structure in the 1930s, Haywood was eventually expelled for his "Negro nationalist" and revolutionary positions following the triumph of revisionist bourgeois reformism within the party. Other black intellectuals and artists attracted to the Communist Party because of its militancy on the Negro question in the 1930s left much earlier because of the twists and turns the party leadership took on pressing national and international issues. However, during its heyday, communist ideology was not only important in defining the politics of black liberation, it was also influential in determining how the black masses would be portrayed in literary works produced by African-American artists.

5

Richard Wright and Zora Neale Hurston

Conflicting Blueprints for Black Writing

—

Perspective for Negro writers will come when they have looked and brooded hard and long upon the harsh lot of their race and compared it with the hopes and struggles of minority peoples everywhere that the cold facts have begun to tell them something. . . . Theme for Negro writers will emerge when they have begun to feel the meaning of the history of their race as though they in one lifetime had lived it themselves throughout all the long centuries.

—RICHARD WRIGHT, 1937

From what little I have been able to learn, I know that goodness, ability, vice, and dumbness know nothing about race lives or geography. I do not wish to close the frontiers of life upon my own self. I do not wish to deny myself the expansion of seeking into individual capabilities and depths by living in a space whose boundaries are race and nation. Lord, give my poor stammering tongue at least one taste of the whole round world, if you please, Sir.

—ZORA NEALE HURSTON, 1941

Photograph
by Carl Van Vechten.
Reprinted courtesy of
the estate of Carl Van
Vechten, Joseph
Solomon, Executor;
and the Schomburg
Center for Black Cul-
ture, New York Public
Library.

Photograph
by Carl Van Vechten.
Reprinted courtesy of
the estate of Carl Van
Vechten, Joseph
Solomon, Executor;
and the Schomburg
Center for Black Cul-
ture, New York Public
Library.

"My FIRST GLIMPSE of the flat black stretches of Chicago depressed and dismayed me, mocked all my fantasies." Richard Wright, who was to become one of the most influential African-American writers in the twentieth century, arrived in Chicago from Memphis in the late fall 1927 with his Aunt Maggie Wilson Hoskins. In his autobiographical work *American Hunger*, written in the early 1940s, he recalled that "Chicago seemed an unreal city whose mythical houses were built of slabs of coal wreathed in palls of grey smoke, houses whose foundations were sinking slowly into the dank prairie. Flashes of steam showed intermittently on the wide horizon, gleaming translucently in the winter sun. The din of the city entered my consciousness, entered to remain for years to come" (*AH*, 1).[1]

The autobiographies of Richard Wright, *Black Boy*, published in 1945, and *American Hunger*, published in 1977 after his death in 1960, have become classics in the African-American autobiographical tradition. *Black Boy* described Wright's early years growing up in Mississippi and other parts of the South; *American Hunger* dealt with his years in Chicago, his interactions with members of the Communist Party, and his profound disillusionment when he was confronted by the anti-intellectualism exhibited by black communists who felt threatened by his desire to become a writer.[2]

Richard Wright was born in Natchez, Mississippi, on September 8, 1908. His father, Nathan Wright, was a farmworker, and his mother, Ella Wilson Wright, was a rural schoolteacher forced into domestic service after the family moved to Memphis. Nathan Wright abandoned the family in 1913, and shortly afterward Ella Wright became ill, and Richard and his younger brother, Leon, were briefly placed in an orphanage. When his mother recovered, they moved to Elaine, Arkansas, with his Aunt Maggie and Uncle Silas Hoskins, who owned a saloon. This was a positive time in Richard's young life that was brought to a traumatic and tragic end when his Uncle Silas was killed by local whites who were after his property. The terror-stricken sisters fled to their mother's home in Jackson, Mississippi, where they remained for only about three months before moving to West Helena, Arkansas. They lived there for over two years, but in 1918 Ella Wright suffered the first of a series of paralytic strokes that made her an invalid through the remainder of her life. Richard at age ten had to leave school and find work, and the family was forced to accept the charity of neighbors until his grandmother arrived to take them back to Jackson.[3]

Because of the illness of his grandfather, his grandmother Wilson was unable to support the two boys, so Leon went to Detroit to live with their Aunt Maggie and her common-law husband, "Professor Matthews," while Richard went to live in Greenwood, Mississippi, with his Uncle Clark Wilson and his wife, Jody. Although the couple was kind to him, Richard felt guilty about his separation from his mother and was allowed to return to Jackson to live in his grandparents' strict religious home. Although Richard was able to attend school regularly for the first time in years, and spent much of his spare time reading, the atmosphere within the household was oppressive due to his grandmother's narrow-minded religious beliefs and practices. Richard was forced to attend the Seventh-Day Adventist church regularly where he was expected to undergo a religious conversion and join the church. This did not occur and in the first part of *Black Boy*, Wright emphasized the negative impact that fundamentalist, evangelical Christianity had on the lives of African Americans.

At this time Wright worked as a newsboy, which gave him access to nonreligious literary materials that were strictly forbidden in his grandparents' home. It was also during this period that he began writing short stories. After finishing the Jim Hill Elementary School, Wright obtained a series of jobs, the longest being one with a friendly white family, the Walls. This steady part-time work allowed Wright to attend the Smith-Robinson School for two additional years. It was during this period that his first short story, "The Voodoo of Hell's Half Acre," was published in the *Southern Register*, a local black newspaper. The use of the word "hell" in the title meant that this, his first published work, was condemned by his overly religious grandmother. After losing several other part-time jobs because of his unwillingness or inability to play the role of the contented southern darky, Wright enrolled in the new Lanier High School in the fall of 1924 to continue his studies.

Wright was determined to leave Mississippi because he was fearful that his inability to conform and accept white authority would lead to terrible consequences in that hostile and highly charged racial environment. After saving money from jobs he obtained in a hotel that catered to white prostitutes and in a local movie theater for blacks, he made his way to Memphis in the fall of 1925. His plan was to secure employment and housing and save money to send for his mother. Within a week of his arrival, he soon found lodgings with a warm and friendly black family and a job in a drugstore. He later worked as a delivery boy for an optical company. Free to explore life on his own, Wright made friends with his fellow black workers and read what he chose, especially the works by contemporary novelists, such as Sinclair Lewis, Theodore Dreiser, and Sherwood Anderson. From H. L. Mencken, the iconoclastic editor of the *American Mercury*, Wright learned that words could be weapons in fighting the injustices of the world. Wright read voraciously: "A vague hunger would come over me for books, books that opened up new avenues of feeling and seeing. . . . I would read and wonder as only the naive and unlettered can read and wonder, feeling that I carried a secret, criminal burden about me each day" (*BB*, 275).

At the same time, this new reading generated new attitudes about life in the young Wright. He tried to write, but nothing would come. "I discovered that more than desire and feeling were necessary to write and I dropped the idea." Wright eventually came to the realization that if he was to become a writer, he would have to know about life and people, but this was virtually impossible in the Jim Crow South. "I now knew what being a Negro meant. I could endure the hunger. I had learned to live with hate. But to feel that there were feelings denied me, that the very breath of life was beyond my reach, that more than anything else hurt, wounded me. I had a new hunger" (*BB*, 274).

Black Boy ended with the arrival of his Aunt Maggie Wilson in Memphis, who had recently lost her job in Detroit. Maggie was anxious to start her own hairdressing salon, but was determined to do it in a northern city; so it was decided that she and Richard would go to Chicago and look for work and later send for his mother and brother, who in the meantime would return to Jackson to live with Grandmother Wilson. Upon arrival in Chicago and finding a room on the South Side, Wright through a friend from Jackson was able to get a job in the cafeteria of the Hotel Patricia on the North Side. He then sent for his mother and brother. The restaurant job lasted until February 1929, when Wright was hired by the central Post Office as a mail sorter and substitute clerk. This was definitely a step up, and the Wrights were able to move into a four-room apartment on the far South Side.[4]

By the spring of 1930, however, the effects of the Depression soon became apparent even in the "metropolis of the Midwest" and not only was Wright again out of work, but his mother had suffered a relapse and his brother had become ill with stomach ulcers. Although he worked temporarily at the Post Office during the summer, by the winter of 1931 the only employment he found was as an insurance agent for a funeral home that often defrauded its poor black clients out of their premiums. He worked briefly for Ben "Doc" Huggins, a Republican ward-heeler on the South Side, who promised him a job in a library; however, after the political campaign he was rewarded with only a temporary job as a street sweeper. The following year he worked for the local Democratic bosses during the election, but this too was a temporary position. By the fall of 1932, the situation for the Wrights had again become desperate.

> One morning I rose and my mother told me that there was no food
> for breakfast. I knew that the city had opened relief stations, but each
> time I thought of going into one of them I burned with shame. I sat

for hours, fighting hunger, avoiding my mother's eyes. Then I rose, put on my coat, and went out. As I walked toward the Cook County Bureau of Public Welfare to plead for bread, I knew I had come to the end of something (*AH,* 42).

"I Tried to Be a Communist"

When Richard Wright went to the public relief office, he felt comforted by the fact that he was not alone in his hunger and desperation; there were thousands of others who were trying to cope with horrendous conditions not of their own making. But what were the alternatives? Many times while walking through Chicago's Washington Park, Wright encountered the soap-box orators who held forth on everything from the need to repent because the end was near to the Garveyites' call for a black exodus to Africa. There he also heard black communists inveighing the assembled black crowds against the crimes of the ruling classes and the need to make a "workers' revolution." Initially, Wright was more impressed by the Garveyites. "The one group I met during those exploring days whose lives enthralled me was the Garveyites, an organization of black men and women who were forlornly seeking to return to Africa." They represented a "passionate rejection of America" on the part of African Americans, and "I understood their emotions, for I partly shared them." He met several UNIA members and Wright knew they "could never understand why I liked them but would never follow them, and I pitied them too much to tell them that they could never achieve their goal, that Africa was owned by the imperial powers of Europe, that their lives were alien to the mores of the natives of Africa, that they were people of the West and would forever be so until they merged with the West or perished" (*AH,* 28–29).

The black communists, on the other hand, "baffled and angered me." Wright was turned off by their purposely disheveled appearance and their phony speech patterns in which they imitated the white communists by rolling their Rs as if they were Russian or Polish immigrants. "'Comrades' became 'cumrrrades,' and 'distribute,' which they had known how to pronounce all their lives, was twisted into 'distrrribuuute,' with the accent on the last instead of the second syllable." Wright believed that "many sensitive Negroes agreed with the Communist program but refused to join their ranks because of the shabby quality of those Negroes whom the Communists had already admitted to membership." The communists often talked about revolution, but it was cloaked in "so many ridiculous overstatements." Wright was attracted by their "readiness to act, but they seemed lost in folly, wandering in a fantasy. For them there was no yesterday or tomorrow, only the living moment of today;

their only task was to annihilate the enemy that confronted them in any manner possible" (*AH,* 38–40).

Moreover, many of their speeches "were downright offensive to lowly,
hungry Negroes." Wright recalled one communist's attack on religion.

> "There ain't no Goddamn God! If there is, I hereby challenge
> Him to strike me dead!"
> He paused dramatically before his vast black audience for God to
> act, but God declined. He pulled out his watch.
> "Maybe God didn't hear me!" he yelled. "I'll give Him two more
> minutes!" Then, with sarcasm: "Mister God, kill me!"
> He waited, looking mockingly at his watch. The audience laughed
> uneasily.
> "I'll tell you where to find God," the speaker went on in a hard
> ranting voice. "When it rains at midnight, take your hat, turn it upside
> down on the floor in a dark room, and you'll have God."
> I had to admit that I had never heard atheism of so militant a na-
> ture, but the Communist speaker seemed to be amusing and frighten-
> ing the people more than he was convincing them.
> "If there is a God up there in the empty sky," the speaker roared
> on, "I'll reach up there and grab Him by his beard and jerk Him down
> here on this hungry earth and cut His throat." He wagged his head.
> "Now let God dare me!"

The crowd was shocked at first, then "yelled with delight. I shook my head and
walked away. That was not the way to destroy people's outworn beliefs. . . .
They were acting like irresponsible children" (*AH,* 40).

Wright, however, felt that the communists were on the right track. "I believed that the Negro could never solve his problem until the deeper problem
of American civilization had been faced and solved. And because the Negro
was the most cast-out of all the outcast people of America, I felt that no other
group in America could tackle this problem of what our American lives meant
so well as the Negro could" (*AH,* 41). Several months after the incident in
Washington Park some white friends he had met while working at the Post Office invited him to a South Side hotel and Wright was surprised to find out that
many of them had joined the Communist Party. Wright mentioned the communists' antics in the park, and his friends said that was merely a tactic they employed to attract attention.

Subsequently, at one of these gatherings a Post Office friend, Abraham
Aaron, announced that one of his short stories had been accepted by Jack Conroy's *Anvil,* a new leftist literary magazine, and asked Wright to attend a meeting of the newly organized John Reed Club in Chicago. Named after the
American journalist who participated in the Bolshevik revolution and wrote the

immensely popular *Ten Days That Shook the World,* the clubs were founded in October 1929 by communist intellectuals and became very successful in attracting young artists and writers. One of the purposes of the clubs was to help create "proletarian culture" in music, plastic arts, dance, and literature. The club's major literary vehicle was the magazine *New Masses,* which was founded in 1926 by leftist literati, but by 1929 under the editorship of Mike Gold had become virtually an organ of the Communist Party committed to the development of "proletarian realism."[5]

Within four years there were over thirty John Reed Clubs throughout the United States, and its members were affiliated with Moscow's International Union of Writers. *Left Front* was started in June 1933 as the literary magazine for the John Reed Clubs in the Midwest and at his first club meeting in Chicago Wright was asked to sit in on the deliberations of the magazine's editorial board. Wright sat in a corner while they discussed the magazine policies and looked over several copies of *New Masses* they had given him. When he returned home that evening he recalled that "I went home full of reflection, probing the sincerity of the strange white people I had met, wondering how they *really* regarded Negroes." That evening Richard Wright underwent a profound ideological conversion experience. "I lay on my bed and read the magazines and was amazed to find that there did exist in this world an organized search for the truth of the lives of the oppressed and the isolated. When I had begged bread from the officials, I had wondered dimly if the outcasts could become united in action, thought, and feeling. Now I knew. It was being done in one-sixth of the earth already. The revolutionary words leaped from the printed page and struck me with tremendous force" (*AH,* 62–63).

Wright joined Chicago's John Reed Club and he submitted several of his poems to *New Masses* and several other party-sponsored publications. To his surprise and delight they all were published. At that time the Chicago John Reed Club was dominated by the painters, and in a move to wrest control away from them, the writers called for the election of a new executive secretary. Wright's name was submitted for the position, but he initially objected, having been in the club less than two months. But in the voting that followed, to his surprise he was elected to the leadership position. "Later I learned what happened: the writers had decided to 'use' me to oust the painters, who were party members, from leadership in the club" (*AH,* 68). The card-carrying communists had organized a separate "fraction" and attempted to draw the organization closer in line with the dictates of the party. The party leaders felt that the club was too involved in the publication of *Left Front,* and spent too little time on the ideological concerns of the world communist movement. The party wanted the magazine dissolved, but Wright and the other writers objected. When the showdown came, it became clear that to remain as club executive secretary, Wright would have to join the Communist Party, which he did in 1933.[6]

he was condem by marxists
& commu-nist

As a member of the party, Wright was assigned to a unit on the South Side made up mostly of African Americans, but from the beginning he felt alienated from them because of their anti-intellectualism. The black communists criticized his reading of "bourgeois books," and they commented negatively on the fact that he wore a clean shirt and tie. "My manner of speech had seemed an alien thing to them. 'He talks like a book,' one of my Negro comrades had said." And Wright, who had only a grammar school education, was accused of being an "intellectual." "The more I learned of the Negro Communists the more I found that they were not vicious, that they had no intention to hurt. They just did not know anything and did not want to learn anything. They felt that all questions had been answered, and anyone who asked new ones or tried to answer old ones was dangerous. The word 'writer' was enough to make a black Communist feel that the man to whom the word applied had gone wrong." What was disturbing about them for Wright was their "militant ignorance" (*AH*, 77–78).

Wright ran afoul of party leaders when he decided he would interview local black communist organizers to profile them and recount their personal paths to communism. He approached a black party member named Ross, who had migrated from the deep South, become involved in party activities, and had been recently arrested for "inciting a riot" during a communist-sponsored protest. After the first interview session, Wright was visited at his lodgings by a black communist official who warned him: "Intellectuals don't fit well into the party." Wright objected, "But I'm not an intellectual . . . I sweep streets for a living." Wright had just been assigned to street-cleaning duties by the city's department of public relief. But the unnamed party member pointed out nonetheless that intellectuals generally drop out or were expelled because of their "general opposition to the party's policies" (*AH*, 79–80).

The party official told Wright that he would be expected to demonstrate "revolutionary loyalty," not by writing, but by getting "whacked over the head by the cops" during a protest or demonstration. Besides, "the Soviet Union has had to shoot a lot of intellectuals." This was what happened to the followers of Leon Trotsky, who after serving as one of the leaders of the new Soviet Union was exiled in 1929 for his ideological deviations. Trotsky opposed the development of the Soviet bureaucracy and Stalin's support for "one-state socialism." Trotsky called for "permanent revolution" in all the advanced capitalist societies under the leadership of the industrial proletariat.[7]

> "You've heard of Trotsky, haven't you?" he asked.
> "Yes."
> "Do you know what happened to him?"
> "He was banished from the Soviet Union," I said.
> "Do you know why?"

"Well," I stammered, trying not to reveal my ignorance of politics, for I had not followed the details of Trotsky's fight against the Communist party of the Soviet Union, "it seems that after a decision had been made, he broke that decision by organizing against the party."

"It was for counterrevolutionary activity," he snapped impatiently; I learned afterwards that my answer had not been satisfactory, had not been couched in acceptable phrases of bitter, anti-Trotsky denunciation (*AH*, 81).

On another occasion when Wright was interviewing Ross for the biographical sketch, a black communist who worked for the International Labor Defense (ILD), which was handling Ross's indictment, stopped in and questioned Wright about his project. "To whom have you shown this material?" Wright responded that he had shown it to no one, but it was clear that the official was suspicious of Wright's motives. Wright understood his caution, but as a writer, he wanted to "make the lives of these men known through the images already accepted as the common coin of communication. I wanted to make them know that they had allies, that more people than they knew, and in ways they did not understand, were their friends, and that I was their friend." But the black communists were afraid of the unfamiliar. "They were more fearful of my ideas than they would have been had I held a gun on them; they could have taken the gun away from me and shot me with it, but they did not know what to do with ideas" (*AH*, 85–86).

The relief authorities assigned Wright to a position in the South Side Boys' Club. There he worked with many homeless black boys, some of whom had recently arrived from the South and were finding it difficult to make it in the Depression-ridden northern city. Wright talked with them for hours about their experiences, taking notes on a yellow notepad all the while. "These boys did not fear people to the extent that every man looked like a spy. The Communists who doubted my motives did not know these boys, their twisted dreams, their all-too-clear destinies; and I doubted if I would ever be able to convey to them the tragedy I saw here" (*AH*, 88). Soon Wright was warned to stay away from Ross, for he was to be put on trial by the party for "anti-leadership tendencies," "class collaborationist attitudes," and "ideological factionalism." Wright protested against their forbidding him to see Ross. "Can't you accept a decision?" the angry communist representative asked. Wright responded that since he felt he had done nothing wrong, he did not feel bound by the party's decisions. "Your attitude does not merit our trust," the representative told Wright and left (*AH*, 87).

At a Midwest writers' conference in August 1934 sponsored by the Chicago John Reed Club, party leaders voted the club's magazine, *Left Front*, out of existence and demanded that the writers spend more time on party activities, such as writing pamphlets and reports. Wright was openly opposed to both proposals and argued that the writers would make even greater contributions to the party through their imaginative work. His objections had no effect on the vote. In frustration Wright offered a resolution that the party dissolve the John Reed Club. "My 'defeatism,' as it was called, brought upon my head the sharpest disapproval of the party leader. The conference ended with the passing of a multitude of resolutions dealing with China, Japan, Germany, and Japan, and conditions afflicting various parts of the earth. But not one idea regarding writing emerged" (*AH*, 90).

At a national congress of the John Reed Clubs held in Chicago in September 1934, Wright got his first chance to meet many well-known leftist writers. Unfortunately, it was also announced at this meeting that the party intended to dissolve all the John Reed Clubs and replace them with a more broadly based writers' organization that would attract noncommunists. A national conference of American writers was held the following spring (1935) in New York City, and Wright was sent as a representative of the Chicago John Reed Club. While he was impressed with New York City, the nightlife, and its wide-ranging theatrical and musical entertainments, he was frustrated and disturbed about his inability to find housing because of his color. "I stood on the sidewalks of New York with a black skin, practically no money, and I was not absorbed with the burning questions of the left-wing literary movement in the United States, but with the problem of how to get a bath." Finally a white comrade from Chicago introduced him to "a big heavy white woman" who said he could stay with her. He went to her apartment and met her husband. They provided him a cot for the night (*AH*, 96).

The next morning Wright went to a park near the apartment to work on his presentation in defense of the continuation of the John Reed Clubs. "But again the problem of the clubs did not seem important. What did seem important was: Could a Negro ever live halfway like a human being in this goddamn country" (*AH*, 96). After the conference sessions that day he went to Harlem in search of a hotel room, but was turned away there as well. Even in Harlem most of the hotels were "for whites only." He finally was told to go to the colored branch of the YMCA where he was able to get a room. The next day he attended the session that made the final decision to dissolve the John Reed Clubs. During the debate "I rose and explained what the clubs meant to young writers and begged for their continuance. I sat down amid silence. Debate was closed. The vote was called. The room filled with uplifted hands to dissolve. Then there came the call for those who disagreed and my hand went up alone. I knew that my stand would be interpreted as one of opposition to the Communist party, but I thought the hell with it. . . . New York held no further interest and the next morning I left for home" (*AH*, 98).

Back in Chicago now that the John Reed Club was dissolved, Wright decided that he would no longer have anything to do with the Communist Party. Unfortunately, he soon learned that he was the object of a whispering campaign and had been labeled a "bastard intellectual" and "smuggler of reaction." In the midst of this growing disenchantment, a communist official came by his room and told him that the new communist leader for the South Side wanted to see him. Harry Haywood (whom Wright identified in *American Hunger* as "Buddy Nealson") had just arrived in Chicago and Wright was told that Haywood wanted to talk with him about his party work. Wright was to meet the new party leader for the South Side at his apartment. Wright was aware of Haywood's high position within the party organization, but he was unaware of the problems Haywood had encountered with party leaders in New York City. "He was the man who formulated the Communist position on the American Negro; he had made speeches in the Kremlin, he had spoken before Stalin himself" (*AH,* 101).

Wright presented a very unflattering portrait of Harry Haywood in *American Hunger.* "He was a short, black man with an ever-ready smile, thick lips, a furtive manner, and a greasy, sweaty look. His bearing was nervous, self-conscious; he seemed always to be hiding some deep irritation. He spoke in short, jerky sentences, hopping nimbly from thought to thought, as though his mind worked in a free, associational manner." Haywood suffered from asthma, "and he would snort at expected intervals. Now and then he would punctuate his flow of words by taking a nip from a bottle of whiskey. He had traveled half around the world and his talk was pitted with vague allusions to European cities." Wright paid close attention to Haywood's every word, "for I knew that I was facing one of the leaders of World Communism" (101).

Haywood asked about Wright's relationship with Ross. "Ross is not particularly a friend of mine," Wright responded, "but I know him well, in fact, quite well." Haywood accused Ross of being a nationalist, and "we communists don't dramatize Negro nationalism." Haywood told Wright the party needed him to organize a committee on the high cost of living. Wright objected, reiterating the point that he was a writer, and if the party did not appreciate his literary abilities,

> "Maybe I don't belong in the party."
> "Oh no! Don't say that," he said snorting. He looked at me. "You're blunt."
> "I put things the way I feel them," I said. "I want to start in right with you. I've had too damn much crazy trouble in the party."
> He laughed and lit a cigarette.
> "Dick," he said, shaking his head, "the trouble with you is that

you've been around those white artists on the North Side too much. . . .
You talk like 'em. You've got to know your own people . . ."

"I think I know them," I said, realizing that I could never really
talk with him. "I've been inside three-fourths of the Negroes' homes
on the South Side . . . "

"But you've got to work with 'em," he said.

"I was working with Ross until I was suspected of being a spy," I
said (105–6).

At that point they were joined by a European white woman who Wright
thought was Haywood's wife. When she asked Haywood what the problem
was, and he explained that Wright was a writer and was working on a book, but
the party wanted him to collect information on the high cost of living, she
commented, "That oughtn't to interfere with his book." Wright objected, "I
work in the day." She lightly responded, "Oh you'll find the time" (106).

During the interview Wright reluctantly agreed to go along with the
party's program for him. He attended the founding meeting of the National
Negro Congress in Chicago in February 1936, which Haywood later detailed
in his autobiography, *Black Bolshevik*. Indeed, Wright wrote an effusive account
of the National Negro Congress meeting that later appeared in the *New Masses*,
but this important historical event is never mentioned in *American Hunger*.[8]
Wright's rapprochement with the Chicago communists was short-lived. Soon
thereafter Wright was asked to a meeting at a Chicago hotel with Haywood and
John P. Davis, the National Negro Congress's executive secretary. Very likely
spurred by Wright's enthusiastic account of the congress meeting, Davis invited Wright to be a Communist Party representative at a Youth Congress to be
held in Switzerland. Wright refused the offer. Davis in frustration shouted,
"Wright, you're a fool." According to Wright, this sealed it and at the next
meeting of his unit, Wright announced that he wished to be dropped from
party's rolls. He told them "no ideological differences impel me to say this. I
simply do not wish to be bound any longer by the party's decisions." Although
Wright left the meeting at that point, he later learned from two communist
friends that Haywood would not accept his resignation. Wright was told he
could be expelled, but he could not resign. They informed him that if he resigned, "people would think that something was wrong if someone like you
quit here on the South Side" (*AH*, 109–11).

Wright then described another experience that further dramatized his growing ideological differences with black and white communists in Chicago. Around
this time public relief officials transferred Wright from the South Side Boys' Club
to the Federal Negro Theater to work as a publicity agent. This was another dis-
appointing encounter for Wright because he clashed with the black actors over

the types of plays to be presented. Whereas the white director assigned to the group insisted upon putting on a series of European plays "revamped to 'Negro style' with jungle scenes, spirituals, and all," Wright saw the Federal Negro Theater as an opportunity to do "worth-while Negro drama." When he took his concerns to white officials of the Federal Writers Project, they agreed to transfer that director and brought in Charles DeSheim, who, although he was white, made it clear he was interested in presenting true Negro drama.

At the cast meeting Wright handed out copies of white playwright Paul Green's *Hymn to the Rising Sun,* a one-act play about the brutal and inhumane conditions for black prisoners forced to work on chain gangs in southern states. Green's play was based on the numerous eyewitness accounts and journalistic investigations of how prison laborers were cruelly exploited by the state-sponsored convict lease system. During the reading of the play, however, some of the actors had difficulty with the lines; others refused to read at all. "We think this play is indecent," one of the actors finally admitted. "I don't think any such conditions exist in the South. I lived in the South and I never saw any chain gangs. Mr. DeSheim, we want a play that will make the public love us." Wright could not believe what he was hearing. "I had assumed that the heart of the Negro actor was pining for adult expression in the American theater, that he was ashamed of the stereotypes of clowns, mammies, razors, dice, watermelon, and cotton fields. . . . Now they were protesting against dramatic realism! I tried to defend the play but was heckled down" (*AH,* 114–15).

A few days later the actors got up a petition that called for the removal of DeSheim, and Wright refused to sign. Wright then informed DeSheim about the petition and suggested that he meet with the actors and try and clear up the misunderstanding.

> "Who told you that we were getting up a petition?" a black man demanded.
>
> DeSheim looked at me and stammered wordlessly.
>
> "There's an Uncle Tom in the theater!" a black girl yelled.
>
> After the meeting a delegation of Negro men came to my office and took out their pocketknives and flashed them in my face.
>
> "You get the hell off this job before we cut your bellybutton out!" they said.
>
> I tried to talk to them, but could not. That day a huge, fat, black woman, a blues singer, found an excuse to pass me as often as possible and she hissed under her breath in a menacing singsong: "Lawd, Ah sho hates a white man's nigger" (*AH,* 116).

Wright immediately asked for a transfer, which he was given; but he was later told that white communists in the Federal Writers Project had put the Negro actors up to this insurrection against him and the white director.

Ross's trial was coming up and two communists came to Wright's home and asked him to attend the proceedings. At first he thought it was a trap, and that he too would be put on trial. "As they talked, my old love of witnessing something new came over me. I wanted to see this trial, but I did not want to risk being placed on trial." They assured him that was not the case; they merely wanted him to be present at the event. Held on a Sunday afternoon in a large meeting hall, there were over four hundred people in attendance. "The trial began in a quiet informal manner. The comrades acted like a group of neighbors sitting in judgment upon one of their kind who had stolen a chicken. Anybody could ask and get the floor. There was absolute freedom of speech. Yet the meeting had an amazingly formal structure of its own, a structure that went as deep as the desire of men to live together" (*AH*, 118–20).

The first speeches by high party officials summed up the world situation and conditions in the Soviet Union. The next two speakers assessed the situation in the United States in general and for African Americans in particular, making the connection with larger struggles for workers' rights. Finally, the specific charges against Ross were stated, not by party leaders, but by friends and comrades of Ross. "It was crushing. Ross wilted." Then came the time for Ross to defend himself. "'Comrades,' he said in a low charged voice, 'I'm guilty of all the charges, all of them . . . ' His voice broke in a sob. No one prodded him. No one tortured him. He was free to go out of the hall and never see another Communist. But he did not want to. He could not. The vision of a communal world had sunk down into his soul and it would never leave him until life left him. He talked on, outlining how he had erred, how he would reform." For Wright, "this . . . was a spectacle of glory; and yet, because it had condemned me, because it was blind and ignorant, I felt that it was a spectacle of horror" (*AH*, 124–25). Overcome by the emotional scene, Wright could stay no longer and when he got up and tried to leave, one party official signaled to open the locked doors and let him go.

When Wright returned to his job at the Federal Writers Project, his former white comrades made it clear he was not wanted. They accused him of incompetence and were attempting to have him removed. He was determined not to be forced to leave, but the worst was still to come. One day when the communist threw up a picket line in front of the building where he worked demanding higher wages from the Works Progress Administration, as Wright left, they shouted, "There's Wright, that goddamn Trotskyite." "That sonofabitch Wright is with them too." "We know you, bastard." "Wright's a traitor too." Wright wanted to confront party officials about the situation and finally got an appointment with one, but did not get to meet him. Wright was stopped by the secretary at the local communist headquarters, who finally told him, "There's nothing we can do for you here" (*AH*, 130).

Despite communist opposition, Wright was elected shop chairman of the local union at the Writers Project. Plans were made for the union to participate in the 1936 May Day parade, but when Wright arrived, his union had already left. An old party friend told him to fall into the parade with them. Wright said he did not think that was a good idea, but his friend insisted, "This is *May Day.*" But when he began to march, a white party official shouted at him, "Get out of our ranks!" Wright tried to explain that he was invited; the official again shouted, "Get out." When Wright did not move, the official and several others grabbed him by his collar, but he resisted, "Turn me loose!" At that point "hands lifted me bodily from the sidewalk; I felt myself being pitched headlong through the air. I saved myself from landing on my head by clutching a curbstone with my hands. Slowly I rose and stood. . . . The rows of white and black Communists were looking at me with cold eyes of nonrecognition. I could not believe what had happened, even though my hands were smarting and bleeding. I had suffered a public, physical assault by two white Communists with black Communists looking on" (*AH,* 132).

This is the final incident in *American Hunger,* completed in 1944. He mentioned that he followed the procession to Grant Park, but sat on a bench during the proceedings. At home later that day he thought over what had occurred. Wright had only sought an example of how to live a human life.

> All my life I had been full of a hunger for a new way of life. . . . Yes, the whites were as miserable as their black victims, I thought. If this country can't find its way to a human path, if it can't inform conduct with a deep sense of life, then all of us, black as well as white, are going down the drain. . . . I picked up a pencil and held it over a sheet of white paper, but my feelings stood in the way of my words. Well, I would wait, day and night, until I knew what to say. Humbly now, with no vaulting dream of achieving unity, I wanted to try to build a bridge of words between me and the world outside, that world which was so distant and elusive that it seemed unreal. I would hurl words into the darkness and wait for the echo, and if the echo sounded, no matter how faintly, I would send other words to tell, to march, to fight, to create a sense of the hunger for life that gnaws in us all, to keep alive in our ears a sense of the inexpressibly human (*AH,* 135).

Richard Wright's autobiographical account of his life in Chicago as a member of the Communist Party, "I Tried to Be a Communist," was first published in *Atlantic Monthly* in August and September 1944, and was not included in *Black Boy,* which was published in 1945 and covered only his early years in Jackson and Memphis. By that time Wright had indeed severed all relations with the Communist Party, but this did not take place until 1942 or 1943, following the publication of his highly acclaimed novel *Native Son* in 1940. In reading the essays that later became *American Hunger,* however, one gets the impression that Wright left the party at that point, but that was not the case.

"The Social Consciousness of the Negro Writer"

RICHARD WRIGHT had received wide praise for the short stories he published in various magazines and anthologies in the mid-1930s and was hard at work on his first novel, "Cesspool" (later published as *Lawd Today*). He was determined to pursue a career as a professional writer. Even though he finally was able to get a regular appointment at the Post Office in 1936, he decided to leave Chicago and go to New York City with only the possibility of an assignment on the Federal Writers Project there. In New York Wright became a prominent member of leftist literary circles, rejoined the Communist Party, and was a regular contributor to the *Daily Worker, New Masses,* and other communist-sponsored magazines and journals. Moreover, it was in this period from 1937 to 1942 that Wright made his most significant contributions to African-American literary theories.

Along with Langston Hughes, Arna Bontemps, Claude McKay, Countee Cullen, Waring Cuney, Owen Dodson, and other young African-American writers and poets, Richard Wright was one of the founders of the literary magazine *New Challenge* in 1937. A successor to Dorothy West's magazine, *The Challenge,* which was published briefly in 1934, the new journal was conceived as a literary vehicle for "New Negroes" of the 1930s. Although its inability to gain sufficient financial support from either the Communist Party or from advertisements meant that only one issue was published, Wright's contribution, "Blueprint for Negro Writing," according to biographer Michel Fabre, is still considered the "most complete, coherent and profound statement of Wright's theories on Afro-American writing" and reflected his attempt to blend Marxist literary approaches with interpretations of black life and culture.[9]

Wright believed that African-American culture was a source upon which the artist could draw for inspiration, but he was more concerned about the social consciousness of the black writer. He argued that while African-American workers had demonstrated a consciousness of the sources of their oppression, the literary works by most African-American writers did not reflect this awareness. "Generally speaking, Negro writing in the past has been confined to humble novels, poems, and plays, prim and decorous ambassadors who went a-begging to white America." In a veiled reference to some black writing in the 1920s, Wright believed that much of it was "the fruit of that foul soil which was the result of a liaison between inferiority-complexed 'Negro geniuses' and burnt-out white Bohemians with money." In order to explore black social consciousness, the artist could draw upon two important elements in African-American culture, the "Negro church and the folklore of the Negro people."[10]

> It was through the portals of the church that the American Negro first entered the shrine of western culture. . . . It was, however, in a folklore moulded out of rigorous and inhuman conditions of life that the Negro achieved his most indigenous and complete expression. Blues, spirituals, and folk tales recounted from mouth to mouth . . . work songs sung in the blazing sun—all these formed the channels through which the racial wisdom flowed.[11]

African-American folklore was also the fountain out of which flowed "Negro nationalism" as well as "the collective sense of Negro life in America. Let those who shy at the nationalist implications of Negro life look at this body of folklore, living and powerful, which rose out of a unified sense of a common life and a common fate." Wright believed that "Marxism is . . . a starting point" for the African-American writer. "It is through a Marxist conception of reality and society that the maximum degree of freedom in thought and feeling is gained for the Negro writer." But Marxism was only a beginning, the social theory that provided the "perspective" from which to view "the revolutionary significance of these nationalist tendencies" in African-American life. A viable social and literary perspective came through an alliance with "world movements," but at its best it was a "pre-conscious assumption, something which the writer takes for granted, something which he wins through his living." Wright trumpeted the "necessity for collective work" among African-American writers based on "ideological unity and the alliance of that unity with all the progressive ideas of our day."[12]

It was this requirement of "ideological unity" among African-American writers and the potential alliance with white progressives that would be the most difficult to attain because of the "enforced exclusion" of the black writer. Wright understood that "this isolation exists *among* Negro writers and *between* Negro and white writers. The Negro writers' lack of a thorough integration with the American scene, their lack of a clear realization among themselves of their possible role, have bred generation after generation [an] embittered and defeated literati."[13] In the period between 1941 and 1945 in two important nonfiction works Richard Wright attempted to follow this blueprint to explore the "truth and humanity" of African-American folk culture.

Native Son, Wright's first and most famous novel, was published in 1940 and examined the life of Bigger Thomas, a Chicago black youth whose rage over his treatment by racist white American society led to two murders, the accidental killing of Mary Dalton, the daughter of his white employer, and the premeditated murder of Bessie, his black girlfriend. Highly praised for its social realism, Wright became the most talked-about black writer in the country, and a star in the Communist Party's literary firmament.[14] On the heels of the success of *Native Son,* Wright collaborated with well-known photographer Edwin Rosakam on an illustrated book that was to be "a folk history of the Negro in the United States." Published in 1941, *12 Million Black Voices* presented Wright's examination of the sociological and historical development of black America from a Marxist perspective. Wright did a great deal of research for the work and called upon his friend, sociologist Horace Cayton, to help him develop the theoretical framework.

In *12 Million Black Voices* Wright described the advent of slavery in the seventeenth and eighteenth centuries when "the slavers continued to snatch us from our native African soil to be used as tools to till the tobacco, rice, sugarcane, and cotton plantations. . . . The gold of slave-grown cotton concentrated the political power of the Old South in the hands of a few Lords of the Land, and the poor whites decreased in number as we blacks increased. To protect their delicately balanced edifice of political power, the Lords of the Land proceeded to neutralize the strength of us blacks and the growing restlessness of poor whites by dividing and ruling us, by inciting us against one another." In the Civil War the "Lords of the Land" were pitted against the "Bosses of the Buildings" who owned the "dwellings, shops, factories, mills, and foundries" in the North. It was the Bosses' desire to protect "their hopes of industrial civilization . . . not the strength of moral ideal alone, that lessened the grip of the Lords of the Land upon us."[15]

Following the Civil War "there were some 4,000,000 of us black folk stranded and bewildered upon the land which we tilled under compulsion for two and a half centuries." Most were forced into "a new kind of bondage: sharecropping." Assigned ten or fifteen acres of land, advanced a mule, seed, fertilizer, tools and clothing, they must make the cotton crop. But each year due to "illness and death, rain and sun, boll weevil and storms," the sharecroppers fell further and further into debt, tying them more tightly to the Lords of the Land. "If we should escape to the city to avoid paying the mounting debts, white policemen track us down and ship us back to the plantation." Sometimes the similarities in the conditions for the poor white farmers

> make us think that perhaps we can join our hands with them and lift the weight of the Lords of the Land off our backs. But, before new meanings can bridge the chasm that has been long created between us, the poor whites are warned by the Lords of the Land that they must cast their destiny with their own color, that to make common cause with us is to threaten the foundations of civilization. . . . The Lords of the Land stand in our way; they do not permit the poor whites to make common union with us, for that would mean the end of the

Lords' power. To ask questions, to protest, to insist, to contend for a secure institutional and political base upon which to fulfill ourselves is equivalent to a new declaration of war.[16]

News of better working conditions and higher wages in the industrial North sparked the southern black migrations. Instead, what those black migrants often encountered was "death on city pavements." Discrimination and racism meant blocked opportunities. "The Bosses of the Buildings decree that we must be maids, porters, janitors, cooks, and general servants" and the migrating blacks are forced to live in "crowded, barn-like rooms in old rotting buildings where once dwelt rich native whites a century ago." Two- and three-room apartments were divided into "kitchenettes" for which they are charged exorbitant rents. "The kitchenette is our prison, our death sentence without a trial, a new form of mob violence that assaults not only the lone individual, but all of us, in its ceaseless attacks."[17]

One of the major reasons for the flight from the South was hope of improvements for the children. But that too generally did not occur. In the city the children became restless and rebellious, and turned their backs on their cultural traditions. "The streets, with their noise and flaring lights, the taverns, the automobiles, and the poolrooms claim them, and no voice of ours can call them back. . . . It is not their eagerness to fight that makes us afraid, but that they go to death on city pavements faster than even disease and starvation can take them." Wright, however, saw some hopeful signs on the horizon. One was the demand that "we form intensely racial and nationalistic organizations and advocate the establishment of a separate state, a forty-ninth state, in which we black folk would live." At the community level, African Americans created and patronized black businesses that kept money in their own hands and gave them greater control of their own destinies. The other positive development was the "widening acceptance of an identity of interests" between black and white workers. "The differences between black folk and white folk are not blood and color, and the ties that bind us are deeper than those that separate us. The common road of hope which we all have traveled has brought us into a stronger kinship than any words, laws, or legal claims. . . . If we black folk perish, America will perish."[18]

What was extremely interesting and important about 12 Million Black Voices, particularly in comparison with his autobiographical work, Black Boy, published three years later, was Wright's respectful and appreciative portrayal of black folk culture. Wright wrote about how under slavery African Americans "stole words from the grudging lips of the Lords of the Land" and developed their own language which carried new meanings, "meanings which enabled us to speak of revolt in the actual presence of the Lords of the Land without their being aware. Our secret language extended our understanding of what slavery meant and gave us freedom to speak to our brothers in captivity." Wright wrote effusively about African-American music and dance and praised black religion because it sustained African Americans by emphasizing the triumph of oppressed peoples over exploitation and subjugation. "The preacher's voice is sweet to us, caressing and lashing, conveying to us a heightening of consciousness that the Lords of the Land would rather keep from us, filling us with a sense of hope that is treasonable to the rule of Queen Cotton." It planted in their hearts

> a possibility of inexhaustible happiness; we know that if we could but get our feet planted firmly upon this earth, we could laugh and live and build. . . . We take this feeling with us each day and it drains the gall out of our years, sucks the sting from the rush of time, purges the pain from our memory of the past, and banishes the fear of loneliness and death. . . . Some say that, because we possess this facility of keeping alive this spark of happiness under adversity, we are children. No, it is the courage and faith in simple living that enable us to maintain this reservoir of human feeling, for we know that there will come a day when we shall pour out our hearts over this land.[19]

Black reviewers heaped praise upon *12 Million Black Voices* for what they considered to be its forthright and truthful portrait of the African-American condition and saw it as a worthy addition to the literature of race vindication. In contrast, from its publication in 1945 to the present, many African Americans have criticized *Black Boy* for its negative assessments of the black masses and African-American culture. Of course the communists, who viewed Wright as a "counterrevolutionary and renegade" following the publication of "I Tried to Be a Communist" in 1944, were critical. Black communist Benjamin J. Davis objected to Wright's suggestion in *Black Boy* that the contemporary South was immune to the progressive movements advancing in the country and the world. Davis was also one of the first black reviewers to criticize Wright for stating that the Negro had no capacity for "genuine emotion and kindness."[20]

For example, early in *Black Boy* Wright made the following observation:

> After I had outlived the shocks of childhood, after the habit of reflection had been born in me, I used to mull over the strange absence of real kindness in Negroes, how unstable was our tenderness, how lacking in genuine passion we were, how void of great hope, how timid our joy, how bare our traditions, how hollow our memories, how lacking we were in those intangible sentiments that bind man to man, and how shallow was even our despair. After I had learned other ways of life I used to brood upon the unconscious irony of those who felt that Negroes led so passional an existence! I saw that what had been taken

for our emotional strength was our negative confusions, our flights, our fears, our frenzy under pressure (*BB,* 45).

In *12 Million Black Voices,* however, Wright had argued that African Americans were in and of Western civilization and that the two thousand years of western civilization have been compressed for African Americans into three hundred years.

Imagine European history from the days of Christ to the present telescoped into three hundred years and you can comprehend the drama which our consciousness has experienced. Brutal, bloody, crowded with suffering and abrupt transitions, the lives of us black folk represent the most magical and meaningful picture of human experience in the Western world. Hurled from our native African homes into the very center of the most complex and highly industrialized civilization the world has ever known, we stand today with a consciousness and memory such as few people possess.[21]

But in *Black Boy,* according to Wright, there was nothing "magical and meaningful" about the African-American experience; indeed Wright argued that blacks had failed to absorb the best elements of Western civilization.

Whenever I thought of the essential bleakness of black life in America, I knew that Negroes had never been allowed to catch the full spirit of Western civilization, that they lived somehow in it but not of it. And when I brooded upon the cultural barrenness of black life, I wondered if clean, positive tenderness, love, honor, loyalty, and the capacity to remember were native to man. I asked myself if these human qualities were not fostered, won, struggled and suffered for, preserved in ritual from one generation to another (*BB,* 45).[22]

Black Boy was definitely *not* an autobiographical work in the African-American intellectual tradition of race vindication. Richard Wright's biographer Michel Fabre suggested that Wright's critical statements about African Americans in *Black Boy* were aimed at the "Uncle Toms" and "good Negroes," but in criticizing conservative black spokespersons, he alienated

those who were insulted by his way of minimizing the actual richness of Afro-American culture on the grounds that it could have been much greater. He in fact regarded submissive members of his race with a certain revulsion (the word *obscene,* which he always used in the moral sense, describes his feeling about them exactly) and with an undisguised scorn, which perhaps led him to minimize and underestimate his cultural heritage, and fail to see that in other cities and states, even in the South itself, there were Blacks who used this very tradition as the basis for their own development. . . . Wright had perhaps used his special experience as a universal example of cultural poverty, when it may have been caused largely by his particular family relationships and atypical religion.[23]

But this does explain why, as one reviewer noted, "Wright in *12 Million Black Voices* identifies his voice with that of the black masses, whereas in *Black Boy* the masses are unconsciously his enemy."[24] The important question to answer is: Did Richard Wright really appreciate "the actual richness of Afro-American culture"? Although Wright wrote poetically about black life in *12 Million Black Voices*, the distinguishing element in that work was its Marxist perspective, not its evocation of African-American cultural beliefs and practices. Moreover, when he wrote *12 Million Black Voices*, he was still a member of the Communist Party and this work clearly reflected the positive assessments of African Americans being expressed by communist writers and leaders.[25] By 1944 and 1945 Wright had broken with the party and it is likely that *Black Boy* reflected more closely his true feelings about the culture of the black masses.

One can gain another perspective on this issue by assessing how Richard Wright actually responded to authors whose literary works were embedded in African-American culture and put to literary use black folk expressions. Zora Neale Hurston's novel *Their Eyes Were Watching God* was first published in 1937 and is generally considered a major contribution to the African-American literary tradition and one of the finest examples of the use of African-American folk expressions in a fictional work. Literary critic Joanne Gabbin declared that "Zora Neale Hurston lays on hands and takes it as her sacred task to keep alive Afro-American oral traditions in the living memories of black people. In her now classic novel of a black women's journey into womanhood and self-possession, *Their Eyes Were Watching God*, she surrounds Janie Crawford's story with the lore she had heard as a child in the all-black town of Eatonville, Florida."[26]

The novel tells the story of the three marriages of Janie Crawford. Janie is raised by her grandmother, who picks Janie's first husband, Logan Killicks, who is much older, because he owns his own home and sixty acres of land. After a brief and loveless marriage, Janie runs away and meets Joe Starks, a striver who eventually acquires over two hundred acres of land and becomes mayor of an all-black town. Over the twenty-year marriage, the romantic spark between the two dies out and their marital difficulties are aired publicly. Joe Starks's death leaves Janie a relatively young widow, and she then takes up with Vergible "Tea Cake" Woods, a young laborer. Janie goes off with Tea Cake and is happy working and being with him. Their idyll is interrupted by a ferocious hurricane and in making their escape, Tea Cake is bitten by a rabid dog. He soon develops rabies and in the madness that accompanies it, he attempts to shoot Janie. She kills him in self-defense. The novel ends with her acquittal for the murder by an all-white jury.[27]

Their Eyes Were Watching God is saturated with black folk traditions. Hurston used the "lying sessions" and folk tales not merely as local color but to develop character and as an integral part of the story. And most astonishing was the language; Hurston's use of the Negro dialect was masterful and achieved a resonance and beauty that has been unsurpassed. This has been the assessment of later critics, but when the novel was published in 1937 most reviewers did not know what to make of it. Some liked the work, but had trouble understanding its major thrust. Very few reviewers realized that it was the chronicle of the growth and development of an African-American woman within a black cultural context and environment. The poet and critic Sterling Brown was one of the few early reviewers of Hurston's work who recognized its significance. In his book *The Negro in American Fiction,* published in 1937, Brown declared that Hurston's novels and short stories "showed a command of folklore and idiom excelled by no earlier novelist."[28]

Richard Wright reviewed *Their Eyes Were Watching God* for *New Masses* in October 1937. While he grudgingly admitted that "Miss Hurston can write," he also found her prose "cloaked in that facile sensuality that has dogged Negro expression since the days of Phillis Wheatley. Her dialogue manages to catch the psychological movements of the Negro folk-mind in their simplicity, but that's as far as it goes." To Wright the novel harked back to

> the minstrel technique that makes "white folks" laugh. Her characters eat and laugh and cry and work and kill; they swing like a pendulum eternally in that safe and narrow orbit in which America likes to see the Negro live: between laughter and tears. . . . The sensory sweep of her novel carries no theme, no message, no thought. In the main, her novel is not addressed to the Negro, but to a white audience whose chauvinistic tastes she knows how to satisfy. She exploits that phase of Negro life which is "quaint," the phase which evokes a piteous smile on the lips of the "superior" race.[29]

In "Blueprint for Negro Writing," published earlier that year, Wright called upon African-American writers to utilize folklore and other cultural expressions in their literary works, but to combine it with a "Marxist conception of reality and society." Zora Neale Hurston's work was completely immersed in African-American cultural expressions, but the "social consciousness" she documented was distinctive and ultimately went beyond the contemporary Marxist theories and concepts.[30] Moreover, in her autobiography, *Dust Tracks on a Road,* published in 1942, Zora Neale Hurston presented an alternative view of black life and culture and the role of the African-American literary artist and made an original contribution to the emerging African-American intellectual tradition.

Beyond Race Vindication:
The Autobiography of Zora Neale Hurston

THE AUTOBIOGRAPHICAL works of Alexander Crummell, Ida B. Wells-Barnett, James Weldon Johnson, and Harry Haywood were the products of individuals who were involved on a day-to-day basis with various aspects of the so-called Negro Problem. As was the case with the authors of the slave narratives, the particular ideological stances they took were not only based on their personal experiences, but often tied to particular *political* movements aimed at African-American advancement. Their ideological expressions were tied to political campaigns in which they took an active part, such as the antebellum anti-slavery movement, Republican Party politics, the anti-lynching crusade, and the Communist Party. Zora Neale Hurston, on the other hand, was not a political activist and she was uninterested in using her autobiography as a vehicle for exploring the "Negro Problem." "Negroes are supposed to write about the Race Problem," she declared in *Dust Tracks on a Road;* however, "I was and am thoroughly sick of the subject. My interest lies in what makes a man or a woman do such-and-so, regardless of his color. It seemed to me that human beings I met reacted pretty much the same to the same stimuli. Different idioms, yes. Inherent difference, no" (151).[31]

Zora Neale Hurston was interested in exploring those elements of her personal experience that defined her as an individual. The work was filled with statements about her ideals; it just did not examine the political ideologies of the day. However, in only the first half of the book did she examine her background and experiences. The largest part of the work consisted of essays on topics that she thought were important and about which she had some personal knowledge. Born in the all-black town of Eatonville, Florida, on January 7, 1891, her father, John Hurston, was a carpenter and Baptist preacher; her mother, Lucy Potts Hurston, was a former schoolteacher. The couple had migrated to Florida in the 1880s and had eight children, six boys and two girls. The family lived in a large house that was the center of community activity, and Zora attended the local black school before she went to Jacksonville for her secondary education. Throughout her formative years, Zora was not exposed to the naked racism and violence that so many southern blacks experienced at the hands of whites. Indeed, the whites with whom she came into contact made favorable impressions upon her.

Hurston tells the story of how when she was born it was "hog-killing time," her father was out of town, and the local midwife was attending a barbecue. Her mother's water broke and she sent the younger children for help, but before anyone arrived Zora was born. "My mother had to make it alone. She was too weak after I rushed out to do anything for herself, so she just was

lying there, sick in the body, and worried in mind, wondering what would become of her, as well as me. She was so weak, she couldn't even reach down to
where I was. She had one consolation. She knew I wasn't dead, because I was
crying strong." At that moment, since it was hog-killing time, a white neighbor who was a friend of the family stopped by with some freshly butchered
meat and other supplies. When he opened the door and "heard me spreading
my lungs all over Orange county," he followed the sound and saw what had
happened. "Being the kind of man he was, he took out his Barlow knife and
cut the navel cord, then he did the best he could about other things. When the
mid-wife, locally known as granny, arrived about an hour later, there was a fire
in the stove and plenty of hot water on. I had been sponged off in some sort of
a way and Mama was holding me in her arms" (21).

While growing up Zora did not get along well with the girls her age in the
neighborhood because she played too rough; so she hung around the boys. "I
was acceptable to them because I was the one girl who could take a good pum-
meling without running home to tell." Her family believed it was "not lady-like
to play with boys," but the things that girls did, such as playing with doll-babies,
she found uninteresting. "Dolls caught the devil around me," Zora recalled.
"They got into fights and leaked sawdust before New Year's. They jumped off
the barn and tried to drown themselves in the lake." Zora was driven inward and
created her own fantasy characters; "I lived an exciting life unseen" (30).

But her one friend during those early years was the old white man who had
helped to bring her into the world. A fairly prosperous farmer with hundreds of
acres of land, he took a special interest in Zora.

When I got old enough to do things, he used to come along some af-
ternoons and ask to take me with him fishing. . . . In between fishing
business, he would talk to me in a way I liked—as if I were as grown as
he. He would tell me funny stories and swear at every other word. He
was always making me tell him things about my doings, and then he
would tell me what to do about things. He called me Snidlits, explaining that Zora was a hell of a name to give a child.

"Snidlits, don't be a nigger," he would say to me over and over.
"Niggers lie and lie!" Any time you catch folks lying, they are skeered
of something. Lying is dodging. People with guts don't lie. They tell
the truth and then if they have to, they fight it out. You lay yourself
open by lying. The other fellow knows right off that you are skeered of
him and he's more'n apt to tackle you. If you don't do nothing, he
starts to looking down on you from then on. Truth is a letter of
courage. I want you to grow guts as you go along. So don't you let me
hear of you lying. You'll get 'long all right if you do like I tell you.
Nothing can't lick you if you never get skeered.

Hurston made it clear that when he told her "don't be a nigger," "the word Nigger used in this sense does not mean race. It means a weak contemptible person of any race" (30–31).

The old white man counseled her to say what she believed and believe what she said because somebody was going to hate her no matter what she said or did. "My idea is to give 'em a good cause if it's got to be. And don't change too many words if you aim to fight. Lam hell out of 'em with the first lick. And keep on lamming. I've seen many a fight finished with the first lick. Most folks can't stand to be hurt. But you must realize that getting hurt is part of fighting. Keep right on. The one that hurts the other one worst wins the fight." The old man was later killed when he was thrown from a horse, and he died "in high favor with everyone." He had taken care of his family, accumulated property, and "nobody thought anything about his going to the county seat frequently, getting drunk, getting his riding mule drunk along with him, and coming down the pike yelling and singing while his mule brayed in drunken hilarity. There went a man!" (32–33).

Hurston also described in detail her encounters with two white women from Minnesota, Mrs. Johnstone and Miss Hurd, who made a surprise visit to Mr. Calhoun's school when she was in the fifth grade. The young Zora was impressed by the way the women looked with their pretty black and white dresses and long white fingers. The students were asked to read; when it came time for Zora to read, it was one of her favorite stories from Greek mythology, which she had read many times. The women were noticeably impressed and Mr. Calhoun proudly had her read the entire story. After the class was dismissed, the two women and Mr. Calhoun held a low-voiced conversation and looked in Zora's direction. "I began to worry. Not only was I barefooted, but my feet and legs were dusty. My hair was more uncombed than usual, and my nails were not shiny clean. Oh, I'm going to catch it now" (38).

Mr. Calhoun called Zora over and she was introduced to them. "They asked me if I loved school, I lied that I did." This was not a complete lie; she liked reading and geography and recess, but hated writing and arithmetic. When school was dismissed, Mr. Calhoun told Zora that she was to go the next afternoon to the Park House Hotel in Maitland, the white town five miles away, and ask for the two women. The next day she was let out of school an hour early, returned home, washed and dressed in her best outfit, warned about her behavior, and taken to the ladies' hotel by her oldest brother, John. Once in the room they gave Zora "strange things, like stuffed dates and preserved ginger," talked with her and asked her to read several paragraphs from *Scribner's* magazine. Then they went outside, took her photograph, and handed her a "cylinder done up in fancy paper, tied with a ribbon, and they told me goodbye, asking me not to open it until I got home" (38).

When she got home and opened the package, "perhaps, I shall never experience such joy again. The nearest thing to that moment was the telegram accepting my first book. One hundred goldy-new pennies rolled out of the cylinder. Their gleam lit up the world. It was not avarice that moved me. It was the beauty of the thing. I stood on the mountain. Mama let me play with my pennies for a while, then put them away for me to keep." Within a few days, Hurston received from the ladies an Episcopal hymnbook and some books of short stories and fairy tales. The next month she received a large box containing clothes and more books of fairy tales, Greek and Norse mythology, and adventure stories. Her mother had made her read the Bible and Hurston became fascinated by the adventures of King David and other heroes of the Old Testament. "Except for the beautiful language of Luke and Paul, the New Testament still plays a poor second to the Old Testament for me." It was this early exposure to Western literature that instilled in her a desire "to be away from the drabness and to stretch my limbs in some mighty struggle" (40–41).

Although these early positive experiences with whites would be replicated throughout her life, Hurston also developed a strong appreciation for African-American folk expressions and cultural practices during these early years. "For me, the store porch was the most interesting place that I could think of." It was there that the men sat around and discussed the ways of the world. "There were no discreet nuances of life on Joe Clarke's porch. There was open kindnesses, anger, hate, love, envy and its kinfolks, but all emotions were naked and nakedly arrived at. It was a case of 'make it and take it.' You got what your strengths would bring you." What was most interesting to Zora were the "lying sessions" where the men would compete with each other in telling folk tales.

> God, Devil, Brer Rabbit, Brer Fox, Sis Cat, Brer Bear, Lion, Tiger, Buzzard, and all the wood folk walked and talked like natural men. The wives of the story-tellers might yell from the backyards for them to come and tote some water, or chop wood for the cook-stove and never get a move out of the men. The usual rejoinder was, "Oh, she's got enough to go on. No matter how much wood you chop, a woman will burn it all up to get a meal. If she got a couple of pieces, she will make it do. If you chop a whole boxful, she will burn every stick of it. Pay her no mind." So the story telling would go right on (47).

Hurston included several of these folk tales in *Dust Tracks*, but in the 1920s when she went to study anthropology at Columbia University with Franz Boas, she traveled throughout Florida and the South, as well as the Caribbean, collecting this folk wisdom and published it in several books, especially *Mules and Men* (1935) and *Tell My Horse* (1938). Novelist Alice Walker declared that *"Mules and Men* is a classic among folklore collections primarily because of Hurston's approach and style. She does not divorce herself from the people she is studying, as traditional folklorists do, nor does she attempt to make people something other than what they are. If the folk are colorist, that is shown; if they harbor self-hatred as well as self-love, that is left clear. At all times Hurston is 'the folk,' a character in the tales or privy to them, just as the people who tell the tales are." What was important about these experiences with black folk culture and expressions was that they instilled in her an appreciation for the intelligence and creativity of the black masses that was in sharp contrast to the contemporary preoccupation with the "pathology of black life" found in the social science literature and the works of some African-American literary artists.[32]

Wanderings of a Motherless Child

THE DEATH of her mother when Zora Neale Hurston was only nine years old was the most critical event in her childhood and is represented as a turning point in *Dust Tracks on a Road*. As the favorite child among her eight children, Zora had a very close relationship with her mother. In the autobiography she observed that her mother's death was "the end of a phase in my life. I was old before my time with the grief of loss, of failure, and of remorse." The reason Hurston was so filled with remorse was her failure to carry out her mother's dying wishes. When Zora came to see her on her death bed, her mother asked her to make sure no one removed the pillow from under her head until she had died. "The clock was not to be covered, nor the looking glass. She trusted me to see to it that these things were not done. I promised her as solemnly as a nine year old can do, that I would see to it." When her mother was near death, several other women came in and moved the bed so her head faced east. Then somebody began to cover the clock and another reached for her mother's pillow. "Don't!" Zora cried, "Don't take the pillow from under Mama's head! She said she didn't want it moved!" Zora was stopped from interfering by her father, as the women began covering the clock and the mirror.

> "Don't cover that clock! Leave that looking glass like it is! Lemme put Mama's pillow back where it was!". . .
> But Papa held me tight and the others frowned me down. Mama was still rasping out the last morsel of her life. I think she was trying to say something, and I think she was going to speak to me. What was she trying to tell me? What wouldn't I give to know! Perhaps she was telling me that it was better for the pillow to be moved so that she could die easy, as they said. Perhaps she was accusing me of weakness and failure in carrying out her last wish. I do not know. I shall never know (63–64).

As an adult Hurston came to understand why her father had restrained her when they were carrying out the rituals of death. But for years afterward Hurston agonized over the event

> in the midst of play, in wakeful moments after midnight, on the way home from parties, and even in the classroom during lectures. My thoughts would escape occasionally from their confines and stare me down. . . . No matter what others did, my mother had put her trust in me. She had felt that I could and would carry out her wishes, and I had not. And then in that sunset time, I failed her. It seemed as she died that the sun went down on purpose to flee from me. That hour began my wanderings. Not so much in geography, but in time. Then not so much in time as in spirit (63–65).

Following her mother's death, Zora Neale Hurston was sent with her sister, Sarah, to a school in Jacksonville. Two months afterward, Sarah got sick and returned home. Two weeks later Hurston received a letter from her sister saying that their father had remarried, and shortly after that Zora learned that Sarah had been put out of the house. Sarah had been their father's favorite child, and when he refused to beat her with a buggy whip for commenting on the marriage taking place so soon after their mother's death, their stepmother insisted that "Sarah must be driven out of town. So Sarah just married and went down on the Manater River to live. She took Everett [their youngest brother] with her. She probably left more behind than she took away" (71).

Hurston remained in school in Jacksonville until one day she was told that her tuition had not been paid and asked what she was going to do. She did not know, and when the money was not forthcoming the school officials continued to harass her. Although the bills were not paid, she was able to remain for the year by working around the school. "I was put to scrubbing down the stair steps every Saturday, and sent to help clean up the pantry and do what I could in the kitchen after school" (77). In the spring Zora was expecting her father to come for her, but the school's assistant principal told Zora she had received a letter from her father saying that he was not coming and the school should adopt her. The school's administrators could not do that so they gave her money to return home.

By that time the four oldest children were gone from their father's home, and the four remaining were one by one sent to live with friends of their mother at the insistence of their father's new wife. For the next five years Hurston was in school on and off and "shifted from house to house of relatives and friends and found comfort nowhere. I was without books to read most of the time, except where I could get hold of them by mere chance. That left no room for selection. I was miserable, and no doubt made others miserable around me, because they could not see what was the matter with me, and I had no part in what interested them" (85). Hurston began to work to support herself. She worked in the homes of whites, and stayed briefly in the home of her brother Dick and his wife, but was soon ordered to return to her father's home.

Shortly after arriving there Hurston had a knock-down, drag-out fight with her stepmother when she called Zora "a sassy impudent heifer" and threw a bottle at her, but missed its target. Although her stepmother was much bigger, Zora soon pinned her against the wall and pounded her with her fists, and the older woman soon gave up. When Zora's father refused to intervene, her stepmother screamed she was going to get the pistol and kill Zora. They started fighting again and soon a neighbor and friend of her stepmother came in. "I grabbed my stepmother by the collar," Zora recalled, "and dragged her to a hatchet against the wall and managed to get hold of it. As Mrs. G. waddled through the living room door, I hollered to her to get back, and let fly with that hatchet with all that my right arm would do. It struck the wall too close to her head to make her happy. She reeled around and rolled down those front steps yelling that I had gone crazy." Zora continued to thrash her stepmother until her father finally pulled her away (75).

Her stepmother wanted Zora arrested, but her father did nothing. When the women in her father's church made it clear that they thought Zora had given her stepmother what she deserved (they were all friends of Zora's mother), the woman left and soon filed for a divorce. After the fight, Zora found a job working in a doctor's office, but soon received a letter from her brother Bob asking her to come and live with him and his family. Zora went to their home in hopes of returning to school, but her brother wanted her to help take care of the children. Before long a white woman she met told her that a singer in a traveling opera company was looking for a lady's maid. When Hurston went for the interview for the position, she tried to lie about her age (she was fifteen); the young singer knew she was lying, but hired her anyway.

Hurston enjoyed working in the opera company, which specialized in Gilbert and Sullivan musicals. And the singers were really taken by Hurston, who was the only black person in the company. The singers, who were all from the North, loved the way Zora spoke because "I was a Southerner and had the map of Dixie on my tongue." Hurston used southern idioms in her speech, which was filled with "images and flavor" as well as "simile and invective."

It was an everyday affair to hear somebody called a mullet-headed, mule-eared, wall-eyed, hog-nosed, 'gator-faced, shad-mouthed, screw-necked, goat-bellied, puzzle-gutted, camel-backed, butt-sprung, battle-hammed, knock-kneed, razor-legged, box-ankled, shovel-footed, un-mated so-and-so! Eyes looking like skint-ginny nuts, and mouth looking like a dish-pan full of broke-up crockery! They can tell you in simile exactly how you walk and smell. They can furnish a picture gallery of your ancestors, and a notion of what your children will be like (98)

The members of the company teased Hurston just to hear her talk, but there was no malice in it. Hurston began keeping a scrapbook and commented upon daily goings-on in the company on sheets pinned to the call-board. Soon others were adding to "Zora's messages." "They would take a pencil to the board and set down their own item. Answers to the wisecracks would appear promptly and often cause uproarious laughter. They always started off with either 'Zora says' or 'The observant reporter of the Call-board asserts'—Lord, Zora said more *things!* I was continually astonished, but always amused" (100–101).

At the end of the run her employer met a man from Newark and soon announced that she would marry and leave the stage. The singer wanted Hurston to return to school and since they were in Baltimore, she looked around for a place for her to enroll. Eventually, Hurston found a job in a restaurant and attended night school and subsequently the high school department of Morgan College (later Morgan State University). There she met Dean William Pickens, who upon hearing that she had no money for school found her a job in the home of Dr. Baldwin, a white clergyman and trustee for the school. The Baldwins had a large library and Hurston read everything that struck her fancy. She remained at Morgan for two years and was encouraged to go on to college. At a chance meeting with Mae Miller, daughter of Dean Kelly Miller of Howard University, Miller suggested that Hurston attend Howard. So Hurston moved to Washington, found a job first in a restaurant and later as a manicurist at the G Street Barber Shop, which catered only to whites, particularly congressmen, senators, and members of the national press corps.

Hurston recounted one particular incident that was revealing about the nature of segregation and race relations at the time. The black owner of the barber shop, Mr. Robinson, owned several establishments throughout the city that employed only blacks. The shop on G Street, however, only served white customers. One day a black man entered the barber shop and asked for a haircut. The manager told him that this shop only served whites, but Mr. Robinson had another shop across town that served black customers. The man refused to leave, saying he had a right to be served there. When he tried to sit in one of the barber's chairs, the barbers, porters, and other men working in the shop rushed him and threw him out of the shop into the street. Even Hurston admitted that she wanted the man thrown out. She later realized that she was "giving sanction to Jim Crow, which theoretically, I was supposed to resist." But the livelihood of the black owner and workers was being threatened by the man's action. "This was the first time it was called to my attention that self-interest rides over all sorts of lines. I have seen the same thing happen hundreds of times since, and now I understand it. One sees it breaking over racial, national, religious and class lines. Anglo-Saxon against Anglo-Saxon, Jew against Jew, Negro against Negro, and all sorts of combinations of the three." Hurston admitted that "I do not know what was the ultimate right in this case. I do know how I felt at the time. There is always something fiendish and loathsome about a person who threatens to deprive you of your way of making a living. That is just human nature, I reckon" (119–20).

Hurston enjoyed her years at Howard and was active in many campus activities. She worked for the student newspaper, *The Hill Top,* joined Zeta Phi Beta Sorority, and belonged to the Stylus, a small literary group on campus, headed by Dr. Alain Locke. A short story that she wrote for the Stylus was later submitted to and published in Charles Johnson's *Opportunity* magazine. Upon finishing Howard, Hurston went to New York City in hopes of becoming a writer and was befriended by the Charles Johnsons. "I won a prize for a short story at the first [*Opportunity*] Award dinner, May 1, 1925, and Fannie Hurst offered me a job as her secretary, and Annie Nathan Meyer offered to get me a scholarship to Barnard. My record was good enough, and I entered Barnard in the fall, graduating in 1928" (122).

While there Hurston became "Barnard's sacred black cow" and was adored by "the Social register crowd." She was invited to all the important social gatherings and took classes in literature and met and studied with the influential anthropologist Franz Boas, whom she came to call "Papa Franz." A few weeks before her graduation from Barnard, Professor Boas informed her that he had arranged for her to get a fellowship to go south and collect Negro folklore. During her first trip south, she remained for six months, but brought back very little material. She recalled that she would ask the people "in carefully accented Barnardese, 'Pardon me, do you know any folk-tales or folk-songs?' The men and women who had whole treasuries of material just seeping through their pores looked at me and shook their heads. No, they had never heard of anything like that around here. Maybe it was in the next county." When she returned to New York with only a few items, Boas understood that Hurston was "green and feeling my oats, and that only bitter disappointment was going to purge me. It did." Subsequent research trips were financed by Mrs. R. Osgood Mason, whom she called Godmother. Mrs. Osgood was not only interested in collecting information and materials on "primitive" peoples, but was also a true "patron of the arts" and gave financial assistance to a number of artists, including the Mexican painter Miguel Covarrubias and poet Langston Hughes. Hurston was able to collect a great deal of information in her later trips to Florida, Louisiana, Alabama, Haiti, Jamaica, and the Bahamas; this was the research published in her books *Mules and Men* and *Tell My Horse*.[33]

The last six chapters of *Dust Tracks on a Road* are essays on specific topics, such as "books and things," "love," and "religion," and only incidentally could they be considered autobiographical. It is because Hurston did not discuss many of her personal experiences during her adult years or political issues that many literary critics have dismissed or expressed their disappointment in the autobiography. But when we examine what Hurston does say about African-American folk culture in this work, especially in comparison with what is found in Richard Wright's *Black Boy,* which was published three years later, important differences emerge, issues and problems that eventually became part of the emerging African-American intellectual tradition.[34]

Although Hurston was critical of many of the "ways of black folk," she clearly did not accept the contemporary social scientific view that black culture and community represented a "pathological version" of white American culture and community. The classic statement of this position was found in Gunnar Myrdal's highly influential work, *An American Dilemma: The Negro Problem and Modern Democracy,* published in 1944. Funded by the Carnegie Foundation, this massive research project was designed to examine "the Negro Problem in the United States." Working with a number of American social scientists, including E. Franklin Frazier, Ralph Bunche, Arnold Rose, Richard Sterner, and Guy B. Johnson, Swedish economist Gunnar Myrdal gathered a great amount of information on black religion, the press, family, community, and culture. Myrdal concluded that the Negro problem created a "moral dilemma" in the minds of white Americans, who subscribed to the "American Creed" or the belief in life, liberty, and equality of opportunity, but supported legal segregation of the races. Myrdal was interested in exposing what he considered were the discrepancies and conflict between honored American cultural ideals and the pervasive practice of racial discrimination.[35]

In the chapters examining African-American life and community, Myrdal and his associates were interested in demonstrating the negative impact of white racism upon black life. In a now famous passage, Myrdal emphasized the "pathological condition" of black culture in the United States.

> In practically all its divergences, American Negro culture is not something independent of general American culture. It is a distorted development or a pathological condition, of the general American culture. . . . This can be said positively: we assume that it is to the advantage of American Negroes as individuals and as a group to become assimilated into American culture, to acquire the traits held in esteem by the dominant white Americans. . . . Also not to be taken in a doctrinal sense is the observation that peculiarities in the Negro community may be characterized as social pathology. As a reaction to adverse and degrading living conditions, the Negro's culture is taking on some

characteristics which are not given a high evaluation in the larger American culture. Occasionally the Negro culture traits are appreciated by the whites.[36]

It is also clear that Richard Wright and a number of other African-American artists and intellectuals in the 1930s and 1940s subscribed to Myrdal's views about the pathological nature of African-American culture.[37] In an article published in *The Atlantic Monthly* in October 1940 following the publication of his highly praised novel *Native Son,* Wright asserted that

> We Negroes have no religion that teaches us that we are "God's chosen people"; our sorrows cannot be soothed with such illusions. . . . What culture we did have when we were torn from Africa was taken from us; we were separated when we were brought here and forbidden to speak our languages. We possess no remembered cushion of culture upon which we can lay our tired heads and dream of our superiority. . . . In *Native Son* I tried to show that a man, bereft of a culture and unanchored by property, can travel but one path if he reacts positively but unthinkingly to the prizes and goals of civilization; and that one path is emotionally blind rebellion.[38]

Richard Wright's acceptance of Marxist cultural theories and his affiliation with the John Reed Club and the Communist Party in the 1930s and early 1940s help explain his positions on African-American culture and provide the historical context for his literary and artistic perspectives. The problem for Wright was his inability to appreciate the artistic creations by African-American writers that utilized African-American folklore, such as Zora Neale Hurston's *Their Eyes Were Watching God,* but did not demonstrate a finely tuned Marxist perspective. On the other hand, when black writers emphasized the pathological nature of black life and culture due to the negative impact of white racism, Wright was laudatory.

When St. Clair Drake and Horace Cayton's famous study, *Black Metropolis: A Study of Negro Life in a Northern City,* was first published in 1945, it included an introduction by Richard Wright, in which he called the book "a landmark of research and scientific achievement." *Black Metropolis* was one of most important works produced by a group of African-American social scientists trained at the University of Chicago during the 1930s and 1940s, including Charles S. Johnson, E. Franklin Frazier, Bertram Doyle, Allison Davis, and Horace Mann Bond. "If, in reading my novel, *Native Son,* you doubted the reality of Bigger Thomas," declared Wright in his introduction,

> then examine the delinquency rates cited in this book; if, in reading my autobiography, *Black Boy,* you doubted the picture of family life shown there, then study the figures on family disorganization given

here. . . . This book assumes that the Negro's present position in the
United States results from the oppression of Negroes by white people,
that the Negro's conduct, his personality, his culture, his entire life
flow naturally and inevitably out of the conditions imposed on him by
white America.[39]

Wright's biographer Michel Fabre has noted that

Wright's conceptual approach to Afro-American culture through the
Chicago School of Social Research led him to emphasize, along with
E. Franklin Frazier, the relative lack of "African survivals" in the
United States. From the start, he thus tended to stress differences,
rather than similarities, between American and African cultures. For
personal reasons, especially because of the oppressive role of religion
in his childhood, he also tended to consider religious beliefs shackles
to individual freedom."[40]

Zora Neale Hurston, on the other hand, learned to appreciate the importance of religion in the lives of the black masses, even though she did not practice religion herself. In the chapter entitled "Religion" in *Dust Tracks on a
Road,* she described in detail what took place during religious services in her
father's church. "It seems to me to be true that heavens are placed in the sky
because it is unreachable. The unreachable and therefore the unknowable always seems divine—hence religion." Given the conditions of life, particularly
for the oppressed, religion provided a sense of personhood and well-being.

People need religion because the great masses fear life and its consequences. Its responsibilities weigh heavy. Feeling a weakness in the
face of great forces, men seek an alliance with omnipotence to bolster
up their feelings of weakness, even though the omnipotence they rely
upon is a creature of their own minds. It gives them a sense of security. . . . It seems to me that organized creeds are collections of words
around a wish. I feel no need for such. However, I would not, by word
or deed, attempt to deprive another of the consolation it affords. It is
simply not for me (201–2).

Hurston also appreciated the gifts of her people, even though she understood that "the Negro race was not one band of heavenly love." In her autobiography in the chapter entitled "My People, My People," Hurston recalled
that "from the earliest rocking of my cradle days, I have heard this cry go up
from Negro lips. It is forced outward by pity, scorn and hopeless resignation. It
is called forth by the observation of one class of Negro on the doings of another branch of the brother in black" (157). Hurston related numerous incidents where lower-class blacks engaged in behavior in public that the upper

class found exasperating and embarrassing. But Hurston eventually came to the conclusion that

> it took more than a community of skin color to make your love come down on you. . . .
>
> Light came to me when I realized that I did not have to consider any racial group as a whole. God made them duck by duck and that was the only way I could see them. I learned that skins were no measure of what was inside people. So none of the Race cliches meant anything any more. I began to laugh at both white and black who claimed special blessings on the basis of race. Therefore I saw no curse in being black, nor no extra flavor by being white.

Ultimately, Hurston believed that it came down to the individual and each individual should be judged by her or his own merits. "If you haven't got it, you can't show it. If you have got it, you can't hide it. That is one of the strongest laws God ever made" (170–71).

Richard Wright and Zora Neale Hurston in their autobiographical works presented very different versions of southern black culture and experience. Wright embraced Marxist literary theories, and even after he left the Communist Party he utilized a class analysis in explaining the oppression and exploitation of African-American people. On the basis of his personal experiences growing up in the South, Wright accepted the idea that there was much that was "pathological" about black life and culture and saw that cultural background as a hindrance to the eventual integration of African Americans into American society on the basis of equality. Zora Neale Hurston also grew up in the South; she, however, developed an appreciation of African-American mass culture, including the religion, and utilized African-American folk expressions in her artistic works. She never subscribed to Marxist theories of literature and culture, but she vehemently opposed "the efforts of any man or community to live and advance their interests at the expense of the lives and interests of others" (207).[41]

The life and writings of Richard Wright and Zora Neale Hurston were significant contributions to the African-American intellectual tradition. In "Blueprint for Negro Writing" Wright's most important essay on literary theory, he insisted that African-American artists

> must accept the concept of nationalism because, in order to transcend it, they must *possess* and *understand* it. And a nationalist spirit in Negro writing means a nationalism carrying the highest possible pitch of social consciousness. It means a nationalism that . . . is aware of the dangers of its position; that knows its ultimate aims are unrealizable within the framework of capitalist America; a nationalism whose reason for

being lies in the simple fact of self-possession and in the consciousness of the interdependence of people of modern society.[42]

Wright's blueprint would serve as an inspiration for the literary works of Amiri Baraka, Larry Neal, Nikki Giovanni, and other black writers associated with the Black Arts Movement of the 1960s and 1970s.

Zora Neale Hurston's use of African-American folk expressions in literary works was the literary fulfillment of the artistic principles advocated by James Weldon Johnson in the early decades of the twentieth century. At the same time, Hurston's focus on the growth and development of an African-American woman in *Their Eyes Were Watching God* inspired an entire generation of black women writers. In 1979 novelist Alice Walker declared that "many of us love Zora Neale Hurston. . . . We love Zora Neale Hurston for her work, first, and then again (as she and all Eatonville would say), we love her for herself. For the humor and courage with which she encountered a life she frequently designed, for her absolute disinterest in becoming either white or bourgeois, and for her *devoted* appreciation of her own culture, which is an inspiration to us all."[43]

6

The Autobiographical Legacy of W. E. B. Du Bois

The split between white and black workers was greater than between white workers and capitalists; and this split depended not simply on economic exploitation but on a racial folk-lore grounded on centuries of instinct, habit and thought and implemented by the conditioned reflex of visible color. This flat and incontrovertible fact, imported Russian Communism ignored, would not discuss. . . .

I was not and am not a communist. I do not believe in the dogma of inevitable revolution in order to right economic wrong. I think war is worse than hell, and that it seldom or never forwards the advance of the world.

On the other hand, I believed and still believe that Karl Marx was one of the greatest men in modern times and that he put his finger squarely upon our difficulties when he said that economic foundations, the way in which men earn their living, are the determining factors in the development of civilization, in literature, religion, and the basic pattern of culture. And this conviction I had to express or spiritually die.

—W. E. B. Du Bois, 1940

Photographer unknown. Reprinted by permission of the Schomburg Center for Research in Black Culture, New York Public Library.

WILLIAM EDWARD Burghardt Du Bois is considered one of the most important American intellectuals of the twentieth century. Within African-American intellectual circles he was without peer. As a scholar, Du Bois made seminal contributions to the fields of history, sociology, literature, and race relations, and as a journalist and publisher his name became a household word among African Americans, particularly between 1911 and 1934 when he served as the editor of *The Crisis* magazine, the official publication of the National Association for the Advancement of Colored People. Born in Great Barrington, Massachusetts, in 1868, Du Bois graduated from Fisk University in Nashville, Tennessee, in 1888 and Harvard University in 1890. He received his Master of Arts degree from Harvard in 1892, and attended the University of Berlin between 1892 and 1894. In 1895 he was the first African American to receive the Ph.D. degree from Harvard University, and his dissertation, *The Suppression of the African Slave Trade to the United States of America, 1638–1870,* was published in 1896 as the first volume in the Harvard Historical Studies. After teaching at Wilberforce University in Ohio between 1894 and 1896, he went to the University of Pennsylvania to conduct research for *The Philadelphia Negro: A Social Study,* published in 1899. He began teaching at Atlanta University in 1897, where he remained until 1910 and conducted the annual conferences on black life and edited the Atlanta University Studies series on the "Negro Problem," which were considered "the most thoroughly scientific studies" on the Negro then available.[1]

It was while he was teaching and working at Atlanta University that Du Bois slowly began to question the positions taken by Booker T. Washington, then considered the leader of his race. Du Bois eventually challenged Washington's leadership in a series of articles that culminated in the essay "Of Booker T. Washington and Others" published in his classic work *The Souls of Black Folk,* published in 1903. As was noted in Chapter Two, Du Bois, Ida Wells-Barnett, William Monroe Trotter, and a number of younger black intellectuals objected to Washington's accommodationist ideological positions in the face of increasing violence, brutality, and discrimination leveled against African Americans in the United States. They opposed Washington's suggestion that "the Negro can survive only through submission." As a leader and spokesperson for African Americans, Washington failed to present the case of the African-American people to the larger American public. Other members of the African-American intelligentsia, known as the Talented Tenth, believed they had to oppose openly Washington's positions, otherwise they would be going against the African-American cultural and intellectual heritage. "In failing thus to state plainly and unequivocally the legitimate demands of their people, even at the cost of opposing an honored leader," declared Du Bois in *The Souls of Black Folk*, "the thinking classes of American Negroes would shirk a heavy responsibility—a responsibility to themselves, a responsibility to the struggling masses, a responsibility to the darker races of men whose future depends so largely on this American experiment, but especially a responsibility to this nation—this common fatherland."[2]

The opponents of Washington met in Niagara Falls, Canada, in July 1905 and formed the Niagara Movement, which had among its objectives the restoration of voting rights, the end of legal segregation in public accommodations, and equal access to public education. The group called for the use of agitation and protest as strategies for bringing about changes in the conditions for African Americans. The Niagara Movement, as had been the case with the National Afro-American League in 1890, was an example of independent black leaders coming together around specific matters of principle to confront the pressing social and political problems facing African Americans in the United States. Du Bois started a magazine, *The Moon: An Illustrated Monthly*, later that year which he hoped would serve as the intellectual outlet for the ideas and ideals of the Niagara Movement. Unfortunately, it was published for only one year. In January 1907 he helped to found *The Horizon*, another monthly magazine, which was somewhat more successful and was published until February 1910. With the formation of the NAACP in 1909, Du Bois was named the director of publications and research. In 1910 he moved to New York City from Atlanta and became editor of the NAACP's *The Crisis* magazine, and remained in that position until 1934.[3]

Although he had become well known for his scholarly works, such as *The Philadelphia Negro* and the Atlanta University Studies, Du Bois from very early in his intellectual career introduced autobiographical elements into his examination of larger social, political, or cultural issues facing the African-American population. Eschewing the position of the detached scholar in many of his works, Du Bois offered his personal feelings, emotions, and responses to the topics under discussion. While a student at Fisk in 1886, he published an essay on his personal experiences as a teacher in rural Tennessee in the student newspaper, the *Fisk Herald;* at the turn of the century he wrote about his travels in England and France for a national publication, and four of the fourteen essays published in *The Souls of Black Folk* were essentially autobiographical.[4]

"The Meaning of Progress," the fourth essay in *The Souls*, was a nostalgic reflection on the rural black folk he encountered in Tennessee during the summers he worked as a teacher though still a student at Fisk. Du Bois wandered far and wide looking for a school, until he met Josie, "a thin homely girl of twenty, with a dark brown face and thick hard hair," who knew of one where he was eventually hired. The essay was a personal portrait of the individuals, families, and communities among rural black folk. When Du Bois returned to the area after a ten-year absence, he was surprised and dismayed by what he found. Josie never married and had died from overwork, and although the log school where he taught was closed and a new one that had replaced it was made of wooden boards, in most of its particulars the conditions were the same. "How shall man measure Progress there where the dark Josie lies? How many heartfuls of sorrow shall balance a bushel of wheat? How hard a thing is life to the lowly, and yet how human and real! And all the life and love and strife and failure, — is it the twilight of nightfall or the flush of some faint-dawning day?"[5]

The essays "Of the Black Belt" and "Of the Quest for the Golden Fleece" were based on research Du Bois conducted in 1898 on black families and conditions in Dougherty County, Georgia. While describing poetically the landscape and history of the area where "ten thousand Negroes and two thousand whites" live, Du Bois recaptured people, places, and conversations that took place as he traveled around. In the woods he encountered "an old, hollow-cheeked man, with a drawn and characterful brown face," who had "a sort of self-contained quaintness and rough humor impossible to describe." He and his wife left another place because "the niggers were jealous" and so they "begged this piece of woods, cleared it and made a tall and rich cotton crop." Unfortunately, a few weeks before, his mule had died, "a calamity in this land equal to a fire in town," but a white neighbor lent him another. "Then he added, eyeing us, 'Oh, I gets along with white folks.'"[6] But the greater part of this essay, "Of the Quest of the Golden Fleece," was devoted to a penetrating analysis of the negative impact of cotton production upon the lives of rural black farmers who are kept in a "slavery of debt" and "modern serfdom" through the operation of the sharecropping and crop lien systems.

The wonderfully perceptive essay on Alexander Crummell was also written in this autobiographical form, based directly on Du Bois' personal encounters with the great man. As was noted in Chapter One, this was an expansion of the eulogy Du Bois prepared upon Crummell's death in September 1898. "Of the Passing of the First Born," a meditation on the brief life and death of his young son, is generally considered the most touching and personal, yet universal, essay in the entire volume. "Within the Veil was he born, said I; and there within shall he live, — a Negro and a Negro's son. Holding in that little head—ah, bitterly—the unbowed pride of a hunted race, clinging with that tiny dimpled hand—ah, wearily—to a hope not hopeless but unhopeful, and seeing with those bright wondering eyes that peer into my soul a land whose freedom is to us a mockery and whose liberty a lie."[7] Du Bois learned to love the young son, but when he was just eighteen months old, he became sick and for ten days he and his wife saw him waste away. Then one night as he tried to sleep, Du Bois recalled hearing a voice, "The Shadow of Death! The Shadow of Death!" Du Bois and wife stayed up all night and the following day. "He died at eventide, when the sun lay like a brooding sorrow above the western hills, veiling his face; when winds spoke not, and the trees, the great green trees he loved, stood motionless."[8]

The bereaved parents decided not to bury him in the alien land of Georgia, but took him to Massachusetts for internment. "All that day and all that night there sat an awful gladness in my heart, — nay, blame me not if I see the world thus darkly through the Veil, — and my soul whispers ever to me saying, 'Not dead, not dead, but escaped; not bond, but free.' " He would be spared the "studied humiliations of fifty million fellows," but he also "might have borne his burden more bravely than we, aye, — and found it lighter some day; for surely this is not the end."[9] Du Bois ended the essay with the most agonizing questions for all parents in this situation, but at the same time he made the connection between his personal experience and that of his people in this country.

If one must have gone, why not I? Why may I not rest me from this restlessness and sleep from this wide waking? Was not the world's alembic, Time, in his young hands, and not my time waning? Are there so many workers in the vineyard that the fair promise of this little boy could lightly be tossed away? The wretched of my race that line the alleys of the nation sit fatherless and unmothered; but Love sat beside his cradle, and in his ear Wisdom waited to speak. Perhaps now he knows the All-love, and needs not to be wise. Sleep, then, child—sleep till I sleep and waken to a baby voice and the ceaseless patter of little feet—above the Veil.[10]

Despite the numerous autobiographical sketches and elements in *The Souls of Black Folk*, Du Bois always claimed that his first major autobiographical work was *Darkwater: Voices from Within the Veil*, written in 1918 and 1919, and published in February 1920. In *The Autobiography of W. E. B. Du Bois: A Soliloquy on Viewing My Life from the Last Decade of Its First Century*, completed in the late 1950s, he wrote that "forty years ago when at the age of fifty, I first essayed a brief autobiography, my memories furnished many details and conclusions which now disappear or return as quite strange. . . . In *Dusk of Dawn* I wrote much about my life as I saw it at age 70, which differs much from what I think at the age of 91." Thus without including *The Souls of Black Folk*, Du Bois completed three full-length autobiographies and each was a significant contribution to the African-American intellectual tradition.[11]

Darkwater: Voices of the Prophet

THE FIRST and what many critics consider to be Du Bois's most significant autobiographical work, *Darkwater* was a unique contribution to the African-American autobiographical tradition primarily because of the numerous "voices" introduced to describe various facets of his life and work. Du Bois decided to include short fiction and poetry, as well autobiographical and semi-autobiographical pieces in the volume, and thus its structure and organization were very different from earlier autobiographical works published by African Americans. As was noted above, Frederick Douglass's *Narrative of My Life As a Slave, My Bondage and My Freedom,* and *The Life and Times of Frederick Douglass* served as the literary models for autobiographical works by enslaved and free African Americans in the late nineteenth and early twentieth centuries. The slave narratives told the personal truth about the realities of slavery in the United States with the additional objective of providing support for the political movement aimed at ending the barbarous practice. They were personal and political documents. On the other hand, the autobiographies by John Lynch, Ida Wells-Barnett, James Weldon Johnson, and Harry Haywood resemble the "Life and Times" approach found in Douglass's second two autobiographies, and emphasized the roles of these individual leaders in larger political campaigns and movements.[12]

Between 1911 and 1920 as editor of *The Crisis* magazine, Du Bois became the most influential journalist and editor among African Americans and he spoke out regularly on the more significant and controversial issues facing his people. Du Bois was relentless in exposing the injustices heaped upon African Americans by the dominant white majority. War, peace, imperialism, colonialism, lynchings, rioting, and mob violence were constantly denounced in editorials and reports published in *The Crisis* and other national publications, while advances and improvements in race relations were hailed to express the hope for the future of Africans in America and throughout the world. Several of the more important and controversial essays published over the two previous decades were included in *Darkwater,* in highly revised and expanded forms.[13]

Du Bois was serious when he announced in the subtitle that he would tell his life story in many voices. The first voice we hear is that of Du Bois in his "Credo," first published in 1904 in *The Independent.* It is a prose poem and prayer containing his ideological principles.

I believe in God who made of one blood all nations that on earth do dwell. I believe that all men, black and brown and white, are brothers, varying through time and opportunity, in form and gift and feature, but differing in no essential particular, and alike in soul and the possibility of infinite development.

Especially do I believe in the Negro Race: in the beauty of its genius, the sweetness of its soul, and its strength in that meekness which shall yet inherit this turbulent world.

I believe in pride of race and lineage and self: in pride of self so deep as to scorn injustice to other selves; in pride of lineage so great as to despise no man's father; in pride of race so chivalrous as neither to offer bastardy to the weak nor beg wedlock of the strong, knowing that men may be brothers in Christ, even though they be not brothers-in-law (*D*, 3).[14]

Darkwater is a classic work in the African-American autobiographical tradition of race vindication, but it was much more than that. Essentially, Du Bois explored his personal background and experiences to illuminate and clarify important matters of principle that he accepted and advanced throughout his life as an intellectual and spokesperson for his people. But the voice through which he explores these issues is sometimes fictive, sometimes scientific and analytical, but always poetic. The historical and analytical pieces are preceded by poems or short stories that were in some way related to the essay that followed it. "The Credo" served as the introduction to the first essay, "The Shadow of the Years," which explored Du Bois's family background and briefly examined his early years in Massachusetts and his schooling at Fisk, Harvard, and at the University of Berlin. He mentioned his stay at Wilberforce University, his marriage in 1896, and the time spent working on *The Philadelphia Negro*. In 1897 he was summoned to work at Atlanta University by the president, Horace Bumstead.

My real life work was done at Atlanta for thirteen years, from my twenty-ninth to my forty-second birthday. They were years of great spiritual upturning, of the making and unmaking of ideals, of hard work and hard play. Here I found myself. I lost my mannerisms. I grew more broadly human, made my closest and most holy friendships, and studied human beings. I became widely-acquainted with the real condition of my people (*D*, 20–21).

During those years Du Bois became a "race leader" after the founding of the Niagara Movement in 1905, and "for the first time I faced criticism and *cared.*" Blacks accused him of being envious and jealous of the power and influence of Booker T. Washington, "while white people said I was ashamed of my race and wanted to be white! And this of me, whose one life fanaticism had been belief in my Negro blood." When he received the call from the white reformers who founded the NAACP to come and work in New York City, he went because he knew they were committed to the "final emancipation of the American Negro" (*D*, 22–23).

This chapter was followed by his now famous poem "Litany for Atlanta," written after he heard the reports of the riot in Atlanta in September 1906. Presented in the form of a prayer, Du Bois asked God to deliver African Americans from "lust of power and lust of gold" as well as the "leagued lying of despot and of brute." The most controversial stanza was his hopeful expression that God was not white.

> *Keep not Thou silent, O God!*
> Sit not longer blind, Lord God, deaf to our prayer and dumb to our dumb suffering. Surely Thou, too art not white, O Lord, a pale, bloodless, heartless thing!
> *Ah! Christ of all the Pities!*
> Forgive the thought! Forgive these wild, blasphemous words! Thou art still God of our black fathers and in thy Soul's Soul sit some soft darkening of the evening, some shadowing of the velvet night.
> But whisper—speak—call, Great God, for the silence is white terror to our hearts! The way, O God, show us the way and point us the path! (*D*, 27).

"The Souls of White Folk" was Du Bois's discussion of the meaning and practice of white supremacy, and was one of the most controversial essays in the book. An earlier essay of the same title was published in *The Independent* in 1910, and dealt with the same issue, the negative impact of white racism on both the black and white worlds as well as on the individual psyches of white Europeans and Americans. In an article entitled "On Being Black," first published in *The New Republic* in February 1920, he included much of the same material, but the "voice" came initially from within the Jim Crow railroad car, ubiquitous in the southern United States during this period. "The 'Jim Crow' car is up next to the baggage car and engine. It stops out beyond the covering in the rain or sun or dust. Usually there is no step to help you climb on and often the car is a smoker cut in two and you must pass through the white smokers or else they pass through your part, with swagger and noise and stares." Then very abruptly in the middle of the essay, the voice shifts to that of the moralizing black prophet, "high in the tower, where I sit above the loud complaining of the human sea, I know many souls that toss and whirl and pass, but none there are that intrigue me more than the Souls of White Folk." Although the whites may "deny my right to live and be and call me a misbirth," the black prophet is clairvoyant and sees in and through them, and knows their thoughts "and they know that I know. This knowledge makes them embarrassed, now furious!"[15]

In the version of this essay that appeared in *Darkwater*, only the voice of the black prophet is heard and the result is a singularly powerful indictment of the ways of white folk. Du Bois explored the lie that all of the accomplishments of civilized society have their origins among white Europeans. "Everything considered, the title to the universe claimed by White Folk is faulty. It ought, at least, to look plausible." The world would very likely be a better place *without* the gifts of white folk. But more importantly, "Europe has never produced and never will in our day bring forth a single human soul who cannot be matched and over-matched in every line of human endeavor by Asia and Africa. Run the gamut, if you will, and let us have the Europeans who in sober truth over-match Nefertari, Mohammed, Rameses and Askia, Confucius, Buddha, and Jesus Christ." Europe is great "because of the foundations which the mighty past have furnished her to build upon" (*D*, 39–40).

White supremacist doctrines were relatively new in the nineteenth century and Du Bois understood that they became increasingly important in gaining the participation of the newly empowered and self-conscious white working classes in the exploitation of darker peoples. Capitalist imperialism presented "a chance for exploitation on an immense scale for inordinate profit, not simply to the very rich, but to the middle class and to the laborers." At the cultural level, these doctrines were "evolving into the theory that the 'darkies' are born beasts of burden for white folk"; and in its everyday expression it is the idea that "everything great, good, efficient, fair, and honorable is 'white'; everything mean, bad, blundering, cheating, and dishonorable is 'yellow'; a bad taste is 'brown'; and the devil is 'black.' " It was the belief that "a White Man is always right and a Black man has no rights that a white man is bound to respect" (*D*, 43–44).

Then came World War I, "where from beating, slandering, and murdering us the white world turned temporarily aside to kill each other, we of the Darker Peoples looked on in mild amaze." They also learned a fateful lesson. "We darker peoples said: This is not Europe gone mad; this is not aberration or insanity; this *is* Europe; this seeming Terrible is the real soul of white culture—back of all culture—stripped and visible today." Warfare erupted when it did for a variety of reasons, old tribal feuds, overarching political ambition; but the "deep interests involved . . . the possession of land overseas, in the right to colonies, the chance to levy endless tribute from the darker world—on coolies in China, on starving peasants in India, on black savages in Africa, on dying South Sea Islanders, on the Indians of the Amazon—all this and nothing more." They fought over "the divine right of white people to steal" (*D*, 47–48).

Given this cultural and military onslaught,

> what is this dark world thinking? It is thinking that as wild and awful as this shameful war was, *it is nothing to compare with that fight for freedom which black and brown and yellow men must and will make unless*

their oppression and humiliation and insult at the hands of the White
World cease. The Dark World is going to submit to its present treatment
just as long as it must and not one moment longer.

Europe was living under a delusion of major proportions if she believed that
the last war was "the war to end all wars." As long as the "despising and rob-
bing of darker peoples" continued, "this is not the end of world war, — it is
but the beginning" (49–50). In a volume full of controversial assessments of
the state of the world, this was the essay that caused most of the anger and
alarm.[16]

The poem that followed complemented both the second and third essays,
and the voice was that of the downtrodden darker peoples, victimized by "the
white world's vermin and filth," and now who await the coming of the black
Christ who will unburden them of poverty, injustice, and sorrow (*D,* 53). In
the preceding essay Du Bois had made it clear that he believed "white Christianity is a miserable failure" (*D,* 36), and in the poem "The Riddle of the
Sphinx" he expressed lyrically his belief that a black version of Christianity will
be the salvation for black and white folk.

The third essay, "Hands of Ethiopia," was an expansion and updating of an
article, "The African Roots of War," first published in *The Atlantic Monthly* in
May 1915. In the earlier version Du Bois contrasted Africa's position in the ancient world where she sustained "the earliest of self-protecting civilizations and
grew so mightily that it still furnishes superlatives to thinking and speaking
men," with the contemporary situation in Africa following its partitioning in
1884 by the Europeans. Using methods that were "contemptible and dishonest beyond expression," white Europeans stole almost an entire continent.
"Lying, treaties, rivers of rum, murder, assassination, mutilation, rape, and torture have marked the progress of Englishmen, German, Frenchmen, and Bel-
gian on the dark continent. The only way in which the world has been able to
endure the horrible tale is by deliberately stopping its ears and changing the
subject of conversation while the deviltry went on." The world war was sparked
by the situation in the Balkans, "that storm-centre in Europe," but "the ownership of materials and men in the darker world is the real prize that is setting
the nations of Europe at each other's throats today." This behavior was not being ignored by the colonized colored peoples and Du Bois made it clear that
unless there is an extension to darker peoples of democratic ideals, wherein
rulers govern by the consent of the ruled, warfare will continue. These colored
nations "are going to endure this treatment just as long as they must and not a
moment longer. Then they are going to fight and the War of the Color Line
will outdo in savage inhumanity any war this world has yet seen. For colored
folk have much to remember and they will not forget."[17]

In 1919 the war was over and in "The Hands of Ethiopia," found in *Dark-*

water, Du Bois puts forward his particular interpretation of the postwar colored situation, and his preferred strategy for extending the doctrine of the "right of self-determination" to the colonized peoples of Africa and Asia. President Woodrow Wilson went to the Paris Peace Conference in 1919 promoting the concept of self-determination, the idea that "no people must be forced under the sovereignty under which it does not wish to live," as part of his Fourteen Point Plan for the postwar world. Du Bois argued that this ideal and objective must be extended to the colonized peoples of Africa and Asia. He presented his plan for a "new African State" that would be carved out of territories previously controlled by Germany, England, France, and Belgium. Initially, it would be controlled "by that which we hope to govern the world for peace," that is, the League of Nations, but ultimately "independence and self-government" were the long-range objectives. The interim governing commission appointed by the League of Nations for this African state "must, naturally, be chosen with great care and thought. It must represent, not simply governments, but civilization, science, commerce, social reform, and religious philanthropy without sectarian propaganda. It must include, not simply white men, but educated and trained men of Negro blood" (*D,* 70–71).

Du Bois recognized that in order for this new African state to become a reality, the "civilized world" must recognize the humanity and equality of African peoples. "Men of education and decency ask, and ask seriously, if it is really possible to uplift Africa. Are Negroes human, or, if human, developed far enough to absorb, even under benevolent tutelage, any appreciable part of modern culture? Has not the experiment been tried in Haiti and Liberia, and failed?" Du Bois reiterates the point he has been making throughout the work, and throughout his life, the idea that the innate inferiority of the Negro is a big white lie, and "rests upon no scientific foundation worth a moment's attention. It is nothing more than a vicious habit of mind." The Old Testament proclaimed that "Ethiopia shall soon stretch out her hands unto God," and Du Bois declared that "they are not mere hands of helplessness and supplication, but rather are they hands of pain and promise; hard, gnarled, and muscled for the world's real work; they are hands of fellowship for the half-submerged masses of a distempered world; they are the hands of helpfulness for an agonized God!" (*D,* 74).

In the essay "Of Work and Wealth" Du Bois discussed the unpaid labor of enslaved African Americans who through their labor created much of the wealth of the United States, and the failure of white workers to join with their black brothers in improving the conditions for the working class. Focusing on the conditions that led to the race riot in East St. Louis in July 1917, Du Bois explored the violence and brutality spawned by race hatred. When black strikebreakers fought back against attacks by striking white workers, "five thousand rioters arose and surged like a crested storm wave from noonday until midnight." Du Bois visited the city in the aftermath of the riot and collected reports from eyewitnesses who claimed that the white rioters "killed and beat and murdered; they dashed out the brains of children and stripped off the clothes of women; they drove victims into the flames and hanged the helpless to the lighting poles. Fathers were killed before the faces of mothers; children were burned; heads were cut off with axes; pregnant women crawled and spawned in dark, wet fields; thieves went through houses and firebrands followed; bodies were thrown from bridges; and rocks and bricks flew through the air" (*D*, 94–95). Over 125 African Americans were killed, but only a handful of white rioters spent any time behind bars.[18]

Black workers were used by industrial capitalists to undercut the organized labor movement, and labor organizations refused to let black workers join. One result of this situation was the rioting in East St. Louis and other industrializing areas. But this racial strife among the working classes prevented the distribution of the world's goods to meet the needs of the mass of humanity. White workers in East St. Louis and throughout the country feared that black workers would take the bread from their mouths.

> Thus the shadow of hunger, in a world which never needs to be hungry, drives us to war and murder and hate. But why does hunger shadow so vast a mass of men? Manifestly because in the great organizing of men for work a few of the participants come out with more wealth than they could possibly use, while the vast number emerge with less than can directly support life (*D*, 99).

Du Bois believed that "all humanity must share in the future industrial democracy in the world. . . . Above all, industry must minister to the wants of the many and not of the few, and the Negro, the Indian, the Mongolian, and the South Sea Islander must be among the many as well as the Germans, Frenchmen, and Englishmen" (*D*, 103–4).

With the coming of industrial society where "the object of life was to make goods," there was a shift in the earlier trend toward universal participation in "The Ruling of Men." In this sixth essay in *Darkwater* Du Bois reminds us that the movement toward democracy began in the eighteenth century in Europe when leading philosophers came to the conclusion that "if All ruled, they would rule for All and thus Universal Good was sought through Universal Suffrage." However, social and economic developments in the nineteenth century slowed campaigns for universal suffrage as Western industrialists demanded more public resources because of the their "technical expertise," and soon after there arose "the old cry of privilege, the old assumption that there are those in the world who know better what is best for others than those others know themselves, and who can be trusted to do this best" (*D*, 140). In the United States the idea that certain groups should be excluded from the democratic process became generally accepted. Women continued to be excluded based on the argument that their interests were being addressed by their fathers, brothers, and husbands; while white southerners "continually insist that a benevolent guardianship of whites over blacks is the ideal thing. They assume that white people not only know better what Negroes need than Negroes themselves, but that they are anxious to supply these needs." But democracy means that "in the people we have the source of that endless life and unbounded wisdom which the rulers of men must have." It is based on the collective intelligence of the people, "and if democracy tries to exclude women or Negroes or the poor or any class because of innate characteristics which do not interfere with intelligence, then that democracy cripples itself and belies its name" (D, 145–46).

Du Bois was well aware of the "tyranny of the majority." At least an aristocracy or an oligarchical political system, where only a few families are in control, can be overthrown through mass rebellion and revolution. But in democracies where "the majority rules," the government often ran roughshod over the rights of minorities. In a true democracy, however, the governmental objectives must also reflect the "consent of the governed." "Granted that government should be based on the consent of the governed, does the consent of a majority at any particular time adequately express the consent of all? Has the minority, even though small and unpopular and unfashionable minority, no right to respectful consideration?" (D, 151). Du Bois made it clear that he placed his faith in parliamentary governments created "by temporary coalitions of small and diverse groups" that came together for the purpose of "expressing the will of man and setting the human soul free." Minorities must be tolerated and considered. "The toleration and encouragement of minorities and the willingness to consider as 'men' the crankiest, humblest and poorest and blackest peoples, must be the real key to the consent of the governed" (D, 152–53).

In the postwar industrial world, "the making of the rules of industry . . . is not in the hands of All but in the hands of a few. The Few who govern industry envisage, not the wants of mankind, but their own wants. They work quietly, often secretly, opposing Law, on the one hand, as interfering with the 'freedom of industry'; opposing, on the other hand, free discussion and open determination of the rules of work and wealth and wages, on the ground that harsh natural law brooks no interference by Democracy." Du Bois recognized that "the problem of the democratization of industry is tremendous," and called for "the careful, steady increase of public democratic ownership of industry" (D, 157–59).

Women must be included in the decision making in industrial society, not merely because they are a large and increasing proportion of the industrial working class, but because they are free and equal citizens in a democracy. "The Damnation of Women" is considered by many the most powerful essay in the volume. The voice is that of the feminist who understood that "only at the sacrifice of intelligence and the chance to do their best work can the majority of modern women bear children. . . . All womanhood is hampered today because the world on which it is emerging is a world that tries to worship both virgins and mothers and in the end despises motherhood and despoils virgins." Du Bois began the essay with a reminiscence about four women from his childhood who were all appendages of their male relations. Their only defense from "the bestiality of free manhood" was "free womanhood," complete with a life work, economic independence, and "the right of motherhood at her own discretion" (*D*, 164).

But Du Bois was even more disturbed by the degradation of "black womanhood."

> I shall forgive the white South much in its final judgment day: I shall forgive its slavery, for slavery is a world-old habit . . . I shall forgive its "pride of race," the passion of its hot blood, and even its dear, old, laughable strutting and posing; but one thing I shall never forgive, neither in this world nor the world to come: its wanton and continued and persistent insulting of black womanhood which it sought and seeks to prostitute for its lust. . . . The result of this history of insult and degradation has been both fearful and glorious. It has birthed the haunting prostitute, the brawler, and the beast of burden; but it has also given the world an efficient womanhood, whose strength lies in its freedom and whose chastity was won in the teeth of temptation and not in prison and swaddling clothes (*D*, 172–73).

Du Bois praised Harriet Tubman, Sojourner Truth and Mary Ann Shadd Cary, exceptionally courageous African-American women, but he emphasized the plight of average black women who "toil and toil hard." "I instinctively feel and know," Du Bois declared almost in an aside, that it is not the men, but "the five million women of my race who really count." He paid homage to black women's beauty, wit, and intelligence, and while he admitted that "we still have our poverty and degradation, our lewdness and our cruel toil; but we have too a vast group of women of Negro blood who for strength of character, cleanness of soul, and unselfish devotion of purpose, is today easily the peer of any group of women in the civilized world" (*D*, 185).

The poem that followed and introduced the eighth essay was titled "Children of the Moon," and the voice was that of those women who participated in the struggles for freedom; "I was a woman born . . . and I brought to Children of the Moon, Freedom and vast salvation." Women protect and bring freedom to "The Immortal Child" in many more ways than men. Du Bois expressed his feelings about the need to protect and assist the development of all children because therein lies our immortality. In some cases the child that one chooses to protect turns out to be a musical genius, like Samuel Coleridge-Taylor, the well-respected British composer of African descent, who was raised by his English mother and escaped poverty and discrimination only because several musical patrons came upon him, recognized his genius, and sponsored his training and education.[19]

"What is the real lesson of the life of Coleridge-Taylor? It is this: Humanly speaking it was sheer accident that this boy developed his genius. We have a right to assume that hundreds and thousands of boys and girls today are missing the chance of developing unusual talents because the chances have been against them; and that indeed the majority of children of the world are not being systematically fitted for their life work and for life itself." Why was this the case? Because the current system of publicly sponsored schooling was geared toward the replication of the social structure rather than social progress and the realization of individual freedom. "Instead of seeking to push the coming generation ahead of our accomplishment, we insist that they march behind." The objective of all education should be "manhood and womanhood, clear reason, individual talent and genius, and the spirit of service and sacrifice" (D, 205–6).

The focus of the educational process must be the child, not the role the child and later adult is to play in the emerging industrial society. "We cannot base the education of future citizens on the present inexcusable inequality of wealth nor on physical differences of race. We must seek not to make men carpenters, but to make carpenters men." We provide just enough training to make good cotton mill operatives and then wonder why when drafted in the armed services "we discover soldiers too ignorant to use our machines of murder and destruction." We train them to use these weapons, but we do not train them "to make a universe intelligent, busy, good, creative and beautiful." Du Bois wanted to give "every single human being college and vocational training free and under the best teaching force procurable for love or money" (D, 212–14).

Darkwater was published in 1920 after Du Bois underwent several life-threatening surgical operations. Biographer Arnold Rampersad in *The Art and Imagination of W. E. B. Du Bois* noted that the operations "caused him to think of an imminent death and to assess the meaning of his life." The poem that follows his discussion of "The Immortal Child" is entitled "Almighty Death," and the poet cries "Softly, full, softly, let me rise and greet the strong, low luting of that long awaited call. . . . Thro' the black kingdoms of eternal death" (D, 219). In the last essay, "Of Beauty and Death," Du Bois asked, "this Death—is this Life? And is its beauty real or false?" (D, 221). Arnold Rampersad believes that in answering this question, "Du Bois composed not only the most complex piece of the book but perhaps his most involved statement on the significance of race in the context of the human experience."[20]

Du Bois was struck by the utter beauty and ugliness in mankind and in nature. "There is not in the world a more disgraceful denial of human brotherhood than the 'Jim Crow' car of the southern United States; but, too, just as true, there is nothing more beautiful in the universe than sunset and moonlight on Montego Bay in far Jamaica. And both things are true and both belong to this our world, neither can be denied" (*D*, 230). Du Bois contrasted the beauty of patriotism with the treatment of black soldiers in Brownsville and Houston and other parts of the South. He described the beauties of London, Paris, and New York. "And then—the Veil. It drops as drops the night on southern seas—vast, sudden, unanswering. There is Hate behind it, and Cruelty and Tears." This Veil is "a thought-thing, tenuous, and intangible" and behind "this vast hanging darkness . . . the Doer never sees the Deed and the Victim knows not the Victor and Each hates All in wild and bitter ignorance. Listen, O Isles, to these Voices from within the Veil, for they portray the most human hurt of the twentieth Cycle of that poor Jesus who was called the Christ!" (*D*, 246).

Throughout this period in his life and work Du Bois likened the pain and suffering experienced by Africans in America to that of Jesus Christ in the New Testament. In *Darkwater* in the short story "Jesus Christ in Texas" and in the poems "Children of the Moon" and "The Prayers of God" and the essay "Of Beauty and Death," Du Bois portrayed the African-American experience in messianic terms, emphasizing the moral superiority as well as the hatred and oppression leveled against African Americans. This theme served as the subtext for "The Comet," the final short story in the volume, in which a rich white woman and poor black janitor believe they are the last people on earth after it is struck by a shooting star. Within a short time the woman comes to appreciate the knowledge and strength of the black janitor, but the two are soon discovered by others who survived the collision and who then suggest that the black man be lynched for being caught alone with a white woman (*D*, 253–73).

Jesus Christ suffered and died to save humanity; Africans in the United States have suffered and died to bring humanity to European Americans. This preoccupation with the messianic aspect of the African-American experience was an important element in Du Bois's understanding of the moral superiority of African Americans and was in keeping with his characterization of himself as "Prophet and Seer." Du Bois understood that he was different, superior to other men and women. He believed in his Negro blood, but he was not a savior. Arnold Rampersad makes it clear that Du Bois accepted his status as a "prophet" to his race but recognized his responsibility to all peoples. "As powerful as Du Bois's attacks are on the white world, his deepest concern in *Darkwater* is ecumenical, interracial, and international in scope."[21] This is clear from the final poem in the volume, "A Hymn to the Peoples," which ended by calling for the "truce of God" among men.

> We see the nakedness of Toil; poverty of Wealth,
> We know the Anarchy of Empire, and doleful Death of Life;
> And hearing, seeing, knowing all, we cry:

Save us, World-Spirit, from our lesser selves!
Grant us that war and hatred cease,
Reveal our souls in every race and hue!
Help us, O Human God in this Thy Truce,
To make Humanity divine! (*D*, 276).

Darkwater's reviewers all agreed that Du Bois's volume was controversial and his views difficult to dismiss. Northern and southern whites, Europeans, and even northern black reviewers expressed alarm at the threats and declarations found in the essays on "The Souls of White Folk" and the "Hands of Ethiopia," where he suggested that the colonized colored peoples should resort to armed struggle to obtain their liberation. Some claimed that he was too militant and bitter about the race situation. M. E. Bailey in the *The Bookman* declared it was "a stern indictment and one to which we cannot close our ears. It is a lesson, however, that cannot be driven home by storming, no matter how righteous be the anger." The reviewer in *The Outlook* agreed and was convinced that "the final solution of the problem of race relationship in America will not be found, must not be found, through the means Dr. Du Bois advocates." Robert F. Foerster in *The Survey* also found that "Dr. Du Bois had overstressed in his book the point of identity, not only of the colored races as such, but of the white and black races especially; yet I am equally sure the white men have overstressed the points of divergence. The signal service of this book is that it quite magnificently points out the white man's error and makes clear as day the fact that the 'race question' is, at least to a great extent, a question of social environment."[22]

Very likely because of its controversial nature, *Darkwater* sold out its first printing by August 1920, and sold well over ten thousand copies in the next few years. But it must be kept in mind that while Du Bois's views were controversial, they were not the most *radical* perspectives on the "Negro Problem" then in circulation. As was mentioned in Chapter Three, socialist and communist New Negroes emphasized the fact that African Americans were workers and that they must join with their white brothers and sisters in bringing about the end of capitalism through a Bolshevik-type revolution in the United States. While Du Bois was very much in favor of socialism, he parted company with those who believed a violent revolution would be necessary to bring it about in Western societies. Black socialist William Colson reviewed *Darkwater* for A. Philip Randolph and Chandler Owens's *The Messenger* and praised it as "primarily a work of *art*," and acknowledged that it was through Du Bois's liberalism and personality "that the awakening of 'The New Negro' had its genesis." But Colson criticized Du Bois's failure to recognize that "freedom will come only when there are no races, no classes, no creeds." Du Bois had declared in 1903 that "the problem of the twentieth century is the problem of the color line." Colson disagreed, "the distribution of wealth and knowledge is the problem of the twentieth century. . . . *Labor* will create a new world, and in the new scheme the Negro must take his place, not as a Negro, but as an equal sharer of all opportunity among equal men."[23]

In *Darkwater* Du Bois called for "Africa for the Africans," but his proposal for the creation of an "African State" under the guardianship of a special commission of the League of Nations was certainly less radical and threatening than Marcus Garvey's and the UNIA's demand that the European imperialist powers immediately relinquish to black men and woman control of their colonial territories in Africa. In August 1920 at the UNIA International Convention held in New York City with over 25,000 delegates in attendance, "The Declaration of the Rights of the Negro Peoples of the World" was issued and later circulated widely. The resolutions called for the right of "self determination for all peoples" and endorsed the position that "the Negro should adopt every means to protect himself against barbarous practices inflicted on him because of color." More importantly, the UNIA condemned European colonialism and called for "Africa for the Africans" and declared that "Negroes, wheresoever they form a community among themselves, should be given the right to elect their own representatives . . . in legislatures, courts of law, or such institutions as may exercise control over that particular community." Thus Du Bois's views on capitalism in the United States and European colonialism in Africa, published in *Darkwater,* were moderate or even conservative compared to those of the black socialists, communists, and Garveyites.[24]

Indeed, as Du Bois moved through his sixth decade, he came to be considered by many younger black intellectuals a spokesperson for the older generation, and in the literary debates over *Nigger Heaven, Home to Harlem,* and "The Criteria for Negro Art," he was labeled a "conservative." Whereas James Weldon Johnson, Alain Locke, and Charles S. Johnson praised and promoted the works of the younger generation, Du Bois denounced writers whom he believed prostituted themselves trying to satisfy the lascivious interests of white publishers and readers. Du Bois's major contribution to the New Negro literary movement was his novel, *Dark Princess: A Romance,* published in July 1928, which he often declared was his favorite work. It dealt sometimes melodramatically with the love affair between a young black medical student and an Indian princess, while the other major characters were a Chicago black politician and an ambitious black schoolteacher caught up in the social and political whirl in the Windy City. In one blurb for the novel written by Du Bois himself, he declared *"Dark Princess* is a story of the great movement of the darker races for self-expression and self-determination. It stretches from Banares to Chicago and from Berlin to Atlanta, but centers in two persons, a princess of India seeking light and freedom for her people and an American Negro seeking first to escape his problem and then to understand it."[25]

The novel's major theme was the movement among the darker peoples to end white political and economic domination. From the Universal Races Conference in London in July 1911 through the Pan-African Congress and his trips to Africa in 1923 and the new Soviet Union in 1926, Du Bois had held the ideal of the colored peoples of the world joining together to help one another gain freedom and independence of the white world. In the novel the dark Indian princess is committed to this movement and eventually convinces her alienated African-American lover to take up the cause. Although southern white reviewers scoffed at Du Bois's fantasies about "dusky solidarity" and complained that "the story blubbers down to drivelings of incoherent hate," most northern black and white reviewers were impressed and favorable in their response. Allison Davis, a social scientist who was later to write *Deep South,* seemed to capture the reading public's ultimate response to the ambitious work. *"Dark Princess* will not appeal to the same public which enjoyed *Nigger Heaven* and *Home to Harlem.* All those who have a high faith in the destiny and nature of the Negro, ought to read it."[26]

While he worked on his novel in the 1920s, Du Bois published autobiographical essays and sketches in his contributions to *The Crisis,* and continued this practice into the 1930s until he left the magazine and the NAACP in 1934 over his public disagreement with the organization's board and officials over the most appropriate economic strategies for African Americans suffering through the Great Depression. Du Bois was growing increasingly frustrated by the NAACP's failure to put forward a plan or program for African Americans to assist themselves economically during the worldwide crisis. While he supported the organization's campaign to monitor the treatment and conditions for African Americans under Democrat Franklin Roosevelt's New Deal programs, Du Bois felt that blacks needed to organize their power as consumers into large cooperatives that would provide employment, training, and financial credit to African Americans. The NAACP board not only refused to endorse these positions, but passed a resolution stating that no salaried officer of the organization could criticize its official policies in the pages of *The Crisis.* After an extended dispute Du Bois resigned his editorship and his membership on the NAACP board in June 1934, and accepted an invitation by his close friend, Atlanta University president John Hope, to return to the school permanently and help develop its department of sociology.[27] While there Du Bois put the finishing touches on his magnum opus on the history of the role of African Americans in the Reconstruction era in the United States.

From as early as his graduate school years at Harvard, Du Bois questioned the popular and scholarly versions of the South under Republican control which claimed that political incompetence, graft, and corruption were the hallmarks of the "radical" regimes of that "Tragic Era." In 1909, Du Bois had written about "Reconstruction and Its Benefits," and in various publications between 1909 and 1935 he challenged the ideological orthodoxy in professional historical circles. With the assistance of a grant from the Rosenwald Fund, he completed the work while in Atlanta and *Black Reconstruction in America, 1860–1880* was published in June 1935. Although the reviews in popular magazines were generally favorable, professional historians tried to ignore the work because of its Marxian approach and revisionist interpretations, while younger Marxists criticized Du Bois because they believed he had played fast and loose with certain fundamental Marxist concepts.[28]

Viewing (incorrectly according to some Marxists) African-American agricultural laborers in the nineteenth-century South as a "black proletariat," Du Bois argued that slavery was the primary cause of the Civil War, and the Union's victory was made possible through the support of the black population, North and South. He viewed black soldiers as an important element in restoring federal control over the former Confederate states, and he considered the enfranchisement of southern black males as a historic step in the expansion of democracy. The disfranchisement movement in the South at the end of the century was a major step backward from these democratic principles. Reconstruction after the Civil War failed not merely because of the extension, then withdrawal of the franchise to black males, but because bourgeois capitalists, North and South, were successful in their campaign to divide the southern working class along racial lines and thus prevent the redistribution of the region's wealth by giving "land to the landless," black and white. "The attempt to make black men American citizens was in a certain sense all a failure, but a splendid failure," Du Bois wrote in the final paragraph. "It did not fail where it was expected to fail. It was Athanasius contra mundum, with back to the wall outnumbered ten to one, with all the wealth and all the opportunity, and all the world against him. And only in his hands and heart the consciousness of a great and just cause; fighting the battle of all of the oppressed and despised humanity of every race and color, against the massed hirelings of Religion, Science, Education, Law, and brute force."[29]

Upon his return to Atlanta University as head of the Sociology Department, Du Bois also undertook a number of other projects that were far less fruitful, but telling in the light they shed on the position he occupied within the emerging African-American intelligentsia. Howard University professor Alain Locke was chair of Associates in Negro Folk Education and he asked Du Bois to contribute a volume to a series he was editing on African-American life and conditions to be published by the American Association for Adult Education. Du Bois agreed and he later recalled that "I think I made a fair and pretty exhaustive study of the experience of the Negro from 1933 to 1936." Du Bois included much of what he had said about the need for African Americans to create cooperative economic institutions along racial lines to cope with the pressing conditions during the Depression. He also highlighted the limitations of integrationist strategies in the "Basic American Negro Creed," which he included in the manuscript. "We repudiate an enervating philosophy of Negro escape into an artificially privileged white race which has long sought to enslave, exploit, and tyrannize over mankind." Despite the fact Du Bois was then *the* major African-American intellectual and his views were gradually becoming accepted by those in positions of authority, Locke and the AAAE executive committee found the manuscript too radical and refused to publish it, though he was paid for completion of the contract.[30]

From as early as 1930 Du Bois had also written to his publisher, Henry Holt, several times about the possibility of issuing an updated version of his book *The Negro*, first published in 1915. After correspondence that stretched over seven years, the new owner of Holt Publishing & Company, Richard H. Thornton, finally in November 1937 wrote Du Bois of his interest in a general book on the Negro, but emphasized that he could "use what material you would like from the other book, but I suspect you will wish to rewrite it in large measure." After the contracts were signed, Du Bois began working on what later became *Black Folk: Then and Now*, published in June 1939. The brief volume was very favorably received by black and white critics for the forthright way the cultures and contributions of African peoples were handled.[31]

The Autobiography of the Race Problem

WHEN DU BOIS celebrated his seventieth birthday on February 23, 1938, two younger colleagues at Atlanta University, Ira De Aldrich Reid and Rayford Logan, organized a university convocation in which Du Bois gave a speech later published in pamphlet form under the title *A Pageant in Seven Decades: 1868–1938*.[32] Shortly thereafter, Du Bois decided to expand and amplify the autobiographical material found in the pamphlet into his second major autobiographical work, *Dusk of Dawn: An Essay Toward an Autobiography of a Race Concept*, published in August 1940.

The speech and pamphlet resembled more a personal reminiscence of "the life and times of Dr. W. E. B. Du Bois," much like the *Soliloquy*, his third major autobiographical work, written in 1958 and 1959. *Dusk of Dawn*, written in 1939, dealt with a very different period in Du Bois's life. He starts off with a brief "Apology" for not writing the kind of autobiography that "assumes too much or too little; too much in dreaming that one's own life has greatly influenced the world; too little in the reticences, repressions and distortions which come because men do not dare to be absolutely frank." Du Bois believed that his life was really a part of a larger problem, and his personal experiences only assume significance in relation to that problem. The race problem was broad, expanding, and dangerous; and he was going to examine "the concept of race . . . by explaining it in terms of the one human life I know best." This work was "meant to bé not so much my autobiography as the autobiography of a concept of race, elucidated, magnified and doubtless distorted in the thoughts and deeds which were mine" (*DD*, 2).[33]

Du Bois unveils "The Plot" in the next section as well as the various levels of analysis to be pursued. There was the ideological superstructure based on physical differences among the peoples of the world that was in place when Du Bois was born in Great Barrington in 1868. The cultural belief in European superiority remained intact for the next seven decades because it was reinforced by the oppressed conditions of colored peoples around the world. The fact that there were economic interests and class considerations underpinning the maintenance of racial subordination made the belief in racial differences even more difficult to eradicate or attack successfully. Even at the personal level, it was difficult to have any great influence because there was "resistance in vast areas of unreason and especially in the minds of men where conscious present motive had been built on false rationalization" (*DD*, 6).

And then there were the victims of racial oppression and the social conditions that existed for them. When he was younger, Du Bois believed it was "a matter of education," "a matter of knowledge . . . a matter of scientific procedure," but he soon came to realize that brute force must be applied to improve the situation. "The black world must fight for freedom. It must fight with the weapons of Truth with the sword of the intrepid, uncompromising Spirit, with organization in boycott, propaganda and mob frenzy." Meanwhile, there was the immediate "problem of securing existence, of labor and income, of food and home, of spiritual independence and democratic control of industry." Du Bois was going to explore these broad social issues through the examination of his life: "the intent in this book is to set forth the interaction of this stream and change of my thought, on my work and in relation to what has been going on in the world since my birth" (*DD*, 5–6).

The first two chapters are mostly autobiographical, examining "A New England Boyhood and Reconstruction," and "Education at the End of the Nineteenth Century." Du Bois recalled that he was "a child of his age," and given his early training in the schools of Great Barrington, where he for many years was the only African-American student, and the time spent at Fisk between 1885 and 1888, he imbibed the contemporary ideals about racial progress and civilization. "I was blithely European and imperialist in outlook; democratic as democracy was conceived in America." He even chose Otto Bismarck, the German chancellor who consciously shaped German unification in racial terms, as the subject for his graduation address at Fisk University in 1888 (*DD*, 32–33).

At Harvard Du Bois applied the lessons he had learned about southern

racial mores to the sometimes inhospitable social environment of Cambridge in
the early 1890s. He chose to remain on the fringes of campus life and sought
social outlets within Boston's African-American community. He made many
friends, and "with them I carried on lively social intercourse, but one which involved little expenditure of money. I called at their homes and ate at their ta-
bles. We danced at private parties. We went on excursions down the Bay. Once,
with a group of colored students gathered from surrounding institutions, we
gave Aristophanes' 'The Birds' in a colored church" (DD, 35–36).

After finishing his bachelor's degree Du Bois decided to remain at Harvard
for additional training in the "knowledge of social conditions" and was appointed Henry Bromsfield Rogers fellow between 1890 and 1892. He also decided he wanted to obtain the doctorate and study in Germany, which was all
the vogue among American researchers in the Gilded Age, and where the best
work in social scientific research was being carried out. The Slater Fund was established in 1882 to support education for southern blacks and Du Bois came
across a statement in the *Boston Herald* in November 1890 from former President Rutherford B. Hayes, its chairman, rhetorically asking: "If there is any
young colored man in the South whom we find to have a talent for art or literature or any special aptitude for study, we are willing to give him money from
the education funds to send him to Europe or give him an advanced education" (DD, 43). Du Bois jumped on this immediately, but Hayes later claimed
he was misquoted and the fund no longer had a scholarship program. But over
the next two years Du Bois persisted and the foundation officials were deluged
with letters from his professors at Harvard supporting his application. The
Slater board finally relented and he was given a $750 grant, half fellowship, half
loan, with the possibility of renewing it for a second year.[34]

Du Bois sailed for Europe in the summer of 1892 and ended up staying almost two years. He landed in the Netherlands, made his way to Berlin where
he enrolled at the university in the seminars offered by Gustav Schmoller, Wil-
helm Dilthey, Max Weber, and other well-known German social theorists and
philosophers. During vacations he traveled cheaply throughout southern Germany and parts of the Austro-Hungarian Empire, and down into Italy. He returned via Paris, staying as long his funds would allow, and was forced to travel
in steerage "having reduced myself to my last cent." He landed in the United
States in July 1894 needing a job quickly, and after sending out numerous in-
quiries he received three offers of employment, at Wilberforce University, Lincoln Institute in Missouri, and Tuskegee Institute. He accepted the one from
Wilberforce in Ohio because it was the first he received. "It would be interesting to speculate," Du Bois remarked at the end of the chapter, "just what
would have happened, if I had accepted the last offer of Tuskegee instead of
that at Wilberforce" (DD, 49).

At this point in his young life Du Bois viewed himself as a scientist and "was determined to put science into sociology through a study of the condition and problems of my own group." Unfortunately, at Wilberforce he was asked to teach every undergraduate subject *except* sociology. Thus when the University of Pennsylvania approached him about undertaking a study of the black population in Philadelphia's Seventh Ward, he accepted despite the low salary. "The Negro problem was in my mind a matter of systematic investigation and intelligent understanding. The world was thinking wrong about race, because it did not know. The ultimate evil was stupidity. The cure for it was knowledge based on scientific investigation" (*DD*, 58).[35]

Dusk of Dawn's fourth chapter, entitled "Science and Empire," described the activities of the "young scholar" as Du Bois pursued a course of "scientific race vindication" over the next thirteen years. With *The Philadelphia Negro* and the Atlanta University Studies Du Bois was able to create "an increasing body of scientifically ascertained fact, instead of the vague mass of the so-called Negro problems" (*DD*, 64). He traveled and lectured widely on his findings, testified before the U.S. Congress, published essays and articles in the leading scholarly and popular magazines and journals; "I began to be regarded by many groups and audiences as having definite information on the Negro to which they might listen with profit." Unfortunately, harsh and unrelenting reality intruded and Du Bois eventually came to realize that "there was no such definite demand for the scientific work of the sort I was doing," and that it would be increasingly difficult for him to remain "the detached scientist when Negroes were lynched, murdered and starved" (*DD*, 67).[36]

The remainder of this discussion of "Science and Empire" is devoted to Du Bois's version of his ideological clash with Booker T. Washington and the Tuskegee Machine. Du Bois emphasized his great admiration for Washington's accomplishments, but made clear his resentment over the methods Washington employed. "These methods have become common enough in our day [1940] for all sorts of purposes: the distribution of advertising and favors, the sending out of special correspondence, veiled and open attacks upon the recalcitrant, the narrowing of opportunities for employment and promotion. All this is a common method of procedure today, but in 1904, it seemed to me monstrous and dishonest, and I resented it" (*DD*, 87). When Du Bois expressed his ideological differences with Washington in *The Souls of Black Folk* and other works, and organized the Niagara Movement in 1905, wealthy white friends of Washington made it difficult for Atlanta University to receive philanthropic funding as long as Du Bois remained on the faculty. "No one ever said this openly to me, but I sensed it in the worries which encompassed the new young president [Edmund] Ware who had succeeded Dr. [Horace] Bumstead. I began to realize that I had better look out for work elsewhere." Thus when William English Walling, Mary White Ovington, and the other liberal white founders of the NAACP asked him to come to New York City in 1910 to serve as the organization's director of research and publications, "I did not hesitate. . . . It was a voice without reply" (*DD*, 93–95).

"The Concept of Race" is the topic in Chapter Five. Here the autobiographical information is minimized, while the social and historical analysis come to the fore. Du Bois reviewed the long history of comparing people with differing physical and cultural traits and the well-known conclusion by white Europeans that they were the most beautiful, intelligent, and civilized people in the world. But he also recognized that "the economic foundation of the modern world was based on the recognition and preservation of so-called racial distinctions. In accordance with this, not only Negro slavery could be justified, but the Asiatic coolie profitably used and the laboring classes in white countries kept in their place by low wages" (*DD*, 103).

Through a genealogical analysis of his personal heritage, focusing on his maternal great-great-grandfather, Tom Burghardt, and his paternal grandfather, Alexander Du Bois, he was able unravel the European and African strands in his personal background. He felt much closer to his African heritage not merely because of "blood" or physical traits, but because of his culture and experiences. "My African racial feeling was then purely a matter of my own later learning and reaction; my recoil from the assumptions of the whites; my experience in the South at Fisk. But it was none the less real and a large determinant of my life and character. I felt myself African by 'race' and by that token was African and an integral member of the group of dark Americans who were called Negroes" (*DD*, 115).

Despite the attitudes and practices of whites, Du Bois also considered himself an "American," and even tried to join the Massachusetts branch of the Sons of the American Revolution, since he was the descendent of Tom Burghardt, who had served in one of the colonial regiments recruited in that commonwealth. When officials at the headquarters in the Smithsonian Institution in Washington found out, they demanded that the branch obtain "proof of marriage" and "record of birth of a son" to allow Du Bois's membership. The secretary, A. Howard Clark, knew "that the birth record of a stolen African slave could not possibly be produced," and thus Du Bois's membership was suspended. So much for being American (*DD*, 115).

In contrast to the white Americans at whose hands he had received frightful treatment, the Africans he encountered on his 1923–1924 trip to Liberia representing President Calvin Coolidge at the inauguration of President Charles D. B. King "showed breeding," kindness, as well as great respect for others. "African life with its isolation has deeper knowledge of human soul," Du Bois observed. "The village life, the forest ways, the teeming markets, bring intimate human knowledge that the West misses, sinking the individual in the social. Africans know fewer folk, but know them infinitely better." But Africa and the Africans were being used and exploited by the Europeans. "I

think it was in Africa that I came more clearly to see the close connection between race and wealth." Racial prejudice and practices had "income bearing
value" and in the United States "the income of the Cotton Kingdom based on
black slavery caused the passionate belief in Negro inferiority and the determination to enforce it even by arms" (*DD*, 128–29).

Du Bois ends his chapter on the race concept by presenting a powerful
metaphor for the situation for people of African descent in the United States
and his own personal relationship to their predicament. Caste segregation was
like a "dark cave in a side of an impending mountain." The people outside pass
back and forth, while those "entombed souls" try to make those outside understand their entrapment in this cave. They speak logically and try to explain
the problem, but those outside barely notice or even bother to look at them.
"It gradually penetrates the minds of the prisoners that the people passing do
not hear; that some thick sheet of invisible but horribly tangible plate glass is
between them and the world. They get excited; they talk louder; they gesticu-
late." Passersby noticing these gesticulations "laugh and pass on. . . . Then the
people within may become hysterical. They may scream and hurl themselves
against the barriers, hardly realizing . . . that these antics may actually seem
funny to those outside looking in. They may even, here and there, break
through in blood and disfigurement, and find themselves faced by a horrified,
implacable, and quite overwhelming mob of people frightened for their very
existence" (*DD*, 131).

It is possible for some of those outside the glass barrier to "assume a facile
championship of the entombed, and gain the enthusiastic and even gushing
thanks of the victims." However, these outsiders can never serve as the interpreters
of the experience of the entombed because they have not lived it themselves
and they are liable to "misinterpret and compromise and complicate matters,
even with the best of will." Moreover, "outside advocacy" will remain unsuccessful
until it has accomplished "the freeing and making articulate the submerged
group." Some of the imprisoned become resentful and hateful of the outside
world, even those outsiders who advocate change. These race-conscious individuals are concerned only with the situation for themselves and their fellow
prisoners. The loyalty of the "race man is unending . . . and balks at almost no sacrifice." Du Bois, however, was no narrow and provincial "race man," but a
prophet who plastered the thick plate glass with brilliantly conceived mani-
festos that at times captured the attention of the outside world and provided
the imprisoned with a better sense of the correctness of their cause. "This was the
race concept which has dominated my life, and the history of which I have
made the leading theme of this book" (*DD*, 132–33).

The next two chapters examine "The White World" and "The Colored
World Within," and they are autobiographical only in the sense that Du Bois
intersperses personal encounters that illustrate the broader issues under exami-

nation. Although the format is different from that used in the essay "The Souls of White Folk" in *Darkwater,* the chapter on the white world covers much of the same territory. Here he re-creates dialogues with white friends about "racial differences," but the important point is the same: the most salient characteristic of white culture is the fact that it is built on a lie. European civilization rests on the cultural and economic contributions of black, yellow, and brown peoples. The widely circulated untruth that whites in Europe originated or created "Western civilization" has been perpetuated by propaganda and art, and raised to a science. Moreover, "the democracy which the white world seeks to defend does not exist" because it not only excludes lower-class whites from "a voice in the control of industry" but also the colored peoples of Asia, Africa, and America. Du Bois reiterated the point he first made over twenty years before: "the progress of the white world must cease to rest upon the poverty and the ignorance of its own proletariat and of the colored world" (*DD,* 171).

When he turns to "The Colored World Within," he takes the opportunity to explain his position in the debate with his former NAACP colleagues over what African Americans should be doing to help themselves given the economic conditions created by the Depression. Du Bois argued that the African American faced two sets of facts: "his present racial segregation which despite anything he can do will persist for many decades; and his attempt by carefully planned and intelligent action to fit himself into the new economic organization which the world faces" (*DD,* 199). Du Bois believed that one major objective must be "full Negro rights and Negro equality in America." But at the same time, African Americans can improve their social status and economic conditions by recognizing their segregated situation and organizing among themselves to provide those things needed for their survival and advancement in American society. In education they must "organize and plan these segregated schools so that they become efficient, well-housed, well-equipped, with the best teachers and with the best results on the children" (*DD,* 201). There was need for a "a racial grouping for the advancement of arts and literature." Du Bois called for a revival of "ancient African art through an American Negro art movement." Black artists must also use "the extremely rich and colorful life of the Negro in America and elsewhere as a basis for painting, sculpture, and literature" and they should "expect support for their art from the Negro group itself" (*DD,* 202).

In the area of health, "what is needed is a carefully planned and widely distributed system of Negro hospitals and socialized medicine with an adequate number of doctors on salary, with the object of social health and not individual income" (*DD,* 203). And given the effects of crime and criminal activities upon African Americans, there was a need to develop rehabilitation programs for youthful offenders and "legal defense organizations" to deal with blacks' problems with the police and court system. The most important area where African

Americans need to come together and organize their own resources to solve some of their own problems was economics. Du Bois examined four economic approaches currently available or advocated to improve the overall conditions for the black population. The Communist Party U.S.A. (CPUSA) wanted black workers to join in a revolution to overthrow capitalism in the United States. Du Bois saw two fundamental weaknesses in this program. First, "the split between white and black workers was greater than that between white workers and capitalists." Besides, white workers benefited from the economic exploitation of black workers. Second, communist attempts to obliterate racist practices within its own ranks, through public pronouncements and in "show trials" against "racial chauvinism," such as the one against August Yokinen in New York City described in Chapter Four, "absolutely blocked any chance they might have had to attract any considerable number of white workers to their ranks" (*DD*, 205).

The second approach was through the organized labor movement. Du Bois argued that given the discrimination leveled against black workers by white workers, the answer is "Negro unionism" and the creation of "United Negro Trades" organizations "to fight for equality and opportunity within the ranks of labor." Of course, this was an example of just the kind of separate racial organization that Du Bois was advocating during this period. The third approach was black capitalism. While he agreed that African Americans must own their own businesses and employ one another, as a strategy for economic advancement it has limitations because it would likely exacerbate "class tensions" among blacks, and "subject the masses of the race to an exploiting capitalist class of their own people." Du Bois advocated a fourth approach: "To use the power of the Negro as a consumer not only for racial uplift but in addition to that, for his economic education." Du Bois wanted a proliferation of "Negro cooperatives" that would buy and sell products produced by black businesses, hire and train black employees, and provide instruction in the development of successful cooperative enterprises. The overall objectives would be "for Negro workers . . . to weave their own cloth, make their own shoes, slaughter their own meat, prepare furniture for their homes, install electrical appliances, make their own cigars and cigarettes" (*DD*, 210–11).

This Negro "cooperative commonwealth" would be led by an "aristocracy of talent" from within the group, but Du Bois began to back away from his earlier advocacy of leadership by the Talented Tenth. "My own panacea of earlier days was flight of class from mass through the development of a Talented Tenth; but the power of this aristocracy of talent was to lie in its knowledge and character not in its wealth." Wealthy blacks often used their power and authority within the group to aggrandize themselves. Successful capitalists certainly were part of the Talented Tenth, but they should not be allowed to assume leadership positions. While Du Bois was clear about who was *not* to be included in the leadership of the new Negro cooperative movement, he provided very little information about the qualities and qualifications of those who *should* be the leaders. He favored "democratic processes" within the group, but he ended the chapter by merely expressing his hope that "when real and open democratic control is intelligent enough to select of its own accord on the whole the best, most courageous, most expert, and most scholarly leadership, then the problem of democracy within the Negro group is solved. . . ." (*DD*, 220).

The eighth chapter, "Propaganda and World War," opened with a reiteration of the point he made in the initial "Apology": *Dusk of Dawn* should not be considered a traditional autobiography. His life experiences were digressions from the main topic under examination, "the concept of race," not the other way around. "I have named and tried to make this book an autobiography of race rather than merely a personal reminiscence, with the idea that peculiar racial situations and problems could best be explained in the life history of one who has lived them" (*DD*, 221). Du Bois reviewed the formation of the NAACP in 1909 and 1910, the attack on black civil rights during Woodrow Wilson's administration, the campaign for a separate black officers' training camp during the war, the postwar racial violence and rioting, and the anti-lynching campaign, all from his own personal knowledge about and participation in these activities. Many of these personal activities became part of "race history": the founding of *The Crisis* magazine in 1910, which achieved a circulation of over 100,000 by 1919, the Races Congress in London in July 1911, the Pan-African Congress he organized in Paris in February 1919. However, his most important activity was travel. "Between 1918 and 1928 I made four trips of extraordinary meaning: to France directly after the close of the war and during the Congress of Versailles; to England, Belgium, France and Geneva in the earliest days of the League of Nations; to Spain, Portugal and Africa in 1923 and 1924; and to Germany, Russia, and Constantinople in 1927." It was the travel that gave him the "depth of knowledge and breadth of view" for judging the problem of race in the modern world (*DD*, 266–67).

As usual Du Bois saved the best for last and in the final chapter he decided to take up the issue of "Revolution." Surprisingly, not only was it filled with numerous personal reminiscences, but Du Bois used it to settle some old scores and to put some important issues into perspective. After the war Du Bois pursued his Pan-African Congresses, the art and literary movement, and black cooperative enterprises as vehicles for "economic rehabilitation and defense of the Negro." He defended his approaches and activities in all three areas. The Pan-African Congresses failed to achieve anything meaningful because the imperialist powers stopped allowing them to take place. Marcus Garvey and his movement's militant demand for an end of white rule in Africa was too much of a threat and the European colonizers banned further Pan-African meetings. Even the one held in New York City in 1927 was basically an "empty gesture to keep the idea alive." The one planned for Tunis in 1929 was never held because "the French government vetoed the project" (*DD*, 279–80).

As was discussed in Chapter Four, African-American intellectuals exhibited diverse responses to the successful Bolshevik Revolution in 1917. While Du Bois was impressed by the achievement of the Russian Revolution, he did not support the American communists' call for a revolution to overthrow the capitalist system in the United States. In 1927 when personally confronted by two Russian revolutionaries who believed that oppressed African Americans should serve as the vanguard for the communist revolution in this country, Du Bois told them in no uncertain terms: "no revolution in America could be started by Negroes and succeed, and even if that were possible . . . after what I had seen of the effects of war, I could never regard violence as an effective, much less necessary, step to reform the American state" (*DD*, 286).

While Du Bois greatly admired the works of Karl Marx and believed he was "one of the greatest men in modern times," he did not share the Communist Party's conclusion that violent revolutionary struggle was inevitable. Nor did he see socialism or communist revolution on the horizon in the America of the 1930s. Meanwhile, the Depression was devastating African Americans and "the essential need was to guard and better the chances of Negroes, educated and ignorant, to earn a living, safeguard their income, and raise the level of their employment. I did not believe that the further prolongation of looking for salvation from the whites was feasible." African Americans needed to "provide for their own social uplift" through independent economic institutions (*DD*, 296).

When he raised these issues in the pages of *The Crisis*, he was criticized by NAACP officials for advocating racial segregation, and denounced by black and white communists for "racial chauvinism" and failing to support the revolutionary working-class movement. James Weldon Johnson pointed out in *Along This Way* that the First Amenia Conference, which was called to iron out differences of opinion and create an ideological consensus among African-American intellectuals and spokespersons following the death of Booker T. Washington in 1915, was a great success. Du Bois agreed. However, the Second Amenia Conference, held at Joel Spingarn's estate in August 1933 to explore the differences of opinion between older and younger, liberal and communist African-American leaders over the best strategies for African Americans facing the economic crisis, Du Bois viewed as a disappointment. Although the participants concluded that the primary problem facing African Americans was economic, they were equally certain "that this economic problem could not be approached from the point of view of race. The only approach to it must be through the white labor masses who were supposed to accept without great reluctance the new scientific argument that there was no such thing as 'race.' " This, Du Bois found, "fanciful and unrealistic" (*DD*, 300–301).[37]

Du Bois used *The Crisis* and other vehicles to hammer his major point home: "agitation against race prejudice and a planned economy for bettering the economic condition of the American Negro were not antagonistic ideals but part of one ideal; that it did not increase segregation; the segregation was there and would remain for many years." When the NAACP Board of Directors issued a resolution stating that no salaried employee could criticize the group's activities within the pages of *The Crisis,* Du Bois had two alternatives at this point, either to keep silent or resign; and he chose the latter because he was "unwilling . . . to be limited in the expression of my honest opinions in the way in which the Board proposes" (*DD,* 313).[38] Du Bois returned to Atlanta, but continued to work on what he believed was needed, "an economic program for the Negro," and other projects. On his seventieth birthday he was asked to give a speech at the university on his "philosophy of life," which in its second version became *Dusk of Dawn.*

When it appeared in June 1940, *Dusk of Dawn* received overwhelmingly favorable reviews. Virtually all the critics agreed that Du Bois had brilliantly expressed the social and economic alternatives for African Americans and the important matters of principle that determined his own ideological stances. Several reviewers expressed the view that there was a great deal more "ideology" than "autobiography" in this volume, as was the case with *Darkwater* twenty years earlier, and they looked forward to some future work that would present a fuller "portrait of the extraordinary man himself."[39]

The Soliloquy: An Exercise in Personal Vindication

DURING WORLD WAR II, despite the fact that he was in his seventies, Du Bois remained as active as ever. While at Atlanta University he not only chaired the Department of Sociology and taught graduate courses, he also founded and edited *Phylon,* a quarterly journal devoted to issues of race and culture. He continued writing his weekly newspaper columns that began in 1934 and appeared in the *Chicago Defender, Pittsburgh Courier, Amsterdam News,* and other black newspapers.[40] When Du Bois returned to Atlanta University, John Hope, the president, was also interested in the possibility of starting up the Atlanta University Studies again, but the two were unsuccessful in gaining philanthropic support. In 1940, however, Du Bois was given a grant from the Carnegie Foundation to hold the First Phylon Conference on Race and Culture and out of that meeting came the suggestion that "state by state social studies" of the black population should be undertaken under the auspices of the local land grant colleges for Negroes.

Under the terms of the Second Morrill Act of 1890, each state with a dual system of public higher education had to designate one black school as the state's black land grant institution, and federal land grant funds for that state were to be shared equitably with the black institution. In the 1940s and before, the black land grant schools received at most five percent of the annual federal grants, and when complaints were filed, southern educational officials argued that the discrepancy existed because the black institutions were not engaged in scientific research. Du Bois proposed to the presidents of the black colleges that they appeal for increased support from the federal expenditure on the basis of their conducting annual social scientific studies of the local black population. Du Bois presented his proposal to the black land grant association in 1941 and the following year it was accepted. Meeting in Atlanta in April 1943, leading social scientists from across the country gave their enthusiastic support for the program of "cooperative social studies" to be carried out by the black land grant colleges, and coordinated by researchers at Fisk, Howard, and Atlanta universities.[41]

Just when this major educational movement had been set in motion and plans were being made for the second national conference in 1944, Du Bois was hit by a bombshell: he was forced into retirement by Atlanta University president Rufus Clement with the consent of the school's Board of Trustees. At the time of his appointment to Atlanta's presidency (1936), Rufus Clement was only thirty-six years old, and had served as the president of the Louisville (Kentucky) Municipal College, the Negro branch of the University of Louisville, since 1931. Clement was university president, but Du Bois was the world-renowned scholar and intellectual and Clement basically ran the institution in the shadow of the great Dr. Du Bois. Over the years there were incidents—differences of opinion with the financially well-connected white dean Florence Read, foot-dragging by Clement in making arrangements to join forces with the black land grant association. Finally in April 1944 at a Board of Trustees meeting, Dean Read submitted a resolution calling for Du Bois's immediate retirement. (He was already ten years past the normal retirement age, and the trustees assumed Du Bois had been consulted and agreed to retire.) President Clement gave his support for the measure and it passed.[42]

All this was done without Du Bois's knowledge. For the aging Du Bois this was traumatic, especially since extending him a pension had *not* been voted on. This incident was one of the most important crises in Du Bois's life in the two decades following the publication of *Dusk of Dawn*. When he was in his ninety-first year, 1958–1959, Du Bois decided it was time for another autobiography. In writing three autobiographies, he suggested that "one must then see these varying views as contradictions to truth, and not as final and complete authority. This book then is a Soliloquy of an old man on what he dreams his life has been as he sees it slowly drifting away; and what he would like others to believe" (S, 13).[43]

The Autobiography of W. E. B. Du Bois: A Soliloquy on Viewing My Life from the Last Decade of Its First Century was Du Bois's third major autobiographical work, published posthumously in 1968 by Herbert Aptheker, his literary executor. In form and organization the *Soliloquy* is very different from the two earlier works, but the closest of the three in form and content to other works in the African-American autobiographical tradition. Neither *Darkwater* nor *Dusk of Dawn* resembled the African-American autobiographical form associated with the slave narratives. As was mentioned above, both these works made unique contributions to the African-American autobiographical form and style and organization. In the case of the *Soliloquy* we find that Du Bois has chosen to write a "personal reminiscence" that resembles "the life and times autobiographies" that trace their origin in the literary tradition to Frederick Douglass's *My Bondage and My Freedom* (1855) and *The Life and Times of Frederick Douglass* (1882, 1892).

The *Soliloquy* begins with a brief discussion of Du Bois's forced retirement from Atlanta University in 1944 and it came to typify his concerns throughout this work. This action hurt him deeply, primarily because it came as such a shock; and throughout the *Soliloquy* Du Bois wanted to make clear how the horrible things that were done to him over the years had affected him personally. When he accepted what he thought was a "life-time job" at Atlanta University at age sixty-five, he was quite healthy and never thought about making provisions for when he was too old to work. "Personally this problem never bothered me until suddenly at 75 I was retired from work with practically no savings, and no pension in view to support me. Failure to give attention to this part of my future was due to no laziness or neglect. I was eager to work and work continuously" (*S*, 13).

Of necessity the *Soliloquy* covered much the same territory as *Darkwater* and *Dusk of Dawn*. But in the earlier works Du Bois consciously eschewed the personal in favor of the prophetic and universal. In the *Soliloquy*, however, his personal experiences were brought to the foreground and systematically evaluated and intellectually engaged. Divided into three parts, the five chapters included in Part One examined his fifteenth trip abroad, and presented his personal impressions of Western Europe in the late 1950s, "the pawned peoples" of East Germany, Poland, Czechoslovakia, the Balkan and Baltic States, and life in the Soviet Union and China. Du Bois was critical of Western Europe, concluding that it was "unprepared to surrender colonial imperialism. It clings desperately to the wealth and power which comes from cheap colonial labor, held in serfdom by modern technique" (*S*, 20–21).

In Moscow Du Bois received the Lenin Peace Prize and met with Soviet leader Nikita Khrushchev. Du Bois hailed the triumph of socialism and communism in Eastern Europe and the Soviet Union, and observed, "here was a people seeking a new way of life through learning the truth, and cooperating with each other and by willing sacrifice" (*S*, 29). In *Darkwater* and *Dusk of Dawn*, he had decried the failure in the United States to make industry and industrial production subject to the democratic control of the mass of workers in the society. In the *Soliloquy* Du Bois heaped praise on the Soviet Union because it "is trying to make the working man the main object of industry. His well-being and his income are deliberately set as the chief ends of organized industry, directed by the state." The developing nations throughout the world, but particularly in Africa, must look to the Soviet Union as a model because it has managed "to conduct a great modern government without autocratic leadership of the rich." Du Bois was also pleased with the Soviet government's policy toward organized religion. Under the czars the Russian Orthodox church was the handmaiden of the autocratic state, but the new Soviet Union did not allow "any church of any kind to interfere with education, and religion is not taught in the public schools. It seems to me that this is the greatest gift of the Russian revolution to the modern world" (*S*, 42–43).

Du Bois was even more impressed by his 1959 visit to China where he met with Chairman Mao Tse-tung, and Du Bois's ninetieth birthday was celebrated with great fanfare. "Many leading nations I have visited repeatedly. But I have never seen a nation which so amazed and touched me as China" (*S*, 47). China had made "the Long March from feudalism, past capitalism and socialism to the communism in our day." The pride and spirit of the Chinese people greatly impressed him: "I saw a happy people"; everything he witnessed undermined the propaganda and distortions about Chinese communist society issued by the U.S. State Department and similar agencies. "Fifteen times I have crossed the Atlantic and once the Pacific. I have seen the world. But never so vast and glorious a miracle as China" (*S*, 53).

Part One is followed by a two-page "Interlude," printed in italics, on communism. In *Dusk of Dawn* Du Bois had presented a lengthy discussion of why he did not support communism and the CPUSA. The problem in the United States was that the white workers used racist beliefs and practices to advance themselves at the expense of black workers, and this limited the possibility of success of any "working class movement" in this country. "This flat and incontrovertible fact, imported Russian Communism ignored, would not discuss" (*DD*, 205). And Du Bois also disagreed with the communists' conclusion that violent revolution was necessary to overthrow capitalism. "I was not and am not a communist. I do not believe in the dogma of inevitable revolution in order to right economic wrong. I think war is worse than hell, and that it seldom or never forwards the advance of the world" (*DD*, 302).

World events and his own personal experiences over the next twenty years forced Du Bois to change his mind. The *Soliloquy* expressed current matters of principle:

I have studied socialism and communism long and carefully in lands where they are practiced and in conversation with their adherents, and with wide reading. I now state my conclusion frankly and clearly: I believe in communism. I mean by communism, a planned way of life in the production of wealth and work designed for building a state whose object is the highest welfare of its people and not merely the profit of a part. I believe that all men should be employed according to their ability and that wealth and services should be distributed according to need (S, 57).

Thus one important reason for a third major autobiographical work was to explain how he arrived at this latest conclusion. *"This is the excuse for this writing which I call a Soliloquy"* (S, 58).

In reviewing the work, however, it becomes clear that Du Bois had also changed his mind about several other issues he had championed throughout his life, including the leadership provided to African Americans by the so-called Talented Tenth, and this soliloquy presented his final assessments.

Part Two begins with a chapter on "My Birth and My Family" and Du Bois includes personal entries from his grandfather Alexander Du Bois's diary during a trip to Haiti in May 1861. In *Dusk of Dawn* Alexander Du Bois was primarily the subject of genealogical analysis, and the discussion of Du Bois's own religious training was confined to one paragraph. In the *Soliloquy* Du Bois goes on for several pages about religious programs and celebrations and the time he spent in Sunday School classes. He loved the "broad and beautiful rooms and sunlit windows" in the new Sunday School building, and in class "I was quite in my element and led in discussions, with embarrassing questions, and long disquisitions. I learned much of the Hebrew scriptures. I think I must have been both popular and a little dreaded, but I was very happy" (S, 89).

There is much overlap with earlier descriptions of his first years in the South as a student at Fisk and teacher in rural Georgia, but the observations in the *Soliloquy* are more personal and pointed. He described southern racial practices as a form of "barbarism," and he was not referring merely to lynchings and mob violence, but everyday encounters between blacks and whites. Once when he was on a Nashville street and he accidentally jostled a white woman, he instinctively begged her pardon and raised his hat. But the woman was furious, and Du Bois could not understand why. "Somehow, I cannot say how, I had transgressed the interracial mores of the South. Was it because I showed no submissiveness? Did I fail to debase myself utterly and eat spiritual dirt? Did I act as an equal among equals? I do not know. I only sensed scorn and hate; the kind of despising which a dog might incur." Du Bois then described the impact that such incidents had on his behavior when interacting with white people. "Thereafter for at least half a century I avoided the necessity of showing them courtesy of any sort. If I did them any courtesy which sometimes I must in sheer deference to my own standards of decency, I contrived to act as if totally unaware that I saw them or had them in mind" (*S,* 121–22).

In the discussion of his years at Harvard and his studies in Europe not only were there more details, but also several personal documents were quoted at length. In *Dusk of Dawn* his Harvard commencement speech on Jefferson Davis, the president of the Confederacy, was merely noted, but he pointed out in the *Soliloquy* that the speech was controversial at the time and presented the text and quotations from newspaper accounts of the stir it caused. In *Dusk of Dawn* he merely summarized his letter in 1890 to former President Rutherford B. Hayes inquiring about the reports that the Slater Fund was financing European study by "colored scholars"; in the *Soliloquy* the main body of the letter was included. And whereas in *Dusk of Dawn* he devoted only part of a paragraph to his relationship with Dora Marbach, the daughter of "Herr Oberpfarrer [Rector] Marbach," with whom he boarded while studying in Berlin, in the *Soliloquy* he provided intimate details about their love affair. The couple spent much time together (always chaperoned, of course). "We confessed our love for each other and Dora said she would marry me '*gleich!*' [at once]. But I knew this would be unfair to her and fatal for my work at home, where I had neither property nor social standing for this blue-eyed stranger. She could not quite understand" (*S,* 161).

Du Bois included pages and pages of descriptions of his student days in Berlin that were taken directly from his personal journals and diaries, and offered lengthy recollections of his travels in Europe and particularly the return voyage on the *Chester* to "nigger-hating America" in 1894. The chapters on "Wilberforce," "University of Pennsylvania," and "Atlanta University" flesh out his years as a "scientist" and covered much the same material as *Darkwater* and *Dusk of Dawn,* but again the discussion was more personalized, and Du Bois included colorful portraits of his wife, Nina Gomer, whom he married in May 1896, AME Bishop Benjamin Arnett of Wilberforce, Horace Bumstead of Atlanta University, and others.

The chapters on "The Niagara Movement" and "The NAACP" contained almost verbatim the same material on these organizations found in *Dusk of Dawn.* Unlike the previous thirteen chapters, there was very little additional documentation included. However, before moving into a discussion of his break with the NAACP in 1934, Du Bois devoted an entire chapter to a discussion of his "character." This topic was completely missing from the two earlier autobiographies and included important information about his life after the publication of *Dusk of Dawn* in 1940.

"When I was a young man, we talked much of character. At Fisk University character was discussed and emphasized more than scholarship." Then Du Bois outlined his personal values. He tried to be honest; "I did not mean to take anything that did not belong to me." He did not gamble, and was careful not to go heavily into debt. However, because he was not overly concerned with his finances, and never received large amounts of money from his employment and publications, he was unable to save much money for his retirement. This discussion of his personal finances is important in conveying the trauma he experienced when forced into retirement by Atlanta University in 1944. When he first arrived in New York City he purchased a home, but in 1925 in hopes of improving his financial situation, he bought a heavily mortgaged building in Harlem containing five apartments. He and his family lived in one, and the other four were rented to provide a permanent source of income, or so he thought. When the Depression hit, and his tenants could no longer pay their rent, "I gave it to the owners of the mortgages and shouldered the loss of all my savings at 60 years of age" (*S*, 278–79).

When Du Bois returned to Atlanta University in 1934, he was out of debt, but had no savings for retirement. "In money matters I was surely negligent and ignorant; but that was not because I was gambling, drinking or carousing; it was because I spent my income making myself and my family comfortable instead of 'saving for a rainy day.' I may have been wrong, but I am not sure of that." Then in keeping with the intention to distinguish this autobiographical work from the earlier ones, Du Bois entered into a discussion of even more intimate subjects: sex and friendships.

Sex was not discussed in his family circle in New England, so when he arrived at Fisk at age seventeen, he confessed not only that he was a virgin, but "I actually did not know the physical difference between men and women." His Fisk classmates, who were much older, thought he was either "a liar or a freak." Unfortunately, his first sexual experience was filled with trauma. While working as a teacher in east Tennessee, "I was literally raped by the unhappy wife who was my landlady." This meant that throughout his years in Cambridge and Boston as well as in Europe, "I went through a desperately recurring fight to keep the sex instinct in control." This sexual sublimation continued when he returned to the United States and took the position at Wilberforce. There, due to the sexual politics on campus, he was literally "frightened into marriage" long before he had enough money to support a family. Du Bois claimed that as soon as he arrived at the school, he was approached by several colleagues and propositioned to sleep with their wives. Du Bois had evidently entered a highly charged sexual environment that challenged his sense of decency, even if he were able to perform. At a small social gathering on campus he met Nina Gomer, a young student from Cedar Rapids, Iowa. Her father was a chef in one of the leading hotels and her recently deceased mother was German, from the Alsace. She was a beautiful dark-eyed mulatto girl of nineteen who knew how to run a family household well after having taken care of her invalid mother for many years. They fell in love and agreed to marry. On May 12,

1896, the young professor and student went to Cedar Rapids to meet Nina's family, "a tall, heavy father, a young stepmother, and a shy fat sister," and he met with their approval. The two were married later that same day, took the train back to Wilberforce that evening, and Du Bois was back in his classroom the next morning (*S,* 187–88).

The detailed and intimate discussion of his married life found in the *Soliloquy* was nowhere found in the earlier autobiographical works. It is clear that the couple loved each other and they had a happy life for most of the fifty-three years they spent together. But Du Bois also gives the impression this was in some ways a joyless marriage because of the pain and hurt both felt over the death of their oldest child. As we have seen, many critics have said that the most touching and universal essay in *The Souls of Black Folk* was "Of the Passing of the First Born," in which Du Bois tenderly expressed the grief any couple would experience at the loss of one so young. But the earlier autobiographical works gave no sense of the impact the child's death had upon the marriage. Even the birth of their daughter, Yolande, in 1901 failed to fill the void. The son's death had already torn their lives apart. "I threw myself completely into my work, while most reason for living left the soul of my wife . . . [who] never forgave God for the unhealable wound" (*S,* 281).

But there was another more intimate problem with the marriage and this added to the personal sadness. Du Bois believed his wife never learned to enjoy the sexual act. "It took careful restraint on my part not to make her unhappy at this most beautiful of human experiences." They were together fifty-three years and Du Bois declared that despite the preponderance of females among his closest friends and associates, "I do not think my women friends ever gave my wife harm or unease." In 1945 Mrs. Du Bois suffered a stroke that made her an invalid until she died on July 11, 1950. Her death was "normal and sad," and left him with a profound feeling of loneliness.[44]

Du Bois's second wife, Shirley Graham, was an accomplished writer, composer, conductor, and theatrical director who began corresponding regularly with him in 1936. Her father was a Methodist minister who greatly admired Du Bois's work for "the race" and had even served as Du Bois's host during a speaking engagement for the NAACP in Colorado Springs, Colorado, in 1920. The great Doctor was quite open and accessible and the thirteen-year-old Shirley Graham plied him with numerous questions, which he answered and then advised her, "Read. Read all you can." She later attended Howard University and Morgan State College, and studied at the Sorbonne in Paris in 1926. Graham received her Master of Arts degree from Oberlin College in music history and wrote several plays and the opera, *Tom-Tom: An Epic of Music and the Negro,* produced in 1932 by the Cleveland Opera Company, and given national attention. In 1942 she became one of the national field secretaries for NAACP, and in 1946 and 1947 her biographies of Paul Robeson and Frederick Douglass appeared. Graham then expressed her interest to Du Bois about doing a biography of him. In 1947 she began working on the biography and with historian Herbert Aptheker on Du Bois's papers.[45]

In the *Soliloquy* Du Bois noted that for many years he served as Shirley Graham's "father confessor in literary affairs and difficulties of life. . . . I knew her hardships and I rejoiced in her successes." Now a young widow with two sons she was raising alone, she had been spending a great deal of time with Du Bois once he returned to the NAACP in 1944. After the death of Mrs. Du Bois in 1950, "Shirley Graham, with her beautiful martyr complex, finally persuaded herself that I needed her help and companionship, as I certainly did" (*S,* 281). They were married a few days after his eighty-third birthday and only two weeks after his indictment by the U.S. Department of Justice as "an agent for a foreign principal."[46]

In *Dusk of Dawn* Du Bois mentioned his close friendship with Atlanta University president John Hope, and with Joel Spingarn, his colleague at the NAACP. This was reiterated in the *Soliloquy,* as well as the claim to personal reticence with most white acquaintances. But Du Bois had very few close friends, black or white. To most whites he appeared arrogant and "hard to know." Du Bois pled guilty to the charges. He claimed that he was religious, but was opposed to most Christian churches because they "defended such evils as slavery, color caste, exploitation of labor, and war." In interactions with his fellow man he only regretted his failure to get to know his students better as individual human beings. He also regretted the firing of a young man who worked with him because he was "arrested for molesting men in public places. I had no conception of homosexuality. I had never understood the tragedy of an Oscar Wilde. I dismissed my co-worker forthwith, and spent heavy days regretting the act" (*S,* 282).

The chapters on "The Depression" and "A New Deal for Negroes" described Du Bois's activities in the 1930s and 1940s, including the break with the NAACP over the absence of an economic program for African Americans trying to cope with the economic crisis. He described the move to Atlanta, and the project he began with the presidents of the black land grant colleges, which came to nothing after he left. After he was forced to retire from Atlanta University, he was first offered temporary and part-time positions at several black colleges. But to his surprise he was asked by NAACP officials, particularly board members Louis Wright and Arthur Spingarn, the brother of his close friend Joel Spingarn, to return to the organization as director of special research. Du Bois was to work with Walter White, who was still executive secretary, but the specific terms of the appointment were left vague and tentative. Du Bois returned to New York City, and even before getting settled, started to work. He participated in the Fifth Pan-African Congress, held in August 1945 in Manchester, England, with many future leaders of the African liberation movements; traveled over twenty thousand miles lecturing for the NAACP; published numerous articles, pamphlets, and newspaper columns; and produced two timely and important books on imperialism and colonialism in the postwar world.

Color and Democracy: Colonies and Peace, published in May 1945, was preceded by two articles, "The Realities in Africa: European Profit or Negro Development?," which appeared in *Foreign Affairs* in July 1943, and "Prospect of a World Without Race Conflict," in the *American Journal of Sociology* in March 1944. Du Bois also was signatory to the "Declaration by Negro Voters" issued at the close of the war by the heads of the largest African-American social and cultural institutions, which contained the recommendation "that political and economic democracy must displace the present system of exploitation of Africa, the West Indies, India, and other colonial areas." Du Bois brought together his writings and ideas on imperialism and colonialism in *Color and Democracy* and argued that democratic institutions and practices must be introduced among the colonized colored peoples throughout the world, and imperial domination must gradually be brought to an end. If these objectives are not pursued by the imperial powers in the postwar period, then they should expect no peace in the colonial territories. As Du Bois put it, "if colonial imperialism has caused wars for a century and a half, it can be depended upon to remain as a continual cause of other wars in the century to come."[47]

In *The World and Africa,* published in January 1947, Du Bois continued and expanded his examination of the impact of "colonial imperialism" on African cultures and societies, but also took time to dispel numerous myths about the Africans' "backwardness" and "cultural inferiority" that had been propagated as the rationale for white domination of the continent. Du Bois clearly delineated Africa's contribution to the modern world; "nothing which has happened to man in modern times has been more significant than the buying and selling of human beings out of Africa into America." This he referred to as "The Rape of Africa." More importantly, Du Bois charted African resistance to enslavement and imperial domination, from the slave revolt on Santo Domingo in 1522 to the role of Africans in the war for Cuban independence from Spain in 1895, and concluded that the Western powers must understand that "democracy is not a privilege—it is an opportunity. Just as far as any part of a nation or of the world is excluded from a share in democratic power and self-expression, just so far the world will always be in danger of war and collapse. If this nation could not live half slave and half free, then the world in which this nation plays a larger and larger part also cannot be half slave and half free, but must recognize world democracy."[48]

Both works were extremely well received by the national and international press, but the success of his literary and scholarly work did little to improve his situation at the NAACP; and from the beginning there were problems. Du

Bois never received the office space he was promised by Louis Wright, Arthur Spingarn, and other NAACP board members. In the *Soliloquy* he complained that "finally I hired offices for myself on Sixth Avenue and 42nd Street in the suite of a friend. I paid $476 for these out of my own pocket" (*S*, 330). There were differences in the understanding of Du Bois's area of activity within the NAACP's administrative structure, which had expanded greatly since he had left ten years earlier. Du Bois was supposed to be concerned with African affairs and issues, and he was admonished by NAACP lawyers when he voiced his opinion about a court case in Dayton, Ohio. But most of his problems stemmed from his clashes with his old nemesis, Walter White.

White had orchestrated the response of the NAACP board to editorials critical of the group's policies that began to appear in *The Crisis* in 1933 and that eventually led to Du Bois's resignation. In *Dusk of Dawn* this entire controversy is described in detail, but Walter White's name is never mentioned; he is referred to only as "the Secretary." In Walter White's autobiography, *A Man Called White,* which appeared in 1948, few references were made to Dr. Du Bois, and there was no mention of any differences of opinion.[49] In 1955 White died of a stroke so Du Bois felt free to express his candid opinion of the NAACP chief executive in the *Soliloquy,* written in 1959.

Du Bois acknowledged that Walter White could be very charming and was a conscientious and hard worker, but "he was one of the most selfish men I ever knew. He was absolutely self-centered and egotistical to the point that he was almost unconscious of it. He seemed really to believe that his personal interests and the interest of the race and organization were identical" (*S*, 293). At times he could be "absolutely unscrupulous," as in the case of his dealing with Du Bois after his return to the NAACP.

The United Nations Organization (UNO), created in the aftermath of World War II, was gearing up for deliberations to take place in San Francisco in April 1945. The NAACP board was asked to furnish a consultant to the UNO meetings, and the board voted Du Bois as the group's representative. Somehow "when final authorization came from Washington, White was set down as consultant and I as assistant." Nonetheless, Du Bois was active at the sessions and penned numerous statements, memoranda, and reports, but was left out of many meetings because White was the official NAACP consultant. Following the San Francisco meetings Du Bois was asked to appear before the U.S. Senate's Committee on Foreign Relations about the proposed UN charter, and did so; but White became outraged because Du Bois did not get his prior approval. Du Bois claimed he testified as an individual, not as representative of the NAACP, and thus did not need White's permission.[50]

Problems continued the next year when Du Bois recommended that "An Appeal on Behalf of American Negroes" be submitted to the UN Commission on Human Rights, similar to, but an expansion upon the one drawn up by the

National Negro Congress in May 1946. A pamphlet would be produced that would include articles by the leaders of the major African-American social and cultural organizations, detailing human rights violations against African people in the United States. Du Bois was to contribute a brief introduction. White decided he wanted to write an introduction as well, but Du Bois objected that such a short work (less than one hundred pages) did not need two introductions. Du Bois prevailed, but when the "Appeal" was officially accepted by the UN commission at a public meeting, "Walter White made the speech of presentation" (*S,* 333).[51]

White told Du Bois to stay out of party politics, that the NAACP was non-partisan. But White did everything he could do to support Harry Truman's presidential campaign in 1948 because of his strong support for civil rights. In contrast, Du Bois "donned a [Henry] Wallace button and let it be known that I was going to support him" (*S,* 334). After he spoke at a political meeting in Philadelphia in support of former Vice President Henry Wallace, the Progressive Party candidate, Du Bois was officially rebuked by White, even though Du Bois prefaced his remarks by pointing out these were his personal views. In April 1947 White decided he would go to the Paris meeting of the UN Commission on Human Rights when it was to review the "Appeal," and asked Du Bois to supply additional memoranda for the meeting. He did. A few months later Du Bois also sent a memorandum to the NAACP board members complaining about White's partisan political activities and his usurpation of authority in areas where Du Bois was placed in charge, namely international affairs. After receiving the memo, the NAACP board voted to dismiss Du Bois from his position, effective December 31, 1948. Du Bois later came to realize that Arthur Spingarn and Louis Wright had agreed at the outset that "at any time White could not get along with me, I was to go" (335).[52]

Du Bois was again out of a job. Although he was almost eighty years old, he was still strong and in good health. This time the Council on African Affairs (CAA) came to his rescue. Formed in 1938 by singer, actor, and political activist Paul Robeson and Max Yergan, the head of the YMCA's Negro Department, the CAA attempted to lobby and generate support for projects involving Africa among African Americans. Unfortunately, in January 1948 the council was added to the list of groups considered "subversive" by the U.S. Department of Justice as part of its campaign to clamp down on communist and "communist-front" organizations. Benjamin Davis, Doxey Wilkerson, Henry Winston, and several other black communists were members of the council, but the organization was never controlled by the Communist Party. When Yergan, the executive director, asked the council members to endorse a statement publicly declaring its "non-partisan stance," Robeson objected strongly, and a split occurred and Yergan was soon ousted from the group. Du Bois had long been a member of the council, and supported Robeson's position that issuing such a statement would mean capitulation to "red baiting reactionaries." In December of that year, when Du Bois was dismissed from his position at the NAACP, the council named him an honorary vice president, offered him an office in their facilities rent-free, and agreed to provide him with clerical assistance.[53]

Unfortunately, the U.S. Justice Department's implication that the CAA was a communist-front organization had a disastrous effect on its ability to raise funds. Du Bois was aware of the CAA's extreme financial straits and in the fall of 1950 offered to give up his office and clerical assistance. Instead council members suggested that since his eighty-third birthday was approaching, the CAA would organize a celebration and solicit contributions that would be used as a "publication fund" to pay for his office and finance the republication of several of Du Bois's early works long out of print. Then, on February 8, 1951, three weeks before his birthday and his marriage to Shirley Graham, Du Bois and four other members of the Peace Information Center were indicted by officials of the Justice Department for failure to register as "agents of a foreign principal" (S, 361).[54]

Abandoned by the Talented Tenth

DU BOIS presented a detailed account of his indictment, trial, and acquittal of the government's charges in his book *In Battle for Peace: The Story of My 83rd Birthday,* published in July 1952; and much of the material found in that work is included in the *Soliloquy.* Du Bois had declared himself to be a "pacifist" several years earlier, and the Peace Information Center was formed in April 1950 to prepare and distribute educational materials, circulate petitions, and lobby government agencies as part of the worldwide peace movement. Du Bois attended the American Congress on Peace that met in New York City in March 1949 and in April he attended the World Peace Congress held in Paris. "I went to what seems to me to have been the greatest demonstration for peace in modern times. For four days witnesses from nearly every country in the world set forth the horrors of war and the necessity of peace if civilization was to survive" (S, 350). The Peace Information Center was subsequently opened by Du Bois and four colleagues to generate support for peaceful solutions to conflicts arising from the increasing military and ideological competition between Western capitalists and Soviet and Chinese communists.[55]

In the United States support for the worldwide peace movement was considered by many politicians and high-ranking government officials support for American disarmament at a time when the military threat from the Soviet Union was considered greatest. The hot war had just ended, but the Americans and West Europeans believed they were engaged in a Cold War with the Soviet Union and the Eastern Bloc, and that the Russian communists were conspiring with sympathetic Americans to destroy American society from within. Communist ideas were infiltrating American society through "card-carrying communists" controlled by Moscow, and numerous "fellow travelers" who in their heart of hearts wanted to see the overthrow of the capitalist system in the United States. The Cold Warriors in the U.S. Congress and state legislatures passed laws requiring teachers to take oaths of loyalty to the government or face dismissal. The State Department denied hundreds of applications for passports for reasons of "national security," and the Justice Department identified, prosecuted, and persecuted members of leftist groups using the provisions of the Foreign Agents Registration Act of 1938 and the Smith Act of 1940.[56]

Both pieces of legislation came about on the heels of the growing number of "fascist" and "communist" groups operating throughout the United States in the late 1930s. The Foreign Agents Registration Act forced all U.S. political groupings receiving financial support from abroad, and attached to some larger "ideological movement," to register with the Department of Justice as "an agent of a foreign principal." The Smith Act sought to identify and prosecute those groups or organizations teaching or advocating the overthrow of the U.S. government by force. As early as 1945 the FBI began putting together evidence for a Smith Act indictment of the leaders of the Communist Party U.S.A., and John F. X. McGohey, the U.S. Attorney for New York City, forced Attorney General Tom Clark to move on the indictment in 1948, given the strength of the evidence. The legendary "Battle of Foley Square," which lasted for nine months beginning in January 1949, pitted the Justice Department lawyers led by McGohey against the defense attorneys, led by Henry Sacher and George Crockett, retained by the eleven communist leaders.[57]

During the winter of 1948–1949 black communist Harry Haywood was without full-time employment so he took a job for thirty-eight days as a waiter on the *Uruguay*, which made its way slowly to Brazil. When he got back in early February 1949, he contacted Communist Party headquarters in New York City and was assigned to help research the briefs for the defense of the two black communists named in the Justice Department indictment, Benjamin J. Davis and Robert Thompson. In his autobiography *Black Bolshevik*, Haywood explained that he worked with Henry Sacher, Abraham Isserman, Louis Cade, and the other attorneys for the communist leaders. "I went to the courtroom every day and sat through the interminable, boring sessions. I saw the viciousness and red-baiting of [Judge Henry] Medina and the prosecutor [John] Francis McGohey, first hand, as well as the unseemly array of stool pigeons the government had mustered to its side." After the jailing of several of the defense attorneys for "contempt of court" in July, the outcome of the trial was a foregone conclusion. "On October 14, 1949, the eleven were convicted. All received five-year sentences, except Thompson [a combat hero] whose sentence was reduced because of his wartime record. The case was appealed all the way to the Supreme Court, where convictions were upheld." Seven began serving their sentences in July 1951, but four went underground briefly before entering the federal prisons.[58]

Du Bois was outraged by the government's anti-communist campaigns and in a article in the *National Guardian,* on October 24, 1950, entitled "U.S. Needs No More Cowards," he observed,

> I never thought I would see the day that free speech and freedom of opinion would be so throttled in the United States as it is today. . . . No man can be sure of earning a living, of escaping slander and personal violence, or even of keeping out of jail unless publicly and repeatedly he proclaims:
> That he hates Russia.
> Than he opposes socialism and communism.
> That he supports wholeheartedly the war in Korea. . . .
> That he is ready to fight the Soviet Union, China and any other country.
> That he believes in the use of the Atom Bomb or any other weapon of mass destruction and regards anyone who is opposed as a traitor.[59]

Du Bois used this statement in much of the campaign literature he distributed when he ran for U.S. senator from New York on the American Labor Party ticket in the fall of 1950. "I went into the campaign for Senator knowing well from the first that I did not have a ghost of a chance for election, and that my efforts would bring me ridicule at best and jail at worse." The American Labor Party was a small New York City–based left-wing organization that included socialists, trade unionists, communists, and progressives. Du Bois had worked with Henry Wallace and the Progressive Party in 1948, and by 1950 many of the former Progressives had joined the American Labor Party. Du Bois enjoyed the campaigning and gave speeches to assemblages of up to seventeen thousand. "I was astonished by a vote of 205,729, a vote from men and women of courage, without the prejudice against color which I always expect and usually receive. . . . For this I was happy" (*S,* 363).

Officials in the U.S. Department of Justice were clearly not happy with Du Bois's activities in support of indicted communists, his leadership of the allegedly Soviet-sponsored worldwide peace movement, and his continual criticism of official U.S. foreign policy. They began in August 1950 demanding that the Peace Information Center, which Du Bois headed, register as the "agent of a foreign principal," and then conscientiously pursued the matter through to the trial of Du Bois and four others (all whites), which began in

November 1951. The Justice Department's case hinged on the hearsay testimony of O. Albert Rogge, an activist in the peace movement turned state's witness. Without corroborating evidence that the Paris-based Defenders of Peace, which received some direct financial support from the Soviet Union, was in any way involved in determining the policies and actions of the Peace Information Center, the judge rendered a directed verdict of acquittal.[60]

Du Bois was not overly surprised at the actions and attack by the Justice Department given the anti-communist hysteria that gripped the government and the nation at the time. What surprised him more was the response of his friends and colleagues to his indictment. In the *Soliloquy* he noted that at the time most "intelligent Americans" knew that the indictment and trial were politically motivated, but

> despite this, most Americans of education and stature did not say a word or move a hand. This is the most astonishing and frightening result of the trial. We five are free, but America is not. The absence of moral courage and intellectual integrity which our prosecution revealed still stands to frighten our own nation and a better world. It is clear still today, that freedom of speech and of thinking can be attacked in the United States without the intellectual and moral leaders of this land raising a hand or saying a word of protest or defense, except in the case of the Saving Few (*S,* 388–89).

Most of the petitions, letters, and declarations of protest against the indictment came from abroad, and the vast majority of the members of the International Committee in Defense of Dr. W. E. B. Du Bois and His Colleagues was from outside the United States. Du Bois was shocked at the high cost of his defense, even though his attorney, Vito Marcantonio, worked for free. He estimated that the costs were over forty thousand dollars. Du Bois knew that the reason his supporters were able to raise the needed funds was because his case became an international *cause célèbre*. But what about the other innocent victims of government repression, many of whom were African American? "We protect and defend sensational cases where Negroes are involved. But the great mass of arrested or accused black folk have no defense. There is a desperate need of nationwide organizations to oppose this national racket of railroading to jails and chain gangs the poor, friendless, and black" (*S,* 390).

The response by African-American elites and their organizations to his indictment led Du Bois to a reassessment of his earlier belief that African-American advancement depended on the work of the Talented Tenth. *In Battle for Peace* contained the first expression of his complete disillusionment with the group with which he was so closely identified. "The reaction of Negroes to this case revealed a distinct cleavage not hitherto clear in American Negro opinion. The intelligentsia, the 'Talented Tenth,' the successful business and professional men, were not, for the most part, outspoken in our defense. There were many notable exceptions, but as a group this class was silent or antagonistic." Some actually believed the government had evidence against Du Bois, but others "had become American in their acceptance of exploitation as defensible, and in their imitation of American 'conspicuous expenditure.' They proposed to make money and spend it as they pleased. They had beautiful homes, large cars and expensive fur coats. They hated 'Communism' and 'Socialism' as much as any white American." Earlier in his career Du Bois had placed his faith in this Talented Tenth; "I now realize that the ability within the people does not automatically work for its highest salvation. On the contrary, in an era like this, and in the United States, many of the educated and gifted young black folk will be as selfish and immoral as the whites who surround them and to whom Negroes have been taught to look for ideals."[61]

Du Bois also came to realize after his indictment and trial something that black communist Harry Haywood had learned early in his life as a result of his experiences with the black working class: "out of the mass of the working classes, who knew life and its bitter struggle, will continually rise the real, unselfish and clear-sighted leadership."[62] In the *Soliloquy*, written six years after *In Battle for Peace*, Du Bois reiterated the same points. In contrast to the "lethargy and fright" of the Talented Tenth during his trial, "the mass support which I gained from Negroes of the nation began to increase slowly as soon as they could understand the facts, and then swelled in astonishing volume as the trial neared. From the beginning of the trial the courtroom was continuously crowded, largely by the out-of-town colored people and white, some of whom came long distances. The coverage by the Negro newspapers attested to the nationwide demand for news and sympathy for the accused." Since the trial Du Bois had become even more conscious of the poor leadership provided by this new Talented Tenth. "I have discovered that a large and powerful portion of the educated and well-to-do Negroes are refusing to forge forward for social leadership of anyone, even their own people, but are eager to fight social medicine for sick whites or sicker Negroes; are opposing trade unionism not only for white labor, but for the far more helpless black worker; are willing to get 'rich quick' not simply by shady business enterprise, but even by organized gambling and the 'dope' racket" (*S*, 393).

Du Bois earlier believed that the black masses and the Talented Tenth shared an "inner Negro cultural ideal" based upon the similarity of background and experiences. "I thought this ideal would be built on ancient African communism, supported and developed by memory of slavery and experience of caste, which drive the Negro group into a spiritual unity precluding the development of economic classes and inner class struggle." This was his dominant ideological perspective while he worked at Atlanta University and his years at *The Crisis*, but by the late 1950s so many members of the Talented Tenth appeared to be betraying that ideal, or acted as if it did not exist. "We must admit that the majority of the American Negro intelligentsia, together with much of the West Indian and West African leadership, shows symptoms of following in the footsteps of western acquisitive society, with its exploitation of labor, monopoly of land and its resources, and with private profit for the smart and unscrupulous in a world of poverty, disease, and ignorance, as the natural end of human culture" (*S*, 391–92).

The black leadership class deserted Du Bois after his trial and former colleagues and acquaintances acted as if they thought the charges brought against him were justified, and were not part of the ongoing attack against the vision and moral leadership Du Bois provided. Du Bois was hated by white Americans for his moral courage and outspoken criticism long before the reign of terror associated with the McCarthy era. His activities in support of socialist and communist groups and objectives in the late 1940s merely served as a useful pretext. "The American Negro must realize that the attack on me for socialism is but the cloaked effort of the Southern whites to deprive Negroes of leadership in my and other cases. I was just as much hated by the white South before the Russian Revolution as now; and feared too by those of the educated and progressive elements who were and are determined to keep the dark world in submission. They have seized on the charge of 'Communism' to silence me just as they once charged 'Abolition' to shut the mouths of Northerners. And just today the thrifty are cowed by the threat of revolution" (*S*, 393–94).[63]

Even though Du Bois was acquitted of all charges,

Colleges ceased to invite my lectures and Negro colleges no longer asked for my lectures or my presence at Commencement exercises. From being a person whom every Negro in the nation knew by name at least and hastened always to entertain or praise, churches and Negro conferences refused to mention my past or present existence. . . . A whispering campaign continually intimated that some hidden treason or bribery could be laid at my door if the government had not been lenient. The central office of the NAACP refused to let branches invite me or sponsor any lectures. I was refused the right to speak on the University of California campus, because of NAACP protest. In fine I was rejected of men, refused the right to travel abroad and classed as a "controversial figure" even after being acquitted of guilt by a Federal court of law (*S*, 394–95).

A small window of opportunity to leave the country was presented in 1958 when the Supreme Court ruled that the U.S. Congress had not given the State Department the authority to demand a political affidavit, attesting to non-membership in the CPUSA, in order to be issued a passport. Du Bois had refused to fill out the affidavit, and was denied the right to travel abroad beginning in 1952, but immediately after the ruling, the State Department issued passports to him and his wife Shirley Graham, as well as Paul and Eslanda Robeson. President Dwight Eisenhower promised to seek such authority for the State Department in new legislation, so the Du Boises decided to leave right away and thus Du Bois was able to make his fifteenth trip abroad, which is described in detail in Part One of the *Soliloquy*.[64]

When the Du Boises returned from China in July 1959, their passports were confiscated by officials of the State Department; however, in June 1960 when they received invitations to the inauguration of Kwame Nkrumah as president of the newly independent nation of Ghana, their lawyers were able to get their passports reissued and they spent six weeks in West Africa. At a meeting with President Nkrumah, Du Bois was asked if he would come to Accra and serve as editor of an "Encyclopedia Africana." Du Bois had been gathering information for just such a project for almost fifty years, but believed that he was then too old to conduct such an enormous activity. Nkrumah continued to push the project, laying out the terms and details of his appointment. Soon Du Bois began to consider the offer seriously, and finally accepted in February 1961.[65]

Four days before he was scheduled to leave for Ghana, on October 1, 1961, Du Bois applied for membership in the Communist Party U.S.A. In his letter of application to Gus Hall, party chairman, he emphasized many of the same points he had made in *Dusk of Dawn* and the *Soliloquy* about the evolution of his appreciation of Karl Marx and Marxist thought. He mentioned that his trips to China, the Soviet Union, and Eastern Europe finally convinced him "that socialism was an excellent way of life" and that there were many promising paths to a socialist economic order. "Communism—the effort to give all men what they need and to ask of each the best they can contribute—this is the only way for human life." On the other hand, "capitalism cannot reform itself; it is doomed to self-destruction. No universal selfishness can bring social good to all." He supported the Communist Party because among other things it supported "public ownership of natural resources and of all capital," "no exploitation of labor," "no dogmatic religion," and "freedom under law." "These aims are not crimes. They are practiced increasingly over the world. No nation can call itself free which does not allow its citizens to work for these ends." Du Bois left New York City and after a brief stopover in London, arrived in Accra, Ghana, on October 7, 1961. He worked on the "Encyclopedia Africana" for the next three years, and became a citizen of Ghana just six months before his death on August 27, 1963.[66]

In the *Soliloquy*, written at age ninety-one, Du Bois presented the final version of the matters of principle that defined his intellectual life. Using a literary form with which he was familiar, Du Bois presented his personal truths on a wide variety of topics, many of which he had dealt with in earlier periods of his life. Thus whether or not his biographers agree with the ideological emphases during the last decade, Du Bois in the *Soliloquy* specifically outlined how and why he supported communist and socialist movements. Given his respect for the accomplishments of Kwame Nkrumah, his treatment by many of his colleagues and peers in the United States, and the fact that he had been working on material for the "Encyclopedia Africana" for many years, the invitation to come to live and work in Ghana was one he found he could not refuse. However, the decision to join the Communist Party was equally as significant and requires further examination.

The statement Du Bois issued on October 1, 1961, gave some of his reasons for joining the party, but his biographers have suggested others. Herbert Aptheker saw the decision to join the party "as embodying the best in the radical and liberating tradition of this country and the best in the egalitarian and militant traditions in humanity." Several years later he added that when the Supreme Court upheld the constitutionality of the McCarran Act upholding the State Department's right to sequester the passports of so-called subversives, "Du Bois was horrified and enraged. . . . Such a state of affairs would jeopardize his cherished plan to go to Ghana at the invitation of President Nkrumah."[67]

Biographers Arnold Rampersad and Gerald Horne argued that since Du Bois had for decades considered himself "a socialist of the path," "the wonder is not that Du Bois joined the party in 1961, but that he had not done so before." In *Dusk of Dawn* he had stated that he opposed the party because of its advocacy of violent revolution, but by 1957, Rampersad noted, he had come to the conclusion that "the violence that accompanies the revolution is not the revolution." The real revolution was the shift in economic power in the society from the capitalists to the workers. Gerald Horne emphasized the fact that American communist leaders had been wooing Du Bois for several years; "the announcement was a significant coup for the party and it broadcast his association broadly." Manning Marable agreed with the assessment of earlier biographers, and added that "another factor influencing Du Bois's decision was the continued anti-Communist stance of the NAACP, and its growing alienation from many domestic progressive currents that were taking the lead in combating segregation." Shirley Graham Du Bois in her personal memoir of Du Bois suggested that the decision to join the Communist Party was a last-minute one and that she was surprised when he showed her the letter, which was, primarily, "a decision declaring his independence."[68]

But it should also be noted that Du Bois was responding to the ideological changes that were forced on the CPUSA by the government's attacks during the early Cold War years. In *Black Bolshevik*, Harry Haywood outlined the options available to Communist Party leaders when they were placed on trial in New York City in 1949. Haywood pointed out that rather than assuming an offensive position and reaffirming their right to freedom of speech and their earlier commitment to "revolutionary change" in the United States, the defense attorneys, and subsequently communist leaders, argued that the party advocated "the theory of peaceful transition to socialism." Party leader William Z. Foster's deposition during the trial "served as one of the Party's main lines of defense. In it he outlines a course of workers' struggle for socialism via a people's front government, the perspective for achieving socialism in the U.S. along constitutional and peaceful channels."[69]

Pressure from Moscow and the international communist movement forced party chairman Foster to recant this position, and in his book, *History of the Communist Party of the United States,* published in 1952, he argued that "the Communist Party, although it does not advocate violence in workers' struggles, cannot, however, declare that there will be no violence in the establishment of socialism in this country. This is because of the certainty of reactionary attacks from capitalists." However, by the mid-1950s Foster had retired from his leadership position in the party. Following Premier Nikita Khrushchev's confirmation of the charges of massive terror, forced labor camps, phony trials, and thousands of deaths due to Stalin's purges of Soviet dissidents, the remaining leaders of the CPUSA announced their support for an "American road to socialism," which would include participation in electoral politics, support of civil rights, and the development of the welfare state. The party also changed its position on the "Negro problem" and endorsed the liberal, integrationist policies of the NAACP, and expelled those Negro nationalists, such as Harry Haywood, who clung to the earlier position supporting "the right of self-determination in the Black Belt."[70]

Thus after 1956 it was not Du Bois who had changed his views to conform with positions associated with the Communist Party, but the party which had been forced to change and accept the Du Boisian positions due to national and international events. In 1940 in *Dusk of Dawn* Du Bois declared that the transition to socialism in the United States must be brought about by constitutional, non-violent means. "I do not believe in the dogma of inevitable revolution in order to right economic wrong" (*DD,* 302). Since American communist leaders had moved to accept Du Bois's position, and had supported him during the years he was harassed and attacked by the U.S. government, he returned the favor by joining the Communist Party before he left in October 1961.[71]

The three major autobiographical works written by Du Bois between 1919 and 1959 described the changes and continuities in his ideological positions over half a century, and were also significant contributions to the African-American literary tradition. In these works Du Bois demonstrated the continuing importance of the autobiography in the development of the distinct African-American intellectual tradition in the United States.

7

The Confessions of James Baldwin

———

Richard [Wright] accused me of having betrayed him, and not only him but all American Negroes by attacking the idea of protest literature. . . . And Richard thought I was trying to destroy his novel [*Native Son*] and his reputation; and yet it had not entered my mind that either of these *could* be destroyed, and certainly not by me. And yet what made the interview so ghastly was not merely the foregoing or the fact that I could find no words with which to defend myself. What made it most painful was that Richard was right to be hurt, I was wrong to have hurt him. He saw clearly enough, far more clearly than I had dared to allow myself to see, what I had done: I had used his work as a kind of springboard into my own. His work was a road-block in my road, the sphinx, really, whose riddles I had to answer before I could become myself. I thought confusedly then, and feel very definitely now, that this was the greatest tribute I could have paid him. But it is not an easy tribute to bear and I do not know how I will take it when my time comes.

—JAMES BALDWIN, 1961

Photograph by Bob Adelman. Reprinted by permission of the Schomburg Center for Research in Black Culture, New York Public Library.

THE YOUNG WRITER James Baldwin almost got to meet the great Dr. Du Bois at Le Congrès des Ecrivains et Artistes Noirs (Congress of African Writers and Artists), held in Paris at the Sorbonne in September 1956. Baldwin attended the meeting as a reporter and his essay, "Princes and Powers," describing the proceedings appeared in *Encounter* magazine in January 1957. Organized by French-speaking Caribbean and African intellectuals residing in Paris, the conference sought to examine those elements of European culture that should be carried over into the new African nation-states that were emerging during the new era of decolonization. To a very great extent the most widely recognized father of the decolonization movement was W. E. B. Du Bois, who during World War I had called for self-determination of colonized peoples in Africa, Asia, and the Caribbean, and had organized the 1919 Pan-African Congress around this issue. Unfortunately, since 1952, following his indictment and trial as an unregistered agent of a foreign power, the U.S. State Department denied Du Bois's applications for a passport. Although he was unable to attend the 1956 meeting in Paris, he sent a message to the delegates that was read at the beginning of the deliberations.[1]

The young Baldwin did not fully understand that the reason Du Bois was unable to attend involved serious matters of principle. Du Bois was prevented from traveling because he refused to declare in writing that he did not belong to the Communist Party, which was indeed the case in 1956. Had Du Bois been allowed to participate in the Paris meeting, he would have insisted that the delegates consider "the socialist road to economic development." Du Bois understood that those African-American leaders and spokespersons who denounced or denied the viability of socialist and communist alternatives for the developing nations were allowed to travel abroad to international meetings, such as the African writers conference in Paris, because government officials assumed that they were proponents of capitalism. In his letter to the conference delegates Du Bois declared, "any American Negro who travels abroad today must either not discuss race conditions in the United States or say the sort of things which our State Department wishes the world to believe."[2]

James Baldwin thought that Du Bois's letter got the conference off to a bad start, particularly for the Americans attending. While Baldwin admitted the greater horror was "the incontestable fact that he [Du Bois] had not been

allowed to leave his country," as was the case for the delegates from South
Africa, who were victimized by their government's official policy of apartheid,
"Du Bois's extremely ill-considered communication" tended to justify the Europeans' distrust toward black Americans traveling abroad and "made yet
deeper, for the five American Negroes present, that gulf which yawns between
the American Negro and all other men of color." "This is a sad and dangerous
state of affairs," Baldwin concluded, "for the American Negro is possibly the
only man of color who can speak of the West with real authority, whose experience, painful as it is, also proves the vitality of the so transgressed western
ideals" (44).

At a time when W. E. B. Du Bois had become completely disillusioned
with the idea that the experience of African peoples in the United States could
serve as a beacon of hope for other oppressed colored peoples around the
world, James Baldwin reiterated that potentiality. African Americans should be
considered "the connecting link between Africa and the West, the most real
and certainly the most shocking of all contributions to Western cultural life,"
declared Baldwin.

> The land of our forefathers' exile had been made, by that travail, our
> home . . . and nothing . . . could take away our title to the land which
> we, too, purchased with our blood. This results in a psychology which
> is very different—at its best and at its worst—from the psychology
> which is produced by a sense of having been invaded and overrun, the
> sense of having no recourse whatever against oppression other than
> overthrowing the machinery of the oppressor. We have been dealing
> with, have been made and mangled by, another machinery altogether.
> It had been a necessity to make the machinery work for our benefit
> and the possibility of its doing so had been, so to speak, built in (45).

One of the major issues addressed at the African writers conference in Paris
was the significance of the role that traditional African cultural practices would
play in the movement toward modern statehood. Most of the artists and writers in attendance felt that despite their training and education in Europe, they
were nonetheless forever linked to their native lands through experience and
cultural background. In the late 1920s and 1930s, Aime Cesaire, Leon Damas,
Leopold Senghor, and other writers and artists launched the Negritude movement, that particular version of the New Negro literary renaissance found in
the French-speaking African world. The emphasis that these poets, playwrights, novelists, and essayists placed on the cultural values, beliefs, and practices of the African masses mirrored that found in the works of Langston
Hughes, Claude McKay, James Weldon Johnson, and Zora Neale Hurston in
the United States. The Negritude writers recognized the richness and wealth of
information about *la condition humaine* that was contained in the folklore,

religious practices, and social interactions of African and Afro-Caribbean peoples.[3]

At the 1956 African writers conference in Paris, however, novelist Richard Wright, who had been living in France since 1946, challenged this particular artistic orientation. On the evening of the first day, Wright was called upon to respond to the charges leveled by Du Bois against the American blacks in attendance. Wright asserted his own "freedom of expression," and like James Baldwin, he emphasized the fact that American blacks' identification with Africa was limited by the fact that they were Westerners. Wright also argued that despite the richness and spontaneity of traditional African cultures, they may have hindered the struggle against colonization and perhaps in the future would retard the movement toward modernization in these societies. In the address given on the third day of the conference, entitled "Tradition and Industrialization: The Historic Meaning of the Plight of the Tragic Elites in Asia and Africa," Wright reiterated this point and called upon African intellectuals to reject their "irrational past" and turn toward rationalism and industrialization. In this instance, however, James Baldwin disagreed with Wright's notion that "what was good for Europe was good for all mankind" (59).[4]

James Baldwin believed that this was "a tactless way of phrasing a debatable idea," but Wright went on to express other ideas that Baldwin found even more bizarre. Wright argued that the European colonizers should turn over the running of these newly independent nations to the African elites whom they had trained, and the former colonizers should not be shocked or dismayed by the dictatorial methods these new leaders might employ to bring about the transition to a modern political economy. Baldwin was highly skeptical of this approach. "Wright said these men, the leaders of their countries, once the new social order was established, would voluntarily surrender their 'personal power.' He did not say what would happen then, but I supposed it would be the second coming" (59). However, "Princes and Powers" was merely the latest public airing of James Baldwin's ideological differences with his literary and artistic mentor, Richard Wright.

Encounters with Father Figures: Richard Wright

THE NOVELIST Richard Wright was sixteen years older than James Baldwin, and when the two first met in 1945, Wright was the most important African-American writer in the United States. Baldwin had read and reread *Native Son* and *Black Boy* when he was young and several biographers have suggested that his literary style, particularly the nonfiction, was greatly influenced by Wright. But despite the fact that they started out as friends, the wide ideological and personal differences between the two writers made it almost inevitable that they would be unable to sustain a long-term friendship or relationship.

James Baldwin was born on August 2, 1924 in Harlem. He was the first child of Emma Berdis James, who later married David Baldwin, with whom she had eight other children. Emma Berdis had migrated to New York City from Deal Island, Maryland, and David Baldwin was from New Orleans. David Baldwin always had great difficulty supporting his large and growing family on the wages he received as an employee of a soda bottling factory on Long Island. But he supplemented the family income with money he received as an itinerant minister. James Baldwin, like Richard Wright, was raised in a sternly religious household that enforced the fundamentalist teachings of the Bible and Protestant Christianity. For both writers the time spent in church became important for learning the myths and symbols associated with African-American religious practices. But whereas Wright resisted his grandmother's attempt to get him to convert to her narrow Seventh-Day Adventist beliefs, Baldwin used his experiences in church and his religious conversion as a weapon in his struggle against his father, who constantly criticized and belittled the little boy, whom he thought was "ugly" and had "frog-eyes."[5]

James Baldwin's decision at age fourteen to begin to preach had as much to do with his desire to outdo his father at his own game as it did with the genuine belief that God had called him to the pulpit during his religious conversion experience. Years later in his autobiographical essay "Down at the Cross," included in *The Fire Next Time* (1963), Baldwin confessed that following his conversion his ego would not allow him to remain in the church "merely as another worshipper," so he decided to become a "Young Minister." "My youth quickly made me a much bigger drawing card than my father. I pushed this advantage ruthlessly, for it was the most effective means I found of breaking his hold over me." His new status provided "immunity from punishment," and an excuse for "the sudden right to privacy" during which he was supposed to be writing his sermons. "I could not be interrupted—not even by my father. I had immobilized him" (345).[6] This youthful experience prefigured Baldwin's relationships with individuals, especially Richard Wright, who represented father figures in his personal and public life.

After about a year in the pulpit Baldwin began feeling "quite dishonest" about his preaching, since it had become more of a performance on his part, and was valued more as a form of entertainment by his parishioners. "Being in the pulpit was like being in the theater; I was behind the scenes and knew how the illusion worked." However, Baldwin used the essay in *The Fire Next Time* not only to confess his deceit and describe his personal disillusionment with the black church congregation he belonged to, but also to bear witness about the nature of Christianity in the United States and other Western societies. The young preacher soon came to realize that the so-called Christians in his congregation (and many congregations like it) did not subscribe to the precept "love thy neighbor." It was not just the fact that the ministers were getting fat and wealthy off the hard labor of their impoverished parishioners; there seemed to be no "loving-kindness" found among them. "I really mean that there was no love in the church. It was a mask for hatred and self-hatred and despair. The transfiguring power of the Holy Ghost ended when the service ended, and salvation stopped at the church door. When we were told to love everybody, I had thought that that meant *everybody*. But no. It applied only to those who believed as we did, and it did not apply to white people at all" (348).

African Americans were no more "simple," "spontaneous," or "Christian" than white Americans, according to Baldwin; they were just more oppressed, and clung to their religious beliefs and practices for their own physical survival and mental stability. "The passion with which we loved the Lord was the measure of how deeply we feared and distrusted, and, in the end, hated almost all strangers, always, and avoided and despised ourselves." But unlike many white Christian churches Baldwin had visited, he greatly enjoyed the activities sponsored by his congregation, and came to appreciate the zest for life among the members because of their shared experience: they all had managed to survive the life-threatening conditions associated with black life in America. Baldwin experienced great joy and happiness at church dinners, picnics, and other outings. "Perhaps we were, all of us—pimps, whores, racketeers, church members, and children—bound together by the nature of our oppression, the specific and peculiar complex of risks we had to run; if so, within these limits we sometimes achieved with each other a freedom that was close to love" (348–49).

On the other hand, in white Christian churches there was too little love and joy because there was too much denial. Baldwin argued that historically the Christian church operated in the "realm of power" more than the "realm of morals" and sanctioned the activities of white supremacists who profited from the practices of slavery, conquest, and colonization. "The Christian church itself . . . sanctioned and rejoiced in the conquests of the flag, and encouraged, if it did not formulate, the belief that conquest, with the resulting relative well-being of the Western populations, was proof of the favor of God." The white Christians' concept of God had to be abandoned and a new morality, based on the truth about the past, must be substituted to achieve a kind of spiritual well-being. Taking seriously his role as "witness" and "prophet," Baldwin declared, "It is not too much to say that whoever wishes to become a truly moral human being (and let us not ask whether or not this is possible; I think we must *believe* that it is possible) must first divorce himself from the prohibitions, crimes, and hypocrisies of the Christian church. If the concept of God has any validity or any use, it can only be to make us larger, freer, and more loving. If God cannot do this, then it is time we got rid of Him" (351–52).

Although James Baldwin and Richard Wright attended segregated public schools, Baldwin also attended integrated schools where his writing talent was cultivated by both his black and white teachers. At Public School 24 Baldwin received the special attention of the black principal, Gertrude Ayer, and a young white teacher, Orilla Miller, who took Baldwin to his first theatrical performance (to the great dismay of his fundamentalist father). At Frederick Douglass Junior High School in Harlem, Baldwin was instructed by Countee Cullen, an important African-American poet, and wrote for the school paper, *The Douglass Pilot.* Baldwin was also among the small number of African Americans who attended Bronx's DeWitt Clinton High School between 1934 and 1938. There he made many lifelong friendships with white classmates, many of whom worked with him on the school literary magazine, the *Magpie.*[7]

After high school and with the assistance of his white classmates, Baldwin landed a job in Belle Mead, New Jersey, as a manual laborer, and it was during this period that Baldwin experienced what southern blacks lived with (or through) all their lives. "Notes of a Native Son," one of Baldwin's most famous essays, was published in 1955 and described in detail his responses to American racial mores and practices "up South." Just like the main character Bigger Thomas in Richard Wright's *Native Son,* the rage that Baldwin felt from his continual confrontations with racist whites and the overt discrimination led to a violent outburst. One evening in 1943 in Trenton, New Jersey, he and a white friend were looking for something to eat and were refused service in the American Diner. "We don't serve Negroes," they were told. When the two were out in the street, somehow Baldwin lost control and suffered a kind of "optical illusion or nightmare"; then he snapped. Baldwin started wandering aimlessly up and down the street. "I wanted to do something to crush these white faces, which were crushing me" (134).[8]

Baldwin then spied a swanky white restaurant where he knew "not even the intercession of the Virgin would cause me to be served." He went in and sat down in a booth. "Whatever I looked like I frightened the waitress who shortly appeared, and the moment she appeared all my fury flowed toward her." When she began to intone the mantra, "We don't serve Negroes," Baldwin heard in his head "a thousand bells of a nightmare," and picked up the only thing on the table, a large mug, and hurled it at the waitress. "She ducked and it missed her and shattered against the mirror behind the bar." Everyone's mouth in the restaurant flew wide open in shock and surprise. As Baldwin made for the exit, "a round pot-bellied man grabbed me by the nape of the neck just as I reached the doors and began to beat me about the face. I kicked him and got loose and ran into the streets. My friend whispered, '*Run,*' and I ran" (134–35).

Baldwin writing in 1955 long before the riot-torn summers of the 1960s recognized that incidents such as this one, which are common experiences for

African Americans, "can wreck more important things than race relations. There is not a Negro alive who does not have this rage in his blood—one has the choice, merely, of living with it consciously or surrendering to it. As for me, this fever has recurred in me, and does, and will until the day I die" (133). Baldwin used autobiographical essays to confess his personal rage at the treatment of Africans and other colored peoples in societies dominated by white Europeans and Americans. These literary acts of confession soon led to his name being placed at the top of best-seller lists throughout the English-speaking world.

The young Baldwin was fired (several times) from his manual laborer's job in New Jersey, and soon returned to live in Harlem with his family and to pursue his literary career. His father had become ill with tuberculosis, deteriorated mentally and physically, and finally died on July 29, 1943, the same day that James's mother gave birth to his youngest sister, Paula. In "Notes of a Native Son" Baldwin presented intimate details about his relationship with his father and the circumstances of his death. Baldwin reluctantly visited his father in the hospital on Long Island with his aunt the day before he died. "I told my mother that I did not want to see him because I hated him. But this was not true. It was only that I *had* hated him and I wanted to hold on to my hatred. I did not want to look on him as a ruin: it was not a ruin I hated. I imagine that one of the reasons people cling to their hates so stubbornly is because they sense, once hate is gone, that they will be forced to deal with pain" (137–38).

With his father's death James Baldwin as the oldest child had to take greater responsibility for his eight brothers and sisters. He worked at several menial jobs, but continued to read voraciously and began to write poems, short stories, and eventually a novel. His friends introduced him to the postwar Greenwich Village literary scene, which was dominated by the editors and publishers of the various avant-garde magazines. Eventually, Baldwin made contact with several of these editors and his reviews began to appear in *New Leader, The Nation,* and *Commentary.* It was during this early Village period that Baldwin met his literary father, Richard Wright. In another of Baldwin's famous acts of confession, written shortly after Wright's death in November 1960, entitled, "Alas Poor Richard," Baldwin detailed his side of the controversial relationship.[9]

Confession Is Good for the Soul

IT WAS IN THE winter of 1945 that the young and aspiring James Baldwin first visited Richard Wright at his apartment in Brooklyn in hopes that the older writer would help him get a grant. Wright was thirty-seven and famous; Baldwin was twenty-one and still unpublished. "It was winter, I was broke, natu-

gay

rally, shabby, hungry, and scared." Wright was very friendly, greeting him, "Hey boy," with a "pleased, surprised expression on his face." He offered Baldwin some bourbon. At this time Baldwin was not much of a drinker, and he was terrified the alcohol on an empty stomach would make him sick. "I was so afraid of falling off my chair and so anxious for him to be interested in me, that I told him far more about the novel than I, in fact, knew about it, madly improvising, one jump ahead of the bourbon, and all the themes which cluttered up my mind" (275). Wright agreed to read the sixty or seventy pages of Baldwin's manuscript, and with Wright's help the young writer was awarded the the Eugene Saxton Fellowship in November 1945, worth $500.

Wright left for Paris in May 1946, and eventually settled there permanently.[10] Baldwin ran into him in the Village where Wright had rented an apartment on Charles Street shortly before Wright and his family left, but for Baldwin the meeting was not pleasant. Wright had done everything he could to assist the young writer and Baldwin felt embarrassed because the outline and first few chapters of his manuscript for his first novel, *Go Tell It on the Mountain,* had been rejected by several publishers. "I was ashamed of myself and I was sure that he was ashamed of me, too. This was utter foolishness on my part, for Richard knew far more about first novels and fledgling novelists than that; but I had been out for his approval. It simply had not occurred to me in those days that anyone *could* approve of me if I had tried something and failed" (276).

Richard Wright fled the limitations placed on him in the United States as a famous *Negro* writer after having been exposed to the relative freedom from racial discrimination he found in Paris. When Wright returned to the United States in January 1947, he was verbally abused regularly by his Village neighbors when he and his wife, Ellen Poplar Wright (who was white), were out together. One time the couple was even attacked by a group of white thugs, and that may have clinched it. In August 1947 Wright left for Europe with no plans to return. James Baldwin, after making arrangements for his family, also escaped to Paris, in November 1948. Although in interviews later in life Baldwin often gave a variety of explanations why he left New York for Paris, in most versions the reasons were similar to those of Richard Wright. The most personally revealing is found in the autobiographical essay entitled "The New Lost Generation," published in *Esquire* magazine in 1961.[11]

It appears that Baldwin believed if he had remained in the United States any longer he would have been killed or would have committed suicide as did his best friend, Eugene Worth. The two young idealists had worked together on various leftist causes in the name of "world socialism." "He and I were Socialists, as were most of our friends, and we dreamed of this utopia, and worked toward it. We may have evinced more conviction than intelligence or skill, and more youthful arrogance than either, but we, nevertheless, had carried petitions about together, fought landlords together, worked as laborers together, been fired together, and starved together" (305).

Baldwin, however, became disillusioned and began to drift away from the movement; and right before Eugene Worth's death, Baldwin quarreled with him about the nature of human nature. His friend believed that "people were good and that one had only to point out to them the right path in order to have them, at once, come flocking to it in loudly rejoicing droves." Baldwin by this time had grown more cynical and jaded. He had learned that, as a Negro, the world "despised and scourged me." "I was different from my friend in that it took me nearly no time to despise the world right back and decide that I would accomplish, in time, with patience and cunning and by becoming indestructible, what I might not, in the moment, achieve by force or persuasion" (305–6).

His friend had fallen in love with a white girl, and her family was trying to have him put in jail. Shortly before Baldwin's final meeting with his friend, the interracial couple had been attacked in the subway by a gang of white teen-agers, and Baldwin's friend was hurt very badly. When his friend asked, "What about love? With the indescribable authority of twenty-two, I snarled, Love! You'd better forget about that my friend. That train is *gone.*" Baldwin regretted the statement almost as soon as he made it. "You're a poet, he said, and you don't believe in love. And he put his head down on the table and began to cry." Baldwin sat there stiffly unable to console his friend. They parted and shortly afterward Baldwin learned that Worth had committed suicide by jumping off the George Washington Bridge (306–7).

It was at this point that Baldwin resolved to leave the country. "There were two reasons for this. One was that I was absolutely certain . . . that I too, if I stayed here, would come to a similar end. I felt then, and to tell the truth, I feel now, that he would not have died in such a way and certainly not so soon, if he had not been black." This death, as well as the changes he had seen in the personalities of Jewish classmates who during the war witnessed the Nazi death camps and subsequently bragged about the number of Germans they "blasted off the face of the earth," convinced Baldwin that he could not remain. "I was afraid that hatred, and the desire for revenge would reach unmanageable proportions in me, and that my end, even if I should not physically die, would be infinitely more horrible than my friend's suicide" (307).

Baldwin arrived in Paris on November 11, 1948, with no funds and few prospects, but saw as a good omen the fact that "the day I got to Paris, before I checked in at the hotel, I was carried to the Deux Magots, where Richard [Wright] sat, with the editors of *Zero* magazine, 'Hey boy!' he cried, looking more surprised and pleased and conspiratorial than ever, and younger and happier" (277). Wright had been in Paris for two years and, given the respectful treatment he received from the French people as a famous writer, he was indeed happy with his personal circumstances and *la vie intellectuelle* in France. James Baldwin's circumstances in Paris in the late 1940s, however, were often desperate and pitiful and in several essays he presented his reflections about his experiences.[12]

In the essay "The New Lost Generation" Baldwin discussed the American expatriates and what they were seeking and finding in postwar Paris. At home often they were fleeing "failure, elimination, and rejection," but somehow managed to make it to Europe and decided to settle there. This certainly was the case for Baldwin, and the glorious new freedom that living in Paris was supposed to bring turned out to be illusory. For Baldwin the real Paris was "a devastating shock." "Paris, from across the ocean, looked like a refuge from American madness; now it was a city four thousand miles from home. It contained—in those days—no doughnuts, no milk shakes, no Coca-Cola, no dry martinis; nothing resembling, for people on our economic level, an American toilet; as for toilet paper, it was yesterday's newspaper." The Paris *gendarmes* harassed American residents with a vengeance, checking to make sure their visas were up to date. "They were not kidding about the three-month period during which every foreigner had to buy a new visa or leave the country. Not a few astounded Americans, unable to call the embassy, spent the night in jail, and steady offenders were escorted to the border" (310).[13]

Paris hotels had no central heating, hot showers, or ham and eggs; and the student hotels did not allow visitors in one's room unless they registered and paid to spend the night. The expatriate writers, artists, and intellectuals who snobbishly thought their fellow Americans at home were particularly juvenile in their unwillingness to confront the ugly realities about themselves and their society found that in Paris they too were considered "immature children" by the more sophisticated Parisians. "We were perfectly willing to refer to all the other Americans as children—in the beginning; we had not known what it meant; we had not known that we were included" (311).

Despite the inconveniences, Baldwin resided in Paris off and on for nine years before returning home for an extended stay. In the 1961 essay on the "new" lost generation he ultimately concluded that "my exile saved my life." The extreme desire for acceptance, to fit in with the crowd, robbed Americans of their individual lives, and kept them from pursuing their own personal vision. "The best thing that happened to the 'new' expatriates was their liberation, finally, from the need to be smothered by what is really nothing more (though it may be something less) than mother love." Baldwin here was referring to "the great emphasis placed on public approval here [the United States], and the resulting and quite insane system of penalties and rewards. It puts a premium on mediocrity and had all but slaughtered any concept of excellence. . . . What Europe still gives an American—or gave us—is the sanction, if one can accept it, to become oneself. No artist can survive without this acceptance. But rare indeed is the American artist who achieved this without first becoming a wanderer, and then, upon his return to his own country, the loneliest and most blackly distrusted of men" (312–13).

James Baldwin became a literary artist despite many unfortunate incidents in Paris and indeed he later used these horrifying personal experiences as material in pursuing his art. Soon after arriving in Paris he was asked to review books and contribute articles to several magazines published in France and the United States. He used these opportunities "to become himself" in literary terms, and in the process alienated the one person Baldwin assumed would understand what he was trying to do. His essay "Everybody's Protest Novel" was first published in *Zero* magazine in Paris in the spring of 1949. In examining what Baldwin considered the poor character development in Harriet Beecher Stowe's classic, *Uncle Tom's Cabin*, he concluded not only that it was "a very bad novel" and presented an incomplete portrait of the people and the times, but it substituted sentimentality, "the ostentatious parading of excessive and spurious emotion," for the revelation of something closer to the truth about human nature. Stowe was more an "impassioned pamphleteer" than a novelist and her book was "a catalogue of violence" that was intended to do nothing more than prove that slavery was wrong. "The virtuous rage of Mrs. Stowe is motivated by nothing so temporal as a concern for the relationship of men to one another—or, even, as she would have claimed, by a concern for their relationship with God—but merely by a panic being hurled into the flames, being caught in traffic with the devil" (30).[14]

The spirit that pervades *Uncle Tom's Cabin*, according to Baldwin, "is not different from that spirit of medieval times which sought to exorcize evil by burning witches; and is not different from that terror which activates a lynch mob." Protest novels often raise "unsettling questions," but the answers provided are "safely ensconced in the social arena, where, indeed, it has nothing to do with anyone, so finally we receive a very definite thrill of virtue from the fact that we are reading such a book at all." Despite the authors' "good intentions" and "lofty purposes," these novels often confuse literature and sociology, degenerate into social fantasies, and "they emerge for what they are: a mirror of our confusion, dishonesty, panic, trapped and immobilized in the sunlit prison of the American dream" (31).

This was also the case with Richard Wright's novel *Native Son*, published in 1940. Baldwin suggested that the life of the main character, Bigger Thomas, is "controlled, defined by his hatred and his fear. And later, his fear drives him to murder and his hatred to rape: he dies, having come through this violence, we are told, for the first time, to a kind of life, having for the first time redeemed his manhood." Baldwin argued that Stowe's and Wright's characters accepted the larger white society's beliefs about "Negro inferiority." "Bigger Thomas is Uncle Tom's descendent, flesh of his flesh, so exactly the opposite a

portrait that, when the books are placed together, it seems that the contemporary Negro novelist and the dead New England woman were locked together
in a deadly, timeless battle; the one uttering merciless exhortations, the other
shouting curses" (33). The tragedy of Bigger Thomas was that "he admits the
possibility of his being sub-human and feels constrained, therefore, to battle
for his humanity according to those brutal criteria bequeathed to him at birth."
Bigger Thomas failed to accept the burden of his humanity or reject society's
cruel and condescending labels. "The failure of the protest novel lies in its rejection of life, the human being, the denial of his beauty, dread, power, in its
insistence that it is his categorization alone which is real and which cannot be
transcended" (33).

Biographer Michel Fabre claimed that Wright endorsed the publication of
"Everybody's Protest Novel" by the editors of *Zero* magazine, but because it
was reprinted in two journals financed by the U.S. Cultural Service, he came to
believe that "Baldwin was letting himself be used in an attempt to destroy
Wright's reputation." Fabre pointed out that "Wright was so irritated at being
singled out by this beginner whom he had recommended for a scholarship that
he did not hesitate to tell him, the day after the article was published, that he
would have no more to do with him." Fabre claimed that while Wright praised
Baldwin's work in public, Wright avoided any personal contact with the young
writer and later privately wrote: "This man disgusts [me] . . . there is a kind of
shameful weeping in what he writes."[15]

In the essay written after Wright's death in 1960, "Alas Poor Richard,"
Baldwin described the meeting at the Brasserie Lipp the day after the earlier essay was published and confirmed that the two men disagreed about the nature
of "protest literature." "'What do you mean, *protest!*' Richard cried. 'All literature is protest. You can't name a single novel that isn't protest.' To this I could
only weakly counter that all literature might be protest but all protest was not
literature. 'Oh,' he would say then, looking as he so often did, bewilderingly
juvenile, 'here you come again with all that art for art's sake crap.' This never
failed to make me furious, and my anger, for some reason, always seemed to
amuse him" (278).

In his defense Baldwin claimed that he was not trying to destroy Wright's
novel or reputation in writing the essay. "It had not entered my mind that either
of these *could* be destroyed, and certainly not by me." Baldwin remorsefully admitted, "Richard was right to be hurt, I was wrong to have hurt him." Baldwin
confessed to what he had done: "I had used [Wright's] work as a kind of springboard into my own. His work was a road-block in my road, the sphinx, really,
whose riddles I had to answer before I could become myself" (277).

But the ideological points over which James Baldwin chose to differ with
Richard Wright in the 1950s closely mirrored the intellectual and artistic dif-

ferences over the "blueprints for Negro writing" that existed between Richard Wright and Zora Neale Hurston earlier in the century. As was discussed in Chapter Five, in his movement away from the positions associated with the Communist Party and advocated in his youth, Richard Wright emphasized the impact of oppression and segregation upon the humanity of southern blacks. In *Black Boy* (1945) and in essays and short stories written in the 1940s and 1950s Wright described the horrors of enslavement and brutalization and "the barrenness of black life" that resulted. Wright agreed with E. Franklin Frazier, Gunnar Myrdal, and other social scientists' view that many African-American cultural practices were pathological versions of those in the larger society, and his books and essays conveyed the heavy toll that oppression had taken on black humanity.

Zora Neale Hurston, on the other hand, accepted southern blacks' basic humanity and their ability individually and collectively to overcome the pathological elements in their lives and surroundings. In *Their Eyes Were Watching God*, *Jonah's Gourd Vine*, and other works Hurston took the humanity of her African-American characters for granted and assumed that they would respond in ways similar to other human beings living under the similar circumstances. But Hurston and other black artists and writers also believed that the religion, values, movements, and cultural practices that evolved over four centuries among African Americans were wonderfully unique in many ways and worthy of serious attention and analysis. This rich folk culture provided the artist with source material for the creation of literary works that drew the universal out of the particular. James Weldon Johnson, Langston Hughes, Sterling Brown, Arna Bontemps, Claude McKay, and other literary artists understood that African-American folk culture reflected the best in humanity and vindicated the race from charges of savagery and inferiority.

James Baldwin's first novel, *Go Tell It on the Mountain*, published in 1952, expressed his belief in the strength and power of African-American religion and its ability to bring about personal liberation. The story is told from the point of view of John Grimes, a fourteen-year-old boy living in Harlem with his family in 1935. The first section, "The Seventh Day," introduced John and described his hatred for his strict and self-righteous father, Gabriel, who favored his younger son, Roy, over John, who is sustained primarily by his mother Elizabeth's love and affection. The various members of the church are also introduced, including Pastor James and Praying Mother Washington, Ella Mae and Elisha, potential young lovers, John's Aunt Florence, Deborah, and Esther. In the religious scenes in the second section, "Prayers of the Saints," it is revealed that Gabriel is not John's real father. Gabriel's illicit affair with Esther, another church member, is also revealed. The third section, "The Threshing Floor," described in vivid and harrowing detail John's conversion experience in which "the Lord . . . laid him out, and turned him around, and wrote his new name down in glory." The visions and revelations he received convinced the boy that he was indeed saved and his sins had been forgiven.[16]

Go Tell It on the Mountain received a very favorable response from the critics, who praised it as "compelling" and full of great "intensity and feeling," and its author as a "promising new addition to the literary scene, and not only the 'Negro literary scene.'" Literary critic Harvey Curtis Webster writing in the *Saturday Review of Literature* found that "Mr. Baldwin's first novel is written as skillfully as many a man's fifth essay in fiction. His handling of the flashbacks so that they show the past without interrupting the drama of the present is masterful. His penetration of the mind of John, especially in the scene of his conversion, is as valid as anything in William James's 'Varieties of Religious Experience' and as moving as the interior monologues in Faulkner's 'As I Lay Dying.'" Critic J. Saunders Redding proclaimed in the *New York Herald Tribune Book Review* that "even the most insensitive readers will put the book down with a troubled feeling of having 'looked on beauty rare.'"[17]

While he was waiting for the publication of *Go Tell It on the Mountain,* and upon his return to Paris in the summer of 1954 after a brief trip to the United States, Baldwin completed his first play, *The Amen Corner,* which was set in the living room and storefront church of evangelist Sister Margaret. Baldwin later claimed that at the time he was afraid to start a new novel. "I did not trust myself to do it. I was really terrified that I would, without even knowing that I was doing it, try to repeat my first success and begin to imitate myself." Although the play also comes out of Baldwin's experiences in the black church, the focus is on the domineering and bigoted Sister Margaret, her tyrannized son, David, and the impact that the return of her husband, Luke, a wandering jazz musician, has on their lives. At the play's climax in the third act, Sister Margaret learns that "To love the Lord is to love all his children—all of them, every-one!—and suffer with them and rejoice with them and never count the cost."[18]

Baldwin was unable to get his play produced by a professional company, but poet and playwright Owen Dodson mounted a student production at Howard University in May 1955, and Baldwin was thrilled. It was not until 1965 that the play was performed by a professional company at the Ethel Barrymore Theater in New York City. Of that production theater critic Harold Clurman declared that "the genuineness the play creates comes from its sure feel for race, place and universality of sentiment. It is folk material unadorned and undoctored. It is the stuff which has made the best in Baldwin. It has heart and reaches the heart."[19] What was clear from these two early fictional works was Baldwin's acceptance of black humanity and his appreciation of African-American folk culture, particularly the religion. James Baldwin may have confessed in his 1961 essay, "Alas Poor Richard," that he knew what he wrote about Wright's *Native Son* in "Everybody's Protest Novel" would hurt the famous author and father figure, but in that 1949 essay he had clearly identified the artistic and ideological differences that would distinguish his fictional works from those of his mentor, Richard Wright.

On the heels of the positive reception of *Go Tell It on the Mountain,* Baldwin's agent, Helen Strauss, was able to get a contract from Beacon Press for a book of essays that would include many of his contributions to magazines and journals over the previous six years. *Notes of a Native Son* was published in November 1955 and was Baldwin's first major contribution to the African-American autobiographical tradition. While some of the essays could be considered social commentary and literary criticism, such as his discussion of "The Harlem Ghetto," his review of Otto Preminger's film *Carmen Jones,* and the account of his brother's 1948 "Journey to Atlanta," they were all highly personalized observations that revealed as much about the ideals and experiences of the author as they did about the social and cultural realities under examination.[20]

In the essay "A Question of Identity," for example, Baldwin observed that "the American in Europe is everywhere confronted with the question of his identity, and this may be taken as the key to all contradictions one encounters when attempting to discuss him." At the personal level (and this certainly was the case for Baldwin), he or she discovers "the terms on which he is related to his country, and to the world. . . . From the vantage point of Europe he discovers his own country. And this discovery which not only brings to an end the alienation of the American from himself, but which also makes clear to him, for the first time, the extent of his involvement in the life of Europe" (99).

This was certainly the case for African Americans in Paris in the postwar period. In the essay "Encounter on the Seine: Black Meets Brown," Baldwin pointed out that, except for the black entertainers, most of the African Americans in Paris lived quite isolated lives because of their desire to escape from things that would remind them of the United States; this included "one's traditional oppressors" as well as "one's traditional kinfolk." Given their small numbers and desire to be forgotten, "the American Negro in Paris is very nearly the invisible man." The Africans in Paris were also to be avoided not merely because of the "gulf of three hundred years" that separates Africans from African Americans, but the reality that the African American in Paris is there for the same reasons as his fellow countrymen. African Americans often come to the realization that it is "in this need to establish himself in relation to his past, he is most American, that this depthless alienation from oneself and one's people is, in sum, the American experience" (39).

It is important to note that Baldwin also included in this volume his essay "Many Thousand Gone," the more lengthy dissection of Wright's *Native Son,* which first appeared in the *Partisan Review* in November 1951. Expanding upon some of the points he made in "Everybody's Protest Novel," Baldwin argued that Bigger Thomas's violence and brutality suggested that "he *is* the

monster created by the American republic, the present awful sum of genera-
tions of oppression." Baldwin accused Wright of presenting "no more than a
single aspect of the story of the 'nigger.' " While he admitted that the novel
was "the most powerful and celebrated statement we have yet had of what it
means to be a Negro in America," Baldwin found it too narrow and superficial
in its presentation of the African-American experience.

> *Native Son* does not convey the altogether savage paradox of the
> American Negro's situation, of which the social reality which we prefer
> with such superficiality to study is but, as it were, the shadow. It is not
> simply the relationship of the oppressed to the oppressor, of master to
> slave, nor is it motivated merely by hatred; it is also, literally and
> morally, a *blood* relationship, perhaps the most profound reality of the
> American experience, and we cannot begin to unlock it until we accept
> how very much it contains of the force and anguish and terror of love
> (69, 76–77).

The remaining essays in *Notes of a Native Son* were autobiographical and
dealt with profound and important personal events, such as his negative experiences as a teenager while working in New Jersey ("Notes of a Native Son"),
his arrest and ten-day jail stay in Paris for being in possession of a sheet stolen
from a Paris hotel ("Equal in Paris"), and his brief stay in a Swiss village where
many of the inhabitants had never before seen an African or African American
("Stranger in the Village"). In the "Autobiographical Notes" at the beginning
of the volume, he mentioned significant literary influences, including the language of Shakespeare, the King James version of the Bible, the novels of Henry
James, as well as "the rhetoric of the store front church." More important, he
made it clear that he accepted and rejoiced in the fact that he was a "Negro"
writer.

> I don't like people who like me because I'm a Negro; neither do I like
> people who find in the same accident grounds for contempt. I love
> America more than any other country in the world, and, exactly for
> this reason, I insist on the right to criticize her perpetually. I think all
> theories are suspect, that the finest principles may be modified, or may
> even be pulverized by the demands of life, and that one must find,
> therefore, one's own moral center and move through the world hop-
> ing that this center will guide one aright. I consider that I have many
> responsibilities, but none greater than this: to last, as Hemingway says,
> and get my work done (4–6).

The reviews of *Notes of a Native Son* were favorable and Baldwin was commended for possessing "a literary style of complexity and power." Langston
Hughes reviewed the volume for *The New York Times Book Review* and de-

clared that "as an essayist [Baldwin] is thought-provoking, tantalizing, irritating, abusing and amusing. And he uses words as a sea uses waves, to flow and beat, advance and retreat, rise and take a bow in disappearing." In a letter to poet Arna Bontemps in February 1953, Hughes had been critical of *Go Tell It on the Mountain* because he believed that Baldwin's poetic language did not suit "the earthiness of the subject-matter." Hughes felt that the novel presented "a low down dirty story in a velvet bag" and claimed that Baldwin "over-writes and over-poeticizes in images way over the heads of the folks supposedly thinking them." Hughes found *Go Tell It on the Mountain* an "art book about folks who are not 'art' folks." In the essays in *Notes of a Native Son*, however, "the words and material suit each other. The thought becomes poetry, and the poetry illuminates the thought." Hughes found that "few American writers handle words more effectively in the essay form than James Baldwin."[21]

By the mid-1950s James Baldwin was beginning to make a reputation for himself as one of the leading "Negro" writers. However, Baldwin also saw himself as an artist, and for this reason (and others), he decided that his next novel would not deal with the black experience. *Giovanni's Room* was one of the most controversial novels published in the United States in the 1950s because it dealt with the then taboo subject of homosexuality. It told the story of David, a clean-cut, middle-class white American who comes to Paris and meets and falls in love with a handsome young Italian bartender named Giovanni. David is engaged to Hella and when she joins him in Paris, he decides to end his relationship with Giovanni. Feeling abandoned, Giovanni goes off on a drunken spree, murders a man after sleeping with him for money, and eventually is caught and guillotined. At the end of the novel David in despair decides not to marry Hella, and runs away to the Côte d'Azur where he picks up sailors he encounters there.[22]

When Baldwin submitted the work to the editors at Beacon, they rejected it, as did Knopf, because of its subject matter. The only other major novel with a homosexual theme to be published and widely read in the United States was Gore Vidal's *The City and the Pillar*. At the time of its publication in 1948 Vidal's novel caused a minor sensation, but most large publishing houses were still reluctant in 1955 to issue works that dealt with this topic. Baldwin sent it to Michael Joseph Publishers in London and it was accepted for publication. Finally, James Silberman, an editor at the Dial Press in New York, read the manuscript, liked it, and recommended its publication to the president, George Joel, who decided to offer Baldwin a contract. This was the beginning of Baldwin's long relationship with Dial.[23]

Baldwin's decision to write and work hard to gain the publication of a novel with a homosexual theme reveals a great deal about his character and personality. Several editors, close friends, and his agent, Helen Strauss, tried to discourage him from attempting to get the manuscript published. On the basis of the positive reception of his earlier works, Baldwin at age thirty-two had an an extremely promising career as a novelist and writer ahead of him, but the publication of *Giovanni's Room*, many thought, would end it. When Baldwin showed the manuscript to the publisher George Knopf, it was reported that Knopf suggested that Baldwin burn it. "They told me to burn it," Baldwin recalled angrily in a later interview. "They said it would ruin me if I tried to get it published. I had turndowns because they treated it like pornography. But I wouldn't accept such treatment."[24]

In several other interviews later in life, Baldwin elaborated on the dangers that were associated with the publication of *Giovanni's Room*. This work, as well as others, represented turning points in his life and career. *"Giovanni's Room* was that at one point, too,"* Baldwin told interviewer Wolfgang Binder in 1980, "because it was such a dangerous thing for me, and I paid for that, too. There were all the obvious condemnations. That's cool." He was condemned "for moral reasons." "That was a put-down, you know, but I survived. And again, that was an important turning point, too, that I survived. I had to get that out of the way in order to get to work. But I think that is finally true for everything I do." But what was striking was the fact that at the time he was emerging as an important "Negro writer," there were no black characters in *Giovanni's Room*. Baldwin was asked about that by Jordan Elgrably in an interview in 1984. "I thought I would seal off Giovanni into a short story, but it turned into *Giovanni's Room,"* Baldwin recalled. "I certainly could not possibly have—not at that point in my life—handled the other great weight, the 'Negro Problem.' The sexual-moral light was a hard thing to deal with. I could not handle both propositions in the same book. There was no room for it. I might do it differently today, but then, to have a black presence in the book at that moment, and in Paris, would have been quite beyond my powers."[25]

The publication of *Giovanni's Room* was necessary and important because James Baldwin wanted to be considered an "artist" as well as a Negro writer. Baldwin was very close to his brother David, who later served as his personal assistant and manager. When David Baldwin was interviewed by Fern Eckman in 1965, he made an insightful observation about his brother. "One thing that Jimmy's got that's good is that he's stubborn. When they said, '*Giovanni's Room* will destroy your career,' he said, 'I'm sorry—that'll have to happen.' If he'd allowed them to frighten him that way, he'd never been able to write again."[26]

Ultimately, Baldwin's faith in himself as an artist was rewarded by the very positive response of the critics to *Giovanni's Room*. William Esty writing in *The New Republic* found it to be "the best novel dealing with homosexuality I have read." In the *New York Times* the well-respected critic Granville Hicks pointed out that "much of the novel is laid in scenes of squalor, with the background of characters as grotesque and repulsive as any that can be found in [Marcel] Proust's *Cities of the Plain,* but even as one is dismayed by Mr. Baldwin's materials, one rejoices in the skill with which he renders them. Nor is there any suspicion that he is working these materials merely for the sake of shocking the reader. On the contrary, his intent is most serious." And David Karp in the *Saturday Review* agreed that although some readers may find some of the characters and scenes "loathesome" and "detestable," they are handled "with a very delicate sense of good taste." Karp ultimately concluded that "Mr. Baldwin has taken a very special theme and treated it with great artistry and restraint."[27]

By the time *Giovanni's Room* appeared, Baldwin was back in Paris and in September 1956 he attended the African writers conference at the Sorbonne. Following the conference he traveled to Corsica where he worked on the early drafts of his next novel, *Another Country.* It was at this time that Baldwin began to read the reports about civil rights protests taking place in the southern United States. In May 1954 the U.S. Supreme Court in its *Brown v. Board of Education* decision had outlawed segregation in public education. Following the decision the NAACP, which had successfully litigated the desegregation suit, sent out directives to its various southern branches to begin to demand the desegregation of public schools in their area. Newspaper and magazine reports were being published about the brave black children who volunteered to be the first to attend previously all-white schools in the face of threats, intimidation, and violence from local whites.[28]

South to a Very Frightening Place

JAMES BALDWIN returned to the United States from Paris in July 1957 for several reasons. He had signed a contract with Dial Press for another book of essays and he and his agent, Helen Strauss, had agreed that he needed several additional articles to complete the volume. Baldwin was also aware that something important was happening in the South and it was difficult to understand from Europe exactly what was going on. When he arrived home, he was commissioned by *Harper's* and *Partisan Review* to go south and report his personal impressions. Baldwin had never been to the South and initially he was somewhat fearful and uncertain about traveling there. After remaining for several months in New York City, he set out on his trip in September 1957 and his first stop was Charlotte, North Carolina, where he interviewed a teenage boy and his family who were caught up in the school desegregation campaign.[29]

"A Hard Kind of Courage" was published first in *Harper's* magazine in October 1958, and was later included in his second book of essays, *Nobody Knows My Name: More Notes of a Native Son,* under the title "A Fly in the Buttermilk." As was the case with many other essays, Baldwin began with a confession. "The South had always frightened me. How deeply it frightened me—though I had never seen it—and how soon, was one of the things my dreams revealed to me while I was there." But he was motivated by his curiosity and his desire to understand what was going on. "I wondered where the children got their strength—the strength in this case, to walk through mobs to get to school." At the same time that Baldwin was heading south (September 1957), President Dwight Eisenhower had to call out the 101st Airborne to enforce the desegregation order at Central High School in Little Rock, Arkansas, and to protect the nine black children who were being prevented from enrolling in the school by violent mobs of angry whites. The "grace under pressure" exhibited by the Little Rock Nine was reported by the news media from all over the world.[30]

Gus Roberts, the boy Baldwin interviewed in Charlotte, was fifteen years old and had recently "integrated" the local all-white high school. At first the boy was silent and his mother did all the talking. "Mrs. R was a very strong-willed woman, handsome, quiet-looking, dressed in black. Nothing, she told me, beyond name-calling, had marked G's first day at school; but on the second day she received the last of several threatening phone calls. She was told that if she didn't want her son 'cut to ribbons' she had better keep him home. She heeded this warning to the extent of calling the chief of police." At the school the white students only attempted to block Gus's entrance until the principal showed up and escorted him in as the students angrily shouted "Nigger-lover!" (163).

When Baldwin asked Gus about his first day, he said that there was mostly name-calling, which didn't bother him. One student tripped Gus in the hall and knocked him down, but later apologized in the presence of the principal. Mrs. Roberts made it clear that the reason she allowed her son to be subjected to this was *not* because she wanted him to be around white people. "You see that boy? Well, he's always been a straight-A student. He didn't hardly have to work at it. . . . Well, when he was to —— High School [the black school], he didn't have no homework or if he did, he could get it done in five minutes. Then, there he was, out in the streets, getting into mischief, and all he did all day in school was to keep clowning to make the other boys laugh. He wasn't learning nothing and didn't nobody care if he *never* learned nothing and I could just see what was going to happen to him if he kept on like that." Baldwin was told that forty-five girls had dropped out of the black school the year before because they had become pregnant, and less than two weeks before Baldwin arrived, eighteen boys from the school had been arrested and sent to work on the chain gang (164–65).

"Don't the teachers care about the students?" Baldwin's inquiry brought laughter. In his essay, he commented: "How could they care? How much could they do if they *did* care? There were too many children, from shaky homes and worn-out parents, in aging inadequate plants. They could be considered, most of them, already doomed. Besides, the teachers' jobs were safe. They were responsible only to the principal, an appointed official, whose judgment, apparently, was never questioned by his (white) superiors or confreres." Baldwin was told that the seventy-five-year-old black principal was a strict disciplinarian who punished students by allowing other students to beat them with leather belts. This had happened once to Gus. "The teachers have themselves arrived at a dead end, for in the segregated school system they cannot rise any higher, and the students are aware of this. Both students and teachers soon cease to struggle" (165).

Baldwin was informed there had been no reprisals against the Roberts family members for their actions, but several whites had made it clear they disapproved. When Baldwin asked if Gus wanted to return to the segregated black high school, he responded in the negative. "I'll make it. I ain't going back." Baldwin understood that pride and silence were Gus's only weapons. "'It's hard enough,' the boy said later, still in control, but with flashing eyes, 'to keep quiet and keep walking when they call you nigger. But if anybody ever spits on me, I *know* I'll have to fight.' His mother laughs, laughs to ease them both, then looks at me and says, 'I wonder sometimes what makes white folks so mean' " (166–67).

Baldwin later got an interview with the principal of the white school, who made it clear that he was no "Nigger-lover," and opposed school desegregation because "it was simply contrary to everything he'd ever seen or believed." The principal claimed that he did not hate black people, but merely expected them to stay in their place. Baldwin commented,

> I certainly did believe him; he impressed me as being a very gentle and honorable man. But I could not avoid wondering if he had ever really *looked* at a Negro and wondered about the life, aspirations, the universal humanity hidden behind the dark skin. As I wondered, when he told me that race relations in his city were "excellent" and had not been strained by recent developments, how on earth he managed to hold on to this delusion (168).

The white principal countered Baldwin's suggestion that the black children were only interested in getting a decent education by suggesting that "the colored school was just as good as the white ones." "Still," Baldwin responded, "I should think that the trouble in this situation is that it's very hard for *you* to face a child and treat him unjustly because of something for which he is no more responsible than *you* are." The principal had to agree, but offered no opinion on what the future held, only pointing out that he was a "religious man" and that he believed "the Creator will always help us find a way to solve our problems. If a man loses that, he's lost everything." Baldwin agreed and when the principal asked if he was from the North, he affirmed it. "Well . . . you've got your troubles too." Baldwin also agreed and ended the essay prophetically. "I did not say what I was thinking, that our troubles were the same trouble and that, unless we were swift and honest, what is happening in the South today will be happening in the North tomorrow" (169).

From Charlotte, Baldwin went to Atlanta, Georgia, to meet with the young minister who had led the successful bus boycott in Montgomery, Alabama, Martin Luther King, Jr. In an essay entitled "The Dangerous Road Before Martin Luther King," published in *Harper's* in February 1961, Baldwin described this meeting. King was holed up in a hotel working on his book, *Stride Toward Freedom*, his autobiographical account of the Montgomery, Alabama, bus boycott that brought an end to the practice of segregation in the city's public transportation system. Baldwin felt guilty about interrupting the young minister, since by this time King had become "a world famous man." Yet King was open and friendly and Baldwin liked him immediately.

> King impressed me then and impresses me now as a man solidly anchored in those spiritual realities concerning which he can be so eloquent. This divests him of the hideous piety which is so prevalent in his profession, and it saves him from the ghastly self-importance which until recently, was all that allowed one to be certain one was addressing a Negro leader. King cannot be considered chauvinist at all, not even incidentally, or part of the time, or under stress, or subconsciously. What he says to Negroes he will say to whites; and what he says to whites he will say to Negroes. He is the first Negro leader, or the first in many generations, of whom this can be said; most of his predecessors were in the extraordinary position of saying to white men, *Hurry,* while saying to black men, *Wait.* This fact is of utmost importance. It says a great deal about the situation which produced King and in which he operates, and of course, it tells us a great deal about the man (246).[31]

After the brief meeting in the hotel room, Baldwin saw King at a party later that evening. Baldwin noted that King remained in a corner, drinking something nonalcoholic, and obviously wanting to get out of there as soon as possible. "I remember feeling, rather as though he were a younger muchloved, and menaced brother, that he seemed very slight and vulnerable to be taking on such tremendous odds" (248). Baldwin left Atlanta for Montgomery the following day, and when he arrived, he made sure he rode the newly desegregated buses. Baldwin was struck by the silence of the bus riders, both black and white. "This silence made me think of nothing so much as the silence which follows a really serious lovers' quarrel: the whites, beneath their cold hostility, were mystified and deeply hurt." The blacks not only refused to stay "in their place," but refused to accept whites' image of them. "Without this image, it seemed to me, the whites were abruptly and totally lost. The very foundations of their private and public worlds were being destroyed" (249).

Baldwin wanted to hear Rev. King preach, so he attended the Sunday morning service at the Dexter Avenue Baptist Church. Baldwin, who had been raised in the black church, felt something new and different about the service at King's church in Montgomery. "Here it was, totally familiar and yet completely new," and when Rev. King rose to preach, Baldwin came to understand what was different. Before, the black church was a sanctuary, and the minister gave his congregation "sustenance for another day's journey." In Montgomery in 1957, however, the people had begun this new civil rights struggle, and the people had chosen King as their leader. Now that King had accepted and taken on this struggle, "the place that they had prepared for him, their struggle, became absolutely indistinguishable from his own, and took over and controlled his life. He suffered with them and thus, he helped them to suffer. The joy which filled this church, therefore, was a joy achieved by people who have ceased to delude themselves about an intolerable situation, who have found their prayers for a leader miraculously answered, and who now know that they can change their situation, if they will" (250).

Baldwin believed that Rev. King's power lay only partly in his brilliance and eloquence. It was King's intimate knowledge of the people he addressed and his forthrightness and willingness to tell the truth that empowered him. "We know," Baldwin recalled King saying that Sunday morning, "that there are many things wrong in the white world. But there are many things wrong in the black world, too. We can't keep on blaming the white man. There are many things we must do for ourselves." Not only must blacks save more of their money and raise their moral standards, "we've got to stop lying to the white man. Every time you let the white man think *you* think segregation is right, you are cooperating with him in doing *evil*. The next time . . . the white man asks you what you think of segregation, you tell him, Mr. Charlie, I think it's wrong and I wish you'd do something about it by nine o'clock tomorrow morning." Baldwin later heard King explain to one of his parishioners that "bigotry was a disease and that the greatest victim of this disease was not the bigot's object, but the bigot himself. And these people could only be saved by love. In liberating oneself, one was liberating them" (250–51).

Following his trip south and meeting with Martin Luther King, James Baldwin became committed to the civil rights movement and in the early 1960s did all he could to promote the campaigns and support the activities of the leaders and organizations. Baldwin was also able to devote more time to his writing because his financial situation was improving. Not only was he receiving money from his books and magazine articles, he received a grant from the Ford Foundation in February 1959 to support him while he worked on his next novel. When he was notified in late 1958 that *Giovanni's Room* was optioned for a Broadway production as a play, he apprenticed himself to director-playwright Elia Kazan to learn all he could about the theater, and worked with Kazan on productions of Archibald MacLeish's *J.B.* and Tennessee Williams's *Sweet Bird of Youth*. At the time Kazan suggested to Baldwin that he consider doing a play on the Emmett Till case. Till was a fifteen-year-old boy from Chicago who was killed in Mississippi in 1955 for allegedly whistling at a white woman. The whites accused of his murder were eventually acquitted following a lengthy trial. Baldwin would use the Till case as the point of departure for his Broadway play, *Blues for Mister Charlie,* produced by the Actors Studio in April 1964.[32]

Baldwin's second volume of essays, *Nobody Knows My Name,* was published in July 1961 and was both a critical and financial success. The book remained on the *New York Times* best-seller list for over six months, and James Baldwin became one of the most famous black writers in the United States, and almost everyone in the country knew his name. The volume included "Princes and Powers," his report on the 1956 African writers conference in Paris; "A Fly in the Buttermilk," his essay on Gus Roberts and public school desegregation in Charlotte; and "Alas Poor Richard," his assessment and personal reminiscence of his relationship with Richard Wright. Other previously published essays included in the volume touched on literary and artistic topics. In "The Discovery of What It Means to Be an American," first published in January 1959, Baldwin compared the status of the writer and artist in Europe and the United States, and concluded that the artist was better off in Europe because "he does not have to pretend to be something that he is not, for the artist does not encounter in Europe the same suspicion he encounters here." American writers went to Europe because they found things that were missing in this country, "a sense of the mysterious and inexorable limits of life, a sense, in a word, of tragedy (173, 176).[33]

"The Male Prison" was Baldwin's 1954 review of *Madeleine,* an autobiographical work by French writer André Gide; and "The Northern Protestant" was Baldwin's report on his visit to Stockholm, Sweden, in December 1959 and his interview with filmmaker Ingmar Bergman. Baldwin also attended the third annual *Esquire* magazine symposium on "The Role of the Writer in America" in San Francisco in October 1960, and "Notes for a Hypothetical Novel" was the talk he gave at that conference. There he emphasized the need for the writer "to describe things which other people are too busy to describe." Baldwin felt that the problem with Americans was that they prefer to live in a world of fantasy rather than confront the painful truth about themselves and their society. Thus the role of the writer is to help the society deal with harsh realities. "A country is only as strong as the people who make it up and the country turns into what people want it to become." The United States was in the process of being transformed, hopefully for the better. "I don't believe any longer that we can afford to say that it is entirely out of our hands. We made the world we're living in and we can make it over" (244).

"Faulkner and Desegregation" was Baldwin's response to the famous southern writer William Faulkner's suggestion that blacks "go slow" in the campaigns for first-class citizenship rights. According to Faulkner, "things are getting better" in the South, and white southerners need more time to work out their "moral identity." Baldwin disagreed. "The time Faulkner asks for does not exist—and he is not the only southerner who knows it. There is never time in the future in which we will work out our salvation. The challenge is in the moment, the time is always now" (151–52).

The essay "The Black Boy Looks at the White Boy" was Baldwin's response to Norman Mailer's essay "The White Negro," first published in 1957; and the assessment of Baldwin as a writer in Mailer's 1959 book *Advertisements for Myself.* As was the case in many other essays, before and after, Baldwin presented his own unique blending of literary criticism and autobiography. Baldwin had met Mailer in Paris in 1956, and they spent some time together debating literary and political issues late into the night at the homes of mutual friends and in bars and cafés. Baldwin claimed that he liked Mailer, admired his work as a novelist, and considered him one of his friends. In "The White Negro" Mailer tried to make the point that the "hipsters" of the Beat Generation were rebels against society, and in their speech, dress, and mannerisms as well as their rejection of the "sophisticated inhibitions of civilization" and strong desire for the "pleasures of the body," they emulated blacks. Mailer believed that alienated white youths of the 1950s had accepted "the black code to fit their facts. The hipster had absorbed the existentialist synapses of the Negro, and for practical purposes could be considered a white Negro."[34]

In the evaluation of James Baldwin in *Advertisements for Myself,* Mailer said he thought *Giovanni's Room* was "a bad book but mostly a brave one," and suggested that Baldwin was "too charming" to be considered a major American writer. In "The Black Boy Looks at the White Boy," Baldwin confessed that he was hurt and disappointed by Mailer's assessment, since he considered Mailer a friend. Regarding "The White Negro," Baldwin noted that while he had liked Mailer's novels *The Naked and the Dead* and *Barbary Coast,* "I could not, with the best will in the world, make any sense of 'The White Negro' and, in fact, it was hard for me to imagine that this essay had been written by the same man who wrote the novels" (296).

Baldwin went on to argue that "The White Negro" had more to do with the white American man's sense of his own masculinity ("I think that I know something about American masculinity which most men of my generation do not know because they have not been menaced by it in the way I have been") than about black men. Baldwin believed that white men were hung up on certain delusions about black male sexuality and that Jack Kerouac and the other Beat poets and writers' preoccupation with the "male mystique" was a "grim system of delusions" that at times was "lewdly vicious" and "infantile." "Why malign the sorely menaced sexuality of Negroes in order to justify the white man's own sexual panic?" Baldwin felt that many writers of the Beat Generation had abdicated their artistic and social responsibilities and built up "fantasy structures" that imprison rather than protect them. "I know that this point of view is not terribly fashionable these days," Baldwin admitted, "but I think we *do* have a responsibility, not only to ourselves and our own time, but to those who are coming after us. . . . And I suppose that this responsibility can only be discharged by dealing as truthfully as we know how with our present fortunes, these present days" (297, 303).

The autobiographical essays "Fifth Avenue, Uptown," "East River, Downtown," and "Nobody Knows My Name" became the most talked-about pieces in the collection because in each one Baldwin predicted the violence and racial rioting that would erupt in American cities in the 1960s. In "Nobody Knows My Name" Baldwin recounted his various trips to Atlanta, Birmingham, and other southern cities in the late 1950s. He noted that the changing attitudes, especially among younger blacks, and failure of southern white politicians to deal with this change,

> is absolutely certain, sooner or later, to create great trouble in these cities. When a race riot occurs in Atlanta, it will not spread merely to Birmingham, for example. (Birmingham is a doomed city.) The trouble will spread to every metropolitan center in the nation which has a significant Negro population. And this is not only because the ties between northern and southern Negroes are still very close. It is because the nation, the entire nation, has spent a hundred years avoiding the question of the place of the black man in it (192).

While the essay "In Search of a Majority," based on an address given at Kalamazoo College in 1960, held out the hope of some kind of reconciliation between black and white Americans on the basis of love for one another, Baldwin was talking about the kind of love that brings liberation from oppression. "Love does not begin and end the way we seem to think it does. Love is a battle, love is a war; love is a growing up. No one in the world—the entire world—knows more—knows Americans better or, odd as it may sound, loves them more than the American Negro." From the beginning of the nation, blacks and whites have been bound together, and "these walls—these artificial walls which have been up so long to protect us from something we fear, must come down . . . to create a country in which there are no minorities—for the first time in the history of the world" (234).

Unfortunately, wherever Baldwin went, he found resistance to the creation of some type of integrated American identity, and given the African-American mood, violence was inevitable. When he witnessed the conditions in Harlem, he found that "the pressure within the ghetto causes the ghetto walls to expand, and this expansion is always violent. White people hold the line as long as they can, and in as many ways as they can, from verbal intimidation to physical violence." In "Fifth Avenue, Uptown," which explored the mental and physical circumstances for the residents of Harlem, Baldwin declared that it was folly for northerners to think that "they can ignore what is happening in northern cities because what is happening in Little Rock and Birmingham is worse." Violence is virtually inevitable because "the spirit of the South is the spirit of America. . . . It is a terrible, an inexorable, law that one cannot deny the humanity of another without diminishing one's own: in the face of one's victim, one sees oneself. Walk through the streets of Harlem and see what we, this nation, have become" (213).

In "East River, Downtown," Baldwin pointed out that American government officials often try to blame the communists for violent protests against American imperialism abroad and racism and discrimination at home. In the South the government blames "outside agitators," in the North "it blames the Kremlin," and "we thus give credit to the Communists for attitudes and victories which are not theirs. We make them champions of the oppressed, and they could not, of course, be more delighted." And all of these actions play into the hands of the Nation of Islam, which becomes more and more powerful everyday. The Black Muslims were calling for a complete separation of the races, they wanted nothing from "American democracy," and the evidence that blacks were unwanted in American society was all on their side. "This is the great power a Muslim speaker has over his audience. His audience has not heard this truth—the truth about their daily lives—honored by anyone else." Baldwin believed that "it is quite impossible to argue with a Muslim concerning the actual state of Negroes in this country—the truth, after all, is the truth." (264–65).

James Baldwin's third novel, *Another Country,* was published in May 1962, and although it received only mixed reviews from the critics, it soon made its way to the top of best-seller lists, assisted greatly by several attacks on it by critics who considered it lewd and pornographic. Set in New York City, the major character, Rufus Scott, a young black drummer in a jazz band, has tortured relationships with Leona, a southern white woman, and Eric, a white homosexual actor. Although Rufus commits suicide early in the novel, the lives of the other characters, including that of Vivaldo Moore, his best friend, who is white, and Ida, his sister, are described in terms of their ultimately destructive relationships with Rufus. Ida and Vivaldo have a love affair, but this interracial romance is doomed because of the guilt and pain over how they had responded to Rufus's self-destructive behavior. The only character who manages to have a somewhat positive and romantic sexual relationship is Eric, who meets and falls in love with a French boy, Yves. Critic Granville Hicks in the *Saturday Review* declared that "James Baldwin's *Another Country* is a novel about love and hate, and more about hate than love. In its totality and with all due allowance for occasional weaknesses in writing, it is one of the most powerful novels of our time. The complexities of love have seldom been explored more subtly or at greater depth, and perhaps the power of hate has never been communicated with more terrifying force."[35]

Even before the publication of *Another Country* James Baldwin had secured for himself a place in the highest echelons of the American literary pantheon. By 1963 he was not only a controversial artist and novelist, but an uncompromising civil rights advocate who excelled at making clear the meanings of explosive current events from the vantage point of the oppressed and rebellious. The public witness was called upon again and again to "go tell it on the mountain," and James Baldwin, the literary artist, testified and was thus transformed simultaneously into James Baldwin, "black spokesman."

Encounters with Father Figures: Elijah Muhammad

FROM THE publication of *Nobody Knows My Name* in 1961 and throughout the 1960s, Baldwin devoted more and more of his time to civil rights causes, speaking and lecturing around the country for the benefit of the Congress of Racial Equality (CORE), the Student Nonviolent Coordinating Committee (SNCC), and other civil rights groups. He was interviewed regularly on radio and television, and at times appeared on the same programs with Malcolm X, the fiery young spokesperson for the Nation of Islam. In September 1962 Baldwin was invited to dinner at the home of Elijah Muhammad, the leader of the Nation of Islam. The article he wrote about the meeting, "Letter from a Region in My Mind," was published in *The New Yorker* in November 1962. This autobiographical essay, along with "A Letter to My Nephew," first published in *The Progressive* magazine in December 1962, became the contents for one of Baldwin's most famous works, *The Fire Next Time*, issued by the Dial Press in May 1963.[36]

In "A Letter to My Nephew," which was titled "My Dungeon Shook" in *The Fire Next Time*, Baldwin provided some advice that he thought would assist the teenager in his movement into manhood. Baldwin wanted his nephew to avoid what ultimately destroyed the boy's grandfather, the sad reality that "he really believed what white people said about him." American racial practices have brought about the destruction of hundreds of thousands of black lives and minds in the enforcement of white supremacy, and the young black male's con-

ditions and future are overdetermined by his color. "You were born into a society which spelled out with brutal clarity, and in as many ways possible, that you
were a worthless human being. You were not expected to aspire to excellence: you
were expected to make peace with mediocrity." Baldwin warned his nephew
not to participate in this socially reinforced self-destruction. "You can only be destroyed by believing that you really are what the white world calls a *nigger.* I tell
you this because I love you, and please don't ever forget it." Baldwin counseled
his nephew to "trust your experience" and "know from whence you came" because
then there will be "no limit to where you can go" (333–36).

The first part of what was now titled "Down at the Cross: A Letter from a
Region of My Mind," dealt with Baldwin's conversion experience when he was
fourteen years old, his time in the pulpit as a child preacher, and his subsequent
disillusionment with the Christians he met and the "prohibitions, crimes, and
hypocrisies of the Christian Church." Baldwin recalled encountering speakers
for the Nation of Islam on street corners in Harlem, but "I have long had a
very definite tendency to tune out the moment I come anywhere near a pulpit
or a soapbox." Baldwin had heard it all before, and "I dismissed the Nation of
Islam's demand for a separate black economy in America . . . as willful, and
even mischievous, nonsense." But when he noticed how the police seemed to
be afraid of the Muslims and the "silent intensity" of the black crowd listening
to their teachings, Baldwin decided he needed to pay more attention (352–53).

The Black Muslims believed that all white people were devils and that
white power and control were coming to an end within ten or fifteen years.
These were not new ideas or concepts in the black community, but why was
the Nation of Islam attracting so many members? Baldwin mentioned a whole
list of reasons and causes for the change in attitude. Europe's loss of her colonial empire in the East and West, the creation of independent black nations in
these former colonial territories, and the African nationalism formed through
experiences in the various wars of liberation certainly had something to do
with it. But primarily the Nation of Islam's beliefs were spreading among
blacks because of the growing disillusionment and fear at the alternatives provided from greater contact with and integration into white, Christian civilization. Violent hostility and oppressive police practices had led to the creation
of governmental agencies working for the extermination of targeted ethnic
groups within white European societies. Genocide as governmental policy was
a very real element in the lives of outcast and marginal groups and individuals
in Europe, the United States, and other parts of the Americas. The southern
government officials gave African Americans little indication that they would
refrain from using genocidal tactics to keep blacks "in their place." Thank
goodness, Baldwin exclaims, these southern politicians had no access to tacti-
cal nuclear weaponry.

"In the end," Baldwin concluded, "it is the threat of universal extinction hanging over all the world today that changes, totally and forever, the nature of reality and brings into devastating question the true meaning of man's history. We human beings now have the power to exterminate ourselves; this seems to be the entire sum of our achievement." This is what the white God had wrought, and the Black Muslims came along and declared, "God is black. All black men belong to Islam; they have been chosen. And Islam will rule the world." The Black Muslims cleaned up in the black lower- and working-class communities. "It is this dream," Baldwin mused, "this sweet possibility, that thousands of oppressed black men and women now carry away with them after the Muslim has spoken, through the dark, noisome ghetto streets, into the hovels where so many have perished. The white God has not delivered them; perhaps the Black God will" (356–57).

Baldwin was not exactly sure why the Honorable Elijah Muhammad had asked him to dinner. In "Down at the Cross" and later in *No Name in the Street*, Baldwin reminisced about his personal meetings and encounters with Malcolm X. Baldwin and the brilliant Muslim spokesperson had appeared together on several radio and television shows and in the discussions Baldwin often seconded the positions put forward by Malcolm. After leaving one of these TV shows, someone came up to him and said, "Goodbye, Mr. James Baldwin. We'll soon be addressing you as Mr. James X." Baldwin thought to himself, "My God, if this goes on much longer, you probably will" (358).

Perhaps Elijah Muhammad had seen these programs and that was the reason for the invitation. In any case Baldwin arrived somewhat fearful about being "summoned into a royal presence," but was soon made to feel welcome by the young disciples who surrounded Mr. Muhammad. Indeed, when the thin, small man with a slender face and winning smile entered the room, "something came into the room with him—his disciples' joy at seeing him, his joy at seeing them." The scene was striking because "it is so rare that people enjoy one another" (359).

At dinner Baldwin sat to the left of Muhammad, who headed the long men's table. Baldwin recalled that "whenever Elijah spoke, a kind of chorus arose from the table, saying, 'Yes, that's right.' This began to set my teeth on edge." And the honorable one tended "to ricochet his questions and comments off someone else on their way to you." Baldwin found this annoying, but through these interchanges he was able to learn the source of the Muslim leader's power and authority. "Elijah's power came from his single-mindedness," Baldwin finally concluded.

There is nothing calculated about him; he means every word he says. . . . "The so-called American Negro" is the only reason Allah has permitted the United States to endure so long; the white man's time was up in 1913, but it is the will of Allah that this lost black nation, the black men of this country, be redeemed from their white masters and returned to the true faith, which is Islam. Until this is done—and it will be accomplished very soon—the total destruction of the white man is being delayed. Elijah's mission is to return "the so-called Negro" to Islam, to separate the chosen of Allah from this doomed nation (361).

There were many areas where Baldwin felt that the position assumed by the Nation of Islam mirrored his own beliefs. Given the brutal and discriminatory treatment of the black man in white-controlled society, "it is not hard for him to think of white people as devils. For the horrors of the American Negro's life there has been almost no language." Baldwin shared much of the Muslim leader's disdain for the practices of so-called Christians. But Baldwin assured Mr. Muhammad, "I left the church twenty years ago, and I haven't joined anything since." This was also Baldwin's way of letting the Muslims know that, despite the fact that he shared the same experiences that led other blacks to join the Nation of Islam, they were not going to convert him. To his way of thinking the black Muslims indulged in too much "fantasy" if they thought the U.S. government was going to turn over "six or seven states" to African Americans. This was not going to happen anytime soon, and if the American empire were going to fall sometime soon, why not stay and help it along its decadent, sleazy way. "If I were a Muslim," Baldwin declared, "I would not hesitate to utilize—or indeed, to exacerbate—the social and spiritual discontent that reigns here, for, at the very worst, I would merely have contributed to the destruction of a house I hated, and it would not matter if I perished, too. One has been perishing here so long!" (365).

James Baldwin could not become a Muslim, but there were more similarities than differences between Elijah Muhammad's black separatism and Baldwin's "so-called integrationism." While Baldwin admitted that he "really wished to be able to love and honor him as a witness, an ally, and a father," his differences with Elijah Muhammad involved matters of principle. "I am very much concerned that American Negroes achieve their freedom here in the United States," Baldwin observed, "but I am also concerned for their dignity, for the health of their souls, and must oppose any attempt that Negroes may make to do to others what has been done to them. I think I know—we see it around us every day—the spiritual wasteland to which this road leads. It is so simple a fact and one that is hard, apparently, to grasp: *Whoever debases others is debasing himself.* This is not a mystical statement, but a realistic one, which is proved by the eyes of any Alabama sheriff—and I would not like to see Negroes ever arrive at so wretched a condition" (369).

Baldwin was attacked later in the decade by young militants who accused him of "loving the white man too much." Black Panther Eldridge Cleaver in his popular 1968 volume, *Soul on Ice,* included an essay entitled "Notes on a

Native Son." Not only did Cleaver argue that Norman Mailer's essay, "The White Negro" was "prophetic and penetrating in its understanding of the psychology involved in the accelerating confrontation of black and white in America," he also claimed that "there is in James Baldwin's work the most grueling, agonizing, total hatred of the blacks, particularly of himself, and the most shameful, fanatical, fawning, sycophantic love of whites that one can find in the writings of any black American of note in our time." And without any indication that he actually read and studied Richard Wright's *Black Boy* and the autobiographical essays later published as *American Hunger*, or Wright's later novels, such as *The Outsider* or *Savage Holiday*, Cleaver claimed that "of all black American novelists, and indeed of all American novelists of any hue, Richard Wright reigns supreme for his profound political, economic, and social reference." In contrast, "it is Baldwin's work which is so void of a political, economic, or even a social reference." What was clear from this essay was Cleaver's strong distaste for the homosexual themes in Baldwin's novel *Another Country* (there is no indication that he even knew about *Giovanni's Room*), and his profound misreading of Baldwin's definition of "love" between black and white Americans.[37]

In *The Fire Next Time*, which Cleaver claimed he read and liked, Baldwin made it clear that he believed that white Americans were lying about themselves and their past and as a result "a vast amount of the energy that goes into what we call the Negro problem is produced by the white's profound desire not to be judged by those who are not white, not to be seen as he is" (374). It is the responsibility of those who love them to tell them the truth, so that they too may be set free. "Love takes off the masks that we fear we cannot live without and know we cannot live within. I use the word 'love' here not merely in the personal sense but as a state of being, or a state of grace—not in the infantile American sense of being made happy but in the tough and universal sense of quest and daring and growth" (375).

James Baldwin understood that "the white man's unadmitted—and apparently, to him unspeakable—private fears and longings are projected onto the Negro." The white man has nothing to teach the Negro, but much to learn. "The white man is himself in sore need of new standards, which will release him from his confusion and place him once again in fruitful communion with the depths of his own being." As far as Baldwin was concerned, "the only thing white people have that black people need, or should want, is power—and no one holds power forever" (374–75).

Thus James Baldwin in *The Fire Next Time* continued to warn white Americans about the alternatives they had created for the African Americans, and predicted the responses of those more militant blacks who would challenge the power and authority of white capitalists and government officials over the affairs of the "emerging black nation" within the United States.

Ideological Brotherhood:
Encounters with Martin Luther King, Jr.

THE FIRE NEXT TIME zoomed to the top of the best-seller lists soon after its publication in May 1963. *Life* magazine did a nine-page spread on Baldwin, and his face appeared on the cover of *Time* magazine on May 17, 1963. A week later Baldwin was scheduled to meet briefly with Attorney General Robert Kennedy at his Virginia home, Hickory Hill, but because Baldwin was late, Kennedy suggested that they meet the next day in New York City. Baldwin showed up at the attorney general's hotel with an entourage that included Lorraine Hansberry, Harry Belafonte, Lena Horne, Rip Torn, Kenneth Clark, and Martin Luther King's lawyer, Clarence Jones. Kennedy was interested in gaining Baldwin's perspective on the current racial crisis, but the meeting turned into a highly emotional shouting match between Kennedy and Baldwin over the failure of the federal government to do all that was necessary to protect the lives of civil rights workers in the South.[38]

The meeting with Robert Kennedy was an exercise in frustration and Baldwin returned to France shortly afterward. But when he learned of plans for the March on Washington on August 28, 1963, to put pressure on the U.S. Congress to pass the civil rights bill then stalled in committee, Baldwin made arrangements to be present. There was some suggestion that he would be one of the speakers on the occasion. But, files recently made available from the Federal Bureau of Investigation not only reveal that Baldwin was the target of FBI surveillance from 1960 (and more intensely so after his meeting with Robert Kennedy in May 1963), but also provide information about the nature of Martin Luther King's private feelings about James Baldwin. FBI wiretaps on King's telephone conversations reveal that King purposely avoided appearing in public with Baldwin because of his homosexuality. Baldwin biographer James Campbell gained access to these files, which totaled over 1,300 pages, and found that the FBI recorded King's view of Baldwin in the summer of 1963.

> A conversation involving King was eavesdropped on by the Bureau on 1 or 2 June, in which a person whose identity was censored asked King if he would be willing to appear on a television programme with Baldwin. King, the FBI agent noted in his report, was "not enthusiastic about the idea because he felt that Baldwin was uninformed regarding his movement." King told his interlocutor that while Baldwin was considered "a spokesman of the Negro People by the Press," he was "not a civil rights leader." The potential embarrassment which Baldwin's unconcealed homosexuality might cause was raised on a separate

occasion; Baldwin was felt to be "better qualified to lead a homosexual movement than a civil rights movement."[39]

Baldwin attended the March on Washington in 1963, but did not address the gathering due primarily to King's opposition. However, King's having to confront the issue of openly homosexual leaders in the civil rights movement was not a new issue, having been a concern from as early as 1960. Bayard Rustin had been a pacifist during World War II and active in leftist and civil rights causes even during the McCarthy era. Rustin became one of the main advisors to King in the early civil rights campaigns and was instrumental in the founding of the Southern Christian Leadership Conference (SCLC). King and labor leader A. Philip Randolph were planning civil rights demonstrations for both the Democratic and Republican national conventions in the summer of 1960 in an attempt to put pressure on both parties to include civil rights planks in their national platforms. However, Harlem Congressman Adam Clayton Powell, Jr., informed King and Randolph that he opposed launching any protests at the 1960 Democratic conclave, and according to Powell biographer Charles V. Hamilton, the congressman was prepared to embarrass King publicly if the demonstrations took place. "Apparently, Powell was prepared to accuse King and Rustin of a homosexual relationship," Hamilton revealed. "Knowing this was blatantly false, King nevertheless was upset and worried about the impact of such a charge. (Rustin was homosexual, though at the time this was not public knowledge. King was not, but he knew of Rustin's sexual orientation.)" King tried to get Randolph to call off the demonstration, but he refused. Rustin, however, decided to disassociate himself from the SCLC and resigned as an advisor to King. The demonstration did take place at the Democratic national convention.[40]

Baldwin publicly denounced King for allowing Rustin to resign. In his essay "The Dangerous Road Before Martin Luther King," published in 1961, Baldwin claimed that King lost a great deal of "moral credit," especially among young people, "when he allowed Adam Clayton Powell to force the resignation of his [King's] extremely able organizer and lieutenant, Bayard Rustin. Rustin, also, has a long and honorable record as a fighter for Negro rights, and is one of the most penetrating and able men around. The techniques used by Powell—we will not speculate as to his motives—were far from sweet; but King was faced with the choice of defending his organizer, who was also his friend, or agreeing with Powell; and he chose the *latter* course" (261).

Although James Baldwin often spoke of his admiration and support for Martin Luther King during the 1960s and afterward, with the increasing violence leveled against civil rights demonstrators, Baldwin began questioning the use and effectiveness of nonviolent protests. The events that pushed him toward greater militancy and away from nonviolence included the assassinations of the NAACP field secretary, Medgar Evers, in Jackson, Mississippi, in June 1963, and Malcolm X in New York City in February 1965, the bombing of the Sixteenth Street Baptist Church in Birmingham, Alabama, in September 1963, the urban riots, and ultimately the murder of Martin Luther King in Memphis in April 1968. Biographer James Campbell and others have suggested that Baldwin's growing militancy in his public statements adversely affected his art and the quality of his writing, including the nonfiction. After 1963, say these critics, James Baldwin became the type of "protest writer" he had criticized Richard Wright for being. "Nineteen sixty-three was the year his voice broke," wrote biographer James Campbell, "and it affected every element of his literary style—his rhythm, his syntax, his vocabulary, the way in which he made discriminations and reached judgments. It was the year Baldwin shifted away from the lyrical cadence that had been his signature tune. In years to come, it would make people wonder: what happened to Baldwin's great style? And it was done on purpose."[41]

Throughout that decade Baldwin remained productive. His play *Blues for Mr. Charlie* was produced and ran on Broadway for six months in 1964. *Going to Meet the Man,* a collection of his short stories, was published in 1965; and the novel *Tell Me How Long the Train's Been Gone* was published in 1968. These fictional works received favorable to mixed reviews from the critics at the time, but those who expressed negative views generally echoed criticism that had been made about his earlier fiction. It was suggested that the descriptions of life and personal experiences attributed to the characters in these fictional works resembled too closely the views and literary style found in Baldwin's nonfiction. In other words, James Baldwin the essayist and civil rights spokesperson was more on display in these fictional works than was James Baldwin the novelist and literary artist.[42]

"Ye Are Liars and the Truth's Not in You!"

WHILE THE literary career and public pronouncements of James Baldwin will be examined and debated by critics and biographers for years to come, when one examines Baldwin's nonfiction after 1963, particularly *No Name in the Street,* published in 1972, one finds great continuity with the style, themes, and ideological perspectives found in the earlier nonfiction works. Like *The Fire Next Time, No Name in the Street* consisted of two essays, "Take Me to the Water" and "To Be Baptized," but these were original and not previously published. The title for the new book was taken directly from a passage in the Bible, rather than from a Negro spiritual or hymn as was the case in the earlier works. In Job 18: 17–18, it is written "His remembrance shall perish from the earth and he shall have no name in the street. He shall be driven from light into darkness, and chased out of the world."[43]

As in *Notes of a Native Son, Nobody Knows My Name,* and *The Fire Next Time,* this new volume contained the intimate confessions of James Baldwin. He began with a reminiscence about his family and growing up in Harlem. Baldwin recalled that in the period before his brothers and sisters were born, he was the only child in the house. "If I remember myself tugging at my mother's skirts and staring up into her face, it was because I was so terrified of the man we called father; who did not arrive on *my* scene, really, until I was more than two years old." When Baldwin was older he recalled that his mother had to protect the children against her husband's rage and "we all, absolutely and mercilessly, united against our father." Baldwin later understood his father's rage: given "his unreciprocated love for the Great God Almighty, it is no wonder our father went mad" (450–51).

No Name in the Street presented a revealing confession about Baldwin's guilt feelings over his celebrity status. A childhood friend had read in the newspaper that Baldwin had said that he could never again wear the suit he bought to attend Martin Luther King's funeral in Atlanta in April 1968. His friend, who was the same size, contacted Baldwin and asked if he could have the suit. They had been very close when they were young and Baldwin felt guilty about his success, about leaving his friends, about his apparent betrayal of his brothers and sisters in the ghetto. When he went to the home of his friend in Harlem, "I was guilty because I had nothing to say to him, and at one time I had told him everything or nearly everything. . . . I was guilty because I knew, at the bottom of my heart, that I judged this unremarkable colored man very harshly, far more harshly than I would have done if he were white, and I knew this to be unjust as well as sinister" (455). When they were young, his friend was a better athlete, handsomer, and more popular than Baldwin; and now he was merely a postal worker, untouched by the events of the world. "And what in the world was I by now," Baldwin confessed, "but an aging, lonely, sexually dubious, politically outrageous, unspeakably erratic freak?—his old friend" (458). The friend tried on the suit, it fit, and Baldwin left.

In his reflections on coming home to the United States in 1952 during the height of McCarthyism, Baldwin not only confessed to having been a Trotskyite at age nineteen, but also explained why he always distrusted white liberals. "Some of the things written during those years, justifying, for example, the execution of the Rosenbergs, or the crucifixion of Alger Hiss (and the beatification of Whittaker Chambers) taught me something about the irresponsibility and cowardice of the liberal community which I will never forget. Their performance, then, yet more than the combination of ignorance and arrogance

with which this community has always protected itself against the deepest implications of black suffering, persuaded me that brilliance without passion is
nothing more than sterility" (464–65).

More important, in condemning white liberals for their hypocrisy and their
"lying about their motives" for turning in their fellow writers and friends during the McCarthy era, James Baldwin stated specifically the matters of principle
that underpinned virtually all of his nonfiction writing, including *No Name in
the Street*. "Intellectual activity, according to me, is, and must be disinterested—the truth *is* a two-edged sword—and if one is not willing to be pierced
by that sword, even to the extreme of dying on it, then all of one's intellectual
activity is masturbatory delusion and a wicked and dangerous fraud" (465).
Thus when Baldwin wrote about his return to the United States in 1952, it was
as a disinterested observer that he told the truth about what white liberal intellectuals had done and were capable of doing. But James Baldwin also had to reveal the truth about all white Americans.

> I have always been struck, in America, by an emotional poverty so bot-
> tomless, and a terror of human life, of human touch, so deep that vir-
> tually no American appears to be able to achieve any viable, organic
> connection between his public stance and his private life. This is what
> makes them so baffling, so moving, so exasperating, so untrustwor-
> thy. . . . If Americans were not so terrified of their private selves, they
> would never have needed to invent and could never have become so
> dependent on what they still call "the Negro problem." This problem,
> which they invented to safeguard their purity, has made them criminals
> and monsters, and it is destroying them; and this is not from anything
> blacks may or may not be doing but because of the role a guilty and
> constricted white imagination has assigned to blacks (477).

Not only have white Americans sinned against African Americans, they
have lied about it. At one point Baldwin noted, "Somewhere in the Bible there
is the chilling observation: 'Ye are liars, and the truth's not in you!' " (510). In
the case of white Americans, "sin has merely been added to sin, guilt piled
upon guilt." Baldwin believed that "people pay for what they do, and still
more, for what they have allowed themselves to become." Thus as far as he was
concerned, "in generality, as social and moral and political and sexual entities,
white Americans are probably the sickest and certainly the most dangerous
people of any color to be found in the world today" (477–78).

Baldwin claimed that he reached this conclusion during his first visit to the
South in 1957 when "I felt as though I had wandered into hell." He confessed,
"I doubt that I really knew much about terror before I went south." But he
also found that "this terror can produce its own antidote: an overwhelming

pride and rage, so that, whether or not one is ready to die, one gives the appearance of being willing to die. And at that moment, in fact, since retreat means accepting a death far worse, one *is* willing to die, hoping merely (God's last small mercy) to drag one's murderer along" (479). Baldwin described what he found menacing and those who were menaced in the white South, and conveyed his awe and admiration for African Americans living in Little Rock, Montgomery, Birmingham, and other cities. "So many of the black men I talked to in the South in those years were—I can find no other word for them—heroic." Their heroism was not demonstrated in large public events, but in small private ways. "What impressed me was how they went about their daily tasks, in the teeth of southern terror" (483–84).

But even more revealing, Baldwin confessed that during one of these trips he was shocked "when I realized that I was being groped by one of the most powerful men in one of the states I visited." This situation created a different kind of terror, but it was no less real because this man was known to have power over life and death in that state. "Therefore, one had to be friendly: but the price for this was your cock." Baldwin recognized this act for what it was— a debasing, loveless violation of the type usually reserved for women by an individual in a position of power.

> That men have an enormous need to debase other men—and only because they are *men*—is a truth which history forbids us to labor. And it is absolutely certain that white men, who invented the nigger's big black prick, are still at the mercy of this nightmare, and are still, for the most part, doomed, in one way or another, to attempt to make this prick their own: so much for the progress which the Christian world has made from that jungle in which it is their clear intention to keep the black man treed forever (482).

A large part of the essay "To Be Baptized" in *No Name in the Street* was devoted to a discussion of Baldwin's attempts to have his friend and former driver, Tony Maynard, released from prison in Hamburg, Germany, following his flight from the United States after being charged with the murder of a marine. Maynard was accused of killing Michael E. Kroll, who intervened in an argument between a sailor, Michael Crist, and two men, one white and one black, on Third Avenue in New York City. The argument allegedly occurred because the sailor rejected an indecent proposal made to him by the black man, who then produced a sawed-off shotgun and killed him. Baldwin was convinced that Maynard had been targeted for the murder by the New York Police Department because "he had a taste for white women (who had a taste for him)" (501).

At the time of Maynard's arrest and flight to Germany, Baldwin was in Hollywood working on the screenplay for a film based on *The Autobiography of*

Malcolm X, written with Alex Haley and published in 1965. (Although the film was never produced because of conflicts that arose between Baldwin and the Hollywood producers, the scenario, *One Day, When I Was Lost,* was published in 1972.) Baldwin immediately left Hollywood for Hamburg to visit his friend in prison. During one of these visits, when Baldwin discovered that Maynard had been severely beaten by German prison guards, he was able to have Maynard extradited to the United States to stand trial. Despite the fact that the evidence against Maynard was flimsy, his first trial ended in a hung jury. After a second trial Maynard was found guilty, but through Baldwin's assistance he was given a third trial and eventually the charges against him were dropped. Baldwin spent years trying to win the exoneration of his friend, but the entire episode convinced Baldwin that for the poor and black in the United States "the administration of justice is a wicked farce" (527).

In the remainder of *No Name in the Street* Baldwin discussed his personal interactions with Martin Luther King, Medgar Evers, Malcolm X, Huey Newton, and Eldridge Cleaver. In the case of Evers, Malcolm, and King, as in earlier works Baldwin described his personal responses to their lives and untimely deaths. Baldwin also examined the emergence of the Black Panthers, and he stressed his belief that their rise was inevitable given the violent attacks on black leaders and the distrust in the black community for the police. Baldwin had met Huey Newton on at least two occasions and liked him very much because of his intelligence and single-mindedness in pursuit of the liberation of his people. In was clear to Baldwin that the police and high government officials were determined "to smash the Panthers in order to hide the truth of the American black situation" (542).

Baldwin mentioned that he also met Eldridge Cleaver on one occasion and found him impressive, "but I felt a certain constraint between us." At that point he had not read what Cleaver had written about him in *Soul on Ice,* but even after he read it, Baldwin understood why Cleaver would consider him "a dangerously odd, badly twisted, fragile reed, of too much use to the Establishment to be trusted by blacks." But Baldwin also felt that "it is a pity that we won't, probably, ever have the time to attempt to define once more the relationship of the odd and disreputable artist to the odd and disreputable revolutionary, for the revolutionary, however odd, is rarely disreputable in the same way that an artist can be." Baldwin suggested that Cleaver's failure to try to understand the artist's vision could result in the revolutionary's betrayal of the people he was trying to lead

> either by sinking to the apathy of cynical disappointment, or rising to
> the rage of knowing, better than the people do, what the people want.
> Ultimately, the artist and the revolutionary function as they function,
> and pay whatever dues they must pay behind it because they are both

possessed of a vision, and they do not so much follow this vision as find themselves driven by it. Otherwise, they could never endure, much less embrace, the lives they are compelled to lead (540).

In the long discussion of the leadership of Malcolm X in *No Name in the Street* Baldwin made it clear that he believed Malcolm was killed because of his vision and love for black people. "Malcolm considered himself to be the spiritual property of the people who produced him. He did not consider himself to be their savior, he was far too modest for that, and gave that role to another; but he considered himself their servant and in order not to betray that trust, he was willing to die, and died." Malcolm told black people the truth and "it was of the utmost importance for black people to hear it, for the sake of their morale. It was important for them to know that there was someone like them, in public life, telling the truth about their condition." Baldwin argued that what made Malcolm X dangerous "was not his hatred of white people but his love for blacks, his apprehension of the horror of the black condition, and the reasons for it, and his determination so to work on their hearts and minds that they would be enabled to see their condition and change their lives." Baldwin predicted, "in some church some day, so far unimagined and unimaginable, he will be hailed a saint" (499).

The most controversial passages of *No Name in the Street* came at the end when Baldwin suggested that black people were justified in their hatred of and desire to kill white people. In the past whites killed blacks for sport or as a way of "affirming their identity as white men, none of these motives appear necessarily to obtain for black men: it is not necessary for a black man to hate a white man, or to have any particular feelings about him at all, in order to realize that he must kill him. . . . White people, after all, have brought this on themselves." Baldwin denied that he was advocating violence, "but the shape and extent of whatever violence may come is not in the hands of people like myself, but in the hands of the American people, who are, at present, the most dishonorable and violent people in the world." Then Baldwin revealed that on more than one occasion when he felt his life was threatened, he was saved by a black man with a gun. And he made a final confession: "I know what I would do if I had a gun and someone had a gun pointed at my brother, and I would not count ten to do it and there would be no hatred in it, nor any remorse. People who treat other people as less than human must not be surprised when the bread they have cast on the waters comes floating back to them, poisoned" (550–51).

As we have seen, some critics have suggested that after 1963 James Baldwin lost his voice and that in his essays he became bitter and intemperate. However, from his earliest essays Baldwin was always willing to confess the truth about himself so he would be free to tell the truth about the world as he witnessed it as a black man and artist living in the middle of the twentieth century. While many earlier African-American intellectuals, including Ida Wells-Barnett, James Weldon Johnson, W. E. B. Du Bois, and others, were committed to telling the truth, very few (if any) adopted a confessional style that exposed so much about their personal lives. Du Bois wrote three autobiographies, and while the third was the most revealing about his personal life, it did not provide the kind of intimate details that James Baldwin presented in the autobiographical essays in *Notes of a Native Son, Nobody Knows My Name, The Fire Next Time,* and *No Name in the Street.*

Earlier autobiobiographies by African-American intellectuals were written to vindicate the race through examinations of their public lives and personal experiences. While Zora Neale Hurston's and Richard Wright's autobiographies were not written to vindicate the race from the charges of intellectual or cultural inferiority, the personal experiences examined and detailed generally revealed more about the culture and social circumstances that helped to form their unique personalities and artistic sensibilities than they did about their personal frustrations, confusions, and weaknesses. James Baldwin's autobiographical essays were intimate confessions of personal frailties and emotions, and derived their power from the fact that they were so revealing. To a very great extent the autobiographical works of Malcolm X, Bobby Seale, Huey Newton, Eldridge Cleaver, Angela Davis, George Jackson, Audre Lorde, and many other African-American artists and intellectuals in the 1960s and 1970s follow the pattern of personal intimacy and confession found in the essays of James Baldwin.

8

Malcolm X and the Resurrection of the Dead

◄━━

Sometimes, recalling all of this, I don't know, to tell the truth, how I am alive to tell it today. They say God takes care of fools and babies. I've so often thought that Allah was watching over me. Through all of this time of my life, I really *was* dead—mentally dead. I just didn't know that I was.

—MALCOLM X, 1964

Photograph by Jack T. Franklin. Reprinted by permission of the Afro-American Historical and Cultural Museum, Philadelphia.

VIRTUALLY ALL studies of American autobiography published after 1965 include some discussion of *The Autobiography of Malcolm X,* which has come to be considered a classic in that literary genre. In the epilogue, Alex Haley, who wrote the work in collaboration with Malcolm X, explained its origins. In 1959 Haley was a journalist who had recently completed twenty years' service in the U.S. Coast Guard and was made aware of the Nation of Islam by friends in Detroit. When he moved to New York City, he proposed to the editors at *Reader's Digest* an article on the group. He interviewed several Muslims in New York City, including Malcolm X, and subsequently went to Chicago where the Nation of Islam's headquarters were located and interviewed the Honorable Elijah Muhammad, the "Messenger of Allah" and leader of the religious sect. Haley's article, "Mr. Muhammad Speaks," appeared in March 1960.[1]

In 1962 Alex Haley and Al Balk wrote an article on the Nation of Islam for the *Saturday Review* and the following year Haley published an interview of Malcolm X in *Playboy* magazine.[2] Early in 1963 Haley's agent informed him that the editors at Grove Press proposed that Haley collaborate with minister Malcolm X on the autobiography of the provocative spokesperson for the Nation of Islam. After some initial skepticism and receiving assurances that the final work would have to meet totally with his approval, Malcolm X agreed to the project. After coming to an agreement about how they were to proceed, Haley began regular interviews with Malcolm that continued for the next year and a half. The book was completed after Malcolm's death on February 21, 1965. Haley had earlier gotten the minister to agree that an epilogue written by Haley would be included that would explain the circumstances surrounding the writing of the work and the nature of their collaboration.

The Autobiography of Malcolm X was published in 1965 and became an immediate best-seller and has remained in print over the last thirty years, attracting larger and larger audiences. Literary critics have suggested several reasons for its immense popularity and importance within the American autobiographical tradition. G. Thomas Couser in *American Autobiography: The Prophetic Mode* found that Malcolm X's self-writing exemplified the "prophetic" tradition, which emphasized "the conflation of the personal and the communal, the conscious creation of exemplary patterns of behavior, and their didactic, even hortatory, impulses." Couser found that Malcolm's "awareness of his prophetic role in life is obvious in the narrative," and evidence in his collabora-tor's epilogue suggests that he was aware that tact and delicacy were required for the successful treatment of that role in autobiography. "He [Malcolm] strove to resist the temptation to attribute too much importance to himself and to write an exemplary and didactic narrative in which his own experience of family instability, poverty, unemployment, and discrimination would stand for the plight of American blacks."[3]

While Couser understood the significance of the "conversion experience" that occurred during Malcolm's incarceration in Massachusetts in the late 1940s for structuring and organizing the autobiography, he did not under-stand the "cultural" and "spiritual" importance of this profoundly religious and ultimately miraculous occurrence. Couser found Malcolm "less successful at communicating a sense of this [conversion] experience than he had been at re-creating his previous life" as high school dropout, street hustler, pimp, and burglar. Malcolm's reticence about "the most liberating experience in his life" suggested to Couser that it was nothing more than "an intellectual and emo-tional commitment to an ideology which offered him a redeeming self-image and a useful mythology. Nor does Malcolm acknowledge at this point that his experience of liberation had made him, in a sense, a prisoner of racist ideology. Instead of indicating the provisional nature of the conversion, he lets it stand as a crucial, if imperfectly communicated experience."[4]

Malcolm, of course, made it clear by the end of the work that during his years with the Nation of Islam his vision was obscured by racist ideological blinders, but Alex Haley in the epilogue also pointed out that he had to con-vince Malcolm not to change the earlier sections of the work relating to his first experiences with the Nation of Islam to conform to the more recent changes in his ideological positions (414). And even though G. T. Couser wanted more discussion of his conversion experience, what Malcolm did say was that it in-cluded events that he considered "miraculous." As we shall see, it was the miraculous element in Malcolm's conversion that helps explain the importance of the *Autobiography* in the African-American intellectual tradition.

Malcolm adopted his particular "prophetic mode" because he had experi-enced mystical encounters in his spiritual journey. Sacvan Bercovitch in *The American Jeremiad* found that at the heart of the "political sermons" preached by Puritan ministers in early seventeenth-century Massachusetts, decrying the settlers' failure to live up to the covenant the colony had made with God, was some "miraculous event" or set of events that demonstrated God's wrath against a sinful people, and their need to repent. Sometimes miracles were as-sociated with prophetic visions about how God would restore his chosen peo-ple to the Promised Land. In the Old Testament the prophet Jeremiah warned the Israelites about their fall and destruction, but he also promised the restora-tion of their kingdom at a future time and place. "Israel's redemption," Bercovitch found, "will come by miracle, though its deeds are to justify the miracle. Although restoration depends on service, it is a foregone conclusion in God's mind and will."[5]

Bercovitch examined the political sermons issued by Puritan and other American Jeremiahs from the seventeenth through the nineteenth centuries and found that these public pronouncements not only underscored the uniqueness and specialness of the American people—"a chosen people"—but also promised death and destruction due to their contemporary decadence and evil practices. John Winthrop, John Cotton, Increase Mather, Ralph Waldo Emerson, Henry David Thoreau, Walt Whitman, Frederick Douglass, and other American Jeremiahs accepted the religious and political destiny of "America," but declared that it could be realized only after the Americans discarded their evil and sinful ways. While some Jeremiahs played down the miraculous nature of the changes necessary to achieve redemption, they all agreed that a fundamental resurrection of the people's spirit must take place for America to achieve its destiny.[6]

Beginning in the early nineteenth century, African-American intellectuals and religious leaders also participated in this distinctly American literary and political tradition. Frederick Douglass, Booker T. Washington, Ida B. Wells-Barnett, W. E. B. Du Bois, Mary McLeod Bethune, and Martin Luther King, Jr., issued jeremiads against white Americans, a chosen people, who were failing to live up to their own religious and political ideals; and against African Americans, another chosen people, who were also failing to act upon their cultural and spiritual destiny. David Howard-Pitney in *The Afro-American Jeremiad: Appeals for Justice in America* identified a "black American jeremiad tradition" that conceives of African Americans as "a chosen people *within* a chosen people" and "addresses *two* American chosen peoples—black and white—whose millennial destinies, while distinct, are also inextricably entwined."[7]

Malcolm X participated in the black jeremiadic tradition when he delivered his "blistering attacks against such signs of black social depravity as drug addiction, family instability, and lack of thrift and enterprise," but according to Howard-Pitney, Malcolm's separatism placed him outside both the American and African-American jeremiad.

Malcolm's rhetoric to whites represented a profoundly "un-American" jeremiad. He castigated whites for wickedly oppressing blacks and predicted Allah's wrathful vengeance against whites, but he did not do so within the framework of redemptive prophecy and faith in America. He prophesied that blacks would shortly repent and realize Allah's plan for world salvation but whites were not an instrument of Providence. White Americans obstructed God's work by imprisoning black chosen people and keeping them from fulfilling their mission. Whites' destruction was a necessary step to achieving the millennium. No salvation but eternal damnation awaited America.

Howard-Pitney believes that "only Douglass, Du Bois, and King consistently used the jeremiad in its pure form, that is, boldly and unrelentingly to lambaste white Americans for violating the national ideals and covenant by their racism."[8]

While Howard-Pitney may characterize Malcolm X's jeremiad as "un-American," the text that he produced, *The Autobiography of Malcolm X,* certainly could *not* be so described. The work fits well within the tradition of "spiritual autobiographies" produced by Americans, black and white, from the colonial era to the present, many of which described miraculous events at the turning point in the author's religious lives. Peter A. Dorsey in *Sacred Estrangement: The Rhetoric of Conversion in Modern American Autobiography* argued that at the heart of almost all "spiritual autobiographies" was the "conversion experience." Among the Puritans and later eighteenth- and nineteenth-century Americans, these spiritual autobiographies or "conversion narratives" were often "purely religious," emphasizing "the relationship between the individual and God," or were self-portraits that described "the conditions of the inner life."[9] In the modern American autobiographical tradition, Peter Dorsey found that conversion narratives may be sacred or secular, and the *conversion* experiences described are as likely to be vivid accounts of "political awakenings" as they are stories of religious enlightenment. More important, these autobiographical works offer profound insights into the larger society and culture in which the individual lived.

> Conversion discourse provides a reliable index of the relationship between the self and the larger cultures because it has traditionally served a socializing function, signifying that one has come into alignment with certain linguistic, behavioral, and cultural expectations. The communal context of the spiritual autobiography was frequently acknowledged (and sometimes celebrated) in many narratives as the authors imbedded the accounts of others who have undergone similar experiences into their own texts. In many such cases "conversion" is actually triggered by reading or hearing the narratives of others.[10]

Although Peter Dorsey presented no detailed analysis of *The Autobiography of Malcolm X* as a spiritual autobiography, the work certainly fits into that literary and cultural category. The work is set within an African-American "communal context," and detailed descriptions of the conversion experiences of others who were influential in Malcolm's life were included in the text. In reading the *Autobiography of Malcolm X* one finds that the narrative is carried along by three voices, those of Malcolm X, Alex Haley, and Elijah Muhammad. Malcolm began the story with his birth in May 1925 in Lansing, Michigan, the death of his father, Earl Little, and the subsequent dispersal of his family after his mother suffered a mental breakdown. Malcolm moved to Boston when he was sixteen and stayed with his half-sister Ella Little, but later moved to Harlem, where he entered a life of violence and crime that culminated in his in-carceration in prison in Concord, Massachusetts, in February 1946. While there, he was introduced to the teachings of Elijah Muhammad by his younger brother Reginald and members of his family.

Malcolm's brothers and sisters in Detroit and Chicago had been converted to "the natural religion of the black man" and Malcolm began to receive letters from them explaining the tenets of their new faith. Eventually, they urged Malcolm to write the Muslim leader. "I did write to Elijah Muhammad," Malcolm recalled in the chapter entitled "Saved," and "Mr. Muhammad sent me a typed reply. It had an all but electric effect upon me to see the signature of the 'Messenger of Allah.' After he welcomed me into the 'true knowledge,' he gave me something to think about. The black prisoner, he said, symbolized white society's crime of keeping black men oppressed and deprived and ignorant, and un-able to get decent jobs, turning them into criminals" (169).

After his introduction to the basic tenets of the Nation of Islam, Malcolm underwent a miraculous experience that came to symbolize the divine element in his conversion. When his brother Reginald was suspended from the Nation because he was found guilty of adultery, Malcolm prayed to Allah for his brother's reinstatement. The next night while lying on his bed in the cell,

> I suddenly, with a start, became aware of a man sitting beside me in my chair. He had on a dark suit, I remember. I could see him as plainly as I see anyone I look at. He wasn't black, and he wasn't white. He was light brown-skinned, an Asiatic cast of countenance, and he had oily black hair. I looked right in his face. I didn't get frightened. I knew I wasn't dreaming. I couldn't move. I didn't speak, and he didn't. I couldn't place him racially—other than that I knew he was non-European. I had no idea whatsoever who he was. He just sat there. Then, suddenly as he had come, he was gone (186–87).

Malcolm later learned that the man he saw in his vision was Wallace D. Fard, who claimed to be God and had taught Elijah Muhammad the religious tenets of the Nation of Islam.[11]

Throughout his remaining years in prison Malcolm read hundreds of books in the prison library and continued to communicate with Elijah Muhammad and the other members of his family. When he was released from prison in the spring of 1952, he went to Detroit and joined his brother

Philbert and the other family members who belonged to the Nation of Islam's Temple Number One. Malcolm found several menial jobs, but spent most of his free time working for the Nation. On Labor Day 1952 the members of the Detroit Temple took a caravan of automobiles to Chicago for a joint meeting, and it was during this trip that Malcolm first met Elijah Muhammad and learned firsthand of the Messenger of Allah's own spiritual awakening. "I have not stopped one day for the past twenty-one years," the Messenger told him. "I have been standing, preaching to you throughout those past twenty-one years, while I was free, and even while I was in bondage. I spent three and one-half years in the federal penitentiary, and also over a year in the city jail for teaching this truth. I was also deprived of a father's love for his family for seven years while I was running from hypocrites and other enemies of this word and revelation of God—which will give life to you, put you on the same level with other civilized and independent nations and peoples of the planet earth. . . ." (196–97).

Malcolm became one of the most active members of the temple in Detroit and eventually began speaking at the religious services. He was so effective in that role that by the summer of 1953 he became an assistant minister at the Detroit Temple and as such traveled to Chicago on various occasions to receive instruction in the faith directly from Elijah Muhammad. It was at this time that Malcolm met Marie Muhammad, the Messenger's mother, and learned more about the Messenger's background and conversion experience. Born in Sandersville, Georgia, one of thirteen children, the young Elijah Poole demonstrated superior intellectual ability and spent many hours studying the Bible and other religious works. Unfortunately, he was unable to attend school beyond the fourth grade before he was forced to work full-time. Elijah met and married his wife, Clara, and they had two children before moving to Detroit, where they had five more. The last child was born in Chicago.

In 1931 Elijah Poole met Wallace D. Fard, who claimed he was born in Egypt of the Koreish tribe of the prophet Muhammad. "Mr. W. D. Fard taught that God's true name was Allah, that His true religion was Islam, that the true name for that religion's people was Muslims" (207). Minister Fard also taught Elijah that the black people of America were descended directly from the Muslims in Africa.

> He taught that Negroes in America were Lost Sheep, lost for four hundred years from the Nation of Islam, and that he, Mr. Fard, had come to redeem and return the Negro to his true religion. No heaven was in the sky, Mr. Fard taught, and no hell was in the ground. Instead, both heaven and hell were conditions in which people lived right here on this planet Earth. . . .
> Master Fard taught that as hell was on earth, also on earth was the

devil—the white race which was bred from the original black man six thousand years before, purposely to create a hell on earth for the next six thousand years. The black people, God's children, were Gods themselves, Master Fard taught. And he taught that among them was one, also a human being like the others, who was the God of Gods: The Most, Most High, The Supreme Being, supreme in wisdom and power—and his proper name was Allah. . . .

Master Fard taught that every religion says that near the Last Day, or near the End of Time, God would come, to resurrect the Lost Sheep, to separate them from their enemies, and restore them to their own people. Master Fard taught that Prophecy referred to this Finder and Savior of the Lost Sheep as The Son of Man, or God in Person, or The Life-Giver, The Redeemer, or The Messiah, who would come as lightning from the East and appear in the West (207–8).

Mr. Muhammad asked Mr. Fard, "Who are you, and what is your real name?" Fard told him, "I am The One the world has been looking for to come for the past two thousand years. . . . My name is Mahdi" (208).[12]

Wallace D. Fard disappeared in 1934, but before then he gathered a group of followers in Detroit and named Elijah Poole, later Elijah Muhammad, "the Messenger of Allah." After the establishment of two temples, Fard's other disciples became jealous of Muhammad and he was pursued from city to city by "hypocrites" who attempted to kill him. After being arrested in 1942 for evading the draft (through the efforts of these hypocrites working with "the white devils"), Elijah Muhammad spent three and a half years in prison, and returned to his religious work in 1946. The story of Elijah Muhammad's conversion and the lessons he taught Malcolm X served to confirm the young minister's belief that his own conversion was divinely inspired. *"I have sat at our Messenger's feet, hearing the truth from his own mouth! I have pledged on my knees to Allah to tell the white man about his crimes and the black man the true teachings of our Honorable Elijah Muhammad. I don't care if it costs my life. . . . "* (210).

While it can be demonstrated that Malcolm's conversion was reinforced by his learning about the conversion of Elijah Muhammad, and that Malcolm and Alex Haley decided to devote a large part of the autobiography to a description of the conversion experiences of others, the true significance of the work lay in its explication of what Peter Dorsey referred to as "the relationship between the self and larger cultures." It was the "communal context" of Malcolm's spiritual autobiography that explains its importance in the African-American intellectual tradition.

Many autobiographical works by African-American intellectuals describe conversion experiences, such as Harry Haywood's political awakening in the early 1920s detailed in *Black Bolshevik* or James Baldwin's religious conversion described in *The Fire Next Time*. In *The Autobiography of Malcolm X*, however, we encounter a type of religious conversion closely identified with the African-American mass experience from slavery to freedom. Malcolm X described his religious conversion, not in terms of a spiritual awakening, but as "a resurrection from the dead." While this concept, the resurrection of the dead, is central to the Christian religion, particularly the evangelical Christianity practiced by many African Americans, and is a very important belief among orthodox Muslims, it is also extremely significant in explaining the success of the Nation of Islam in bringing into its movement young African Americans who were considered "the walking dead."

"Can These Dry Bones Live?"

THE STORIES in the Old and New Testaments describing the resurrection of the dead have always had particular significance to Africans living in the United States. Just as African Americans identified with the enslaved Children of Israel in the Old Testament and African-American Christianity is replete with references to Moses and God's intervention to save the ancient Hebrews, the story of Ezekiel in the valley of the "Dry Bones" found in the Old Testament has been sermonized regularly by African-American preachers of every Christian denomination from at least the 1860s.[13]

When the Lord spoke to the prophet Ezekiel (37:1–14), he found himself in an open valley "full of bones" where an ancient battle had taken place. The Lord told Ezekiel, "prophesy upon these bones, and say unto them, O ye dry bones, hear the word of the Lord." When he began to prophesy, "there was a noise, and behold a shaking, and the bones came together, bone to his bone." Ezekiel was told to "prophesy unto the wind . . . and breathe upon these slain, that they may live"; when he did, "the breath came into them, and they lived, and stood up upon their feet, an exceeding great army." In this Old Testament passage the dry bones referred to the "whole house of Israel"; however, for the Revs. C. L. Franklin, Martin Luther King, Jr., Jesse Jackson, and hundreds of other black ministers from the mid-nineteenth century to the present day, the "dry bones" were those African Americans who were "spiritually dead" and did not recognize that they were among God's chosen people. "I will open your graves, and cause you to come up out of your graves . . . and shall put my spirit in you and ye shall live." This idea of breathing new life into the "dry bones" to bring about the resurrection of the dead is an important concept associated with African-American Christianity.[14]

In the New Testament the raising of Lazarus from the dead was one of the central events in Jesus Christ's public ministry. Found only in the Gospel of St.

John (11:11–45), it tells of Jesus being informed of Lazarus's illness, but Christ was delayed in his trip to Bethany and Lazarus died in the interim. On the road to the home of Martha and Mary, the sisters of Lazarus, Jesus met Martha, who told him, "Lord, if thou hadst been here, my brother had not died. But I know, that even now, whatsoever thou wilt ask of God, God will give it thee." Jesus responded, "Thy brother shall rise again."

This incident has become central to Christian doctrine because it demonstrated that love and faith will bring about the resurrection of the dead. Jesus said to Martha, "I am the resurrection, and the life: he that believeth in me, though he were dead, yet shall he live: And whosoever liveth and believeth in me shall never die. Believest thou this?" Martha said, "Yea, Lord: I believe that thou art the Christ, the Son of God, which should come into the world." After seeing Mary weeping over her dead brother, Jesus also wept and "groaned in the spirit" because he too loved Lazarus. Jesus went to the grave, which was inside a cave, and told them to roll away the stone. When Martha, who followed, mentioned that Lazarus's body smelled, having been in the grave for four days, Jesus said to her: "Said I not unto thee, that, if thou wouldest believe, thou shouldest see the glory of God?" They took away the stone and Jesus said, "Lazarus, come forth." Lazarus rose from the dead "bound hand and foot with graveclothes" with a large cloth covering his face. Jesus said, "Loose him, and let him go."

While virtually all Christians recognize the significance of the story of the raising of Lazarus to their religious faith, in African-American Christianity the incident was often associated with the conversion experience. Before being converted or saved, the individual is like Lazarus in the tomb, spiritually dead, but through love and faith in Jesus Christ, the sinner is resurrected and "saved." When death came to those who were saved, the rebirth in Christ that came with the conversion experience guaranteed eternal salvation and the triumph over the "second death" on the Day of Judgment. The Second Coming of the Messiah or Judgment Day would bring about the collective resurrection of the dead. In Revelations (20:4–15; 21:1–8), Saint John prophesied Christ will come again and rule for a thousand years during which time the righteous ones "lived and reigned with Christ a thousand years. But the rest of the dead lived not again until the thousand years were finished. This is the first resurrection. Blessed and holy is he that hath part in the first resurrection; on such the second death hath no power; but they shall be priests of God and of Christ and shall reign with Him a thousand years."

Saint John prophesied that following the thousand years of Christ's reign, Satan will be unleashed and allowed to wreak havoc upon the world for a millennium. The devil would find work deceiving the various nations and would move throughout "the breadth of the earth," sowing death and destruction, until he happened upon "the camp of the saints." When the devil tried to destroy this community of the faithful, however, "fire came down from God out of heaven, and devoured them. And the devil that deceived them was cast into the lake of fire and brimstone."

Judgment Day followed, according to Saint John, and what had to be determined was who would be joining the devil in the lake of fire and brimstone. "I saw a great white throne, and Him that sat on it, from whose face the earth and the heaven fled away. . . . I saw the dead, small and great, stand before God; and the books were opened: and another book was opened, which is the book of life: and the dead were judged out of those things which were written in the books, according to their works." The description of the resurrection of the dead on Judgment Day is quite vivid. "The sea gave up the dead which were in it; and death and hell delivered up the dead which were in them: and they were judged every man according to their works."

For those saints whose life work merited entrance into the heavenly city, the "new Jerusalem," God "will dwell with them, and they shall be his people, and God himself shall be with them, and be their God." There will be no tears or sorrow, pain or death, "for the former things are passed away." Those who were likely candidates for eternal perdition were also listed and their fate was described. "The fearful, and unbelieving, and the abominable, and murderers, and whoremongers, and sorcerers, and idolaters, and all liars, shall have their part in the lake which burneth with fire and brimstone: which is the second death."

When African Americans enslaved in the United States were introduced to Christianity and allowed to read the very same King James version of the Bible quoted above, they added one additional group to those listed as destined for eternal hellfire. According to the enslaved, if God did not punish the evil slaveholders in this world, come Judgment Day they will all get their just deserts. Sarah Fitzpatrick, a former slave interviewed by the Federal Writers Project in the 1930s, put it this way; "De lawd's got a han' in workin' this thing out, cause you know it says in the Bible, 'Dat de bottom rail will become the top one fo' de end uv times.' "[15]

The God of the spirituals and African-American Christianity will in His justice punish with fire and brimstone those found guilty of the sin of "man-stealing." According to one spiritual, "Just as you live, just as you die, and after death, Judgment will find you so." A central tenet in the version of Christianity adhered to by enslaved African Americans was that slavery was sinful. "Sin is the nature of the act which created it, and in the elements which constitute it," wrote fugitive slave Aaron in 1843; "Sin, because it converts persons into things; men into property; God's image into merchandise."[16]

The God of enslaved African Americans was a just God who would come again in glory to judge the living and the dead. He will reward the good and punish the evil. "Come Along Moses" was among the first spirituals ever published in the United States (1867), and it not only spoke of God's justice on

Judgment Day, but also proclaimed African Americans' strong identification with the enslaved Children of Israel in the Old Testament.

> Come along, Moses, don't get lost
> Don't get lost, don't get lost,
> Come along, Moses, don't get lost
> We are the people of God.
>
> We have a just God to plead our cause,
> Plead our cause, plead our cause,
> We have a just God to plead our cause,
> We are the people of God.
>
> He sits in heaven and He answers prayer
> Answers prayer, answers prayer;
> He sits in heaven and He answers prayer,
> We are the people of God.[17]

"God Struck Me Dead"

BECAUSE AFRICAN AMERICANS were enslaved by white Christians who also believed they were "saved," who claimed that during their conversion experience God had "washed their sins away," many blacks remained skeptical about the truth of Christianity. It was only when they were able to bear witness personally about how and when God made His presence known in their lives that they truly considered themselves Christians. Paul Radin, a white anthropologist, along with his student A. P. Watson, collected between 1927 and 1929 fifty accounts of "conversion experiences" from African Americans living in Nashville, Tennessee. Radin found that the purpose for which black and white Christians sought God was completely different. "The white Methodist and Baptist was asked to prove that Christ had forgiven his sins; the Negro Methodist and Baptist was asked to prove that Christ had recognized him and that he had recognized Christ. In fact, it was not so much the Negro who sought God as God who sought the Negro."[18]

The fifty or more religious conversion experiences Radin and Watson collected bear this out. These African Americans were spiritually struck dead by God, who subsequently resurrected them. The resurrection of the dead was part and parcel of the conversion experience for these African Americans. For example, Martha, a former slave, was sitting at home and felt "burdened down" and that the world had turned against her. "I reached for a drink of water and the water cried out, 'Unworthy! Unworthy!' I run in the other room and fell across the bed. There I declare unto you, I was killed dead to sin and made alive again in Jesus Christ." When Martha's husband arrived, he asked her what was happening. "I could neither speak nor move. My jaws were locked and my tongue was stuck to the roof of my mouth." In this state she had several visions. One was of hell with a host of people "groaning and wandering around as if in pain and sorrow. My heart became heavy and I prayed." She then saw a man who said, "Follow me." Then a voice said, "Come into Father's welcome home." There was a table in the room with many children surrounding it who bowed three times when she entered and cried in unison "Glory be the Lamb that was slain for the sins of the world." A voice then said "Amen."[19]

What was extremely interesting was the impact that Martha's death and resurrection had upon her mental and physical state. "When I left heaven I didn't walk. I seemed to have been rocking along. When I came to I looked at myself and I was all new all over. I looked at my hands and my hands looked new; I looked at my feet; my feet looked new. I began shouting and praising God. I loved everybody and every creeping thing." Martha ended her description of her conversion experience by declaring, "when God got through with me I spoke out of a full heart and said things that I didn't know I had in me."[20]

Although each of the fifty accounts of the conversion experience was different, there were many similarities in the descriptions of events and visions the converts experienced. Black sociologist Charles S. Johnson, in his introduction to *God Struck Me Dead,* the published version of these conversion experiences, pointed out that each individual went through "a dramatic experience—sudden sickness, blurring of vision, painful pressure of heart followed by a 'death' experience in which one sees hell but is saved by the grace of God, or is shown a 'big glorious city' wherein resides a man who commands him to 'go tell others of your experience.' Finally they are brought to life—or rebirth experience."[21]

What was important about this "change in mind and body" was its association with the convert's resurrection from the dead. As one of these reborn Christians put it, when she was raised from the dead, "I started to shouting in the spirit and haven't stopped yet. I died the sinner's death and ain't got to die no more."[22]

The Coming of the Mahdi

THE BELIEF in the resurrection of the dead is also an important concept in the religion of the Nation of Islam. But what is significant is that this concept among the Black Muslims is closer to that of black Baptists and Methodists than it is to the tenets of orthodox Islam. Whereas orthodox Muslim and Christian doctrines focus on the resurrection of the dead at Judgment Day in the hereafter, Black Muslims and Christians look to the resurrection of the dead in the here and now.

The belief in the unity of God (Allah), the prophethood of Muhammad, and the resurrection of the dead on the Day of Judgment are three fundamental articles of faith in the Islamic religion. Islamic scholars have argued that the belief in the Day of Resurrection, or "the Hour," serves as a safeguard and a way of insuring devotion to God and his prophet. On Judgment Day the faithful will be rewarded for their devotion to God and Islam, and unbelievers will be punished. Jane I. Smith and Yvonne Yaazbeck Haddad pointed out in *The Islamic Understanding of Death and Resurrection* (1981) that "despite certain variations in interpretation among modernists and traditionalists, the basic message to which all contemporary Muslims attest is that God has created humanity for a purpose, for the continuation of life and for ultimate accountability. In the next world injustices will be corrected and God will lead us to a perfected existence."[23]

The Quran describes the "signs of the Hour," or Judgment Day, which will include cataclysmic events, such as earthquakes, disruptions in the state of nature ("when the stars shall be thrown down"), and increasing moral degeneracy in Muslim societies. The lowering of moral standards among Muslims signals the "closeness of the Hour" and the coming of the Mahdi, or Messiah, who will teach religion as did the Prophet Muhammad. According to Muslim scholar al-Barzinji, "he will return Muslims their blessedness and well-being and will fill the world with justice." The "evil ones" (those who despise the people of Muhammad) will be destroyed and the Mahdi will reign until the Hour of Judgment.[24]

In the Nation of Islam, the adherents are taught that the Mahdi, or Messiah, has already come into the world under the name of Wallace D. Fard. In *Message to the Blackman in America* (1965), Elijah Muhammad described his meeting with Fard in 1931. Fard told him, "I am God, I came to guide you into the right path that you may be successful and see the hereafter." Fard said the world had been controlled by devils for the last six thousand years, and their time ran out in 1914. Judgment Day will come when the "so-called Negroes" in America are no longer separated from one another and have accepted the teachings of Islam. These so-called Negroes are really the members of the Tribe of Shabazz who have been lost and kept from knowledge about themselves for four hundred years, the period of enslavement in America. The Mahdi, Wallace D. Fard, sent his Messenger, Elijah Muhammad, to teach the truth to "God's despised and rejected in America."[25]

In *Message to the Blackman*, Elijah Muhammad declared that "the principles of belief in Islam are: One God, His Prophets, His Scriptures, His Judgment, [and] His Resurrection [of the mentally dead]." In every issue of the newspapers published by the Nation of Islam, from *Muhammad Speaks* in the 1960s to *The Final Call* today, there is a statement explaining "What the Muslims Believe." Number five among the twelve points listed states: "We believe in the resurrection of the dead—not in physical resurrection—but in mental resurrection. We believe that the so-called Negroes are most in need of mental resurrection; therefore, they will be resurrected first."[26]

The Autobiography of Malcolm X contains numerous references to Malcolm's belief that his conversion experience represented his resurrection from the dead. At the end of the chapter where Malcolm presented the grim details about his life as a hustler, he commented, "sometimes, recalling all of this, I don't know, to tell the truth, how I am alive to tell it today. They say God takes care of fools and babies. I've so often thought that Allah was watching over me. Through all of this time of my life, I really *was* dead—mentally dead. I just didn't know that I was" (125).

When Malcolm went to retrieve a watch he had stolen in one of his burglaries and left at a jewelry repair shop in Boston, the police were waiting for him. Another black man entered the store just as Malcolm was about to pull his gun and shoot the police detective. "There I was, wearing my gun, and the detective talking to that Negro with his back to me. Today I believe that Allah was with me even then. I didn't try and shoot him and that saved my life." There was another policeman in the back of the store ready to shoot Malcolm had he fired. "One false move, I'd have been dead." And even if he had escaped the police trap, "I could have been dead another way. [His white girlfriend] Sophia's husband's friend had told her husband about me. And the husband arrived that evening, and had gone to the apartment with a gun, looking for me. He was at the apartment just about when they took me to the precinct." Malcolm again noted, "I have thought a thousand times, I guess, about how I so narrowly escaped death twice that day. That's why I believe that everything is written" (148–49).

After having been exposed to the teachings of Elijah Muhammad while in prison, Malcolm began to read the Bible and saw a striking similarity between his personal experiences and those of Paul in the New Testament. "I remember how . . . reading the Bible in the Norfolk Prison Colony library, I came upon, then I read over and over, how Paul on the road to Damascus, upon hearing the voice of Christ, was so smitten that he was knocked off his horse, in a daze. I do not now, and I did not then, liken myself to Paul. But I do understand the experience." He went on to discuss the truth he gained from his experiences. "I have since learned—helping me to understand what then began to happen within me—that the truth can be quickly received, or received at all, only by the sinner who knows and admits that he is guilty of having sinned much.

Stated another way: only guilt admitted accepts truth. The Bible again: the one people whom Jesus could not help were the Pharisees; they didn't feel they needed any help" (163).

After his mystical experience in his prison cell, when the spirit of Wallace D. Fard visited him, Malcolm became all the more convinced of the rightness of his new cause. When he was released from prison, and met Elijah Muhammad in Chicago for the first time, "Elijah Muhammad spoke of how in this wilderness of North America, for centuries the 'blue-eyed devil white man' had brainwashed the 'so-called Negro.' He told us how, as one result, the black man in America was 'mentally, morally and spiritually dead' " (199). Elijah Muhammad explained to him that "Master W. D. Fard taught that every religion says that near the Last Day, or near the End of Time, God would come, to resurrect the Lost Sheep, to separate them from their enemies, and restore them to their own people" (207).

Later, when Minister Malcolm was sent to Atlanta in 1955 to help open the newest Muslim temple there, Number Fifteen, a funeral parlor was the only place they could rent for the services. Just before the Muslims entered, a "Christian Negro's funeral" was ending and the mourners were filing out. "'You saw them all crying over their physical dead,' I told our group when we got inside. 'But the Nation of Islam is rejoicing over you, our mentally dead. That may shock you, but oh, yes, you don't realize how our whole black race in America is mentally dead. We are here today with Mr. Elijah Muhammad's teachings which will resurrect the black man from the dead. . . .' " (223). Muslim funerals were very simple, and meant for the dead, not the living. "As Mr. Muhammad had taught me, I would start by reading over the casket of the departed brother or sister a prayer to Allah. Next I read a simple obituary record of his or her life. Then I usually read from Job; two passages, in the seventh and fourteenth chapters, where Job speaks of no life after death. Then another passage where David, when his son died, spoke also of no life after death" (224).

In addition Malcolm used this concept to explain the success of the Muslims in bringing about miraculous changes in the personality and behavior of black prison inmates. The federal government's investigative agencies sent blacks to spy on the Muslims to determine what went on at temple meetings. But "the second major concern was the thing that I believe still ranks today as a big worry among America's penologists: the steadily increasing rate at which black convicts embrace Islam." While still in prison, these "mentally dead" converts accepted the Muslims moral laws, and when they left prison "they entered a Temple fully qualified to become registered Muslims." It was not like joining a Christian church. "One did not merely declare himself a follower of Mr. Muhammad, then continue leading the same old, sinful, immoral life. The

Muslim first had to change his physical and moral self to meet our strict rules. To remain a Muslim he had to maintain those rules" (258).

The reason for the success of the Muslims in rehabilitating longtime drug addicts was the fact that those who were involved in the program had been "raised from the dead." "Our cure program's first major ingredient was the painfully patient work of Muslims who previously were junkies themselves." Malcolm described in detail the "Muslim six point therapeutic process" for curing black drug addicts. The junkies were "fished" out of the ghetto by former junkies. Groups of junkies were then told why they were in that condition and "they listen only because they know the clean-cut proud Muslim had earlier been like them." The Muslims explained to drug addicts that they were trying to "narcotize themselves against being a black man in the white man's America. But, actually, the Muslim says, the black man taking dope is only helping the white man to 'prove' that the black man is nothing" (260).

Sometimes after several months in these sessions and the addict has been introduced to the positive activities sponsored by the Muslims, then he or she develops enough self-confidence to kick the habit. "As the addict's new image of himself builds, inevitably he begins thinking that he can break the habit. For the first time he is feeling the effects of black self-pride. That's a powerful combination for a man who has been at the bottom. I call myself the best example of that." The last step in the process is going "cold turkey" to completely kick the drug habit and this is done with the help and "around-the-clock shifts" of the Muslims. "He will never forget that it was the Nation of Islam's program which rescued him from the special hell of dope" (261).

Even after the rumors of Elijah Muhammad's adulterous affairs with his secretaries had become public and Malcolm's failure to acknowledge what everyone else already knew made him look like "a total fool," Malcolm went to discuss the matter with his spiritual father because "he had virtually raised me from the dead. Everything I was that was creditable, he has made me. I felt that no matter what, I could not let him down" (296). Eventually, Malcolm learned not only that Elijah Muhammad had betrayed his followers by his adultery, but that Muhammad had also approved the earlier attempts made on Malcolm's life. During his trip to Mecca in 1964 Malcolm underwent his final spiritual change. In the first letter from Mecca to his wife, Betty, he explained that "I had been blessed by Allah with a new insight into the true religion of Islam, and a better understanding of America's entire racial dilemma" (339). When Malcolm returned to the United States, "every free moment I could find, I did a lot of talking to key people in and around Harlem, and I made a lot of speeches, saying: 'true Islam taught me that it takes *all* of the religious, political, economic, psychological, and racial ingredients, or characteristics, to make the Human Family and Human Society complete. Since I learned the *truth* in Mecca, my dearest friends have come to include *all* kinds—Christians, Jews,

Buddhists, Hindus, agnostics, and even atheists! I have friends who are called capitalists, Socialists, and Communists! Some of my friends are moderates, conservatives, extremists—some are even Uncle Toms! My friends today are black, brown, red, yellow, and *white!* (375).

Ideological Continuity Within Change

MALCOLM'S BIOGRAPHERS and other commentators have taken a number of stances on the great changes that occurred during his life. Some believe that his assassination made him a martyr, and that his entire life was interpreted from the perspective of his violent death. This has led to his canonization and the development of the cult of "Saint Malcolm." Others have argued that the final religious conversion may have been only superficial, and that had he lived, he may have reverted to his earlier "black racist ideology" that came to characterize many black militants associated with the Black Power movement of the second half of the 1960s. Still others believe that even in his final stage of ideological development, Malcolm had not gone far enough in identifying those things that needed to be changed in American society in general and among African Americans in particular. These critics point to Malcolm's failure to develop a "feminist perspective" on the particular conditions facing women in American society and throughout the world. His final trips to the Middle East and Africa tended to reinforce his male chauvinist views about the need for black men to "give" black women their equal rights.[27]

When we examine *The Autobiography of Malcolm X* to assess its contribution to the making of the African-American intellectual tradition, we find that it offered many ideological continuities despite the dramatic changes taking place in Malcolm's life. For example, while Malcolm's views about white Americans changed from hatred and total rejection to tolerance and acceptance of some as close friends, his beliefs about white liberals did not change, and in many ways mirrored the views of James Baldwin. In the third chapter where Malcolm described the breakup of his family following his mother's mental collapse, and his stay as a foster child in the home of Mr. and Mrs. Swerlin, who were white, he recalled "one of their favorite parlor topics was 'niggers,' " even when Malcolm was standing right there. "It just never dawned upon them that I could understand, that I wasn't a pet, but a human being. They didn't give me credit for having the same sensitivity, intellect, and understanding that they would have been ready and willing to recognize in a white in my position." What he disliked most was the "kindly condescension which I try to clarify today, to these integration-hungry Negroes, about their 'liberal' white friends, these so-called 'good white people'—most of them anyway" (27).

In the fifteenth chapter, in discussing the positions he took on various civil rights issues and campaigns, Malcolm explained why he felt the northern Freedom Riders in 1961 were hypocrites. Why should they be taking buses to integrate Mississippi, when "ultra liberal New York had more integration problems than Mississippi." When he suggested that northern white liberals go into the black ghettos where there were "enough rats and roaches to kill to keep all the Freedom Riders busy," he was roundly denounced. "Snakes couldn't have turned on me faster than a liberal. Yes, I will pull off the liberal's halo he spends such efforts cultivating! The North's liberals have been for so long pointing accusing fingers at the South and getting away with it that they have fits when they are exposed as the world's worst hypocrites" (271).

In the final pages of the last chapter, Malcolm reiterated: "I never really trust the kind of white people who are always so anxious to hang around Negroes, or to hang around Negro communities. I don't trust the kind of whites who love having Negroes always hanging around them." He traced this belief to his experiences with whites throughout his life, particularly in Boston and Harlem. He also opposed letting whites into black organizations.

> I know that every time that whites join a black organization, you watch, pretty soon the blacks will be leaning on the whites to support it, and before you know it the black may be up front with a title, but the whites because of their money, are the real controllers. . . . Let sincere white individuals find all other white people they can who feel as they do—and let them form their own all-white groups, to work trying to convert other white people who are thinking and acting so racist. Let sincere whites go and teach non-violence to white people! (376–76).

At various times during his public career, Malcolm X was accused of preaching anti-Semitism. In *The Autobiography* Malcolm stated over and over that his assessments of Jews and their behavior were based, not on his Islamic religious beliefs, but completely on his experiences with Jews in Boston, New York, and other places. The first personal reference to Jews came in the chapter describing his life as a hustler in New York City. Malcolm got a job with a Jewish merchant, Hymie, who bought, refurbished, and resold at a profit bars and restaurants in Harlem. "Hymie really liked me, and I liked him. He loved to talk. I loved to listen. Half his talk was about Jews and Negroes. Jews who anglicized their names were Hymie's favorite hate. Spitting and curling his mouth in scorn, he would reel off the names of people he said had done this. Some of them were famous names whom most people never thought of as Jews" (123). Malcolm's major job was transporting Hymie's bootleg liquor that had been funneled into brand name bottles. Unfortunately, something happened involving the State Liquor Authority. "One day Hymie didn't show up where he had told me to meet him. I never heard from him again . . . but I did hear that he was put in the ocean and I knew he couldn't swim" (124).

After Malcolm's conversion and public career as spokesperson for the Nation of Islam, his views were often challenged by Jewish people in his audiences. He always found the Jews to be "the most subjective" and "hypersensitive" about his attacks on whites. "I mean you can't even say 'Jew' without him accusing you of anti-Semitism. I don't care what a Jew is professionally, doctor, merchant, housewife, student, or whatever—first he, or she, thinks Jew." Malcolm believed that Jewish support of black causes had a very practical side: "all of the bigotry and hatred focused upon the black man keeps off the Jew a lot of the heat that would be on him otherwise." Malcolm sometimes would mention that Jewish merchants in black communities siphoned out money,

> which helped the ghetto stay poor. But I doubt that I have ever uttered this absolute truth before an audience without being hotly challenged, and accused by a Jew of anti-Semitism. Why? I will bet that I have told five hundred challengers that Jews as a group would never watch some other minority systematically siphoning out their community's resources without doing something about it. I have told them that if I tell the simple truth, it doesn't mean that I am anti-Semitic; it means merely that I am anti-exploitation (283).

In the final chapter, where he complained about his "constant surveillance," he described how he guessed that the one government agent who had been following him most of the time was Jewish. Malcolm confronted him. "I told him all I held against the Jew was that so many Jews actually were hypocrites in their claim to be friends of the American black man, and it burned me up to be so often called 'anti-Semitic' when I spoke things I knew to be the absolute truth about Jews." Malcolm told the agent that he gave the Jews credit for supporting the civil rights movement, but they did this to divert the prejudices of Gentiles away from them. Malcolm believed the Jews were insincere in this support for civil rights because "so often in the North the quickest segregationists were the Jews themselves. Look at practically everything the black man is trying to 'integrate' into for instance, if the Jews are not the actual owners, or are not in controlling positions, then they have major stock holdings or they are otherwise in powerful leverage positions—and do they really sincerely exert these influences? No!" (372–73).

Malcolm believed that the Jews' true beliefs about blacks were demonstrated "whenever a Negro moved into a white residential neighborhood that was thickly Jewish. Who would always lead the whites' exodus? The Jews! Generally in these situations, some whites stay put—you just notice who they are: they're Irish Catholics, they're Italians; they're rarely Jews. And, ironically, the Jews themselves often still have trouble being 'accepted' " (373).

The greatest degree of continuity in the ideological positions presented in *The Autobiography of Malcolm X* came regarding his beliefs about the hypocrisy of white American Christianity. However, while this has been a theme in the works of African-American intellectuals from Frederick Douglass in the early nineteenth century through the denunciations of white Christian practices by James Baldwin in *No Name in the Street* (1972), Malcolm never agreed with these others that African-American Christianity, which had justice for the oppressed as a defining principle, was a distinct version of the Christian religion. As he put it, "the white man's Christian religion further deceived and brainwashed this 'Negro' to always turn the other cheek, and grin, and scrape, and bow, and be humble, and to sing, and to pray, and to take whatever was dished out by the devilish white man; and to look for his pie in the sky, and for his heaven in the hereafter, while right here on earth the slavemaster white man enjoyed *his* heaven." (163). In the last chapter, he declared that he knew that "Negroes would not rush to follow me into the orthodox Islam which had given me the insight and perspective to see that the black men and white men truly could be brothers. America's Negroes—especially the older ones—are too indelibly soaked in Christianity's double standard of oppression. . . . Since the Civil War's 'freedom,' the black man has gone down so many fruitless paths. His leaders, very largely, had failed him. The religion of Christianity had failed him. The black man was scarred, he was cautious, he was apprehensive" (364–65).

Malcolm X also pointed out that he was often denounced by whites for "stirring up the Negroes," but the historical reality was that Martin Luther King, Jr., and many other Christian leaders of the civil rights campaigns were as often, or more often, accused of "stirring up the Negroes" as well. However, Rev. King built his nonviolent protest movement by appealing to the basic tenets of African-American Christianity. The only indication in the *Autobiography* that Malcolm understood that Martin Luther King and the black Christians in the civil rights movement were also interested in achieving "social justice" for the African-American and other oppressed people came in the final pages.

> Sometimes, I have dared to dream to myself that one day, history may even say that my voice—which disturbed the white man's smugness, and his arrogance, and his complacency—that my voice helped to save America from a grave, possibly even fatal catastrophe. The goal has always been the same, with the approaches to it as different as mine and Dr. Martin Luther King's non-violent marching, that dramatizes the brutality and the evil of the white man against defenseless blacks. And in the racial climate of the country today, it is anybody's guess which of the "extremes" in approach to the black man's problems might *personally* meet a fatal catastrophe first—"nonviolent" Dr. King, or so-called "violent" me (377–78).[28]

Malcolm and the Black Pharisees

THE IDEOLOGICAL POSITIONS put forward about white liberals, Jews, and white and black American Christianity were basically consistent from the beginning to the end of the *Autobiography,* with only minor changes and clarifications following Malcolm's split with the Nation of Islam. This was also the case with another major topic: educated or middle-class blacks, integrationist black leadership, and "Negro intellectuals." What little change there is centers on those educated blacks and African-American intellectuals who also began to question "integration" as the appropriate objective for African Americans in the United States. It is clear that in the *Autobiography* Malcolm saved his harshest criticism, not for bigoted white Americans, but for educated, middle-class blacks in general, and integrationist black spokespersons in particular. In this instance *The Autobiography of Malcolm X* presented a classic statement of the relationship between ideology and experience in the African-American intellectual tradition.

In the early chapters, long before his conversion experience and when he still viewed most whites in a positive light, Malcolm voiced his extreme dislike (hatred almost) for upwardly mobile blacks. He commented that when he was only fifteen and visited his half-sister Ella who lived among the Hill Negroes in Boston, "I saw those Roxbury Negroes acting and living differently from any black people I'd ever dreamed of in my life. This snooty-black neighborhood; they called themselves the 'Four Hundred,' and looked down their noses at the Negroes in the black ghetto, or so-called 'town' section where Mary, my other half sister, lived." These Hill Negroes in Roxbury considered themselves "'cultured,' 'cultivated,' 'dignified' and better off than their black brethren down in the ghetto," even though they were employed "in finance" as bank janitors, "in government" as messenger boys, or "with an old family" as butlers, cooks, and maids (40–41).

In 1943 during his hustler years Malcolm received "Uncle Sam's greetings" and was told to report to the draft induction center in New York City. He decided to run a scam on the officials and pretend that he was eager to join. Malcolm put on a superb performance for the army psychiatrist, whispering to him at one point, "I want to get sent down South. Organize them nigger soldiers, you dig? Steal some guns, and kill up crackers!" The psychiatrist was shocked and dismissed him. He received his 4-F classification as unfit for military service within weeks. The receptionist at the psychiatrist's office was a black nurse who took an instant disliking to Malcolm. He read her immediately as a "Negro Firster." "Negroes know what I'm talking about. Back then the white man during the war was so pressed for personnel that he began letting some Negroes put down their buckets and mops and dust rags and use a pencil, or sit at some desk, or hold some twenty-five cent title. You couldn't read the Negro press for the big pictures of smug black 'firsts.' " Malcolm believed that it was the attitude of the educated Negroes that kept blacks from uniting and dealing with their mutual predicament. "So many of these so-called 'upper-class' Negroes are so busy trying to impress on the white man that they are 'different from those others' that they can't see they are only helping the white man to keep a low opinion of *all* Negroes" (106).

The chapters on his years in prison and subsequent conversion to Islam were peppered with statements about those "brainwashed black Ph.D.s" who resisted the teachings of the Honorable Elijah Muhammad. But it is clear that these references were related to experiences with "so-called Negro intellectuals" after he became a spokesperson for the Nation of Islam. In the chapter titled "Black Muslims," where he described the early responses to his public statements by reporters from the white press, he made it clear that he was more shocked and disturbed by the vehemence of the attacks that came from black leaders. "My bitterness was less against the white press than it was against the Negro 'leaders' who kept attacking us. Mr. Muhammad said he wanted us to try our best not to publicly counterattack the black 'leaders' because one of the white man's tricks was keeping the black race divided and fighting against each other" (243).

Unfortunately, the "black puppets continued ripping and tearing at Mr. Muhammad and the Nation of Islam" and Malcolm was finally given permission to fight fire with fire.

> Today's Uncle Tom doesn't wear a handkerchief on his head. This modern, twentieth-century Uncle Thomas now often wears a top hat. He's usually well-dressed and well-educated. He's often the personification of culture and refinement. The twentieth-century Uncle Thomas sometimes speaks with a Yale or Harvard accent. Sometimes he is known as Professor, Doctor, Judge, and Reverend, even Right Reverend Doctor. This twentieth-century Uncle Thomas is a *professional* Negro . . . by that I mean his profession is being a Negro for the white man (243).

As the attacks continued, Malcolm became more incensed and lashed out regularly at the "black heads with white minds." At radio and television studios he would be paired in debate with "the devils and the black Ph.D. puppets" who got along so well together that "it made me sick to my stomach" (245). During these programs Malcolm stressed the point that it was "the white man's puppet Negro 'leaders,' his preachers and the educated Negroes laden with degrees, and others who have been allowed to wax fat off their black poor brothers" who have been keeping the "black masses quiet until now" (247).

In speech after speech Malcolm attacked "integration-mad Negroes" for taking the position that the reason why African Americans were in the United States was to become integrated into American society. "The Honorable Elijah Muhammad teaches us that since Western society is deteriorating, it has become overrun with immorality, and God is going to judge it, and destroy it. And the only way the black people caught up in this society can be saved is not to *integrate* into this corrupt society, but to *separate* from it, to a land of our own, where we can reform ourselves, lift up our moral standards, and try to be godly." When the Muslims were accused of supporting "segregation," the legal separation of the races in American society, Malcolm made the distinction clear.

> We reject *segregation* even more militantly than you say you do! We want *separation,* which is not the same! The Honorable Elijah Muhammad teaches us that *segregation* is when your life and liberty are controlled, regulated, *by someone else.* To *segregate* means to control. Segregation is that which is forced upon inferiors by superiors. But *separation* is that which is done voluntarily, by two equals—for the good of both! (246).[29]

Opposition to integration as the primary objective for African Americans was an important continuity in the ideological change from Malcolm X to "El Hadj Malik El Shabazz." When he returned to the United States following his trip to Mecca, Malcolm established the Organization of Afro-American Unity (OAAU), which was to be "a non-religious and non-sectarian group organized to unite Afro-Americans for a constructive program toward the attainment of human rights." In the epilogue, Alex Haley noted that the new organization represented a kind of "militant black nationalism" that was interested in converting African Americans "from non-violence to active self-defense against white supremacists across America" (416).

When "El Shabazz" was asked by reporters whether nonblacks would be allowed into the new organization, he responded, "they can't join us," and explained that he felt those whites who might be interested in joining would only be trying to "salve their consciences" by attempting to "prove" that they were "with us."

> But the hard truth is this *isn't* helping to solve America's racist problem. The Negroes aren't the racists. Where the really sincere white people have got to do their "proving" of themselves is not among the black *victims,* but out on the battle lines of where America's racism really *is*—and that's in their own home communities; America's racism is among their fellow whites. That's where the sincere whites who really mean to accomplish something have got to work (376).

Malcolm X pointed out that as a result of his experiences, he came to like and respect certain whites because they liked and respected him. "Irv Kupcinet in Chicago, and Barry Farber, Barry Gray and Mike Wallace in New York—people like them. They also let me see that they respected my mind—in a way I know they never realized" (380). In the epilogue, Alex Haley made a similar observation. "Malcolm X's growing respect for individual whites seemed to be reserved for those who ignored on a personal basis the things he said about whites and who jousted with him as a *man*." Haley noted that the white reporter Malcolm came to respect the most was M. S. Handler of the *New York Times*, who was subsequently asked to write an introduction to the *Autobiography* when it appeared in 1965. Haley recalled:

> The first time I ever heard Malcolm X speak of Handler, he began, "I was talking with this devil"—and abruptly he cut himself off in embarrassment. "It's a reporter named Handler from the *Times*—" he resumed. Malcolm X's respect for the man steadily increased, and Handler, for his part, was an influence upon the inner Malcolm X. "He's the most genuinely unprejudiced white man I ever met," Malcolm X said to me, speaking of Handler months later. "I have asked him things and tested him. I have listened to him talk closely" (400).

Malcolm also moderated his sweeping condemnation of *all* "educated Negroes" as a result of his personal experiences with C. Eric Lincoln, a black professor and author of *The Black Muslims in America* (1963) and journalist Louis Lomax, the author of *When the Word Is Given* (1961). He developed a close relationship with the highly esteemed actor Ossie Davis, and greatly admired the work of James Hicks and James Booker, writers for New York's *Amsterdam News*. What is most interesting was Malcolm's great admiration for the writer James Baldwin, who in the early 1960s was considered by many the leading black intellectual in the "integrationist" camp. "He's so brilliant," Malcolm exclaimed, according to Haley, that "he confuses the white man more than anybody except The Honorable Elijah Muhammad" (401).

As was discussed in Chapter Seven, James Baldwin also greatly admired Malcolm X and devoted a great part of *No Name in the Street* to an explication of Malcolm's importance as a black leader. The mutual admiration between the two spokespersons is understandable when we recognize that both believed in black self-determination, and that Baldwin's ideological version of "integration" resembled very closely the advice Malcolm gave to "sincere white people" before he was assassinated in February 1965. In *The Fire Next Time* (1963) Baldwin argued that the only way to save white American society *from itself* was to give the nonwhite peoples in the United States equal rights.

> What it comes to is that if we, who can scarcely be considered a white nation, persist in thinking of ourselves as one, we condemn ourselves, with the truly white nations [of Europe], to sterility and decay,

whereas if we could accept ourselves *as we are,* we might bring new life to the Western achievements, and transform them. The price of this transformation is the unconditional freedom of the Negro; it is not too much to say that he, who has been so long rejected, must now be embraced, and at no matter what psychic or social risk.[30]

African Americans are not interested in imitating white people, declared Baldwin: "There is certainly little enough in the white man's public or private life that one should desire to imitate. White men, at the bottom of their hearts, know this." But the reason that white Americans have been reluctant to extend equal rights to African Americans was, according to Baldwin, "the white man's profound desire not to be judged by those who are not white, not to be seen as he is, and at the same time a vast amount of the white anguish is rooted in the white man's equally profound need to be seen as he is, to be released from the tyranny of his mirror. All of us know, whether or not we are able to admit it, that mirrors can only lie, that death by drowning is all that awaits one there."[31] In the final pages of his autobiography Malcolm declared that he hoped to be remembered in history because "my voice helped save America from a grave, possibly even fatal catastrophe" (377). In *The Fire Next Time* Baldwin declared "the only thing white people have that black people need, or should want, is power—and no one holds power forever."[32]

Malcolm X believed that "guilt admitted accepts truth" and can bring about the resurrection of the dead. As a result of his experiences with a few educated blacks and "Negro intellectuals," Malcolm ultimately concluded that not all of them were like the Pharisees in the New Testament who could not be saved because "they didn't feel they needed any help" (163). Had he lived, Malcolm may have further changed his views about educated and middle-class blacks because in the second half of the 1960s, it was highly educated black writers, artists, and middle-class students who led the movement for Black Power and the creation of a distinct black aesthetic in arts and letters. In the autobiographies of Gwendolyn Brooks and Amiri Baraka we find vivid and profound descriptions of the ideological and artistic changes that occurred for them when they confronted, or were confronted by, the militant black nationalism that Malcolm X, more than any other black intellectual, represented.

9

Gwendolyn Brooks
and Amiri Baraka

The Creation of a Black Literary Aesthetic

◆

MALCOLM X

Original.
Ragged-round.
Rich-robust.

He had the hawk-man's eyes.
We gasped. We saw the maleness.
The maleness raking out and making guttural air
and pushing us to walls.

And in a soft and fundamental hour
a sorcery devout and vertical
beguiled the world.

He opened us—
who was a key,

Who was a man.

—GWENDOLYN BROOKS, 1968

Photograph by Roy Lewis.
Reprinted by permission of Roy
Lewis Photography, Hyattsville,
Maryland.

Photographer
unknown. Reprinted by
permission of the
Schomburg Center
for Research in Black
Culture, New York
Public Library.

The purpose of our writing is to create a nation. (The advanced state of creation. Create an individual ego, that is one measure. . . . Create the nation and the muscle of that work is, you see?, a gigantic vision . . . the difference between building a model airplane and the luftwaffe.) In this grand creation and the total light of man in heaven—himself realized—as the expanded vision of the angel.

We want a nation of angels. The illuminated. We are trying to create in the same wilderness, against the same resistance. The fire is hot. Let it burn more brightly. Let it light up all creation.

—Amiri Baraka, 1969

FOR BLACK WRITERS and other creative artists of the 1960s and 1970s, the major social disruption with which many tried to deal in their art was the Civil Rights–Black Power movement. In the 1920s, the artists of the Lost Generation in Europe and the United States felt the need to confront the reality of world war in their artistic works, and African artists in the Americas, the Caribbean, and on the African continent confronted the various subtleties and shading that went into the term "New Negro." The worldwide depression of the 1930s shaped the sensibilities of artists attracted to the idea of social realism, and American and African-American writers approached their literary activities ideologically refracted through a Marxist lens. Artists who lived through World War II not only assessed the impact of worldwide death and destruction on the lives of individual human beings, but in the postwar era also confronted through their art the reality of organized genocide and the possibility of the total destruction of the human species.

For African-American artists and intellectuals the preoccupation with race vindication in the late nineteenth and early twentieth centuries began to be superseded in the 1920s by a broader concern with the lived experiences of "the folk." In 1926 Langston Hughes trumpeted the younger poets' and writers' need to get beyond the barriers and limitations presented by the "Racial Mountain." The old attitude about "white is best" in all things literary was being replaced by a desire to tell the truth about the lives of the rural and urban black masses. "They furnish a wealth of colorful, distinctive material for any

artist because they still hold their individuality in the face of American stan-
dardization. And perhaps these common people will give to the world its truly
great Negro artist, the one who is not afraid to be himself."[1]

In the midst of the Great Depression Richard Wright offered a "Blueprint
for Negro Writing" that endorsed Hughes's, Claude McKay's, Sterling
Brown's, and Arna Bontemps's use of African-American cultural beliefs and
practices, "the Negro church and the folklore of the Negro People," in their
literary creations. Wright called for the employment of Marxist conceptions of
history and society for framing their art. "It is through a Marxist conception
of reality and society," Wright declared in 1937, "that the maximum degree of
freedom in thought and feeling is gained for the Negro writer." In the 1920s
James Weldon Johnson had called for a fusion of black folk materials with universal themes and broad human concerns in an attempt to reach both a black
and white audience. "When a Negro author does write so as to fuse white and
black America into an interesting and approving audience," wrote Johnson in
"The Dilemma of the Negro Artist" (1928), "he has performed no slight feat,
and has most likely done a sound piece of literary work."[2] To a very great extent, Richard Wright in his novel *Native Son* was able to accomplish this fusion, and subsequent black writers were able to follow in his literary footsteps.
Gwendolyn Brooks's *Annie Allen* (1949), Ralph Ellison's *Invisible Man*
(1952), and James Baldwin's *Go Tell It on the Mountain* (1953) were met by
an "interested and approving" black and white audience that shared an integrationist ideological perspective and saw these works as important additions
to "American" arts and letters.

The response of the federal and local governments, organized religion, and
lower- and middle-class white people to the African-American demand for first-
class citizenship rights and the end of "American apartheid" served as the backdrop for the rejection of integrationist values and the espousal of militant black
nationalism by African-American artists associated with the Black Arts Movement. While younger literary artists, such as Don L. Lee, Sonia Sanchez, Carolyn Rodgers, Larry Neal, Mari Evans, Nikki Giovanni, and Ntozake Shange,
came to adulthood during this period and viewed the Civil Rights–
Black Power Movement as part of their generational experience, the established black writers and poets responded in a variety of ways to the new black-
nationalist-defined objectives for art. Whereas James Baldwin embraced and
was embraced by these younger black artists, Ralph Ellison kept them and their
literary movement at arm's length, perhaps to the detriment of his own creative
energies. Gwendolyn Brooks and LeRoi Jones, two of the most admired and
respected poets among both black and white literary critics in the early 1960s,
responded differently. There were striking similarities in the social background
and literary experiences of Gwendolyn Brooks and LeRoi Jones/Amiri Baraka,
and their autobiographies, like those of Ida Wells-Barnett, Harry Haywood,

and Malcolm X, presented important literary statements about the relationship between experience and ideology. Both Brooks and Baraka described "artistic" and "ideological" conversion experiences in their autobiographies and explored their personal transformations during the turbulent decade of the 1960s.

"To Weave the Coat That I Shall Wear": Gwendolyn Brooks

MOST LITERARY critics consider Gwendolyn Brooks one of the most important American poets of the twentieth century. Brooks was born in Topeka, Kansas, rather than in Chicago, Illinois, where she has spent virtually all of her life, only because her parents, David and Keziah Wims Brooks, had decided that the expectant mother would do better in the home of her parents. In her autobiography, *Report from Part One,* published in 1972, Brooks described her parents' background and the circumstances surrounding her birth. David Brooks was born in 1883 in Atchison, Kansas, one of twelve children, and following the death of his father, Lucas, became the male head of the large family. David Brooks worked at numerous trades, and in hopes of pursuing a career in medicine enrolled at Fisk University at the turn of the century. Unfortunately, he could afford to remain only one year, and decided to head for Chicago. There he managed to get a job as a janitor at the McKinley Music Publishing Company, where he remained for over thirty years. In 1914 at the age of thirty-one David Brooks met Keziah Wims, who was born in Topeka and had graduated from Emporia Normal School, and taught music there. The couple carried on a lengthy courtship and were married in July 1916.[3]

Keziah Brooks became pregnant later that year, and Gwendolyn was born on June 7, 1917, and by July the family was reunited in Chicago. The second child, Raymond, was born sixteen months later. Gwendolyn attended Forrestville Elementary School (all black), Hyde Park Branch High School (predominantly white), Wendell Philips High School (predominantly black), and Englewood High School (predominantly white), graduating in February 1934. Brooks's writing talent was "discovered" early, when she was seven years old, by her mother, who did much to encourage her to write. In *Report from Part One,* Brooks recalled that she read the Emily books by L. H. Montgomery when she was quite young and began to keep notebooks like the heroine in one of the adventure stories. "I loved the little adventures—yearning to meet their splendid creator." Her parents had already introduced her to the poetry of Paul Laurence Dunbar. " '*You,*' my mother announced, 'are going to be the *lady* Paul Laurence Dunbar. I still own the Emily books and the 'Complete Paul Laurence Dunbar' " (56).

Gwendolyn Brooks's first published poems appeared in a neighborhood paper in 1928, when she was eleven. When she was thirteen, Brooks discovered the *Writer's Digest,* which she described as "a milestone" in her life. "Why there were *oodles* of *other* writers! They, too, suffered and had suffered. They, too, ached for the want of the right word—reckoned with mean nouns, virtue-less adjectives. They, too, sent Things out, got Things back. They, too, knew the coldness of editors, spent much money on stamps, waited, loud-hearted, for the postman" (56). Throughout her high school years Gwendolyn filled notebooks with poetry and prose, and published several pieces in local magazines as well as in the Englewood High School paper.

The second edition of James Weldon Johnson's *The Book of American Negro Poetry* was published in 1931, and as was noted in Chapter Three, Johnson included several works by Langston Hughes and Sterling Brown, younger poets who were trying to "create an authentic black voice in American poetry." In 1933, at age sixteen Gwendolyn Brooks wrote Johnson to have him comment on her poetry. In a 1971 interview included in *Report from Part One,* Brooks recalled that "what made 16 important for me was that I decided to write James Weldon Johnson. . . . He told me that I was talented but that I needed to read modern poetry. This was a great help to me. I already knew the work of such people as Langston Hughes and Countee Cullen. Then I began to read others, T. S. Eliot, Ezra Pound, and e.e. cummings. . . ." Brooks even met Johnson at one of his lectures in Chicago. Her mother, Keziah, led them through the crowd after his speech, and seeing that Gwendolyn was too shy to say anything, "she said, 'This is my daughter,' and told him my name. Then she said, 'she is the one who sent you those poems, and you wrote to her.' And he replied, 'I get so many of them, you know.' And that was all he had to say. So we came away disgruntled, chastised, properly put in our places" (173–74).

Not long afterward, Brooks met Langston Hughes at a poetry reading in Chicago and this was the beginning of a long and close association. Brooks found Hughes "altogether different" from Johnson. "We went through the same rigmarole. I hadn't written to him, but my mother had brought a whole pack of stuff, and showed it to him. He read it right there; he said that I was talented and must go on writing. He was really an inspiration" (174). Indeed, Hughes was as great an influence on Brooks after his death in 1967 as he was before. To some extent the significance of the poetic legacy of Langston Hughes for Gwendolyn Brooks helps explain the conversion experience recounted in *Report from Part One.*[4]

Upon graduation in February 1934 from Englewood High School, Brooks enrolled in the newly opened Wilson Junior College (later Kennedy-

King College), while she worked on and off as a domestic. In 1937 two of her poems were included in anthologies of American poetry. That same year she met Henry Lowington Blakely, Jr., at a poetry reading at the YMCA in downtown Chicago. Blakely, another aspiring poet, had come to the Windy City from Kentucky with his mother, father, and two brothers. Unfortunately, his father abandoned them when Henry, the oldest, was thirteen, and his single-parent household had a difficult time struggling through the lean years of the Depression. Despite these disadvantages, Henry Blakely graduated from Samuel Tilden High School in Chicago and also took courses at Wilson Junior College. He found work as an insurance salesman during the day, while in the evenings he worked on his own poetry or attended readings. Henry met Gwendolyn at one of these readings at the YMCA and they fell in love, and were married on September 17, 1939.

The young couple moved into a "bleak kitchenette" on Chicago's South Side, but they enjoyed life and attracted numerous young writers to their home for poetry readings and parties. "It is not true that the poor are never 'happy,'" Brooks declared in *Report from Part One*, "I believe a giggle or two may escape into the upper air of a Dachau, or a Buchenwald." After the birth of their two children, Henry Jr. in October 1940 and Nora in September 1951, their apartment was always filled with the sounds and laughter of the children.

> My husband and I were married for thirty years. We were very poor, underwent strains, as will all young couples, but chiefly had a [great] deal of fun, sharing our growth. There were discovery, friends, movies, children, picnics, long drives in a succession of old cars that often stopped and had to be pushed by the then formidable strength of Henry Lowington Blakely the Second, writing, reading, spirited conversation (especially did we both seriously enjoy, even in times of woe, breakfast talks in whatever we happened to be living in—garage, kitchenette, room, or, finally, this small house) (58).

In 1941 Inez Cunningham Stark decided to offer a poetry workshop at Chicago's South Side Community Arts Center. Stark was a poet who also happened to be white, wealthy, and well-connected and served on the board of directors for the influential *Poetry* magazine. She was part of the modernist movement of T. S. Eliot, Ezra Pound, e.e. cummings and others who sought to rearrange the words and structures of the English language to create new meanings. Brooks's biographer George Kent emphasized that Stark instilled in her students the "fear of the cliche, the necessity to twist language and put it under strain in communicating meaning, and writing about the experience that is really known." Brooks and her husband, Henry Blakely, Edward Bland, Margaret Burroughs, Margaret Danner, and John Carlis were among the students in the workshop.[5]

In *Report from Part One* Brooks recalled that Inez Stark "did not care to be regarded as a teacher, but as a friend who loved poetry and respected our interest in it." Stark's aristocratic friends had cautioned her about going to "the very *buckle* of the Black belt" among the "savages." "*Poetry?* Rhymes, perhaps. You may teach them to pair rhymes. You'll never teach them to write poetry. They haven't it in them" (65). Inez Stark brushed off these uninformed and racist warnings and proceeded with the class, entering each time with a new pile of books brought from her own personal library. She lent books to the students and at the beginning she read passages relevant to the topic under discussion that week. "When she had finished, it was not necessary for her to ask questions. A burst of excitement met her full blast. The 'students' evaluated, criticized, praised, tore. They treated similarly their own precious creations, laboriously evolved during the seven days since the last meeting. Sometimes what we said to each other hurt or stung" (66).

The young black poets not only differed with one another, they differed with their instructor as well. "If, in spite of everything that she could tell us, we often so clung to our own ways and words, and we often so clung, she bowed gracefully and let us alone, trusting to time to further instruct us, or trusting to the possibility that she herself might be wrong" (67). Inez Stark submitted the work of her students to regional poetry competitions, and in 1943, 1944, and 1945 Gwendolyn Brooks won the Midwestern Writers' Conference poetry prizes. After winning the poetry prize in 1943, Brooks was asked by Emily Morison of Knopf Publishers to submit her poems for possible publication. "Very soon I had packed off at least forty—love poems, war poems, nature poems, patriotism poems, 'prejudice' poems. Eventually, Emily Morison replied. She liked the 'Negro poems.' She hoped that, when I had a full collection of these, I would try Knopf again" (71).

Brooks rushed to complete more "Negro poems," and when she had enough for a book, she submitted them to Harper Brothers, rather than Knopf, "I was too shy to approach that door again," and the work was sent to novelist Richard Wright for comments. In his letter to Harpers, Wright was effusive in his praise for Brooks's poetry.

> There is no self-pity here, nor a striving for effects. She takes hold of reality as it is and renders it faithfully. There is not so much an exhibiting of Negro Life to whites in these poems as there is an honest human reaction to the pain that lurks so colorfully in the Black belt. A quiet but hidden malice runs through most of them. She easily catches the pathos of petty destinies; the whimper of the wounded; the tiny accidents that plague the lives of the desperately poor, and the problem of color prejudice among Negroes. There are times when open scorn leers through. Only one who has actually lived and suffered in a

kitchenette could render the feeling of lonely frustration as well as she does—of how dreams are drowned out by the noises, smells, and the frantic desire to grab one's chance to get a bath when the bathroom is empty. Miss Brooks is real and so are her poems.

Wright concluded by affirming that "she is a real poet; she knows what to say and how to say it. I'd say that she ought to be helped at all costs. America needs a voice like hers and anything that can be done to help her to bring out a good volume should be done."[6]

A Street in Bronzeville was published by Harpers on August 15, 1945, and received enthusiastic responses from black and white critics. The volume included her prize-winning poem, "Gay Chaps at the Bar." It began:

> We knew how to order, Just the dash
> Necessary. The length of gaiety in good taste.
> Whether the raillery should be slightly iced
> And given green, or served up hot and lush.
> And we knew beautifully how to give to women
> The summer spread, the tropics, of our love.
> When to persist, or hold a hunger off.
> Knew white speech. How to make a look an omen.
> But nothing ever taught us to be islands.
> And smart, athletic language for this hour
> Was not in the curriculum. No stout
> Lesson showed how to chat with death. We brought
> No brass fortissimo, among our talents,
> To holler down the lions in this air.[7]

In her autobiography, Brooks recalled that the poet and teacher Paul Engle reviewed the volume for the *Chicago Tribune*.

> I'll never forget how my husband and I, returning from yet another Saturday night movie, bought the *Tribune* and ripped it open to the book pages. "For Heaven's sake!" There, prominently situated, was the review that initiated My Reputation! Henry and I read the entire review on the midnight street, then waited in ecstasy (forgive me, students whom I've cautioned against the use of that weak word) for the bus (72).

Beginning in 1948 Gwendolyn Brooks was asked to review books on a regular basis for the *Chicago Daily News* and *Chicago Sun-Times,* and later periodically for the *New York Times, New York Herald Tribune,* and *Negro Digest* (later *Black World*). "I was exuberant. I remember with what joy I received those packages, wondered what was inside, found out, ate eagerly. Then came the responsibility of analysis, the serious responsibility of careful reportage on the year-long—perhaps five year-long or twenty-year-long—ache and toil and fright of some earnest soulexhauster" (73). Brooks reviewed books by Japanese, Hungarian, Russian, European-American, and African-American artists.

In May 1949 Brooks's second book of poetry appeared, *Annie Allen*. Earlier that year *Poetry* magazine had published several sonnets that were included in the volume, including one entitled "Children of the Poor."

> What shall I give my children? who are poor,
> Who are adjudged the leastwise of the land,
> Who are my sweetest lepers, who demand
> No velvet and no velvety velour;
> But who have begged me for a brisk contour,
> What that they are quasi, contraband
> Because unfinished, graven by a hand
> Less than angelic, admirable or sure.
> My hand is stuffed with mode, design, device.
> But I lack access to my proper stone.
> And plentitude of plan shall not suffice
> Nor grief nor love shall be enough alone
> To ratify my little halves who bear
> Across an autumn freezing everywhere.[8]

Literary critic J. Saunders Redding reviewed *Annie Allen* in the *Saturday Review* in September 1949 and declared that "if *A Street in Bronzeville* indicated that the author, Gwendolyn Brooks, possessed valuable poetic gifts, her second volume goes a long way toward proving them. *Annie Allen* . . . is as artistically sure, as emotionally firm, and as aesthetically complete as a silver figure by [Benvenuto] Cellini. Nor is the comparison so incongruous as it seems. The same liquid lyricism, momentarily held in delicate static poise, that informs a Cellini informs the pieces in Miss Brooks's new work." In April 1950 Brooks was notified by *Poetry* magazine that she had been awarded the Eunice Tietjens Prize for the poems that appeared in the March 1949 issue. Then on May 1, 1950, she was notified that she had won the 1950 Pulitzer Prize for poetry. Among the other poets nominated that year were Conrad Aiken, Robert P. T. Coffin, William Carlos Williams, and Robert Frost. After the announcement Brooks telegraphed her editor, Elizabeth Lawrence, at Harpers that she was "sick with happiness." Langston Hughes, who had helped to get some of Brooks's poems published in the *Negro Quarterly*, and had very favorably reviewed *Annie Allen*, telegrammed congratulations to Brooks and later declared in the *Chicago Defender*, "for almost ten years now, I have been hailing Miss Brooks as one of the most important literary talents in America. Naturally I am delighted to see my own contentions vindicated."[9]

In the December 1950 issue of *Phylon* magazine, founded by W. E. B. Du Bois at Atlanta University in 1940, both Langston Hughes and Gwendolyn Brooks participated in a symposium devoted to the topic "The Negro Writer Looks at His World." In an interview Hughes commented on the "many encouraging aspects which were not present twenty, or ten, or even five years ago." For Hughes, "the most heartening thing for me . . . is to see Negroes writing works in the general American field, rather than dwelling on Negro themes solely." Hughes mentioned novelists Ann Petry, Frank Yerby, and Dorothy West as writers who presented "non-Negro subjects." Paul Laurence "Dunbar, of course, and others wrote so-called 'white' stories, but until this particular period there have not been so many Negroes writing characters not drawn from their own race."[10]

Gwendolyn Brooks wrote poems on "non-Negro subjects," but it was her use of black subject matter in poems well grounded in modern poetic techniques and forms that paved the way for her receiving the Pulitzer Prize. In her brief contribution to the symposium, entitled "Poets Who Are Negroes," Brooks championed the use of black subject matter in poetic expression. "Every Negro poet has 'something to say.' Simply because he is a Negro he cannot escape having important things to say. His mere body, for that matter is an eloquence. His quiet walk down the street is a speech to the people. Is a rebuke, is a plea, is a school." But the poet must work and rework these cultural materials like a baker who must properly cook his dough to make bread that will be appetizing. "It is like throwing dough to the not-so-hungry mob. . . . You have to cook the dough, alter it, until it is unrecognizable. Then the mob will not know it is accepting something that will be good for it. Then it will eat, enjoy and prosper." But Brooks's final plea to the younger poets was that they not give up their artistic vision. "No real artist is going to be content with offering raw materials. The Negro poet's most urgent duty, at present, is to polish his technique, his way of presenting his truths and his beauties, that these may be more insinuating, and, therefore more overwhelming."[11]

Prefiguring Black Feminism

GWENDOLYN BROOKS'S reputation as a poet, not just a "Negro poet," was secured with the awarding of the Pulitzer Prize in 1950, and thus she had the freedom to be creative, experimental, and expansive in her literary horizons. In 1953 she published *Maud Martha,* which she called an "autobiographical novel." Delving into the daily life of a dark-skinned girl and showing her movement into womanhood, the novel was written in a kind of "poetic prose" that resembled the language found in *A Street in Bronzeville* and *Annie Allen.*

Maud Martha is a short novel, and the story is told in short chapters, some less than three pages, that examine people, "kitchenette folks"; places, "at the Burns-Coopers"; and events, "Mother comes to call" and "a birth." The novel covered Maud's brief courtship and marriage to Paul Phillips, her life as a housewife, and the birth of her daughter, Paulette. Maud is a nonheroic figure whose interior life is the most fulfilling. The narrative evoked Maud Martha's suppressed rage over her treatment as "an old black gal" in a community that values light skin color, as well as the subtle silences over slights and disappointments in Maud's life and marriage. This was in keeping with the "feminine mystique" of the 1950s, which stressed "housewifely eminence." As was made clear throughout *Maud Martha,* "what she wanted was to donate to the world a good Maud Martha. That was the offering, the bit of art, that could not come from any other. She would polish and hone that."[12]

When *Maud Martha* appeared in 1953, it received highly favorable reviews. In *The New York Herald Book Review,* Coleman Rosenburger found that although "it is small book, within the compass which Miss Brooks has set for herself, it is a superb achievement." Hubert Creekmore in the *New York Times* found that "Miss Brooks's prose style here embodies the finer qualities of insight and rhythm that were notable in her two earlier books of poetry, and gives a freshness, a warm cheerfulness as well as a depth of implication to her first novel. In technique and impression it stands virtually alone of its kind."[13] While reviewers were virtually unanimous in praising Brooks's poetic language and characters "whose validity is beyond question," *Maud Martha* evoked differing responses from feminist literary critics Mary Helen Washington and Barbara Christian.

Mary Helen Washington was most struck by the "rage and silence" in *Maud Martha,* but was disappointed that Maud did not exhibit the kind of "freedom" of Janie Starks, the female heroine of Zora Neale Hurston's novel *Their Eyes Were Watching God.* "I only wish Brooks had found a way for Maud to know that someone in the community had grown ten feet higher from listening to her story." Barbara Christian, on the other hand, argued that *Maud Martha* was a highly nuanced story of the sensitivity and individuality of an "ordinary black girl" and thus prefigured the female characters in novels by Paule Marshall, Toni Morrison, Alice Walker, and other black women novelists in the 1970s. "As a prose piece, *Maud Martha* is a fusion of these two qualities, the sensitive and the ordinary, not only in its characterization of its protagonist, but also in the moments the writer chooses to include in her compressed rendition of an urban black life. Yet these moments, as they form a whole, both look back to the novels of the 1940s and towards black women's novels of the 1960s and 1970s." Christian believes that Brooks presented a "heroic celebration" of "an unheroic ordinary black girl from Chicago." "Through her use of nuance," Christian concluded, "Brooks is able to present this celebration in its essential form, suggesting that Maud Martha is one of any number of ordinary people who, against the limits of mundane life, continue to create themselves."[14]

It should be noted that neither Mary Helen Washington nor Barbara Christian suggested that *Maud Martha* prefigures the kind of "feminist consciousness" found in black women's novels in the 1960s and 1970s. However, in her autobiography Brooks included a discussion of feminism in the same section that included her reflections on *Maud Martha*. Brooks revealed that *"Maud Martha*, my one novel, is not autobiographical in the usual sense. Much that happened to Maud Martha has not happened to me—and she is a nicer and better coordinated creature than I am. But it is true that much in the 'story' was taken out of my own life, and twisted, highlighted or dulled, dressed up or down" (191). Brooks also said that when she was younger, she subscribed to what Mary Helen Washington referred to as the 1950s cult of housewifely eminence. "A truly horrible thing was that I grew up to womanhood believing that the gleaming white family life on the motion picture screens *should be* my model" (213).[15]

In a 1971 interview with Ida Lewis included in *Report from Part One*, however, Brooks clarified what she viewed as the positive and negative elements in the "women's liberation movement."

> LEWIS: Does the black woman have a special responsibility to be independent, to redefine her role in life?
>
> BROOKS: I feel that she does, and that it's not an easy job in these strange days. The men are forging "forward" now, too. They have a new belief in themselves, and one of the things many of them are determined not to be loaded with is conventional attachments to women—like marriage.
>
> Relations between men and women seem disordered to me. I was asked recently how I felt about Women's Lib. I think Women's Lib is not for black women for the time being, because black men *need* their women beside them, supporting them in these tempestuous days. I made this comment in Horace [Mann] Bond's class [at Atlanta University] as well, and a young man asked me, "What do you mean 'for the time being'?"
>
> I said, "Well, that will depend on how you men treat us. As our struggle goes on, if you treat us considerately, we may never need to subscribe to 'the movement.' But if you don't, who knows what we'll have to do in the future." I did say that it is entirely wrong, of course, for women to be denied the same job income men have. When it comes to that, black women should be fighting for equal pay just as white women should (179–80).

In the section in *Report from Part One* entitled "Collage," Brooks elaborated on these points, making it clear that in the midst of "tragedy and hatred and neglect," and "her own efforts to purify," that the black woman must "mightily enjoy the readily available. . . ."

> Black women must remember, through all the prattle about walking or not walking three or twelve steps behind or ahead of "her" male, that her personhood precedes her femalehood; that, sweet as sex may be, she cannot endlessly brood on the Black Man's blondes, blues, blunders. She is a person in the world—with wrongs to right, stupidities to outwit, *with* her man when possible, on her own when not. And she is also here to enjoy. She will be here, like any other, once only (204).[16]

The nonviolent direct-action protests of the late 1950s and early 1960s served as the backdrop for Gwendolyn Brooks's next book of poems, *The Bean Eaters*. Published in 1960, the volume included poems that dealt with black women as well as racial themes taken from the ongoing civil rights struggle, such as "A Bronzeville Mother Loiters in Mississippi. Meanwhile, A Mississippi Mother Burns Bacon." This poem was a response to the murder of Emmett Till, the black boy from Chicago who was killed in 1955 while visiting his grandmother in Mississippi.

> The fun was disturbed, then all but nullified
> When the Dark Villain was a blackish child
> of fourteen, with eyes still too young to be dirty,
> And a mouth too young to have lost every reminder of its
>   infant softness.
>
> That boy must have been surprised! For
> These were grown-ups. Grown-ups were supposed to be
> wise.
> And the Fine Prince—and that other—so tall, so broad,
> so
> Grown! Perhaps the boy had never guessed
> That the trouble with grown-ups was that under the
>   magnificent shell of adulthood, just under,
> Waited the baby full of tantrums.[17]

And there was "We Real Cool," which was a reflection on the youth gangs that dominated many inner-city neighborhoods in Chicago and other northern cities. This became one of Brooks's best-known and most recited and anthologized poems.

> THE POOL PLAYERS.
> SEVEN AT THE GOLDEN SHOVEL.
>
> We real cool. We
> Left school. We

> Lurk late. We
> Strike straight. We
>
> Sing sin. We
> Thin gin. We
>
> Jazz June. We
> Die soon.[18]

The explicit racial themes in *The Bean Eaters* disturbed many critics, both black and white, who suggested that Brooks's "impressionistic method" was inadequate for her "protest mission," or that the poems contained an "unseemly social emphasis." Literary critic Maria K. Mootry argued that "one reason *The Bean Eaters* aroused such a range of disparate critical assessments was the way Brooks yoked her 'social' message to a variety of classic high modernist techniques."[19] In a 1969 interview with George Stavros included in *Report from Part One,* Brooks was asked whether she felt her later poems were more "socially aware."

> Yes, although many people hated *The Bean Eaters*, such people as would accuse me of forsaking lyricism for polemics despised *The Bean Eaters* because they said that it was "getting too social. Watch it, Miss Brooks!" (Laughs) They didn't like "The Lovers of the Poor"; they didn't like "The Chicago Defender Sends a Man to Little Rock: Fall 1957," which I don't care overmuch about—or at least I'd like to remove that last line ("the loveliest lynchee was our Lord"). . . . I just feel that they're poems. I think that the wonderment or resentment is inside the person who is making the accusation, if it is an accusation, and usually when people talk about the "social content" of the poems, they are accusing you of doing something dastardly (165).

In 1963 Brooks published *Selected Poems* and in the section "New Poems," the one that best reflected this new social consciousness, was the long poem "Riders to the Blood-Red Wrath," which in part declared:

> The National Anthem vampires at the blood.
> I am a uniform. Not brusque. I bray.
> Through blur and blunder in a little voice!
> This is a tender grandeur, a tied fray!
> Under macabre, stratagem and fair
> Fine smiles upon the face of holocaust,
> My scream! unedited, unfrivolous.
> My laboring unlatched braid of heat and frost.
> I hurt. I keep that scream in at what pain:

At what repeal of salvage and eclipse.
Army unhonored, meriting the gold, I
Have sewn my guns inside my burning lips.[20]

"Poetry For the People"

WHEN CIVIL rights activists rushed to Greenwood, Mississippi, in June 1966 to complete the march across the South started by James Meredith, who in 1962 was the first African American to be enrolled in the University of Mississippi, the African-American objective of civil rights was almost overnight replaced by the demand for Black Power. The purpose of Meredith's "Memphis to Mississippi March" was to encourage intimidated southern blacks to overcome their fears and to register to vote. Unfortunately, on the second day of Meredith's march, he was ambushed and received two shotgun blasts in the back. Within days Martin Luther King, Jr., announced that the Southern Christian Leadership Conference (SCLC) would now take up Meredith's march, and subsequently Floyd McKissick, the North Carolina attorney, who became national chairman of the Congress of Racial Equality (CORE) in January 1966; Stokely Carmichael, the new chairman of the Student Nonviolent Coordinating Committee (SNCC); and other civil rights leaders agreed to join. As a result of the continuing violence leveled against SNCC workers and other civil rights activists, many who agreed to participate in the march pledged that they were not going to allow what happened to Meredith to happen to them. As Martin Luther King recalled in *Where Do We Go from Here?: Chaos or Community,* he heard one of the SNCC workers proclaim, "If one of them damn Mississippi crackers touches me, I'm gonna knock the hell out of them."[21]

Although King was able to extract a pledge from Stokely Carmichael, who was becoming increasingly militant, that the march would be nonviolent, Carmichael used the event to announce the new thrust for his organization. As the march got underway on June 15, 1966, rallies were held by Carmichael and other SNCC leaders in which they introduced the slogan "Black Power." "This is the 27th time I've been arrested," Carmichael told the crowd on the evening of June 16, "I ain't gonna be arrested no more. . . . [Police Chief] Buff Hammond has to go. I'm gonna tell you, baby, that the only way we're gonna get justice is when we have a black sheriff. . . . Every court house in Mississippi should be burnt down tomorrow so we can get rid of the dirt." The following day, Carmichael exhorted the marchers, "What do we want?" The loud rejoinder was "Black Power." "When do we want it?" "Now!"[22]

For many the call for Black Power was initially interpreted as black self-defense against violent attack, but even in this limited context the new rallying cry signaled the end of the type of nonviolent protest associated with Martin Luther King. While King, Roy Wilkins, James Farmer, and other civil rights leaders publicly denounced Black Power because of its "anti-white" overtones, just as they had earlier opposed the militant black nationalism of Malcolm X, the slogan was taken up by the black students in SNCC because nonviolent protests had not brought about the social changes for which they had been struggling. As the word was spread by newspapers, television, and magazines black activists, intellectuals, and artists across the country began to spell out what they thought the Black Power slogan meant. As was the case with the New Negro Movement of the 1920s, there were as many definitions of Black Power as there were individuals who talked or wrote about it.[23]

For students and other activists who had worked for black civil rights in the South during the 1960s, Black Power came to mean black political empowerment. Flamboyant and controversial Harlem Congressman Adam Clayton Powell, Jr., was the first to convene a Black Power Conference with the specific objective of increasing black political power. Held in his congressional office in September 1966, the meeting was boycotted by Stokely Carmichael and other SNCC activists because they believed (incorrectly) that Congressman Powell was interested in increasing black power within the Democratic Party, rather than developing an *independent* black political movement. In the book *Black Power: The Politics of Black Liberation in America,* which Carmichael co-authored with political scientist Charles V. Hamilton and published in 1968, the view was expressed that Black Power meant the creation of independent political institutions and expanding to other black communities, north and south, the type of political organizing carried out by SNCC and local activists in the Lowndes County, Mississippi, Freedom Party, formed in March 1966. "We see independent politics . . . as the first step toward implementing something new. Voting year after year for the traditional party and its silent representatives gets the black community nowhere," Carmichael and Hamilton concluded. The supporters of Black Power had to make "the move in the direction of independent politics—and from there, the move toward the development of wholly new political institutions."[24]

For other civil rights activists the new Black Power slogan was interpreted to mean black economic development. In September 1962, the Southern Christian Leadership Conference had created its economic arm at the suggestion of Philadelphia's Rev. Leon Sullivan. Following a series of protests and Selective Patronage Campaigns in Philadelphia in 1961 and 1962, Rev. Sullivan had launched Operations Industrialization Centers (OIC) for the purpose of training blacks for jobs opening up in industry after the several successful boycotts of local businesses. Operation Breadbasket was created in 1962 by the SCLC with Fred Bennette as director for the purpose of expanding economic opportunities for blacks. Rev. Jesse Jackson headed up the SCLC's Operation Breadbasket in Chicago beginning in February 1966 and won a number of major victories. In November 1966 Jackson became the SCLC director of economic development and promoted black capitalist enterprises and alliances between black businesses and large white corporations. By 1969 newly elected President Richard Nixon came to embrace Black Power when it meant black capitalism because he was aware that the development of black business was no real threat to the existing political and economic structures in American society.[25]

Whereas black capitalists opposed the calls for a "socialist revolution" that would lead to a redistribution of wealth in the United States, many revolutionary black nationalists, such as Huey Newton, Bobby Seale, Eldridge Cleaver, and the members of the Black Panther Party, called for a socialist revolution in the United States similar to that which occurred in China under the leadership of Mao Tse-tung in the 1940s and 1950s. The Black Panthers in alliance with other anti-capitalist groups also wanted to launch a "cultural revolution" in this country modeled after the contemporary movement taking place in China. The Panthers demonstrated that they were willing to take up arms to bring about revolutionary social and economic change in the United States.[26]

Other militant black nationalists who received their inspiration from the teachings of Malcolm X were more interested in launching a revolutionary movement based on black culture. As historian William Van Deburg pointed out, for "cultural nationalists," such as Larry Neal, LeRoi Jones, and Ron Karenga, "black power *was* black culture. By asserting their cultural distinctives via clothing, language, and hairstyle and by recounting their unique historical experiences through the literary and performing arts, cultural nationalists sought to encourage self-actualization and psychological empowerment." While the cultural nationalists were accused of "racial chauvinism," they believed that their cultural thrust would serve to underpin black political liberation as well. "It was believed that the subordination of culture to economics or politics would eviscerate the revolution by denying its supporters access to the movement's life-blood."[27]

Cultural nationalists were in the forefront of what was known as the Black Arts Movement, which poet Larry Neal defined in a seminal essay first published in 1968. "Black Art is the aesthetic and spiritual sister of the Black Power concept," wrote Neal.

> As such, it envisions an art that speaks directly to the needs and aspirations of Black America. . . . The Black Arts and Black Power concept both relate broadly to the Afro-American's desire for self-determination and nationhood. Both concepts are nationalistic. One is concerned with the relationship between art and politics; the other with the art of politics.

Neal argued that the two movements were beginning to converge and the "political values inherent in the Black Power concept are now finding concrete expression in the aesthetics of Afro-American dramatists, poets, choreographers, musicians, and novelists."[28]

Along with this new self-definition came a reevaluation of Western aesthetics and the development of a distinctive black aesthetic. Western aesthetics, according to Neal, were based on European and white American cultural sensibilities, and in dealing with non-Western peoples this tradition has been "anti-human in nature" and a "source of oppression." The younger black artists were therefore interested in pursuing a black aesthetic in various areas of creative endeavor.

> When we speak of a "Black aesthetic" several things are meant. First, we assume that there is already in existence the basis for such an aesthetic. Essentially, it consists of an African-American cultural tradition. But this aesthetic is finally, by implication, broader than that tradition. It encompasses most of the elements of Third World culture. The motive behind the Black aesthetic is the destruction of the white thing, the destruction of white ideas, and white ways of looking at the world. The new aesthetic is mostly predicated on an Ethics which asks the question: whose vision of the world is finally more meaningful, ours or the white oppressors'? What is truth? Or more precisely, whose truth shall we express, that of the oppressed or of the oppressors. These are basic questions. Black intellectuals of previous decades failed to ask them.

Neal concluded that "the Black Arts movement believes that your ethics and aesthetics are one. That the contradictions between ethics and aesthetics in western society is symptomatic of a dying culture."[29]

Literary critic Addison Gayle, Jr., in his introduction to the anthology *The Black Aesthetic*, published in 1972, asserted that the black artist who subscribed to this new ideological perspective produced his or her works for a black audience.

> The black artist of the past worked with the white public in mind. The guidelines by which he measured his production was its acceptance or rejection by white people. To be damned by a white critic and disavowed by a white public was reason enough to damn the artist in the eyes of his own people. The invisible censor, white power, hovered over him in the sanctuary of his private room—whether at the piano or the typewriter—and, like his black brothers, he debated about what he could say to the world without bringing censure upon himself.

Gayle made it clear that this involved significant matters of principle and that the contemporary black artist "has given up the futile practice of speaking to whites, and has begun to speak to his brothers" and sisters.[30]

The fundamental difference between the artists associated with the Black Arts Movement and earlier black novelists, poets, and writers was not really their preoccupation with black subject matter and themes or even black forms and standards. As we have seen, from the 1920s there was greater and greater awareness among African-American artists of their rich cultural heritage and the need to create art that utilized African-American folk materials. As Gwendolyn Brooks had pointed out in 1950, "Every Negro poet has 'something to say.' Simply because he is a Negro; he cannot escape having important things to say." But Brooks, Richard Wright, Zora Neale Hurston, Ralph Ellison, James Baldwin, and other black artists of the 1940s and 1950s were primarily interested in attracting a white audience. Thus when Gwendolyn Brooks discovered that there was a large and growing black audience being developed by the poets, playwrights, and novelists associated with the Black Arts Movement, she underwent a profound ideological conversion experience.

In April 1967 Brooks was asked to attend a Black Writers Conference, held at Fisk University in Nashville; she found "suddenly there was [a] New Black to meet." In *Report from Part One* she described what happened.

> Coming from white white white South Dakota State College I arrived in Nashville, Tennessee, to give one more "reading." But blood-boiling surprise was in store for me. First, I was aware of a general energy, an electricity, in look, walk, speech, *gesture* of the young blackness I saw around me. I had been "loved" at South Dakota State College. Here, I was coldly Respected. Here, the heroes included the novelist-director John Killens, editors David Llorens and Hoyt Fuller, playwright Ron Milner, historians John Henrik Clarke and Lerone Bennett (and even poor Lerone was taken to task, by irate members of a no-nonsense young audience, for affiliating himself with *Ebony Magazine*, considered at the time a traitor for allowing skin-bleach advertisements in its pages, and for over-featuring light skinned women). Imamu Amiri Baraka, then "Leroi Jones," was expected. He arrived in the middle of my offering, and when I called attention to his presence there was jubilee in Jubilee Hall (84).

Before this dramatic incident in Nashville in 1967 Brooks had collected "helpful materials: hints, friendly *and* inimical clues, approximations, statistics, 'proofs' of one kind or another; from these I am trying to weave the coat that I shall wear." But the encounter with the younger artists pushed Brooks into "some inscrutable and uncomfortable wonderland" (85). When she returned to Chicago she was asked by playwright Oscar Brown, Jr., to attend the preview of the play *Opportunity Please Knock,* which he had produced with the help of several members of a Chicago street gang, the Blackstone Rangers. Brooks was impressed by the talent exhibited by these teenagers, and asked if there were any writers or poets among them. Brooks decided to start a creative writing workshop in the South Side Community Center for some of the Rangers and others who were interested. Among the participants in the workshop were Don L. Lee (later Haki Madhubuti), Mike Cook, Jewel Lattimore (later Johari Amini Konjufu), Jim Rodgers, Carolyn Rodgers, and others (193–94).

Jump Bad, the book of poetry produced by the young poets in the workshop, was published in 1971, with an introduction by Brooks that she also decided to include in *Report from Part One.*

> With the arrival of these young people my neatly-paced life altered almost with a jerk. Never did they tell me to change my hair to a "natural." But eventually I did. Never did they tell me to look about me, open my eyes. But soon I did. Never did they tell me to find them sane, serious, substantial, superseding. But soon I did.
>
> I am proud of these young people. . . . They scratch out roads for themselves, are trying to BE themselves. They do not mind making "mistakes." In a new nation, what *are* the offenses against standards? What are the standards? Who decides? Are the rulers of *other* nations to decide?

Brooks concluded her introduction to the volume by the young poets by declaring that they were "blackening English. Some of the results are effective and stirring. Watch for them in the months and years ahead. True black writers speak *as* blacks, *about* blacks, *to* blacks" (194–95).[31]

Gwendolyn Brooks published in 1968 one of her most important volumes of poetry, *In the Mecca,* based on her experiences at age nineteen in the Mecca Building, a tenement occupied by blacks and a few whites, where she worked for Prophet Williams, a "spiritual advisor" and "faith healer." In an interview included in *Report from Part One* she recalled that "he had a fantastic practice; lucrative. He had us bottling medicine as well as answering letters. Not real medicine, but love charms and stuff like that he called it, and delivered it through the building; that was my introduction to the Mecca building." Brooks began "In the Mecca" as a novel in the late 1950s, but it was immediately rejected by her publishers at Harpers. In 1968 "In the Mecca" was transformed into poetry that reflected Brooks's new black consciousness.

> I wish to present a large variety of personalities, against a mosaic of daily affairs, recognizing that the *grimmest* of these is likely to have a streak or two streaks of sun. In the Mecca were murders, loves, loneliness, hates, jealousies. Hope occurred, and charity, sainthood, glory,

shame, despair, fear, altruism. Theft, material and moral. "Mental cruelty" (189–90).

There were poems on "The Blackstone Rangers," "Medgar Evers," the slain black civil rights leader in Mississippi, and "Malcolm X." The poem "The Wall" dealt with a mural that was painted on the side of run-down tenement building, and two "Sermons on the Warpland" (the United States) moved beyond complaints about victimization to a more pluralistic view of the American future. Literary critic D. H. Melhem found that *In the Mecca* "marks a creative prime meridian for the poet. There the oracular voice, prescriptive and prophetic, is clearly heard. Fact, fiction, strangers, friends, history and personal narrative, past, present, future are caught in a dynamo of refining energy."[32]

In the last poem in the volume, "The Second Sermon in the Warpland," Brooks described "Big Bessie," who maintains her dignity despite her oppressive surroundings.

> The time
> cracks into furious flower. Lifts its face
> all unashamed. And sways in wicked grace.
> Whose half-black hands assemble oranges
> is tom-tom hearted
> (goes in bearing oranges and boom).
> And there are bells for orphans—
> and red and shriek and sheen.
> A garbageman is dignified
> as any diplomat.
> Big Bessie's feet hurt like nobody's business,
> but she stands—bigly—under the unruly scrutiny, stands in the
> wild seed.
>
> In the wild weed
> she is a citizen,
> and, in a moment of highest quality, admirable.
>
> It is lonesome, yes. For we are the last of the loud.
> Nevertheless, live.
>
> Conduct your blooming in the noise and whip of the whirlwind.[33]

After her "conversion experience" in 1967, Gwendolyn Brooks became more intimately involved with the black literary renaissance taking place in Chicago in the late 1960s and early 1970s. The Organization of Black American Culture (OBACC) was formed in Chicago in 1966 under the leadership of Hoyt Fuller, editor of *Negro Digest* (later *Black World*), and sponsored several Artists Workshops in which Brooks participated with the younger writers. Poet

Dudley Randall was a close associate of Brooks and in 1966 he started Broadside Press in Detroit to publish the works of the young black poets and writers. In 1969 Broadside published her long poem *Riot*, which described Brooks's response to the assassination of Martin Luther King, Jr., in April 1968. Then at a conference on black women artists held at Yale University in December 1970 Brooks announced that she was switching from Harpers to the new Broadside Press because it was a black owned and operated publishing company.[34]

Brooks made a trip to "Mother Africa" in July 1971 that reinforced her evolving "blackness." In Kenya and Tanzania, while she was impressed by the dignity and self-assurance the people projected, she was also made aware of the enormous impact European colonization had upon these Africans. Brooks was informed by black Americans living there that the Africans were not interested in black Americans coming over to try and "take over." "THE AFRICANS!" she was told, "they insist on calling themselves Africans and their little traveling brothers and sisters 'Afro-Americans' no matter *how* much we want them to recognize our kinship" (130).[35]

Report from Part One was published in 1972 when Gwendolyn Brooks was fifty-five years old and considered one of the most important poets in the United States. While the text of the autobiography included information about her youth and schooling, artistic training, encounters with the politically new and different, and her "conversion experience," the structure and organization—with its prefaces by poet Don L. Lee and literary critic George Kent, fragments, interviews, marginalia, and collages—resembled more W. E. B. Du Bois's *Darkwater* (1921) and Zora Neale Hurston's *Dust Tracks on a Road* (1942) than the autobiographies of fellow poets James Weldon Johnson and Langston Hughes, both of whom she admired greatly. Johnson's *Along This Way* and Hughes's *The Big Sea* (1940) and *I Wonder as I Wander* (1956) described important events in their lives in chronological order, focusing on crossroads and turning points that ultimately came to determine their personal identity as artists and poets.[36]

In Du Bois's *Darkwater* the structural complexity was achieved by the inclusion of poems, short stories, political as well as autobiographical essays, with a number of voices interspersed throughout the text to carry the narrative along. In *Dust Tracks on a Road* Hurston's narrative voice told the story of her life primarily in the first half of the text, while the remaining chapters presented her views on "Books and Things," "Love," "Religion," and "My People, My People." In *Report from Part One* the complexity was achieved through Brooks's use of several voices, including those of Don L. Lee, George Kent, and her interviewers, that tend to confirm the images of the "self" Brooks was presenting; as well as through the use of the narrative form of the "prose poem" that Brooks had employed earlier in her novel, *Maud Martha*. Literary critic Nellie Y. McKay pointed out that "in their autobiographies, Hurston and

Brooks have created alternative versions of the black female self that go well beyond refuting the negative stereotypes of black women in American literature." McKay concluded that "what both books demonstrate is an independence on the part of their writers to disregard external expectations and shape their autobiographical selves in images of their own making. They empower themselves to name themselves in their own voices."[37]

In the interview with George Stavros included in *Report from Part One* Brooks was asked what the younger writers thought of the work of older poets.

> STAVROS: How about poets who are more widely known? How do you
> fit Leroi Jones among these writers?
> BROOKS: Oh, he is their hero! He's their semi-model, the one they
> worship. I personally feel that he is one of the very good poets of
> today, and people hearing this who have no real knowledge of his
> work, but have merely a couple of "inflammatory" passages in the
> newspapers, might say, "Well, what in the world do you mean?
> That's no poet." But he is a most talented person. His work *works*.
> STAVROS: What do you feel makes Jones' a voice of his generation?
> BROOKS: Well, first of all he speaks to black people. They appreciate
> that. And he's uncompromising in his belief that the black people
> must subscribe to black solidarity and black self-consciousness.
> STAVROS: Is it his message or poetic method that makes his poetry appeal particularly to blacks?
> BROOKS: If it is a "method," it comes just from the sincere interest in
> his own people and in his desire to reach them, to speak to them
> of what he believes is correct (150–51).

If You're Brown, Stay Around: LeRoi Jones

MORE THAN any other writer, LeRoi Jones (later Imamu Amiri Baraka) presented in his poems, plays, and nonfiction the new black consciousness of the 1960s and 1970s. Born Everett Leroy Jones in Newark, New Jersey, on October 7, 1934, his parents, Coyette Leroy Jones and Anna Lois Russ Jones, were able to provide him and his younger sister, Elaine, a relatively secure and stable home environment. Indeed, Jones's lower-middle-class family background was very similar to that of Gwendolyn Brooks. Only a high school graduate, Jones's father, Coyt, worked as a barber and truck driver, and finally was able to secure a position in the Post Office, while his mother, who had attended the high school division of Tuskegee Institute, and later Fisk University, worked as a secretary. Jones's extended household while growing up included his mother's parents and an uncle who was a Pullman porter. Jones characterized his family as "lower middle class" with bourgeois pretensions on his mother's side, primarily because before the Depression her father, Tom Russ, had been the director of his own funeral parlor.

Jones grew up in a black neighborhood, but attended integrated schools in Newark, and at the time, the early 1940s, both McKinley Junior High School and Barringer High School were predominantly Italian. He attended Bethany Baptist Church regularly with his family, where his grandfather was one of the church trustees. Although he had many close friends with whom he shared numerous adventures as "the Secret Seven," in *The Autobiography of LeRoi Jones/Amiri Baraka,* published in 1984, he recalled that "one emotional center of my earlier life was my special relationship with my father. My father loved sports and playing sports was the prerequisite for being part of the community of youth I ran with. I'd read the *Daily News* sports pages from way back in grammar school. And he'd take me to football games, baseball games, I mean real pros." At these sports events Jones felt a "special *grandeur*" when someone said, "You look just like your father." "There was pride in that, I mean for the persons saying that, not just for my old man and me. But in the people it seemed to be a kind of high joy that such a genetic miracle could be produced. And that it was a sleek brown kid that had been produced—Eureka!—down to the sky-drinking eyes" (33).[38]

When his family moved to the racially mixed Hill section in Newark in the late 1940s, Jones began seriously to get an education in things "Black Brown Yellow White." Black represented "fundamental black life, the life of blues people"; and "the yellow, the artificial, the well-to-do, the middle class really," was the "petty bourgeoisie." Jones was brown and developed a "brown sensitivity." "The brown, caught between the black and the yellow, did not, in spite of themselves, like the yellow. They hated it, them, even worse than white . . . (normally) because white folks didn't exist with the same day-to-day common reality. The yellow would be around bugging you, having a haircut neatly parted with well-greased legs and knees. . . . They would be laughing and having always good exclusive times, usually at your expense, even if it didn't have nothing to do with you" (43). But when brown Jones left his brown house, "there was nowhere to go but the black streets and the people who ran those streets and set the standards of our being were black. And no matter where we would go and what we would get into, when we were true to ourselves, when we were actually pleasing our deepest selves, being the thing we most admired and loved, we were black (and blue)" (47).

The spirituals, gospel, jazz, blues, and popular songs were all part of Jones's home life while growing up. Through the "All-City Chorus" he was exposed to "the Classics." But it was at the weekend canteen dances at the Masonic Temple on Belmont Avenue that Jones first developed a soulful appreciation of black music. "The canteen was our world," and Jones would slide in there with his friends, "dressed to the nines," and ready to "suck it all in."

> As young people we were blues people, it is and remains African American popular music. It was the most natural element in our lives, the sound of those lives, as they were lived. In the late 40's and 50's the whole of the US was going through changes and we were going through changes with it. What the blues said and says is the flow of our blood and the flow of us through this world. The music took on everything we ever did, which is why we loved it and made it (being us) (54).

Bebop, the music of Dizzy Gillespie, Miles Davis, Thelonius Monk, Charlie Parker, Maynard Ferguson, and Stan Getz, presented "a new language a new tongue and vision for a generally more advanced group of our generation." For Jones, "the music took me places I'd never been. Literally." And the fact that many of the Beboppers were white "meant nothing to me. What they were playing was linked to something I dug" (60). Not only did Jones seek out the music and the musicians, he also took up the trumpet, and studied with an "Italian classicist." But that was not what Jones wanted. "I wanted to play like Miles Davis, so I had to slide the horn to the side of my mouth sort of to try to get that sound. Because the way the trumpet teacher was teaching me only the big old round notes would come out and I thought that was square." The music was *"frantic*. In sharp endless motion. But even frantic was cool in the blues sense." At the dances and parties

> we was cool we moved through those blue lights under those red lights trying to sidestep the ugliest parts of our ghetto reality. . . . Where I was comin' from, the brown side, we just wanted to keep steppin. The black had shaped us, the yellow had taunted us, the white had terrified and alienated us. And cool meant, to us, to be silent in the face of all of that, silent yet knowing. It meant being smart, intelligent, too. So we hooked up the weirdness and the intelligence. Dizzy's hornrim BeBop glasses, the artist's tam, these spelled some inner deepness to us. It was a way into ourselves further, and sometimes because we went into ourselves, we seemed quiet on the street (61–62).

Upon graduation from predominantly white Barringer High School (Brooks had earlier graduated from predominantly white Englewood High School in Chicago), Jones enrolled for one year at the Newark campus of Rutgers University, but he found the all-white environment too much like high school, so he decided to transfer to Howard University, sometimes (derisively) referred to as "the Capstone of Negro Education." Passing himself off as a premed major, Jones made new friends, many of them from Newark and other parts of New Jersey. The "Jersey boys" were relatively high on the social pecking order, behind the "New York cats," "Philly cats," and "Chi cats." Jones and his roommates considered themselves "outlaws" who were on the fringes of campus social life, which was dominated by the "yellow parties" sponsored by the Greek letter sororities and fraternities. "Neither school nor mainstream HU yellow-ass social functions were our real thing. Our real thing was hanging out, bullshittin—talking bad to each other and about everything else" (77).

Jones did pledge Alpha Phi Alpha fraternity, but he was never admitted. When he refused to go downtown to buy donuts for one of his "big brothers," he was beaten black and blue during the hazing. Jones was on the track team at the time and was unable to compete in the next meet because his legs had been so badly beaten. His roommates were furious and a few days later during another hazing session the pledges, or "sphinxes," set up an ambush and "generally whaled the daylights out of the big brothers under the cover of night and confusion." That was the end of "fraternity life" for Jones. At the end of the school year he returned home to Newark, worked in a grocery store and took a class in "scientific German" at Seton Hall University. It was also during this summer vacation that he got "wobbly spitting-up drunk," for the first time, much to the chagrin of his parents (89).

When "LeRoi" Jones (around this time he changed the spelling of his first name) returned to Howard in the fall, he did not hang out as much with his buddies and became more introspective, spending large amounts of time in the library reading Gertrude Stein, Ezra Pound, and even the Elizabethans. He also spent more time off campus, exploring the city, attending shows at the Howard Theater. The second semester he moved off campus into a house rented by some West Indian students attending Howard. In his room Jones could "look at stuff and think about stuff, maybe read something, or maybe go for a walk or eat or drink a beer, or just let strange stuff fill up my head in absolute silence." But he was also flunking the courses in his major and finally realized he was going to have to leave. During the summer of his junior year he spent some time in New York City, in the Village, where he ran into a friend from Newark, Steve Korret, and his black Canadian wife, Lita. The couple gave Jones his first taste of "black bohemia." Although he returned to campus in the fall of 1954, he was not allowed to enroll because of his grades and merely said goodbye to some of his friends.

After a brief time in Newark, Jones decided to join the air force (which in his autobiography he called the "Error Farce"). He was not sure why; it was merely something to do. His first stop was Sampson Air Force base in upstate New York, "cold, gray, ugly, resembling nothing but hopelessness," for basic training. "In Basic I found myself with bloods from South Jersey mostly, for some reason. Dudes from Camden and Trenton, mostly black dudes looking for a way off the streets" (97). Following Basic, Jones was sent to Chanute Field in Rantoul, Illinois, for training as a weatherman. There were only whites in his unit; "it felt like Barringer again." But Jones did run into several "base intellectuals," who like him resented the "Nazi," "fascist" types in the unit. On trips to Chicago on weekends he discovered bookstores and bought whatever struck his fancy. After Chanute, Jones signed up to go to Ramey Air Force Base in Puerto Rico (because he heard it was a "country club") to be, not a normal weatherman, but a *"weather gunner."* But once there he met several airmen who were into jazz, poetry, and other esoteric things, and together they considered themselves members of the "Ramey Air Force Base Intellectuals' Salon" (113).

"We had the jazz foundation mixed with concern for the graphic arts—painting and photography—a couple of academics ensconced among us for laughs, and a few of us interested in literature" (113). It was at this time that Jones began to write poetry more regularly. He started writing during his last year at Howard, "but now I was more serious (though still not together) with what I was doing. I was at least trying to put down what I knew or everything I thought I felt. Straining for big words and deep emotional registration, as abstract as my understanding of my life" (117). He even began to read the *New York Times Book Review* and *The New Yorker* magazine. One day Jones had been reading "one of the carefully put together exercises *The New Yorker* publishes constantly as high poetic art, and gradually I could feel my eyes fill up with tears, and my cheeks were wet and I was crying, quietly softly but like it was the end of the world." This became a turning point for Jones.

> I had been moved by the writer's words, but in another, very personal way. A way that should have taught me even more than it did. Perhaps it would have saved me many painful scenes and conflicts. But I was crying because I realized that I could never write like that writer. Not that I had any real desire to, but I knew even if I had had the desire I could not do it. I realized that there was something in me so *out,* so unconnected with what this writer was and what that magazine was that what was in me that wanted to come out as poetry would never come out like that and be *my* poetry (118).

During the Christmas break, Jones went home to Newark and visited his friend Steve Korret in Greenwich Village and found that Korret had become a Zen Buddhist and worked in an Eastern bookstore called Orientalia. Jones went to the store and perused the books on Eastern thought. "I was swept up." And his friend had become a writer. "The idea of this made me drunk with wonder. A writer! What a thing to be—so weird—so outside of the ordinary parade of gray hellos and goodbyes I could begin to measure my life with.

A writer. In the mysterious jumble of Greenwich Village" (119). This made his life in the air force "even sadder and more hopeless." In the gunnery schools at Tampa, Florida, and Shreveport, Louisiana, Jones became more "disconnected." He read everything. He was trying to become "an intellectual." "I was being drafted into the world of Quattrocentro, vers libre, avant-garde, surrealism and dada, New criticism, cubism, art nouveau, objectivism, 'Prufrock,' ambiguity, art music, rococo, shoe and non-shoe, Highbrow vs. Middlebrow, and I didn't realize the significance of it" (121). The air force facilitated Jones's move into the intellectual arena by giving him an "undesirable discharge" once it was discovered he read subversive literature, such as the *Partisan Review*. Although his friends at home were upset when they learned of his discharge, Jones's response was "hey, I wanted to get out . . . Out! Undesirable or Not, here I come" (123).

Brown to Black in Bohemia

LeRoi Jones headed straight for the Village upon his discharge and almost immediately got caught up in the hip world of bohemianism. After he managed to get a job as a clerk in a record store specializing in jazz, the Record Trader, his life stabilized and he started to go to poetry readings regularly. At these gatherings Jones met and bedded several white women, including "Nellie Kohn" (Hettie Cohen), who was the quintessential Village bohemian, black leotards and all. At the time she was unemployed, but later got a job with a publishing company as an editor. The two began a long-term relationship that would eventually lead to marriage and two children.[39]

In 1958 the two decided to start a literary magazine, *Yugen* (in his autobiography, Baraka calls it "Zazen"), which would publish the works of some of the better known poets and writers of the Beat Generation, including Allen Ginsberg, Philip Whalen, Gregory Corso, William Burroughs, and Jack Kerouac. What Jones and Kohn shared with these writers was a sensibility that rejected the received literary and political ideas of the decade. "We saw 'the man in the grey flannel suit' as the enemy, an agent of Dwight Eisenhower whose baby-food mentality we made fun of. We could feel, perhaps, the changes that were in motion throughout the whole society. We reflected some of that change. Though, in those days, I was not political in a conscious way, or formally political at any rate" (152). Jones published some of his earliest poetry in *Yugen*, and the nonpolitical element was apparent, as in the poem "Slice of Life."

> The train pulled in to Hartsville, S.C. and an angel jumped out . . .
> It was dark and he was scared

> And the only sound was the noise
> The moonlight makes when it strikes the rails.
>
> He picked himself up, brushed off his wings, and looked
>   around for the "John" . . .
> There were three of them, "Johns"
> That is, one marked MEN, one
> Marked WOMEN, and the third marked OTHERS.
>
> He hesitated momentarily, checked his credentials
>   and murmured,
> "I wonder, could they have known?"[40]

Jones expanded his literary horizons through the writers he met and their works. He was impressed by the poetry of Charles Olson, who was at one time the director of the artist colony known as Black Mountain in North Carolina. He met Frank O'Hara and Kenneth Koch, the leading lights in the New York School of Poets, whose works appeared in the *Evergreen Review,* where some of Jones's early poems also appeared. Jones was particularly drawn to the poetry of Allen Ginsberg, who had recently published the volume *Howl.*

> Allen Ginsberg's *Howl* was the first thing to open my nose, as opposed to, say, instructions I was given, directions, guidance. I dug *Howl* myself, in fact many of the people I'd known at the time warned me off it and thought the whole Beat phenomenon a passing fad of little relevance. . . . I could see the young white boys and girls in their pronouncement of disillusion with and "removal" from society as being related to the black experience. That made us colleagues of the spirit. Yet I was no stomp-down bohemian. I had enough of the mainstream in me, of lower-middle-class craving after order and "respectability," not to get pulled all the way over to Wahooism. Yet as wild as some of my colleagues and as cool as I usually was, the connection could be made because I was black and that made me, as Wright's novel asserted, an *outsider.* (To some extent, even inside those "outsider" circles) (156–57).[41]

Jones's first book of poetry, *Preface to a Twenty-Volume Suicide Note,* published in 1961, reflected the Beat intellectual and literary influences, but also an alienation from his own African-ness, such as in "Notes for a Speech."

> Africa blues
> does not know me. Their steps, in sands
> of their own
> land. A country
> in black & white, newspapers

blown down pavements
of the world. Does
not feel
what I am.
                   Strength
in the dream, an oblique
suckling of nerve, the wind
throws up sand, eyes
are something locked in
hate, of hate, of hate, to
walk abroad, they conduct
their deaths apart
from my own. Those
heads, I call my "people."[42]

The first of several ideological conversion experiences described in *The Autobiography of LeRoi Jones/Amiri Baraka* came in July 1960 when Jones was asked to join a group of African-American writers on a trip to Fidel Castro's Cuba. Having successfully overthrown the U.S.-backed government of Fulgencio Batista, Castro had established a Marxist-Leninist regime on the island in 1959 and extended an invitation to visit to several African-American writers and artists. Among those writers and intellectuals who made the trip were Harold Cruse, Julian Mayfield, John Henrik Clarke, and Robert Williams, the head of the Monroe, North Carolina, NAACP branch who would later call for "black self-defense" against white attacks. In Havana Jones met "the great Afro-Cuban poet Nicolas Guillen, who asked me straight out where was Langston [Hughes], and did I think that Langston had gotten more conservative. I smiled, but I did not know then that Langston had testified, under duress, before HUAC [House Un-American Activities Committee], denouncing some of his own earlier work, to keep great patriots like the filthy Cracker bastard James Eastland off his back" (164).[43]

Jones toured several parts of the island with the other visitors and was present when Castro gave a speech in Yara, a small town in Oriente Province, to over sixty thousand supporters. "I heard Fidel Castro speak for perhaps two hours nonstop, relating the entire history of the revolution to *campesinos,* soldiers, intellectuals, and foreign visitors," Jones recalled. "I even got to meet him and say a few words" (165). The entire experience had a profound impact on Jones. "When I returned I was shaken more deeply than even I realized. The arguments I'd had with my old poet comrades increased and intensified. It was not enough just to write, to feel, to think, one must act! One *could* act" (166).[44]

This was the beginning of a prolonged period of social activism as well as literary accomplishment for LeRoi Jones. He became active in Richard Gibson's Fair Play for Cuba Committee and started the Organization of Young Men (OYM), which was an attempt by black writers and artists in the Village to come together to raise one another's political consciousness about the social changes affecting the African-American community. He wrote articles on jazz and other types of music for *Metronome* and other music magazines. When he got a job with Prestige Records writing liner notes for jazz albums, this drew him closer into the jazz circles in the Village, and brought him into direct contact with the leading jazz innovators, including John Coltrane, Cecil Taylor, Charlie Mingus, Sonny Murray, Jackie McLean, Eric Dolphy, Ornette Coleman, Sonny Rollins, Max Roach, and Horace Silver. Writing the liner notes and music columns laid the foundation for one of Jones's most influential books, *Blues People,* published in 1963. In that work he argued that the transformation of African peoples from African to American can be traced in the development of black American music from the spirituals to gospel to blues and finally jazz. "There are definite *stages* in the Negro's transmutation from African to American," Jones wrote in the Introduction,

> or, at least, there are certain very apparent changes in the Negro's re-
> actions to America from the time of his first importation as slave until
> the present that can, I think, be seen—and again, I insist that these
> changes are most graphic in his music. I have tried to scrutinize each
> one of these stages as closely as I could, with a musical as well as soci-
> ological and anthropological emphasis.[45]

Blues People was very well received in most literary and music circles. The major criticism of Jones's approach and conclusions came from novelist Ralph Ellison, who was becoming more and more disturbed by what he considered to be the increasingly "ideological" bent of works by black artists. In his review of *Blues People* Ellison argued that Jones's theory about the evolution of African-American music suggested a kind of "cultural separation" between blacks and whites in the United States that Ellison believed did not exist. In the case of the blues, for example, Ellison felt that they

> speak to us simultaneously of the tragic and the comic aspects of the
> human condition and they express a profound sense of life shared by
> many Negro Americans precisely because their lives combined these
> modes. . . . For the blues are not primarily concerned with civil rights
> or obvious political protest; they are an art form and thus a transcen-
> dence of those conditions created within the Negro community by the
> denial of social justice. As such they are one of the techniques through
> which Negroes have survived and kept their courage during that long
> period when many whites assumed, as some still assume, they were
> afraid.

Ellison ultimately concluded, "it is unfortunate that Jones thought it necessary to ignore the aesthetic nature of the blues in order to make his ideological point, for he might have come much closer had he considered the blues not as politics but as art."[46]

In his review of *Blues People* Ellison raised an important issue that would be taken up by younger black artists in the second half of the decade: the nature of the "black literary aesthetic." LeRoi Jones/Amiri Baraka would become the leader of that group of black artists who came to the conclusion that the only way to understand and interpret the literary art created by African Americans was through an analysis of their social, economic, and political conditions. These artists believed that there can be no separation between art and politics. Indeed, for them a measure of the significance of a literary work was the extent to which it was successful in raising the political consciousness of its black (or white) audience.[47]

After participating in the drama workshops organized by playwright Edward Albee at the Cherry Lane Theater in the Village, Jones saw his play *Dutchman* performed there, and it received favorable reviews. The short, two-act play focused on a confrontation on a New York subway between Clay, an Ivy League black man, and a white woman, Lula, whom he tries to pick up. When Lula comes to realize that Clay is an "intellectual Negro," not a "hip field nigga," she taunts him into revealing his previously submerged hatred of white people. After this revelation, she kills him. Jones won an Obie Award for the best Off-Broadway play of the 1964 season, and in the process established his reputation as an "angry Negro writer."[48]

In the essay "LeRoi Jones Talking," published in 1964, he responded to the criticism that the crazy, neurotic Lula was meant to represent *all* white people. "How can one white person be all white persons, unless all white persons are alike. Are they? Similarly, it is equally stupid to think of the Negro boy as all Negroes, even though, as I've said, most white people do think of black men simply as Negroes, and not as individual men." The characters were not symbols, they were meant to be two real people. *"Dutchman* is about the difficulty of becoming a man in America. It is very difficult, to be sure, if you are black, but I think it is now much harder to become one if you're white. In fact, you will find very few white American males with the slightest knowledge of what manhood involves. They are too busy running the world, or running from it."[49]

Jones wrote several other plays, *The Baptism, The Toilet,* and *The Slave,* all performed in 1964; and published another volume of poetry, *The Dead Lecturer.*[50] His increasing militancy and "anti-white" public pronouncements led to an estrangement from his white wife because he was unable to live with the contradiction between his pro-black rhetoric and integrated, personal reality.

Even before the death of Malcolm X in February 1965, Jones could no longer live with this cognitive dissonance and decided to move uptown to Harlem. "The middle-class native intellectual, having outintegrated the most integrated, now plunges headlong back into what he perceives as blackest, native-est. Having dug, finally, how white he had become, now, *classically,* comes back to his countrymen charged up with the desire to be black, uphold black, etc. . . . a fanatical patriot!" (202). Jones rented a brownstone in Harlem that would become the center of the Black Arts Movement in New York City.

Black Arts Impresario

ON THE first floor of the brownstone he rented on West 130th Street, Jones opened the Black Arts Repertory Theater/School with the assistance of several black artists, writers, and hangers-on from downtown. Arts programs, forums, and theatrical productions were mounted during the summer of 1965 with financial assistance from the Harlem Youth Opportunities Unlimited Act, the Haryou Act, which created New York City's federal anti-poverty agency. "Haryou was the first anti-poverty program set up by Lyndon Johnson in his continuing assault on the Great Society. They were trying to set-up a stop-riot program for the summer of '65, the summer after the 'long hot summer' of '64" (211). Jones received funds for a summer arts and culture program. A Jazzmobile traveled throughout the neighborhoods and presented musical concerts nightly for Harlem residents. Street corner poetry readings were offered, dance and drama productions were mounted, and at the theater/school itself classes were offered in history, poetry, music, painting, and martial arts. Unfortunately, throughout the summer despite the success of many of the programs, the Black Arts Center was racked by internal and external conflicts.[51]

When Sargent Shriver, the national director of the anti-poverty program, was not allowed to visit the center during a trip to New York City because he was white, the program developed a reputation for "teaching racism with government funds." This diminished the likelihood that it would receive future funds from the anti-poverty agency. Confrontations between Muslims and non-Muslims, Sunni Muslims and Black Muslims, cultural nationalists and revolutionary nationalists, each one assuming a "blacker-than-thou" posture, at times exploded into open violence.

> There were gangsters and hoodlums and people in "the life" and all kinds of people who had been overlooked or peeped or popped. There was, as in any large urban black community, all kinds of promise and all kinds of frustration and bitterness. The sickness, the pathology that

[Frantz] Fanon talks about in the communities of the oppressed, it was all full out and openly roaring around and over and through and within us. The Black Arts itself was a pastiche of so many things, so many styles and ideologies. We had no stated ideology except "black," and that meant many things to many people, much of it useful, much of it not. But we shot from the hip, came always off the top or near the top of our heads. Our sincerity was our real ideology, a gestalt of our experience, an eclectic mixture of what we thought we knew and understood. What we wanted. Who we thought we were. It was very messy (221).

After several violent incidents and threats from militants, Jones decided he had had enough; and when he visited his parents in Newark over the Christmas (1965) holidays, he decided not to return to Harlem. Guilt feelings were mixed in with Jones's sense of frustration. "The guilt I carried about my life in the Village always undermined the decisive actions I had to take to preserve any dynamic and productive development in the Black Arts" (232). This was one of the major reasons he allowed obviously disturbed, though "militant," individuals from his Village days to bring about the destruction of the Harlem Black Arts project. But there was much that was positive about the activities in Harlem. Other cities started Black Arts programs modeled after the one in New York City, and the Black Arts Movement had been launched.[52]

After finally getting over his initial feelings of depression, Jones located and rented a house on Stirling Street in the downtown area and quickly became involved in bringing the Black Arts to Newark. In the summer of 1966 Jones organized an Afro-American Festival of the Arts, which brought Stokely Carmichael to Newark from Greenwood, Mississippi, right after he issued the call for Black Power. Jones recalled that when he read about the confrontation in Mississippi in the *New York Times* "next to the article I penned: 'God bless you, Stokely Carmichael' " (236). Two new plays by Jones, *A Black Mass* and *Jello,* were first performed in Newark at what was now dubbed Spirit House.[53] It was during the production of *A Black Mass* that Jones met Sylvia Wilson (Sylvia Robinson), an actress, dancer, and mother of two. She became Jones's partner and significant other in the various enterprises he undertook in Newark, and eventually they were married and had five children.

Spirit House not only sponsored many arts and cultural programs, but it also published a magazine, *Afro-American Festival of the Arts,* that included works by Larry Neal, Sonia Sanchez, Ben Caldwell, Clarence Reed, and other younger poets and writers. Many of these poets were included in *Black Fire: An Anthology of Afro-American Writing,* co-edited by Jones and Larry Neal, and published in 1968. In that work and in the collection of essays he published that year, *Black Music,* Jones emphasized his belief that the innovations made in Bebop and jazz by black musicians such as Ornette Coleman, Sonny Rollins, Cecil Taylor, and particularly John Coltrane, were what the poets, playwrights, and other writers were trying to do with black literature. In his autobiography Jones declared that

> the fact of music was the black poet's basis for creation. And those of us in the [Black Arts Movement] were drenched in black music and wanted our poetry to *be* black music. Not only that, we wanted that poetry armed with the spirit of black revolution. An art that could not commit itself to black revolution was not relevant to us. And if the poet that created such art was colored, we mocked him and his inspiration as brainwashed artifacts to please our beast oppressors! (237).[54]

LeRoi Jones's Spirit House also published a community newsletter, the *Stirling St. Newspaper.* The information was gathered and compiled by the young people who worked at the center. It was through the newsletter that the issue of black political power in Newark was raised. "In our kid-operated *Stirling St. Newspaper,*" Jones recalled, "we began to raise the fact that Newark was over 60 percent black. We asked, 'What do you think of having a black mayor?' " (246). By 1970 Spirit House would become the operations center for the campaign that led to the election of the first black mayor of any city in the northeastern United States.[55]

In 1966 Jones became acquainted with Maulana Ron Karenga, the founder of US, a cultural nationalist group centered in Los Angeles. Karenga had developed a system of cultural practices and beliefs for African Americans based on certain East African languages and cultures. Aimed at producing a Chinese-style cultural revolution among Africans in the United States, the "Kawaida doctrine" (African traditionalism) was expressed through the "Nguzo Saba," or Seven Principles: Umoja (Unity), Kujichagulia (Self-Determination), Ujima (Collective Work and Responsibility), Ujamaa (Collective Economics), Nia (Purpose), Kuumba (Creativity), and Imani (Faith). It was through Karenga and US that Kwanzaa came to be celebrated by thousands of African Americans throughout the United States.[56]

On a trip to Los Angeles early in 1967, Jones was able to observe firsthand the practices of US. That spring he was serving as a visiting professor of literature at San Francisco State College. Following a student protest at the school in the fall of 1966, a demand was made for more courses on the black experience. Nathan Hare, a sociologist from Howard University, was brought in to direct the establishment of what came to be the first Black Studies Program in the country. Jones, along with poets Marvin X and Sonia Sanchez, were among the first professors in the program. Marvin X and playwright Ed Bullins had been instrumental in the creation of Black Arts West, modeled after Jones's centers in Harlem and Newark. Jones participated in poetry readings, and directed productions of plays by Bullins, Ben Caldwell, and his own *Madheart*.[57]

The Bay Area was also the center of the Black Panther Party, and Jones met Eldridge Cleaver, the Panther minister of information and author of *Soul on Ice*, and several other leading Panthers, during his stay. Jones was informed that Cleaver had been attending meetings of the (white) Socialist Workers Party, but Jones was more disturbed by Cleaver's decision to remove all the artists from Black House, the Oakland black cultural center, for being too "reactionary." In any case, Jones at this point was more attracted to Karenga's cultural nationalism than the Panthers' hand-me-down Marxism because "Karenga's US was a perfect vehicle for working out the guilt of the overintegrated" (255).[58]

Jones returned to Spirit House in Newark in July 1967 only to be confronted by the increasing tensions between the black community and the local police, the same conditions that preceded the Watts riot in 1965 and the Chicago and Cleveland riots in 1966. Demonstrations had been organized by Newark's CORE branch over the brutal beating of a black taxicab driver, John William Smith, and Jones and other Spirit House workers joined the picket lines. Later that day (July 14, 1967), as Jones and his family were sitting down to dinner, some young boys rushed in. "They're breaking windows on Springfield Avenue." Jones and two others hopped into their van and headed in that direction.

> When we got there the shit was already on! Further up the street you could see figures moving fast. We could see some smoke, hey, then glass started to break close to where we were.
>
> The spirit and feeling of the moment a rebellion breaks out is almost indescribable. Everything seems to be in zoom motion, crashing toward some explosive manifestation. As Lenin said, time speeded up, what takes years is done in days, in real revolution. In rebellions life goes to 156 rpm and the song is a police siren accompanying people's breathless shouts and laughter (259–60).

As Jones and his friends in the van headed down Belmont Avenue and came upon a man who had been brutally beaten by the police, they stopped, put him into the van and took him to the city hospital where the atmosphere resembled a war zone. Later that evening as they were heading home, they came upon a wall of police cars, and policemen armed with shotguns and rifles. They could not turn around. The police surrounded the van, and Jones heard one shout, "these are the bastards who've been shooting at us." Another shouted, "Where are the guns?" Jones recognized one of the policemen, just before he smashed Jones's forehead with his gun, and others started beating him with nightsticks. "The blood felt hot in my face. I couldn't see, I could only feel the wet hot blood covering my entire head and face and hands and clothes. They were beating me to death" (262).

Several people witnessed the attack from their windows and started shouting at the police, who then shoved Jones into a police car; he was still semiconscious. Taken to the police station, he was dragged up the steps; and in the station he recognized Dominick Spina, the police director. "Hello, Mr. Spina." He turned and smiled and said, "They got you." "I'm alive . . . You didn't kill me!" From the police station Jones was taken to the city hospital, where the white doctor on duty recognized him and asked if he was a poet. "He said, 'Well, you'll never write any more poetry!' Then he gave me fifteen stitches in my forehead and another five in the hairline, with no anesthetic, like some primitive Gestapo butcher." Jones was left in the hallway handcuffed to a wheelchair, and when Sylvia arrived, she started screaming, and the police acted as if they were going to strike her. "Are you going to make *me* look like this?" The intervention of a black policemen kept her from being attacked (265).

Jones was locked up and later taken to Newark City Jail and placed in solitary confinement. From their cells the prisoners could see National Guardsmen shooting at rioters in the streets; some Guardsmen even started firing into the prison. During the three days of rioting, twenty-six people were killed, mostly by the police and the National Guard. A week later an even more violent riot erupted in Detroit where forty-five people were killed and federal troops had to be brought in.[59] Subsequently, Jones was released on $25,000 bail, which was raised only by putting his parents' and friends' houses up as collateral. "For me, the rebellion was a cleansing fire," Jones recalled. "I felt the clubs, the guns; they had even bashed one of my teeth out and loosened some more with fists and clubs. I would be scarred for life. The hottest rage had become a constant of my personality" (266).

Shortly after the riot, a group of Sunni Muslims came to Spirit House, led by Hajj Heesham Jabbar. "It was Heesham who gave me the name Ameer Barakat (The Blessed Prince). Sylvia was named Amina (faithful) after one of Muhammad's wives. Later, under Karenga's influence, I changed my name to Amiri, Bantuizing or Swahiliizing the first name and the pronunciation of the last as well." Jones, now "Amiri Baraka," felt that the name change symbolized the reality that "I was now literally being changed into a blacker thing. I was discarding my 'slave name' and embracing blackness" (267). At Baraka's subsequent trial, Judge Leon W. Karp not only sentenced him to jail for possession of two guns, but also read one of his poems into the proceedings as evidence against him. Although Baraka spent a week in Trenton State Penitentiary, on appeal the conviction was overturned primarily because the judge had made the poem part of the reason Baraka had been convicted of "criminal activity" (270).[60]

Black Politics: Detour on the Road to Black Liberation?

THE RIOT added urgency to the Newark black community's demand for black political power. The Committee for a United Newark (CFUN) was organized, under the influence of Ron Karenga, who visited the city several times. The CFUN was active in organizing the Black Power Conference that took place in Philadelphia in July 1968, but Karenga's US played only a marginal role in the proceedings because of its ongoing conflicts with the Black Panthers in Los Angeles (often fomented by agents from the FBI). The 1969 Black Power Conference took place in Bermuda, but Baraka and other black "radicals" were not allowed to attend by the Bermudian government. Meanwhile, the CFUN made preparations for challenging the corrupt city government under Mayor Hugh Addonizio. Rallies and fund-raising events brought James Brown, Leontyne Price, Bill Cosby, Adam Clayton Powell, Jr., Jesse Jackson, and other celebrities and national figures to Newark.[61]

Kenneth Gibson, a black City Hall civil engineer, had run for mayor in 1966 and eventually became the CFUN candidate in the 1970 mayoral election. Baraka was unimpressed by Gibson, but he hoped that with the people's movement behind him, he would be transformed. "I thought he had some loyalty and feeling for black people. He was so dull I could not see beneath that bland exterior there was a truly dull mind, a mind so dull that it had not yet even aspired to embrace the collective energy of black struggle except in the most opportunistic and low-level careerist way" (284). Gibson's campaign was also boosted by the fact that Mayor Addonizio was indicted a week before the election on corruption charges. On election day Anthony Imperiale, the corrupt head of Newark's Democratic machine, used his "thugs" and "goons" to try to intimidate black voters, but to no avail; and Gibson won the July election, and most of the black and Puerto Rican community-endorsed candidates were also victorious. Blacks in Newark were literally dancing in the streets in celebration.[62]

Because of the continuing confrontations between the Black Panthers and US in Los Angeles, Ron Karenga was rendered almost dysfunctional at the Black Power Conference in Atlanta in August 1970, where the main focus was the formation of the Congress of Afrikan Peoples (CAP), which was conceived as a national black united front.[63] Haywood Henry, a young Unitarian minister, was elected CAP's chairman and plans were made for the creation of CAP branches throughout the country. The convention also issued a call for a National Black Political Convention to be held in 1972 "to choose candidates to run in major elections and to give black people a unified voice in dealing with the presidential election" (292).

Meanwhile, in Newark problems arose over the decisions and policies pursued by Mayor Kenneth Gibson. Although plans had been dropped for the construction of a medical center downtown that would have displaced thousands of black residents, the mayor caved in when executives from the Prudential Insurance Company, the city's largest employer, opposed a proposal for a downtown cultural center. In each subsequent conflict over plans for changes in the city's social and economic policies or practices, when white businessmen objected, Gibson sided with the businessmen. "He [Gibson] gradually moved from being some kind of spokesperson for an independent black community to being a messenger to black people for the federal government" (295).

In 1972 plans moved ahead for the National Black Political Convention to be held in Gary, Indiana. "Electoral politics had become an obvious arena for the struggle for Black Power" (295). At planning sessions for the convention, representatives from the newly formed Congressional Black Caucus, as well as the NAACP, Urban League, and National Urban Coalition, pledged their participation. Baraka, Richard Hatcher, the newly elected mayor of Gary, and Detroit Congressman Charles Diggs became the co-conveners of the meeting, which took place in May 1972, with over nine thousand delegates in attendance. The convention issued the National Black Agenda, which offered a program for black political empowerment. Baraka was even appointed to go to the Democratic National Convention in Miami to present the document. "But once in Miami, the majority of the black politicians who were talking much militant shit in Gary had reverted to character and were simply scrambling to get on some candidate's payroll. Jesse Jackson, Shirley Chisholm, Ken Gibson, and most of the Congressional Black Caucus, were whoring like nobody's business" (296).[64]

Although Baraka and the CFUN were able to open an Afrikan Free School, which served as the model for many black independent schools across the country, and Spirit House continued to offer a wide array of cultural programs, Baraka was becoming more and more disillusioned with cultural nationalism, electoral politics, and black politicians. He found that in too many instances "cultural nationalism" served as an excuse for "male chauvinism." Amina (Sylvia), whom Baraka had married in 1970, voiced continual objections to the militants' male chauvinist practices supposedly in the name of "black revolution."

> The women in those 60s and early 70s black nationalist organizations (and even, I'm told, those further to the left) had to put up with a great deal of unadulterated bullshit in the name of revolution. My own wife, who first came into contact with me in what appeared to be the dying days of my bohemianism, really had got to me when bohemianism had changed its color. It is my contention that much of the cultural nationalism young people fervently believe is critically important to the struggle is just a form of black bohemianism. Take away the at-

tention to Africa, and the "weird" clothes, and "communalism" can be found in any number of white hippie communities. Some of the cultural nationalists we began to recognize when we started to read the history of the Communist Party (Bolshevik). These old Russian hippies and cultural nationalists were called Narodniks. When we read that, we recognized ourselves so clearly (300–301).

Baraka began to study Marxist thought, scientific socialism, because by 1973 he believed that "cultural nationalism was a dead end." At a regional meeting in Chicago of the Congress of African Peoples, Baraka made a speech on "National Liberation and Politics" and called for "the inclusion of Marx's theories and the teaching of Lenin and Mao as part of the Revolutionary Kawaida" (306). At this point Jitu Weusi from New York and Haki Madhubuti (formerly Don L. Lee) from Chicago resigned from the organization, and it was never to recover from the split. At the National Black Political Convention, held in Little Rock, Arkansas, in April 1974, Baraka made a speech calling for "socialist revolution." "It stunned quite a few people in the National Political Assembly and at that point I'm certain that more conservative factions in the organization vowed to get me out of the secretary-general's post" (306). In May 1974 in Washington at a meeting sponsored by the African Liberation Struggle Committee, which had been responsible for organizing the African Liberation Day marches and rallies, a number of Pan-African, cultural-nationalist, and revolutionary-nationalist groups participated. Baraka gave a speech in which he tried to reconcile Marxism and cultural nationalism, but the long diatribe convinced very few people, not even himself. "If we believed that socialism, scientific socialism, was the direction our people had to seek, then we should quit obstructing their progress in that direction" (308).[65]

In Newark Baraka felt that his latest ideological shift was further vindicated by the actions of the black mayor, Kenneth Gibson. When several young Puerto Ricans were brutalized by two white policeman, protests were held on the steps of City Hall by members of the African American and Puerto Rican communities. After Baraka and several others met with the mayor, who promised nothing, Baraka was coming down the steps, "suddenly from around the corner, police on horses and in patrol cars. The whole front of City Hall got shattered and the crowd went surging up the street. The police then did what police of any white racist monopoly capitalist government would do, they tried to kill the people. They roared down the street, one car slamming on brakes just a few yards from the crowd of us." One young demonstrator "was slammed high into the air but did not get hurt. Later two Puerto Rican brothers were killed." After this initial violence, Mayor Gibson came out and issued a ban on further demonstrations. "He was playing the 'white boy' to the

Puerto Ricans like Addonizio to the bloods. I hated the feeling this gave me, I could understand what radical whites must feel when white racists and white supremacy freaks are running their usual hate everybody oppress everybody bullshit" (304–5).

Baraka attended the Sixth Pan-African Congress, held in Dar es Salaam in July 1974, and organized by Tanzanian President Julius Nyerere. It was the first Pan-African Congress to be held on the African continent. Representatives of black groups from around the world, including delegates from the African liberation movements then involved in revolutionary struggles in Angola, Mozambique, and other parts of Africa, made it clear that "anti-imperialism" was the thrust of their activity, not "narrow nationalism."[66] As a result of his experiences with black nationalism in the United States, Baraka fully agreed with this ideological position. More importantly, Baraka came to many of the same conclusions about black liberation as Malcolm X had following his trips to Asia and Africa in 1964.

> I realized, also, that the US was my home. . . . I realized that the 30 million African Americans would play a major role in the transformation of black people's lives all over this planet. It was no mere truism, we lived where the head of world oppression lived and when the people of the world united to bring this giant oppressor to its knees we would be part of that contingent (of not only blacks, but of other oppressed nationalities and workers of all nationalities) chosen by the accident of history to cut this thing's head off and send it rolling through the streets of North America (311).

As was the case with Ida Wells-Barnett, Harry Haywood, W. E. B. Du Bois, Malcolm X, and Gwendolyn Brooks, the autobiography of LeRoi Jones/Amiri Baraka clarified the relationship between the ideological changes he underwent throughout his life and his personal experiences. His shift to a more "political" emphasis in his poetry and other writings after 1960 was one of the results of his trip to post-revolutionary Cuba. Baraka's adoption of a cultural-nationalist ideology came about as a result of his experiences in Greenwich Village and Harlem during the mid-1960s. And his latest ideological conversion to "Marxist-Leninist-Maoism" came about as a result of his political activities in Newark.

> When I returned to the US . . . I was no longer a nationalist, I knew that just black faces in high places could never bring the change we seek—all of us who are conscious or describe ourselves as advanced or progressive. I could see my own life and those tasks I had declared for myself in a new light. I had seen [Kenneth] Gibson and domestic "neo-colonialism," I had been to Africa and seen that same boy at

work over there holding the people down. It was clearer to me that only socialism could transform society, that the whole world must be at the disposal of the whole world, that all of us must benefit by each other's existence, a few billion primates of an arguably advanced species in a world dominated by insects (311).

Gwendolyn Brooks, LeRoi Jones/Amiri Baraka, and the other poets and writers active in the Black Arts Movement of the 1960s and early 1970s were inarguably successful in creating a black literary aesthetic. The most important element in this literary concept was the idea that black artists should participate in the movement for Black Power or black revolution by creating art for and about black people. African-American artists should use the experience and culture of peoples of African descent in the United States in the creation of distinctly African-American art and literature. This issue had first come up in the 1920s and most younger poets and novelists saw the advantages of using the rich cultural heritage—the folklore, music, religious practices—as a source for their creative works aimed at both black and white audiences. Black writers of the 1930s, 1940s, and 1950s, writing sometimes under the ideological sway of the white left, understood that most of their audience would be white, although some, like Langston Hughes, particularly with his Jesse B. Semple stories, consciously sought to expand their black readership by choosing subject matter that would have mass appeal.

With the coming of the Civil Rights–Black Power movement, however, the poets, writers, and other artists saw as the major objective the creation of poetry and other literary works that would raise the political consciousness of the black masses. While the literary Garveyites in the 1920s had also wanted to create art for the black masses that would raise their political consciousness, they were uninterested in using African-American cultural forms. The Garveyites avoided "Negro dialect" in their poetry, and believed that the only reason the black masses liked the spirituals, blues, jazz, and other forms of "Negro music" was because they did not know or had not been exposed to "higher" (classical European) forms of music.[67] The artists of the Black Arts Movement, however, built their art upon precisely these African-American cultural forms, particularly the language and music; and through their participation in street corner poetry readings, Black Arts festivals, drama workshops, and theatrical productions sponsored by black cultural centers demonstrated their commitment to bringing their art to the people and developing the creative talents within the black community.

Black art was an important element in the movement for Black Power because a "cultural revolution" was necessary for the creation of a new black consciousness. For many black artists this became a matter of principle. At the same time, these artists also believed that with black political and economic empowerment would come an expansion in the size and number of independent black cultural institutions. However, to the extent that black artists were supported by institutions outside the black community, particularly the federal and local governments, their independence could be compromised, and they would be dependent on the political strength of the black community to maintain the cultural institutions that would support their artistic endeavors. The election of African Americans to political office was seen as necessary for the maintenance of black cultural institutions; black politicians, however, had divided loyalties and were often unable (or unwilling) to guarantee the support of artists in the black community.

Adam Clayton Powell, Jr., the only black elected official closely associated with the Civil Rights–Black Power movement, was keenly aware of the limitations placed on black politicians in either the Democratic or Republican Party. After serving over twenty-five years in elective office, Powell came to the conclusion that neither party was concerned with the improvement in the status of African Americans if that objective was in conflict with the goals of another constituency these politicians viewed as more important. Thus if black leaders were truly interested in advancing African-American interests, then they would have to remain independent of the dominant political establishment that was committed to maintaining the social, economic, and cultural status quo. A status quo that kept African Americans at the bottom of the socioeconomic ladder.

10

Adam Clayton Powell, Jr.

The Need for Independent Black Leadership

The black masses should follow only those leaders who can sit at the bargaining table with the white power structure as equals and negotiate for a share of the loaf of bread, not beg for crumbs. We must stop sending little boys whose organizations are controlled and financed by white businessmen to do a man's job. Because only those who are financially independent can be men. This is why earlier I called for black people to finance their own organizations and institutions. In so doing, the black masses guarantee the independence of their leadership.

—ADAM CLAYTON POWELL, JR., 1971

Photograph by Jack T. Franklin. Reprinted by permission of the Afro-American Historical and Cultural Museum, Philadelphia.

THE BEHAVIOR exhibited by Kenneth Gibson once he was elected mayor of Newark, and that was denounced by Amiri Baraka in his autobiography, has been typical of black elected officials before and after 1970. Baraka complained that Gibson could not conceive of "black people having to make their own way, of self-determination and self-sufficiency. A government check is the only way we'll make it. So he gradually moved from being some kind of spokesperson for an independent black community to being a messenger to black people for the federal government" (294–95). Oftentimes African Americans had gone to great measures to secure the election of one of their own to political office, only to find that once in office that individual acted no differently than other Democratic or Republican politicians and was all too willing to compromise on important issues facing the black community. It was the rare exception when independent political activity within the black community resulted in the election to public office of individuals, such as Adam Clayton Powell, Jr., who consistently maintained their independence and placed the collective interests of African Americans above those of the political party to which they belonged.

The earliest group of African Americans elected to political office were those members of the Republican Party in the former Confederacy during Congressional, or "Radical," Reconstruction. While some black elected officials were former slaves and Union war veterans, others were free before the Civil War. Some came from a background in business, while others were professionals, such as journalists and educators. Some were considered "charismatic leaders" whose intellect and speaking ability were well recognized in both the black and white communities, while others kept a low profile and were known for their more conservative beliefs and practices. Despite the fact that these black politicians were elected from areas that were virtually all black, or at least had a substantial black majority, and forged political alliances with sympathetic whites in the party, they wielded very little political influence or power. In summarizing much of the scholarly research on the subject, historian August Meier suggested in *Southern Black Leaders of the Reconstruction Era* several reasons for this state of affairs. One was the nature of American politics. "American politics is a politics of compromise between competing and varied interest groups," Meier declared; thus the "radical step of enfranchising the freedmen was likely at best to produce only limited advances for them." Moreover, black politicians functioned in a "white-dominated society" and the national government failed to give its "unequivocal support to Radical Reconstruction." Even in states where blacks were the majority, "influential whites, with their connections to higher federal authorities or for other reasons, retained much of the power." And while many of these men were sincerely interested in "serving the race," others entered politics for personal gain, and "like so many of their white counterparts, blacks did support legislation for their own direct economic interest." Meier concluded that in many instances the role of the black politician was "symbolic" and "many of the Negro political leaders were able to give the impression of influence and power, when actually they may, in many cases, have had relatively little of it."[1]

With the overthrow of Radical Reconstruction in 1877, black politicians were not even able to give the impression of wielding some kind of political power within the Republican Party. In instance after instance, the civil rights guaranteed by the Fourteenth and Fifteenth Amendments to the Constitution were undermined not merely by the Democratic Party in the South, but by the Republican Party as well. Black Republican politicians were powerless to influence these political decisions. As was described in Chapter Two, when the Republican-dominated Supreme Court in 1883 declared unconstitutional the Civil Rights Act of 1875, which had banned discrimination in theaters, railroads, hotels, and other public accommodations, black preachers, professors, and publishers throughout the country denounced the decision. These black spokespersons were particularly disturbed by the fact that the justices who voted against the civil rights law were Republicans. Even Frederick Douglass, who by this time had received several political appointments from Republican presidents, had to denounce the Supreme Court's ruling. "This decision has inflicted a heavy calamity upon seven millions of people of this country, and left them naked and defenseless against the action of a malignant, vulgar, and pitiless prejudice." Douglass believed that the Republican justices had acted "in utter and flagrant disregard of the objects and *intentions* of the National legislature by which [the civil rights law] was enacted, and of rights plainly secured by the Constitution."[2]

It was also a Republican-dominated Supreme Court that upheld the constitutionality of the clauses written into the Mississippi state constitution in 1890 instituting poll taxes and literacy tests as requirements for the right to vote. In the case of *Williams v. Mississippi* (1898), the Court ruled that since the Mississippi constitution did not state that blacks must pay poll taxes and take literacy tests, but that *all* citizens were subject to these requirements, these new qualifications were not considered violations of the Fifteenth Amendment, which prohibited infringements on the right to vote on the basis of race, creed, color, or previous condition of servitude. The result was that these and other voting requirements were used to remove southern blacks from the electorate, not just in Mississippi, but throughout the South, and by 1901 there were virtually no black elected officials in any of the states of the former Confederacy.[3]

The Illusion of Service: Black Politics in the North

ALTHOUGH A FEW African Americans were elected to political office in northern states between 1901 and 1928, no blacks served in the U.S. Congress during that entire period. Oscar De Priest was the first African American elected to the U.S. Congress in the twentieth century, and the first to be elected from a northern state. Born of ex-slaves in Florence, Alabama, on March 9, 1871, De Priest, along with his family, joined the Black Exodus to Kansas in 1878 and settled in Salina. After attending school in Kansas, Oscar De Priest migrated to Chicago in 1889, worked as a house painter, and soon became involved in Republican politics. In 1904 with the support of Republican leaders, De Priest was elected to the Cook County Commission, the major governing body that included the city of Chicago. Although he was renominated in 1908, factionalism within the Republican Party prevented his reelection.[4]

Out of politics temporarily, De Priest became involved in real estate, taking advantage of the fact that the large numbers of southern blacks migrating to Chicago needed housing. De Priest organized the Chicago branch of Booker T. Washington's National Negro Business League. Using the rhetoric of "racial solidarity," according to political scientist Ira Katznelson, De Priest "made his fortune by the technique known as 'block busting'. . . . He purchased buildings of flats that were occupied by white families and then rented vacant apartments to Negroes. The building's whites usually moved out, the building became all-black, and rents were promptly raised." The exploitative rents that were charged to black tenants were used "to invest in securities, more real estate, and to finance his political career."[5]

Although De Priest shifted his support from Republican to Democratic candidates when it was to his advantage, in December 1914 he received the support of the Republican Party for the councilmanic seat from Chicago's Second Ward. His election to office was assured in the heavily black, Republican district. Once in office De Priest became closely associated with the vice and gambling interests in his ward. On January 18, 1917, De Priest was indicted by grand jury on conspiracy to allow gambling and houses of prostitution in his district, and bribery of police officers. Although his trial resulted in his acquittal through the efforts of the nationally known lawyer Clarence Darrow, he failed in his attempts at reelection to the City Council. De Priest decided to rebuild his political organization, this time in the city's Third Ward, and continued to support candidates who promised him the most once elected.[6]

In 1926 De Priest's organization backed former Mayor William "Big Bill" Thompson's bid for reelection, and in the 1928 Republican primary De Priest was elected Third Ward committeeman. Congressman Martin Madden won the nomination for the U.S. Congress from the Ilinois Second District in 1928, but soon died. De Priest moved quickly, gained the support of the Thompson political machine, and won the nomination in the heavily black and Republican congressional district. De Priest was elected to the U.S. Congress in 1928 and served two additional terms.[7]

While at one time Chicago was often hailed as the center of black political activity in the North, later research has revealed that black voters received very few benefits from their close relationship with the Republican machine during the years of Oscar De Priest's political prominence. While blacks did receive city patronage jobs, these were primarily as cooks, janitors, messengers, and garbagemen. In many city departments those blacks who received patronage positions were segregated and became the victims of discriminatory treatment, such as the first blacks appointed in the Chicago Fire Department. While black elites directly tied to the Republican Party benefited from their political connections, the black masses were often placed in a worse situation. Ira Katznelson found that "the black-Thompson alliance did nothing to improve the shocking condition in the black-belt's housing, schools, recreational facilities, and welfare services. In fact, the Thompson-black alliance may have actually led to a deterioration in living conditions as a result of the collusion of the Mayor with the underworld which permitted vice to flourish in black neighbourhoods."[8]

The entire orientation of black politics in Chicago during this period was individualistic, rather than collective, and the black politicians in effect served as messengers and buffers between the black community and the city's white leadership. "The black political machine was co-opted into the Thompson machine and lost its independence." Other scholars, including Harold Gosnell, James Q. Wilson, and Harold Cruse, agreed with the conclusions of Ira Katznelson about the nature of Chicago black politics during this era. "The black politicians had the potential to exercise group power on behalf of solutions for the group; instead, the generalized capacity of the group, based on assent of the votes of the masses, was used to obtain individual solutions. . . . And for the masses, the political gains were almost non-existent."[9]

With the coming of the Great Depression and the election of Democrat Franklin Roosevelt to the presidency in 1932, African-American voters in the North said "farewell to the party of Lincoln" because Democratic politicians decided to include blacks in the various New Deal programs. In many cities black politicians en masse shifted to the Democratic Party and those who did not were defeated by black Democrats. In the 1934 congressional elections in Chicago, Oscar De Priest was defeated by Arthur W. Mitchell, a black Democrat who had never served in elective office before. Campaigning as a fervent "New Dealer," Mitchell benefited from the fact that De Priest took his reelection for granted and refused to debate Mitchell in public. De Priest lost his congressional seat by over three thousand votes.[10]

Unfortunately, Arthur Mitchell was even more conservative on racial issues than De Priest, and Mitchell's voting record was regularly attacked by black leaders across the country and particularly by Walter White and other officials of the NAACP. The legislative issue dominating NAACP lobbying efforts during the early 1930s was the passage of a bill making lynching a federal crime. Not only did Congressman Mitchell initially refuse to support the anti-lynching legislation introduced by Congressman Joseph Gavagan of New York and supported by the NAACP, Mitchell introduced a much weaker bill that was then supported by southern Democrats. The entire House voted down Mitchell's substitute bill, and when the Gavagan bill was forced out of committee, Mitchell reluctantly supported it. The Gavagan bill eventually passed the House, only to be subsequently blocked in the Senate by conservative southern Democrats.[11]

In subsequent years Congressman Mitchell introduced legislation for the desegregation of interstate transportation and for civil service reform, as well as a bill creating a federal Commission on Negro Affairs, none of which was passed by Congress. In 1942, Mitchell decided not to run for reelection, and his congressional seat went to Democrat William Dawson, who became the third African American elected to the U.S. Congress in the twentieth century. Unlike Mitchell, Dawson was a career politician in Chicago. In the 1928 Republican primary in the Illinois Second District, Dawson came in second, behind Martin Madden. But Oscar De Priest outmaneuvered Dawson within the Republican organization and captured the nomination. Dawson went on to develop his own "sub-machine" on the South Side and was elected Republican state committeeman in 1932 and to the Chicago City Council in 1933, where he served until 1939. Dawson was the Republican candidate who challenged Democrat Arthur Mitchell in the 1938 congressional election, but lost in the heavily Democratic Second District. In 1939 Dawson switched to the Democratic Party, then under the leadership of Chicago Mayor Edward Kelly. Dawson then began developing his own "sub-machine" within the Democratic organization, and when Mitchell announced his retirement in 1942, Dawson won the Democratic nomination in the primary. In the fall election Dawson defeated Republican William King by over three thousand votes.[12]

William Dawson became the classic example of the "Negro machine politician." Dawson introduced very few bills in Congress, instead focusing his energies and efforts on building and maintaining his political organization on Chicago's South Side. Spending much more time in his home district than most congressmen, Dawson oversaw political patronage, made sure that blacks running for election met with his approval, and distributed the material benefits stemming from his growing political power to individuals loyal to his organization. James Q. Wilson in his 1960 book *Negro Politics: The Search for Leadership* described Chicago black politics in the era of William Dawson.

> The Dawson machine, like all machines, is an organization whose purpose is the election of men to office and which is sustained mainly through the distribution of tangible incentives to its members. To a greater extent than any other Negro organization which acts in the public or civic arena, it is "issue-free." It holds the loyalties of the voters in large part by virtue of their commitment to the Democratic Party, but also in part by providing services (or the illusion of services) to the voter and by personal relationships of loyalty and mutual favors which exist between the voters and precinct captains. Although in its formative years, the Dawson organization—and Dawson personally—used appeals to race pride and race unity as a technique for building strength and gaining adherents, the organization has for some time been in a position of security and established success which have made such appeals unnecessary.[13]

Subsequent research on black politics and politicians in New York, Philadelphia, Detroit, Cleveland, and other northern cities in the first half of the twentieth century has documented a pattern similar to that in Chicago. Black politicians were generally more devoted to the advancement of their own political careers than the collective interests of the black community. The black political bosses used their power and positions to maintain black support for the local (white) political machine of which they were a part, and only secondarily (if at all) to improve the social and economic status of their black constitutency. Chuck Stone in his book *Black Political Power in America,* published in 1968, examined the relationship between blacks and machine politics in the North before 1950 and concluded that "no matter how stained his hands, how sullied his reputation, or how unpopular his manner, if the black politician has played power politics with the same relentless and unconscionable efficiency as white politicians, he will soon be accepted by black people as have the most important power brokers in society."[14]

With the election of Rev. Adam Clayton Powell, Jr., to political office in 1941, however, an alternative model for black political activity was created that demonstrated the collective advantages that were possible through the support of a politician who was independent and committed to the advancement of African Americans as a group.

Breaking the Political Mold: Adam Clayton Powell, Jr.

DURING THE 1960s when the Civil Rights–Black Power movement reached its peak, Rev. Adam Clayton Powell, Jr., was the most powerful black politician in the United States. Powell often referred to himself as "Mr. Civil Rights" and became an early supporter of Black Power. Although he was eventually stripped of his powerful position as chairman of the House Committee on Education and Labor, and was defeated (some say through political corruption and fraud) in his bid for reelection to his thirteenth term in Congress in 1970, throughout his political career Powell ran and behaved as a political independent, and used his political power to advance African Americans, not just in Harlem, but throughout the country. In his autobiography, *Adam by Adam,* published in 1971, Powell not only sought to explain his side of the controversial issues that led to his ouster from the U.S. Congress in 1967, but also demonstrated his commitment to the matters of principle that came to define the African-American intellectual tradition in the United States. More important, Powell presented an eloquent plea for African Americans to support only those leaders who were independent of the dominant political and economic interests in American society.[15]

Adam Clayton Powell, Jr., was born on November 29, 1908, Thanksgiving Day, in New Haven, Connecticut. He was the younger child of Mattie Fletcher Schaefer Powell and Adam Clayton Powell, Sr., who was then pastor of Immanual Baptist Church in New Haven. Powell Sr. was born in Soak Creek, Franklin County, Virginia, in 1865, and received his early education there and in West Virginia where his mother and stepfather, Anthony and Sally Dunning Powell, moved in 1875. Powell Sr. also attended Rendville Academy in Perry, Ohio, and graduated from Wayland Seminary and College in Washington, D.C., in 1892. In July 1889 Powell Sr. married Mattie Schaefer of West Virginia, whose father was Jacob Schaefer, a German brewmaster, and whose mother was black (Powell Jr. never knew his maternal grandmother's name). After graduating from Wayland Seminary in 1892, Powell Sr. served as pastor of the Ebenezer Baptist Church in Philadelphia, and in 1893 he was called to Immanual Baptist Church in New Haven; in 1895 and 1896 he took courses at Yale University. Adam and Mattie Powell's first child, Blanche, was born in New Haven in 1898. One month after the birth of Adam Jr. in 1908, Powell Sr. was called to the pastorship of the Abyssinian Baptist Church, one of the oldest churches in New York City, established in 1808 by Thomas Paul.[16]

The church was then located on 40th Street in a deteriorating neighborhood, but the family moved into a brownstone on West 134th in Harlem, which in 1909 was an upper-middle-class, predominantly Jewish area. Powell Jr. admitted that while growing up he was spoiled by the three women in his life, his mother, older sister, and their maid, Josephine. When Powell Jr. was six years old, he had a serious respiratory infection and was nursed backed to health by the women in the household. In his autobiography Powell Jr. recalled that "because of my illness I was in the attentions of the three women who figured so importantly in my childhood. What a wonderful womb to live in. It made the cutting of the umbilical cord later in life so difficult. But I have not a single criticism" (20).

Adam Jr.'s fair skin and straight hair was the result of the mixed racial heritage of both his parents. Powell Jr. confessed in his autobiography that at times both he and his sister, Blanche, passed for white. However, he also described the childhood experience that awakened his consciousness about racial realities in American society. After the family had moved from 134th to 136th Street in Harlem, Powell Jr. was sent by his father for the evening paper, and he was stopped by a group of black boys, who asked, "Are you white or colored?" He looked at his skin and said, "white," The boys proceeded to beat him up. The next night he was stopped on Eighth Avenue by a gang of white boys who asked, "What are you?" Recalling the incident the night before, he answered, "Colored," and the white boys beat him up. On a third night another group of black boys stopped him on the street and asked, "What are you." "Remembering once more my previous experiences, I said, 'Mixed!' One of the boys yelled, 'Oh, he's a Mick!' And I was sent home crying for a third time." Powell concluded, "this was my first real brush with racism. It sowed the seeds of my belief that it's not the color of your skin but the way you think that makes you what you are" (24).

Powell Jr. attended P.S. 5 in Harlem for his elementary schooling and Townsend Harris High School, a college preparatory secondary school associated with the City College of New York (CCNY). Powell played on the school's basketball team, and when he entered CCNY in 1925 at age sixteen, he played on the freshman squad. He enjoyed his first semester, spending more time on extracurricular activities—"parties, drinking, smoking, being spoiled by women in many ways"—and after failing three subjects, it was only through the intervention of his father that he was able to return for the second semester. Unfortunately, during the spring semester (1926) his sister, Blanche, died after her attack of appendicitis was misdiagnosed. Powell was very close to his sister and her death greatly affected him. That semester he failed all his courses at CCNY. "This particular death, this shock, this particular moment in my life turned me against everything and everyone without reason or logic," he later recalled. "I began to hate, mistrust. God was a myth, the Bible a jungle of lies. The church was a fraud, my father was the leading perpetrator, my mother a stupid rubber stamp. The smiling good people of the church were grinning fools" (30).

Powell got several jobs that summer, including one at the San Remo Hotel, which catered to a Broadway clientele. As a bellhop he made over sixty-five dollars a week, but he was broke all the time because he lost his money gambling. A family friend recommended that he go to a school far away from the city where he was less likely to get into trouble, Colgate University, an all-male school in upstate New York. The president at the time, Dr. George Barton Cutten, had worked with his father in New Haven. Powell soon grew accustomed to Colgate, made many friends, and did well in his course work. The only racial incident he mentioned was when his father was asked to deliver a lecture at the school, and his white roommate learned that he was not white. The roommate demanded that Powell be moved out of the dorm room. "This was the first time in my life that deep discrimination had touched me directly. It came as a tremendous shock" (32).

During his senior year after he had made plans to attend medical school, Powell had a "mystical experience," similar to that of Malcolm X during his incarceration in Massachusetts, that led to his decision to enter the ministry. In the middle of the night while Powell was lying in bed, "suddenly there was a voice. Something like my father's, but softer, and yet more insistent. A still, small voice: 'Whom shall I send? Who will go for me?' And there in that room, in that quiet, for the first time in my life God talked to me. That day I began my first steps in the area of mysticism. And ever since, in every way, I've tried to maintain a sensitivity and an awareness so that this voice would always be heard" (34). When he told his parents of his decision to become a minister, they were overcome with emotion. Powell Jr. gave his trial sermon on Good Friday in 1930 in his father's pulpit, and the congregation was filled with many of his nightclub friends, who were quite surprised, to say the least. After graduation and a three-month trip to Europe, Egypt, and Palestine, he joined the Abyssinian Baptist Church as an assistant minister and began taking courses at Union Theological Seminary and Teachers College, Columbia University.[17]

Within a few months of his return, however, Powell's father suffered a nervous breakdown from overwork and was told to refrain from all church activities for several months. Thus the supervision of the over-five-thousand-member congregation fell upon the shoulders of the twenty-one-year-old seminarian. "With no experience, I had to step in and take my father's place all through that winter. I knew that my preaching was far below what the church was accustomed to, but was pleased when the crowds did not fall off and offerings maintained their usual level" (36).

It was also in 1930 that Powell received his political baptism, when a group of black physicians who had recently been banned from practicing at Harlem Hospital by the white administration came to him for assistance. Powell soon became fired up by the issue and led a delegation of over six thousand in a march to City Hall. The Board of Estimate was in session, and one member, Joseph V. McKee, demanded that young Rev. Powell be heard. Powell spoke and as a result the Board of Estimate launched an investigation; shortly thereafter the five black doctors were reinstated, and eventually Harlem Hospital had a completely integrated staff. Powell learned an important lesson from this incident: "When I stood before the Board of Estimate and stated our demands, I knew at least the power of the masses—as long as I could keep the thousands on my side united, it mattered not who opposed us because we would win" (58–59).

With this first success behind him, the young minister was called upon by other groups. Those unemployed by the Depression were being evicted from their homes and apartments, and young Rev. Powell worked with the Consolidated Tenants League to force landlords to allow those unable to keep up with their rents to remain in their homes. The Harlem Riot in March 1935 was sparked by rumors that a Puerto Rican boy who was caught allegedly stealing from a five-and-dime store on 125th Street had been beaten by the white store owner. Mobs gathered and violence and looting soon erupted. Over two hundred store windows were smashed and three blacks were killed. Damage from the riot was estimated at over a million dollars. Powell gained much notoriety when he published a series of articles on the riot in the *New York Post* and blamed the supposedly liberal administration of Mayor Fiorello La Guardia for allowing horrible living conditions to exist in Harlem. While some commentators tried to blame the communists for the violence, Powell disagreed. "It was not a riot; it was an open, unorganized protest against empty stomachs, overcrowded tenements, filthy sanitation, rotten foodstuffs, chiseling landlords and merchants, discrimination on relief, disfranchisement, and against a disinterested administration. It was not caused by the Communists."[18]

Powell was instrumental in the formation of the Greater New York Coordinating Committee for Employment, whose mission and slogan was "Jobs for Negroes." Stores operating on Harlem's 125th Street that employed no blacks were targeted for boycotts. The group managed to gain some jobs from local merchants as well as from the Consolidated Edison (Electric) Company and the New York Telephone Company. The greatest success came after the group organized protests at the site of the upcoming New York's World's Fair. Over two hundred blacks gained employment as a result of the protests.[19] Then on September 25, 1941, Rev. Powell announced his candidacy for the City Council, and although he was approached by both Republican and Democratic leaders, he decided to run as an independent. Using primarily his own money and the voluntary efforts of members of his own congregation, Powell took to the political trail. "When the vote was counted, I had come in third out of ninety-nine candidates and had the right to sit on the council of the largest city in the world as an independent" (69).

Powell's autobiography presented no information about the four years he served on the City Council, probably because almost none of the legislation

Councilman Powell introduced was passed during the years he served. Maurine Christopher noted in *Black Americans in Congress* that Powell's critics declared that "while he talked a great deal, he accomplished nothing concrete in the city council where every Powell-advanced measure was either emasculated or defeated. His explanation was that as a nonpartisan independent he got no cooperation from party regulars. He did, however, focus on wrongs that needed righting, and eventually many of his suggestions were enacted." And after he launched his own newspaper, *The People's Voice,* he used his "Soap Box" column to make sure that the people in Harlem knew where he stood on pressing social and political issues, and to keep himself and his views before the people.[20]

"The First Bad Nigger in Congress"

WHEN A NEW congressional district was created in 1944 that encompassed Harlem, Councilman Powell announced his candidacy for the seat. Although he still campaigned as an independent, Powell entered his name in four primaries and actually won the nomination for the Democratic, Republican, and American Labor parties. In the November election he ran unopposed. In January 1945 when Powell was sworn in, William Dawson from Chicago was the only other black in the U.S. Congress. Later in 1945 Congressman Powell published his first book, *Marching Blacks: An Interpretive History of the Rise of the Black Common Man,* which presented a brief history of African peoples in the United States, not from Jamestown, Virginia, in 1619, but from 1526 when enslaved Africans were first brought to North America by Vásquez De Allyon. "The slaves immediately revolted, killed the slave traders, plunged into the interior of the Carolina coast and mixed with the Indian tribes. Today [1945] remnants of this African-Indian culture can be found along the Carolina coast."[21]

Powell described the black struggle for freedom in *Marching Blacks,* pointing out that "organized Negroes, of course met their greatest successes in the North, but here and there in the deep South the power of the black mass was making itself felt."[22] Powell believed that the fight for civil rights during World War II was "a war within a war," and declared that "the Negro demanded—in a word—EQUALITY! Not only economic and political, but educational, religious *and social equality* as well."[23] Even more controversial than his claim that blacks wanted "social equality" (meaning legalized intermarriage) was his suggestion that all of the oppressed blacks in the South should migrate to the North. "The people must move—and NOW! This is the only answer to the South's inhumanity to man. Migration does not mean running away from the problem. It represents the considered conclusion that some portions of the South are hopeless. It will serve notice that it must change immediately."[24] The publication of *Marching Blacks* gave the flamboyant young congressman from Harlem the national attention he sought.[25]

In *Marching Blacks* Powell described his campaigns for black social and economic advancement in Harlem in the 1930s and early 1940s, and in his autobiography, *Adam by Adam,* he presented lengthy discussions of the important pieces of legislation that he introduced or supported. The most significant was the bill calling for the creation of a permanent Fair Employment Practices Commission (FEPC). In 1941 when A. Philip Randolph threatened to bring 100,000 blacks to Washington to demand an end to discriminatory practices by employers receiving government contracts during the wartime mobilization, President Franklin Roosevelt issued Executive Order 8802, which banned discriminatory hiring practices by federal contractors. The order also created the Fair Employment Practices Commission, whose role was to investigate charges of discrimination in hiring on the basis of race, creed, color, or nationality by employers with government contracts. The executive order was considered a wartime measure and Congressman Powell beginning in January 1945 co-sponsored legislation for a permanent FEPC, "a permanent act of this Congress which will forever, in wartime and peacetime, rule out discrimination in public and private employment" (77).[26]

Congressman Powell was appointed to the House Committee on Labor and Education and it took four years before the FEPC bill was actually brought to the floor of the House for debate, due primarily to the opposition from southern congressmen from his own party. In January 1950 an attempt was made to bypass the House Rules Committee, which determined whether or not bills voted out of committee would be considered by the entire House. "By the rules of the House, the Rules Committee may be bypassed and bills [could be] presented directly to the House on Calendar Wednesday." Each House committee was assigned a Calendar Wednesday when its bills could be considered, "and finally our day came. My FEPC bill was called up, and debate began at last. we did not adjourn until close to four o'clock in the morning, when Republican [Samuel] McConnell, with the support of Richard Nixon, killed the Powell FEPC bill. A toothless substitute that killed the FEPC drive prevailed" (84). The U.S. Congress never passed permanent FEPC legislation.[27]

The young congressman from Harlem had more success with what came to be known as the Powell Amendment. The purpose of the measure was to end federal support for programs that at the state and local level discriminated against African Americans. The first application of the amendment came with the federally sponsored school lunch program proposed in 1946.

With the support of my colleagues, the first civil rights amendment, attached to the school lunch program, was passed. It is Public Law 396,
enacted by the 79th Congress, June 4, 1946. From then on I was to
use this important weapon with success, to bring about opportunities
for the good of man and to stop those efforts that would harm democracy's forward progress. Sometimes I used it only as a deterrent against
the undemocratic practices that would have resulted if that amendment had not been offered (81).[28]

In the summer of 1952 as the time for the Democratic National Convention approached, Congressman Powell threw his support behind New York's
W. Averell Harriman, who during his term as Secretary of Commerce in Harry
Truman's administration had authorized the desegregation of National Airport
in Washington, D.C. Powell wanted the Democratic Platform Committee to
issue a strong plank on civil rights that endorsed the passage of FEPC legislation, a federal anti-lynching law, and the abolition of legal segregation in the
District of Columbia. Congressman William Dawson was the only black on the
Platform Committee, but according to Senator Hubert Humphrey, who also
served on the committee, Dawson supported the weak statement that was issued instead. "Incredible as it may seem, rumors began to spread that the sole
Negro committee member and head of the big black Second Ward of Chicago,
Bill Dawson, was the one who compromised the issue." When black newspapers began to spread the word that Dawson had killed the strong civil rights
plank, "Dawson at first denied this, but he later issued a statement carried by
the Associated Negro press on August 2 [1952]: 'I am very proud of the civil
rights plank as a whole.' " Powell left the Democratic Convention in disgust,
and Illinois Governor Adlai Stevenson was nominated for president, with Senator John Sparkman of Alabama as his running mate.[29]
    Congressman Powell subsequently met with Governor Stevenson in
Springfield, Illinois, and asked him to take a stronger position on civil rights,
which he did. Afterward, Powell issued a statement announcing his "one hundred percent support for Stevenson." A few days before the November election, Governor Stevenson campaigned in New York City, and Powell appeared
with him at rallies in Harlem. Stevenson, however, lost the election to Republican Dwight Eisenhower by a wide margin. Powell was apprehensive about
Eisenhower's approach to civil rights issues, but once he was in the White
House, Eisenhower may have accomplished more for black advancement than
had either Roosevelt or Truman. The veterans hospitals across the country
were desegregated, as were public places in the District of Columbia and the
schools on U.S. Army bases. The segregation of black workers on federal property, including the Navy yards in Norfolk, Virginia, and Charleston, South Car-

olina, was ended. Nevertheless, the Congressman and the President came to a parting of the ways in 1956 over federal support for the construction of public schools following the Supreme Court's *Brown v. Board of Education* in May 1954 outlawing segregation in public education. Despite objections from the White House, the Powell Amendment was attached to the school construction bill, and was passed by the House of Representatives in July 1956.[30]

As the national political conventions approached in the summer of 1956, Congressman Powell wanted to meet with Governor Stevenson to discuss the need for a strong statement by the Democratic Party condemning southern state officials who were dragging their feet on the implemention of the Supreme Court's *Brown* decision. Tammany Hall—New York City's Democratic organization—leader Carmine De Sapio tried to arrange a meeting during one of Stevenson's trips to New York City, but "Stevenson refused to see De Sapio." Philadelphia Congressman William Green was a close associate of Stevenson's campaign manager, James A. Finnegan, and both men tried to arrange a meeting, but Stevenson still refused. In the fall, however, White House aide Charlie Willis offered to arrange a meeting between Congressman Powell and President Eisenhower, and on October 11, 1956, the two met at the White House. When Eisenhower agreed to support a civil rights bill, to be drawn up by Attorney General Herbert Brownell, that would place the resources of the Justice Department at the disposal of plaintiffs in legal suits aimed at public school desegregation, Powell agreed to support the President's bid for reelection. "I campaigned for him from coast to coast. After Eisenhower won, he lived up to each of the pledges and the nation received its first civil rights law in eighty-two years," the Civil Rights Act of 1957. (130).[31]

The decision in 1956 to support Republican President Dwight Eisenhower's bid for reelection had serious repercussions for Democratic Congressman Adam Clayton Powell, Jr. Powell was attacked by the leaders of *both* parties for his independence. "There was definite resistance on the part of Republican leaders because they resented the fact that I had come out for Eisenhower. Basically, I think it was a combination of the Democratic and Republican leadership in New York City, which often worked hand-in-glove on many things, deciding that there was no place in their program for anyone who was an independent, even if that independence favored one of them." Two of Powell's patronage appointees in New York City were fired by the Democratic leadership. Powell was denied the chairmanship of a subcommittee within the Committee on Education and Labor, despite his seniority. And in 1958 the leaders of Tammany Hall let it be known that they were not interested in supporting Powell for reelection to Congress in the fall. The official reason given was his support for Eisenhower in 1956, but it was Powell's independence on so many other issues as well that galled leaders within the Democratic Party.[32]

When Harlem Democratic leaders met in May 1958 and voted not to back

Powell's reelection, the problem was to find someone to support against Powell in the Democratic primary. After much delay Carmine De Sapio, the Tammany Hall leader, convinced Harlem City Councilman Earl Brown to enter the primary with the official party endorsement. The campaign was nasty with charges and countercharges hurled by both candidates. Powell made it clear to his constituents that Democrats in New York had conspired with southern Dixiecrats to deprive him of his committee chairmanship. He accused Brown of being an Uncle Tom who was doing the bidding of Carmine De Sapio, the "plantation boss." Although Powell was guaranteed a place on the ballot in November because he ran unopposed in the Republican primary as well, he wanted the Democratic nomination. His reelection bid was endorsed by labor leader A. Philip Randolph, Jackie Robinson, the baseball player, and the young leader of the successful bus boycott in Montgomery, Alabama, Rev. Martin Luther King, Jr. On August 12, 1958, primary day, Powell triumphed over Brown by a three-to-one margin. Although Earl Brown was on the ballot in the November election as the Liberal Party candidate, Powell was the nominee for both the Democratic and Republican parties and was easily reelected. Thus in his campaign of 1958, where he was deprived of the backing of the Democratic Party, Adam Clayton Powell demonstrated a degree of political independence rarely duplicated by black politicians before or after.[33]

After the primary election, Powell agreed to endorse the Democratic candidate for governor, Averell Harriman, and the Tammany Hall leadership reciprocated by agreeing to assist Powell in regaining his seniority once he returned to Congress. However, the Democratic leadership was unable (or unwilling) to use its influence in Powell's behalf regarding the charges of income tax evasion leveled by the Internal Revenue Service. Although there is no direct evidence, there are indications that the decision to initiate these proceedings against Powell was politically motivated. In December 1956, a grand jury was empaneled to investigate the tax returns of Congressman Powell and his wife, Hazel Scott, an internationally known concert pianist, for six years, 1950 through 1955. Powell complained several times to officials in the White House about what he termed "harassment" by the IRS. However, in May 1958 the grand jury entered a three-count indictment against Powell, and after several postponements, primarily due to Powell's operation for removal of a stomach tumor, the trial began in March 1960. Powell's legal team, led by well-known attorney Edward Bennett Williams, made clear their belief that the indictment was politically motivated. During the trial Williams emphasized this question before the all-white jury: "I ask you if they were conducting an investigation into his taxes, or if they were waging a political vendetta designed to destroy him?" (159).

Judge Frederick Van Pelt Bryan eventually dismissed the charge that Powell "understated" his income in 1951 once evidence was presented that he had really *overstated* it; he also dismissed the charge that the Powells attempted to evade taxes in 1952 because the government attorneys presented insufficient evidence to make this case. The third charge, that the Powells had knowingly sought to defraud the government, went to the jury. After several days of deliberation, the jurors were unable to agree on a verdict and they were finally dismissed by the judge. After the trial, attorney Williams went to the judge and asked that the remaining charge be dismissed because several members of the jury had been contacted by reporters for the right-wing magazine *National Review,* which had been editorializing for Powell's conviction for over a year. Judge Bryan refused, but a year later, on April 13, 1961, the case was dismissed by the Federal Court when the government said it would not proceed because of "insufficient evidence." In *Adam by Adam* an entire chapter was devoted to the income tax trial, describing the great amount of time, energy, and money Powell expended on the case. He presented a statement from *New York Daily News* reporter Edwin Murray, dated March 16, 1961, that reflected what Powell believed had happened and why. "It is outrageous to think that our government would spend $100,000 to prosecute a man like Powell for $3000. There must be something more than that behind this unwarranted scheme" (182).[34]

Congressman Adam Clayton Powell, Jr., paid a heavy price for his political independence, but he had weathered the storm. In 1960 he worked hard for the election of John Kennedy and Lyndon Johnson, and following the Democratic victory in November, Powell became one of the most powerful members of Congress. Later, as chairman of the House Committee on Education and Labor, he became the key figure in the passage of Johnson's Great Society and War on Poverty legislation. In his autobiography, Powell included a letter from President Johnson dated March 18, 1966, the fifth anniversary of his committee chairmanship, in which Johnson congratulated Powell for his "brilliant record of accomplishment" and "the successful reporting to the Congress of 49 bedrock pieces of legislation." Johnson concluded "only with progressive leadership could so much have been accomplished by one Committee in so short a time. I speak for the millions of Americans who benefit from these laws when I say that I am truly grateful" (204).

Throughout the early 1960s Congressman Powell closely identified himself with the nonviolent direct-action protests launched by Martin Luther King's Southern Christian Leadership Conference and the various other civil rights groups. When African Americans' demand for first-class citizenship rights was replaced by calls for Black Power, Powell organized the first Black Power Conference, in Washington in September 1966. Powell's close association with Black Power would fuel another round of attacks on him by Republicans and southern Democrats who resented his increasing political power. But unlike earlier attacks, these latest ones would lead to his political downfall.[35]

Throughout his years in Congress, Powell had been criticized for his high

rate of absenteeism and poor voting record. Powell defended himself by pointing out that his level of production of important legislation was better than
most of the congressmen who had perfect voting records. Powell was chided
for his junkets to exotic places around the world with "lovely ladies" who were
putatively members of his staff. Threats were made by members of Congress
who wanted to cut his committee's huge budget, but these actions were opposed by officials in both the Kennedy and Johnson administrations. Powell
had also made many enemies in New York City because of his exposure of gambling and racketeering operations in Harlem. In March 1960 when he was a
guest on a television talk show, Powell accused Esther James, a sixty-six-year-
old domestic, of serving as a "bag woman" for numbers runners in Harlem.

Powell was sued by Esther James for libel in 1961 and she asked for over
$1 millon in damages. In *Adam by Adam* he admitted, "at this point I made a
grave mistake, one that would eventually cost me a large sum of money. I did
not take the threatened lawsuit seriously. I thought it was just another of the
smear tactics being employed against me" (157). When the case went to court
in New York City in April 1963, Powell failed to appear. The court ordered
him to pay over $200,000 in damages to James, and Powell's attorneys imme-
diately filed for an appeal. A second suit was brought by James's attorneys
when they learned that Powell was transferring property out of his name to
that of his new wife, Yvette, and her relatives. The state court reduced the dam-
ages to $46,500, but when Powell failed to turn over financial records re-
quested by the courts, two civil contempt warrants were issued. Taking
advantage of the state law that civil warrants could not be served on Sundays,
Powell started going to New York only on Sundays to preach, and returning to
Washington by the end of the day. This went on for over a year. Finally, in November 1966 Powell was ordered to appear before the court under penalty of
arrest, and his lawyers began to enter into serious negotiations with James's
lawyers for the $46,500 judgment against him. Although the parties reached a
settlement, it was too late to affect proceedings underway in the House to strip
him of his committee chairmanship, and his eventual removal from his congressional seat.[36]

In September 1966 Congressman Powell was accused by several House
members of using committee funds for private trips. Powell's wife, Yvette, was
placed on his payroll as a staff member, a common practice among House
members; but Powell himself was accused of cashing her paychecks. In September 1966 a House subcommittee was formed, chaired by Congressman
Wayne Hays of Ohio, to investigate the charges against him, and on January 3,
1967, the subcommittee reported that Powell had misused committee travel
funds and that although his wife received a salary as a staff member, she did not
work in either Harlem or Washington. In January 1967, the House Democratic caucus voted to strip Powell of his committee chairmanship. A new

House committee was formed, chaired by Congressman Emanuel Celler of New York, to investigate the charges against Powell, and voted that he be fined and censured, but not removed from his seat in Congress. On March 1, 1967, the entire House went further and voted to deny Powell his seat in Congress.[37]

In the special election that was called for April 11, 1967, to fill the vacancy left by the congressman's removal, Powell ran again and received over seventy percent of the vote. However, rather than return to Congress, Powell filed an appeal to regain his seat and salary as of November 1966. He ran for reelection in November 1968 and won overwhelmingly, and the U.S. Supreme Court agreed to hear his suit for full reinstatement. On June 16, 1969, the Supreme Court ruled that the House had acted improperly in excluding him from membership for reasons other than age, inhabitancy, or citizenship. In subsequent proceedings the Federal Court of Appeals ruled that not only was Powell entitled to reinstatement to his seat in Congress, but he was also entitled to court costs of the Supreme Court litigation. In the primary election in June 1970, Powell was defeated by Councilman Charles Rangel by 150 votes. In his autobiography Powell claimed that his precinct workers found gross improprieties at the polling places. "My workers found machines with more votes recorded than the total of voters who had signed in to vote. They found voting machines that had not been guarded by police before and/or after the polling (to prevent additional, illegal votes from being registered on the machine)." They even found that "twenty-seven dead men had faithfully cast their vote for Rangel!" (241). Powell appealed the election results to federal courts. With the appeal still pending, Rangel went on to win the election in November 1970, and in December the court declared that Powell's appeal had been filed too late.[38]

In October 1971 Powell's autobiography, *Adam by Adam,* appeared; and while some reviewers felt that there was insufficient analysis of the social and personal factors that were important in the development of his personal political style, others found that this "impenitent apologia" presented a viable explanation of the forces of "bigotry and bureaucracy" that were arrayed against him. The reviewer in *The New Yorker,* for example, noted that "Mr. Powell insists that the various moves against him were retaliation for his pertinacious pursuit of racial equality—a plausible point, inasmuch as the actions, including a suit by the Internal Revenue Service and the House of Representatives' refusal to seat him, were not sustained."[39]

The autobiography of Adam Clayton Powell, Jr., addressed many of the important matters of principle that defined the African-American intellectual tradition in the United States. As was the case with Alexander Crummell, Powell understood the importance of vindicating the *black* race. He mentioned that when he was a young child Marcus Garvey came to his home to visit with his father. "One of the greatest thrills of my life when I was about ten or twelve years was to sit at Garvey's feet, or roll down Seventh Avenue with him as he paraded in his white-plumed hat." Powell understood Marcus Garvey was important because he sought "to make 'black' Negroes proud of their color" (51). The final chapter of the autobiography was devoted to an examination of "Black Power and the Future of America," and Powell pointed to Garvey's movement as an important example of Black Power. "Black Power means black dignity. Pride in being black. Pride that black is beautiful. Pride that blacks are not second-class citizens as our forefathers were" (245).

As was the case with Ida Wells-Barnett and many other spokespersons for African Americans, Powell understood the need to be committed to telling the truth. In the chapter devoted to a discussion of "My Religion," Powell explained that once one has come to the conclusion that God created all things, then one will realize that "all things have within them some element of beauty." One must seek the truth,

> not the truths that the world proclaims as truths, for these truths are relative, but the truths that are absolute, the truths that one must find because only through finding the absolute can one be free. . . . One looks for beauty in all things because all things come from the Creator of beauty. A chain reaction is set up, not the chain reaction that comes from the beauty of the superficial nor the truth of the popular word, but a chain reaction that leads to goodness from the beauty that is within and the truth that makes one free, rather than the truths that make one captive. This is the eternal struggle of man against the unliberating truths that are self-evident, and toward the freedom-giving truths that must be agonizingly sought after (41).

Powell understood and appreciated the importance of African-American folk culture, particularly the religion. "The Negro is no better than the white man, but his awareness of God, his techniques to approach His nearness, and his unsegregated church undeniably indicate that his religion is more mature." While many "objective thinkers" looked down on the African-American's religion because it was considered too emotional, "emotionalism has its place in religion, for it is a part of the drive, the dynamism. Religion is a joyful thing. . . . The white man's Christianity has become ritualized; ferment of the religion of the Pilgrim Fathers has been aborted." God is sought primarily in times of crisis, "when there is not a crisis, [Americans] merely 'belong.' But the reason the Negro is more mature in his religion than the white man is that because of the white man's oppression of him, the Negro has been forced to make the search for God an everyday, twenty-four hour job" (42).

In the 1930s Powell worked closely with communists and noncommunists alike in defense of the rights of the black worker. The Jobs for Negroes program and the Don't Buy Where You Can't Work campaigns sought the "inte-

gration of people on the basis of ability, not on the basis of color." In obtaining
this goal, Powell was willing to work with whoever was willing to put themselves on the picket lines.

> My critics have often cited the names of many Communist-front orga-
> nizations with which my name was associated. Let it be a matter of
> record that no man ever used me, but in order to help my people I
> used everyone that had any strength whatsoever, including the Com-
> munists. The proof of this is that the membership of the Communist
> Party in Harlem never exceeded five hundred out of the section's three
> thousand Negroes. Yet there were times when I could get a thousand
> or two Communists to picket for our cause (67).[40]

As was the case in the autobiographies of Harry Haywood, Richard
Wright, W. E. B. Du Bois, Malcolm X, Gwendolyn Brooks, and Amiri Baraka,
Adam by Adam presented a detailed description of a profound ideological conversion experience. The Bandung Conference, a gathering of the leaders of the
newly idependent, nonaligned nations in Asia and Africa, was scheduled to be
held in April 1955. Powell was shocked when he learned that the U.S. State
Department decided that the United States would not send a representative or
observer to the international meeting. He believed this was a great mistake,
and decided to go with or without the support of the U.S. government. "Why
did the Department of State not want an American to go to what has now become the most important conference in modern times? Simply because we did
not have an adequate foreign policy for Asia and Africa." U.S. foreign relations
were focused too heavily on the "existing colonial powers" and the American
leaders did not realize that "three-fifths of the free peoples of the world are colored" (104). Powell understood that the failure of the United States to send a
representative would give the Soviet Union, the People's Republic of China,
and the Communist Bloc a propaganda field day, and allow them "to smear the
United States of America on the race question before twenty-nine colored nations of the world" (108).

Congressman Powell traveled to the conference at his own expense and
met with many of the anti-colonial leaders from around the world, including
Moses Kitani from the African National Congress in South Africa, Mohammed
Ali from Pakistan, Kojo Botsio from the Gold Coast, West Africa, and Chou
En-lai of the People's Republic of China. While there Powell held a news conference for the world's press and was able to deflect the anti-American propaganda being spread by representatives from the Communist Bloc. Powell wrote
later that he told reporters that "racism and second-class citizenship are on
their way out in the United States and [I] pointed pridefully to the number of
Negroes who are holding public office" (107–8).

"Bandung had completely changed my thinking," Powell wrote in his autobiography. "It made me over into an entirely new man." He explained that before traveling to the conference in Indonesia, he considered himself a "nationalist" and had focused on the attainment of equal rights for African Americans.

> Whereas previously I thought of civil rights in terms of rights for Negroes only, I now thought of civil rights as the sole method by which we could save the entire United States of America. Throughout the land, I began to speak on the subject "The Fight to Save the United States." I called on Negro people to take the leadership in this fight and urged them to get out of the rut of thinking that I had once been in: that the fight for civil rights was their fight alone; they must realize that it was also America's fight. They were the yardstick by which not only black Africa and brown Asia, but also white Europe were measuring our land (118–19).[41]

By Any Means Necessary?

IN THE DEBATES among African-American intellectuals in the 1950s, 1960s, and 1970s over the answer to the question "Why are we here?," those spokespersons in the nationalist ideological camp argued that African Americans were here to save themselves, and to serve as a model of resistance for other oppressed people in the United States and around the world. In the liberation struggle, saving America was a secondary concern (if at all), and according to Malcolm X, black freedom was to be achieved "by any means necessary." Integrationists, on the other hand, believed that Africans were in the United States as part of a larger plan to save America from itself and make the powerful whites who controlled the society live up to their self-professed creed of "liberty and justice for all." Thus for integrationists the means by which black liberation was brought about were as important as the end.

This ideological difference of opinion involved matters of principle as was clear in James Baldwin's encounter in 1962 with one of his father figures, Elijah Muhammad. While Baldwin understood and appreciated the Muslim leader's separatist position (and had himself been accused by some whites of being a Black Muslim), he could not support any program that resulted in the debasement of African Americans through actions that mimicked those of their oppressors. As Baldwin put it in *The Fire Next Time* (1963)

> I am very much concerned that American Negroes achieve their freedom here in the United States, but I am also concerned for their dignity, for the health of their souls, and must oppose any attempt that

Negroes may make to do to others what has been done to them. I think I know—we see it around us every day—the spiritual wasteland to which this road leads. It is so simple a fact and one that is hard, apparently, to grasp: *Whoever debases others is debasing himself.* This is not a mystical statement, but a realistic one, which is proved by the eyes of any Alabama sheriff—and I would not like to see Negroes ever arrive at so wretched a condition.[42]

What defined the ideological differences between James Baldwin and Elijah Muhammad, between Martin Luther King, Jr., and Malcolm X, was the acceptance or rejection of the belief that black liberation was to be achieved "by any means necessary," including violence. Martin Luther King, in his last book, *Where Do We Go from Here?: Chaos or Community* (1967) addressed this point. He noted that Malcolm X and the supporters of Black Power who advocate violence for use in "self-defense" were not the issue. "In a sense this is a false issue, for the right to defend one's home and one's person when attacked has been guaranteed through the ages by common law." The real issue was the attainment of power through violence. This was the case historically for white Europeans and Americans, and this cannot be imitated by African Americans. "The ultimate weakness of violence is that it is a descending spiral, begetting the very thing it seeks to destroy. Instead of diminishing evil, it multiplies it. Through violence you may murder the liar, but you cannot murder the lie. Through violence you may murder the hater, but you cannot murder the hate." King quoted the poet Henry Wadsworth Longfellow: "In this world a man must either be an anvil or a hammer."

We must be hammers shaping a new society rather than anvils molded by the old. This not only will make us new men, but will give us a new kind of power. It will not be Lord Acton's image of power that tends to corrupt or absolute power that corrupts absolutely. It will be power infused with love and justice, that will change dark yesterdays into bright tomorrows, and lift us from the fatigue of despair to the buoyancy of hope. A dark, desperate, confused and sin-sick world waits for this new kind of man and this new kind of power.[43]

After Malcolm X traveled to Asia and Africa, he became more aware of the international dimensions of the black liberation struggle in the United States, and his public positions came to resemble those of Martin Luther King. Malcolm understood that indeed "the whole world is watching," and African Americans could not adopt strategies that had been used against them for decades by their oppressors. In the final chapter of his autobiography, Malcolm X concluded that "both races, as human beings, had the obligation, the responsibility, of helping to correct America's human problem. The well-meaning white people . . . had to combat, actively and directly, the racism in other white people. And black people had to build within themselves much greater awareness that along with equal rights there had to be the bearing of equal responsibilities."[44]

Adam Clayton Powell's participation at the Bandung Conference also made him more of an internationalist in the struggle for freedom and equal rights. The travel abroad in 1955 and meetings with other nonwhite leaders from Asia and Africa had the same ideological effect on Powell as it would later have on Malcolm X and Amiri Baraka. And the reason Powell was able to make this important ideological conversion was because he was an independent and more like other independent black leaders, such as W. E. B. Du Bois, James Baldwin, Martin Luther King, and Malcolm X, than he was like traditional black politicians, such as Oscar De Priest, Arthur Mitchell, and William Dawson. When Powell announced he was going to attend the Bandung Conference, State Department officials William Lacy and Thurston Morton came to his office and tried to convince him not to attend. "Lacy and Morton told me that they had stopped Chester Bowles, our great Ambassador to India, from attending and they did not want me to go because I would be 'persona non grata.' " When Powell explained that this was not the case and the Indonesian government had made arrangements for his transportation and was planning an official dinner for him, "the Administration virtually ordered me to stay away from the United States Embassy, the United States Ambassador, and all United States employees in Indonesia." Powell told them he would be more than happy to do that "because I am ashamed of the Department of State's and the White House's attitude toward the Bandung Conference" (105).

And there is other evidence that the independent Adam Clayton Powell, Jr., was not like other black politicians before or after. When he first ran for the New York City Council in 1941, he ran as an independent and was able to secure the support of *both* the Democratic and Republican parties in his election bid. When he announced his candidacy in 1944 for the newly created seat in Congress representing the people of Harlem, he ran as an independent and was the nominee of *both* political parties. In 1958 when he was dropped by Democratic Tammany Hall in the primary election for his support of Republican Dwight Eisenhower's reelection campaign in 1956, Powell was immediately offered the congressional nomination by Republican leaders, but he also wanted the Democratic nomination. He defeated Earl Brown, the candidate supported by the Democratic Party in the primary, and in the November 1958 congressional election in Harlem, Powell was the nominee of *both* the Democratic and Republican parties in New York City. How many black politicians, before or after, could make the claim that their political independence could not be compromised by their partisan affiliation?

As was the case with James Baldwin, Adam Clayton Powell, Jr., believed that "confession was good for the soul," and in his autobiography he admitted that in many ways it was his personal behavior that paved the way for his political downfall. After presenting a detailed account of the numerous women with whom he had affairs, Powell confessed

> I have been criticized during my life for admitting that I enjoyed the company of women. And there have been times when I have been told that it would be better not to let photographers shoot me with a glass in my hand. I have been accused of almost everything—of being a black racist, an Uncle Tom, a rabble-rouser, a pleasure seeker, a slanderer, and much more. But I have never been accused of being a hypocrite, of saying anything that I did not believe in, or doing anything I did not enjoy (235).

The final chapter of *Adam by Adam* was devoted to an examination of Black Power, and among the many important issues addressed was Powell's belief in the need for black leaders to be independent. He presented his version of an encounter with Martin Luther King and his SCLC associate Ralph Abernathy in which "King told me that he was giving up the concept of total nonviolence." When reports were leaked about this possible ideological change, "King immediately called his own press conference and denied that he had made such a statement. My puzzlement over this action was dispelled several days later when he received a foundation grant for several hundred thousand dollars" (242–43). On numerous occasions Powell made it clear that he had the greatest respect for Dr. King's accomplishments in the field of civil rights. However, in the "Black Power Position Paper" included in this chapter, Powell also argued that "we must stop sending little boys whose organizations are controlled and financed by white businessmen to do a man's job. Because only those who are financially independent can be men" (248).

Powell believed that the black masses must support financially their own independent institutions and leaders. "Blacks must reject the white community's carefully selected 'ceremonial Negro leaders' and insist that the white community deal instead with the black leadership chosen by black communities. For every 'ceremonial Negro leader' we permit to lead us, we are weakened and derogated just that much." Through the support of independent black institutions, "the black masses guarantee the independence of their leadership" (249).

Adam Clayton Powell, Jr., ended his autobiography with advice and counsel that is as appropriate in the 1990s as it was in the 1970s.

> Black people must discover a new and creative total involvement with ourselves. We must turn our energies inwardly toward our homes, our churches, our families, our children, our colleges, our neighborhoods,

our businesses, and our communities. Our fraternal and social groups must become an integral part of this creative involvement by using their resources and energies toward constructive fund-raising and community activities. This is no time for cotillions and teas. These steps I urge all of America's 25 million black people to take as we begin the dawn of a new day by walking together. And as we walk together hand in hand, firmly keeping the faith of our forebears, we glory in what we have become and are today (249–50).

NOTES

Introduction

1. Frederick Douglass, *Narrative of the Life of Frederick Douglass, An American Slave* (1845; reprinted New York, 1968); Lorene Cary, *Black Ice* (New York, 1991); Brent Staples, *Parallel Time: Growing Up in Black and White* (New York, 1994); Stephen Butterfield, *Black Autobiography in America* (Amherst, Mass., 1976), pp.1–7; William L. Andrews, "The First Fifty Years of the Slave Narrative, 1760–1810," in John Sekora and Darwin T. Turner, eds., *The Art of the Slave Narrative: Original Essays in Criticism and Theory* (Macomb, Ill., 1982), pp. 6–24; and *To Tell a Free Story: The First Century of the Afro-American Autobiography, 1760–1865* (Urbana, Ill., 1986), pp. 2–31.

2. Marva J. Furman, "The Slave Narrative: Prototype of the Early Afro-American Novel," in Sekora and Turner, eds., *The Art of the Slave Narrative,* pp. 120–26; and Marion Wilson Starling, *The Slave Narrative: Its Place in American History* (Boston, 1981), pp. 294–310.

3. Henry Louis Gates, Jr., "Introduction: On Bearing Witness," *Bearing Witness: Selections from African American Autobiography in the Twentieth Century* (New York, 1991), pp. 3–9; see also, Roger Rosenblatt, "Black Autobiography: Life as the Death Weapon," in James Olney, ed., *Autobiography: Essays Theoretical and Critical* (Princeton, N.J., 1980), pp. 169–80.

4. The three autobiographies of Frederick Douglass have recently been reprinted by the Library of America; see Henry Louis Gates, Jr., ed., *Autobiographies: Narrative of Frederick Douglass; My Bondage and My Freedom; and The Life and Times of Frederick Douglass* (New York, 1994). For a discussion of the recent critical analyses of Douglass's autobiographies by Stepto, Baker, Gates, O'Meilly, and others, see William L. Andrews, "African American Autobiography Criticism: Retrospect and Prospect," in Paul John Eakin, ed., *American Autobiography: Retrospect and Prospect* (Madison, Wisc., 1991), pp. 195–215.

5. Waldo E. Martin, *The Mind of Frederick Douglass* (Chapel Hill, N.C., 1984), p. 219; Frederick Douglass, "The United States Cannot Remain Half-Slave and Half-Free," in Philip S. Foner, ed., *The Life and Writings of Frederick Douglass,* Volume 4 (New York, 1955), p. 370.

6. Martin, *The Mind of Frederick Douglass,* pp. 220, 224; Douglass, "The Future of

the Colored Race," *North American Review,* May 1886, reprinted in Foner, ed., *The Life and Writings of Frederick Douglass,* Volume 4: 348–49. See also, Douglass, "Our Composite Nationality," 7 December 1869, in John W. Blassingame et al., eds., *The Frederick Douglass Papers,* Series One, Volume 4 (New Haven, 1991), pp. 240–59. Douglass demonstrated that he practiced what he preached when he married his white secretary, Helen Pitts, in January 1884. For a discussion, see William S. McFeely, *Frederick Douglass* (New York, 1991), pp. 318–23.

7. W. E. B. Du Bois, *The Souls of Black Folk* (1903; reprinted New York, 1969), pp. 45–46.

8. George M. Fredrickson, *The Black Image in the White Mind: The Debate on Afro-American Character and Destiny, 1817–1914* (New York, 1971), pp. 43–70. See also, William Stanton, *The Leopard's Spots: Scientific Attitudes Toward Race in America, 1815–1859* (Chicago, 1960); and John Haller, *Outcasts of Evolution: Scientific Attitudes of Racial Inferiority, 1859–1900* (Urbana, Ill., 1971).

9. Harold Cruse, *The Crisis of the Negro Intellectual* (New York, 1967), pp. 544–65.

10. Peter A. Dorsey, *Sacred Estrangement: The Rhetoric of Conversion in Modern American Autobiography* (University Park, Pa., 1993), p. 9.

Chapter 1: Alexander Crummell: Defining Matters of Principle

1. Alexander Crummell, *Jubilate: The Shades and Lights of a Fifty Years' Ministry, 1844–1894* (Washington, D.C., 1894), p. 20. Page numbers for quoted material are placed in parentheses in the text.

2. Crummell's three most recent biographers are Gregory U. Rigby, *Alexander Crummell: Pioneer in Nineteenth Century Pan-African Thought* (Westport, Ct., 1988); Alfred Moss, Jr., "Alexander Crummell: Black Nationalist and Apostle of Western Civilization," in Leon Litwack and August Meier, eds., *Black Leaders of the Nineteenth Century* (Urbana, Ill., 1988), pp. 237–51; and Wilson J. Moses, *Alexander Crummell: A Study of Civilization and Discontent* (New York, 1989).

3. For recent essays on the effects of the slave trade on Africa, see David Northrup, ed., *The Atlantic Slave Trade* (Lexington, Mass., 1994), pp. 133–74.

4. Arthur Zilversmit, *The First Emancipation: The Abolition of Slavery in the North* (Chicago, 1967), pp. 175–84.

5. Leon Litwack, *North of Slavery: The Negro in the Free States, 1790–1860* (Chicago, 1961), pp. 20–24.

6. James Forten and Peter Williams quoted in Benjamin Quarles, *Black Abolitionists* (New York, 1969), pp. 4–7.

7. For the history of the American Colonization Society, see Philip J. Staudenraus, *The African Colonization Movement, 1816–1865* (New York, 1961). See also, V. P. Franklin, "Education for Colonization: Attempts to Educate Free Blacks in the United States for Emigration to Africa, 1822–1832," *The Journal of Negro Education* 43 (Winter 1974): 91–103; and Floyd L. Miller, *The Search for Black Nationality: Black Emigration and Colonization, 1787–1863* (Urbana, Ill., 1975), pp. 82–90.

8. For biographical information on John Russwurm, see Rayford Logan and

Michael Winston, eds., *Dictionary of American Negro Biography* (New York, 1981), hereinafter *DANB*, pp. 538–39.

9. *Freedom's Journal* 27 March 1827, reprinted in Martin Dann, ed., *The Black Press, 1827–1895: The Quest for National Identity* (New York, 1971), pp. 33–34.

10. *Walker's Appeal* (1829) reprinted in Sterling Stuckey, ed., *The Ideological Origins of Black Nationalism* (Boston, 1972), pp. 39–117.

11. *DANB*, pp. 538–39.

12. Litwack, *North of Slavery*, pp. 19–23; Carol V. R. George, *Segregated Sabbaths: Richard Allen and the Rise of the Independent Black Churches, 1760–1840* (New York, 1973), pp. 135–59.

13. *Minutes of the Proceedings of the National Negro Conventions, 1830–1864*, edited by Howard H. Bell (New York, 1969); see also, Howard Bell, *A Survey of the National Negro Conventions, 1830–1865* (New York, 1969).

14. Moses, *Alexander Crummell*, pp. 16–17.

15. Alexander Crummell, "Eulogium on Henry Highland Garnet," in *Africa and America: Addresses and Discourses* (Springfield, Mass., 1891), pp. 273–75.

16. John Hope Franklin and Alfred Moss, Jr., *From Slavery to Freedom: A History of Negro Americans*, sixth edition (New York, 1988), pp. 180–86; John L. Thomas, *The Liberator: William Lloyd Garrison, A Biography* (Boston, 1963), pp. 114–28.

17. George M. Fredrickson, *The Black Image in the White Mind: The Debate over Afro-American Character and Destiny, 1817–1914* (New York, 1971), pp. 27–42.

18. Crummell, "Eulogium on Henry Garnet," pp. 279–80.

19. Moses, *Alexander Crummell*, pp. 34–51, provides a detailed discussion of "the struggles of the young priest."

20. For a detailed examination of the debate between black Philadelphians and New Yorkers over the advisability of "caste" or "complexional" institutions, see V. P. Franklin, *Black Self-Determination: A Cultural History of African-American Resistance* (Brooklyn, N.Y., 1992), pp. 90–95.

21. *DANB*, pp. 252–53.

22. Joel Schor, *Henry Highland Garnet: A Voice of Black Radicalism in the Nineteenth Century* (Westport, Ct., 1977), pp. 28–46.

23. *DANB*, pp. 181–82; see also, Frederick Douglass, *Narrative of the Life of Frederick Douglass, An American Slave* (1845; reprinted New York, 1968).

24. Garnet, "Address to the Slaves in the United States" (1843), reprinted in Stuckey, *The Ideological Origins of Black Nationalism*, pp. 168–70.

25. The ideological differences among black abolitionists in the 1840s and 1830s are examined in Franklin, *Black Self-Determination*, pp. 90–96.

26. *Proceedings of the National Convention of Colored People and Their Friends, Held in Troy, New York, 6th, 7th, 8th, and 9th October, 1847*, pp. 47–48. Crummell's report on the black college was not published with the proceedings.

27. R. J. M. Blackett, *Building an Antislavery Wall: Black Americans in the Atlantic Abolitionist Movement, 1830–1860* (Baton Rouge, La., 1983) is an important work devoted to this topic.

28. Moses, *Alexander Crummell*, pp. 31–32, 69–70.

29. Rigsby, *Alexander Crummell*, pp. 58–59.

30. Alexander Crummell, *The Future of Africa: Being Addresses, Sermons, Etc. Delivered in the Republic of Africa* (New York, 1862), p. 285.

31. Stanley Campbell, *The Slave Catchers: Enforcement of the Fugitive Slave Law, 1850–1860* (Chapel Hill, N.C., 1970).

32. Franklin, *Black Self-Determination,* pp. 96–102.

33. Crummell to John Jay, 12 September 1851, quoted in Moses, *Alexander Crummell,* p. 81.

34. Tom Shick, *Behold the Promised Land: A History of Afro-American Settler Society in Nineteenth Century Liberia* (Baltimore, 1980), pp. 42–58; J. Gus Liebenow, *Liberia: The Quest for Democracy* (Bloomington, Ind., 1987), pp. 25–29.

35. Rigsby, *Alexander Crummell,* pp. 93–94.

36. Shick, *Behold the Promised Land,* pp. 42–58.

37. The discussion of the conflicts between Bishop Payne and Rev. Crummell is based on information found in Moses, *Alexander Crummell,* pp. 89–118, 179–95.

38. Rev. Crummell's assessment of the native African peoples may be found in "Report from Caldwell, Liberia, on a Journey through the Dey and Vai Countries," *Spirit of Missions* 36 (1871):485–89.

39. For an examination of the deteriorating conditions for free blacks in the United States on the eve of the Civil War, see Franklin, *Black Self-Determination,* pp. 96–102.

40. Crummell, *The Future of Africa,* pp. 3–4.

41. *DANB,* p. 49; Hollis Lynch, *Edward Wilmot Blyden: Pan–Negro Patriot, 1832–1912* (New York, 1967), pp. 26–31.

42. Crummell stressed these points in the essays that appeared in *Africa and America: Addresses and Discourses* (1891, reprinted New York, 1969), pp. 127–96, 405–54.

43. Rigsby, *Alexander Crummell,* pp. 95–124; Lynch, *Edward Wilmot Blyden,* pp. 123–45.

44. Moses, *Alexander Crummell,* pp. 156–58.

45. Crummell to Rev. Tracy, 24 August 1866, in Moses, *Alexander Crummell,* p. 160.

46. The discussion of Crummell's flirtation with Eli Stokes's campaign to create a black–controlled Liberian church is based on information found in Rigsby, *Alexander Crummell,* pp. 73–89.

47. Ibid., pp. 84–85.

48. The following incident involving Sydney Crummell is examined in detail in ibid., pp. 89–92; and Moses, *Alexander Crummell,* pp. 173–77.

49. Rigsby, *Alexander Crummell,* pp. 90–92; Moses, *Alexander Crummell,* pp. 176–77.

50. Crummell, "Our National Mistakes," in *Africa and America,* pp. 170–73.

51. Rigsby, *Alexander Crummell,* pp. 128–33; Moses, *Alexander Crummell,* pp. 190–95; Lynch, *Edward Wilmot Blyden,* pp. 48–53.

52. There are minor differences in the accounts of Rigsby and Moses about Rev. Crummell's flight from Liberia in 1871, see Rigsby, *Alexander Crummell,* pp. 130–33; and Moses, *Alexander Crummell,* pp. 192–95.

53. Rigsby, *Alexander Crummell,* p. 139; Moses, *Alexander Crummell,* pp. 196–222.

54. Alexander Crummell, "The Race Problem in America," in *Africa and America,* pp. 41–49.

55. Ibid., p. 45.

56. Ibid.

57. Ibid., p. 46.

58. Alexander Crummell quoted in Alfred Moss, Jr., *The American Negro Academy: Voice of the Talented Tenth* (Baton Rouge, La., 1981), pp. 20–21.

59. Crummell to John E. Bruce, 7 April 1896, quoted in ibid., p. 22.

60. Moss, *The American Negro Academy,* pp. 13–14.

61. Ibid., pp. 31–32.

62. Ibid., p. 61.

63. James D. Anderson, *The Education of Blacks in the South, 1860–1935* (Chapel Hill, N.C., 1988), pp. 33–109.

64. Crummell, "The Dignity of Labor," in *Africa and America,* pp. 381–82.

65. Crummell, "Civilization the Primal Need of the Race," *Occasional Papers, American Negro Academy,* Number 3 (Washington, D.C., 1898), pp. 3–4.

66. Ibid., p. 4.

67. Ibid.

68. Ibid., pp. 4–5.

69. Ibid., p. 5.

70. Crummell, "The Attitude of the American Mind Toward the Negro Intellect," *Occasional Papers, American Negro Academy,* Number 3, p. 10.

71. Ibid., pp. 14–16.

72. Ibid., p. 16.

73. W. E. B. Du Bois, "Of Alexander Crummell," in *The Souls of Black Folk* (1903; reprinted New York, 1969), pp. 234–42.

74. Ibid., p. 249.

Chapter 2: Ida B. Wells-Barnett:
To Tell the Truth Freely

1. Ida B. Wells-Barnett, *Crusade for Justice: The Autobiography of Ida B. Wells,* Alfreda M. Duster, ed. (Chicago, 1970). Page numbers for quoted material are placed in parentheses in the text.

2. John R. Lynch, *The Facts of Reconstruction* (1913; reprinted Indianapolis, 1970), pp. 9–10.

3. Biographical information on Ida Wells-Barnett may be found in Thomas Holt, "The Lonely Warrior: Ida B. Wells-Barnett and the Struggle for Black Leadership," in J. H. Franklin and A. Meier, eds., *Black Leaders in the Twentieth Century* (Urbana, Ill., 1982), pp. 39–61; and Mildred I. Thompson, *Ida B. Wells-Barnett: An Exploratory Study of an American Black Woman, 1893–1930* (Brooklyn, N.Y., 1990), pp. 1–24.

4. *Chesapeake & Ohio & Southwestern Railroad Company v. Wells. Tennessee Reports: Cases Argued Before the Supreme Court of Tennessee . . . 1887,* p. 615.

5. Bertram Wyatt-Brown, "The Civil Rights Act of 1875," *Western Political Quarterly* 18 (1965): 763–75; James M. McPherson, "Abolitionists and the Civil Rights Act of

1875," *The Journal of American History* 52 (1965): 493–510; and James M. McPherson, *Ordeal by Fire: The Civil War and Reconstruction* (New York, 1982), pp. 575–78.

6. *New York Globe,* 20 October 1883.

7. Henry McNeal Turner quoted in *Christian Recorder,* 8 November 1883. See also, Edwin Redkey, *Black Exodus: Black Nationalist and Back-to-Africa Movements, 1890–1910* (New Haven, Ct., 1969), pp. 23–31.

8. Emma Lou Thornbrough, *T. Thomas Fortune: Militant Journalist* (Chicago, 1970), pp. 123–25.

9. Frederick Douglass, "Preface" to Ida B. Wells, *Southern Horrors* (1892), reprinted in *On Lynchings: Southern Horrors, A Red Record; Mob Rule in New Orleans* (New York, 1969), p. 4.

10. Social Gospeler Dwight Moody and his religiously inspired reform movement is described in R. C. White and C. H. Hopkins, *The Social Gospel: Religion and Reform in Changing America* (Philadelphia, 1976), pp. 199–201.

11. Ruth Bordin, *Women and Temperance: The Quest for Power and Liberty, 1873–1900* (Philadelphia, 1981); and *Frances Willard: A Biography* (Chapel Hill, N.C., 1986).

12. Frances Willard quoted in Ida B. Wells-Barnett, *A Red Record: Lynchings in the United States—1892, 1893, 1894,* in *On Lynchings,* pp. 126–27. For a brief discussion of the Wells-Willard debate, see Mildred I. Thompson, *Ida B. Wells-Barnett,* pp. 56–61.

13. Wells-Barnett, *A Red Record,* pp. 82–83.

14. Ibid., p. 33.

15. Ibid., p. 89.

16. Ibid., pp. 89–90.

17. Jennie J. Croly, *The History of the Women's Club Movement in America* (New York, 1897); Mary I. Wood, *History of the General Federation of Women's Clubs* (New York, 1912).

18. Fannie Barrier Williams quoted in Paula Giddings, *When and Where I Enter: The Impact of Black Women on Race and Sex in America* (New York, 1984), p. 98.

19. Philip Bruce, *The Plantation Negro As a Freeman* (1889), quoted in Beverly Guy-Sheftell, *Daughters of Sorrow: Attitudes Toward Black Woman, 1880–1920* (Brooklyn, N.Y., 1990), pp. 42–43.

20. For a recent detailed discussion of the formation of the National Association of Colored Women, see Dorothy Salem, *To Better Our World: Black Women in Organized Reform, 1890–1920* (Brooklyn, N.Y., 1990), pp. 12–28.

21. C. Vann Woodward, *The Origins of the New South, 1877–1913* (Baton Rouge, La., 1951), pp. 333–38.

22. Philip S. Foner, *Organized Labor and the Black Worker, 1619–1973* (New York, 1974), pp. 77–81, 103–8.

23. I. Garland Penn, *The Afro-American Press and Its Editors* (1891; reprinted New York, 1969), pp. 523–24.

24. Fortune quoted in ibid., pp. 528, 532. See also, Emma Lou Thornbrough, "The National Afro-American League, 1887–1908," *The Journal of Southern History* 27 (February 1961): 494–512.

25. Harold Cruse in his recent work, *Plural but Equal* (New York, 1987), discusses

the league in detail, but concludes that it shared the integrationist goals and objectives of the NAACP; see pp. 8–16, 77–78.

26. T. Thomas Fortune, "The Afro-American League," *AME Church Review* 7 (July 1890): 2–5.

27. Ibid., pp. 4–5. These core values of the southern black masses during this period are examined in detail in V. P. Franklin, *Black Self-Determination: A Cultural History of African-American Resistance* (Brooklyn, N.Y., 1992), pp. 177–85.

28. Thornbrough, "The National Afro-American League," pp. 500–501; and "T. Thomas Fortune: Militant Editor in the Age of Accommodation," in Franklin and Meier, eds., *Black Leaders in the Twentieth Century,* pp. 26–27.

29. Alexander Walters to T. Thomas Fortune, March 1897; and Fortune to Walters, 24 August 1898; quoted in George M. Miller, "A This-Worldly Mission: The Life and Career of Alexander Walters, 1858–1917" (unpublished Ph.D. dissertation, State University of New York at Stony Brook, 1984), pp. 165–66.

30. "The Aims and Objectives of the National Afro-American Council," quoted in ibid., p. 166.

31. Louis Harlan, *Booker T. Washington: The Making of a Black Leader, 1856–1901* (New York, 1972), pp. 204–8; "Booker T. Washington and the Politics of Accommodation," in Franklin and Meier, eds., *Black Leaders in the Twentieth Century,* pp. 1–18.

32. Thompson, *Ida B. Wells-Barnett,* pp. 75–77.

33. Salem, *To Better Our World,* pp. 32–34; Duster, *Crusade for Justice,* pp. 258–63. It is interesting that in her autobiography, *A Colored Woman in a White World* (1940; reprinted New York, 1980), Mary Church Terrell claimed that the Chicago meeting was the most successful during her presidency, and she made no mention of the problems created over the appearance of Wells-Barnett; see pp. 152–53.

34. Mary Church Terrell, "First Presidential Address to the National Association of Colored Women," reprinted in Beverly Jones, *Quest for Equality: The Life and Writings of Mary Eliza Church Terrell, 1863–1954* (Brooklyn, N.Y., 1990), pp. 137–38.

35. Beverly Jones, ibid., p. 24; see also Joanne Braxton, *Black Women Writing Autobiography: A Tradition Within a Tradition* (Philadelphia, 1989), pp. 132–38.

36. Wells-Barnett, *Crusade for Justice,* pp. 261–62; Alexander Walters, *My Life and Work* (New York, 1917), pp. 112–13.

37. Harlan, *Booker T. Washington: The Making of a Black Leader,* pp. 264–67.

38. Ibid.; see also, Louis Harlan, "Booker T. Washington and the National Negro Business League," (NNBL) in William G. Shade and Roy C. Herrenkohl, eds., *Seven on Black* (Philadelphia, 1970), pp. 75–91.

39. Harlan, "Booker T. Washington and the National Negro Business League," pp. 75–78.

40. Wells-Barnett, "Booker T. Washington's New Movement," *Chicago Conservator* 7 July 1900.

41. Booker T. Washington (BTW), "Speech Before the NNBL," 23 August 1900; and "The Closing Address Before the NNBL," in Louis Harlan et al., eds., *BTW Papers,* Volume 5 (Urbana, Ill., 1976), pp. 600–605.

42. BTW, "Interview in the Boston *Journal,*" 11 August 1900, ibid., pp. 594–95.

43. Harlan, *Booker T. Washington: The Making of a Black Leader*, pp. 268–71.

44. BTW, "An Address at the Metropolitan A.M.E. Church," 22 May 1900, in *BTW Papers* Volume 5, p. 530. According to Louis Harlan, this same speech was given in Indianapolis at the council meeting, ibid., p. 630.

45. John Colburn to BTW, Indianapolis, 3 September 1900, in *BTW Papers* Volume 5, pp. 629–31.

46. Harlan, *Booker T. Washington: The Making of a Black Leader*, pp. 271–75.

47. Thornbrough, *T. Thomas Fortune*, pp. 204–7.

48. W. E. B. Du Bois, *The Souls of Black Folk* (1903; reprinted New York, 1969), p. 86.

49. Thompson, *Ida B. Wells-Barnett*, p. 79.

50. BTW, "The Tuskegee Idea," *World Today* 6 (April 1904): 512.

51. Ibid., pp. 513–14.

52. W. E. B. Du Bois, "The Parting of the Ways," ibid., pp. 521–22.

53. Ibid., p. 522.

54. Ibid., p. 523.

55. Ibid.

56. Ida B. Wells-Barnett, "Booker T. Washington and His Critics," ibid., p. 519.

57. Ibid.

58. Ibid. Carl R. Osthaus, *Freedmen, Philanthropy, and Fraud: A History of the Freedmen's Savings Bank* (Urbana, Ill., 1976).

59. Wells-Barnett, "Booker T. Washington and His Critics," p. 519.

60. Ibid., p. 520.

61. Ibid., p. 520.

62. Ibid., p. 521.

63. Charles Crowe, "Racial Massacre in Atlanta, September 12, 1906," *The Journal of Negro History* 54 (April 1969): 150–73.

64. Ann Lane, *The Brownsville Affair: National Crisis and Black Reaction* (Port Washington, N.Y., 1971).

65. Louis Harlan, *Booker T. Washington: The Wizard of Tuskegee, 1901–1915* (New York, 1983), pp. 322–23.

66. William English Walling, "Race War in the North," *Independent* 65 (3 September 1908): 529–34.

67. Charles F. Kellogg, *NAACP: A History of the National Association for the Advancement of Colored People, 1901–1920* (Baltimore, 1967), pp. 9–30. The "Call for the Conference" (January 1909) is reprinted on pp. 297–99.

68. Harlan, *Booker T. Washington: The Wizard of Tuskegee*, pp. 32–62; Stephen Fox, *The Guardian of Boston: Willian Monroe Trotter* (New York, 1971), pp. 127–29.

69. Kellogg, *NAACP*, pp. 21–22.

70. For a discussion of her activities after 1910, see Thompson, *Ida B. Wells-Barnett*, pp. 85–126.

Chapter 3: James Weldon Johnson: The Creative Genius of the Negro

1. James Weldon Johnson (JWJ), *Along This Way: The Autobiography of James Wel-*

don Johnson (New York, 1933). Page numbers for quoted material are placed in parentheses in the text.

2. JWJ, *The Autobiography of an Ex-Colored Man* (1912; reprinted New York, 1960), p. 87.

3. For biographical information on Johnson's contributions to African-American life and letters, see Eugene Levy, *James Weldon Johnson: Black Leader, Black Voice* (Chicago, 1973); Eugene Levy, "James Weldon Johnson and the Development of the NAACP," in John Hope Franklin and August Meier, eds., *Black Leaders of the Twentieth Century* (Urbana, Ill., 1982), pp. 85–103; Robert E. Fleming, *James Weldon Johnson* (Boston, 1987); and Rayford Logan and Michael Winston, eds., *Dictionary of American Negro Biography* (New York, 1982), hereinafter *DANB*, pp. 353–57.

4. *DANB*, pp. 353–54.

5. JWJ, "Tunk," in *Fifty Years and Other Poems* (Boston, 1917), pp. 66–68.

6. See also, Levy, *James Weldon Johnson*, pp. 49–70; and Fleming, *James Weldon Johnson*, pp. 7–14.

7. Quoted in Levy, *James Weldon Johnson*, pp. 71–72.

8. Booker T. Washington's personal secretary sent a letter to Johnson commenting on the popularity of his song for Teddy Roosevelt; Emmett Jay Scott to JWJ, 18 January 1905, in Louis Harlan and Raymond Smock, eds., *Booker T. Washington Papers*, Volume 8 (Urbana, Ill., 1979), pp. 178–79.

9. Booker T. Washington (BTW) to Elihu Root, U.S. Secretary of State, 23 February 1906; BTW to Charles Anderson, 5 March 1906; BTW to Charles Anderson, 8 March 1906, in ibid., pp. 532–33, 538, 541–42.

10. JWJ to Booker T. Washington, 9 April 1908, in ibid., Volume 9 (Urbana Ill., 1980), pp. 494–95.

11. Karl Berman, *Under the Big Stick: Nicaragua and the United States Since 1848* (Boston, 1986), pp. 154–66.

12. Kathleen L. Wolemuth, "Woodrow Wilson and Federal Segregation," *The Journal of Negro History* 44 (April 1959): 158–73; Henry Blumenthal, "Woodrow Wilson and the Race Question," ibid. 48 (January 1963): 1–21; Nancy J. Weiss, "The Negro and the New Freedom: Fighting Wilsonian Segregation," *Political Science Quarterly* 84 (March 1969): 61–79.

13. JWJ, "Mother Night" and "O Black and Unknown Bards," in *Fifty Years and Other Poems*, pp. 7, 22.

14. "Fifty Years," in ibid., pp. 2–3.

15. I. A. Newby, *Jim Crow's Defense: Anti-Negro Thought in America, 1900–1930* (Baton Rouge, La., 1965), pp. 113–68; George M. Fredrickson, *White Supremacy: A Comparative Study in American and South African History* (New York, 1981), pp. 239–82.

16. August Meier, "Booker T. Washington and the Negro Press," *The Journal of Negro History* 38 (January 1953): 67–90.

17. JWJ's column, "Views and Reviews," first appeared in the *New York Age* on 15 October 1914. Fred Moore in an editorial on "Our New Acquisition" pointed out that "one of his latest literary efforts to attract general attention is 'The Autobiography of an Ex-Colored Man.' "

18. JWJ, "White Witch," in *Fifty Years and Other Poems,* pp. 19–21.

19. The NAACP's campaign against *The Birth of A Nation* is discussed in Charles F. Kellogg, *NAACP: A History of the National Association for the Advancement of Colored People* (Baltimore, 1967), pp. 142–45.

20. Levy, *James Weldon Johnson,* pp. 149–50.

21. Kellogg, *NAACP,* pp. 87–88; B. Joyce Ross, *J. E. Spingarn and the Rise of the NAACP, 1911–1939* (New York, 1972), pp. 46–48.

22. Levy, *James Weldon Johnson,* pp. 183–89; Kellogg, *NAACP,* pp. 113–14.

23. Kellogg, *NAACP,* pp. 92–115.

24. August Meier and Elliott Rudwick, "The Rise of the Black Secretariat in the NAACP, 1909–35," in *Along the Color Line: Explorations in the Black Experience* (Urbana, Ill., 1976), pp. 103–5.

25. Kellogg, *NAACP,* pp. 112–15.

26. John Hope Franklin and Alfred Moss, Jr., *From Slavery to Freedom: A History of Negro Americans,* sixth edition (New York, 1988), pp. 326–27.

27. W. E. B. Du Bois, "Special Report: Massacre in East St. Louis" (September 1917), reprinted in Julius Lester, ed., *The Seventh Son: The Thought and Writings of W. E. B. Du Bois,* Volume 2 (New York, 1971), pp. 80–106; Elliott W. Rudwick, *Race Riot in East St. Louis, July 2, 1917* (Carbondale, Ill., 1964).

28. Robert V. Haynes, *A Night of Violence: The Houston Riot of 1917* (Baton Rouge, La., 1976).

29. Walter White, *A Man Called White: The Autobiography of Walter White* (New York, 1948), p. 36.

30. Walter White, *Rope and Faggot: A Biography of Judge Lynch* (New York, 1929), contains White's findings during the 1920s.

31. John Shillady quoted in Levy, *James Weldon Johnson,* pp. 211–12.

32. Robert Zangrando, *The NAACP Crusade Against Lynching, 1909–1950* (Philadelphia, 1980).

33. "Lily-white Republicanism" helped drive black voters into the Democratic party; see Richard B. Sherman, *The Republican Party and Black America: From McKinley to Hoover, 1896–1933* (Charlottesville, Va., 1973), pp. 258–89; Nancy Weiss, *Farewell to the Party of Lincoln: Black Politics in the Age of FDR* (Princeton, N.J., 1983), pp. 5–12.

34. "A Poetry Corner," *New York Age,* 7 January 1915; JWJ, ed., *The Book of American Negro Poetry* (1922, 1931; reprinted New York, 1959).

35. JWJ, "Preface to First Edition," in *The Book of American Negro Poetry,* pp. 9–10.

36. Ibid., p. 10.

37. Ibid., p. 14.

38. Ibid., pp. 18–20.

39. Ibid., p. 34.

40. Ibid., p. 36.

41. Ibid., pp. 41–42.

42. Ibid., p. 42.

43. Theodore G. Vincent, "Preface," *Voices of a Black Nation: Political Journalism*

in the Harlem Renaissance (San Francisco, 1973), pp. 19–38. This anthology contains a generous sampling of New Negro literature produced by militant black editors and publishers of various ideological persuasions.

44. Theodore L. Kornweibel, *No Crystal Stair: Black Life and the Messenger, 1917–1928* (Westport, Ct., 1975). The relationship between white socialists and communists and black intellectuals during this period is examined in detail in Chapter Three, pp. 66–104.

45. V. P. Franklin, *Black Self-Determination: A Cultural History of African-American Resistance* (Brooklyn, N.Y., 1992), pp. 196–201.

46. The "Garvey Must Go" campaign is detailed in Kornweibel, *No Crystal Stair,* pp. 132–75; and in Tony Martin, *Race First: The Ideological and Organizational Struggles of Marcus Garvey and the Universal Negro Improvement Association* (Westport, Ct., 1976), pp. 316–33. Dozens of reports by special agents for the Department of Justice's Bureau of Investigation on Marcus Garvey and the UNIA are published in Robert A. Hill, ed., *Marcus Garvey and Universal Negro Improvement Association Papers,* Volumes 1, 2, 3 (Berkeley, Ca., 1983, 1984).

47. W. E. B. Du Bois, "Back to Africa," *Century* (February 1923), reprinted in John Henrik Clarke, ed., *Marcus Garvey and the Vision of Africa* (New York, 1974), pp. 105–19.

48. Ibid., pp. 105, 118; Martin, *Race First,* pp. 22–37; Franklin, *Black Self-Determination,* pp. 198–200.

49. Marcus Garvey, "W. E. B. Du Bois As Hater of Dark People," *Negro World* 13 February 1923. See also, Du Bois, *Darkwater: Voices from Within the Veil* (1920; reprinted New York, 1969), p. 9.

50. Garvey, "W. E. B. Du Bois as Hater of Dark People," *Negro World,* 13 February 1923; Du Bois, "A Lunatic or Traitor," *Crisis* 28 (May 1924): 8–9.

51. David Levering Lewis, *When Harlem Was in Vogue* (New York, 1981), pp. 120–21.

52. JWJ, "Preface to First Edition," *The Book of American Negro Poetry,* p. 41.

53. Bruce Kellner, *Carl Van Vechten and the Irreverent Decades* (Norman, Okla., 1968), pp. 195–208.

54. "The Negro in Art: How Shall He Be Portrayed—A Symposium," *Crisis* 31 (March 1926): 219.

55. Carl Van Vechten, in ibid., p. 219; see also Kellner, *Carl Van Vechten,* pp. 218–20; and Arnold Rampersad, *The Art and Imagination of W. E. B. Du Bois* (Cambridge, Mass., 1976), pp. 207–26.

56. Carl Van Vechten, *Nigger Heaven* (1926; reprinted New York, 1971).

57. Lewis, *When Harlem Was in Vogue,* pp. 180–89.

58. W. E. B. Du Bois, "Review of *Nigger Heaven,*" *Crisis* 33 (December 1926): 81–82.

59. JWJ, "Romance and Tragedy in Harlem—A Review," *Opportunity* 4 (October 1926): 316–17, 330.

60. Ibid., p. 330.

61. W. E. B. Du Bois, "Review of Locke's *The New Negro,*" *Crisis* 31 (January 1926): 140–41. Du Bois contributed an essay, "The Negro Mind Reaches Out," to this influential volume; see Alain Locke, ed., *The New Negro: An Interpretation* (1925; reprinted New York, 1969) pp. 385–414.

62. W. E. B. Du Bois, "The Criteria of Negro Art," *Crisis* 32 (October 1926): 294, 296.

63. Ibid., p. 296.

64. Ibid., p. 297.

65. Tony Martin, *Literary Garveyism: Garvey, Black Arts, and the Harlem Renaissance* (Dover, Mass., 1983), p. 57.

66. Marcus Garvey and William Ferris quoted in ibid., pp. 8, 13.

67. Ibid., pp. 46–47. For additional information on Garvey's objections to dialect poetry and black folk practices in general, see Robert A. Hill, "General Introduction," *The Marcus Garvey and Universal Negro Improvement Association Papers,* Volume 1 (Berkeley, Ca., 1983), pp. xxxix–l.

68. JWJ, "Views and Reviews," *New York Age,* 20 May 1922.

69. Claude McKay, *Home to Harlem* (1928; reprinted New York, 1965).

70. W. E. B. Du Bois, "Review of *Home to Harlem,*" *Crisis* 33 (June 1928): 202.

71. *Negro World,* 29 September 1928. Reviews of *Home to Harlem* published in black newspapers are discussed in Wayne F. Cooper, *Claude McKay: Rebel Sojourner in the Harlem Renaissance* (New York, 1987), pp. 243–45.

72. Langston Hughes, JWJ, and Claude McKay quoted in Cooper, *Claude McKay,* pp. 242–46.

73. JWJ, "Preface," *The Book of American Negro Spirituals* (New York, 1925), pp. 12–13.

74. JWJ, "Preface," *God's Trombones: Seven Negro Sermons in Verse* (New York, 1927), pp. 7–8.

75. JWJ "Preface to the Second Edition (1931)," *The Book of American Negro Poetry,* pp. 4–5.

76. JWJ, "The Dilemma of the Negro Artist," *American Mercury* 15 (December 1928): 478–81.

77. Ibid., pp. 480–81. Johnson made the same point in other essays in the 1920s; see "The Negro Artist and Race Prejudice," *Harper's* 157 (December 1928): 769–76; and "Negro Authors and White Publishers," *Crisis* 36 (July 1929): 228–29.

78. JWJ, *Negro Americans, What Now?* (New York, 1934), pp. 18, 74–75.

Chapter 4: Harry Haywood: In Defense of the Black Working Class

1. Harry Haywood, *Black Bolshevik: Autobiography of an Afro-American Communist* (New York, 1978). Page numbers for quoted material are placed in parentheses in the text.

2. African-American leaders' support for the interests of black workers is examined by Charles Wesley in his classic work, *Negro Labor in the United States, 1850–1925: A Study in American Economic History* (Washington, D.C., 1927), pp. 156–91.

3. The socialist writings of Holly, Ransom, and Woodbey are reprinted in Philip S. Foner, ed. *Black Socialist Preacher* (San Francisco, 1983). See also, Philip S. Foner, *American Socialism and Black Americans: From the Age of Jackson to World War II* (Westport, Ct., 1977), pp. 94–127; R. Laurence Moore, "Flawed Fraternity: American

Socialist Response to the Negro, 1901–1912," *Historian* 26 (November 1969): 19–25; and Sally M. Miller, "The Socialist Party and the Negro, 1901–1920," *The Journal of Negro History* 56 (July 1971): 220–39.

4. For the history of the CPUSA, see Theodore Draper, *The Roots of American Communism* (New York, 1957); Theodore Draper, *American Communism and Soviet Russia: The Formative Years* (New York, 1960); and Bert Cochran, *Labor and Communism: The Conflict That Shaped American Unions* (Princeton, N.J., 1977). Documents on the communists' early preoccupation with the "Negro Question" are reprinted in Philip S. Foner and James S. Allen, eds., *American Communism and Black Americans: A Documentary History, 1919–1929* (Philadelphia, 1987), pp. 3–9.

5. Robert V. Haynes, *A Night of Violence: The Houston Riot of 1917* (Baton Rouge, La., 1976).

6. Arthur Barbeau and Florette Henri, *The Unknown Soldiers: Black American Troops in World War I* (Philadelphia, 1974); Jack Foner, *Blacks and the Military in American History: A New Perspective* (New York, 1974), pp. 109–32.

7. For a discussion of this pamphlet distributed by the U.S. Army, see John Hope Franklin and Alfred Moss, Jr., *From Slavery to Freedom: A History of Negro Americans*, sixth edition (New York, 1988), pp. 298–304.

8. The most detailed study of the Chicago Riot of 1919 is the official riot report by the Chicago Commission on Race Relations, *The Negro in Chicago: A Study of Race Relations and a Race Riot* (Chicago, 1922). See also, William M. Tuttle, *Race Riot: Chicago in the Red Summer of 1919* (New York, 1970).

9. William Graham Sumner, *Social Darwinism: Selected Essays* (Englewood Cliffs, N.J., 1963); see also, Richard Hofstader, *Social Darwinism in American Thought* (Boston, 1955); Cynthia E. Russett, *Darwin in America: The Intellectual Response, 1865–1912* (San Francisco, 1976); and Robert C. Bannister, *Social Darwinism: Science and Myth in Anglo–American Social Thought* (Philadelphia, 1979).

10. For information on the Industrial Workers of the World, see Paul F. Brissenden, *The I.W.W.: A Study in American Syndicalism* (1919, reprinted New York, 1957); and Patricia Renshaw, *The Wobblies: The Story of Syndicalism in the United States* (Garden City, N.Y., 1967), pp. 159–60, 182–84.

11. "Biographical Supplement: Cyril V. Briggs," in Robert A. Hill, ed., *Marcus Garvey and Universal Negro Improvement Association Papers*, Volume 1 (Berkeley, Ca., 1983), pp. 521–27.

12. Ibid., pp. 523–25; see also, Draper, *American Communism and Soviet Russia*, pp. 315–56; Robert K. Murray, *The Red Scare of 1919: A Study in National Hysteria, 1919–1920* (New York, 1955); and William Preston, *Aliens and Dissenters: Federal Suppression of Radicals* (Cambridge, Mass., 1963), pp. 208–37.

13. Poet and novelist Claude McKay also attended the Comintern Congress in Moscow in 1922 as an "invited delegate"; see his autobiography, *A Long Way from Home* (New York, 1937), pp. 154–68; and Wayne Cooper, *Claude McKay: Rebel Sojourner in the Harlem Renaissance* (Baton Rouge, La., 1987), pp. 171–92.

14. *Summary of the Program and Aims of the African Blood Brotherhood* (1920), quoted in Robert A. Hill, "Racial and Radical: Cyril V. Briggs, *Crusader*, and the African Blood Brotherhood, 1918–1922," in *Crusader*, Volume 1, facsimile edition (New York, 1987) p. xxviii.

15. Rose Pastor Stokes, "The Cause of Freedom: Blacks and Communists," *Negro World* 21 August 1921, reprinted in Theodore Vincent, ed., *Voices of a Black Nation: Political Journalism in the Harlem Renaissance* (San Francisco, 1973), pp. 131–32.

16. *Negro World* 8, 15, and 22 October 1921; see also, "Biographical Supplement: Cyril V. Briggs," p. 524.

17. Documents on the African Blood Brotherhood are reprinted in Foner and Allen, *American Communism and Black Americans,* pp. 16–23, 38–40, 102, 112.

18. Philip S. Foner, *Organized Labor and the Black Worker, 1619–1973* (New York, 1974), pp. 148–49; and *American Socialism and Black Americans,* pp. 309–11.

19. For the two sides of this split in the CP leadership, see Charles E. Ruthenberg, *From the Third Through the Fourth Convention of the Workers (Communist) Party* (New York, 1925), pp. 10–15; and William Z. Foster, *History of the Communist Party of the United States* (New York, 1952), pp. 211–23.

20. The proceedings, resolutions, and editorials on the ANLC convention in Chicago in October 1925 are reprinted in Foner and Allen, eds., *American Communism and Black Americans,* pp. 109–29.

21. Ibid., pp. 78–79; James Ford, *The Negro and the Democratic Front* (New York, 1938), pp. 81–83; Foner, *Organized Labor and the Black Worker,* pp. 171–72. For favorable contemporary statements on the formation of the ANLC, see *Opportunity* 3 (December 1925): 354; and *Crisis* 31 (December 1925): 60.

22. For information on Ernst Thaelmann and the German Communist Party in the 1920s, see Otto Friedrich, *Before the Deluge: A Portrait of Berlin in the 1920s* (New York, 1972), pp. 982–84; and Eberhard Kolb, *The Weimar Republic* (London, 1988), pp. 71–76, 107–22.

23. V. I. Lenin, "The Discussion on Self-Determination Summed Up," in *National Liberation, Socialism, and Imperialism: Selected Writings* (New York, 1968), pp. 151–58.

24. V. I. Lenin, *The Right of Nations to Self-Determination* (Westport, Ct., 1977). See also Irving Fletcher, "The Development of Marxism," and David Lane, "Leninism," in Tom Bottomore et al., eds., *A Dictionary of Marxist Thought* (Cambridge, Mass., 1983), pp. 279–81, 309–12.

25. It should be noted that despite his absence from the country, Harry Haywood had been elected to the national committee of the Young Communist League; see *Black Bolshevik,* p. 218.

26. For a more recent restatement of this position, see James Forman, *Self-Determination and the African American People* (Seattle, Wash., 1981).

27. Harry Haywood's report to the Comintern Congress in 1928 on "The Negro Problem and the Tasks of the Communist Party of the United States" is, according to Philip S. Foner, one of the "earliest published expositions on the position finally adopted by the Communist International." It is reprinted in Foner and Allen, eds., *American Communism and Black Americans,* pp. 172–78. See also, Jay Lovestone, "The Sixth World Congress of the Communist International," *Communist* 7 (November 1928): 673–74.

28. "Communist International on the Negro Question in the United States," *Communist* 9 (January 1930): 48–55.

29. "A Trade Union Program of Action for Negro Workers," *Communist* 9 (January 1930): 42–43. This unsigned article was very likely written by George Padmore.

30. James R. Hooker, *Black Revolutionary: George Padmore's Path from Communism to Pan–Africanism* (New York, 1967), pp. 17–38.

31. Wilson Record, *The Negro and the Communist Party* (New York, 1971), pp. 77–78.

32. Otto Huiswood, "World Aspects of the Negro Question," *Communist* 9 (February 1930): 132–47; Harry Haywood, "Against Bourgeois-Liberal Distortions of Leninism on the Negro Question in the United States," ibid. (August 1930): 694–712. See also, Joyce Moore Turner, "Richard B. Moore and His Works," in W. B. Turner and Joyce Moore Turner, eds., *Richard B. Moore: Caribbean Militant in Harlem—Collected Writings, 1920–1972* (Urbana, Ill., 1988), pp. 56–57.

33. For contemporary information on the Gastonia textile strike, see Cyril Briggs, "The Negro Question in the Southern Textile Strikes," *Communist* 8 (June 1929): 324–8; and "Further Notes on the Negro Question in the Southern Textile Strikes," ibid. (July 1929): 364–74; and William F. Dunne, "Gastonia—The Center of the Class Struggle in the New South," ibid., pp. 375–83. See also, Liston Pope, *Millhands and Preachers: A Study of Gastonia* (New Haven, 1942), pp. 239–73.

34. Documents on the activities of the LSNR are reprinted in Philip S. Foner and Herbert Shapiro, eds., *American Communism and Black Americans: A Documentary History, 1930–1934* (Philadelphia, 1991), pp. 122–24, 162–63, passim. See also, Arthur Simpson, "The Communists and Black Liberation, 1930–1932," *Political Affairs* 31 (February 1975): 7–15.

35. August Yokinen quoted in Mark Naison, *Communists in Harlem During the Depression* (New York, 1983), p. 47.

36. Documents related to the Yokinen trial are reprinted in Foner and Shapiro, eds., *American Communism and Black Americans,* pp. 147–77.

37. This was the case for George Padmore, who was expelled from the Communist International in June 1934; see Hooker, *Black Revolutionary,* pp. 31–38. See also, Harry Haywood, "The Struggle for a Leninist Interpretation of the Negro Question in the United States," *Communist* 12 (September 1933): 890–94.

38. Dan T. Carter, *Scottsboro: A Tragedy of the American South* (Baton Rouge, La., 1969); William Nolen, *Communism Versus the Negro* (Chicago, 1951); Record, *The Negro and the Communist Party,* pp. 86–92; Record, *Race and Radicalism: The NAACP and the Communists in Conflict,* (Ithaca, N.Y., 1964); Naison, *Communists in Harlem,* pp. 57–94; Harvey Klehr, *The Heyday of American Communism: The Depression Years* (New York, 1984), pp. 329–48.

39. Harry Haywood, "The Scottsboro Decision: Victory of Revolutionary Struggle over Reformist Betrayal," *Communist* 11 (December 1932): 1068–74.

40. Ronald L. Lewis, *Black Coal Miners in America: Race, Class, and Community Conflict, 1790–1980* (Lexington, Ky., 1987), pp. 143–64.

41. Angelo Herndon, *Let Me Live* (New York, 1937); Benjamin J. Davis, *Communist Councilman from Harlem* (New York, 1969), pp. 53–81; and Charles H. Martin, *The Angelo Herndon Case and Southern Justice* (Baton Rouge, La., 1976). Documents related to the Angelo Herndon case are reprinted in Foner and Shapiro, eds., *American Communism and Black Americans,* pp. 320–51.

42. Robin D. G. Kelley, *Hammer and Hoe: Alabama Communists During the Great Depression* (Chapel Hill, N.C., 1990), pp. 34–55.

43. Davis, *Communist Councilman from Harlem*, pp. 82–100; Naison, *Communists in Harlem*, pp. 109–11, 313.

44. For information on African Americans in Memphis during the 1930s, see William D. Miller, *Mister Crump of Memphis* (Baton Rouge, La., 1964), pp. 206–10; David M. Tucker, *Black Pastors and Leaders: Memphis, 1819–1972* (Memphis, 1975), pp. 101–18; and Roger Biles, *Memphis in the Great Depression* (Lexington, Ky., 1986), pp. 102–7.

45. Excerpts from Haywood's *The Road to Negro Liberation* (1934), are reprinted in Foner and Shapiro, eds., *American Communism and Black Americans*, pp. 125–46.

46. See also, Harry Haywood, "The Crisis of Jim Crow Nationalism of the Negro Bourgeoisie," *Communist* 10 (April 1931): 330–38.

47. For a detailed discussion of James Ford's activities in Harlem at this time, see Naison, *Communists in Harlem*, pp. 95–114.

48. Fernando Claudin, *The Communist Movement: From Comintern to Cominform—Part One: The Crisis of the Communist International* (New York, 1975), pp. 184–95; Record, *The Negro and the Communist Party*, pp. 129–33.

49. For a discussion of blacks and the Chicago political scene in the 1930s, see Roger Biles, *Big City Boss in Depression and War: Mayor Edward J. Kelly of Chicago* (DeKalb, Ill., 1984), pp. 92–96.

50. Accounts of the "Hands Off Ethiopia" demonstration may be found in *Daily Worker* 2 September 1935; and *Chicago Defender* 7 September 1935.

51. This controversy is examined in detail in Chapter Six.

52. For information on the origins of the National Negro Congress, see Record, *The Negro and the Communist Party*, pp. 153–62; Horace Cayton and George S. Mitchell, *Black Workers and the New Unions* (Chapel Hill, N.C., 1939), pp. 410–29; Raymond Wolters, *Negroes and the Great Depression: The Problem of Economic Recovery* (Westport, Ct., 1970), pp. 353–76; and Harvard Sitkoff, *A New Deal for Blacks: The Emergence of Civil Rights as a National Issue—The Depression Decade* (New York, 1978), pp. 55–57.

53. Record, *The Negro and the Communist Party*, p. 117. At one point poet Langston Hughes was made president of the LSNR, but at that time the group was basically inactive. See Arnold Rampersad, *The Life of Langston Hughes, Volume I: I, Too, Sing America* (New York, 1986), pp. 217–18, 240.

54. Paula F. Pfeffer, *A. Philip Randolph: Pioneer of the Civil Rights Movement* (Baton Rouge, La., 1990), pp. 32–43. Randolph was unable to deliver the keynote address in person. He was ill and it was read by another delegate.

55. Foner, *Organized Labor and the Black Worker*, pp. 204–37.

56. Klehr, *The Heyday of American Communism*, pp. 365–85; Harvey Klehr and J. E. Haynes, *The American Communist Movement: Storming Heaven Itself* (New York, 1992), pp. 84–95.

57. For a discussion, see Hugh Thomas, *The Spanish Civil War* (New York, 1961); Burnett Bolloten, *The Grand Camouflage: The Spanish Civil War and Revolution, 1936–1939* (New York, 1961); Burnett Bolloten, *The Spanish Revolution: The Left and the Struggle for Power during the Civil War* (Chapel Hill, N.C., 1979); Burnett Bolloten, *The Spanish Civil War: Revolution and Counterrevolution* (Chapel Hill, N.C., 1991); and Arthur Landis, *The Abraham Lincoln Brigade* (New York, 1967).

58. After Haywood's return to the United States, the civil war continued for eigh-

teen more brutal months. In March 1939 General Franco's forces defeated the Loyalists and imposed a fascist dictatorship upon Spain that would last until Franco's death in 1975. See R. Dan Richardson, *Comintern Army: The International Brigades and the Spanish Civil War* (Lexington, Ky., 1982), pp. 47–80; and J. W. D. Trythall, *El Caudillo: A Political Biography of Franco* (New York, 1970), pp. 101–54, passim.

59. Klehr and Haynes, *The American Communist Movement*, pp. 96–109; Joseph Starobin, *American Communism in Crisis, 1943–1967* (Cambridge, Mass., 1972).

60. Haywood, *Negro Liberation* (New York, 1948).

61. Starobin, *American Communism in Crisis*, pp. 230–35; Cedric Belfrage, *The American Inquisition, 1945–1960* (Indianapolis, 1973), pp. 51–116, 118–232; Peter Steinberg, *The Great "Red Menace": United States Prosecution of American Communists, 1947–1952* (Westport, Ct., 1984), pp. 157–80.

62. Hosea Hudson reached this same conclusion; see Nell Irvin Painter, *The Narrative of Hosea Hudson: His Life as a Negro Communist in the South* (Cambridge, Mass., 1979), pp. 27–28.

63. Haywood, *Negro Liberation*, p. 216.

Chapter 5: Richard Wright and Zora Neale Hurston: Conflicting Blueprints for Black Writing

1. Richard Wright, *American Hunger* (New York, 1977). Page numbers for quoted material are placed in parentheses in the text (*AH*).

2. Richard Wright, *Black Boy: A Record of Childhood and Youth* (New York, 1945). Page numbers for quoted material are placed in parentheses in the text (*BB*).

3. The most important and useful biographical studies of Richard Wright are Constance Webb, *Richard Wright: A Biography* (New York, 1968); Russell C. Brigano, *Richard Wright: An Introduction to the Man and His Works* (Pittsburgh, 1970); John A. Williams, *The Most Native of Sons: A Biography of Richard Wright* (Garden City, N.Y., 1970); Keneth Kinnamon, *The Emergence of Richard Wright* (Urbana, Ill., 1972); Michel Fabre, *The Unfinished Quest of Richard Wright* (New York, 1973); Addison Gayle, *Richard Wright: Ordeal of a Native Son* (New York, 1980); and Margaret Walker, *Richard Wright, Daemonic Genius: A Portrait of the Man, a Critical Look at His Work* (New York, 1988).

4. Fabre, *The Unfinished Quest*, pp. 77–78.

5. Daniel Aaron, *Writers on the Left* (New York, 1965), pp. 86–104; Harvey Klehr, *The Heyday of American Communism: The Depression Decade* (New York, 1984), pp. 69–74.

6. The exact date that Wright joined the Communist Party is unknown, but biographer Michel Fabre placed it "at the end of 1933 at the earliest." See Fabre, *The Unfinished Quest*, p. 103.

7. Leon Trotsky, *History of the Russian Revolution* (New York, 1932–33); Leon Trotsky, *The Revolution Betrayed* (New York, 1937). See also, Isaac Deutscher, *The Prophet Armed: Trotsky, 1879–1921* (New York, 1954); Isaac Deutscher, *The Prophet Unarmed: Trotsky, 1921–1929* (New York, 1959); and Isaac Deutscher, *The Prophet Outcast: Trotsky, 1929–1940* (New York, 1963).

8. Wright's report on the founding meeting of the National Negro Congress was

entitled "Twelve Million Black Voices," *New Masses* 18 (25 February 1936): 16. This also was used as the title for the book on black history he did with photographer Edwin Rosakam in 1941.

9. Richard Wright, "Blueprint for Negro Writing" (1937), reprinted in Ellen Wright and Michel Fabre, eds., *Richard Wright Reader* (New York, 1968), pp. 36–49. All references to this edition, *RWR*. A slightly longer version of this essay was published in John A. Williams and Charles F. Harris, eds., *Amistad 2: Writing on Black History and Culture* (New York, 1971), pp. 3–20; Fabre, *The Unfinished Quest*, pp. 143–44.

10. *RWR*, pp. 37–38.

11. Ibid., pp. 39–40.

12. Ibid., pp. 41, 44, 49.

13. Ibid., p. 48.

14. Wright, *Native Son* (New York, 1940). For a detailed examination of the critical response to the novel, see Fabre, *The Unfinished Quest*, pp. 176–87.

15. Wright, *12 Million Black Voices: A Folk History of the Negro in the United States* (1941), reprinted in E. Wright and Fabre, *The Richard Wright Reader*, pp. 151–52.

16. Ibid., pp. 174–75.

17. Ibid., p. 212.

18. Ibid., pp. 233, 238, 240.

19. Ibid., pp. 169, 192–93.

20. Benjamin J. Davis, "Richard Wright in Retreat, " *Sunday Worker* 8 April 1945, quoted in Fabre, *The Unfinished Quest*, p. 280.

21. Wright, *12 Million Black Voices*, pp. 239–40.

22. For a defense of Richard Wright's *Black Boy*, see Ralph Ellison, "Richard Wright's Blues" (1945), reprinted in *Shadow and Act* (New York, 1964), pp. 78–93.

23. Fabre, *The Unfinished Quest*, pp. 280–81.

24. Yoshinobu Hakutani, "Introduction," *Critical Essays on Richard Wright* (Boston, 1982), p. 20.

25. In the 1930s and early 1940s many communists were effusive in their analyses of black life and culture because they were interested in attracting African Americans to the party. See Chapter Four of this study and Wilson Record, *The Negro and the Communist Party* (New York, 1971), pp. 80–85.

26. Joanne V. Gabbin, "A Laying On of Hands: Black Women Writers Exploring the Roots of Their Folk and Cultural Traditions," in Joanne M. Braxton and Andree N. McLaughlin, eds., *Wild Women in the Whirlwind: Afra-American Culture and the Contemporary Literary Renaissance* (New Brunswick, N.J., 1990), p. 248.

27. Zora Neale Hurston, *Their Eyes Were Watching God* (1937; reprinted New York, 1991).

28. Sterling Brown, *The Negro in American Fiction* (Washington, D.C., 1937), p. 159. The reviews of Hurston's *Their Eyes Were Watching God* are discussed in Robert E. Hemenway, *Zora Neale Hurston: A Literary Biography* (Urbana, Ill., 1977), pp. 240–43. See also, Michael Awkward, ed., *New Essays on Their Eyes Were Watching God* (New York, 1990).

29. Richard Wright, "Between Laughter and Tears," *New Masses* 25 (October 1937): 22, 25.

30. Zora Neale Hurston got back at Richard Wright for his negative review of her novel when she reviewed Wright's book of short stories, *Uncle Tom's Children,* published in 1938. Hurston noted that "the reader sees the picture of the South that the Communists have been passing around of late. A dismal, hopeless section ruled by brutish hatred and nothing else. Mr. Wright's author's solution is the solution of the Party—State responsibility for everything and individual responsibility for nothing." See *Saturday Review* (12 April 1938): 32.

31. Zora Neale Hurston, *Dust Tracks on a Road* (1942; reprinted New York, 1991). Page numbers for quoted material are placed in parentheses in the text. Hurston's autobiography, which was her most commercially successful work, is discussed in Hemenway, *Zora Neale Hurston,* pp. 276–91.

32. Zora Neale Hurston, *Mules and Men* (Philadelphia, 1935); Zora Neale Hurston, *Tell My Horse* (Philadelphia, 1938); Alice Walker, ed., *I Love Myself When I Am Laughing: A Zora Neale Hurston Reader* (New York, 1979), p. 27.

33. Hemenway, *Zora Neale Hurston,* pp. 84–103, 246–72.

34. Poet and writer Maya Angelou in her foreword to the 1991 edition of *Dust Tracks* said that "this puzzling book was written during 1940 and 1941 but for the most part deals with the early part of the twentieth century. . . . There is, despite its success in certain quarters, a strange distance in this book. Certainly the language is true and the dialogue authentic, but the author stands between the content and the reader. It is difficult, if not impossible, to find and touch the real Zora Neale Hurston"; pp. x–xii.

35. Gunnar Myrdal, *An American Dilemma: The Negro Problem and Modern Democracy* (New York, 1944). See also, David W. Southern, *Gunnar Myrdal and Black–White Relations: The Use and Abuse of an American Dilemma, 1944–1969* (Baton Rouge, La., 1987); and Walter A. Jackson, *Gunnar Myrdal and America's Conscience: Social Engineering and Racial Liberalism, 1938–1987* (Chapel Hill, N.C., 1990).

36. Myrdal, *An American Dilemma,* pp. 928–30.

37. Biographer Michel Fabre makes it clear that Wright read and recommended Myrdal's *An American Dilemma* to others. In the 1940s Wright began a lifelong correspondence with Myrdal, whom he admired greatly. See Fabre, *The Unfinished Quest,* pp. 586, 591, passim.

38. Richard Wright, "I Bite the Hand That Feeds Me," *Atlantic Monthly* 165 (25 October 1940): 826–28.

39. Richard Wright, "Introduction" to St. Clair Drake and Horace R. Cayton, *Negro Metropolis: A Study of Negro Life in a Northern City* (1945; reprinted New York, 1961), pp. xx, xxiv. For information on the Chicago School of Social Research and black sociologists of the period, see Robert Faris, *Chicago Sociology, 1920–1932* (San Francisco, 1967); Fred Mathews, *Quest for an American Sociology: Robert E. Park and the Chicago School* (Montreal, Can., 1977); and James Blackwell and Morris Janowitz, eds., *Black Sociologists: Historical and Contemporary Perspectives* (Chicago, 1974).

40. Michel Fabre, "Wright, Negritude, and African Writing," in *The World of Richard Wright* (Jackson, Miss., 1985), p. 192.

41. Biographer Robert Hemenway claims that Hurston disliked white communists and was "suspicious of the party"; see Hemenway, *Zora Neale Hurston,* pp. 334–35.

42. Wright, "Blueprint for Negro Writing," p. 42.

43. Alice Walker, "Dedication—On Refusing to Be Humbled by Second Place in a Contest You Did Not Design: A Tradition Now," in *I Love Myself When I Am Laughing*, pp. 1–2.

Chapter 6: The Autobiographical Legacy of W. E. B. Du Bois

1. The more useful biographies of W. E. B. Du Bois are Francis L. Broderick, *W. E. B. Du Bois: Negro Leader in a Time of Crisis* (Stanford, Ca., 1959); Elliott M. Rudwick, *W. E. B. Du Bois: Propagandist of Negro Protest* (Philadelphia, 1960, 1968); Shirley Graham Du Bois, *His Day Is Marching On: A Memoir of W. E. B. Du Bois* (Philadelphia, 1971); Arnold Rampersad, *The Art and Imagination of W. E. B. Du Bois* (Cambridge, Mass., 1976); Manning Marable, *W. E. B. Du Bois: Black Radical Democrat* (Boston, 1986); and David Levering Lewis, *W. E. B. Du Bois: Biography of a Race, 1868–1919* (New York, 1993). See also, John Henrik Clarke et al., eds., *Black Titan: W. E. B. Du Bois* (Boston, 1970); and Rayford Logan, ed., *W. E. B. Du Bois: A Profile* (New York, 1971).

2. W. E. B. Du Bois, *The Souls of Black Folk* (1903; reprinted New York, 1969), p. 91.

3. For a generous sampling of Du Bois's writings in the *Crisis,* organized chronologically and topically, see Daniel Walden, ed., *W. E. B. Du Bois: The Crisis Writings* (Greenwich, Ct., 1972).

4. William L. Andrews, "Checklist of Du Bois's Autobiographical Writings," in William L. Andrews, ed., *Critical Essays on W. E. B. Du Bois* (Boston, 1985), pp. 226–30.

5. Du Bois, *The Souls of Black Folk,* pp. 107–8.

6. Ibid., pp. 157–58.

7. Ibid., pp. 227–28.

8. Ibid., pp. 228–29.

9. Ibid., p. 231.

10. Ibid., p. 232.

11. The three major autobiographical works by Du Bois to be discussed are *Darkwater: Voices from Within the Veil* (1920; reprinted New York, 1972); *Dusk of Dawn: An Essay Toward an Autobiography of a Race Concept* (1940; reprinted New York, 1971); and *The Autobiography of W. E. B. Du Bois: A Soliloquy on Viewing My Life from the Last Decade of Its First Century* (New York, 1968). Another major autobiographical work, *In Battle for Peace: The Story of My 83rd Birthday* (1952; reprinted Millwood, N.Y., 1976) deals primarily with the years 1950 and 1951, and is also discussed below.

12. See Introduction, pp. 13–14.

13. Herbert Aptheker identified where each previously published essay, story, or poem can be found; see *The Literary Legacy of W. E. B. Du Bois* (White Plains, N.Y., 1989), p. 150.

14. Du Bois, *Darkwater: Voices from Within the Veil*. Page numbers for quoted material are placed in parentheses in the text (*D,*).

15. W. E. B. Du Bois, "The Souls of White Folk," *Independent* 69 (18 August 1910): 339–42; and W. E. B. Du Bois, "On Being Black," *New Republic* 21 (18 February 1920): 338–41.

16. The controversy really began on a smaller scale a little earlier when much of this material appeared in an article entitled "Of the Culture of White Folk" in *The Journal of Race Development* 7 (April 1917): 434–37. For discussion, see Aptheker, *The Literary Legacy of W. E. B. Du Bois,* pp. 143–54. This work contains the introductions to many of the volumes in *The Complete Published Works of W. E. B. Du Bois,* edited by Aptheker (Millwood, N.Y., 1975–89).

17. W. E. B. Du Bois, "The African Roots of War," *Atlantic Monthly* 65 (May 1915): 707–14.

18. W. E. B. Du Bois and Martha Gruening, "The Massacre of East St. Louis," *Crisis* 14 (September 1917): 219–38. See also, Elliott M. Rudwick, *Race Riot in East St. Louis, July 2, 1917* (Carbondale, Ill., 1964).

19. For information on the life and work of Samuel Coleridge-Taylor, see Eileen Southern, *Biographical Dictionary of Afro-American and African Musicians* (Westport, Ct., 1982), pp. 78–79; and William Tortolano, *Samuel Coleridge-Taylor: Anglo–Black Composer, 1875–1912* (Metuchen, N.J., 1977).

20. Rampersad, *The Art and Imagination,* p. 178.

21. Ibid., p. 183.

22. M. E. Bailey, "Review of *Darkwater,*" *Bookman* 52 (January 1921): 304; *Outlook* 126 (15 December 1920): 690; Robert F. Foerster, "Review of *Darkwater,*" *Survey* 44 (12 June 1920): 384.

23. William Colson, "Phases of Du Bois—Review of *Darkwater,*" *Messenger* 11 (April–May 1920): 10–11.

24. "The Declaration of the Rights of the Negro Peoples of the World" (August 1920), reprinted in Theodore G. Vincent, *Black Power and the Garvey Movement* (San Francisco, 1971), pp. 257–65. See also, Tony Martin, *Race First: The Ideological and Organization Struggles of Marcus Garvey and the Universal Negro Improvement Association* (Westport, Ct., 1976), pp. 11–19.

25. Du Bois quoted in Aptheker, *The Literary Legacy of W. E. B. Du Bois,* p. 197.

26. Allison Davis, "Review of *Dark Princess,*" *Crisis* (October 1928): 39–40. See also, Rampersad, *The Art and Imagination,* pp. 202–18.

27. Du Bois's letters of resignation from the NAACP and *Crisis* (21 May and 26 June 1934) are published in Herbert Aptheker, ed., *The Correspondence of W. E. B. Du Bois* Volume 1, Selections, 1877–1934, hereinafter *Du Bois Correspondence* (Amherst, Mass., 1973; Vol. 2, 1976; Vol. 3, 1978), pp. 478–80.

28. W. E. B. Du Bois, *Black Reconstruction in America, 1860–1880* (1935; reprinted New York, 1992). For a discussion of the reviews and significance of this seminal work, see Aptheker, *The Literary Legacy of W. E. B. Du Bois,* pp. 228–43.

29. Du Bois, *Black Reconstruction,* p. 708. For an excellent examination of *Black Reconstruction* and Du Bois's original contributions to Marxist thought, see Cedric Robinson, *Black Marxism: The Making of the Black Radical Tradition* (London, 1983), pp. 277–91.

30. Du Bois's "Basic American Negro Creed" is included in *Dusk of Dawn,* pp. 320–22. Letters between Du Bois and Locke concerning the manuscript are included in *Du Bois Correspondence,* Volume 2, 1934–1944, pp. 78–86. Another failed project of the decade was the Phelps–Stokes Foundation decision to fund the publication of an *Encyclopedia of the Negro* with Du Bois as editor. Limited funds were provided to sup-

port the project until 1946, and a preliminary bibliography was published in 1945; see W. E. B. Du Bois and Guy B. Johnson, *Encyclopedia of the Negro: Preparatory Volume with Reference Lists and Reports* (New York, 1945). Du Bois found out in 1948 that the General Education Board was thinking of taking over the project with Frederick Patterson, the president of Tuskegee Institute, as editor–in–chief. Nothing more came of either project; see *Du Bois Correspondence,* Volume 3, 1944–1963, pp. 191–95.

31. W. E. B. Du Bois, *Black Folk: Then and Now* (1939; reprinted Millwood, N.Y., 1975); Richard H. Thornton quoted in Aptheker, *The Literary Legacy of W. E. B. Du Bois,* p. 260. Aptheker also discusses the reviews of *Black Folk: Then and Now;* see pp. 264–71.

32. W. E. B. Du Bois, *A Pageant in Seven Decades: 1868–1938* (1938) was reprinted in Aptheker, ed., *Pamphlets and Leaflets by W. E. B. Du Bois* (White Plains, N.Y., 1986), pp. 244–74.

33. Du Bois, *Dusk of Dawn.* Page numbers for quoted material are placed in parentheses in the text (*DD*).

34. Aptheker, *Du Bois Correspondence,* Volume 1, p. 10. The regular reports Du Bois sent back to the Slater Fund trustees between 1890 and 1892 are also included; see pp. 19–29.

35. W. E. B. Du Bois, *The Philadelphia Negro: A Social Study* (1899; reprinted New York, 1967).

36. Twelve of the Atlanta University Publications were reprinted in 1968 by Arno Press. Du Bois's editorship began with the third study, *Social Efforts of the American Negroes for Their Own Betterment,* published in 1898, and Du Bois and A. G. Dill co-edited volumes fifteen through eighteen. See Ernest Kaiser, "Introduction" to the reprint edition, p. vii.

37. The ideological differences between the "young radicals" and "older race men" at the Second Amenia Conference in September 1933 are examined in James Young, *Black Writers in the Thirties* (Baton Rouge, La., 1973). The ideological dichotomy that James Young identified had little basis in reality. Du Bois had more in common with the radicals at the meeting than this author suggests.

38. Letters between Du Bois and the NAACP officers, including his letter of resignation of 11 June 1934, are reprinted in *Du Bois Correspondence,* Volume 1, pp. 478–81.

39. For a discussion of the reviews of *Dusk of Dawn,* see Aptheker, *The Literary Legacy of W. E. B. Du Bois,* pp. 270–81. Quotation taken from *Nation* 151 (23 November 1940): 512.

40. Selections from Du Bois's newspaper columns during this period are reprinted in Herbert Aptheker, ed., *Newspaper Columns by W. E. B. Du Bois,* Volume 1 (Millwood, N.Y., 1986). For a discussion, see V. P. Franklin, "W. E. B. Du Bois As Journalist," *The Journal of Negro Education* 56 (Spring 1987): 240–44.

41. Correspondence relevant to the First Phylon Conference may be found in *Du Bois Correspondence,* Volume 2, pp. 232–34. See also, Frank Davis, "The Nature, Scope and Significance of the First Phylon Institute," *Phylon* 2 (Third Quarter, 1941): 280–87.

42. *Du Bois Correspondence* Volume 2, pp. 390–97.

43. Du Bois, *The Autobiography of W. E. B. Du Bois: A Soliloquy.* Page numbers for quoted materials are placed in parentheses in the text (*S*).

44. Nina Gomer Du Bois's death was reported in several black newspapers and was

noted in Du Bois's correspondence. See, for example, *Du Bois Correspondence*, Volume 3, pp. 289–90.

45. Shirley Graham Du Bois, *His Day Is Marching On*, p. 24; *Du Bois Correspondence*, Volume 3, pp. 130–31. Shirley Graham's memoir about Du Bois is an excellent source for details about Du Bois's daily activities, particularly between 1944 and 1963.

46. Elizabeth Brown–Guillory, "Shirley Graham Du Bois 1896–1977," in Darlene Clark Hine et al., eds., *Black Women in America: An Historical Encyclopedia* (Brooklyn, N.Y., 1992), pp. 357–58; *Du Bois Correspondence*, Volume 3, pp. 130–31.

47. Du Bois, *Color and Democracy: Colonies and Peace* (1945; reprinted Millwood, N.Y., 1975), p. 113. For a discussion of the enthusiastic response to the work from reviewers, see Aptheker, *The Literary Legacy of Du Bois*, pp. 283–96.

48. Du Bois, *The World and Africa* (1947; reprinted Millwood, N.Y., 1976), pp. 44, 256.

49. Walter White, *A Man Called White* (New York, 1948), pp. 60–61, 107, 174, 358–59.

50. *Du Bois Correspondence*, Volume 3, pp. 6–16.

51. Letters and memoranda between White and Du Bois about the "Appeal" on behalf of the "Human Rights of American Negroes" may be found in ibid., pp. 160–66, 178–89.

52. For letters to and from Du Bois relevant to his eventual dismissal from the NAACP in September 1948, see ibid., pp. 236–54.

53. W. Alphaeus Hunton, who served as the CAA's executive secretary, wrote "A Note on the Council on African Affairs," which was included as an appendix to Paul Robeson's autobiography, *Here I Stand*, first published in 1958 (New York), pp. 117–19. See also, Martin B. Duberman, *Paul Robeson: A Biography* (New York, 1989), pp. 330–33.

54. Shirley Graham Du Bois presented a detailed account of the impact of the indictment and trial upon her and her husband in *His Day Is Marching On*, pp. 140–48.

55. W. E. B. Du Bois, *In Battle for Peace: The Story of My 83rd Birthday* (1952; reprinted Millwood, N.Y., 1976).

56. David Caute, *The Fellow–Travelers; A Postscript to the Enlightenment* (New York, 1973), pp. 147–49; Cedric Belfrage, *American Inquisition, 1945–1960* (Indianapolis, Ind., 1973), pp. 60–103; Stanley Kutler, *The American Inquisition: Justice and Injustice in the Cold War* (New York, 1982), pp. 152–63.

57. See sources cited in note 56 above; see also, Alan D. Harper, *The Politics of Loyalty: The White House and the Communist Issue, 1946–1952* (New York, 1969), pp. 145–48; David A. Shannon, *The Decline of American Communism: A History of the American Communist Party of the United States Since 1945* (1959; reprinted Chatham, N.J., 1971), pp. 196–201; Joseph R. Starobin, *American Communism in Crisis, 1943–1957* (Cambridge, Mass., 1972), pp. 205–7; and Harvey Klehr and J. E. Haynes, *The American Communist Movement: Storming Heaven Itself* (New York, 1992), pp. 126–28.

58. Harry Haywood, *Black Bolshevik: Autobiography of an Afro-American Communist* (New York, 1978), pp. 574–75.

59. W. E. B. Du Bois, "U.S. Needs No More Cowards," *National Guardian*, 25 October 1950, in Aptheker, ed., *Newspaper Columns by Du Bois*, Volume 2, p. 878.

60. Du Bois, *In Battle for Peace,* pp. 146–47. For letters relevant to his indictment and trial, see *Du Bois Correspondence,* Volume 3, pp. 306–23.

61. Du Bois, *In Battle for Peace,* pp. 76–77.

62. Ibid., p. 77.

63. Du Bois's conclusion about the nature of black leadership was one of his most important intellectual legacies. For a discussion, see Vincent Harding, "A Black Messianic Visionary," in Rayford Logan, ed., *W. E. B. Du Bois: A Profile* (New York, 1971), pp. 274–93; and Sterling Stuckey, "W. E. B. Du Bois: Black Cultural Reality and the Meaning of Freedom," in *Slave Culture: Nationalist Theory and the Foundations of Black America* (New York, 1987), pp. 245–302.

64. For letters regarding this trip abroad in 1958–1959, see *Du Bois Correspondence,* Volume 3, pp. 432–34.

65. Letters to and from President Kwame Nkrumah are included in ibid., pp. 443–44.

66. Du Bois to Gus Hall, 1 October 1961, in ibid., pp. 439–40. Although the "Encyclopedia Africana" was never completed, Du Bois did finish his last book, *ABC of Color,* while in Ghana and it was published in Berlin in the summer of 1963. For letters about this work, see ibid. pp. 461–44.

67. Aptheker, "On the Passing of Du Bois," *Political Affairs* 42 (October 1963): 35–41; and *Du Bois Correspondence,* Volume 3, p. 438.

68. Rampersad, *The Art and Imagination,* pp. 262–63; Gerald Horne, *Black and Red: W. E. B. Du Bois and the Afro-American Response to the Cold War, 1944–1963* (Albany, N.Y., 1986), p. 310; Marable, *W. E. B. Du Bois: Black Radical Democrat,* p. 211; Shirley Graham Du Bois, *His Day Is Marching On,* p. 325.

69. Haywood, *Black Bolshevik,* pp. 574–75; Shannon, *The Decline of American Communism,* pp. 196–201; Starobin, *American Communism in Crisis,* pp. 205–7; Klehr and Haynes, *The American Communist Movement,* pp. 126–28.

70. William Z. Foster, *History of the Communist Party of the United States* (1952; reprinted New York, 1968), p. 552; Shannon, *The Decline of American Communism,* pp. 262–65; Klehr and Haynes, *The American Communist Movement,* 142–47.

71. Gus Hall's enthusiastic response to Du Bois's application for membership is reprinted in Clarke et al., *Black Titan,* pp. 306–8.

Chapter 7: The Confessions of James Baldwin

1. James Baldwin, "Princes and Powers," *Encounter* (January 1957): 52–60. This essay was reprinted in *Nobody Knows My Name: More Notes of a Native Son* (New York, 1961) and *The Price of the Ticket: Collected Nonfiction, 1948–1985* (New York, 1985). Page numbers for quoted material are placed in parentheses in the text and refer to this later volume.

2. Du Bois's letter to the Congress of African Writers and Artists in September 1956 was printed in *Présence Africain* 8–10, Numero Special, (Juin–Novembre 1956).

3. For information on the Negritude movement and its founders, see Lilyan Kesteroot, *Black Writers in French: A Literary History of Negritude* (Washington, D.C., 1991); James A. Arnold, *Modernism and Negritude: The Poetry and Poetics of Aime Cesaire* (Cambridge, Mass., 1981); Janet G. Vaillant, *Black, French, and African: A Life of*

Leopold Sedar Senghor (Cambridge, Mass., 1990); Daniel L. Racine, *Leon–Gontran Damas, 1912–1978: Founder of Negritude: A Memorial Casebook* (Washington, D.C., 1979); and Ellen Conroy Kennedy, *The Negritude Poets: An Anthology of Translations from the French* (New York, 1975).

4. Richard Wright, "Tradition and Industrialization: The Historic Meaning of the Plight of the Tragic Elites in Asia and Africa," in *White Man, Listen!* (New York, 1958), pp. 44–68. See also, Michel Fabre, *The Unfinished Quest of Richard Wright* (New York, 1973), pp. 435–41.

5. For biographical information on James Baldwin, see Fern Marja Eckman, *The Furious Passage of James Baldwin* (New York, 1966); W. J. Weatherby, *James Baldwin: Artist on Fire* (New York, 1989); James Campbell, *Talking at the Gates: A Life of James Baldwin* (New York, 1991); and David Leeming, *James Baldwin: A Biography* (New York, 1994). Literary studies of the works of James Baldwin also include some biographical information; see Stanley Macebuh, *James Baldwin: A Critical Study* (New York, 1973); Louis H. Pratt, *James Baldwin* (Boston, 1978); and Carolyn Wedin Sylvander, *James Baldwin* (New York, 1980).

6. James Baldwin, *The Fire Next Time* (1963), reprinted in *The Price of the Ticket,* p. 345.

7. For detailed information about Baldwin's schooling and his interactions with his black and white instructors, see Eckman, *The Furious Passage,* pp. 34–65. See also, Alan R. Shucard, *Countee Cullen* (Boston, 1984); and Blanche E. Ferguson, *Countee Cullen and the Negro Renaissance* (New York, 1966).

8. James Baldwin, "Notes of a Native Son" (1955), reprinted in *The Price of the Ticket,* p. 134.

9. James Baldwin, "Alas Poor Richard," *Reporter* (16 March 1961), reprinted in *Nobody Knows My Name* (New York, 1961) and *The Price of the Ticket.* Page numbers in parentheses in the text refer to the later volume.

10. For a discussion of Richard Wright's move to Paris in 1946, see Fabre, *The Unfinished Quest,* pp. 294–301.

11. James Baldwin, "The New Lost Generation," *Esquire* (July 1961), reprinted in *The Price of the Ticket,* pp. 305–13.

12. For a discussion of Richard Wright, James Baldwin, and other African-American writers and expatriates in Paris, see Michel Fabre, *From Harlem to Paris: Black American Writers in France, 1840–1980* (Urbana, Ill., 1991).

13. "The New Lost Generation," *Esquire* (July 1961), reprinted in *The Price of the Ticket,* pp. 305–13.

14. James Baldwin, "Everbody's Protest Novel," *Zero* (Spring 1948) and *Partisan Review* (June 1949), and *The Price of the Ticket.* Page numbers in parentheses in the text refer to the later volume.

15. Fabre, *The Unfinshed Quest,* pp. 362–63, 602. See also, Horace A. Porter, *Stealing the Fire: The Art and Protest of James Baldwin* (Middletown, Ct., 1989), pp. 67–96.

16. James Baldwin, *Go Tell It on the Mountain* (New York, 1952).

17. Harvey Curtis Webster, "Review of *Go Tell It on the Mountain,*" *Saturday Review of Literature* 14 (16 May 1953): 36; J. Saunders Redding, "Review of *Go Tell It on*

the Mountain," *New York Herald Tribune Book Review* (17 May 1953): 5. See also, Michel Fabre, "Fathers and Sons in James Baldwin's *Go Tell It on the Mountain,"* in Keneth Kinnamon, ed., *James Baldwin: A Collection of Critical Essays* (Englewood Cliffs, N.J., 1974), pp. 120–38; Shirley S. Allen, "The Ironic Voice in Baldwin's *Go Tell It on the Mountain,"* in Therman B. O'Daniel, ed., *James Baldwin: A Critical Examination* (Washington, D.C., 1981), pp. 30–37; Shirley S. Allen, "Religious Symbolism and Psychic Reality in Baldwin's *Go Tell It on the Mountain,"* in Fred L. Standley and Nancy V. Burt, eds., *Critical Essays on James Baldwin* (Boston, 1988), pp. 166–87.

18. James Baldwin, *The Amen Corner* (1968; reprinted New York, 1990), pp. xv, 134.

19. Harold Clurman, "The Amen Corner," *Nation* 200 (1965): 514–15, reprinted in Standley and Burt, eds., *Critical Essays on James Baldwin,* pp. 295–96.

20. James Baldwin, *Notes of a Native Son* (New York, 1955). The essays in that volume were reprinted in *The Price of the Ticket.* Page numbers in parentheses in the text refer to the later volume.

21. Langston Hughes to Arna Bontemps, 18 February 1953, quoted in Arnold Rampersad, *The Life of Langston Hughes: Volume II: 1941–1967: I Dream a World* (New York, 1988), p. 205; and Langston Hughes, "From Harlem to Paris," *New York Times Book Review* (26 February 1956): 26, reprinted in Standley and Burt, eds., *Critical Essays on James Baldwin,* pp. 226–26. For a discussion of other reviews of *Notes of a Native Son,* see Weatherby, *James Baldwin,* pp. 128–31; and Campbell, *Talking at the Gates,* pp. 93–94.

22. James Baldwin, *Giovanni's Room* (New York, 1956).

23. Weatherby, *James Baldwin,* pp. 133–47; Campbell, *Talking at the Gates,* pp. 102–6. See also, Roger Austen, *Playing the Game: The Homosexual Novel in America* (Indianapolis, Ind., 1977), pp. 149–52; Georges–Michel Sarotte, *Like a Brother, Like a Lover: Male Homosexuality in the American Novel and Theatre from Herman Melville to James Baldwin* (New York, 1978), pp. 22–6, 170–77.

24. Weatherby, *James Baldwin,* p. 136. See also, Eckman, *The Furous Passage,* pp. 137–39.

25. Wolfgang Binder, "James Baldwin: An Interview" (1980), and Jordan Elgrably and George Plimpton, "The Art of Fiction LXVIII: James Baldwin" (1984), in Fred L. Standley and Louis H. Pratt, eds., *Conversations with James Baldwin* (Jackson, Miss., 1989), pp. 204–5, 239.

26. Eckman, *The Furious Passage,* p. 139.

27. For reviews of *Giovanni's Room,* see *New Republic* 135 (17 December 1956): 26; *New York Times* (14 October 1956): 5; *Saturday Review* 39 (1 December 1956): 34.

28. Richard Kluger, *Simple Justice: The History of Brown v. Board of Education and Black America's Struggle for Equality* (New York, 1976); Mark Tushnet, *NAACP's Legal Strategy Against Segregated Education, 1925–1950* (Chapel Hill, N.C., 1987).

29. Eckman, *The Furious Passage,* pp. 144–48; Weatherby, *James Baldwin,* pp. 153–60; Campbell, *Talking at the Gates,* pp. 117–25.

30. James Baldwin, "A Fly in the Buttermilk," in *Notes of a Native Son* and *The Price of the Ticket.* Page numbers in parentheses in the text refer to the later volume. For

accounts of the desegregation of Little Rock's Central High School in September 1957, see Daisy Bates, *The Long Shadow of Little Rock* (New York, 1962); Elizabeth Huckaby, *Crisis at Central High School, Little Rock, 1957–1958* (Baton Rouge, La., 1980); and Juan Williams, *Eyes on the Prize: America's Civil Rights Years, 1954–1965* (New York, 1987), pp. 92–119.

31. Baldwin, "The Dangerous Road Before Martin Luther King," *Harper's* (February 1961), reprinted in *The Price of the Ticket*. Page numbers in parentheses in the text refer to the later volume.

32. Weatherby, *James Baldwin*, pp. 166–69; Campbell, *Talking at the Gates*, pp. 125–27. See also, James Baldwin, *Blues for Mister Charlie* (New York, 1964).

33. James Baldwin, *Nobody Knows My Name: More Notes of a Native Son* (New York, 1961), reprinted in *The Price of the Ticket*. Page numbers in parentheses in the text refer to the later volume.

34. Norman Mailer, "The White Negro," in *Advertisements for Myself* (New York, 1959), pp. 337–58.

35. James Baldwin, *Another Country* (New York, 1962); Granville Hicks, "Outcasts in a Caldron of Hate," *Saturday Review* 45 (7 July 1962): 21, reprinted in Standley and Burt, *Critical Essays on James Baldwin*, p. 149. See also, George E. Kent, "Baldwin and the Problem of Being," in Kinnamon, ed., *James Baldwin: A Collection of Critical Essays*, pp. 16–27; and Eugenia W. Collier, "The Phrase Unbearably Repeated," in O'Daniel, ed., *James Baldwin: A Critical Evaluation*, pp. 38–46.

36. James Baldwin, *The Fire Next Time* (New York, 1963), was reprinted in *The Price of the Ticket*. Page numbers in parentheses in text refer to the later volume.

37. Eldridge Cleaver, *Soul on Ice* (New York, 1968), pp. 96–107.

38. The meeting with Robert Kennedy in May 1963 is detailed in Eckman, *The Furious Passage*, pp. 180–97; Weatherby, *James Baldwin*, pp. 249–68; and Campbell, *Talking at the Gates*, pp. 163–66. See also, Arthur M. Schlesinger, *Robert Kennedy and His Times* (Boston, 1978), pp. 355–59.

39. Campbell, *Talking at the Gates*, p. 175. Campbell presents a detailed discussion of the FBI's surveillance of Baldwin based on these files; see pp. 167–76.

40. Charles V. Hamilton, *Adam Clayton Powell, Jr.: The Political Biography of an American Dilemma* (New York, 1991), pp. 336–37. See also, Wil Hapgood, *King of the Cats: The Life and Times of Adam Clayton Powell, Jr.* (Boston, 1993), p. 265–66; David J. Garrow, *Bearing the Cross: Martin Luther King, Jr., and the Southern Christian Leadership Conference* (New York, 1986), pp. 138–40; and Adam Fairclough, *To Redeem the Soul of America: Martin Luther King Jr., and the Southern Christian Leadership Conference* (Athens, Ga., 1987), pp. 72–73.

41. James Campbell, *Talking at the Gates*, p. 181. Campbell's version of Baldwin's life and writings contains many subjective assessments that unfortunately do not move beyond exhibiting the revenge of the white liberals Baldwin so often criticized. For a detailed analysis of the flaws and weaknesses of the biographies of James Baldwin by Weatherby and Campbell, see Ekwueme Michael Thelwell, "A Prophet Is Not Without Honor," *Transition* 58 (1992): 90–113.

42. Criticisms and evaluations of the fictional works Baldwin published in the late 1960s may be found in volumes by Kinnamon, ed., *James Baldwin: A Collection of Crit-*

ical Essays; O'Daniel, ed., *James Baldwin: A Critical Edition*; and Standley and Burt, *Critical Essays on James Baldwin*.

43. James Baldwin, *No Name in the Street* (New York, 1972), reprinted in *The Price of the Ticket*. Page numbers in parentheses in the text refer to the later volume.

Chapter 8: Malcolm X and the Resurrection of the Dead

1. Malcolm X and Alex Haley, *The Autobiography of Malcolm X* (New York, 1965). Page numbers for quoted material are placed in parentheses in the text. See also, Alex Haley, "Mr. Muhammad Speaks," *Reader's Digest* 76 (March 1960): 100–4.

2. Alex Haley and Alfred Balk, "Black Merchants of Hate: Black Muslims," *Saturday Review* 236 (6 January 1963): 68–74; Alex Haley, "*Playboy* Interview: Malcolm X," *Playboy* 10 (May 1963): 53–54.

3. G. Thomas Couser, *American Autobiography: The Prophetic Mode* (Amherst, Mass., 1979), pp. 1, 165.

4. Ibid., p. 168. For similar observations about Malcolm's reticence about his conversion in prison, see Carol Ohmann, "*The Autobiography of Malcolm X*: A Revolutionary Use of the Franklin Tradition," *American Quarterly* 22 (Summer 1970): 131–49; and Paul John Eakin, "Malcolm X and the Limits of Autobiography," in James Olney, ed., *Autobiography: Essays Theoretical and Critical* (Princeton, N.J., 1980), pp. 181–93.

5. Sacvan Bercovitch, *The American Jeremiad* (Madison, Wis., 1978), p. 31. See also, Perry Miller, *The New England Mind: From Colony to Province* (1953; reprinted Boston, 1961); Perry Miller, *Errand into the Wilderness* (Cambridge, Mass., 1958); and Ernest L. Tuvesen, *Redeemer Nation: The Idea of America's Millennial Role* (Chicago, 1968).

6. Bercovitch, *The American Jeremiad*, pp. 176–210.

7. David Howard–Pitney, *The Afro-American Jeremiad: Appeals for Justice in America* (Philadelphia, 1990), p. 15.

8. Ibid. See also, Leonard Sweet, *Black Images of America, 1784–1870* (New York, 1976), pp. 148–67; and Wilson Jeremiah Moses, *Black Messiahs and Uncle Toms: Social and Literary Manipulations of a Religious Myth* (University Park, Pa., 1982), pp. 207–25.

9. Peter A. Dorsey, *Sacred Estrangement: The Rhetoric of Conversion in Modern American Autobiography* (University Park, Pa., 1993), pp. 8–9.

10. Ibid. See also, Albert E. Stone, "Individual Stories and Cultural Narratives: Autobiography in Modern America," in *Autobiographical Occasions and Original Acts: Versions of American Identity from Henry Adams to Nate Shaw* (Philadelphia, 1982), pp. 1–27.

11. For discussions of Wallace D. Fard, Elijah Muhammad, and the development of the theology of the Nation of Islam, see C. Eric Lincoln, *The Black Muslims in America* (Boston, 1961); E. U. Essien-Udom, *Black Nationalism: A Search for an Identity in America* (Chicago, 1962); and Louis E. Lomax, *When the Word Is Given: A Report on Elijah Muhammad, Malcolm X, and the Black Muslim World* (Cleveland, 1963).

12. Essien-Udom presents the most detailed discussion of Wallace D. Fard; see *Black Nationalism*, pp. 18, 55–75.

13. For a detailed discussion of the significance of the Exodus story to African-American Christianity, see V. P. Franklin, *Black Self-Determination: A Cultural History of African American Resistance* (Brooklyn, N.Y. 1992), pp. 34–67.

14. C. L. Franklin, "Dry Bones in the Valley," in Jeff Todd Titon, ed., *Give Me This Mountain* (Urbana, Ill., 1989), pp. 80–88; Keith D. Miller, *Voice of Deliverance: The Language of Martin Luther King, Jr. and Its Sources* (New York, 1992), pp. 23–28.

15. Sarah Fitzpatrick quoted in Franklin, *Black Self-Determination*, p. 60.

16. Aaron, *The Light and Truth of Slavery* (1843), quoted in ibid., p. 53.

17. "Come Along Moses" in ibid., p. 61.

18. Paul Radin, "Status, Phantasy, and the Christian Dogma: A Note About the Conversion Experiences of Negro Ex–Slaves," in Clifton H. Johnson, ed., *God Struck Me Dead: Religious Conversion Experiences and the Autobiographies of Ex-Slaves* (Philadelphia, 1969), pp. vii–viii.

19. "I Came from Heaven and Now Return," in *God Struck Me Dead*, pp. 23–25.

20. Ibid., p. 25.

21. Charles S. Johnson, "Introduction to *God Struck Me Dead,*" pp. ii–iii.

22. *God Struck Me Dead*, p. 56.

23. Jane I. Smith and Yvonne Yaazbeck Haddad, *The Islamic Understanding of Death and Resurrection* (1981), p. xi.

24. Al-Barzinji quoted in ibid., pp. 66–67.

25. Elijah Muhammad, *Message to the Blackman in America* (Chicago, 1965), pp. 17–19.

26. Ibid., pp. 83, 243.

27. Peter L. Goldman, *The Death and Life of Malcolm X* (New York, 1973); Eugene V. Wolfenstein, *The Victims of Democracy: Malcolm X and the Black Revolution* (Los Angeles, 1981); and Bruce Perry, *Malcolm: The Life of the Man Who Changed Black America* (New York, 1991). See also, John Henrik Clarke, ed., *Malcolm X: The Man and His Times* (New York, 1969); and Joe Wood, ed., *Malcolm X: In Our Own Image* (New York, 1992).

28. For a detailed discussion of Martin Luther King's appeals to the value of "resistance" in African-American Christianity, see Franklin, *Black Self-Determination*, pp. 48–67. For an excellent analysis of the ideological similarities and differences between King and Malcolm X, see James Cone, *Martin and Malcolm and America: A Dream or a Nightmare* (Maryknoll, N.Y. 1991).

29. In their autobiographies NAACP executive secretary Roy Wilkins and Congress of Racial Equality chairman James Farmer discuss their responses to the separatist ideology of Malcolm X and the Nation of Islam; see Roy Wilkins with Tom Matthews, *Standing Fast: The Autobiography of Roy Wilkins* (New York, 1982), pp. 314–17; and James Farmer, *Lay Bare the Heart: An Autobiography of the Civil Rights Movement* (New York, 1985), pp. 223–36. See also, Nancy J, Weiss, *Whitney Young, Jr., and the Struggle for Civil Rights* (Princeton, N.J., 1989), pp. 122–24.

30. James Baldwin, *The Fire Next Time* (New York, 1963), reprinted in *The Price of the Ticket* (New York, 1985), p. 374.

31. Ibid., pp. 374–75.

32. Ibid., p. 375.

Chapter 9: Gwendolyn Brooks and Amiri Baraka:
The Creation of a Black Literary Aesthetic

1. Langston Hughes, "The Negro Artist and the Racial Mountain," (1926), reprinted in Michael Peplow and Arthur P. Davis, eds., *The New Negro Renaissance: An Anthology* (New York, 1975), p. 472.

2. James Weldon Johnson, "The Dilemma of the Negro Artist," *American Mercury* 15 (December 1928): 480. See also Chapters Three and Five.

3. Gwendolyn Brooks, *Report from Part One* (Detroit, 1972). Page numbers for quoted material are placed in parentheses in the text.

4. The close association between Gwendolyn Brooks and Langston Hughes is described by Arnold Rampersad,*The Life of Langston Hughes; Volume II 1941–1967: I Dream a World* (New York, 1988), pp. 115–17, 172–73, passim.

5. George E. Kent, *Gwendolyn Brooks: A Life* (Lexington, Ky., 1990), p. 60.

6. Richard Wright (18 September 1944) quoted in ibid., pp. 62–63.

7. Gwendolyn Brooks, *A Street in Bronzeville* (1945), reprinted in *The World of Gwendolyn Brooks* (New York, 1971), hereinafter *WGB*, p. 49.

8. *WGB*, p. 100.

9. J. Saunders Redding, "Cellini-Like Lyrics," *Saturday Review* (17 September 1949): 23; Kent, *Gwendolyn Brooks*, pp. 88–89; Langston Hughes, *Chicago Defender* (13 May 1950), quoted in Rampersad, *The Life of Langston Hughes*, II, p. 179. See also, Houston A. Baker, Jr., "The Achievement of Gwendolyn Brooks," in Maria M. Mootry and Gary Smith, eds., *A Life Distilled: Gwendolyn Brooks, Her Poetry and Fiction* (Urbana, Ill., 1987), pp. 21–29.

10. Langston Hughes and the Editors, "Some Practical Observations: A Colloquy," *Phylon* 11 (December 1950): 310–11.

11. Brooks, "Poets Who Are Negroes," ibid., p. 312.

12. Gwendolyn Brooks, *Maud Martha* (New York, 1953), p. 22.

13. Coleman Rosenburger, "Review of *Maud Martha*," *New York Herald Tribune Book Review* (18 October 1953): 11; Hubert Creekmore, "Review of *Maud Martha*," *The New York Times* 4 October 1953.

14. Mary Helen Washington, "'Taming All That Anger Down': Rage and Silence in Gwendolyn Brooks's *Maud Martha*," in Henry Louis Gates, Jr., ed., *Black Literature and Literary Theory* (New York, 1984), pp. 259–60; Barbara Christian, "Nuance and the Novella: A Study of Gwendolyn Brooks's *Maud Martha*," in Mootry and Smith, eds, *A Life Distilled*, pp. 252–53.

15. For discussions of black feminism in the works of black women writers, see Barbara Christian, *Black Feminist Criticism: Perspectives on Black Women Writers* (Elmsford, N.Y., 1985); and Cheryl A. Wall, ed., *Changing Our Own Words: Essays on Criticism, Theory, and Writing by Black Women* (New Brunswick, N.J., 1989).

16. For other literary works that reflect Brooks's feminist perspective, see Rita B. Dandridge, *Black Women's Blues: A Literary Anthology* (New York, 1992), pp. 233–88.

17. *WGB*, p. 318.

18. Ibid., p. 315.

19. Maria K. Mootry, " 'Tell It Slant': Disguise and Discovery as Revisionist Poetic Discourse in *The Bean Eaters*," in Mootry and Smith, eds., *A Life Distilled*, p. 178.

20. Gwendolyn Brooks, "Riders to the Blood–Red Wrath," in *Selected Poems* (New York, 1963), pp. 115–16. See also, George Kent, "The Poetry of Gwendolyn Brooks," in *Blackness and the Adventure of Western Culture* (Chicago, 1972), pp. 125–26.

21. Martin Luther King, Jr., *Where Do We Go from Here?: Chaos or Community* (New York, 1967), p. 25.

22. Stokely Carmichael quoted in Adam Fairclough, *To Redeem the Soul of America: The Southern Christian Leadership Conference and Martin Luther King, Jr.* (Athens, Ga., 1987), p. 316.

23. For a sampling of the early interpretations of Black Power, see Floyd B. Barbour, ed., *The Black Power Revolt: A Collection of Essays* (New York, 1968).

24. Stokely Carmichael and Charles V. Hamilton, *Black Power: The Politics of Liberation in America* (New York, 1967), pp. 176–77. Congressman Powell's version of Black Power is discussed in Chapter Ten.

25. Leon Sullivan, *Build Brother Build* (Philadelphia, 1969), pp. 76–77; Theodore L. Cross, *Black Capitalism: Strategy for Business in the Ghetto* (New York, 1969), pp. 3–12; Fairclough, *To Redeem the Soul of America,* pp. 285, 349–54, 394.

26. For information on the background and activities of the Black Panther Party, see Gene Marine, *The Black Panthers* (New York, 1969); Earl Anthony, *Picking Up the Gun: A Report on the Black Panthers* (New York, 1970); Philip S. Foner, ed., *The Black Panthers Speak* (Philadelphia, 1970); Bobby Seale, *Seize the Time: The Story of the Black Panther Party and Huey P. Newton* (New York, 1970); Huey P. Newton, *To Die for the People: The Writings of Huey P. Newton* (New York, 1972), and Huey P. Newton, *Revolutionary Suicide* (New York, 1974).

27. William E. Van Deburg, *New Day in Babylon: The Black Power Movement and American Culture, 1965–1975* (Chicago, 1992), p. 171.

28. Larry Neal, "The Black Arts Movement" (1968), reprinted in Addison Gayle, Jr., ed., *The Black Aesthetic* (New York, 1972), pp. 272–73.

29. Ibid., pp. 274–75. See also Neal's essays in *Visions of a Liberated Future: Black Arts Movement Writings* (New York, 1989), pp. 7–61, 107–17.

30. Gayle, introduction to *The Black Aesthetic,* p. xxi.

31. Gwendolyn Brooks, "Introduction," *Jump Bad: A New Chicago Anthology* presented by Gwendolyn Brooks (Detroit, 1971), pp. ii–iv. In subsequent interviews Brooks also described her ideological conversion; see, for example, Claudia Tate, ed., *Black Woman Writers at Work* (New York, 1983), pp. 40–41; and D. H. Melhem, *Heroism in the New Black Poetry: Introductions and Interviews* (Lexington, Ky., 1990), pp. 31–36.

32. D. H. Melhem quoted in Kent, *A Life of Gwendolyn Brooks,* p. 219. See also D. H. Melhem, *Gwendolyn Books: Poetry and the Heroic Voice* (Lexington, Ky., 1987), pp. 153–89.

33. *WGB,* p. 426.

34. Gwendolyn Brooks, *Riot* (Detroit, 1969); Kent, *A Life of Gwendolyn Brooks,* pp. 231–32. See also, William H. Hansell, "The Poet-Militant and Foreshadowings of a Black Mystique: Poems in the Second Period of Gwendolyn Brooks"; and Norris B. Clark, "Gwendolyn Brooks and a Black Aesthetic," in Mootry and Smith, eds., *A Life Distilled,* pp. 71–99.

35. Kent, *A Life of Gwendolyn Brooks,* pp. 233–34.

36. See Chapters Three and Six; Langston Hughes, *The Big Sea* (New York, 1940); and *I Wonder as I Wander: An Autobiographical Journey* (New York, 1956).

37. Nellie Y. McKay, "The Autobiographies of Zora Neale Hurston and Gwendolyn Brooks: Alternate Versions of the Black Female Self," in Joanne M. Braxton and Andree N. McLaughlin, eds., *Wild Women in the Whirlwind: Afra-American Culture and the Contemporary Literary Renaissance* (New Brunswick, N.J., 1990), pp. 279–80.

38. LeRoi Jones/Amiri Baraka, *The Autobiography of LeRoi Jones/Amiri Baraka* (New York, 1984). Page numbers for quoted material are placed in parentheses in the text.

39. Baraka changed the names of his two wives, and very likely his other friends, acquaintances, and lovers in his autobiography. Where they have been determined, the real names of persons mentioned will be given in parentheses in the text.

40. LeRoi Jones, "Slice of Life," *Yugen* 1 (1958): 16. In his autobiography, Baraka calls the magazine *Zazen.* For a discussion of Jones's life as "Die Schwartz Bohemien," see Henry C. Lacey, *To Raise, Destroy, and Create: The Poetry, Drama, and Fiction of Imamu Amiri Baraka (LeRoi Jones)* (Troy, N.Y., 1980), pp. 1–41.

41. Fielding Dawson, *The Black Mountain Book* (New York, 1970); and Martin Duberman, *Black Mountain: An Exploration in Community* (New York, 1972). For information on the New York School of Poets, see John Bernard Myers, ed., *The Poets of the New York School* (Philadelphia, 1969), pp. 7–29; and Geoff Ward, *Statutes of Liberty: The New York School of Poets* (New York, 1993), pp. 1–9, 135–36. For biographical information on the individual poets, excluding LeRoi Jones, see Ron Padgett and David Shapiro, eds., *Anthology of New York Poets* (New York, 1970), pp. 545–72.

42. LeRoi Jones, "Notes for a Speech," (1961), reprinted in William J. Harris, ed., *The LeRoi Jones/Amiri Baraka Reader* (New York, 1991), pp. 14–15.

43. For a detailed examination of this unfortunate episode, see Rampersad, *The Life of Langston Hughes, II,* pp. 207–22.

44. LeRoi Jones, "Cuba Libre" (1960), in *Home: Social Essays* (New York, 1966), pp. 11–62.

45. LeRoi Jones, *Blues People: Negro Music in White America* (New York, 1963), p. x.

46. Ralph Ellison, *Shadow and Act* (New York, 1964), pp. 256–58. Ellison's review of *Blues People* was first published in *The New York Review of Books,* 6 February 1964.

47. Baraka declared that "our art shd [sic] be our selves as self–conscious with a commitment to revolution. Which is enlightenment. Revolution is enlightenment." See "The Black Aesthetic," *Negro Digest* 18 (September 1969): 5.

48. LeRoi Jones, *Dutchman* (1964), reprinted in Harris, ed., *The LeRoi Jones/Amiri Baraka Reader,* pp. 76–99. See also, Sherley Anne Williams, "The Search for Identity in Baraka's *Dutchman,*" in Kimberly Benston, ed., *Imamu Amiri Baraka (LeRoi Jones): A Collection of Critical Essays* (Englewood Cliffs, N.J., 1978), pp. 135–40.

49. LeRoi Jones, "LeRoi Jones Talking" (1964), reprinted in *Home: Social Essays,* pp. 187–88.

50. LeRoi Jones, *Dutchman and The Slave* (New York, 1964); *The Dead Lecturer* (New York. 1964); *The Baptism & The Toilet* (New York, 1967).

51. For a discussion of the programs of the Haryou Act, see Peter Marris and Martin Rein, *Dilemmas of Social Reform: Poverty and Community Action in the United States* (Chicago, 1973), pp. 51–52, 183–85. See also, Daniel P. Moynihan, *Maximum Feasible Misunderstanding: Community Action in the War on Poverty* (New York, 1969), pp. 109, 122, 130–38; and William Ryan, *Blaming the Victim* (New York, 1971), pp. 53–56.

52. Larry Neal in his 1968 article on "The Black Arts Movement" discussed in detail the impact Jones's efforts in Harlem had upon Black Arts programs around the country; see Gayle, ed., *The Black Aesthetic,* pp. 277–87.

53. Jones's plays *A Black Mass* and *Jello* are included in *Four Black Revolutionary Plays* (New York, 1969). See also, Jones's essay "Black Revolutionary Poets Should Also Be Playwrights," *Black World* 21 (April 1972): 4–6.

54. *Afro-American Festival of the Arts* (Newark, 1966); LeRoi Jones, *Black Music* (New York, 1968); LeRoi Jones and Larry Neal, eds., *Black Fire: An Anthology of Afro-American Writing* (New York, 1968). Kimberly Benston emphasizes the point that "Black music has long represented for Baraka the model and in some ways even the means for attaining the desired Afro-American cultural independence"; see *Baraka: The Renegade and the Mask* (New Haven, Ct., 1976), p. 69. For a comprehensive listing of the anthologies and collections of black writing associated with the Black Arts Movement, see Carolyn Fowler, *Black Arts and Black Aesthetics: A Bibliography* (Atlanta, 1976), pp. xxxvii–xlii.

55. For an excellent report on Jones/Baraka's work at Spirit House, see David Llorens, "Ameer (LeRoi Jones) Baraka," *Ebony* 24 (August 1969): 75–78.

56. Amiri Baraka, "7 Principles of US Maulana Karenga & The Need for a Black Value System," in *Raise Race Rays Raze: Essays Since 1965* (New York, 1971), pp. 133–46; Clyde Halisi, ed., *The Quotable Karenga* (Los Angeles, 1977), pp. 8–14; Van Deburg, *New Day in Babylon,* pp. 171–74.

57. Robert Smith, Richard Axen, and Deve Pentony, *By Any Means Necessary: The Revolutionary Struggle at San Francisco State* (San Francisco, 1970), pp. 130–35, 149–56. Jones's play *Madheart* is included in *Four Black Revolutionary Plays*.

58. The twists and turns in Black Panther ideology during this period are examined in Van Deburg, *New Day in Babylon,* pp. 155–67.

59. There were several detailed investigations of the causes and consequences of the Newark riot in July 1967; see Tom Hayden, *Rebellion in Newark: Official Violence and Ghetto Response* (New York, 1967), pp. 9–36; Nathan Wright, Jr., *Ready to Riot* (New York, 1968), especially pp. 1–10; and Governor's Select Commission on Civil Disorder, *Report for Action* (Trenton, N.J., 1972), pp. 104–25.

60. Theodore R. Hudson, "The Trial of LeRoi Jones," in Benston, ed., *Imamu Amiri Baraka,* pp. 49–53.

61. The Black Power Conferences in the 1960s are discussed in Manning Marable, *Race, Reform, and Rebellion: The Second Reconstruction in Black America, 1945–1982* (Jackson, Miss., 1984), pp. 104–10.

62. Kenneth Gibson's successful mayoral campaign, and the great assistance he received from Amiri Baraka, is discussed in Ron Porambo, *No Cause for Indictment: An Autopsy of Newark* (New York, 1971), pp. 329–44.

63. For a discussion of the conflicts between US and the Black Panthers, see John Bracey, "Black Nationalism Since Garvey," in N. Huggins, M. Kilson, and D. Fox, eds., *Key Issues in the Afro-American Experience* (New York, 1971), pp. 276–79; Marable, *Race, Reform, and Rebellion,* pp. 134–41; and Van Deburg, *New Day in Babylon,* pp. 174–76.

64. Baraka wrote a long and detailed analysis of the National Black Political Convention in Gary in May 1972; see "Toward the Creation of Political Institutions for All African Peoples," *Black World* 21 (October 1972): 54–78.

65. Baraka, "The National Black Political Assembly and the Black Liberation Movement," *Black World* 24 (March 1975): 22–27.

66. For an examination of the history and activities of the Pan–African Congresses, see P. Olisanwuche Esedebe, *Pan-Africanism: The Idea and the Movement, 1776–1963* (Washington, D.C., 1982). The Dar es Salaam meeting in 1974 is discussed on pp. 233–35.

67. The Garveyite literary aesthetic is discussed in Tony Martin, *Literary Garveyism: Garvey, Black Arts, and the Harlem Renaissance* (Dover, Mass., 1983), pp. 8–24; and V. P. Franklin, *Black Self-Determination: A Cultural History of African-American Resistance* (Brooklyn, N.Y., 1992), pp. 196–201. See also Chapter Three.

Chapter 10: Adam Clayton Powell, Jr.: The Need for Independent Black Leadership

1. August Meier, "New Perspectives on the Nature of Black Political Leadership during Reconstruction," in Howard N. Rabinowitz, ed., *Southern Black Leaders of the Reconstruction Era* (Urbana, Ill., 1982), pp. 400–403.

2. Frederick Douglass, "Speech at the Civil Rights Meeting Held at Lincoln Hall, October 22, 1883 (Washington D.C.)," in Philip S. Foner, ed., *The Life and Writings of Frederick Douglass,* Volume 4 (New York, 1955), p. 400.

3. The Supreme Court's *Williams v. Mississippi* (1898) is examined in Donald G. Nieman, *Promises to Keep: African-Americans and the Constitutional Order, 1776 to the Present* (New York, 1991), pp. 111–13.

4. For biographical information on Oscar De Priest, see Rayford Logan and Michael Winston, eds., *Dictionary of American Negro Biography* (New York, 1982), pp. 173–74; and Maurine Christopher, *Black Americans in Congress* (New York, 1976), pp. 168–75.

5. Ira Katznelson, *Black Men, White Cities: Race, Politics, and Migration in the United States, 1900–1930, and Britain, 1948–68* (Chicago, 1976), p. 98.

6. Harold Gosnell, *Negro Politicians: The Rise of Negro Politics in Chicago* (1935; reprinted Chicago, 1967), pp. 173–74.

7. Christopher, *Black Americans in Congress,* pp. 168–70.

8. Ibid., pp. 177–84; Katznelson, *Black Men, White Cities,* pp. 101–2.

9. Katznelson, *Black Men, White Cities,* p. 103; see also, Gosnell, *Negro Politicians,* pp. 190–95; James Q. Wilson, *Negro Politics: the Search for Leadership* (New York, 1960), pp. 50–51; 130–32; and Harold Cruse, *The Crisis of the Negro Intellectual* (New York, 1967), pp. 7–8.

10. Christopher, *Black Americans in Congress,* pp. 176–77; Nancy J. Weiss, *Farewell to the Party of Lincoln: Black Politics in the Age of FDR* (Princeton, N.J., 1983), pp. 80–86.

11. Christopher, *Black Americans in Congress,* pp. 178–79; Robert L. Zangrando, *The NAACP Crusade Against Lynching, 1909–1950* (Philadelphia, 1980), pp. 141–43.

12. Christopher, *Black Americans in Congress,* pp. 185–86; Wilson, *Negro Politics,* pp. 48–50; Weiss, *Farewell to the Party of Lincoln,* pp. 89–90.

13. Wilson, *Negro Politics: The Search for Leadership,* p. 53.

14. Chuck Stone, *Black Political Power in America* (Indianapolis, 1968), p. 10. See also, John C. Walter, *The Harlem Fox: J. Raymond Jones and Tammany, 1920–1970* (Albany, New York, 1989), pp. 33–54; John Hadley Strange, "The Negro and Philadelphia Politics," in Edward Banfield, ed., *Urban Governance* (Glencoe, Ill., 1969), pp. 408–21; V. P. Franklin, *The Education of Black Philadelphia: The Social and Educational History of a Minority Community, 1900–1950* (Philadelphia, 1979), pp. 67–71, 121–26; Kenneth Kusmer, *A Ghetto Takes Shape: Black Cleveland, 1870–1930* (Urbana, Ill., 1976), pp. 140–47; and Raymond R. Fragnoli, *The Transformation of Reform: Progressivism in Detroit and After, 1912–1933* (New York, 1982), pp. 271–74.

15. Adam Clayton Powell, Jr., *Adam by Adam: The Autobiography of Adam Clayton Powell, Jr.* (New York, 1971). Page numbers for quoted material are placed in parentheses in the text.

16. For biographical information, see Claude Lewis, *Adam Clayton Powell* (Greenwich, Ct., 1963); Christopher, *Black Americans in Congress,* pp. 194–208; Martin Kilson, "Adam Clayton Powell, Jr: The Militant As Politician," in John Hope Franklin and August Meier, eds., *Black Leaders of the Twentieth Century* (Urbana, Ill., 1982), pp. 259–75; Charles V. Hamilton, *Adam Clayton Powell, Jr.: The Political Biography of an American Dilemma* (New York, 1991); and Wil Hapgood, *King of the Cats: The Life and Times of Adam Clayton Powell, Jr.* (New York, 1993). See also, Adam Clayton Powell, Sr., *Against the Grain: An Autobiography* (New York, 1938).

17. On the basis of an interview with Ray Vaughn, a classmate of Powell at Colgate, Charles Hamilton questions Powell's version of why he entered the ministry. See *Adam Clayton Powell, Jr.,* pp. 50–51.

18. Powell, *New York Post* 27 March 1935, quoted in Hamilton, *Adam Clayton Powell, Jr.,* p. 60. See also, E. Franklin Frazier, *The Complete Report of Mayor La Guardia's Commission on the Harlem Riot of March 19, 1935* (1935; reprinted New York, 1969), pp. 7–19. For a recent analysis of the Harlem Riot of March 1935, see Cheryl Lynn Greenburg, *Or Does It Explode?: Black Harlem During the Great Depression* (New York, 1991), pp. 3–5, 136–37, 193.

19. The Greater New York Committee on Employment is discussed in detail in Hamilton, *Adam Clayton Powell, Jr.,* pp. 95–106; see also, Hapgood, *King of the Cats,* pp. 75–78, and Greenburg, *Or Does It Explode?,* pp. 133–37.

20. Christopher, *Black Americans in Congress,* p. 197. Powell's weekly newspaper, *The People's Voice,* is discussed in Hamilton, *Adam Clayton Powell, Jr.,* pp. 119–25, passim; and Hapgood, *King of the Cats,* pp. 88–94.

21. Powell, *Marching Blacks: An Interpretive History of the Rise of the Black Common Man* (New York, 1945), p. 9.

22. Ibid., p. 104.

23. Ibid., p. 135.

24. Ibid., p. 183.

25. Powell's *Marching Blacks* was reviewed widely. See *New York Times* (3 February 1946), p. 3; *Nation* 162 (16 February 1946): 201; *New Yorker* 21 (26 January 1946): 86; and *Saturday Review of Literature* 29 (9 February 1946): 34.

26. The national campaign for a permanent Fair Employment Practices Commission, and Powell's role in it, are examined in Herbert Garfinkel, *When Negroes March: The March on Washington Movement in the Organizational Politics for FEPC* (1959; reprinted New York, 1969), pp. 130–33.

27. Ibid., pp. 148–77; see also, Hamilton, *Adam Clayton Powell, Jr.,* pp. 188–92; and Hapgood, *King of the Cats,* pp. 154–56.

28. Hapgood, *King of the Cats,* pp. 134–35.

29. Hamilton, *Adam Clayton Powell, Jr.,* pp. 196–98; Hapgood, *King of the Cats,* pp. 169–75.

30. Robert Fredrick Burk, *The Eisenhower Administration and Black Civil Rights* (Knoxville, Tenn., 1984), pp. 157–58.

31. The version of the civil rights bill that was passed in 1957 was much weaker than the one supported by Powell. It created the Civil Rights Division in the Justice Department and the U.S. Commission on Civil Rights which was to investigate charges of discrimination in voting rights. But it said nothing about supporting plaintiffs in public school desegregation cases. See Burk, *The Eishenhower Administration and Black Civil Rights,* pp. 204–27; and Nieman, *Promises to Keep,* pp. 161–62.

32. Hamilton, *Adam Clayton Powell, Jr.,* pp. 301–6; Hapgood, *King of the Cats,* pp. 239–42.

33. For a detailed examination of this 1958 congressional campaign, see David Hapgood, *The Purge that Failed: Tammany v. Powell* (New York, 1960). See also, Hamilton, *Adam Clayton Powell, Jr.,* pp. 306–12; and Hapgood, *King of the Cats,* pp. 243–50.

34. "Wheels of Justice Stop for Adam Clayton Powell, Jr.," *National Review* 4 (14 December 1957): 537–41; Hamilton, *Adam Clayton Powell, Jr.,* pp. 313–25; Hapgood, *King of the Cats,* pp. 252–62.

35. The "Black Power Conference" in September 1966 is examined in Hamilton, *Adam Clayton Powell, Jr.,* p. 28; and Hapgood, *King of the Cats,* p. 325. Powell introduced his "Black Power Position Paper" into the *Congressional Record* during the 89th Congress in 1966. It is reprinted in Floyd Barbour, ed., *The Black Power Revolt* (New York, 1968), pp. 305–9. This is shorter and somewhat different from the version included in *Adam by Adam,* pp. 247–50.

36. The libel suit brought by Esther James is discussed in Hamilton, *Adam Clayton Powell, Jr.,* pp. 434–38; and Hapgood, *King of the Cats,* pp. 252–55; 319–22; 371–72.

37. The most thorough account of the machinations to remove Powell from his seat in Congress and the subsequent litigation is Kent M. Weeks, *Adam Clayton Powell and the Supreme Court* (New York, 1971).

38. Weeks includes a chronology of events leading up to the Supreme Court decision on 16 June 1969 and the Democratic primary on 24 June 1970; see ibid., pp.

247–49. See also, Hamilton, *Adam Clayton Powell, Jr.,* pp. 474–78; and Hapgood, *King of the Cats,* pp. 400–404.

39. For reviews of *Adam by Adam,* see *Library Journal* 96 (15 October 1971): 3319; *The New Yorker* 47 (13 November 1971): 202; and *New York Times Book Review* (7 November 1971): 4.

40. For an extensive examination of Powell's work with the Communists in Harlem during the 1930s, see Mark Naison, *Communists in Harlem During the Depression* (New York, 1983), pp. 79, 87–88, 148–49, passim.

41. Powell's visit to Indonesia to attend the Bandung Conference in 1955 is discussed in Hamilton, *Adam Clayton Powell, Jr.,* pp. 237–48; and Hapgood, *King of the Cats,* pp. 200–203.

42. James Baldwin, *The Fire Next Time* (1963), reprinted in *The Price of the Ticket* (New York, 1985), p. 369.

43. Martin Luther King, Jr., *Where Do We Go from Here?: Chaos or Community* (New York, 1967), pp. 55, 62, 66.

44. Malcolm X and Alex Haley, *The Autobiography of Malcolm X* (New York, 1965), p. 375.

INDEX